Ás
Grýtubakki
Möðruvellir
Lögmannshlíð
Munkaþverá
Grund
Möðruvellir
Eiðar
Ketilsstaðir
Skriða
Bjarnanes
Svinafell
Kirkjubær

Property and Virginity

To my sons,
Tómas Óskar, Rúnar and Stefán

AGNES S. ARNÓRSDÓTTIR

Property and Virginity

The Christianization of Marriage in Medieval Iceland 1200-1600

Aarhus University Press

Property and Virginity

Layout: Grafisk SIGNS, Denmark
Cover Design: Grafisk SIGNS
Cover: Sixteenth century Icelandic engagement ring.
Background: Marriage contract from 1380.
Printed in Denmark by Narayana Press, 2010
ISBN 978 87 7934 513 3
This book is published with the generous financial support of
Aarhus University Research Foundation

AARHUS UNIVERSITY PRESS

Langelandsgade 177
8200 Århus N
Denmark
www.unipress.dk
Fax 89 42 53 80

Gazelle Book Services Ltd.
White Cross Mills
Hightown
Lancaster, LA1 4XS
United Kingdom
www.gazellebooks.co

The David Brown Book Co. (DBBC)
P.O. Box 511
Oakville CT 06779
USA
www.oxbowbooks.com

Denne afhandling er af Det Humanistiske Fakultet ved Aarhus Universitet
antaget til offentligt at forsvares for den filosofiske doktorgrad.
Århus, den 25. maj 2009

Bodil Due,
Dekan

Forsvaret finder sted fredag den 19. marts 2010, kl. 13
Auditorium I, Bygning 1441
Aarhus Universitet

The love between husband and wife is nowhere warmer and deeper than in Iceland

Qualiscunque descriptio Islandiae
(from the end of the sixteenth century,
probably by Bishop Oddur Einarsson)

Preface

The idea for this study came during the winter of 1992 to 1993, when I was living in Grenoble in France, mostly taking care of my first born son and finishing a book on gender relations in Iceland in the twelfth and thirteenth centuries. As a result of Sverre Bagge's encouraging response to my initial drafts of the present work, I decided to apply for a Research Fellowship from the Norwegian Council of Science. I was aware of course that being abroad when writing the application and having Icelandic citizenship might limit my chances of success, so needless to say I was overjoyed when, just before Christmas 1993, I received a letter from the Council granting the fellowship. Therefore my deep gratitude must go to Norges forskningråd (the Norwegian Council of Science), for their support of this project, and for having previously given me a one-year student scholarship during my stay in Bergen from 1989 to 1990.

Secondly, my sincere thanks to the University of Oslo, which also partly funded this project. Particular thanks are due to the History Department, which provided my workplace from 1994 to 1997.

Other institutions that have given support to the project are: Arnamagnæanske Samling (the Arnamagnæan Institute) in Copenhagen, Senter for Universitet og Høyskole samarbeid med Frankrige (the Norwegian-French collaboration of Universities), Fondet for Dansk-Norsk Samarbejde (the Danish-Norwegian Collaboration Foundation) and Aarhus Universitets Forskningsfond (Aarhus University Research Foundation). I wish to thank all of them for their support.

I started work on this project under the doctoral program of the University of Oslo in 1994, and worked on the project while also teaching from May 1994 to August 1999, with the exception of nine months maternity leave in 1996. During the year 1998 to 1999 I was also a visiting fellow at the History Department of the University of Tromsø. The last part of this project has been completed at the University of Aarhus, where I became an assistant professor in Danish and European medieval history in August 1999, and later associate professor in 2002. Because of this, it has been possible to extend work on the project to coincide with my teaching, which provides the greatest inspiration for my historical research.

The first empirical research was finished in 2002. Since then I have managed to read through all the material again, and have therefore used more of the latest international literature on the subject. Special thanks go to Bodil Due, leader of the Faculty of Humanities at Aarhus University, for making funding available for one term of leave from teaching in the spring term of 2006, which made it possible to finish the editing of the work. No publications released after 2006-2007 have been used in this study.

I am greatly indebted to my colleagues in the History Departments of Oslo and Aarhus Universities who so warmly welcomed me. There are also many individuals to thank for inspiration, supervision, and assistance. First I wish to thank Arnved Nedkvitne in Oslo, for being the formal supervisor of this project under the doctoral program and for all his support and critical comments. Thanks also to Lars Ivar Hansen for supervision and many stimulating discussions during my stay in Tromsø. To the leader of the doctoral seminar in Oslo, Leif Ahnström, along with Knut Kjeldstadli and many other friends and doctoral fellows at the Faculty of Humanities in Oslo, thanks for providing a wonderful atmosphere and great inspiration. Thanks also to all my students in Oslo, Tromsø and Aarhus for many joyful moments and interesting discussions, and finally to Jill Farleigh Wolfe, Caroline Smith and Mary Waters Lund for their invaluable help in correcting my English.

Without the assistance and support of my Icelandic colleagues and friends, working on Icelandic history would not have been possible. I am enormously grateful to Auður Magnúsdóttir, Árni Daníel Júlíusson, Gunnar F. Guðmundsson, Gunnar Karlsson, Helgi Þorláksson, Lilja

Árnadóttir, Magnús Stefánsson, Mjöll Snæsdóttir, Orri Vésteinsson, Ragnheiður Mósesdóttir, Sveinbjörn Rafnsson, and especially to Hrefna Róbertsdóttir for her sincere and warm friendship. And, last but not least, to my husband Per Ingesman, my warmest thanks for his welcome criticisms and encouragement and for helping with the book's Danish summary. Needless to say, however, I alone am responsible for any errors.

Working on this book has meant that too much time has been spent away from my family. The summer holidays usually spent visiting my mother and sisters in Iceland have grown shorter and shorter. And since their birth my sons have been used to sharing their mother with the discipline of History. The book is therefore dedicated with love to them: Tómas Óskar born in 1991, Rúnar born in 1995 and little Stefán born in 2004.

Agnes S. Arnórsdóttir
Aarhus, December 2009

Contents

Preface 7

Contents 11

CHAPTER 1

Introduction 21

1.1 Historiographical background to this study 23

1.2 Symbols and social relations 29

1.2.1 Bilateral and patrilineal structures of social organization 30

1.2.2 Marriage and inheritance strategies 34

1.3 Property and gender 36

1.4 Interpretation and the content of the chapters 41

CHAPTER 2

Historical and historiographical background 45

2.1 Iceland and its history 45

2.2 Icelandic sources about marriage in the Middle Ages 52

2.2.1 Law codes and other legal documents 53

2.2.2 Marriage contracts: From oral to written tradition 56

2.2.3 Other source material 60

2.3 Problems related to the use of the sources 61

Part I Legal aspects of marriage 63

CHAPTER 3

Consent in canon law and Icelandic marriage legislation 67

3.1 *Consent in canon law: A European background* 67

3.1.1 *Marriage in canon law* 69

3.1.2 *What consequences did the consent theory have for the further development of marriage legislation?* 71

3.1.3 *The two models of marriage* 75

3.2 *Marriage law in twelfth- and thirteenth-century Iceland* 77

3.2.1 *The early influence of canon law in Iceland* 80

3.2.2 *The compromise between the two models of marriage* 86

3.2.2.1 The marriage legislation of Bishop Árni Þorláksson 87

3.2.2.2 Marriage law in *Jónsbók* 94

3.2.2.3 The correction in the *réttarbætur* of the late thirteenth and early fourteenth century 101

3.3 *The wider discursive context of the consent theory in Iceland* 104

3.4 *Conclusion* 109

CHAPTER 4

The regulation of Icelandic marriage 1300-1600 113

4.1 *The definition of legal marriage according to the royal and ecclesiastical authorities* 115

4.1.1 Réttarbætur *from the late thirteenth and early fourteenth centuries* 115

4.1.2 *The bishops' statutes of the fourteenth century* 118

4.2 *Change in marriage regulation in the sixteenth century* 122

4.3 *The era of practical change* 132

4.3.1 *The local courts* 132

4.3.2 *The late fourteenth and early fifteenth centuries* 134

4.3.3 *The role of the bishops after the Reformation* 141

4.4 *Conclusion* 150

CHAPTER 5

The local knowledge of canon law and the internalization of new norms 153

5.1 *Judgement of legal marriage* 154

5.1.1 *Legitimacy and the question of inheritance* 156

5.1.2 *Control of illegitimacy and the question of sin* 160

5.2 *Drawing the lines: Local people's use of the law* 166

5.2.1 *The narrative use of canon law* 167

5.2.2 *Rumor* 176

5.2.3 *The forbidden degrees of marriage* 179

5.3 *Penance, confession and sexual crimes* 195

5.3.1 *The rules about penance for different sins* 196

5.3.2 *Sin no more and the letters of confession* 200

5.3.3 *From sin to crime* 206

5.4 *Conclusion* 212

Part II Ritual aspects of marriage 217

CHAPTER 6

The marriage ritual: The entry into marriage 221

6.1 *Linguistic change in the marriage contract* 222

6.2 *The spoken and written words of marriage* 230

6.1.1 *Formulae* 231

6.2.2 *The witnesses and the role of the priest* 236

6.3 *The form of the written contract* 239

6.4 *Conclusion* 243

CHAPTER 7

Christian influence and change in the form of the written contract 247

7.1 *The earliest evidence of written contracts* 248

7.2 *Property agreements and marriage according to the law of God. The evidence from the marriage contracts in the fifteenth century* 251

7.3 *Financial and religious aspects in the fifteenth and sixteenth century* 256

7.3.1 *The role of the priest* 257

7.3.2 *The clerical entrance into holy matrimony* 260

7.3.3 *Parental control* 264

7.4 *Conclusion* 269

CHAPTER 8

The making of holy bonds and human bonds 271

8.1 *Change in terminology – change in bonding agreements?* 273

8.2 *The sacred marriage* 277

8.2.1 *The bed and the bride* 278

8.2.2 *Virginity and the legal consequences of the "joining of minds"* 283

8.3 *New gender relations – freedom not force?* 286

8.4 *Conclusion* 292

Part III Property aspects of marriage 295

CHAPTER 9

Marital property and marriage strategy 299

9.1 *Regional differences in forming marriage practice* 300

9.2 *Two types of Icelandic marriage contracts:* máli *and* helmingarfélag 303

9.2.1 *From* kvennagiptingar *to marital arrangements* 307

9.2.2 *The different principles of property transfer* 312

9.3 *Property strategies of the aristocracy in the fifteenth and sixteenth centuries* 323

9.4 *Conclusion* 333

CHAPTER 10

Exchange of marriage gifts and the problem of inheritance 337

10.1 *Historical background* 339

10.1.1 *Canon law influence on gift-giving in the twelfth and thirteenth century* 339

10.1.2 *Gift-giving in Iceland during the Late Middle Ages* 346

10.2 *Reciprocal exchange of gifts* 350

10.2.1 *The institution of dowry* 351

10.2.2 *The indirect dowry* 356

10.2.3 *The morning gift and the* bekkjargjöf 361

10.3 *"Legal gifts" and the meaning of the exchange between the spouses* 366

10.4 *Conclusion* 373

CHAPTER 11

Transfer of property and property right 377

11.1 *Marital property and the question of inheritance* 379

11.1.1 *The limitation of the property rights of the husband* 381

11.1.2 *The property rights of the wife* 388

11.1.3 *The rights of the relatives of the wife* 393

11.2 *The consequences of the new marriage practice for property transfer* 397

11.2.1 *The consent of heirs to property transfer* 397

11.2.2 *Adoption and legal gifts as means by which to transfer property* 400

11.2.3 *Preliminary conclusion* 406

11.3 *Patrilineal strategy* 406

11.3.1 *Patrilineal ideology and bilateral inheritance practice* 407

11.3.2 *The influence of the* óðalsréttur *in Icelandic legal thinking* 411

11.3.3 Höfuðból 418

11.4 *Conclusion* 424

CHAPTER 12

Conclusion and discussion 427

12.1 *Conclusion* 428

12.2 *Discussion: Christian influence on property rights and gender relations* 435

Bibliography		443
Unprinted sources		443
Printed primary sources		445
Unpublished theses and papers		447
Secondary sources		448

Appendices		471
Appendix I.	*Marriage contracts 1351 to 1600*	471
Appendix II.	*Contract of* helmingarfélög *1402-1567*	488
Appendix III.	*Marriage gifts*	490
Appendix IV.	*List of Icelandic bishops appointed directly by the Papacy*	501

List of abbreviations	503
Glossary and explanation	505
Danish summary	513
Index of Persons	523
Geographical Index	531

* * * *

List of Tables

Table I.	*Marriage contracts 1300-1600*	59
Table II.	*Marriage dispensations and cases about the forbidden degrees of marriage*	181
Table III.	Máli *and* helmingarfélag *in the Diplomatarium Islandicum*	305
Table IV.	*Morning gifts and gifts of the bench in marriage contracts 1405-1505*	364
Table V.	*The gifts of the bench in marriage contracts 1402-1505*	365
Table VI.	*Gifts given at marriage 1380-1590*	367

List of Figures

Plate section, Part I

Figure 1. A drawing of a slaughtered cow.
Figure 2. Map of land belonging to the powerful families in fourteenth- and fifteen-century Iceland.
Figure 3. *Kaupbréf.*
Figure 4. A Roman church bell.
Figure 5. Late sixteenth-century wedding celebration.
Figure 6. Royal document from 1545.
Figure 7. Judgement on marriage from 1559.
Figure 8. Crucifix from Húsavík.
Figure 9. The seal of Bishop Gissur Einarson.
Figure 10. The seal of the island of Iceland from 1592.
Figure 11. The tradition of *Festaröl.*
Figure 12. Marriage dispensation from 1535.
Figure 13. Map of the property belonging to Vatnsfjarðar-Kristín.
Figure 14. Family tree of the most powerful families in fourteenth- and fifteenth-century Iceland.

Plate section, Part II

Figure 15. Two drunken woman.
Figure 16. Two drunken men.
Figure 17. Marriage contract of Þórður Bessason and Járngerður Gilsdóttir from 1380.
Figure 18. Ring-shaped buckle from fifteenth- or sixteenth-century Iceland.
Figure 19. Silver and gold rings found in Iceland.
Figure 20. Golden ring of medieval type.
Figure 21. Drinking horns from the fourteenth- and fifteenth-century.
Figure 22. The tapestry from Draflastaðir.
Figure 23. Embroidery, silk on linen.
Figure 24. Renaissance-style chest from 1578.

Plate section, Part III

Figure 25. Seal of Vigfús Hólm.
Figure 26. Map showing the property belonging to Guðmundur ríki.

Figure 27. Family tree.
Figure 28. Altar frontal.
Figure 29. The bench of the bride from ca. 1600.
Figure 30. Judgement on the gift of one-fourth.
Figure 31. Seal of Bishop Jón Arason.
Figure 32. Ring-shaped buckle from late Medieval Iceland.
Figure 33. Drawing of a manor.

Note about cover illustrations

The engagement ring, probably from sixteenth-century Iceland, was found at the excavation in Skálholt, 2002-2007. *National Museum of Iceland.* The ring shows the joining of two hands around a heart. Similar ring types were known also in other parts of Europe in the Late Middle Ages and Early Modern times.
For the cover background, see Fig. 17.

Note about Icelandic terms

In the main text, the spelling of Old Icelandic terms has been changed according to modern grammatical rules to make the text more readable. The same applies to names of people and places. Thus *réttarbætr* becomes *réttarbætur*, *mundr* becomes *mundur*, and, for example, the male name of *Guðmundr* is written *Guðmundur* in modern Icelandic.

CHAPTER I

Introduction

The oldest information concerning marriage agreements in Iceland emanates from the late twelfth and early thirteenth century. At that time marriage agreements were made by way of an oral statement, the relatives of the couple having arranged the marriage which was as much an economic agreement as a political one.[1] During the thirteenth and fourteenth centuries, however, marriage came to be something more. The change was not only related to the economic agreement, but also to the marriage rituals, something which, as time went by, also changed the meaning of marriage.

The change was brought about by the Church and its canon law, which had great impact on marriage during this period. Traditionally in a European context there has been a tendency to understand this process of change as a conflict between secular and ecclesiastical ideas. An example can be taken from Georges Duby's famous study of marriage in twelfth-century France. According to him, there were two models of marriage: an ecclesiastical and a lay model.[2] The ecclesiastical model was based on the consent of both spouses, and it criminalized adultery. The lay model on the other hand was based on the consent of the parents, because above all it was an alliance between two families, and it was based on an economic agreement that could be cancelled.

1 This information is to be found in the marriage legislation of the oldest Icelandic law, *Grágás*. The oldest part of it cannot be traced further back than to the early twelfth century. See Agnes S. Arnórsdóttir 1986, pp. 24, 25-26, compare to *Grágás* Ib, pp. 29-75, II, pp. 152-209.

2 Duby 1991a, pp. 1-22.

Duby himself saw this change in medieval marriage as a struggle between the two models of marriage.[3] Here examples from Icelandic court cases from the Late Middle Ages will be used to explain this development from another point of view. Instead of focusing on how laymen did not follow the ecclesiastical model of marriage as soon as it was established on the legal level, I shall ask how marriage actually changed slowly towards the Christian doctrine. This change in marriage practice is related to general change in moral codes and sexual behavior, but here we shall also focus on how the property arrangement became affected by this process of Christianization.[4] The Church's influence will thus be the principal subject of this study, which aims to examine its effects on Icelandic marriage practice and theory. Changes in these areas will be examined by looking at marriage legislation,[5] alongside other documents that provide information on theory and practice in the making of marriage.[6]

The process of change can be divided into three stages. The first stage dates from the time of the episcopacy of Bishop Þorlákur Þórhallson (1178-1193).[7] Þorlákur placed great emphasis on persuading couples to be joined in holy matrimony, and as Auður Magnúsdóttir's study has showed, the Church increasingly influenced the marital arrangements of

3 See for instance Duby 1991a, p. 3, "the conflict between two radically different and antagonistic models – the lay model of marriage, created to safeguard the social order, and the ecclesiastical model, created to safeguard the divine order." His approach on these "competing" models has been criticized for being taken too directly from economic literature. See Helmholz 2004, p. 522, with reference to Herlihy 1987, pp. 3-17, and Brook 1991, pp. 119-43. Another approach on the nature of marriage in the Christian tradition is for instance to be found in Reynolds 1994, p. xviii, "Marriage in the Christian tradition was both sacred and secular", as well as on p. xix, "Christianization did not remove the secular dimension of marriage, and this twofold aspect remained a formative principle throughout the Middle Ages and beyond."

4 Definition of the process of Christianization of marriage is to be found in Reynolds 1994, p. xiv. He argues that: "Christianization was the process by which marriage became differentiated from its non-Christian origins and environment under the influence of Christianity itself. The peoples of the early Church and of the early Middle Ages brought with them into the Church their own, pre-Christian laws and customs of marriage, and to a large extent these laws and customs endured. Insofar as the influence of the Christian faith (that is, of the Christian Scriptures and of specifically Christian beliefs and ideals) caused marriage to become distinguished from the relevant pre-Christian traditions, we may say that marriage had become Christianized."

5 These are mainly: the old collection of laws called *Grágás*, as well as the late thirteenth century legislation of the royal and Church authorities. See the *New Christian law* printed in *NgL*, V, and in *Járnsíða og kristinréttur Árna Þorlákssonar*, pp. 145-90, published 2005, and the law of *Jónsbók* from 1281, published 1904.

6 These sources are mainly charters. The Icelandic charters have been published in 16 volumes. See *DI: Diplomatarium Islandicum*, 1857-1972.

7 See Sveinbjörn Rafnsson 1982, p. 114 and forward.

Icelandic chieftains in the twelfth and thirteenth centuries.[8] The second stage involved changes at the legal level. In the thirteenth century, the marriage legislation changed under the influence of canon law. Documentary evidence of this phenomenon can be found in *Grágás*,[9] the oldest collection of Icelandic laws from the twelfth and early thirteenth centuries, as well as in the legislation of the late thirteenth century. The third stage of development in regard to the formation of marriage might be called the internalization of Christian norms. It is not until the Late Middle Ages that we have enough evidence from surviving sources to understand this last change.[10] Because not much has been written about Icelandic marriage contracts in the Late Middle Ages, this book is going to concentrate mainly on the second and third stage of change.

1.1 Historiographical background to this study

The main part of this study has to do with the source material about marriage in Iceland from the fourteenth to the sixteenth century. It is partly a continuation of my study of kinship and gender in Iceland in the High Middle Ages,[11] with a special focus on change in marriage in the Late Middle Ages. It is a study of continuity as well as change over time, and shares some features with other current research on the history of marriage in other regions of Europe.[12] An example can be taken from Joel F. Harrington's book, *Reordering Marriage and Society in Reformation Germany* (1995), which studies the nature and the origins of sixteenth-century marriage reform, the roots of which are traced from the twelfth

8 Auður G. Magnúsdóttir 1988, pp. 4-12. See especially pp. 11-12, and Auður Magnúsdóttir 2001, pp. 162-71, especially 169-71.

9 There are changes in the marriage laws of *Grágás*, which can be explained by the influence of canon law. See Agnes S. Arnórsdóttir and Thyra Nors 1999, p. 34.

10 As James Brundage has indicated, it is only from the Late Middle Ages that enough court material survives that can inform us about the practical formation of marriage. He states: "We are far better informed about the actual practices of European courts, both secular and ecclesiastical, during the years between 1348 and 1517 than for any earlier period of human history." See Brundage 1990, p. 547.

11 See unpublished thesis Agnes S. Arnórsdóttir 1990. That study was published in a wider context in Agnes S. Arnórsdóttir 1995.

12 One good example of a similar approach can be found in McCarthy 2004. This book on medieval marriage in England, gives an overview of marriage in England in the entire medieval period, and discusses themes such as the importance of consent, as well as property and alliance policy.

century onwards. According to Harrington's study the ecclesiastical authorities sought to ensure a holy, indissoluble, and consensual definition of the conjugal bond. But from the fifteenth century the secular authorities attempted to intervene in the ecclesiastical jurisdiction over marriage.[13] Harrington's work illustrates that change in marriage must be seen as a long-term process.[14] For instance, according to the Icelandic historian Loftur Guttormsson, marriage in nineteenth-century Iceland still kept some traditions from the Middle Ages, e.g. that people did not get married during Lent.[15] At the same time, however, a study of marriage practices of the fourteenth to sixteenth centuries should also be studied in the light of earlier marriage legislation, because changes on the judicial level originated further back, in the late twelfth and early thirteenth centuries.

Internationally, much has been written about family history and the history of marriage as such.[16] Some of this literature provides comparative information and raises questions relevant to this study.[17] Studies exist about marriage according to canon law,[18] about the exchange of marriage,[19] as well as the political and economic importance of mar-

13 Harrington 1995, pp. 103-104.

14 See other studies also, which clearly give valuable information about marriage in a long term perspective, such as Helmholz 1974, and Helmholz 2004, pp. 521-64, see especially on p. 522: "the requirement of solemnization of marriages *in facie ecclesiae* ... took centuries to work their way into popular mores. Roman and Germanic traditions, which had treated questions of marriage formation as private matters, seem almost to have lived on long after the formation of the classical canon law on marriage and its implementation in court practice."

15 Loftur Guttormsson 1992, pp. 160-61, 163. See also Gísli Ágúst Gunnlaugsson, 1988, p. 86-87 about marriage in Iceland 1780-1900.

16 Bibliographical information about marriage is to be found in Sheehan and Murry 1990, pp. 17-39. Regarding earlier works, a valuable introduction to Christian marriage is to be found in Joyce 1933 and a fundamental work on the canon law of marriage is Esmein, 1929-35. The reference work and examination of canon law and marriage, which has proved most useful for this study, is Brundage 1990. An interesting book on the medieval teaching on virginity is Crouzel 1963.

17 As a general background to this study see especially: Helmholz 1974, as well as Helmholz 2004, pp. 519-64, Duby 1984, Goody 1988a and 1988b, Herlihy 1985, Casey 1989, Brooke 1991, Gies 1989, Duby 1991a, Brundage 1990, Bonfield 1992, Molho 1994, Brundage 1995a, Harrington 1995, Sheehan 1996, Witte 1997, Dean & Lowe 1998, Howell 1998, and Pedersen 2000.

18 See for example Brooke 1991, Brundage 1990, Sheehan 1996, and Pedersen 2000. In Helmholz 2004, p. 521, quotation 1, there is detailed information about studies of marriage practice in the English spiritual courts, as well as on p. 526, quotation 18, about the pattern of litigation in other parts of the Western Church. Reynolds 1994 gives detailed information about marriage in the Western Church during the patristic and early medieval period.

19 See Howell 1998.

riage.[20] There are not many studies, however, that aim at explaining the role of the Church in the wider process of social change, related to how canon law influenced both the social organization of family relations, as well as gender relations.[21] In this study therefore, Icelandic sources from the Middle Ages will be used to analyze this change.

As mentioned previously, Georges Duby's studies about marriage in France has been a great source of inspiration for studying family relations in the Middle Ages. In my earlier book I used his work as well as the work of Jack Goody, Christopher Brooke and James Casey.[22] In the present book, I have been inspired by scholars of canon law. Especially James Brundage's book *Law, Sex and Christian Society in Medieval Europe* (1990) has been most useful when discussing the general development of marriage and canon law, as has the work of Richard Helmholz when discussing marriage litigation in court records.[23]

In the European context marriage remained very important for political alliances.[24] Marriage and inheritance strategies are closely related to the political culture of the Late Middle Ages and Early Modern time.[25] Recent reflections on the more traditional way of writing about marriage as an important political institution have forced me to rethink some of the results of my earlier works on twelfth and thirteenth century Iceland. *Marriage in Italy 1300-1650*, edited by Trevor Dean and Kate Lowe (1998), can be mentioned as one of the contributions that challenge current ideas about medieval marriage, and Trevor Dean's own work in that book: "Fathers and daughters: marriage laws and marriage disputes in

20 See for example Duby 1984 and 1991a, Casey 1989. See also the more recent study by Napran [unpublished thesis] 2001.

21 One new exception is Vogt 2005. This study is about the function of kinship in High Medieval Nordic legislation – especially focusing on the relation of canonical legal ideology and peacemaking legislation.

22 See Agnes S. Arnórsdóttir 1995.

23 See Helmholz 1974, as well as 2004. Even if his work is basically about English court cases, and the court system of Iceland and England during Medieval Ages were quite different, his work has much valuable information about the influence of canon law at a court level.

24 See for instance discussion about this in Dean and Lowe 1998, pp. 7-12.

25 A similar approach is found in Rian 1990, pp. 471-72. He argues that the seventeenth-century family strategy in Norway played an important role in the shaping of political life. See also Benadusi 1995, and Nors 1998b and 2000. Their approach is more related to analyzing political stratification than the type or size of the family as such. It is thus a very different approach than we find in the older traditional studies of family history as, for instance, in the studies about the formation of a pre-industrial household system. See for instance in Hajnal 1982, pp. 449-94, which can be traced back to the study of Le Play in 1871, who was the first to make a typology of different types of families.

Bologna and Italy, 1200-1500", has especially been useful for gaining a better understanding of the process of mutual and parental consent of marriage in the Late Middle Ages.[26]

I have also indirectly been inspired by the works of French scholars of historical anthropology.[27] The work of these scholars especially that of Christiane Klapisch-Zuber based mainly on empirical studies from France and Italy, has been used as a methodological framework on how to analyze the exchange of marriage gifts, and different forms of making contracts. The Icelandic and Norse sources are, however, more similar to the marriage tradition of England and Germany.[28] The literature used, as well as my comparative approach, will be discussed further in relation to each chapter of the book. It has especially been important to focus on the studies which have been published lately about the canon law influence on marriage.

There is no doubt that the history of medieval marriage has been a flourishing field in Western European scholarship, and ongoing research in this field is dynamic. But among historians in the Nordic countries there has not been the same interest in the history of marriage in the Middle Ages, and no comparative studies have been done on the history of marriage in particular.[29] The relationship between the Nordic

26 See chapter 3 below on consent in marriage, which is the basis for further discussion in other parts of the book on viewing parental consent not only as an old tradition of Pre-Christian marriage, but actually as a strong tradition in late medieval Christian culture. See also Laiou 1993, and Agnes S. Arnórsdóttir 2006.

27 See, for instance, André Burguière, Christiane Klapisch-Zuber and Martine Segalen *Histoire de la famille*, which they edited with Francoise Zonabend, Paris 1986. In 1995 I was privileged to obtain a short visiting scholarship to the Maison des Sciences de l'Homme in order to obtain a better knowledge of the work of these people. See also Klapisch-Zuber 1990, pp. 285-311, and Segalen 1996, pp. 13-137.

28 See Erickson 2005, Maurer 1855-1856, and 1878, Lehman 1882, Hertzberg 1889.

29 There are no books about the history of marriage in the Middle Ages in the Nordic countries. There are a few short articles about some aspects of the marriage tradition: see Frank 1973, Jochens 1986b. For books on marriage in medieval Sweden see Carlsson 1965, Patersson 1973 and Korpiola 2004 (now published in a new edition from 2009). For books on the family: see Gaunt 1983, and for books on women and family and inheritance policy: see Sawyer 1998 and 2000, Hansen 2000, and Kleven 2001. Books on gender relations and sexuality: see Agnes S. Arnórsdóttir 1995, Holtan 1996, and Bandlien 2001, 2005. For a book about concubines and married women see Auður Magnúsdóttir 2001. There are articles about concubinage and marriage such as Auður Magnúsdóttir 1988 and 1996, and Nors 1987, 1996, Damsholt 1999, for articles about the influence of canon law in the Nordic countries: see Agnes S. Arnórsdóttir 1999, Korpiola 1999a and 1999b, for articles about property management and inheritance see: Andersen 1981, Græsdal 2000, Lahtinen 2000, Ormøy 2000. Part of Jacobsen's 1995 book is about married women in Danish towns: see pp. 145-202. A book about the history of women, family and property law in Denmark also discusses marriage agreements in the Middle Ages, see Dübeck 2003, pp. 15-171.

development and the general development has not been studied thoroughly enough, neither in general European history nor in Nordic history. Regional differences have not been fully explored,[30] and most of the studies that exist are related to a special region. This is a problem therefore, because we cannot translate patterns from one region to another, because of immense historical and regional differences in making marriage contracts.[31] When scholars write about European marriage or family patterns, as Jack Goody does in his book,[32] their work is often based on the idea that, historically/culturally, the whole of Europe is similar to the central and western part of the continent, thereby resulting in source material from the Nordic countries not being included in these studies of so-called 'Northern Europe'.

No book has been written on marriage in medieval Iceland as a subject in its own right.[33] Neither has there been any study of all the surviving marriage contracts. Icelandic historians of the medieval period have not used source material from the Late Middle Ages to analyze systematically the changes in social structures.[34] There have been only partial efforts to explain the political strategies of Iceland's ruling families

30 Recently there has been a stronger emphasis on studying marriage in the Nordic countries as part of broader European culture. See Agnes S. Arnórsdóttir and Nors 1999, compare to Agnes S. Arnórsdóttir 2001a, as well as Hansen 2000, pp. 9-10. In the book *Mariage et sexualité au Moyen Age* 2000, papers on marriage in Scandinavia are also among the contributions, see especially the articles by Jean-Marie Maillefer and Jenny Jochens. This tendency can be found also in the studies of gender and religion in a European perspective in Børresen & Cabibbo & Specht 2001.

31 On the general differences in making marriage contracts, see the preface in Reynolds and Witte 2007, p. ix "the relationship between written marriage contracts and the contract of marriage *per se* varied considerably over time and across cultures."

32 Even though Jack Goody in the beginning of his study talks about Europe both in the meaning of Western Europe, North-West Europe; and even England, his empirical discussion is mainly based on Europe in the traditional meaning of the term as Western Europe. See Goody 1988b, p. 1, and chapter two about the two sides of the Mediterranean, and chapter three about the change in the German lands.

33 Gunnar F. Guðmundsson has written short chapters about marriage in Iceland in the Middle Ages, see Gunnar F. Guðmundsson 2000, p. 257 ff, and about marriage after the reformation see Björn Björnsson 1989.

34 An exception, however, is Árni Daníel Júlíusson's work. See his PhD thesis, published in 1996 as well as his articles from 1990, 1998a, and 1998b. More studies exist for the High Middle Ages; see for example Orri Vésteinsson 2000, whose study concerns the period 1100 to 1300.

through an examination of their financial affairs.[35] Even though there are no standard works on marriage contracts, these studies of Late Medieval history have been useful for my work.[36] Especially the works of Magnús Már Lárusson and Hrefna Róbertsdóttir have inspired me to further study the strategy of the ruling families of the Late Middle Ages. Lárusson has studied inheritance practices concerning manors in the Late Middle Ages.[37] His work will be used as a basis for further studying how the Christianization of marriage might have influenced the inheritance practice, especially the question of how these manors were transferred from one generation to the next. Róbertsdóttir's short article on the marriage contract of *helmingafélag*[38] from 1986 still represents the only effort to analyze marriage contracts from both a political and social point of view, as well as from the standpoint of women's history.[39] There has thus been a need to further study all the marriage contracts emanating from the late medieval Iceland, and it has been especially interesting to examine more fully which influence canon law actually did have on the rules about jointly owned property in marriage.

Because of this lack of existing research it has been necessary for this study to use almost all relevant Icelandic source material relating to marriage litigation and marriage practice. To some degree also, my case study needed to be related to the wider "marriage pattern" of Western Europe. Therefore my study of canon law's influence on marriage regulation in Iceland during the Middle Ages includes a comparative approach. As Robert Bartlett has written in *The Making of Europe* (1994), Latin Christianity was one of the sharing elements in the culture of the Middle Ages.[40] The discussion here must therefore be understood in relation to

35 The works on this period that have had special relevance for my study are: Arnór Sigurjónsson 1967, and 1973, pp. 74-115, and 1975. Björn Lárusson 1961, pp. 34-64, and 1967. Einar Bjarnason 1960-63, pp. 371-411, and 1971, pp. 286-92, and 1969-1972. Jón Jóhannesson 1956-58. Magnús Már Lárusson 1971, pp. 40-90. Magnús Stefánsson 1975, pp. 57-144, and 1978, pp. 111-260, and 2000. Ólafur Lárusson 1934, pp. 49-88. Páll Vídalín 1854. See also the several papers and work by the legal historian Einar Arnórsson published from 1912-55.

36 Magnús Stefánsson's study of the *Staðir*, is of great importance for the understanding of the property rights of the Church during the Late Middle Ages. See Magnús Stefánsson 2000.

37 Magnús Már Lárusson 1971, p. 40-90, compare to Magnús Már Lárusson 1961, pp. 707-710.

38 *Helmingarfélag* was jointly owned property in marriage, where each spouse owned 50% of the property.

39 Hrefna Róbertsdóttir 1986.

40 Bartlett 1994, p. 269.

the question of how the different regions of Latin Christianity shared the same culture. At every ecclesiastical court in Western Europe marriage cases that were similar in nature were discussed and judged. Canon law culture was, however, not a homogeneous culture.[41] Even if each region became influenced by the same set of norms, sexual behavior was not the same. That is why, under a comparative point of view, it is interesting to do regional studies on the canon law culture of Europe.

To be able to explore how different the canon law culture was, we need to examine the relation between the reception of canon law and the marital culture of each region, and for the purpose of this study this will be done by employing historical anthropology and gender studies as points of departure.

1.2 Symbols and social relations

My main concern is to study the influence of canon law on marriage in Iceland during the High and, especially, the Late Middle Ages. The aim is to discuss how change in the definition of legal marriage was related to the marriage policy of the ruling elite, as well as how change in the symbolic meaning of marriage affected the wider understanding of marriage. Here it is of special relevance to study how the Church influenced the meaning of gender. Anthropological and historical writing on gender has approached the subject from two perspectives: gender as a symbolic construct, and gender as a complex set of social relations.[42] I will argue that through the Christian doctrine, which saw marriage as a sacrament, new gender symbols were created, where the pureness of the virgin was accorded an exceptional value. The focus will be on the relation between these new symbols and the older gender understanding, with its remnants of pre-Christian values. Secondly, this study will discuss how the introduction of Christianity influenced the social relations of couples and their wider kin-groups, as reflected in the marriage contracts concerning property. It has been stated that two main principles existed

41 Agnes S. Arnórsdóttir 2001a, p. 174, compare to Bartlett 1994, p. 269.

42 Barnard 2000, pp. 146-47. A similar approach is found in the writings of historians of gender. See Scott 1996, p. 152, Wiesner-Hanks 2001, p. 2.

in Europe during the Late Middle Ages concerning property transfer through marriage. In northern Europe, especially England, the north of Germany and the north of France, property policy was based on a joint principle, aiming at the maintenance of the household after the death of either the husband or the wife. The other principle, which was more common in the south of Europe, especially in the Mediterranean, was more kin-based. It meant that property should be transferred via either the female or male lines as soon as one of the spouses died, especially if they did not have children.[43]

1.2.1 Bilateral and patrilineal structures of social organization

In this book I examine the change in the definition of legal marriage in relation to the older existing marriage and inheritance strategies[44] of the ruling elite. My thesis is that principles for organizing property transfer came into effect with the Christian doctrine of marriage. But to be able to study the Christian influence it is necessary to define what kind of kinship structure provided the foundations for the general social structure, in Europe as well as in the Nordic countries.

Even if kinship (as a blood relationship), seems to be a product more of nature than culture, in anthropological terms kinship refers to a different way of organizing social bonds.[45] The term 'kinship system' refers thus to the organization of social relations. At the same time a biological process such as reproduction is not only a physical act of sexual intercourse, but also connected to the cultural system of kinship and marriage that unites and orders the relationship of individuals

43 Howell 1998, pp. 31, 198-99.

44 On the term "strategy", see Bonfield and Poos 1988, p. 403, note 2: "The term 'strategy' has been widely used as a means of conceptualizing individual and group behavior. We hear of strategies of heirship: fertility strategies, marriage strategies, etc."

45 The social anthropologist David M. Schneider has underlined the importance of understanding the term "kinship" primarily as an analytic term. However, the idea of pure social kinship according to him "could never be completely freed of its defining feature, human sexual reproduction or the folk theory of it". He asserts the importance of being aware of the dual meaning of the concept. The definition of kinship as genealogy "presupposes that kinship derives from biological processes – reproduction, birth, and sexual intercourse – which yield indissoluble relations, that is, relation of *being*, not *doing*." See Schneider 1992, pp. vii, 111, 131.

to groups.[46] Thus, in a society different forms of transferring property cannot be understood without also examining the complex relationship between various cultural and biological factors.

Those who have studied the kinship system of the Nordic countries in the Middle Ages agree that the system was one of bilateral kindred with a weak tendency towards patrilineal organization. What is characteristic of a society which is organized in this way is that both women and men receive inheritance from their parents, and in those cases where women were not inheritors, they were given their share of property as a direct dowry from their parents.[47] In a society that is patrilineally organized, the property is more often transmitted strictly between generations within the same family. This is called a patrimonial inheritance system. On the other hand the bilateral inheritance system is based on transmitting property between family groups inside the same generation, which happen through marriage. And very often it involves gifts being given from both the family of the bride and of the bridegroom.[48] The difference between the two systems is evident. In the patrimonial system the transmission of property is determined from the time a person is born. The bilateral system is more flexible, and it is more common in societies where marriage serves strategic goals, since it can give political, economical, and military advantage.[49]

Marriage strategies in Icelandic society are to be understood in the bilateral context. It means that upon marriage property was transferred from both the families of the bride and the bridegroom. This equal weight given to maternal and paternal kinship in Iceland, and generally in the Scandinavian countries, can have prevented the development of the so-called *lineage*, of the kind Georges Duby identified in France.[50] But a *lineage* is a descent group with a focus on the transmission of

46 Duby 1994, p. 3.

47 Dowry means the wealth given to the bride by her family at marriage. This amount was often under the guardianship of her husband during their marriage life.

48 Vestergaard 1988, pp. 190-91.

49 The legal historian William Ian Miller has underlined the importance of bilateral kinship by tracing relationships through links of both sexes in the medieval society of Iceland. It means that the kin group was never a closed corporation of determinate membership as it depended on the "ego" to recruit kin for different purposes. See Miller 1990, p. 155.

50 Sawyer and Sawyer 1993, p. 185.

patrimony, which ensures greater control of the line of descent.[51] It is, however, important to underline that the bilateral structure of twelfth and thirteenth century Iceland did not exclude the ideology about the solidarity of the patrilineal kindred. The stronger kinship ties could easily be based on a bilateral kinship system where the emphasis on "ego" is very strong. An example of this can be taken from the studies of the American historian Tamara K. Hareven on the relations between the family and the wider kin-group in Northern Europe during the Middle Ages. She states that "rather than being isolated, nuclear households" the families were "embedded in kinship ties outside their confines."[52] This means that individuals or small groups of family members from the bilateral kindred made alliances with other individuals from other families. Thus the family was at the centre of social interaction. These social ties could take different forms, such as marriage or other types of family relationships.[53] This should be understood in such a way that, even if the structure was thus basically bilateral, it was possible to find ways and means to organize the property transfer according to a patrilineal ideology.

According to my own research on the kinship structure of twelfth- and thirteenth-century Iceland, the inheritance rules were bilaterally organized with a patrilineal tendency.[54] My present study argues that this weak tendency towards patrilineal organization can be understand as a reaction to the canon law influence on marriage legislation.[55] One of the main conclusions of my earlier work was that the bilateral system (through which property could be transferred via both the female and male lines), did not lead to concentration of property, because both women and men could receive property by way of inheritance or

51 See Casey 1989, p. 195.

52 Hareven 1991, pp. 95-124, compare to 108-109, see especially footnote number 40 and pp. 110-111.

53 Hareven 1991, p. 108. She mentions Richards Smith's study of Suffolk in the thirteenth century as an example, see Smith 1979.

54 Agnes S. Arnórsdóttir 1990, pp. 81-82, compare to Agnes S. Arnórsdóttir 1995, chapter 4. However, when focusing on the transmission of status (such as the right to be chieftain) kinship was more patrilineal. On tendencies toward primogeniture, see Jochens 1986a, pp. 35-50, modified again in Agnes S. Arnórsdóttir 1995, pp. 79-85.

55 Compare to Lars Ivar Hansen's analyses of the canon law influence on the Norwegian provincial laws. See Hansen 1996, p. 151.

marriage gifts. As a consequence of the bilateral kinship structure, other types of social relationships, such as friendships, could take on great importance.[56] However, this will not be the focus of the present study, which is instead concerned with the question of the relationships within the kinship structure and the different ways of making marriage agreements involving property. Kinship organization in a society is based on sets of norms, roles, values, groups and categories. Therefore change in the definition of what constituted a legal marriage must have affected the social relations. One of the main questions here is thus how the changes in the marriage rules influenced the kinship structure.

In his book, *The Development of the Family in Europe*, first published in 1983, Jack Goody discussed the influence of the Church on the kinship structure and the family. The Church's role in defining marriage as a sacred union was an important factor in changing the nature of kinship structures of the medieval period. According to Goody this led to looser kinship ties.[57] He has been criticized for giving a too simplistic explanation of the relationship between the Church and the aristocracy, the social group to whom the new rules had the most profound consequences.[58] His response to this critique has partly been to argue that "the brotherhood of the Church was encouraged in preference to that of the family, and brotherhood meant economic interest as well as sentiment and theology."[59] Thus the Church attempted to let its own "spiritual kinship" with its wider social bonds, substitute the so called "natural kinship", at least according to Goody. Although several of Goody's explanations of the Church's strategy in property matters are questionable, it is reasonable to accept his arguments concerning the connection between the policy of the Church and change in the making of marriage contracts. The strength of his work is that it gives an idea of *how* the

56 See Jón Viðar Sigurðsson 1989, pp. 33-34. See also Jón Viðar Sigurðsson 1995b, pp. 311-30, and 1998, pp. 107-16.

57 Goody 1988b, pp. 24-26. See also his final conclusion on p. 221: "For the Church to grow and survive it had to accumulate property, which meant acquiring control over the way it was passed from one generation to the next. Since the distribution of property between generations is related to patterns of marriage and the legitimization of children, the Church had to gain authority over these so that it could influence the strategies of heirship."

58 Compare to Brooke 1991, pp. 134-36.

59 Goody 1996, p. 172.

Church managed to influence the everyday life of medieval people. But the weakness of his theory is related both to the motive behind the efforts of the Church, as well as to the question of which consequences it had.

I agree with Goody that the Church's definition of holy matrimony, and the consequences of this in guaranteeing the legitimacy of children, did affect the social structure. As we have just seen, Goody argued that since the distribution of property between generations was related to the pattern of marriage and the legitimacy of children, the Church had to gain authority over these factors so that it could influence strategies of inheritance.[60] My thesis is, however, that the Church did not necessarily loosen kinship ties, but rather as time passed strengthened the awareness of kinship solidarity. This was the consequence of the canon law influence on marriage legislation, especially the strengthening role of the husband over his wife's belongings, which in the Late Middle Ages resulted in stronger awareness of the consent of the closest heir to all the property transfer.[61] On this basis inheritance and marriage strategies can be seen as part of the political strategy of ruling families,[62] and clearly these strategies became influenced by the canon law rules on marriage. The remaining question is *how* it happened. Let us look at some studies which have treated this question.

1.2.2 Marriage and inheritance strategies

The term "strategy" is used here to conceptualize the kinship principles underlying the different ways of making marriage agreements. In this context both inheritance strategies and marriage strategies are important.[63] This implies that because canon law influenced marriage regulations, the institutions that the aristocracy used to regulate these strategies also changed. These were marriage gifts and different forms of marriage contracts. The Norwegian historian Lars Ivar Hansen has suggested using

60 Goody 1988b, p. 221.
61 This problem is discussed in chapter 11.1 and 11.2.
62 Compare to Benadusi 1995.
63 Compare Bonfield and Poos 1988, p. 403.

the theory of kinship systems in order to understand different strategies for social reproduction. He uses Pierre Bourdieu's concept of the "social field",[64] and proposes that one can see the inheritance system as a social field.[65] In this field you find different actors, different social groups and positions, and different institutions that struggle to put their different inheritance policies into action. Marriage strategy is one part of this field. Hansen proposes that we use the different principles of kinship – in the context of this study the bilateral and the patrilineal principles – as a dynamic tool for explaining change in both the property system and in social relations more generally. This method may help to solve the traditional actor/structure controversy in social analysis.[66]

What do these strategies reveal? Other studies have underlined different aspects of this interaction between family stratification and inheritance policy. The Danish historian Thyra Nors' investigation of the marriage policy of the Danish royal house as described in the chronicler Saxo's *Gesta Danorum* from around 1220, shows that Saxo wrote in favor of the newly established Christian monarchic order of succession in Denmark. She states that, "the political conflicts of the twelfth century as described by Saxo were in fact internal family conflicts."[67] In an article on Tuscany in the early modern period, Giovanna Benadusi argued that changes in the matrimonial and hereditary strategies of elite families were at the same time a product of and a catalyst for larger socio-economic and political developments.[68] The "social field" here is thus not only the inheritance strategy of the ruling elite, but also the meaning of this strategy both for themselves and for the whole society. That is probably why Benadusi thinks that this approach also provides a means of analyzing how the elite perceived itself.[69] Thus analyzing marriage as a transaction involving both social and economic resources will provide opportunities to see how these resources were distributed with reference to both gender and kinship.

64 Hansen 1996, pp. 105-107, 151. "Field" here means historically constituted areas of activity with their specific institutions and their own laws of function.

65 Ibid., p. 103-104. In Hansen 2005 there is a historiographical overview over the latest trends in the studies of the kinship in the old Scandinavian law. See pp. 170-79.

66 Compare to Bourdieu 1995, pp. 72-95.

67 Nors 1998a, p. 33.

68 Benadusi 1995, p. 160.

69 Ibid., p. 162.

Goody has been criticized for his functionalistic approach to the role of the Church in changing the kinship structure of medieval Europe. Thus it is necessary to study further what effect the Church had on marriage and inheritance strategies among the land owning elites. One of the few scholars who have worked on this problem is the Danish historian Michael Gelting. He argues that canon-law culture actually did strengthen the solidarity of the kin during the High Middle Ages, something which can be seen in the provincial laws of the Nordic countries.[70] Partly I am following in his footsteps when arguing that changes in marriage practice occurred because of canon law, and that it should be obvious that those changes could not have occurred without some effect on the wider organization of family relations as well as kinship organization. Therefore, to be able to explain how canon law influenced the wider social structure, a gender approach will be of special importance.

1.3 Property and gender

In a study of marriage regulations it is clear that a gender-based approach is of special importance. Here this approach will be used to study which change the Church regulations of sexuality inside and outside marriage had on gender relations. It will also have great value for understanding how the Christian marriage doctrine influenced change in the understanding of property rights. What characterizes institutions such as marriage, for instance, that regulate sexuality in a given society, depends on the aims of the collective strategies of the social group involved.[71] One of those strategies in the Middle Ages was related to the question of inheritance rules and property rights as mentioned previously. David Warren Sabean's definition of the concept of property suggests how it is possible to study social relations empirically. He states:[72]

70 See for instance Gelting 1999, pp. 118-19, as well as Gelting 2003. This is studied in more detail in Vogt 2005.

71 Bourdieu 1995, p. 58.

72 Sabean 1990, p. 184.

> Property is nothing apart from the set of relations of which it is composed. That is to say, it is the complex totality of rights, claims, duties and obligations between people with regard to things. Although we loosely speak of things or objects as property, what makes them so is not the relationship between themselves and persons, but that between persons.

In this study property has important value for the way social relations were based on affinity through marriage. The focus here, however, will be more on different ways of *thinking* about how landed property should be transferred, than actually how property came to be transferred. Those relations were not only made by owning together property as a married couple did, but they were also made by claiming right to it after the death of the spouses.

For the most part this study will concentrate on those who owned landed property. The reason for this is simple: these are the people concerning whom information has survived. It has survived in documents kept precisely because they would be useful in property disputes. As will be argued, the definition of what constituted a legal marriage had great significance for both the inheritance practice, as well as the exchange of marriage gifts. I want to look at the relationship between the definition of legal marriage and the transaction of property through marriage.[73] This means, however, that I am more interested in the change of meaning in the understanding of marriage, than in analyzing how much property people actually owned or transferred.[74] My study gives no information on how much land was exchanged through marriage, but it analyses how the understanding of making a property contract became influenced by the sacred meaning of marriage.[75]

The concept of gender is not understood as a natural category, but

73 On this method to analyze the meaning of property, see Sabean 1990, p. 18 and forward. In the second volume of his village study of Neckerhausen, from 1998, he rethinks the categories of earlier studies of social historians, both in relation to gender and from the point of view of cultural studies.

74 Though I am mostly interested in landed property (because it was through landed transactions that the strongest social reciprocity bindings were formed inside the group of ruling families), it does not mean that other types of property were not important factors for social bounding and for economic means. See Jón Jóhannesson 1958, pp. 144-45; and Olaus Magnus 1555, who describes how much butter the monastery of Helgafell owned.

75 This discussion is mainly to be found in chapter 3 on the sacramental character of marriage, and in all of part III of this book, which cover property matters.

rather as a social construct based on the physical differences of the sexes. The concept will thus be used as a theoretical concept.[76] As such, gender can be understood as one of many bases for social power relations.[77] The law codes of Medieval Europe for instance, clearly seem to have favored men's property rights over women's. But these relations need to be studied better in the light of women's economic rights. According to the English historian Amy Louise Erickson, the second wave of women's history in the later twentieth century in England concentrated on the representation of women and ideology, while the first wave, in the early twentieth century, had focused on women's political, legal and economic position. The most frequently discussed component of women's "status" was therefore ideology – that is, how people (most men and some women) thought women ought to behave.[78] Here the difference between law and practice in a society becomes very important, and some authors have argued that because of legal limitations women in Pre-industrial Europe used different types of strategies to those of men in order to achieve their goals.[79] It is, however, not the primary aim of this book to study these different strategies, although the way in which property rights in the Middle Ages were influenced by gender relations is one of its central concerns.

76 The American historian Joan Scott, with her poststructuralist project, has been the main practitioners of this approach; see Scott 1988, pp. 28-50, and Scott 1996, pp. 152-80. (See also Scott's revision of her theories in the second edition of her book *Gender and Politics of History*, from 1999). In a Scandinavian context a similar discussion is to been found in Nilsen 1992, pp. 7-34 see especially pp. 7, 12, 25. A debate in *Sign*, vol. 15, no. 4, 1990, between two of the leading historians in women's history in the USA, Joan Scott and Linda Gordon, pp. 848-60, gives a good view about the two main positions of women's history or gender history at that time.

77 Blom 1990, p. 425, compare to Dauphin 1986.

78 Erickson 1995, pp. 8-11.

79 This argumentation can be found in Amy Louise Erickson's introduction to the book *Women and Property in Early Modern England*, see Erickson 1995, pp. 3-20, especially pp. 17-20. This approach is also to be found in the writing of Inger Dübeck in relation to Danish history, see for instance in Dübeck 2005, p. 127: "it is clear that women *did* act economically outside the household; for instance they conducted trade and they made wills. Therefore, the early nineteenth-century interpretation of women as having been barred from public authority to act since time immemorial is clearly erroneous, but it fits in with the new way of conceptualizing "economy" in liberal society." See also Hilde Sandvik's arguments on this approach related to the women's juridical situation in eighteenth century Norway. See also Sandvik 1992, pp. 174-75: "Ved systematisk å studere rettspraksis trer et annet bilde av kvinnenes rettslige stilling fram, enn det bildet de normative lovene og den normative kommentarlitteraturen gir. Fram kommer også bildet av en økonomisk aktiv kvinnerolle i et fattig før-romantisk samfunn. 'Umyndighed' er et utilstrekkelig begrep for å beskrive disse kvinnenes rettlige stilling bl.a. fordi det vi i dag assosierer med en umyndig person ikke er dekkende for deres situasjon." See also Sandvik 2005, pp. 111-26.

It is possible to say that in the Nordic countries medieval women's history became inspired by a gender approach later than the women's history of the nineteenth and twentieth centuries did.[80] The focus on making women visible in medieval history has, however, been important in a series of anthologies from historians dealing with women's history of the Middle Ages published during the 1980s.[81] These studies are based on the viewpoint that the roles of women and men have throughout history been complementary. At the same time the tradition of studying medieval history from a female or gender point of view has, however, often presented women as passive historical actors.[82] This and similar approaches to the complementary role of the sexes have been criticized for not seeing the "real" dominance of men in gender relations.[83] However, on the other hand, also theories about the patriarchy have been criticized for not being based on the fact that the gender relations are changeable over time.[84] To avoid taking an anachronistic approach to gender relations, it is thus important to look behind the representation of the restricted position of women often presented in some literature and law codes.

To be able to see women as part of a wider gender structure I have used established theories of gender relations.[85] I find it challenging to try to combine the various traditions of seeing women as a complementary

80 Øye 1990, pp. 435-54.

81 See the anthologies edited by Gunneng & Birgit Strand 1981, and Silja Aðalsteinsdóttir & Helgi Þorláksson 1983, as well as Andersen 1985 and Gunneng 1989.

82 See this tradition in European context: Ennen 1989, p. 23. She writes: "Precisely because women had less direct influence on their environment and their fate than men, it is essential to discuss their changing legal situation, their social position, their everyday economic context, in terms of temporal change and regional differences."

83 Nielsen 1992, p. 12, compare to Dauphin 1986, pp. 271-93. See also the debate in Sweden in Anderson and Ågren 1996, Anderson 1997, and Sjöberg 1997.

84 Natvig Aas 1993, pp. 27-44.

85 Apart from Joan Scott's work on gender, the work of the Swedish historian Yvonne Hirdman has especially been useful for understanding how important the gender approach is for the study of marriage. She developed a theory about the system of gender, which she calls *genussystem*. Her theory is a general one that can explain why the structure of gender is stabilized over time. The systems of gender are an order, what provide the starting point for all human organizations: social, economical and political. This structure is built on two principles: that the categories of male and female should not be mixed, and secondly that man is higher in the hierarchy than women, and that the male category is the norm. See Hirdman 1988, pp. 49-63, especially p. 51. Both Lena Sommerstadt, and Christina Carlson Wetterberg have criticized Hirdman's theory for not being able to explain changes, from the actor's point of view in particular. See Sommerstadt 1994, p. 108, and Wetterberg 1992. Compare to response in Hirdman 1993.

part of male history in the Middle Ages, as well as to use the theories of gender as a framework for empirical studies. By doing so I wish to argue that the differences between male and female are performed through social practices that need to be studied historically over long periods of time and on a regional basis.[86] My approach has some similarities with Judith Butler's theory about gender as performative, in the meaning that we are all constantly performing our gender in a way that produces our gender identity.[87]

In my studies this performance will be traced by examining how Christian ideas about gender relations and gender performance affected ideas about property transfer through marriage.[88] According to Amy Louise Erickson's research on early modern England, patterns of property distribution can form a basis for generalizations about social relations. Erickson argues that:

> Property offers an excellent means of comparing the theoretical ideal, in the form of the law, with actual practice, in terms of ordinary women's ownership. While gender has been expertly analyzed in legal philosophy, tracing the exclusion of women from concepts of "the individual" since the later seventeenth century, no connection has been made between the theoretical individual and real individuals making property decisions in their daily lives. Even in social history, the prescriptive evidence of the law is still taken largely as reflective.[89]

One does not need to do much research in the Icelandic sources from the Late Medieval and Early Modern period to draw a similar conclusion.[90] My work should be understood in this context. There are thus three levels of gender approach in this work. First, I shall study the role of the Church in creating new ideas and meaning on gender relations. Second, the study will deal with the way change in gender relations formed the

86 So even if we assume as a starting point that man is higher in the political hierarchy than women during the medieval ages, it is only through empirical studies of the gender relation that we can say anything about the social formation of those relations.

87 Butler 1999, pp. xiv-xv, and p. 33.

88 This can especially be seen here in the discussion about how wives became formal partners in selling and buying property during the Late Middle Ages. See pp. 381 ff.

89 Erickson 1995, p. 4.

90 See for instance the discussion of the difference between the inheritance rules of *Grágás* and the information that *Sturlunga saga* gives on this issue in Agnes S. Arnórsdóttir 1995, p. 98.

wider organization of family relations.[91] And third, the discussion is about how the medieval property right was profoundly affected by gender related topics and relations: relations which were much more complicated than the laws about the limitation of women's property rights describe.

1.4 Interpretation and the content of the chapters

There are three main strands in my analysis in the book. The first, which can be found in chapter three, four and five, is the legal aspect of marriage presented through a discussion of legal regulation and the relationship between the changes in marriage regulation and marriage strategies. The second approach of this book, found in chapter six, seven and eight, is the ritual aspect of marriage, which will investigate the role of ritual for entry into marriage and the making of the marriage contract. The form of the contracts will be analyzed to discern how change in making the contract occurred. Changes in the form of contracts could also express change in the meaning of marriage. The third strand of my approach, found in chapters nine, ten and eleven, is about the property aspect of marriage. Questions will be asked concerning, for example, how the more general exchange of marriage gifts affected the inheritance practice. What relationship was there between the rights to own and dispose of property, and where was the line drawn between the legal and illegal transfer of property through marriage?

All three approaches have their roots in different kinds of interpretations. The aim of the first is to describe the public discourse on marriage, influenced by the Church, the royal authority and the Icelandic elite. The second perspective is based on a symbolic analysis, which aims to identify and explain mechanisms of change. Both the words and actions in the formulae for marriage will be analyzed. The last part should not be seen as separate from the symbolic analysis in the second section, or the presentation of legal aspects in the first part. The last approach raises the possibility of observing the molding power of the

91 Here I am not discussing kinship structure as the main framework for gender relations, but I am trying to go behind the organization of kinship and see the formation of gender relation as something that changed the way kinship was constructed.

law and the actors behind it, as well as the close relationship between marriage symbols and property strategy. Of the three key moments in life: birth, death and marriage, it is only the last that can occur in compliance with the wishes of those involved.[92] For these reasons the study of marriage contracts can also be a study of the property strategy of the ruling elite.

Before examining the three aspects mentioned above, I present a brief history of Iceland in the Middle Ages in chapter 2, as well as the sources used in my study.

Chapter 3 describes changes in the definition of marriage according to canon law. It focuses on the issue of who should consent to and arrange marriages, and what consequences the consent theory had on the regulation of marriage laws and practice.

Chapter 4 will consider what constituted a legitimate marriage according to the legal regulations of the Late Middle Ages, especially the law amendments called *réttarbœtur* and the bishops' statutes of the fourteenth century, as well as changes in this legislation after the Reformation. The chapter will provide an overview of marriage legislation from 1280 to 1600.

In chapter 5 court cases will be studied which give information about the acceptance of new Christian norms concerning marriage and sexuality, an acceptance which did not dismiss the old marriage custom, but was simply added to them. It is also concerned with the way in which local authorities defined legal marriage in the courts, as well as how the laws and courts were used to ensure legal marriage. It will consider the regulation of sexuality within and outside marriage, and the question of who attempted to control sexual behavior and how was it controlled.

Chapter 6 deals with marriage ritual and the way in which the Church involved itself in the ritual of the wedding ceremony and in marriage contracts, thereby changing their meaning. This issue is related to the question of how change in social relations occurred over a longer period.

In chapter 7 all the marriage contracts from the late fourteenth till the end of the sixteenth century are studied in light of Christian influence,

92 Loftur Guttormsson 1992, p. 157.

thereafter chapter 8 investigates the way in which secular rituals slowly became more sacred in character, and how this affected the content of the marriage contract and gender identity.

The regional differences in forming Icelandic marriage practice are studied in chapter 9, which will examine the different types of contracts, as well as the way in which they were related to the property strategies of the local aristocracy.

Chapter 10 concerns the gifts given when a marriage contract was concluded. It will consider general changes in the custom of marriage gifts in the Middle Ages and the influence of canon law in this area. Change in Icelandic gift-giving practice will be discussed, as well as the issue of whether there was any change in the type of gifts given under different types of marriage contracts.

In chapter 11 my examination will focus on the principles behind the transfer of property in marriage and in relation to inheritance. It will consider the different means of transferring property, especially through the institutions of adoption and legal gifts. This issue is related to the way in which the new definition of marriage affected the kinship structure and the patrimonial inheritance rules.

My study of Icelandic marriage contracts and inheritance practice is not meant to be an isolated study of marriage ritual in the more private sense of the word. Consequently the last chapter of the book, chapter 12 sums up the discussion in the context of political developments. What relationship, therefore, can we find between Christian marriage doctrine and the Icelandic society of the Middle Ages? The answer to this question is related to the greater issue of the similarities and differences in the national and regional Christian cultures of late medieval Europe.

CHAPTER 2

Historical and historiographical background

To be able to understand this work in its wider context, some information is needed about the history of Iceland in the Middle Ages. Therefore I shall first present the main historical facts from the earliest settlement to the end of the sixteenth century, and secondly, I shall discuss in more detail the sources used for this study and especially give an overview of how these sources will be used for the different parts of the analysis.

2.1 *Iceland and its history*

Iceland was first populated as late as the Viking Age, and for centuries the Icelandic society existed without any central power after Christianity had brought the art of writing on parchment to the country. Therefore Iceland has produced literature about a society that was without a monarch or any central authority.[1] From around 930 a general assembly, *Alþingi*, convened at Þingvellir. With this establishment the Icelanders developed both a legislative and a judiciary system. They did not, however, create any centralized mechanism for enforcing the law.

Around the year 1000, the assembly of *Alþingi* decided that Iceland should become Christian. The first Icelandic bishop was ordained in the year of 1056, and in 1096 the Icelanders agreed to pay tithe to the Church. There were two bishoprics in Iceland, the most important in Skálholt, the other in Hólar. They were under the Norwegian

1 Gunnar Karlsson 2000a, pp. 4-5. On the development on the earliest Icelandic constitution, see Gunnar Karlsson 2000b, pp. 20-27.

archbishop in Niðarós from 1153, when the archiepiscopal seat was established.

The constitution of Iceland was similar to other Norse governing systems of the Viking settlements. What was unique to Iceland was that Christianization and a consolidation of royal power did not go hand in hand.[2] "Iceland thus offers a rare example of a society that tried to preserve law and order without a ruler."[3] In 1262-64 Iceland came under Norwegian dominance by entering into a union with Norway. By the *Gamli Sáttmáli*, the "Old Covenant", the country became a tributary province in the Norwegian monarchy. Thereby the Icelanders accepted the authority of the Norwegian king.

Political development in the Late Middle Ages in Iceland followed general trends in the Nordic countries. Thus when the kingdom of Norway entered a union with Denmark in 1380, Iceland also came under the Danish king. Two terrible plague epidemics devastated Iceland in 1402-04 and 1494-95, and the country's ecological system gradually deteriorated under a colder climate and an over-exploitation of the vegetation, leading to depletion of the birch woods and soil erosion. Jón Egilsson, in his *Biskupa annálar*, gives a description of an alarming situation after the plague in 1402-04. People were lying dead everywhere: women were found dead in their kitchens, alongside the cows they had been milking, or on the road carrying their milk churns.[4]

Animal husbandry was the foundation of the Icelandic economy. In the early fifteenth century English fishermen began to frequent Icelandic waters – this has been called the beginning of the "English Age."

2 The study of Orri Vésteinsson has, however, provided valuable information about how important the Christianization became for the later political development. See Orri Vésteinsson 2000, especially p. 238 and forward.

3 Gunnar Karlsson 2000b, p. 21. In Gunnar Karlsson 2004, chapter V. 4, on pp. 429-58 (p. 485 in the English summary), the author argues that it is likely that the absence of this common executive authority in Iceland encouraged interest in stories of personal disputes and ways to resolve them. Discussions about similar matters can also be found in Axel Kristinsson 2003, and Byock 2001, pp. 343-44, especially p. 344. Byock argues that the patronage of medieval books often had political as well as aesthetic goals. He argues further that "*Stórbændr* used the family sagas to verify the local history of their families and districts. In this way the family sagas served as tools for laying historical claims to local leadership." This tradition of using texts as tools for political leadership has some relevance for understanding how the local leaders of the Late Middle Ages used written property documents, such as marriage contracts, for similar purposes.

4 Here after Björn Þorsteinsson and Guðrún Ása Grímsdóttir 1989, p. 70.

During the sixteenth century Iceland became closer tied to the Danish monarchy, and in the middle of the century, the Icelanders converted to Lutheranism under pressure from the royal government in Copenhagen. The Lutheran Reformation was completed in Iceland in November 1550 with the execution of the last Catholic bishop, Jón Arason, in Hólar. This enhanced the authority of the Danish king in Iceland, because from now on the Church was a state institution, under the direct control of the king and his officials. Furthermore, the confiscation of the property of the Icelandic monasteries made the king the single largest landowner in the country.[5] This strengthened the royal authority in Iceland, but clearly royal influence had already at the end of the Commonwealth period (930-1262/64) started to influence the social structure of the ruling families in Iceland. One of Orri Vésteinsson's conclusions about social change in Iceland between 1000 and 1300 is that the few local families who survived the upheavals of the thirteenth century became the basis for the ruling elite of the Late Middle Ages.[6] The established families disappeared almost from the political map around 1300.

This can be seen in a *réttarbót* (law amendment) of 1302, where the aristocrats legitimated their new status by claiming that they descended from the ruling elite of the Commonwealth period. Genealogies from around 1300 also demonstrate this.[7] This new aristocracy, which emerged only partly from the previous elite, often after two, three or four generations, had new names, which generally came from the names of their farms. The identity of the elite of the Late Middle Ages was thus very much related to the land on which they lived. In contrast to the European nobilities which had both power and privilege, the position of the Icelandic aristocracy was very different. Landed property was one of its main sources of power. This can be illustrated by mentioning that almost all measurements of wealth were based on the value of land and of livestock. Even if those units did not remain totally stable

5 This general description of the development of the Icelandic society is to be found in Guðmundur Hálfdánarson 1997.

6 Orri Vésteinsson 2000, pp. 238-39.

7 Jón Viðar Sigurðsson 1995a, p. 160, compare to DI III, pp. 5-8 [c. 1290], pp. 10-13 [c. 1310], DI I, pp. 501-506 [1230].

during the Middle Ages,[8] they continued to be the most common value to measure wealth.[9] What was also special with this Icelandic society, was that at the end of the Middle Ages, in the years 1540-50, it is assumed that 53% of the land was private property, while the Church owned 45%, and the Crown only 2%.[10] The position of the Icelandic landowners was based on their ability to acquire landed property: they had few privileges and as such were in a very different position from that of the continental feudal landlords whose power was based to a much greater degree on those in more privileged positions. The most powerful member of the Icelandic elite, was in many ways in the same position as any other farmer in the country, the most important difference being that the elite ruled over the other or owned more landed property than him. This position of the Icelandic ruling elite can help us to understand why we have so many property documents preserved from the Late Middle Ages in Iceland.

At the end of the sixteenth century an interesting view on the historical development in Iceland can be found in a description of the land, called *Qualiscunque descriptio Islandiae.* It is stated here that only a few families at this time owned all the principal properties in the country. The richest men from these families could own as much as twenty farms each as well as the main manors they usually lived on themselves. According to this description the situation had been different in the fourteenth century. Then the elite had been formed largely by obtaining offices from the king. They had been "honored as noble men with their own coats of arms" because they were related to the mightiest families of the Norwegian aristocracy. These families still existed at the end of the sixteenth century according to author of the *Qualiscunque descriptio Islandiae*, but they no longer had their leading role because they had lost their property to families of lower status.[11]

8 See Helgi Þorláksson 1991, pp. 523-26.

9 The normal measure of land was called *hundrað.* One hundred was the same as 120 ells, and that was equal to 60 metres of *vaðmál,* which was equal to one cow, which was equal to six sheep, also named *kúgildi,* cow's value, which was the same as 240 fish.

10 Björn Lárusson 1967, p. 122. On change in the value of landed property and the Church ownership of property see Magnús Már Lárusson 1962c, pp. 671-77, Þorkell Jóhannesson 1965, pp. 34-35 and Björn Þorsteinsson and Sigurður Líndal 1978, p. 79.

11 *Íslandslýsing* 1971, pp. 88-89.

Some historical truth lies behind this description in *Qualiscunque descriptio Islandiae.* After Iceland was united with Norway, the Icelanders demanded that officials in Iceland should be Icelandic, in order to safeguard the existence of the aristocracy.[12] The claim that officials should be of Icelandic origin had its roots in the Old Convention, *Gamli sáttmáli* of 1262-4[13] and was repeated again in the *réttarbætur* of the early fourteenth century.[14] The Icelanders insisted that all royal officers should be Icelandic and the demands were presented as a condition for accepting the king of Norway.[15] According to King Hákon V's *réttarbót* from 1308, a person who wanted an office during his reign needed to have a declaration from the *sýslumaður*, the district commissioner, concerning his financial status.[16] Those who became royal officers were, thus, mostly from distinguished Icelandic families and were financially stable.[17]

In this way the Icelandic elite of the Late Middle Ages strongly constructed their identity as the leading families of the country through ownership of landed property. Secondly, ancestry was obviously used to justify their status, as the genealogical evidence proves and, thirdly, it was true that a royal office was also important for legitimating one's position of power during the thirteenth and fourteenth century. Later, in the fifteenth century, the royal administration in Iceland got stronger,[18] and by the end of the sixteenth century the Icelanders had stopped demanding that the highest royal officer should be Icelandic.[19] This meant lesser opportunities for local Icelandic leaders to obtain the highest royal

12 Jón Jóhannesson 1958, p. 301 compare to: DI I, p. 676: "Item at jslendzkir se logmenn og hirdstiorar og suo syslumenn ä landi voru af þeirra ætt sem at fornu hafa godordin upp gefit." See also DI II, p. 497, DI XI, p. 2, from ca. 1320 it says: "Og ad jslendsker sieu laugmenn og syslumenn. og aller valldzsmenn ä landinu". See also more generally the discussion in Gunnar Karlsson 1999, pp. 141-78, about national identity in a non-national period of Icelandic history.

13 DI I, p. 635: "Item at islenskir se logmenn [ok syslumenn] aa landi voro af þeirre ætt sem at fornv hafa godordin upp gefit."

14 DI II, pp. 333-36, and DI XI, pp. 2-3. See also Jón Jóhannesson 1958, p. 83.

15 Compare to DI XI, p. 2, *Réttarbót* ca. 1320. On the royal officer in Iceland before 1400, see also Axel Kristinsson 1998b, pp. 113-152.

16 This rule is dated to 7 July 1308, and is to be found in NgL III, number 25, pp. 74-81.

17 Jón Jóhannesson 1958, pp. 49-58.Jón Viðar Sigurðsson 1995, p. 160. Legitimating one's position by claiming descent from the ruling families of the past has also been seen as one of the motives for the writing of *Landnámabók* and some of the *Íslendingasögur*. See Sveinbjörn Rafnsson 1974 and Durrenberger 1992.

18 An example can be taken from the *Langaréttarbót* of 1450 made by the Danish King Christian I. See DI V, pp. 62-69; see specially p. 63 on the definition of the king's role.

19 Helgi Þorláksson 2003, p. 29.

positions in Iceland. Thus, it seems that the political climate had changed in relation to acquiring power from royal authorities, while claiming property rights to the wealthiest manors in Iceland continued to be the most important political strategy of the aristocracy.[20] This was the historical background behind the description in *Qualiscunque descriptio Islandiae* about how the "old nobility" of Iceland had lost its status to a new ruling elite.[21]

These changes can be traced back to the fifteenth century where land became concentrated in fewer hands. It was a century of general demographic instability, not only with the two above-mentioned epidemics, but also with two great volcanic eruptions taking place.[22] No specific study of the social consequences of the plague on family structure has been undertaken for Iceland,[23] although there have been some studies of how the plague came to Iceland and discussions about the demographic consequences of it.[24] The high mortality levels during the plague meant that all landed property passed into the hands of a few people, and in some cases one person could inherit almost all his/her kinsfolk's property, resulting in wealth being concentrated in a much smaller number of hands than before.[25]

Factors other than demographical change clearly affected the situation, as well as marriage strategy especially. The principles governing inheritance and property devolution became an important issue. Social

20 Compare to Björn Þorsteinsson 1956, p. 5.

21 See also Axel Kristinsson 1998a, pp. 70-82, about the ruling elite of the thirteenth and fourteenth century.

22 Björn Þorsteinsson and Guðrún Ása Grímsdóttir 1989, pp. 70-71.

23 The Black Death brought great changes in social structure throughout Europe, as Frances and Joseph Gies have underlined. See Gies 1989, p. 234: "From one end of Europe to the other, the Black Death, often in combination with other factors, powerfully influenced the family, its size and shape, economic basis, social conditions, and inter – and intra – family relations in a variety of ways, some already determined, some yet to be discovered."

24 Þorkell Jóhannesson was first to write in 1928 an article about the Blach Death 1402-1404. See reprinted version in Þorkell Jóhannesson 1965, pp. 68-87. Árni Daníel Júlísson has studied change in the economic and social structure after the Black Death 1402, and 1495, and Loftur Guttormsson has written about change in the marriage structure in the Early Modern period. See Árni Daníel Júlíusson 1990. Loftur Guttormsson 1992. Gunnar Karlsson and Helgi Skúli Kjartansson, wrote in 1994 an article where they argued that the Medieval Plague in Iceland is an example of a plague causing several epidemics without being spread by rat fleas. In 1996 Jón Ólafur Ísberg argued, however, that the plague in Iceland was a bubonic plague and the bearers of the plague were rat fleas. This debate continued in Gunnar Karlsson 1997, and Jón Ólafur Ísberg 1998. See also in English, Gunnar Karlsson 1996, pp. 263-84.

25 No statistical information exists from Iceland until the seventeenth century. Around 1700, fifteen people owned 12.6% of all the landed property in Iceland. See Magnús Már Lárusson 1962c, p. 673.

ties were reinforced by the transmission of wealth, by inheritance, gifts, selling and buying, renting, marrying and so on. Families with sons and daughters to give in marriage tried to obtain the most advantageous terms possible.[26] The most powerful families managed to acquire great quantities of landed property.[27] According to Hrefna Róbertsdóttir the richest families used the marriage contract of *helmingarfélag* that is jointly-owned property in marriage, to bring as much property as possible to their new households.[28] Thus, after the plague the Church and a small number of wealthy families acquired most of the available land. The Church benefited because many people donated their belongings to ecclesiastical institutions, in the hope of gaining salvation for their souls during difficult times.[29]

However, not only internal factors like marriage strategy and demographical change can explain how the new ruling elite came to power. As mentioned before, in the early fifteenth century English fishermen and merchants, started to come to Iceland,[30] something which the Icelandic elite soon used to its own benefit. This development was strengthened by increasing German interest in the Icelandic fish banks at the end of the fifteenth century. Change in the export and trading culture meant that the coastal manors became more profitable than before. The period 1412 to 1490 was one of great change in property values and ownership patterns.[31] This economic growth was mainly found in the area of Vestfirðir because the later plague of 1494-95 never reached this part of the country, while the situation was very severe in the rural farming areas in the north and east of Iceland.[32] In general the fifteenth century saw great changes in the structure of Icelandic society. New commercial relations were established, especially with England. New families came to

26 Jón Guðmundsson 1902, p. 709. According to the seventeenth century writer Jón Guðmundsson, property that became available after the Black Death was quickly concentrated in a few hands.

27 Magnús Már Lárusson 1962c, pp. 671-77; Þorkell Jóhannesson 1965, pp. 34-35; Björn Þorsteinsson and Sigurður Líndal 1978, p. 79.

28 Hrefna Róbertsdóttir 1986, p. 33, in which she mentions that many of those families who made a contract of *helmingarfélag* were related.

29 Jón Jóhannesson 1958, p. 156.

30 Björn Þorsteinsson 1970, p. 31 and forward.

31 Jón Jóhannesson 1958, pp. 174-75.

32 *Íslenskur söguatlas* I, pp. 134-35.

prominence after the plague, increasingly basing their wealth and power on manors near the coast, rather than inland manors as the aristocratic families previously had done.[33] During the earlier Commonwealth period (930-1262/64), the mightiest chieftains had lived in the agricultural hinterland areas, in Haukadalur in Árnessýsla, Oddi in Rangárvellir, and Svínafell in Öræfi. In the Late Middle Ages the coastal manors of Strönd in Selvogur, Bjarnanes in Hornafjörður, Hóll in Bolungavík, Vatnsfjörður in Ísafjarðardjúp, Reykhólar in Reykjanes and Skarð in Skarðsströnd, were the homes of the ruling elite, (see Figure 2). Only some few of these manors, such as Vatnsfjörður and Skarð, had previously been important.

Iceland's small population, calculated to have been around 40,000-60,000, and its wealth of documents and written sources from the Middle Ages make it an ideal setting for a case study of medieval marriage, particularly for a study of how family and gender relations changed over time. But a case study of Icelandic marriage contracts cannot be understood without an assessment of the special character of Icelandic society described above. Though highly literate, Icelandic society nevertheless remained decentralized: it had no towns, and a royal administration that was far away. This is important to bear in mind when considering the question of the representation of the sources in this book, as well as the comparative European approach. The next section will give further information about the main character of the source material used in this study.

2.2 *Icelandic sources about marriage in the Middle Ages*

Written marriage contracts, as well as the legal regulation of marriage, are the main sources for this study, but because most of the Icelandic sagas were written during the thirteenth and fourteenth centuries they can be used as sources when it is relevant.[34] Information about both the

33 See Björn Þorsteinsson 1956, p. 4. According to Þorkell Jóhannesson the price of stockfish rose by about 33% between 1350 and 1400, and by 71% in the fifteenth century. See Þorkell Jóhannesson 1950, pp. 188-94.

34 The sagas of Bishop Lárentíus and Bishop Árni are especially relevant, as well as the sagas of the Icelanders that were written in the late thirteenth and fourteenth centuries. See *Laurentius saga biskups* 1969, and *Árna saga biskups* 1972. For more details, see below section 2.2.3.

period of the Icelandic settlement, as well as the Commonwealth period (930-1262/64), is to be found in the contemporary sagas of the twelfth and thirteenth century, as well as in the oldest law codes. Great changes occurred in the legal system in Iceland in the thirteenth century. These changes were related to changes in the political structure of the country which in the year 1262/64 had become part of the Norwegian kingdom. My study uses source material that is mainly based on legal regulations and charters concerning marriage after Iceland had become a province under Norwegian, and later Danish, rule: transactions such as debts, sales, marriage contracts, and gifts of property were all recorded in writing.[35]

2.2.1 *Law codes and other legal documents*

The law code of the Commonwealth, called *Grágás,* formulated rules of behavior for a society with a weak central authority. *Grágás* contained rules, which provided answers to individual problems; thus it was casuistic in its nature. According to the law the *lögsögumaður,* the lawspeaker, announced which laws would be deemed correct in the country. The nature of these laws was thus to a large extent based on customary law. However, because *Grágás* was a collection, it also contained many rules that had their origin in the contemporary Church laws of the eleventh and twelfth centuries.[36]

In 1275 *New Christian Law* was accepted in Iceland, and through this, canon law gained a more formal status in Iceland than before. This was very much the work of Bishop Árni Þorláksson, who became bishop of Skálholt in 1269,[37] and he worked hard to make people accept the canon law rules of marriage. The thirteenth century's law regulations were thus both strongly related to the changes in the ecclesiastical as well as the political structure of the country. Shortly after Iceland had become part of the Norwegian kingdom, the king started working on a compilation of the Norwegian law. This affected the making of new legislation for the

35 Björn Þorsteinsson and Guðrún Ása Grímsdóttir 1989, p. 61, see also Björn Þorsteinsson and Sigurður Líndal 1978, p. 28 ff.

36 Sveinbjörn Rafnsson 1990, p. 131. Agnes S. Arnórsdóttir and Nors 1999, pp. 33-35.

37 Sigurður Líndal 1976a, p. 498.

Icelanders.[38] In 1281 a new law was issued for Iceland called *Jónsbók*.[39] This law code, as well as the corrections of the law called *réttarbætur* (law amendments) of 1294,[40] 1305,[41] 1306[42] and 1314,[43] are our main sources for Icelandic secular law for the next four hundred years.

The royal authorities saw Iceland as a special province in legal matters. The law of the Norwegian King Magnús *lagabætir* (Law-Reformer) served as a model for the formation of *Jónsbók*,[44] but the law was also founded on the earlier law of *Járnsíða* (a law code for Iceland dating from 1270 that was used for a very short time),[45] as well as on *Grágás*, the earlier law of the Icelandic Commonwealth. However, after law amendments were undertaken at the end of the thirteenth and the beginning of the fourteenth century to correct some of the laws in *Jónsbók*, few formal changes were made by the royal authority. *Jónsbók* was thus still the law code of the Icelanders in 1600. Although different copies of the law reflect that some changes occurred in the legislation during the Late Middle Ages,[46] these changes did not happen because of formal decisions by royal authority. Changes in the legislation were rather the result of some judicial case decisions, which gained the status of law codes. Or that some elements were taken from certain Norwegian or Danish laws and used in Icelandic judgments. Even to the present day some of the rules from *Jónsbók* are law in Iceland.[47] This law was, to a higher degree than *Grágás*, a law code containing general rules about behavior. It also reflected the establishment

38 Sigurður Líndal, 1982, pp. 182-95.

39 *Jónsbók og réttarbætr*, 1904.

40 Ibid., pp. 281-89, *réttarbætur* for Iceland, given by King Eirikur Magnússon.

41 Ibid., pp. 289-92, the first *réttarbót* for Iceland, given by King Hákon Magnússon.

42 DI II, pp. 347-49, *réttarbót* of King Hákon about marriage agreement of joint possession. This was a Norwegian law amendment about the joint possessions of spouses, but was also referred to and used in Iceland. Compare to DI II, p. 348.

43 *Jónsbók og réttarbætr*, pp. 293-99, the second *réttarbót* for Iceland, given by King Hákon Magnússon in 1314, compare a part of the Norwegian *Retterbød* 2 May 1313, NgL III, pp. 99-102.

44 When King Magnús was working on the compilation of the Norwegian law the archbishop in Niðarós Jón rauði protested. He wanted the Church to gain jurisdiction over its own affairs. The king was only allowed to rewrite the secular part of the law. See Jón Jóhannesson 1958, pp. 16, 20-21. The new law code *Jónsbók* got its name from the lawman Jón Einarsson (d. 1306). The original version is lost, but over 200 copies have survived from before the Reformation.

45 *Járnsíða eður Hákonarbók*, 1847. See also NgL I, pp. 259-300, and NgL V, pp. 13-15.

46 See Már Jónsson 2001, p. 375. He mentions that over 300 manuscripts of *Jónsbók* exist, including also copies from the Early Modern time.

47 Einar Laxness 1995, vol II, pp. 28-30.

of the Church as a key power in Late Medieval Iceland,[48] as well as the growing role of the Norwegian king and his representatives in Iceland. *Jónsbók* was thus supported by an executive power, and as such represented a more centralized rule than that which had produced *Grágás.*

The original Icelandic documents preserved from the Middle Ages number approximately two thousand, the oldest of which are written on parchment while the more recent ones are on paper. Icelandic original documents from the period before 1450 have been published in the *Islandske Originaldiplomer.*[49] Icelandic charters and other written documents increased in number after 1400. The documents older than 1570 are all published in the *Diplomatarium Islandicum* (DI) I-XVI.[50] Only some of the documents after 1570 have been published in the *Alþingisbækur Íslands.*[51] A number of unpublished charters are used in this study; they date mainly from the period 1570 to 1600, and have been registered in the *Arnamagnæan Institute* in Copenhagen.[52]

All the marriage contracts that survive from the Middle Ages are published in the *Diplomatarium Islandicum.* The surviving marriage contracts are both preserved in original versions,[53] and in later copies.[54] *Diplomatarium Islandicum* contains also many property contracts, called *kaupbréf,* which concern the transfer of landed property in general.[55] Both the existence of *kaupbréf* and *kaupmálabréf* can be traced back to a legal rule in *Jónsbók,* stating that it was obligatory to make this kind of agreement if one bought property for the value of six hundred or more.[56]

48 Orri Vésteinsson 2000, p. 83. Vésteinsson says, for instance, that the tithe law should be interpreted in this way.

49 IO: *Islandske Originaldiplomer indtil 1450,* Copenhagen 1963. There original charters from before 1450 number 352.

50 DI: *Diplomatarium Islandicum,* Copenhagen and Reykjavík 1857-1972.

51 Compare to Einar G. Pétursson 1997, pp. 26-29, especially p. 27.

52 See especially Am. dipl. isl. fasc: LXV, 2 – LXX, 31. This material includes both original documents as well as copies made by Árni Magnússon. These charters were registered in 1982 and 1994 by Jóhannes Þorsteinsson, and again in 1997 by Ragnheiður Mósesdóttir.

53 For instance DI VI, pp. 547-49.

54 For instance DI VI, pp. 660-61, which is originally from 1489 but was written on a copy of the manuscript of *Jónsbók* in the year 1600. It is the marriage contract of Sigurður Þorleifsson and Kristín Finnbogadóttir from 24 June 1489.

55 See for example DI III, p. 649 from 1399.

56 Magnús Már Lárusson 1962c, pp. 671-77, especially 675; compare to *Jónsbók,* p. 222. He states that the reason for this was the existence of many strict rules about making the written contract: Compare also to *Grágás,* Ib, pp. 80, II, p. 418 and *Jónsbók,* pp. 221-22. See also Figure 3.

These property contracts will be used to analyze changes in the making of marriage agreements in Late Medieval Iceland. The contracts reflect the marriage strategies of the leading Icelandic families, and provide information about changes in the ownership rights of spouses. They will also be used to study changes in the ritual associated with marriage, and its symbolic meaning.

2.2.2 *Marriage contracts: From oral to written tradition*

The law code of *Grágás* and the sagas record the making of oral marriage contracts. These contracts included information about property transfer. In the twelfth and thirteenth centuries, property rights were defined legally in *Grágás*, but it was not always easy to prove one's right to the land in question.[57] This problem of verifying oral testimony in the law courts was common during the medieval period, as Richard Helmholz has shown in his study about English marriage litigation.[58] When the tradition of making written contracts was established, these contracts were thus commonly used as proof of property rights. The use of all kinds of written documents increased in Iceland from the late fourteenth century onwards.[59] The oldest surviving written marriage contracts date from that time.

From the fourteenth century onwards the royal and ecclesiastic authorities increasingly used records in their administration, and written documents became important evidence in all forms of legal disputes. The ruling families that had previously recorded their rights in written

57 The Icelandic historian Sveinbjörn Rafnsson assumed this could have been one of the reasons behind the writing of the Book of Settlement, *Landnámabók*. He argues for the idea that *Landnámabók* was written because of the need of the thirteenth-century elite to define their inheritance rights to land. This is why the genealogical evidence from colonial times was known and later written down. See Sveinbjörn Rafnsson 1974 and further in Sveinbjörn Rafnsson 2001, p. 10. And the social anthropologist E. Paul Durrenberger argues that this explains why many of the sagas of the Icelanders were in written form, such as *Njáls saga, Egils saga, Gísla saga Súrssonar, Eyrbyggja saga* and *Laxdæla saga*. Durrenberger 1992, pp. 5-7, 14-15, 22-24. It would be a functionalistic explanation to assume that this was the only reason for the writing of the sagas. Writing in the vernacular in other European countries probably stimulated such writing in Iceland also, compare to Guðrún Nordal, Sverrir Tómasson, Vésteinn Ólason 1992, p. 309.

58 Helmholz 2004, pp. 529-30. There he discusses the problem of oral testimony for obtaining right information about impediments to marriage for instance.

59 Sveinbjörn Rafnsson 1990, pp. 2, 15. Compare to Orri Vésteinsson 1994.

genealogies gained a new political weapon. The use of more formal documentation provided new and better proof of land-ownership rights.[60]

The transition from oral tradition to written documents in Iceland did not happen overnight, and the oral tradition lived on alongside the written one.[61] Ownership rights could, for instance, be claimed by calling on the memory of the oldest people or by reference to written genealogies.[62] Written documents became more and more common, however, as evidence in all forms of disputes. When using these documents as historical sources, it is important to note that many of the preserved documents from the late medieval period emanate from the same group of property owners. The absence of a strong common executive authority in Iceland seems to have encouraged interest in documents about personal disputes and property rights. Written documents were commonly used as evidence to verify ownership rights to landed property. Such late medieval legal documentation and interest in written testimony about property matters did not happen in isolation from the production of more literate manuscripts. It has, for instance, been argued that there was a clear connection between the writings of the monastery of Helgafell in Snæfellsnes and the most powerful families that owned the wealthiest manors in Skarð in Skarðströnd, Reykhólar, Vatnsfjörður and generally in other parts of Breiðafjörður, and in the district of Vestfirðir.[63] It is clear that the local leaders of the Late Middle Ages used written property documents, such as marriage contracts, for strategical purposes, and this can explain why so many documents related to marriage disputes have been preserved.[64] This is important to bear in mind before we start to analyze the marriage contracts.

60 Sveinbjörn Rafnsson 1974, p. 109 ff.

61 It is clear from written documents that ownership rights could also be proved orally. The oldest extant document about property transfer contains such information. See DI III, p. 9. It is a document dated 23 June 1309 concerning boundary definitions testified by old men. Another document about boundary definitions from 1354 mentions both the boundary and the purchase of property. See DI III, pp. 54-55. It is about a man who bought landed property from a woman. Afterwards the people who had made the agreement rode together to the piece of land, and the oldest men that were there explained what the boundary definition of the land was.

62 DI III, pp. 5-8, the genealogy from 1290, *Ættartala Hauks lögmanns Erlendssonar og konu hans Steinunnar*, pp. 10-13 and another genealogy from 1310, *Pétur Jónsson and Þorleifur ens haga Eyvindarson.*

63 Vésteinn Ólason 1993, p. 16. See also Figure 2, map of the most powerful families of the Late Middle Ages.

64 Compare to the discussion here on p. 46 in note 3, about the relationship between local leadership and writing.

My study is concerned with surviving marriage contracts that were made during the period of major changes in Icelandic marriage legislation. It starts by focusing on the change following the *New Christian law* of 1275 and the new law of *Jónsbók* from 1281, and ends with the Marriage law of King Frederik II from 1587.[65] To be able to study short-term change after the legislation of 1587, contracts up to 1600 are included.[66]

Almost all existing contracts provide information about landed property as well as other wealth. Legally two main types of marriage contracts during the Late Middle Ages were defined: contracts made by separate ownership rights of the wife, called *máli*, or contracts of jointly-owned property of the spouses, called either *hjónafélag* or *helmingafélag*. The first type of *félag* was a financial agreement where the wife owned a third part of the property, but in *helmingarfélag* husband and wife each owned a half share of their belongings. The contracts can tell us who brought property into a marriage and provide information about the portion that each family could expect to receive in inheritance after the death of the couple if there were no offspring. Thus, they are a very important source material, although they do not provide the same information as, for instance, the marriage registers of priests from the late eighteenth and early nineteenth centuries.[67]

65 A register of surviving marriage contracts and other charters concerning marriage in DI, as well as in unpublished charters from the period 1570-1600 can be found in appendix I.

66 Many contracts are extant from the Early Modern period. The late sixteenth century tradition of making marriage contracts continued into the seventeenth century and after. Analysis of those marriage contracts should be a subject of another study. They have partly been examined by Loftur Guttormsson, but his study is more concerned with the contracts of the eighteenth century than the seventeenth. When I was working on the unpublished contracts from 1570-1600, I did some registration also of the contracts from the seventeenth century. See for instance: AM dipl.isl.fasc. LXI, 7 from 1619, contract of Jón Gissurarson and Þóra Ólafsdóttir. AM dipl.isl.fasc. LXI, 9 from 1629, contract of Magnús Gissurarson and Þórkatla Snæbjarnardóttir. AM dipl.isl.fasc. LXI, 17 from 1629, contract of Snorri Hákonarson and Þórkatla Bjarnadóttir. AM dipl.isl.fasc. LXII, 6 copies from 1657 of the contract of Bjarni Snorrason and Ólöf Guðmundsdóttir, and a letter concerning the inheritance of Guðmundur Þorleifsson the father of Ólöf. AM dipl.isl.fasc. LXX, 31 from 1648-49, contract of Gísli Magnússon (Björnsson) and Þuríður Þorleifsdóttir (Magnússon) (1) contract and (2) witness to the contract. AM dipl.isl.fasc. LXXVI, 61 from 1674, copy of the contract of Ásbjörn Guðmundsson and Guðrún Ormsdóttir.

67 The oldest Church register of marriage from the late seventeenth century is to be found in the National Archives of Iceland (Þjsks: Þjóðskjalasafn Íslands), called *Prestþjónustubækur* where the *Prestþjónustubók Reykholts, Borg, 1664-1788*, is the oldest one. It was not common, however, to register marriage until the late eighteenth and early nineteenth century, as the *Ministerialbók fyrir Reykjavíkurdómkirkju (Prestþjónustubók), 1816-1838*, as well as *Sóknarmanntöl: Húsvitjunarbækur*, illustrate.

Table I	Marriage contracts 1300-1600[68]
1301-1350	0
1351-1400	5
1401-1450	18
1451-1500	39
1501-1550	66
1551-1600	65
	Total: 193

Sources: See Appendix I

The total number of contracts registered is 193. This number includes both contracts, letters of witnesses concerning contracts and, in some cases, summaries of judgements or declarations about contracts. Table I shows how many contracts can be found from each fifty-year period.

Certain patterns emerge from the surviving documents. One of these is that the making of oral marriage contracts probably became less common after written documentation came to be favored.[69] The contracts involved people who owned property, mainly the ruling elite. They vary in form and should be understood primarily as non-standardized documents that were drawn up by the families involved and kept in their family archives. These contracts reflect the first stage in the process of a shift from oral to written marriage contracts, as there was normally a person related either to the royal or the ecclesiastical administration who informally authorized the contract, either by writing it or by serving as a member of the group of witnesses.

The contracts, as well as other charters about marriage matters, are used as the primary source material in all three parts of this study. The first and second part also uses information about the older oral contract, while the written contracts are used more in the second and third part. In the second part, they are used to give valuable information about the

68 There is reason to believe that more contracts exist from this last period of the sixteenth century, because few of the charters after 1570 have been published, compare to footnotes 65-66.

69 The quantity of documents from the earliest period compared to the latest period indicates this.

development of the marriage ritual, such as changes in the meaning of the marriage formulae. The written contracts are the main source for the last part of the book, covering property strategy.

2.2.3 Other source material

Information on the situation in the early thirteenth century is based to a great extent on my own research on *Sturlunga saga* and *Grágás*. The Icelandic sagas, especially the Sagas of the Icelanders, *Íslendinga sögur*, mainly written in the thirteenth and fourteenth century are used as a supplement to the sources of the *Diplomatarium Islandicum* in places where it has special relevance. This applies also to the *Biskupa sögur*. There are two main bishops' sagas that are important to this study: *Laurentius saga biskups* [70] and *Árna saga biskups*.[71] The sagas of the bishops make it possible to cover the period from the middle of the thirteenth century to the period from which more information is available from charters.[72] Information from chronicles that were written in the sixteenth and seventeenth centuries is also valuable to this study,[73] even if they are mainly written and preserved in more recent manuscripts.[74] Some sources from medieval Norway and Denmark will be used to make general comparisons.[75] Statutes both from the archbishop of Niðarós and the bishops of Skálholt and Hólar have also been studied. After the Reformation, sources relating to the new Protestant religion were produced. Many kinds of written sources have also survived from the last part of the sixteenth century. One of these is the before-mentioned

70 *Laurentius saga biskups*, 1969. This is the saga of Bishop Lárentíus Kálfsson in Hólar. The author is not named but is probably the priest Einar Hafliðason in Breiðabólsstaður in Vesturhópi (1307-93), see Jón Jóhannesson 1958, p. 227, and Árni Björnsson's introduction to the *Laurentius saga biskups*, pp. lxv-lxvii. See also the introduction to the newest edition of this saga, in *Íslenzk fornrit* XVII, 1998, pp. lviii-cii.

71 *Árna saga biskups* 1972. See also *Íslenzk fornrit* XVII, 1998, pp. v-lvii.

72 Compare to Guðni Jónsson 1962, pp. vii-ix, especially p. vii.

73 All the chronicles are published in: *Annálar 1400-1800*, vol. 1-6, Reykjavík 1922-88, as well as in *Islandske Annaler indtil 1578*, Christiana 1888.

74 Examples are *Nýi annáll*, describing the period 1393 to 1430, but preserved in a copy from the late sixteenth century, and *Skarðsárannáll*, written in 1639-40.

75 Especially the law codes of twelfth- to fourteenth-century Norway published in NgL: *Norges gamle love indtil 1387*, Christiania 1846-95. See also Norwegian charters in *DN: Diplomatarium Norvegicum*, Christiania/ Oslo 1847-1976. From the fifteenth and sixteenth century we have Danish royal documents about Iceland published in *Lovsamling for Island*, I, 1096-1720, Copenhagen 1853.

description of Iceland, that is assumed to have been written either by the Lutheran Bishop of Skálholt Oddur Einarsson (1559-1630) or by Sigurður Stefánsson (1570-95), rector of the seminary in Skálholt. It is assumed that the work is written at the end of the sixteenth century.[76] Valuable information about the continuation of marriage rituals is found in this account. Other legal documents of importance for the end of the sixteenth century are agreements and judgements from the general assemble in Þingvellir called *Alþingisdómar*.[77]

2.3 *Problems related to the use of the sources*

Even though many sources about Icelandic marriage legislation and practice in the Late Middle Ages exist, there is nevertheless a problem in analyzing this material in its wider context because of a general lack of studies in the social and cultural history of late medieval Iceland. Not much has been written about this period despite the existence of rich source material, and almost all the sources have been published. More studies in the history of the Late Middle Ages are greatly needed. First, the development of Church organization from the fourteenth century until the Reformation has not been fully analyzed, and there is especially need for studies of the ecclesiastic court material, as well as other sources related to the bishoprics.[78] Second, a wider study on general property transfer is also needed. That includes analyses of how much land was sold and bought, and by whom, as well as which type of land. And third, studies are lacking of the political culture of Iceland after the Commonwealth period, and this obviously limits the possibilities here for explaining fully the marriage strategy of the ruling elite.

It has also been difficult to do a field study in the canon law culture of Europe, because the secondary international literature about marriage

76 *Íslandslýsing. Qualiscunque descriptio Islandiae.* In translation by Sveinn Pálsson, Reykjavík 1971. Latest, Einar Sigmarson has written about the author of this description, see Sigmarson 2003, pp. 97-133, especially pp. 126-27 where he argues that it is not beyond doubt that Oddur Einarsson was the original author of the description.

77 *Alþingisbækur Íslands* I (1570-81), Reykjavík 1912-14, *Alþingisbækur Íslands* II (1582-94), Reykjavík 1915-16, *Alþingisbækur Íslands* III (1595-1605), Reykjavík 1917-18.

78 Recently though, valuable research on excommunication in Iceland in the late medieval period has been done. See Lára Magnúsardóttir, 2007.

has its roots in two different traditions. The first one is a part of the tradition of ecclesiastical history, especially canon law studies. The other is more related to the tradition of social history as well as the tradition of historical anthropology. At the same time there are many problems related to the terminology of the marriage studies, as many scholars have already indicated. A wealth of literature exists on the exchange of marriage gifts, but also, unfortunately, great confusion about the terminological meaning. Here, original terms from the primary Icelandic sources are used, for instance in relation to the different types of marriage gifts, as well as concepts used in the formulae of entrance into marriage. I have attempted to translate the meaning into English, but not without difficulties however – especially when comparing the results with other studies. At the same time it is important to remember that the same terms can change in meaning over time. Therefore the terms must always be studied in close relation to their context.

Part I
Legal aspects of marriage

The ecclesiastical model of marriage took different forms in different regional law codes, and it is thus reasonable to assume that marriage practices also were dependent on regional customs. Therefore it is important to study empirically regional differences in marriage legislation. When doing so we need to distinguish between the reception of canon law in the written law codes and the real influence that the Church exerted on behavior and ideas. Part I of this study about the legal aspects of marriage, uses information about legal regulations as evidence for the development of marriage law, and is intended to provide the legal framework of the book. It deals with the way in which the Christian understanding of marriage formed the marriage legislation of the Icelanders. It focuses on the theory of consent in law, and especially asks what influence it had on Icelandic legal thinking during the twelfth and thirteenth century. This first part of the book is also about how the knowledge of canon law and internalization of new norms can be traced in the Icelandic documents, especially in documents from the fifteenth and sixteenth century, where the influence of the Church on the question of penance and the question of sexual crimes is of special importance. This part of the book is very much about how canon law became implemented in the existing legal regulation of marriage and in sexual behavior, and thereby slowly changing the making of marriage.

CHAPTER 3

Consent in canon law and Icelandic marriage legislation

By changing the rules about what made marriage valid, the Western Church in the twelfth century began a process that not only affected the institution of marriage, but also the wider social structure. My discussion of the process in an Icelandic context concerns both the impact on wedding customs, and the influence of Christian doctrine on the institution of marriage as a whole, for example on the exchange of gifts. That is why it is also necessary in this context to discuss other legal changes that occurred as a result of the fact that the mutual consent of the couple became the criterion for a valid marriage.

This chapter describes the change in the definition of marriage according to canon law, and its influence on marriage in the Middle Ages in Iceland. At the heart of this discussion is the question who should consent to and arrange marriage. The chapter will consider the rules concerning consent to marriage that were introduced in the twelfth century, and study the consequences of the consent theory on the regulation of marriage laws and practice. Changes in marriage legislation in Iceland can be seen as part of general change elsewhere in the Christian world. That is why this issue will first be considered from a wider European perspective. It will then be asked how the marriage policy of the Church influenced marriage regulation in Iceland.

3.1 Consent in canon law: A European background

Great changes occurred in marriage legislation in Western Europe during the twelfth and thirteenth centuries because of canon law. This was the result of stronger papal control as well as developments in Church legislation. Canon law was a series of laws emanating from Church authorities such as ecclesiastical councils, and the pope himself. Significantly, these legal rules were written down, which gave them more force at least in Northern Europe in an age when written records and legal rules were few.[1]

Canon law was not a coherent law until the thirteenth century. Gratian finished his compilation known as the *Decretum* around 1140. This was a harmonization of the existing legal texts and documents of the Church, including extracts from Christian writers and Church council decisions.[2] Gratian's work was highly influential. From this time onwards canon law implied acceptance of the pope's right to rule over the Church, and the clerics' right to administer the institutions of the Church. Most of these laws took the form of *decretals*, papal letters that decided particular cases and also enunciated legal rules applicable to other cases of a similar type.[3] Both Pope Alexander III (1159-81) and his successors as Pope Innocent III (1198-1216) supplemented canon law and were the most prolific writers of *decretals* in the period between Gratian and Pope Gregory IX (1227-41). Councils and synods also added to the canon law, and here especially the Third Lateran Council (1179) and the Fourth Lateran Council (1215) were of great importance. No system existed though for collecting and distributing copies of the law. As a result, *decretals* began to be collected by law teachers and other practitioners, such as judges, and these collections started to be circulated amongst the legal elite.[4] Five of the collections became the basis for an official new collection of 1234, which Pope Gregory IX had commissioned to be prepared as an official new Church law. The resulting text became known as the *Liber Extra* or the *Decretals of Gregory IX*. Further in the period 1190-1234 many learned commentaries on canon law were produced. The majority of the glossaries and commentaries made by the so-called

1 On how canon law might have influenced the writing of the provincial laws of the Nordic countries, see Fenger 1983, pp. 71, 78 ff, and more generally Sandvik 1989, pp. 238, 242.

2 Brundage 1990, p. 229 ff.

3 Ibid., p. 325, he refers to the work of Fransen 1972, pp. 12-15 about the collections of the decretals.

4 Ibid., p. 325.

decretalists, were not only explanations to the legal text of the *decretal* collections, but also an effort to cohere better the existing law. After the work of Pope Gregory IX the Church law was based on papal law books, of which his *Liber Extra* was the first. Little information survives about how courts applied canon law prior to the beginning of the thirteenth century. Court records for the period after 1200 are, however, more common, since the Fourth Lateran Council decided that ecclesiastical courts were to document their actions and file them.[5] Matter of marriage was an important part of these new regulations of the ecclesiastical courts.

3.1.1 Marriage in canon law

From the twelfth century onwards the Church asserted a claim to jurisdiction over matters related to marriage. It was first in the course of that century that canon law was used to regulate wedding rites at ecclesiastical courts and used to define what a valid and indissoluble marriage was.[6] Early canon law had no clearly articulated concept of marriage, but was based on the Roman legal tradition.[7] Canonists from the early Church reform period of the eleventh and twelfth centuries borrowed the concept of consent from Roman law, which allowed a couple to make their own marriage by free mutual consent.[8] The canonists of the twelfth century made this a prerequisite for a valid marriage. In so doing they followed in the footsteps of the Church fathers, which had used this idea long before this time. Marriage by consensus had also been practiced in southern Germany and elsewhere long before the Church reformists of the twelfth century made it a cornerstone of their program to reshape the institution of marriage.[9]

Two theories about what constituted a valid marriage were established during the twelfth century. Peter the Lombard (1095-1160), bishop

5 Ibid., pp. 327, 330.

6 Helmholz 2004, p. 524.

7 Brundage 1990, p. 140, compare too pp. 142, 172. See also in Nordic context, Nylander 1963, pp. 222-24 and Jørgensen 1976, p. 483.

8 Consent of the spouses or mutual consent meant that both the woman and the man accepted the marriage freely. Generally on the historical development of the consent theory from Roman law to later medieval time, see Laiou 1993.

9 Brundage 1990, pp. 187-89.

of Paris, stated that marriage should be one of the seven sacraments. In his work the theory of consent was so central to a valid marriage that consent alone almost constituted a valid marriage.[10] In the eyes of God and the Church only the consent of the partners mattered.[11] The Bolognese lawyers, in contrast to the Paris theologians insisted that marriage was a two-stage process. It began with consent and was completed by consummation. This was Gratian's own position on the matter: without sexual union there was no binding marriage contract.[12]

Those of Gratian and Peter the Lombard became the two dominant views of marriage within the Church, and the notion of marriage as a sacrament was forcing its way into the law courts. This happened mainly because of the work of Pope Alexander III (1159-81) and his successors, which both supplemented these rules and changed them. Alexander's ruling on a marriage case from 1180 was definitive. The pope decided that couples could contract a valid marriage in two ways. Either they might freely and voluntarily agree to marry at once by mutual consent (marriage *per verba de presenti*), and by doing so the marriage was valid at once. After the couple had consented to marry they were bound together in matrimony as long as both partners lived. Another way to contract a marriage was that the couple might freely and voluntarily agree to marry at some future time (marriage *per verba de futuro*). This type of marriage was first valid after the future consummation. In either situation, consent was the essential element in the marriage, and no church ceremony was necessary for making it valid. This decision of Pope Alexander III from 1180 became the ruling authority in Western marriage law throughout the rest of the Middle Ages until the Council of Trent in 1563.[13]

The legacy of Roman law dictated that consensus should lie at the heart of marriage. The mutual consent of the parties was all that mattered to the question of a union's validity.[14] In the tradition of the papal court this was defined as consent between both male and female partners.

10 Brundage 1993, p. 247.

11 Gies 1989, pp. 137, 138, Brooke 1991, pp. 137, 138.

12 Brundage 1993, pp. 246-47, compare to the *Decretum* of Gratian at C. 27, in *Corpus iuris canonici.* See also Brundage 1990, pp. 235-39.

13 Brundage 1993, pp. 247-48.

14 Helmholz 2004, p. 524.

However, it is important to note that this discussion among the canonists did not mean that parents could no longer influence the marriage of their children. On the contrary, most parents saw this as a matter to be decided by them, not their children. As we shall see this could be a practical problem for having the new marriage rules accepted.

3.1.2 What consequences did the consent theory have for the further development of marriage legislation?

The consensual theory produced some legal problems. The new marriage rules could stimulate clandestine marriage, since consent was the only essential requirement for a valid marriage. At the Fourth Lateran Council in 1215 this problem was discussed and it was stated that marriage must be public and announced in advance to all parties. However, this attempt, which also included efforts to make the celebration of marriage public, failed to solve the problem of clandestine marriage. Even if clandestine marriages were condemned, such unions were nonetheless valid. What happened was that a distinction between a valid and a legal marriage came into operation. James Brundage has stated that for "nearly half a millennium European marriage law wrestled with this tension between the insistence on preserving the couple's right to contract freely by simple consent and society's interest in requiring persons to marry openly."[15] Another problem faced by the council was the clarification of the process of terminating unsuccessful unions, either through separation of the parties without the right to remarriage or by declaring the marriage never to have taken place because certain formalities had not been performed, such as the mutual consent, or if the couple were related within the forbidden degrees of consanguinity.

The work of the Fourth Lateran Council can be seen as a result of a compromise between secular and ecclesiastical definitions of what constituted a valid marriage. The marriage regulations were finally fixed by the time of Pope Gregory IX's decretals in 1234, which made the decisions by Pope Alexander III and the Fourth Lateran Council part

15 Brundage 1990, p. 415.

of an official papal law book. From that time onwards Christian marriage doctrine was fully developed, with the free consent of the couple providing the basis for a valid marriage.[16]

Related to the issue of a valid marriage were the rules made by the Fourth Lateran Council, which reduced the forbidden degrees of consanguinity and affinity from seven to four.[17] The absence of impediments such as close kinship between the spouses, or to spiritual relatedness (*cognatio spiritualis*), which baptism and confirmation created, also became necessary conditions for a valid marriage.[18] There were rules, which stated that people related through blood ties or connected as in-laws or baptismal sponsors could not marry. The aim of these measures was to prevent incest and some scholars, especially Jack Goody, have argued that the new incest laws were designed to benefit the Church financially.[19]

From 1215 onwards a couple should not be married until after the publication of the banns of marriage. Otherwise the agreement was considered clandestine. Even if clandestine marriages were condemned, such unions were nonetheless valid. To be sure that a valid marriage of this sort also became legal for the outside world, it became common in Europe during the thirteenth century to publish the banns of marriage on the doorstep of the church. This aimed to prevent the marriage of persons closely related and to avoid clandestine marriage. Many Church leaders were also opposed to the remarriage of widows and widowers.[20] So, by the mid-thirteenth century Western churchmen had arrived at a fairly clear consensus about the Church's sexual policy, and canon law had devised workable solutions to many of the most common difficulties.[21]

Even if the canonists were able to secure the Church's claims to jurisdiction over marriage without great conflict,[22] it did not mean that

16 Safley 1984, pp. 16-18.
17 Brundage 1990, pp. 355-56.
18 Gies 1989, pp. 218-19.
19 Compare to the discussion in chapter I on pp. 33-34. Goody has been criticized for this functional explanation; see Appendix 2 in Brundage 1990, pp. 606-607 and Herlihy 1985, pp. 11-13. See also Brundage 1990, p. 88, compare to Goody 1988, pp. 42-47.
20 Brundage 1990, pp. 142, 199 ff, 242-45.
21 Ibid., p. 485.
22 Brundage 1995a, pp. 71-72.

secular marriage legislation was in full harmony with the developments in canon law. This can be explained by the slow adoption of the law in practice. So, even as James Brundage has explained, the royal and municipal lawmakers had just begun to interest themselves in issues of sexual behavior in the Late Middle Ages, the goals of the municipal lawmakers were not always identical with those of the Church leaders. This is one of the reasons why great differences can be found between the civil law and canon law as regards sexual matters.[23] For instance, a clerical blessing was required according to canon law, but it was not a common practice during the Middle Ages, and even in canon law the wedding ceremony first became a legal requirement after the decision of the Council of Trent in 1563.[24] The consent of the couple was thus enough to make a Christian marriage valid throughout the Middle Ages. Any Christian man was able to marry any Christian woman provided that they were past puberty, that they were not too closely related to each other, that neither had taken a vow of chastity, and that the man was not in major orders and required to be celibate.[25]

What influence did the consent theory have on more general marriage regulation and practice? A radical change in marriage practice gradually followed the decisions taken in the twelfth century, when the Church gained stronger formal control of marriage and imposed its rule of monogamy.[26] In this way one might say that the Church had a great indirect influence on marriage practice. Gradually the Church came to be involved in the betrothal and the handing over of the bride.[27] Christian marriage reflected the sacred union of Christ and the Church.[28] Divorce was forbidden, although there were legal reasons which would allow separation. One of these reasons was impotence.[29] Only the Church

23 Brundage 1990, p. 485. In the next section of this chapter, marriage regulation will also be considered from the point of view of the civil law and the practicalities of married life.

24 Reynolds 1994, p. 362.

25 Donahue 1992, pp. 339-40.

26 Brooke 1991, p. 263.

27 Goody 1988, p. 146.

28 Gies 1989, p. 97.

29 In the Western Church during the early medieval periods there had been an ongoing discussion about the conjugal debt related to the question of consummation. See Reynolds 1994, pp. 346-47 and forward. He argues that some "early medieval canonical sources decree or presume that a marriage may be dissolved on the ground either of non-consummation or of the impossibility of coitus."

could give permission to dissolve marriage and this was normally possible only if the marriage had not been made in the right way. Even then the marriage was not considered as "dissolved" but rather "annulled" since it had not been established according to the right criteria. This was the consequence of the fact that marriage was in the Christian meaning a union of two in one flesh. It was created by God and it was thus indissoluble.[30]

Consensus marriage also had great consequences for kinship and family structure. One of the reasons for this was the effect on inheritance rules. James Brundage says on this matter:

> Civil law also surrounded marriage with formal, contractual rituals. A dowry agreement became, at least for a time, a legal necessity. Both civil and religious authorities not only encouraged but even required a property agreement as a condition for recognizing a union as a marriage with full legal consequences. At the same time, the marriage market was changing, too. The value of dowries offered by the families of prospective brides was apparently rising, and in consequence men tended to marry earlier than they had in previous centuries, while the family of nubile women often postponed their daughters' marriages until later than had been customary.[31]

At the same time, marriage became a formal contract. The rules of monogamy secured transfer of property to certain groups of inheritors, namely the children born in valid marriage. Other rules were also added; for instance, the children of unmarried parents could be legitimized and thus get full inheritance rights if their parents married later.[32]

It is important to underline that these changes in inheritance practices were related to the consequences of the consent theory. Let's consider further how this new understanding of marriage influenced the rules concerning the transfer of property through marriage, as well as the inheritance rules.

30 Reynolds 1994, pp. 327, 337.
31 Brundage 1990, p. 88.
32 Casey 1989, p. 74. Sandvik 1989, pp. 247-48.

3.1.3 *The two models of marriage*

The ecclesiastical model of marriage was based on the consent of both spouses. According to Georges Duby it promoted marriage outside the family or kin group (exogamy) and monogamy. The lay model, on the other hand, was according to Duby based on the consent of the parents, and marriage within the same family or kin group (endogamy).[33] As mentioned in the introduction, this understanding of marriage formation during the Middle Ages did not make a discrepancy between canon law and layfolk's practice of marriage. Originally the lay model of marriage was a matter of family policy, not of individual choice. It was a sealed marriage contract, symbolized by a sexual relationship between the parties and dissoluble at will.[34] Marriage was thus above all an alliance between two families, and it was based on a financial agreement that could be cancelled. During the High Middle Ages, when the Church gradually gained jurisdiction in matters pertaining to marriage and morality, this secular contract changed.[35] What was the nature of this change?

It has been argued that the acceptance of the mutual consent of the couple (also named principal consent) was a step towards the creation of the conjugal family. This has been understood as a threat to the existing patrilineal family structure.[36] Studies have shown that some matrimonial cases were brought to the law courts to overcome the opposition of family and friends.[37] Lay society thus continued to view parental consent as essential and defended paternal authority.[38] During the second half of the eleventh century some Christian authors included parental consent as one of the requirements for a valid marriage. This view aroused little enthusiasm among reform-minded canonists who wished to minimize the role of the parents in arranging marriage because these unions should not be dissoluble.[39] The mutual gift giving of the spouses

33 Duby 1991a, pp. 1-22.

34 Brundage 1990, pp. 134-35.

35 Gies 1989, p. 116.

36 In a patrilineal family structure property is transferred between generations through the patrilineal kin, excluding or giving the female side of the kin group less rights.

37 See for instance studies of English cases in Helmholz 2004, p. 527.

38 Goody 1988b, p. 15. See also in a Scandinavian context Helander 1969, pp. 665-68, Sigurður Líndal 1974, pp. 282-83, and Gunnes and Vogt 1979, p. 190.

39 Brundage 1990, pp. 187-88.

and the exchange of promises or an oath should satisfy these purposes. Parental consent was thus in their minds not an acceptable basis for an ecclesiastically valid marriage.[40] However, in practice the fathers of the bride and bridegroom continued to arrange marriages, and if the spouses later gave their consent to the agreements, the marriage became defined valid as a Christian marriage.

In this way marriage *continued* to be a financial and political contract, arranged by the families of the two people who were to become husband and wife. It continued to be a contract between two families, not only a personal contract between the spouses as the Church had insisted.[41] On the other hand, only a monogamous marriage could secure a legitimate heir, which made it easier to keep the estates involved within the family for the future. This encouraged many members of the aristocracy to accept marriage as an institution of the Church.[42]

The role of the Church was to define marriage as a sacred union. Canonical authorities, moreover, were willing to compromise with the civil authorities on some issues involved in marriage jurisdiction. They did not attempt to resolve disputes over the division of marital property, as these matters lay within the competence of the civil courts. This may be one of the reasons why the Church was able to secure its claims to jurisdiction over marriage without major conflict.[43]

In summary, a consequence of the growing influence of canon law on marriage was, on the symbolic level, a greater emphasis on marriage as a personal contract between a woman and a man. The importance of the mutual consent of the spouses is one example of this. However, the two models of marriage, the ecclesiastical and the secular, existed nowhere as social practice in their pure forms and that is why the models should not be regarded as being in complete opposition.[44] Great variations in

40 Ibid., pp. 188, 190. Brooke 1991, pp. 129-30.

41 An example of this strong parental control is, according to Jack Goody, that if daughters opposed the marriage wishes of their fathers they risked losing their dowry. See Goody 1988b, pp. 152-53.

42 Brooke 1991, pp. 120, 142. See also the same attitude in Sandvik 1989, p. 248.

43 Brundage 1995a, pp. 71-72, 74-75.

44 Brooke, and Brundage have partly criticized Duby for his dichotomizing and have attempted a richer analysis of the character of marriage practice, see Brooke 1989, pp. 119-20, 126, 141-42, and Brundage 1990, p. 194. Brooke on p. 126 underlines that it is during the twelfth century that the "lay aristocracy of Europe allowed the Church to take over almost completely the jurisdiction of the law of marriage."

marriage practice reflect differences in the ways of using the principles of inheritance and marriage regulation. When the Church gained jurisdiction over marriage, and the Church courts became established in every part of Western Christianity, the process of change in marital life according to canon law had just started.

3.2 *Marriage law in twelfth- and thirteenth-century Iceland*

> Neither medieval medical theory nor canon law had much effect on Icelandic behavior. The situation in Iceland may be taken as representative of what happened in other rural districts of medieval Europe where both the Church and the world of classical letters were remote.[45]

This statement by Roberta Frank from 1973, illustrates how some scholars have assumed that the Church did not succeed in influencing the marriage practices of the Icelanders in the twelfth and thirteenth century. She is not alone in suggesting that Icelandic society as a whole was not as influenced by Christian thought during the Middle Ages in the same way as the rest of Europe.[46] However, this picture of the relation between the periphery and the centre in the medieval period, seeing the districts of the North as not touched by the great learned culture of the south, has partly been challenged during recent years. As the legal historian Peter Landau has written recently: "Despite some resistance, mainly in the twelfth century, there was no permanent opposition against the influence of canon law in the Scandinavian kingdoms."[47] Thirteen papal *decretals* sent by the popes to the archbishops of Niðarós in the years of 1160-1200, further underline the close contact of the papacy with the newly established Norwegian archbishopric, and some of these also included Icelandic matters.[48]

45 Frank 1973, p. 473.

46 See for instance Leclercq 1991, p. 242: "La sexualité n'y est pas du tout dévalorisée ni disciplinée; la virginité et le modéle monastique n'y ont pas de succés."

47 Landau 2005, p. 39. On the issue of consent theory in Norway and Iceland, see Bandlien 2000, pp. 55-79.

48 Landau 2005, p. 32-37. See the edition of those decretals in Holtzmann 1938, pp. 383-400. Eleven of them are preserved in two English manuscripts in the British Library and in Cambridge. These collections are *Collectio Cottoniana*, and *Collectio Petrihusensis*. On Icelandic manuscripts in English collections, see more generally Jón Þorláksson 1892, pp. 217-35.

In this context it is important to discuss the influence on behavior and on legislation or literature separately. The written sources give a clear picture that Iceland actually was a part of the Christian culture of the High Middle Ages. The Icelandic historian Sveinbjörn Rafnsson has indicated that it is easy to identify the ecclesiastical influence from continental Europe in Icelandic sources from the twelfth and thirteenth century. According to him:

> The Icelanders were actively adopting the European or Roman-Catholic ideology and policy. This comes through by reading the known Icelandic law codes from this time. What characterises it is the reception of the canon law from the South, but the codes were also shaped by the Icelandic society in its manifold.[49]

Sveinbjörn Rafnssons's interpretation is in agreement with both earlier and more recent research.[50] Firstly, it is widely accepted that the Icelanders of the twelfth and thirteenth centuries had a good knowledge of canon law. Early in the last century Einar Arnórsson, a specialist on law, indicated that the Icelanders of the twelfth century made a distinction between the law of God and human law.[51] Torfi Tulinius has contributed to this discussion and has among other things been studying the implication of canon law for the understanding of both the life and writings of Snorri Sturluson.[52] Further, the legal historian Sigurður Líndal has studied the canon law literature mentioned in Icelandic charters, mainly those from the registers of Church property called *máldagi* (a charter which contains an endowment agreement). His research shows that the Icelanders owned and copied manuscripts containing canon law, and his

49 Sveinbjörn Rafnsson 1990, p. 131: "Tímabilið [12. og 13. öld] einkennist að vissu leyti af örri aðlögun Íslendinga að evrópskum eða rómversk-kaþólskum viðhorfum og stjórnháttum. Þetta kemur ekki síst fram í lögum og lagagreinum sem varðveitt eru frá þessum tíma. Einkenni þeirra er viðtaka (*receptio*) lærðs réttar sunnan úr álfunni, sem mótaðist af íslensku samfélagi í margbreytileik sínum."

50 This research is mostly done by Icelandic scholars, while the view that sees Iceland as a peripheral backwater in relation to the rest of the Christianity, is mainly to be found in the work of foreign scholars. These "outsider" views are also related to the tradition of the old Germanic school of law from the last century. According to that tradition the Icelandic society in the early twelfth and thirteenth century could be understood as representative of some older Germanic culture. On this view and its influence on the understanding of the oldest legal documents from Iceland, see Norseng 1987, pp. 54-57.

51 Einar Arnórsson 1912, pp. 3, 5-6.

52 Torfi Tulinius 1996, pp. 31-40.

conclusion is that during the Central and Late Middle Ages canon law knowledge among Icelanders was as great as among other contemporaries in Western Europe.[53]

Secondly, there seems to be no reason to believe that the Icelandic knowledge of canon law was only theoretical. The Church seems actually to have managed to change the everyday life of the Icelanders. As an example I can mention that Sverrir Jakobsson's study of thirteenth century conflict resolution among warring chieftains by clerics clearly identifies the influence of the Church on the behavior of the chieftains.[54]

In addition Sveinbjörn Rafnsson states that the authors of the sagas written in the thirteenth century were interested in matters of marriage, concubines, and the rights of illegitimate children. He claims that the influence of canon law was most strongly evident in relation to women's consent. He explains this not only as a result of a change in legal knowledge, but also as a result of a radical change in the relationship between men and women in Iceland taking place during the thirteenth century.[55] This change was related to the Church's attempt to alter the sexual behavior of Icelandic chieftains in the thirteenth century. The practice of living openly with concubines was an old custom among Icelandic aristocrats but Auður Magnúsdóttir's study has shown that the Church actually managed to influence sexual practices in Iceland: the chieftains of the thirteenth century accepted the monogamy of marriage and would no longer have both wives and concubines, as had been the case earlier.[56]

53 Sigurður Líndal 1997. Icelandic medieval sources provide information about the libraries at the sees of Hólar and Skálholt, where many books on canon law are found in the registers. Sigurður Líndal also states that Bishop Árni probably had the *Liber extra* with him when he came to Iceland in 1269, and the influence of canon law can also be found in the penitence practice of the bishops. See also Magnús Lyngdal Magnússon 2002, p. 44 (an unpublished M.A. thesis).

54 Sverrir Jakobsson 1998a, pp. 7-46. See also Sverrir Jakobsson 1998b, pp. 117-34.

55 Sveinbjörn Rafnsson 1982, pp. 119-21.

56 Auður Magnúsdóttir 1996, pp. 93-113, see especially p. 95. See also Auður Magnúsdóttir 2001, p. 56, about the difference between Jón Loftsson and his sons Ormur and Sæmundur. The father had both concubine and a wife, while the sons only had concubines.

3.2.1 The early influence of canon law in Iceland

There is no doubt that from an early date canon law influenced the Icelandic legal activities. This can at least be seen in the twelfth century legislation. Here, I shall discuss how the marriage law of *Grágás* reflects a process of change towards a Christian understanding of marriage[57] that was evident in the letters of popes and archbishops by the end of the twelfth century.[58] In 1173 Archbishop Eysteinn of Niðarós wrote a letter to the leaders of the Icelanders. He complained about the behavior of the people in the country; he had heard that there were men in Iceland who had beaten clerics, wounded them, and even killed them. The married life of the inhabitants was no better. According to the archbishop

> some men have left their wives and taken mistresses instead. Some keep both their wives and mistresses under their roof and live such unholy lives that it tempts all Christian men to sin.[59]

Seven years later the archbishop wrote again to the Icelandic Bishop Þorlákur and the most powerful chieftains of the country,[60] blaming them for their unchristian behavior:

> You … the most noble of men, disgracefully lead lives of beasts, paying no heed to matrimony, although you know that it is a holy bond that must not be broken, except if yours wives live in adultery.[61]

Condemnation of the sexual morality of Icelanders was part of a wider discourse amongst the clerical elite of Western Europe. In the early

57 This process of change will be discussed further on pp 84 ff.

58 I have discussed this before in Agnes S. Arnórsdóttir 1999, compare to the discussion of marriage legislation in Denmark and Iceland in a European context, in Agnes S. Arnórsdóttir and Nors 1999.

59 DI I, p 221: "svmer hafa konvr sinar latit. ok horkonur under þær tekit. svmer hafa hvarartveggiu jnan hus [med] sier og lifa so ogæzskv life. er alla kristna menn dregur til synda." The translation in the main text is taken from Jochens 1995, pp. 40-41.

60 DI I, pp. 260-64. The men were Jón Loftsson (d. 1197), Böðvar Þórðarson (d. 1187), Ormur Jónsson (d. 1191), Oddur Gizurarson (d. 1180) and Gizur Hallson (d. 1206).

61 Ibid., pp. 262-63: "En þier … ener agætustu menn. lifit bufiar life. rekit eigi hiuskap. ne þat helga samband er eigi ma slitna. nema kona manz hore under hann."

twelfth century Bernard of Clairvaux, when describing the Irish, wrote about their "barbarism" and their "beastlike" behavior. He also criticized their marriage customs and their failure to conform to correct ecclesiastical practices.[62] Bernard and the archbishop of Niðarós must have received their information from the local bishops in Ireland and Iceland.[63] It can indicate that the local Church authorities had started to define their own societies from the canon law point of view.

The Icelandic clergy underlined that the canon law regulations of marriage should be respected and some of them, like Bishop Þorlákur, took an active part in the reform policy of the twelfth-century papacy. This does not mean that change in actual behavior was as sudden as maybe the law codes could indicate. But we do know that Icelandic Church leaders began to interfere in divorce cases and marriages between close relatives as early as the end of the twelfth century.[64] Especially Bishop Þorlákur is reported to have put great emphasis on keeping married spouses together who had been joined in holy matrimony, and he broke up all those unions, which he knew to be illegal.[65]

It is a fact that from the end of the twelfth century a number of Norwegians studied canon law in France,[66] and that Gratian's *Decretum* was known and used in Norway from 1160 onwards.[67] When from 1152-53 Icelandic bishops had a legal duty to obey the archbishops of Niðarós, the Icelandic Church came under the authority of both canon law and

62 Bartlett 1994, p. 22. According to Jacqueline Murry the idea of bestiality underwent a profound transformation between the Early and Later Middle Ages. See Murry 2005, pp. 144-45, compare to Salisbury 1991, pp. 173-86.

63 See Agnes S. Arnórsdóttir 2001a, p. 185.

64 Magnús Stefánsson 1978, pp. 150-51, 252. Jón Jóhannesson 1956, pp. 193-94. Magnús Stefánsson 1975, pp. 57, 68.

65 Orri Vésteinsson 2000, pp. 167-68. He referred to Bsk. Bmf I, p. 107. Here it says in Orri Vésteinsson and Peter Foote's translation: "[Þorlákur] broke up all those unions in his days which he knew to be illegally joined whether greater or lesser men were involved. ... He [Þorlákur] saw no reason to think that those who already had great fortune from God in both wealth and prestige should have more indulgence for not refraining from disobedient acts." According to Orri Vésteinsson those phrases are clearly a part of the hagiographical character of the story about Bishop Þorlákur. The letters of Archbishop Eysteinn from 1179-80, show, however, that the bishop actually was highly involved in matters of morality.

66 Helle 1993, pp. 29, 46. See also Jón Jóhannesson 1958, p. 228, about Norwegians who studied canon law in France around 1300.

67 This was one of Archbishop Eystein's weapons against King Sverrir, see Sandvik 1989, p. 245. See also about the Norwegian provincial law and canon law, Ivarsen 1997, pp. 69-87. In Ivarsen 2005, pp. 75-90 he argues for strong influence from Gratians *Decretum* on the oldest law of *Gulathing* as well as on the oldest Norwegian province statute *Canones nidrosiensis*, probably from 1163, or latest from 1170.

the diocese of Niðarós in Norway.[68] This is indicated both by letters from the archbishops[69] and later from Pope Innocent III.[70] In one of the letters presented by Pope Alexander III to Archbishop Eysteinn,[71] the pope begins his statement with a particular remark about marriage. The papal *decretal* concerns the very rigid law prohibiting marriage between relatives up to the seventh degree of consanguinity. In Archbishop Eysteinn's original report to the pope he refers to the inhabitants of an island about 12 days travel by boat from Norway, who were so much related to each other that they could not find a marital partner on the island itself. The distance of the island from Norway leads one to identify it with Iceland or Greenland. What is of special interest here is that the pope allows the archbishop to grant dispensation to those people wanting to get married but being prevented from doing so because of the fifth, sixth or seventh degree of consanguinity.[72] This means, as Peter Landau has underlined, that the later legislation of the Fourth Lateran council from 1215 limiting the marital impediments to the fourth degree was introduced to Iceland or Greenland 40 years before. In Landau's interpretation this means that these islands seem to have had a pioneering role in the development of canon law at that time.[73] He argues that the correspondence between the Norwegian Archbishop Eysteinn and the Papacy, could have influenced the productions of decretals, which later became two chapters out of five in the title "De feriis" in the *Liber Extra* of Gregory IX in 1234.[74]

Even if the marital impediments to the fourth degree may have been practiced at a early stage at the archbishopric in Niðarós, the important issue of mutual consent to marriage in Iceland was for the first time raised

68 Guðrún Ása Grímsdóttir 1982, pp. 61-62. See also Magnús Stefánsson 1975, p. 5.

69 See DI I, pp. 218-23, 258-59, 260-64 the letters of Archbishop Eysteinn from the years 1173, 1179 and 1180, and see DI I, pp. 284-89, 289-91 the letters of Archbishop Eiríkur from 1189 and 1190.

70 See DI I, pp. 298-302. Pope Innocent III sent an open letter on 30 July 1198 to the Icelandic bishops, Páll Jónsson in Skálholt and Brandur Sæmundsson in Hólar, and in DI I, p. 302, to the "chieftains and the common people in Iceland" as it says in the letter.

71 About Archbishop Eysteinn and his legal affair, see Gunnes 1983, pp. 94-109.

72 Landau 2005, p. 34, who refers to S. Chodorow and Ch. Duggan (ed.), *Decretales ineditae saeculi XII* (MIC, Ser. B. vol. 4 (Città del Vaticano 1982), p. 149 (no. 86).

73 Landau 2005, p. 34.

74 Ibid., p. 36. The two chapters are X 2.9.2 and X 2.9.3.

in a letter of Archbishop Eiríkur in 1189 to the Icelandic bishops.[75] In this letter the archbishop announced that, as soon as a man betrothed a woman, with her approval and in the presence of witnesses, matrimony was established. But, he also stressed the necessity of gaining the consent of the woman's kinsmen, because her relatives knew more clearly what was best for her.[76] The principle of *consensus de praesenti, samþycktt of nalægd,* is present in this letter of the archbishop as well as *consensus de futuro, samþycktt af okomnv,* which was a contract made, for instance, by the parents of the couple. Such an agreement would not be valid without the later consent of the couple.[77]

Thus the consent theory was known in Iceland from the end of the twelfth century but it was not included in the oldest marriage legislation in *Grágás* from the twelfth and early thirteenth century.[78] There are no rules about marriage in a section dealing with matters of the Church and religious practice, except a regulation which says that weddings are not to be held on holy days.[79] Canon law's influence on marriage legislation can, however, be found in other sections of *Grágás.*[80] One of the best examples is the above-mentioned rule about the forbidden degree of marriage,[81] which traditionally has been thought to have its origin in the changes of marriage legislation from the Fourth Lateran Council of 1215. It has been estimated that two years later this resolution had reached the Icelandic lawmen, and resulted in a prompt amendment of the legislation to allow the obtaining of dispensation for marriage between fourth

75 DI I, pp. 284-89, especially p. 287.

76 Ibid., p. 287: "En vm fastnadar mal. þegar madr fastnar sier konu med jaquede hennar sialfrar. og er [samþycktt af nalægd og eigi af okomnv þa er þat fast svo sem fullr hiuskapur ef vottar vitv. Nv fullnast þetta at gudz logum. En þo er hitt bodit at þat skal giora med frænda rade ... þviat optast er þat. at þeir sia betur firir. en þær sialfar."

77 Ibid., p. 287. See also in Gunnar F. Guðmundsson 2000, p. 258, compare to NgL V, p. 38, and the discussion earlier in this chapter about canon law practice.

78 An overview of the marriage legislation in *Grágás* can be found in Gunnar Karlsson 1986, see especially pp. 52-60.

79 *Grágás,* III, p. 592, *Brúðhlaup,* compare to Ib, pp. 39, 241, II, 167-68, III, 35. The marriage rules of *Grágás* are found both in the Christian law, *Kristniréttur eldri,* and in the section about betrothal, *Festaþáttr. Kristniréttur eldri* was written 1122-1133.

80 Agnes S. Arnórsdóttir and Nors 1999, pp. 34-35, compare to Sveinbjörn Rafnsson 1982, p. 121, compare to Sigurður Líndal 1976a, p. 498. See also Sigurður Líndal 1997.

81 See p. 82.

cousins.[82] However, as discussed earlier, this rule of limiting the marital impediments to the fourth degree was already known in a *decretal* from 40 years earlier, so there could be reason to study closer the dating of the relevant rules in *Grágás*.[83]

As we know from the story about Bishop Þorlákur, Church leaders began interfering in matters of divorce and the marriage of close relatives at the end of the twelfth century in Iceland. Rules about this are also to be found in *Grágás*, which says that the bishop can allow a couple to separate, but the earlier custom had been that divorce was possible without the interference of the clerics.[84] Other examples exist of the influence of Church law related to the publicizing of marriage. Thus, *Grágás* brings the rule that in the spring following an agreement for marriage, the bridegroom should swear at the assembly of *Alþingi* that the betrothal between the couple had taken place and that they were not related.[85]

The great stress on *the public aspect of the contract* was a continuation of the old marriage contract. This is a similar pattern to what can be identified in other parts of Northern and Western Europe.[86] By comparing the rules for marriage in *Grágás* with other contemporary law codes, these similarities become obvious. Both Norman laws from the early thirteenth century and the law of Sicily from 1231 concentrate more on the financial aspects of marriage contracts, such as the amount of the dower and dowry, than on the question of consent.[87] The Sicilian law stated how marriages should be contracted:

82 *Grágás* III, p. 613, *Frændsemi*. See also Grágás Ia, p. 37. That this happened in 1217 is provided in DI I, p. 373, compare to pp. 376-81. See also Magnús Már Lárusson 1962a, pp. 374-75.

83 The dating of these rules has its roots in the text in *Grágás* Ia, p. 37, where it says that this *nýmæli* about the change of the rules of impediment came when Magnús Gissurarson was bishop that is in the period of 1216-37.

84 *Grágás*, Ib, pp. 39-44. See also other paragraphs about separation or divorce in *Grágás*: Ib, p. 44 that a woman can divorce a man if he tries to take her out of the country against her will. Ib, 55, and II, pp. 168-73, here it is stated that a women can separate and take her property back home with her if her husband has not entered her bed for three years. In II, pp. 203-204, it is stated that a disagreement can be a reason for separation or even divorce. See also Gunnar Karlsson 1986, p. 58.

85 *Grágás* Ib, p. 37 and thereafter: II, p. 164, compare to Magnús Már Lárusson 1959a, pp. 236-40.

86 On the practice of betrothal in the older Germanic law, for instance the Visigoth, see Reynolds 1994, p. 88 and forward.

87 *Women's Lives in Medieval Europe*, 1993, pp. 53-78.

By the present law, we order that all the men of our kingdom and especially the nobles who desire to contract marriage must have the marriage celebrated solemnly and publicly, with due solemnity and a priestly blessing, after the betrothal has been solemnized.[88]

Not a word about the mutual consent of the partner's marriage is found in these laws, and generally it was not until later that the doctrine of consent became part of the regional law codes of medieval Europe. It was after the Black Death, especially in the fifteenth and early sixteenth centuries, that royal and municipal laws first became seriously involved in the legal control of marriage and sexual behavior.[89] This was partly a response to the social and demographic problems after the epidemics, but it also reflects the strengthening of political and constitutional institutions in the Late Middle Ages.[90]

The marriage regulations contained in the betrothal section of *Grágás* are, thus similar to the regulations issued on the Continent during the same period. They mainly reflect an old secular marriage institution which the Church was only gradually beginning to change. In *Grágás* marriage customs are described in some detail. For example the suitor or his representative should make a proposal to the woman's legal guardian. The ceremonies needed to be performed in the presence of witnesses to ensure the legality of the marriage and the legitimacy of any offspring. First the formal betrothal statement comes, sealed by a handshake between the guardian and the suitor or his representative.[91] On this occasion the amount of the marriage gifts was fixed, and it is stated that the couple needed to have a minimum level of wealth in order to be allowed to marry.[92] However, the rules about not performing marriages on holy days, and that divorce should not be possible without a dispensation from

88 Ibid., p. 66. According to Reynolds' study of the early medieval marriage practice in the Western Church, marrying for instance in the Frankish Church, after the Carolingian reforms, remained for centuries very much domestic, a matter for the spouses and their families, or even for the spouses alone. See Reynolds 1994, pp. 410-11.

89 Brundage 1990, p. 546.

90 Ibid., pp. 546-47.

91 During the Middle Ages formulae were used in all kinds of legal acts and documents. They were highly stylized and stereotypical. For a discussion about the role of formulae in the Middle Ages, see: Boyle 1976, p. 86.

92 *Grágás* Ib, p. 38, compare too *Grágás*, II, p. 167.

the bishop, indicate a beginning of ecclesiastical influence on *Grágás*. These rules, which produced a limited ability to get a divorce, must be understood in relation to the consent theory.[93]

3.2.2 The compromise between the two models of marriage

It is indeed difficult to find any evidence for marriage practices in the Icelandic documents that have not been influenced in some way or another by the ecclesiastical regulation of marriage. At the same time it is obvious that the first step towards changing the marriage rules must have happened in some kind of coexistence with older marriage customs. The Norwegian historian Bjørn Bandlien has published an interesting analysis of the consent issue based on a close reading of Icelandic sagas. He argues for the existence in this source material of two types of women's consent: the original, so-called heroic type that is found in the oldest saga literature, and the mutual consent of the spouses that appears in the sagas of the late thirteenth and early fourteenth centuries. Heroic consent was related to the honor of warriors and the women's acceptance of them. Bandlien's study strongly emphasizes that before the Church introduced the theory of woman's consent, there was an awareness of the importance of women's approval in marriage. His thesis is that before the canonists presented their legal ideas, there existed a local tradition, which placed women at the centre of the process of gaining approval to marriage.[94] Bjørn Bandlien's results can be supported by other sources which show that the old heroic structure survived alongside new ones. As late as in 1433, according to one of the Icelandic annals, *Skarðsárannáll*, a woman declared that she would not get married to any man other than the one who would avenge her brother's death.[95] This narration written down in the middle of the seventeenth century indicates that the old idea of "heroic" consent with the honor of the parties playing an important role, survived or existed alongside the sacred meaning of female consent. Although these two traditions of consent could thus exist side by

93 Agnes S. Arnórsdóttir and Nors 1999, pp. 32-39.

94 Bandlien 1997, compare to Bandlien 2001, pp. 138-43.

95 *Annálar 1400-1800*, vol. 1, p. 57: "vildi engan eiga nema þann, sem hefndi bróður hennar."

side for centuries, legally it was the Christian tradition that mattered, at least after 1275. The law codes, as well as the sagas of the thirteenth century, reflect a process of change in the understanding of what made a marriage valid. As has been mentioned before, the concept of consent to marriage was first introduced to Iceland in a letter from Archbishop Eiríkur in 1189.[96] In Iceland it was not until the end of the thirteenth century that this new understanding of marriage was legitimated. This happened when two different law codes were officially recognized at the assembly of *Alþingi.* These were the *New Christian Law* of Bishop Árni Þorláksson, which was accepted in 1275, and the new civic law code of *Jónsbók*, which was recognized in 1281.

3.2.2.1 The marriage legislation of Bishop Árni Þorláksson

Canon law was formally acknowledged in Iceland when the *New Christian Law* was accepted at the assembly of Þingvellir in 1275.[97] It is clear, therefore, that even if the consent theory had first appeared in Iceland almost one hundred years earlier,[98] it was not until the end of the thirteenth century that this principle was accepted as a legal rule.

The *New Christian Law* was the work of Árni Þorláksson, who became Bishop of Skálholt in 1269. He was elected by Archbishop Jón *rauði* ("the red" 1268-82) and his clerics in Niðarós, and came to Iceland in the year of his election. According to the saga of Bishop Árni Þorláksson he brought with him several books on canon law as well as a number of Church statutes.[99] The saga does not, however, give a clear picture of which legal documents the bishop brought with him to Iceland. One of them seems to have been the *Skipan Árna biskups Þorlákssonar*, the

96 DI I, p. 287.

97 Sigurður Líndal 1976a, p. 498. This was different in Norway, where the central authority seems to have been much stronger than in Iceland. In 1268 the *New Christian Law* of the Norwegian Archbishop Jón was written, in which the consent of the couple was one of the requirements for a valid marriage. On the other hand, this law was not accepted by the royal authority in Norway until a century later. Recently Magnús Lyngdal Magnússon has argued that the *New Christian Law*, was accepted for both the sees of Skálholt and Hólar in 1275. See the discussion later in this chapter on pp. 89-90.

98 DI I, pp. 284-89. This letter from Archbishop Eiríkur Ívarsson to the Icelanders, concerns the canon law relating to marriage. This document has been discussed earlier in this chapter on pp. 82-83.

99 ÍF XVII 1998, p. 13.

Episcopal statute of Árni from 1269.[100] This statute is very similar in content to the *New Christian Law* that was acknowledged six years later.[101] According to the saga of Bishop Árni he brought with him also a text referred to as *Decretales cum apparatu*, a book on Church law which was a gift from the archbishop.[102] The legal historian Sigurður Líndal has argued that this was probably the law book *Liber extra*,[103] but Magnús Lyngdal Magnússon has argued that it also might have included the *Decretum Gratiani*.[104] Árni also brought with him some penitentiary rules *Skriftarboð Árna biskups*, also dated to 1269.[105] These rules are mainly concerned with the issue of consummation, and the paternity of children.[106] The last formula about the paternity of children can also have its origins in the provincial law of Norway, or even from *Grágás*.[107]

Árni's penitentiary and the statute from 1269 is evidence of his active interest in matters related to marriage. His statute does not only contain rules about consent and consummation, it also stresses that marriage banns should be published on three Sundays before a wedding. Each

100 Magnús Már Lárusson 1959a, p. 238. The whole statute is published in DI II, pp. 23-37, under the name *Skipan Árna biskups Þorlákssonar*. The document is dated to 1269 in Skálholt.

101 See discussion about the relation between this statute and the *New Christian Law* in Magnús Lyngdal Magnússon 2002, p. 44, and Lára Magnúsardóttir 1998, p. 212. It was in this statute that the importance of the consent of the woman was first strongly asserted by an Icelandic bishop. It states that a priest should hear the woman consent, without her being forced to do so.

102 Jón Jóhannesson 1958, p. 94. See *Árna saga* in ÍF XVII 1998, p. 13. This was a collection of canon law, and it seems that the archbishops in Niðarós were concerned with giving the Icelandic bishops books, which included canon law. Compare to a later gift, which Bishop Lárentíus got from Archbishop Eilífur. See ÍF XVII 1998, p. 423.

103 Sigurður Líndal 1997, pp. 241-73, see especially p. 262.

104 Magnús Lyngdal Magnússon 2002, p. 44.

105 DI II, pp. 37-42. See also ÍF XVII 1998, pp. 15-16, and note 5. The editor of *Árna saga* writes that from the time Árni Þorláksson became bishop there existed several statutes and orders, which are all printed in DI II, pp. 23-61, 192-94, and 210-19. Some of these documents contain the same information as found in *Árna saga* related to the announcements of the archbishops. The editor of the saga, Guðrún Ása Grímsdóttir underlines that, *The New Christian Law* of 1275 also contains those main announcements from the archbishop in Niðarós, compare to chapter 29 and 32 in *Árna saga*.

106 DI II, pp. 43-49. These penitentiary rules contain formulas for oaths which reflect canon law thinking related to themes such as the consummation of marriage, and impotence. One of those formulas was prepared for a man to swear that he had stopped living with a woman with a "bodily desire". There are other rules about how to prove: that a man had not had intercourse with a woman so that she became pregnant; that a man had not had intercourse with a woman against the laws of God; and that a man had not had intercourse with a woman, nor tried to have intercourse with her. Another formula was for an oath to be sworn by a man who no longer made love to his wife. The third formula was for an oath to be sworn by a woman to prove the paternity of her child.

107 This can be related to the rules about bringing illegitimate children into the kin group of the father. See Agnes S. Arnórsdóttir 1995, pp. 56-57.

parish priest should announce the marriage of a couple in public.[108] This is clearly a reflection of the rules intended to prevent clandestine marriage, which had been introduced by Pope Innocent III at the Fourth Lateran Council of 1215. Both the rules concerning the publication of marriage banns and concerning the woman's consent, which can be found in the *New Christian Law* of 1275, are the same as those in the statute of Árni.[109]

The *New Christian Law* exists in more than 200 manuscripts, about 50 of which predate the Reformation. According to the study of Magnús Lyngdal Magnússon Árni's work is based on the *Christian Law* of the Norwegian Archbishop Jón *rauði* and on the *Old Christian Law* of *Grágás*, as well as on the *New Christian Law* of *Gulating* in Norway from ca. 1270. The content is derived largely from canon law, – from *Liber Extra* as well as *Decretum Gratiani* – but it was probably incorporated into Icelandic law through the Norwegian laws.[110]

Thus, in 1275 the Church's jurisdiction over marriage received formal acceptance in the diocese of Skálholt in southern Iceland.[111] Scholars have traditionally agreed that the *Old Christian Law*'s sections from *Grágás* were still regarded as valid in the diocese of Hólar in Northern Iceland until 1354.[112] Recently Magnús Lyngdal Magnússon has on the contrary argued, however, that the *New Christian Law* was accepted for the whole country, although it had not been easy to get full acceptance for the law. Magnússon assumes then that the *New Christian Law* was valid for the whole country from 1275 until the end of the Middle Ages, when in connection with the Reformation the Church ordinance of King Christian the third became Icelandic law in 1541 in Skálholt, and in 1551 in Hólar.[113] No matter whether the *New Christian Law* was accepted in both of the dioceses or not, the law council at *Alþingi*

108 Gunnar F. Guðmundson 2000, p. 258, compare to NgL V, pp. 36-37.

109 Magnús Már Lárusson 1959a, p. 238, compare to NgL V, pp. 36-39.

110 Magnús Lyngdal Magnússon 2002, pp. 4, 134.

111 Sigurður Líndal 1976a, p. 498. See also DI III, pp. 98-99, *Lovsamling for Island I, Kong Magnus Eirikssons Anordning for Holum Stift, om Kristenrettens Gyldighed*, pp. 33-34.

112 This could explain the existence of a number of manuscripts from the fourteenth century that contain the Christian law section of *Grágás*, as Orri Vésteinsson has pointed out. These manuscripts are printed in *Grágás* III, see Orri Vésteinsson 1996, pp. 36-37.

113 Magnús Lyngdal Magnússon 2002, pp. 3-4, 135.

accepted that jurisdiction was transferred to the Church in 1275.[114] Thus the *New Christian Law* actually had the status of Church law, and was presumably also accepted by the king.[115] The new Icelandic legislation was closely related to the reshaping of Norwegian legislation initiated by King Magnús *lagabætir* ('Law-Reformer') Hákonarson (1263-80). Although the Norwegian royal authorities did not accept Archbishop Jón *rauði's*, *New Christian Law* made for Norway, it had provided the model for the *New Christian Law* of Bishop Árni, which was accepted for Iceland.

The text of the *New Christian Law* of 1275 reflects a process of redefining the meaning of marriage. It begins with the declaration that a marriage is sacred if it is made according to the rules of God and is legally made. The text reflects some of the redefinition:

> Marriage was created because of the sinful life of man and woman, and God created it himself... and it should be without all uncleanness and burning desire and all sorrow...
>
> Everyone who wants to get married to a woman shall ask for that maiden or woman with a wise and honest thought so that no known reason makes the marriage illegal. And if he makes an agreement with her guardian, then he, who wants to get the woman, shall name two or more witnesses that this agreement shall be completed at the agreed time and according to the laws of God ... and not later the priest shall see whether any hindrance existed for the marriage, and if they are found the priest shall forbid the couple to be bound, until it has been found out what could be done about the matter.[116]

The new requirement of mutual consent was here presented alongside the requirement of parental consent.

> But if no hindrance is found, then he [the bridegroom] shall hold the hand of the maiden or woman who he shall betroth, and name two or more witnesses. And he shall say

114 Sigurður Líndal 1976a, p. 498. See especially chapter 41 of the *New Christian Law*. See also DI II, p. 125, a letter from the bishop and the chieftains in the South of Iceland to King Magnús that the *New Christian Law* had been accepted by the *Alþingi*. Compare to *Árna saga biskups*, p. 47.

115 See the arguments for the king's acceptance in Orri Vésteinsson 1996, p. 36.

116 NgL V, p. 36: "var hann af ondverðo fyrir syndina scipaðr millum karls oc kono. af gude sialfum ... utan allrar saurganar oc bruna losta girnðar oc allrar sorgar ... Enn hverr sem sér vill kvanfangs læita. þa scal biþia þeirrar meyiar eða cono með hygli oc goðri forsea sem eigi se meinbugir á suo at viti. Oc ef honom semz um þat mál við þa sem raða eigu. þa scal sa sem kono vill fá nefna uatta tva eða fleiri. at þessor rað scolo tacaz at holldnom scildaga [oc akveðnom tima forfalla laust eptir guds laugom ...oc eigi siþr leiti prestarnir eptir ef þat megi nacqvað talma. oc ef þat finnz þa scal prestrin fyirr bioða saman at binda. fyrr en provat er hvat af þui megi geraz."

> these or similar words: "I betroth you to be my wife according to the laws of God and the words of the Holy Fathers, and from now on you are my legal wife." Because it is forbidden by the law of God to marry a maiden or woman with force, some kind men shall hear the free consent of the maiden or woman to be married, and guardians shall study the conditions. The father or other kinsmen can also marry the maiden or woman off, if that is her wish during the betrothal. Later the priest shall bless the couple. But if a man betroth a woman according to the law of God and with the mutual consent of both of them all their children are legal heirs, no matter whether they were born before the wedding or after.[117]

Behind this consensual theory, first proposed by Peter Lombard and his Parisian scholars in the twelfth century and now promoted by Norwegian and Icelandic clerics, lay an understanding, which stressed the importance of making marriage agreements with the full acceptance of all the parties involved.

According to the *New Christian Law* of 1275 the following categories of men were not allowed to have sexual relationships or to get married: those that entered monasteries, priests, deacons, sub-deacons, mentally sick men, and men that had been castrated. This was the law but, of course, the social practice was a different matter. The theory that both priests and bishops should live in celibacy never became a reality for all churchmen during the Middle Ages.[118] Priests were living with concubines, even if the accepted norm was that a priest should not get married.[119]

After the *New Christian Law* had received formal acceptance, Bishop Árni Þorláksson worked diligently to put the law into practice. An open letter to the people of the Diocese of Skálholt in 1284 declared which cases were under the jurisdiction of the Church, and one of these was

117 Ibid., p. 37: "En ef ongir finnaz a meinbugir. þa scal sa hallda i hönd meyio eða kono sem ser scal hana festa. oc nefna vatta tva eða fleiri. oc mæla þessor orð. eða onnor þvilic. Ec festi þic mer til eiginnar kono eptir guds logum oc heilagra feðra setning. oc ertu min loglig eigin kona heþan af. heyra scolu oc goðir menn iayrdi meyiar þeirrar eþa kono sem fest verðr. oc scilord þess er festir. fyrir þvi at þat er forboðat af guðs halfu at noccor maðr festi mey eða cono naudga. Rætt er oc at fadir eda annarr frendu festi mey eda kono ef þat er hennar vili þa er festar fara fram. Siþan skal prestr syngia yfir hionom. Enn þegar sem maðr festir ser kono at guðs laugum oc með samþyct beggia þeirra. þa ero born oll scilgetin þau sem hann a við þeirri cono. hvart sem þar voro getin fyrir festing eða eptir."

118 Vauchez 2001, pp. 21-32. See especially p. 31: "on estime à environ 20% le nombre des clercs concubinaires dans les diocèses de l'actuelle région Rhone-Alpes, à la fin du XIVe et au début du XVe siècle, et à 40 à 50% dans d'autres parties de la chrétienté."

119 NgL V, p. 38.

the matter of the secular rules of the contract of betrothal, called *festar*.[120] The betrothal and the wedding ceremony should now be joined as one act instead of two as had been the case under the old law.[121] According to *Grágás* there could, for instance, be twelve months between the betrothal contract and the wedding feast, and the bedding ceremony. Another change concerned the rules, which under the older law had required a couple to have a certain amount of wealth in order to be allowed to marry. These rules were excluded from the new marriage law.[122] However, if a betrothal, *festar*, had been legally made, but a wedding was not held, no one could separate the spouses.[123] This must be seen as a direct consequence of the consent theory, because even if the acts of marriage, the betrothal and the wedding, should be joined in one act, it was the consent, which made the marriage valid.

According to the new model established by Bishop Árni marriage should normally be celebrated on the same day on which the contract was made. However, a wedding ceremony could occur almost one year after the betrothal without any punishment being imposed.[124] It was consent and publicity that made a marriage valid. If both the man and the woman agreed to the marriage it was valid immediately (*sponsalia per verba de præsenti*).[125] The priest should hear the free consent of the woman, but the agreement was also valid if the fathers of the couple made it, and the couple later consented to it (*sponsalia per verba de futuro*).[126] This was the only case in which the betrothal could be seen as a separate act from that of the wedding. A marriage could also be acknowledged as valid if a man and woman confirmed that they had lived together for ten years or more, and their relationship was publicly known.[127]

120 Magnús Már Lárusson 1959a, pp. 238-39, compare to DI II, pp. 243-44.

121 NgL V, pp. 37-38.

122 Sigurður Líndal 1976a, p. 498.

123 NgL V, pp. 38-39: "Nu er hiuskapr karlmanz oc cono logligt samband. oc ma þetta samband engi maðr scilia. þo at eigi se brullaup gert ef loglig festing er á."

124 Magnús Már Lárusson 1959a, p. 239.

125 NgL V, pp. 36-38.

126 Ibid., p. 38

127 Sigurður Líndal 1976a, pp. 498-99.

The general rule about publication of marriage banns was reproduced almost without change in the *New Christian Law* of Bishop Árni Þorláksson. Another statute of Bishop Árni survives in the form of a clerical statement on different aspects of Church law.[128] This statement gives valuable information about how rules from Church law in general were adopted and could be enforced. Thus a parish priest, who attended a wedding that had not been publicized, should not be allowed to sing mass for the next three nights.[129] According to the *New Christian Law* of Bishop Árni a priest was also supposed to bless each couple in church.[130] Secret marriages were nevertheless regarded as valid,[131] something which could create problems for the children of such a couple, as a secret marriage was difficult to prove. These children could be seen as illegitimate and therefore without rights of inheritance.[132]

One of the consequences of the new Christian understanding of marriage was that no sexual relationships could be accepted alongside the official marriage. The general canon law forbidding bigamy was also included in the new Icelandic marriage law.[133] This was partly a result of the definition of marriage as a sacred agreement based on the mutual consent of the wife and the husband. When discussing how the new Christian understanding of marriage was not only introduced in the law but also put into practice, a study of the content of the different copies of the legal rules can indicate changes over time in social practice. An example can be taken from the content of the original statute of Bishop Árni from 1269, which differs from later copies that have been preserved. A manuscript of this statute of 1269 in a copy from around 1350 says that the marriage banns should be announced at the door of the church

128 DI II, pp. 58-61. *Skipan Árna biskups Þorlákssonar eða samþykt lærðra manna um ýmislegt í kirkjulögum.*

129 The penalty for marriage without publicity was to pay the bishop twelve ounces of silver. If a man delayed legal marriage, he should pay twelve ounces of silver for every year delayed and the penalty for single adultery was three pounds, but for double adultery twice as much should be paid, as well as confession of the sins made. See DI II, pp. 59-60.

130 NgL V, p. 37

131 Ibid., p. 39.

132 Gunnar F. Guðmundsson 2000, p. 258, with a reference to DI VII, pp. 603-606, especially p. 605.

133 See here for instance the later statute of Archbishop Árni Einarsson ca. 1346-49. DI II, p. 837 and forward. Rules declaring that priests were not allowed to get married and that divorced people were not allowed to remarry, were also taken up in the *New Christian Law*, see Sigurður Líndal 1976a, p. 498. See also Magnús Már Lárusson 1959a, p. 238.

choir, *savnghus*, where it should be said that a particular man wanted to have a particular woman.[134] A copy from 1480 reads:[135]

> If a priest shall bless a couple, he shall publish the wedding on three successive Sundays in front of the people of the parish, and if any reasons exist that make this marriage illegal, such as affinity or consanguinity, then this should be told to the priest.[136]

These manuscripts seem to reinforce different parts of the statute of 1269, reflecting the way in which the document was interpreted in different periods. An act should be published in the choir in the middle of the fourteenth century, while at the end of the fifteenth century it was emphasized that it was the duty of every member of that community to tell the priest whether the marriage could go ahead or not.[137] The people of the parish seem thus to be made responsible for the marriage. This reflects not only how the new understanding of marriage came to be understood and formed over time, but can perhaps also give some indications of change in parish culture. At the end of the fifteenth century the community of the parish had become the appropriate social sphere for this kind of announcement. The different copies of the bishop's statute can thus reflect the different ways they were used and understood over time.[138]

3.2.2.2 Marriage law in *Jónsbók*

The change in the thirteenth century marriage rules about mutual consent to marriage also had influence on the more secular contract of marriage. The first rule from the secular marriage law, in a section called *Kvennagiptingar* (marrying of women) in *Jónsbók*, refers to the close connection between inheritance law and what constituted a legal marriage. It says: "This is the first rule of inheritance that the children born in a legal

134 DI II, p. 29.

135 The statute in DI II, pp. 23-37 is printed after the manuscript of AM 456 from around 1480.

136 DI II, pp. 26-27: "Hann baud ok svo prestum. ef þeir skulu hion saman vigia at presturinn skal lysa. [iij. drottins daga fyri sinum kirkiu soknar monnum fyr en brudkaup giorizt [ok ef nockur er so vid staddr] at [um nockura meinbugi viti þar a uera frændsemi eða sifskapi. þa segi presti til fyrr en brudlaup fullgiorizt."

137 Evidence of this practice can be found in charters from the Late Middle Ages. These state that people from the parish made statements that they had never heard this or that. See discussion about rumors here in chapter 5.

138 The same is true of the many surviving manuscripts of *Jónsbók*.

marriage shall inherit from their father and mother who are legally born after the rules of God and humans."[139] The legal heirs were the children born in a marriage made with the mutual consent of the spouses, as well as also some other customary rules of contracting marriage. This is what is meant by 'the rules of God and humans'.

The marriage law of *Jónsbók* had many elements from the old law in *Grágás*, as well as from the laws of King Magnús the Law-Reformer from 1274.[140] According to the Norwegian law of King Magnús, a woman could lose her right to inherit if she married without the consent of her relatives.[141] The same law is found in *Jónsbók*.[142] The marriage law in *Jónsbók* begins:

> A father and mother shall decide on the marriage of their daughters, if they are alive. But if they are missing then the relatives of the father or the mother who are most closely related should decide. If her brothers are the closest relatives and they do not agree, then the one who follows her wishes shall choose if the couple seems to be of equal heritage … The guardian shall arrange the dowry and the countergift for his female relative in the way they agree … The woman shall not receive more than one-third of the dowry in clothes. And what the guardian gives in addition to that, shall be mainly things that the future husband can also make some use of.[143]

According to this, a woman's guardian, called *giftingar-* or *festamaður*, discussed with the husband-to-be the amount of the dowry called *heimanfylgja*, and what the husband should pay in countergift (the contribution from himself and his family), which was called *gagngjald* or *tilgjöf*.[144]

139 *Jónsbók*, p. 78: "Sú er erfð hin fyrsta, er börn skilgetin taka arf eptir föður sinn ok móður skilfegna at guðs lögum ok manna".

140 Magnús Már Lárusson 1959a, p. 238.

141 Sandvik 1976, p. 494.

142 *Jónsbók*, p. 71.

143 *Jónsbók*, p. 70: "Faðir ok móðir skulu ráða giptingum dætra sinna, ef þau eru til. En ef þeira missir, þá skulu föður frændr ok móður frændr hinir nánustu giptingum ráða. Nú eru bræðr til nánastir, ok skilr þá á, þá skal sá ráða er hennar ráði fylgir, ef þat þikkir jafnræði… Giptingarmaðr skal skilja heimafylgju ok tilgjöf fyrir frændkonu sinni svá sem þeim kemr ásamt, …Eigi skal í klæðum meira heiman gefaz með konu en þriðjungr; en þat sem giptingarmaðr gefr meira, þat skal vera í þeim hlutum, at þat megi vera þeim til þarfa eða afla er konu fær."

144 Ibid., pp. 70-71, chapter 1, *Kvennagiptingar*, compare to chapter 13, *Um úmagaeyri ok mála konu manns*, pp. 89-90.

If a woman marries without the consent of her father, brother or mother, or the person that shall be her guardian, she loses all her rights to the property that she should otherwise inherit, and the closest relative shall take that portion … A widow can marry whom she likes, with some consent of her relatives.[145]

These rules are interesting when compared to the older law of *Grágás*. According to *Grágás*, a woman should inherit even if she married against the will of her parents.[146] This rule, referred to as *nýmæli* (the new law) in *Grágás*, must have been due to canon law, as the consent of women without parental interference was strongly underlined in the twelfth century canon law discourse. Bishop Árni tried to hold to this principle in his demands for accepting *Jónsbók* in 1281. He demands that "women who got married without the consent of her relatives should not lose her right to inheritance."[147] Both the law paragraphs of *Grágás* and the policy of the bishop reflected the canon law understanding of the rights of women in relation to consent to marriage. The understanding of the new law present in *Grágás* was, however, not included in *Jónsbók*, which instead strongly emphasizes parental control. We can thus sum up by saying that in the law of *Jónsbók* these two traditions of mutual and parental consent were presented side by side, and the parental principle in relation to inheritance rules was strengthened compared to *Grágás*. How can this be explained?

The law regarding the marrying of women and the general jurisdiction over marriage was a matter that Bishop Árni Þorláksson and other clerics wanted to be part of the *New Christian Law*.[148] However, the Icelandic aristocracy had demanded that the rules governing marriage and inheritance continued to be part of the civil law, but nonetheless accepted the Church's jurisdiction over marriage. There were no rules about entering into marriage in *Jónsbók*, as they were contained in the *New Christian Law*.[149] *Jónsbók* did, however, contain a chapter on the

145 Ibid., p. 71: "En ef kona giptiz utan ráð föður síns, bróður eða móður, eða þess er giptingarmaðr er fyrir ráði hennar, hafi fyrirgert öllum örfum þeim er undir hana kunnu at falla þaðan frá, ok taki sá þann arf allan er næstr er erfðum…. Ekkja má gipta sik sjálf hverjum sem hon vill við nokkurs frænda síns ráð."

146 Agnes S. Arnórsdóttir and Nors 1999, p. 35.

147 DI II, p. 209: "at su cona sem giptist firi utan frænda Rad misti ei arfa sinna." See also ibid., pp. 206-208, list of items in *Jónsbók*, which Bishop Árni Þorláksson did not want to accept.

148 Ibid., pp. 206-208.

149 Sigurður Líndal 1976a, pp. 495-501.

financial contract of marriage, the rules for the exchange of matrimonial gifts and the rules for inheritance.[150] The economic rules concerning marriage thus came from *Jónsbók*. The rule stating that women should lose their share of inheritance if they did not accept the marriage their fathers proposed should be understood as a part of this compromise.[151] With these legal regulations of *Jónsbók* it was made clear that marriages should not be arranged against the will of the parents. Thus a compromise was obtained between the early canon law understanding of consent and the more customary practice, which the provincial law expressed.[152]

This compromise also included the rules about property transfer. New explicit rules about the jointly-owned property of the spouses cannot be understood in isolation from the consent issue.[153] Paragraph 3 of *Jónsbók*, concerning jointly-owned property and the rights of the women, *hjónafélag ok rétt konu*, opens with the rule that no man can take a woman's wealth out of the country against her will. Although her right to consent in this area was strong, other arguments were included that aimed to limit her rights. The paragraph continues:

> No woman shall deny her husband joint ownership, but they can make an agreement for jointly-owned property by both including in the agreement what they own or will get by inheritance, or in another way ... The one who contributes more to the jointly-owned property shall also get more in inheritance as shall his or hers heirs. If the spouses had lost their wealth the debt should be divided into two parts. But if their wealth has grown, the man or his heir shall receive two-parts and the wife only one-third of their belongings. They do not need to have the accept of anyone for this type of jointure. If the spouses have made the agreement in another way, then it shall not be followed, even if the relatives wish it, because law dissolves such an agreement for jointly-owned property. If there is no agreement for jointly-owned property between the spouses, then the countergift that was publicly given to the woman on the wedding day, according to witnesses, shall belong to the wife if she lives longer than he does. The marriage of women shall be published regularly every tenth year, and the countergift they receive,

150 *Jónsbók*, pp. 70-119.
151 Compare to ibid., p. 71.
152 See generally Brundage 1990, and in a Scandinavian context Agnes S. Arnórsdóttir and Nors 1999, pp. 32-39.
153 *Jónsbók*, pp. 73-74. The law of King Magnús the Law-Reformer includes the same rules.

and this can be done either at the assembly or in church. If the man becomes a widower, the heirs of the wife shall get the dowry, but not the countergift.[154]

These rules show that the possessions of a couple's two families should not be mixed, in case one of the spouses died while they were still childless. It was even thought necessary to state that in the situation in which a husband died and there were not sufficient possessions to pay his widow her portion of their property, his relatives would not be obliged to pay her from their belongings:

> But if a man marries by the law of the country and gives her countergift (*tilgjöf*) and he later dies, then she should be paid her personal things (*þing*), and dowry (*heimanfylgja*) from these belongings, as long as he has enough property. But if that is not enough, then his heirs shall not pay from their possessions, because no one shall buy himself a woman with others' wealth.[155]

The rules in *Jónsbók* about marriage contain another understanding compared to the older legislation of *Grágás*. There the separate property of the couple had great importance. According to the rules in *Grágás* a wife did not need to share the property of the household jointly with her husband if she did not wish to do so.[156] Precisely the opposite is the case in *Jónsbók*, which explicitly states: "No wife shall deny her husband joint ownership."[157] This can be used as an evidence for the fact that even if part of the marriage legislation continued to be in the secular laws of *Jónsbók*, those rules as compared with older legislation reflect a new understanding

154 Ibid., pp. 73-74: "Engi kona á at synja bónda sínum félags; en með því móti megu þau leggja félag sín á millum, at hvárt þeira leggi til félags alt þat er þá á eða eiganda verðr með erfðum eða öðrum hlutum … En þat hjóna, sem meira hafði til félags, skal meira upp taka eða þess erfingjar: sé síðan skipt í helminga, þó at eyðz hafi; en ef aflaz hefir, þá skal karlmaðr eða hans erfingi taka tvá hluti afla, en kona þriðjung; þurfu þau engan mann at þessu félagi at spyrja. En ef þau leggja annan veg, þá skal eigi haldaz, þó at erfingi kunni eigi eða vili eigi rjúfa, því at lög rjúfa þat félag. Nú er eigi félag hjóna í millum, þá skal sú tilgjöf konu heimil vera, er til hennar var gefin ok váttar vitu ok lýst var á giptingardegi, ef hon lifir honum lengr. Lýsa skal giptingum kvenna ok tilgjöfum á hverjum. x. vetrum, ok lýsa í fjölda, hvárt er vill á þingi eða at kirkju. En ef hann missir hennar við, þá taki arfar hennar heimanfylgju, en tilgjöf falli niðr."

155 Ibid., pp. 77-78: "En ef maðr fær konu at landslögum réttum, ok gefr í móti henni tilgjöf, ok fellr hann í frá síðan, þá skulu lúkaz henni þing sín ok heimanfylgja af sjálfs hans fé, meðan þat vinz til. En ef þat vinz eigi, þá skulu erfingjar ekki lúka af sínu fé, því at engi skal sér konu kaupa með annars fé."

156 *Grágás* Ib, pp. 45-46, II, p. 175. See especially in Ib, p. 46: "E*igi* a kona ibve me*ð* boanda sino*m* ne*m*a ho*n* iati þ*v*i."

157 *Jónsbók*, p. 73: "Engi kona á at synja bónda sínum félags".

of marriage. These opposing rules regarding the rights (or lack thereof) of wives to deny joint ownership to their husbands tell us something about different types of marriage law in *Grágás* and *Jónsbók*. In both cases, the property was at the husband's disposal. But a major difference appears in the legal status of the woman. The rule in *Grágás* established separate ownership as the norm: at any time, a wife could take her property and return to her own family or relatives. The rule in *Jónsbók*, on the other hand, strengthened the husband's control over the wife, while the influence of the woman's kin diminished. As a consequence, the husbands gained a stronger right to have their wives' property at their disposal.[158] Thus the thirteenth-century legislation was aimed at strengthening the legal position of the relatively recent conjugal family against the couple's parents or kin group. Based on the evidence of the Norwegian legislation, Randi Andersen has argued that joint ownership of marital property should be seen as the consequence of a stronger position of the Church and the king, "who wanted to break down a family right, appropriate to an older social organization."[159] This explanation can be questioned,[160] but what is important here is that both in Norway, Iceland and Denmark, the institution of *félag* (Danish *fællig*) became stronger under the influence of canon law. The joint principle behind the institution of *félag* could be characterized as a joint principle of sharing wealth between the spouses, instead of having separate belongings. This joint principle strengthened the new institution of marriage, which according to canon law should be based on the spouses' personal relationships.[161]

The principle behind the rule of separate belongings was that separate ownership was the norm, so that the wife could always take her property and go back to her own family or relatives. This was the result of a kin-based principle, understood as a principle based on the bilateral structure of the Icelandic kinship system. The woman did not leave her family at

158 See Andersen 1981, pp. 81-88.

159 Ibid., p. 117.

160 On similar grounds as the critic against Goody's theory about the Church's influence on kinship structure: see my discussion in chapter 1, p. 33 ff.

161 See also here in relation to Danish law: Iuul 1940, Pedersen 1992 and Dübeck 2003, pp. 57, 77-90. An important difference was, however, that in Iceland the family land (inherited property) was included in the *félag*, while in both Norway and Denmark it was a separate property.

marriage, but continued to be both a member of her new conjugal family as well as of the family of her parents.[162] The second rule was based on a more household-orientated principle. It was a principle, which strengthened the position of the newly established conjugal family, in relation to the parents or the kin group of the couple. This new marriage agreement could not be dissolved if it was correctly made. *Jónsbók* has, however, a chapter which refers to ways in which the marriage could be annulled or the couple could be separated.[163]

> If a woman has intercourse with a man other than her husband, or if she becomes separated from him without a reason according to the law of God, she loses the right to her countergift (*tilgjöf*).[164]

This rule about adultery was connected to the belief that a woman who had consented freely to marriage, was obliged to follow the rules of marriage and this included also the economic agreement. If she broke this contract, she no longer had a right to the countergift from her husband, later in life. There are also rules on how their property should be divided if they separated or if they separated and were subsequently reunited.[165]

We can sum up by saying that *Jónsbók* is a result of a compromise between ecclesiastical and secular views on marriage. This stated that marriage should be made according to the rules in *Jónsbók*, but that the Church would have full jurisdiction over marriage.[166] The need to define the rights of the bride's family became important in the wake

162 Because of weak kinship organization, marriage was very important for making political alliances. As mentioned here in the first chapter, many have studied the kinship system of Iceland. The oldest study is that of Philpot from 1913, where she underlined that the kinship organization was not very strong, and the kinship was organized after bilateral principle. Later studies have further illustrated this, see Hastrup 1985, and Miller 1990. On the political importance of marriage, see Agnes S. Arnórsdóttir 1995, and Byock 2001.

163 *Jónsbók*, pp. 75-77: "Um legorðssakir eiginkvenna ok skilnaðarsök við eiginkonur."

164 Ibid., p. 75: "Nú ef kona legz með manni undir bónda sinn, eða skilr hon við hann saklaust móti guðs lögum, þá hefir hon fyrirgert tilgjöf sinni."

165 Ibid., pp. 75-76.

166 DI II, pp. 209-10, compare to: "var þa gör at bæn Biskups midlan á milli Biskups oc konungs vm … sva oc ef menn töpuðu sier sialfum. at minna felli undan erfingium en bok segir … herra Biskup samdi oc. at kvennagiptingar færi eptir bok at hölldnum hans Retti til doma yfir hiuskapar malum. þat var oc bæn þeirra at su cona sem giptist firi utan frænda Rad misti ei arfa sinna." See also Figure 5, an illustration from *Jónsbók*.

of this new understanding of marriage law. In the previous system, the bride's family could more easily have control over her separate property because the economic agreement was arranged before a couple had been married. Thus the parental influence was weakened by the law of *Jónsbók*. The joint ownership of possessions could for instance be arranged after the marriage, without the woman's relatives taking part in the agreement. Secondly, the rules of *félag* gave the husband greater right to rule over their belongings after the couple got married. According to the rules of *þriðjungsfélag* (jointly-owned property in marriage where the woman owned one-third and the husband owned two-thirds), the husband and the wife could each own what they had brought into the marriage, while joint ownership applied to what they earned or lost during their married life. If their fortune increased, the husband would get two-thirds and the wife one-third. If they lost wealth, the debt would be shared equally between them.[167] What matters here is that the husband could decide which parts of their property were his wife's, and which parts were his.

3.2.2.3 The correction in the *Réttarbætur* of the late thirteenth and early fourteenth century

The property aspect of marriage will be discussed in more detail in the last part of this book. Here we need only be mindful of the fact that in practice the financial contract gradually became influenced by the consent theory. According to a *réttarbót* of 1294 a husband could not sell the property of the spouses without the wife's consent.[168] This assertion that a husband needed to ask his wife's permission to sell land was a radical change. This can partly be explained by the fact that the woman's kin became less influential in her life after the acceptance of the new marriage legislation at the end of the thirteenth century. Previously, the family of a bride had protected her property rights, but from this time onwards it was the bride herself who should ensure that her husband did not abuse his rights.

167 Hrefna Róbertsdóttir 1986, p. 34.

168 The origin of this rule is to be found in a *réttarbót* of 1280, see NgL III, pp. 3-12, see especially p. 8, but it was later also accepted in Iceland. See DI II, pp. 196-206, 282-88.

The practical consequences of the new understanding of property rights will be discussed in more detail in chapter 11. Here the main point is to underline that the power of the wife's relatives in relation to the financial arrangements of her household had become limited because the institution of *félag* strengthened the position of the newly married couple, in relation to that of their closest heirs. This must be the reason why some of the law regulations of the early fourteenth century aimed to minimize this freedom of the newly married couple. The *réttarbót* of King Hákon Magnússon of 1305 stated that it was important that the parents or other close relatives of the couple should continue to give consent to the contract. The creation of jointly-owned property by *helmingarfélag* was only allowed with the consent of the spouse's closest kin.[169] This was made even more explicit in another *réttarbót* of the same king from 1306 concerning the jointly-owned property of couples, *félagsgerð hjóna*. This law was made in response to a query over the appropriate rules concerning jointly-owned property. It was probably originally issued for Norway, but it was included in many manuscripts of *Jónsbók*.[170] The 1306 *réttarbót* contains two rules concerning the making of marriage contracts. The first stated that it was important to establish the jointly owned possessions with the consent of the closest kin. The second rule stated that if a man married a maiden or a woman and gave her the gift of countergift *tilgjöf*, they could make an agreement of joint possession, *helmingarfélag*, when they had children as heirs if both parties wanted this, and if the woman was married with the consent of her relatives. All their property and wealth (including what they owned at the outset and what they would acquire later) would be included in the joint possessions.[171]

What do these new rules mean? The institution of *helmingarfélag* ensured that the closest relatives were again more involved in contract making. At the same time this institution gave the household of the newly-married couple more freedom to use the property that was transferred into the new household than the contract of *máli* (contract

169 *Lovsamling for Island* I, pp. 25-26.
170 DI II, p. 348.
171 Ibid., pp. 347-49.

of separate belongings), which was a contract based on the rules of separate possessions of the wife. At the same time, the relatives had more influence over the transmission of property if the couple made *helmingarfélag* rather than *hjónafélag*, because the former agreement should be made with the consent of the closest heirs. It can thus be said that the rules concerning *helmingarfélag* defined in the *réttarbætur* of the fourteenth century were made to secure more firmly the rights of the wife's heirs. But those regulations do not seem to have solved all the problems.

In a *réttarbót* of King Hákon Magnússon of 1314,[172] it was claimed that the lawmen in Iceland did not follow the rules concerning the joint possessions of married couples correctly. The *réttarbót* says that a legal marriage was made if fathers gave their children in marriage and if both they and their children were together when the agreements were concluded. The legal agreement should be made on the wedding day, whether the contract was one of *máli* or *helmingarfélag*. The agreement should be made with the full consent of the couple and sealed by the handshake of all the partners involved in the making of the contract. It was not allowed to make *helmingarfélag* if the couple had children they could not support. Generally, though, the couple could make *helmingarfélag* if both the husband and the wife wished to do so, if they had legitimate children, and if the closest heirs also approved the agreement.[173]

In *Jónsbók* the principle of *helmingarfélag* was only referred to in relation to the situation in which one of the partners died. In these cases the surviving partner should pay half of all their debts.[174] It was thus the rules from the *réttarbætur*, which provided the foundation for the making of *helmingarfélags* contracts in Iceland in the centuries to follow.

It should thus be seen that the *réttarbætur* of 1305, 1306 and 1314,[175] were modifications of the new marriage rules put forward in the *New*

172 *Jónsbók*, pp. 293-300.

173 *Lovsamling for Island* I, pp. 27-31, DI II, p. 395, *Jónsbók*, pp. 293-300.

174 Ibid., p. 90.

175 Hrefna Róbertsdóttir 1986, p. 34.

Christian Law and *Jónsbók*. They were a revision of the original version of *Jónsbók* made at the request of the Icelanders. The strengthening of parental consent and influence in these regulations of the fourteenth century was of greatest importance in this process. The *réttarbót* of 1306 said that if a woman was married with the consent of her relatives, she and her husband could make an agreement for jointly-owned property, *helmingarfélag*, after they had children. If they had children from earlier marriages, their consent was also necessary for such agreements.[176] This type of jointly-owned property secured the interests of the closest heirs better than agreements of *hjónafélag*. By giving consent to these contracts the interests of family lines were also secured. The changes in marriage legislation of the early fourteenth century are thus only understandable as a reaction against the change that occurred in the late thirteenth century. Because of the requirement for the mutual consent of the couple made by the *New Christian Law*, and the strengthening of the institution of *félag* in *Jónsbók*, the principle of keeping the family property under the control of the closest kin of the married couple was strengthened in the corrections of the law at the beginning of the fourteenth century.

3.3 *The wider discursive context of the consent theory in Iceland*

It should now be clear that the consent theory of marriage did not have *direct* influence on the marriage legislation of the twelfth and early thirteenth centuries and the requirement for women's consent to property transfers was first legally introduced in the *réttarbætur* of 1280 and 1313.[177] As Jenny Jochens has stated, neither *Grágás* nor the oldest provincial laws of Norway required women's approval for marriage, but they ensured that fathers or other male relatives were responsible for the betrothal and marriage of women.[178] She has emphasized that the consent of the

176 Here, after ibid., p. 36.

177 Sandvik 1994, p. 102.

178 Jochens 1986b, p. 144. In the older Law of *Gulating* and the older Law of *Borgarting* the wife's consent to marriage is absent, while it can be found in both the oldest Law of *Frostating* and *Eidsting*. See also Jochens 1993, pp. 271-89.

couple was not necessary for a valid marriage during the period of the Icelandic Commonwealth:

> The contemporary historical sagas and the law codes furnish virtually no evidence that churchmen were able to modify the matrimonial regime by introducing the woman's right to approve the choice of her spouse. On the contrary, male force predominated despite the efforts of the clergy.[179]

Jochens also bases her statement that consent did not influence the marriage legislation of the late twelfth and early thirteenth centuries by referring to later court cases from 1429 concerning forced marriage. She refers to a case where it is said that a women would not marry against the will of her father, because she was afraid of him.[180] This case can, however, not be used as an evidence to say that the consent theory was not followed. According to canon law it was important that the woman not only consented to marriage, but also did so without any force. When force was used as an argument in a court case, it meant that the people involved actually did have knowledge of the meaning of the consent theory. Jochens does not seem to be aware of this canon law discourse, since she used the case as well as the legal rules that women should lose their share of inheritance if they did not accept the wishes of their father in marriage questions, as argument for her theory. Jochens interprets these regulations as demonstrating that lay society needed to protect itself against the undesirable consequences of the new success of the ecclesiastical authorities.[181] We find this strong continuity of parental authority demonstrated in many late medieval Icelandic documents, for instance a judgment from 1526, where it was judged, with reference to the *New Christian Law,* that the parents of a woman could marry her off to whom they wished with her consent.[182]

179 Jochens 1986a, p. 44.

180 DI IV, p. 394, where it says that the woman married a man because she was afraid of her father.

181 Jochens 1986b, p. 145. See also Jochens 1980, p. 377, about the growing influence of the Church, "which was attempting to introduce clerical celibacy and marital fidelity into Iceland."

182 DI IX, pp. 374-75. This case attempted to resolve an interesting problem: the husband of the bride claimed that he had never consented to this marriage.

I agree with Jochens that it is hard to find any evidence before the *New Christian Law* of Bishop Árni of 1275 that the mutual consent of the couple was necessary for making a legal marriage. However, rather than finding rules about consent to marriage in *Grágás,* we find as I have been demonstrating in this chapter many rules which were made *as a result* of the Christian understanding of marriage. Because marriage was made by consent, divorce should not be allowed and it was necessary to make the contract public. Thus, *Grágás* gives us indirect information about legal changes as a result of the consent theory.

Later legislation continues to give information about the indirect influence of the consent theory. In the law amendment, *Réttarbót* of 1294, it was stated that it was no longer necessary to own the minimum sum of five hundred to get permission to start living on a farm.[183] This meant that the financial restrictions associated with starting a farming life were removed. The need for such measures may be explained by changes in living conditions at the time: the need for labour around the small fishing villages, which were seasonal rather than permanent, required that it should be easier to establish new farming households. This has been the most frequent explanation for this law.

It should be emphasized, however, that this change can be explained in another way also, namely as a result of the canon law definition of marriage. According to this definition the consent of the bride instead of the marriage gift of *mundur* (the sum, of at least one *mark* paid by the prospective husband at the betrothal) became the most important criteria for a legal marriage. The old rules from *Grágás* requiring a minimum level of wealth in order to marry were thus no longer criteria for a legal marriage contract. At the same time it was seen as important to reinforce the tradition of sealing a marriage by the handshake of the involved partners should continue to be performed. There are other paragraphs in the *réttarbót* of 1294, related to the transfer of property in general. It says that guardianship over other person's property would be unacceptable if it was not made in front of witnesses and confirmed

183 DI II, p. 285: "Su klausa er ór tekin bókinne. er fyri býðr at hafa dilkfe. oc þat capitulum er fyri byðr at þeir menn reisi bunað er minna fe eiga en.v. hundrat."

by handshaking.[184] The paragraphs reflect the need to reinforce the importance of the old customs, such as the parental consent, which can be understood as one part of the discourse of change in legal regulation in the late thirteenth century.

Truly, the mutual consent of marriage became legally accepted in the late thirteenth century. At the same time as the mutual consent of the couple became the requirement for a valid marriage, the legal regulations from the late thirteenth and early fourteenth centuries show that the custom of parental consent continued to be enforced.[185] For a long time after consent had become the norm for contracting marriage, parental consent continued to be an important factor in the validity of such a contract. This compromise between the Church and the secular authorities is evident in documents from the fourteenth century. It is stated in the ordinance of Archbishop Árni Einarsson in Niðarós of 1346-49 that if a man wanted to marry he should first talk to the father and mother of the maiden or woman, but more particularly with the woman he wanted to marry by the law of God.[186] Secondly, the desire for parental authority was not actually in opposition to the Church's desire for the mutual consent of the couple, as this ordinance of Archbishop Árni Einarsson illustrates. Mutual consent and parental consent were further closely related in the legal discourse of the fifteenth and sixteenth century.[187] The existence of the parental consent, or the more general

184 *Lovsamling for Island* I, pp. 19-20: "Eigi er umboð fullt, utan með váttum ok handsölum." Every young man who owned landed property had the right to get back his land if his guardian had sold it, compare to *Lovsamling for Island* I, p. 20. This was called *brigð til þess lands*, which means to have the right to claim the land back to the family, compare to: "Hvar sem úngum manni tæmist land í erfð eða at gjöf, í vígsbætr eða réttarfar, ok selr fjárhaldsmaðr hans í brott, þá á hann brigð til þess lands." On the other hand, the young man could give away his own property called *málaland*. See *Lovsamling for Island* I, p. 21: "Sektalaust er manni at kjósa undan sér málaland sitt". These detailed regulations reflect the need to make the rules for division of property as clear as possible. These rules reinforce the idea that the transmission of property could not be executed without an element of publicity and that the individual's freedom to control *málaland* should be unlimited. The issue of the guardianship of young people was also related to the issue of the guardianship of unmarried women, as well as the husband's right to control his wife's property. It also had implications for the making of marriage contracts.

185 Agnes S. Arnórsdóttir 1996, pp. 82-83.

186 DI II, pp. 837-38.

187 One example can be taken from a marriage agreement from 1553. Þorsteinn Guðmundsson and Þórunn Jónsdóttir in Grund made a marriage contract, but they needed a dispensation to be allowed to carry it through, see DI XII, pp. 502-503. Two documents have survived concerning this matter. The first is a testimony from the lawman Ormur Sturluson and six other witnesses regarding the contract; see ibid., p. 504. A separate declaration from the same Ormur also exists concerning this subject; see ibid., pp. 507-509.

consent of the closest relatives of the couple, was, however, not only a result of the long enduring rules from *Grágás* or even the oldest provincial Norwegian laws, which ensured that fathers or other male relatives were responsible for the betrothal and marriage of their women.[188] The need for parental consent was also something, which represented a new understanding of marriage. According to this understanding, the mutual consent of the spouses was accepted as a form for making marriage contracts, but the parental consent continued also to exist. And what was even more important, because the lack of a wife's consent made her marriage contract invalid, it could be used as the main criterion for annulling the agreement.[189]

We can conclude that the Church authorities introduced the ecclesiastical model of marriage at an early stage, and that local bishops were active in urging people to live according to the new rules. There was no lack of knowledge of Christian doctrine, and canon law affected the Icelandic marriage legislation from the twelfth and thirteenth centuries.[190] The new marriage rules found in *Grágás*, the so-called *nýmæli*, can be seen as a result of this work, and it is possible to track changes in the sexual behaviour of the chieftains of the early thirteenth century. Other changes to be found in the legislation were those which altered the forbidden degrees of marriage and rules concerning divorce. All these rules were adopted by Icelandic legislation as potential solutions to the problems which arose because of clandestine marriage. These rules, along with more explicit rules later concerning consent to marriage, did not remove the role of parental consent to marriage. Further, the rules about the change in rules of joint possession of property in marriage in the *réttarbætur* underline how the theory of consent could

Ormur was a primary witness to this contract. According to him Þorsteinn did: "betroth himself to … the wife … with the consent of her brother, to be his legal wife according to the law of God and the Holy Fathers". See ibid., p. 508: "festi … hvstrv … med hennar jayrdi og samþycki henar brodur.. sier til logligrar eiginkonv. epptter gvdzs logum. og heilagra fedra setningum." Ormur's role as a primary witness was related to the fact that he was a relative of the husband, see ibid., pp. 508-509. The free consent of all the parties involved was stated in two places.

188 Jochens 1986b, p. 144.

189 Studies from courts other than Icelandic support this: See Helmholz 2004, p. 527, as well as Donahue 1976, pp. 267-69, about the policy of Pope Alexander III on consent theory.

190 Sigurður Líndal 1976a, p. 498, Sveinbjörn Rafnsson 1990, p. 131, Agnes S. Arnórsdóttir 1999, pp. 81-82.

have wide impact on property agreements. This was also partly related to the interest of the closest heirs of a couple to interfere in the matters of the couple.

Secondly, parental consent continued to be a strong force and even strengthened in Iceland as well as in many other rural parts of Europe during the Middle Ages. As Trevor Dean has underlined, the role of the Church courts in late medieval Europe in reinforcing parental authority over the marriage of their children has been a subject of debate.[191] Parental control over marriage did not disappear because of the canon law influence on marriage, partly because that was not the intention of the clergy in the different regions of Europe. After the mutual consent of the couple had become a part of the legal discourse, the parental consent became *even more important* for both securing the inheritance right as well as the Christian character of the contract, as will be argued here in the next two chapter of this book.

Thus, even if court cases from the Late Middle Ages can illustrate conflict between the new rule of consent of the spouses and the older rule of parental consent, their importance as an explanation for the development of real change in marriage practice during the Middle Ages should not be overstated: the court cases represent, rather, the change in the legal culture. The family of a bride did not lose all of its authority because she got the right of consent. Even if the idea of mutual consent to marriage was presented in the legal regulation as being in opposition to parental consent, the contrast was never so pronounced at the level of the local courts.

3.4 Conclusion

I have been discussing the way in which the ecclesiastical model of marriage was introduced into Norway and Iceland during the late twelfth and early thirteenth centuries. Change in marriage regulation in Iceland during this time illustrates that the ecclesiastical model of marriage became the main basis for deciding the legality of a marriage contract. The

191 Dean 1998, p. 85. See note 1, which refers to the discussion between C. Donahue, A. J. Finch and F. Pedersen.

new rules that were introduced existed alongside the older tradition of making marriage contracts. Evidence for this process was first found in the letters of popes and archbishops of this period. This resulted in new marriage legislation, which was strongly influenced by canon law. However, as we shall see in the next chapters of this book, it is first from the fourteenth century and onwards that law court material exists from which the implementation of these new ideas can be examined. It is evident that ecclesiastical authorities underlined the need for the double consent of parents and spouses as the correct principle to follow in marriage formation. The idea of the Christian marriage was thus introduced alongside the existing secular custom. However, churchmen proclaimed that if the woman's consent was absent, marriage had not been performed. This provided a satisfactory reason for separation and remarriage. In the thirteenth century the mutual consent of the couple thus became the main criterion for a valid marriage. This did not mean that the consent of parents to the marriage of their children was no longer important. In legal texts and formulas, the wishes of the couple to be married were placed before the wishes of their parents. In everyday life women continued to be given away by their fathers, mothers or other relatives, and a newly married couple received financial support from the previous generation because of parental consent. This chapter has argued that the change in the understanding of marriage during the Middle Ages was thus not necessarily a shift from the secular to the ecclesiastical model of marriage. Rather, it could be said that there was a slow movement in favor of Christian doctrine. Many aspects of the secular model were included in the ecclesiastical model, and the whole idea of marriage as an institution changed.[192]

The marriage legislation of the Icelanders was as much influenced by the Church as was the case in other regions of Europe in the Middle Ages. It is interesting that different sections of *Grágás* reflect the regulation of marriage and inheritance in different periods, although most of the *nýmæli*, the new law, was related to a change similar to that which took place in other European countries at the same time. Therefore

192 Compare to Agnes S. Arnórsdóttir 1999.

Grágás cannot be used solely as an example of the secular model of marriage, for it also reflected ongoing changes towards an ecclesiastical model. It is also important to note that the canonists from the eleventh and twelfth centuries discussed changes in the marriage law, and this discussion gradually changed the marriage regulation included in different law codes. A comparison of marriage law in the earlier *Grágás* with the later *Christian Law* of Bishop Árni from 1275 and *Jónsbók* from 1281 is therefore a study of gradual change in marriage regulations. The marriage regulations in *Grágás* and *Jónsbók* were both influenced by canon law. And these rules did not only come from the Church and the central authority in Norway, but were also shaped by marriage practices in Iceland.

To sum up, it can be said that both mutual and parental consent to marriage were a necessary part of making a legal marriage during the High and Late Middle Ages. This was not only a question of change in the law and statutes, but also changes in interpreting or using these rules. The marriage regulations in the *New Christian Law* of 1275 should thus not be interpreted only as canon law received from abroad, but also as a text 'translated' into a context that made it understandable for those who should follow it. At their most basic level the resulting laws were born by an interaction between clerical and secular traditions, which became accepted by the law council at the assembly at *Alþingi* in 1275 and 1281.

With the change in defining what constituted a legal marriage, changes followed also in the rules about property transfer. To be valid a marriage needed to have mutual consent. The key to developments in social relations at this time was that the changes which took place not only concerned who should give consent, but also what effect this had on wider family relations. The emphasis on mutual consent strengthened the conjugal bonds. This came to be reflected in the stronger control that spouses gained over their possessions. At the end of the thirteenth century rules concerning joint ownership in marriage became dominant in the legislation, while the role of separate ownership started to become less important legally. Instead of looking at this change as a conflict between two models of marriage, we should rather try to understand it as a compromise between the old and new rules. This compromise between old and new rules did not mean, however, that it was always clear what a legal marriage was. The next chapter will discuss this problem, a problem which continued to shape legal culture throughout the medieval period.

CHAPTER 4

The regulation of Icelandic marriage 1300-1600

Even though *Jónsbók* was the formal law code of the Late Middle Ages in Iceland, it is clear that it was only after the changes made in the *réttarbætur* that the marriage legislation fully and formally developed in accordance with the royal authorities. In the prologue to the *réttarbót* of 1294, which was made by King Eiríkur Magnússon especially for Iceland, we find information about the process of creating *réttarbætur*.[1] The king changed the law in compliance with the wishes of the Icelanders. One of these was the demand that property contracts continued to be made by the handshake of the involved partners.[2] Such regulations of the law continued until the end of the reign of King Hákon Magnússon (d. 1319).[3] After this period the marriage legislations, which had been introduced by *Jónsbók* and the *New Christian Law,* were finally and fully developed according to the royal authority.

The ecclesiastical authorities continued, however, to regulate marriage in the church statutes, and these changes were closely related to the

1 *Lovsamling for Island* I, pp. 17-22: "Kong Eirik Magnusson Retterbod, angaaende nogle ændringer i den islandske lov Jónsbók. Tunsberg 15. júlí 1294." See also DI II, pp. 282-88.

2 See the discussion here on this law amendment on pp. 106-107.

3 *Lovsamling for Island* I, pp. 23-24: "Fornyelse af Overkomsten med Norge vedtaket på altinget 1302": *Lovsamling for Island* I, pp. 24-26, see also *Jónsbók*, pp. 289-92, DI II, pp. 342-45, "Kong Hakon Magnussons Retterbod om adskillige punkter i den islandske Landslov. Tunsberg 23 juni 1305": Ibid., pp. 347-49,"Um félagsgerð hjóna." Ibid., pp. 379-86. "Réttarbót Hákonar konungs háleggs um arftökur og annað fleira Niðarósi 1313." *Lovsamling for Island* I, pp. 27-31, DII, p. 395, "Réttarbót Hákonar konungs háleggs um félagsgerð hjóna."*Jónsbók*, pp. 293-300. "Kong Hakon Magnussons Retterbod om adskillige punkter i den islandske Landslov. Bergen 14 juni 1314." *Lovsamling for Island* I, pp. 31-32."Kong Hakon Magnussons Retterbod, at den gamle Kristenret skal indtil videre være den gjeldende. Bergen 28 juli 1316". DI II, pp. 411-14. „Réttarbót Hákonar konungs háleggs um arftökur ættleiðinga", 28 mars 1318 i Tunsberg. Ibid., p. 418, AM 458. 12 mo bls. 79-80 skinnkver c. 1570. "Réttarbót Hákons konungs háleggs um eiða 1318".

problem of clandestine marriage. In a statute by Bishop Jón Halldórsson (1322-39) in Skálholt from 1326, clandestine marriage was forbidden,[4] and the importance of making the contract public was emphasized. The role of witnesses had long been important in securing the legality of marriage. Publicity had also been the criteria for the oral marriage contracts of *Grágás*. However, from the fourteenth century onwards, both the witnesses and the priest should be certain that there were no objections to the marriage and that it was legally made.[5] Here I shall focus both on the legislation of the amendments to the law, *réttarbætur*, from 1280 to 1320, along with the archbishops' and bishops' statutes of the fourteenth century. One of the principal aims of these regulations was to define what made a legal marriage. In addition new legislation was introduced in the sixteenth century, after the Reformation, in the form of new Church ordinances and these too will be discussed. The aim of the chapter is to give an overview of changes in marriage regulations from 1280 to 1587.

The laws and Church statutes from the early fourteenth century onwards, defined what constituted a legal marriage and how it could be legitimately made. However, in determining what constituted a legal marriage, it is not enough only to study the legislation of the authorities, since judgements passed in local courts sometimes attained the status of law. Therefore this chapter also deals with the way the judgements of the local courts became shaped by the canon law practice in Iceland. At the end of the sixteenth century this also included stronger control of sexuality according to the new rules of the judgement called *Stóridómur* (the "Great" or "Long Judgement"), a statute passed at the assembly at Þingvellir in 1564, as well as the marriage regulation of King Frederik II from 1587.

Sources for this chapter are thus both the legislation of the authorities, as well as material relating to local law courts preserved in charters, letters and written judgements. The following sources will be used: bishops' copybooks, judgements from the assembly of *Alþingi* and other

4 See DI II, pp. 582-94: "Bannsakabréf Jóns biskups Halldórssonar." See especially p. 593: "Fyrirbioðum ver ok öllum leikmonnum bæði karlum ok konum. at gera leynilegar festingar eða hionalags band eða heit."

5 Compare to ibid., p. 803, paragraph 73.

documents related to the law courts' definition of what constituted a legal marriage. This material reveals changes in the understanding of a legal marriage from the royal point of view, as well as from the differing policies of the bishops. For the later period the Danish Church ordinance of 1537 survives, which was given by King Christian III. In addition there is an ordinance of King Frederik II from 1587 concerning marriage in Iceland. The redefinition of the penal code for moral offence in the judgment of *Stóridómur* from 1564-65 was also of great importance for the institution of marriage.

4.1 The definition of legal marriage according to the royal and ecclesiastical authorities

Several Church statutes exist from the fourteenth century. These, together with the royal law codes and the *New Christian Law,* contain the official rules covering the institution of marriage in the Middle Ages. No Church statutes or royal legislation concerning marriage exist from the late fourteenth and early fifteenth centuries, but bishops' copybooks provide a good picture of the kind of problems the bishops actually dealt with. These copybooks show that the bishops were actively interfering in the way people lived their married life.

Change in the legislation occurred therefore in relation to local practice. In this chapter we shall primarily study this interaction from the authorities' point of view.

4.1.1 Réttarbætur *from the late thirteenth and early fourteenth centuries*

The changes of greatest interest in the marriage rules are to be found in the *réttarbætur* from the years 1280,[6] 1294,[7] 1305,[8] 1306,[9] and 1314.[10] In the earlier *réttarbætur* we find a definition of what constituted a legal

6 Ibid., pp. 196-206.
7 *Jónsbók og réttarbætur,* pp. 281-89.
8 Ibid., pp. 289-92.
9 DI II, pp. 347-49.
10 *Jónsbók og réttarbætur,* pp. 293-300

marriage, as well as rules concerning concubines and the need for a wife's consent to be given if her husband wished to sell her property.[11] We have earlier discussed that several of the rules are about marriage and property distribution.[12] Among other concerns of the *réttarbót* of 1294, however, are the issues of gifts,[13] and inheritance.[14] Thus the contents of the *réttarbót* reflect both the problems of consent and clandestine marriage, as well as the issue of property division. In the later *réttarbætur* of 1303, 1306 and 1314, the focus is even stronger on the economic elements of the marital contract. New and clearer rules defined the contract, especially in relation to the joint ownership in marriage.[15] The practical consequences of the regulations concerning property transfer and the making of joint possessions will be discussed in detail in chapter nine. What is important here is to underline that the regulation of marriage concerned both the question of consent, and how the spouses would share their property. It is in this context, and especially in relation to the question of inheritance, that clandestine marriage continued to be a problem.

A relationship with a concubine could fulfill the criteria for a valid marriage if the relationship had been made in accordance with the rules requiring both consent to marriage and consummation. In practice, however, marriage in this situation rarely happened automatically. According to the 1280 *réttarbót* of King Eiríkur Magnússon, no man could be forced to marry his concubine.[16] This rule was made for Norway but was later included in *Jónsbók*, and was also partly incorporated in another *réttarbót* given to Iceland by King Eiríkur in 1294. The rule probably assisted those who did not want to marry their concubine. For those who were both married and had a concubine this act provided a means by which to relinquish the concubine.

11 DI II, pp. 196-206, see especially paragraphs 7, 21 and 22. This *réttarbót* is also printed in *Jónsbók og réttarbætur*, pp. 281-89.

12 See discussion here on pp. 94 ff.

13 *Jónsbók og réttarbætur*, p. 286.

14 Ibid., p. 284.

15 *Réttarbætur* of King Hákon from 1302-18 were equally concerned with general property matters.

16 DI II, pp. 196-206, see especially p. 197: "Þat er oc firir boðet at menn se nauðgaðr til þess eiðs at hann skal eiga þa kono sem hann hafðe firir friðlu en hann legzt með henne siðan hann gek til skripta oc ifirbota." Also printed in NgL III, pp. 3-12.

Furthermore, how did the *réttarbætur* of the fourteenth century deal with the definition of what constituted a legal marriage? Apart from rules intended to define the property elements of the contract discussed above in chapter three, there were provisions that ruled that if the couple had been living together for more than ten years the relationship was a legal marriage. Paragraph 4 of the *réttarbót* from 1305 says:

> And if either he or she passes away, and they have been living together for a longer period than ten years, and if they always have regarded themselves as a legally married couple, even if the marriage has not been legally declared, and no rumors spread while they both were alive that she had been his concubine or his mistress, then their children, if there are any, shall be their heirs, and they shall be seen as legitimate, even if the witnesses of the betrothal are no longer alive.[17]

These statements about legal marriage are repeated in the *réttarbót* of 1314. They provide a clear definition of what made a legitimate marriage, and their presence can only be explained by a need for greater clarity in the law.[18] An oath from the fourteenth century (probably the early fourteenth century), gives an even clearer picture of the need. The oath indicates what a man should do if he breaks his marriage contract and starts living with another woman.[19]

To sum up we can say that the *réttarbætur* aimed (amongst other things) to define what constituted a legal marriage. They were concerned with the problem of clandestine marriage, as well as with clarifying the rules about inheritance and property division. These rules were given by royal authority, but were made in accordance with the needs of the local aristocracy. However, members of the aristocracy and the king were not the only important forces in the shaping of the law. The Church was also promoting the ecclesiastic model of marriage that had been introduced in the thirteenth century. The statutes of bishops and archbishops display their efforts and, together with the *réttarbætur*, these statutes demonstrate

17 *Lovsamling for Island* I, pp. 25-26: "Ok ef annathvárt þeirra kann frá at falla, þeirra sem x vetr eða lengr hafa saman verit, ok hafa þau jafnan haldit sik fyri lögleg hjón, þó at hjúskapr þeirra hafi eigi lögliga verit ámálgaðr, ok eigi bygðarfleygt meðan þau lifðu bæði, millum skilríkra manna, at hon væri hans frilla eða hórkona, þá skal barn eða börn, ef til eru, í arf setjast ok haldast fyri skilgetin, þó at eigi lifi festarváttar."

18 Ibid., pp. 28-29.

19 DI II, pp. 508-509.

clearly how the question of what constituted a legal marriage continued to be a central theme in the fourteenth century.

4.1.2 The bishops' statutes of the fourteenth century

Several bishops' statutes exist from the fourteenth century and demonstrate how the Church attempted to put its marriage policy into practice. Elements of the ecclesiastical model of marriage were reiterated in the statutes. For instance, rules forbidding marriage between people related in the fourth degree were frequently repeated.[20] However, the Church statutes were not only concerned with legal questions but also the liturgy of marriage, something to which we will return in a later chapter.

The attempt to avoid clandestine marriage became related in the statutes to the rule that the priest should bless the couple. There is little evidence of the practice of *kirkjuvígsla* (marriage in church) in Icelandic charters before the sixteenth century. But some bishops' statutes state that the priest should bless the couple, for instance the statute of Bishop Jón Sigurðsson (1343-48) in Skálholt from 1345. According to this statute, the priest on the three Sundays prior to the blessing of the spouses should announce that a marriage is to be contracted, and that he should ensure that the woman freely gave her consent to marry the man. If the marriage banns had been published three Sundays before the wedding feast, then the woman's children would be legitimate. These rules are also found in the *New Christian law* of 1275, but the rule that the wedding would be held no later than twelve months after the betrothal, which also is mentioned in this statute of Bishop Jón Sigurðsson, is a rule which has its origin in *Grágás*.[21] According to the statute, the wedding should also not be held "on a day or night that is holy or on a Friday."[22] The same rule is found in a fourteenth century copy of the older *Christian Law* of *Grágás*.[23] It may have its origin in this statute of 1345, but because this

20 See, for instance, in the statute of Bishop Jón Halldórsson from 1326, DI II, pp. 590-91, and the statute of Bishop Jón Sigurðsson from 1345, ibid., p. 812.

21 Ibid., p. 803, paragraf 73 and 76. See also the discussion about marriage rules in *Grágás*.

22 Ibid., p. 812: "Brullaup skulu eigi giorazt þann dag oc nott sem logheilagr dagur eda fostudagur er eptir."

23 See Agnes S. Arnórsdóttir and Nors 1999, p. 33, compare to *Grágás* III, p. 592, compare to *Grágás* Ib, p. 39 and 241, *Grágás* II, pp. 167-68, *Grágás* III, p. 35.

rule is also found in early twelfth-century continental law, it can also have an older origin.[24]

Remarriage was a theme often discussed by canonists in the Central Middle Ages. Their views differ greatly,[25] though in practice remarriage was an accepted and common practice almost everywhere. Bigamy was, however, strongly forbidden. This topic was included in the archbishop of Niðarós's statutes for Iceland. According to the statute of Archbishop Eilífur III of 1327, it was forbidden to make *twenn festmál edr tuennan hiuskap*, which means that once one had made a legal contract of betrothal or a marriage contract, one could never do that again.[26] The subject was taken up again in the statute of Archbishop Páll III from around 1340.[27]

The content of the statutes of Icelandic bishops was often identical to the statutes of archbishops.[28] According to the statute of Bishop Jón Halldórsson of Skálholt of 1326 different liturgies were used for marrying widows and maidens. It was not allowed for priests *sub pena suspensionis* to sing *pussunar messo,* over widows. Churchmen had created the term *púsa,*[29] or "to marry", used as a verb meaning to espouse, as a noun connoting the marriage ceremony. The ceremony could also be called *púsan* or *púsunarmessa,* "nuptial mass", to clarify the role of the priest and that this new ceremony probably should be added to the more traditional making of marriage agreement.[30] The same rule was present in the statute of Archbishop Ólafur of 1351 and again repeated in the statue of Bishop Jón Sigurðsson of Skálholt from 1345.[31] According to this same statute the priest could only marry those couples who had not been married before.[32] This idea had already been stated in a statute of

24 Brundage 1990, p. 191.

25 Brundage, 1995b, pp. 33-48.

26 DI II, pp. 628-29.

27 Ibid., pp. 752-53.

28 An example can be taken from the statute of Bishop Jón Halldórsson, which was from 1326, but in many ways included the same issues as the statute of Archbishop Jón from 1280. See DI II, p. 582.

29 Guðbrandur Vigfússon 1957, p. 480. The word *púsa* comes from the Latin word *sponsa* which is *espouse* in French.

30 Jochens 1995, p. 51. This is known in the Norwegian charters, DN IV, p. 132 from 1320. There it is named that *pusdar messor* are made. See also discussion about the ceremony in Jochens 1993, p. 289.

31 DI III, p. 64, compare to DI II, p. 812.

32 Ibid., p. 812.

Bishop Árni Þorláksson from the year 1292, probably following the advice of Archbishop Jörundur.[33] From the bishop's point of view widows and widowers were thus not supposed to remarry, but in practice things were very different.

The statute of Archbishop Eilífur of 1327 considered the custom of giving property to illegitimate sons or daughters.[34] Living with a concubine and in adultery was forbidden according to the statutes of the same archbishop from 1323. At the same time it was emphasized that every man betrothed to a woman was obliged to marry her before a year had passed from the publishing of the marriage banns in church.[35] The statute ruled that no man could take a woman to church for the ceremony of purification after childbirth if she was a concubine, a mistress, or a woman with whom he had had children in spite of their relationship being within the forbidden degrees.[36]

Archbishop Árni Einarsson's statute of 1346-49 was a manifesto for the ideal virtuous life. According to the statute there were different forms of virtue in life. Virtue could be achieved in widowhood, and in faithful marriage followed by celibacy. Those who did not conform to this manner of life could not expect to receive God's mercy. Living with a concubine and all other expressions of bodily desire outside marriage were forbidden and banned by God himself and the holy Church. If a man wished to be married, he must first speak with the father and mother, or other males related to the maiden or woman concerned. According to the law of God it was particularly important for him also to speak to the woman he intended to marry. If all parties agreed to the marriage the betrothal would be witnessed according to the law and the custom of the country. Afterwards the marriage banns would be published on three consecutive Sundays in the church of the parish where the parties had been born or where they lived. If an objection was raised because the couple was related to each other within the forbidden degrees, the parish priest would not allow the marriage to continue.

33 Ibid., pp. 279-80.
34 Ibid., p. 628.
35 Ibid., pp. 517-18.
36 Ibid., p. 570.

If nobody disagreed to the prospective marriage, the couple would be allowed to marry according to the law and the customs of the country. After this the couple would receive the holy blessing of the church and later consummate the marriage. If a woman became pregnant she could be saved after childbirth by confession and prayer.[37] And, "because we all hardly ever escape from this sorrowful valley, without the knowledge of pain and sickness, crying and sadness," God has, according to the archbishop, given us salvation in baptism.[38]

The statute of Archbishop Árni Einarsson demonstrates how the two models of marriage existed side by side, though not surprisingly it has a stronger emphasis on Christian liturgy than on secular practices. The contents of the statute were one element of the general policy of the Church at this time. The general message of the Church as it was presented in the statutes of the Icelandic bishops was addressed to a specific community, though of course members of this community did not always follow the rules in every respect. The rules of Bishop Gyrðir Ívarsson (1350-60) of Skálholt in a statute of 1354 can probably be used as an example of this. It stated that if a woman had a child with a priest, she should not be allowed to stay in his parish unless she herself owned a landed property in that parish.[39] The rule was adapted to fit the reality of a situation in which many people lived outside matrimony.

As the royal *réttarbætur* of the late thirteenth and early fourteenth century, the Church statutes were thus dealing with marriage from two different angles: i.e., whether a marriage was valid according to the law of God, and whether a marriage was legal according to the custom of the country.[40] Because marriage was a matter that should be dealt with by the jurisdiction of the Church, as well as according to regional custom (because of the issue of determining inheritance rights), both the secular and the ecclesiastical authorities continued to be equally involved in defining the institution. It is thus interesting to

37 Ibid., pp. 836-44. See also NgL III, pp. 295-301.

38 DI II, p. 839: "Oc af þui at mer komum allir swa nauðligha i þenna sorghadall at engi kemir utan verk ok syukdom grat oc vesold."

39 DI III, p. 94.

40 On this division of the law of the country from the law of God, see the discussion here in chapter 3.

further study whether the Reformation changed anything with regard to the regulating of marriage.

4.2 Change in marriage regulation in the sixteenth century

A new Church ordinance for Denmark was written in 1537, approved by Martin Luther, given by King Christian III, and published in Latin in the same year.[41] The ordinance was translated into Danish in 1539 and, on 14 June of that year, became the official law.[42] This version was first printed in Danish in 1542.[43]

The Danish ordinance was declared as Church law in Iceland at the see of Skálholt in 1541, but in the see of Hólar it was not declared law until 1551.[44] It was translated into Icelandic by Bishop Gissur Einarsson in 1541,[45] no doubt from the Latin text of 1537.[46] Another Icelandic translation exists from the later sixteenth century, which is longer than that of Bishop Gissur, probably because it is a translation of the Danish version.[47]

The portion of the text relating to marriage is very short.[48] It concerns the role of the priest in blessing the couple; marriage within the forbidden degrees; publications of the marriage banns in church; and confirmation of the secular authority's jurisdiction over marriage. A new thing in the Church ordinance was that clerics were also allowed to marry.[49]

Except for saying that priests should marry people and help married couples when they faced difficult times, only some few other direct

41 See Ingesman 1991, p. 164, compare to *Ordinatio Ecclesiastica,* 1537.

42 Ibid., p. 165.

43 Ibid., p. 165. Compare to *Kirkeordinansen 1537/39* in Martin Schwarz Lausten 1989.

44 *Lovsamling for Island* I, p. 43. Printed in Danish in short version in ibid., pp. 43-54, and the whole Ordinance in Icelandic in the translation of Bishop Gissur Einarson in DI X, pp. 117-67, and in a later Icelandic translation in ibid., pp. 167-256.

45 Ibid., pp. 117-67.

46 Ibid., p. 122. The argument in favour of the translation from the Latin text rather than from the Danish, is that Gissur's Icelandic version contains the foreword of the Latin text which is missing from the Danish translation by Peder Palladius from 1539.

47 Ibid., pp. 167-255. The Latin version is in ibid., p. 255-328, compare to: *Ordinatio Ecclesiastica – Regnorum Daniæ & Norvegiæ et Ducatuum Slesvicensis, Holsatiæ etc. etc. Anno Domini M.D. XXXVII.*

48 Ibid., p. 143.

49 Compare to the letter of King Christian III of 13 March 1545, printed after the original *Bisk. Skalh. Fasc. I,* original pargament with the seal of the king, DI XI, pp. 379-81.

changes occurred in relation to the marriage laws according to the Church ordinance. The role of the priests was that of ensuring that members of their communities followed Christian doctrine. At the same time the right to judge and punish sexual crimes should become a matter for civil courts.[50] In this way the Church should lose its formal jurisdiction over marriage to the civil courts and the role of clerics should be limited to performance of the liturgical service and pastoral care. This change was related to the new theological meaning of marriage after the Reformation: the Protestants denied the sacramental status of marriage.[51]

These rules about civil courts taking over marital litigation were accepted already in 1542 in Denmark, according to new royal legislation from Copenhagen called *Riparartiklar*. The name of this legislation is related to the fact that it was accepted in the town of Ribe, and it established again that the clerical courts should take care of matters related to marriage. That law also reached Iceland, but it is uncertain whether these rules were specially accepted in Iceland as Church law. What is certain, however, is that they are to be found in many Icelandic translations and copies.[52]

The later text of the Church ordinance is longer but the instruction concerning marriage is the same.[53] According to the chapter about marriage a couple was allowed to proceed with their wedding if there was nothing to hinder the marriage. They should be blessed while a congregation was present and the marriage ceremony should be conducted in accordance with the old custom, as well as the above-mentioned changes.[54]

There is a clear continuation of marriage rituals from those of earlier Church law. The forbidden degrees continued to exist but they were changed from the fourth to the third degree. Clandestine marriage was still forbidden, but the marriage banns needed only to be read in church

50 DI X, p. 143.

51 Peters 2000, p. 64.

52 See for instance DI X, pp. 720-30, *Riparartiklar*, and in ibid., pp. 730-51 in Icelandic translation. These rules changed some of the rules from the Church ordinance of 1537/39. They were accepted as law in Ribe on 4 May 1542 and became known in Denmark as the rules of the *Tamperretten*.

53 DI X, pp. 167-255, see also *Lovsamling for Island* I, p. 45: "Hvorledis man skal samle Folk udi Egteskap."

54 DI X, pp. 143, 199.

once or twice according to the new Church ordinance, rather than three times as required by earlier Church law.[55]

The Icelandic priests had not been living in celibacy before the Reformation. Many of them were living with women, known as *fylgikonur,* female followers of priests.[56] After the Reformation many of these female followers became their legal wives. The authorities in Copenhagen sent orders to Iceland concerning the issue of the right of inheritance of concubines and their children, once they had been married to the priest.[57] From the royal authorities, clear rules were issued about the matrimonial position of clerics, and these were copied and used in Iceland.[58] The *hirðstjóri* Otte Stigsen brought a letter from King Christian III to Iceland in 1545 about clerical marriage, *Konungsbréf um kvonfang klerka,*[59] and in July 1550 a general agreement was made in the assembly of *Alþingi* about priests who lived with their concubines, stating that after receiving absolution, they could be legitimately married to them.[60] This solution was related to earlier practice. Priests were openly living with women and sometimes making property agreements with them in a way that reminds us of formal marriage contracts.[61]

In Iceland it was especially common that clergy, including bishops, did not follow the canon law requirement of celibacy. Many examples can be found of priests who lived with concubines in the Late Middle Ages. Some of these partnerships appear very similar to contracted marriage. For instance, in 1383 the priest Guðbjartur flóki Ásgrímsson made such a contract with Þorbjörg Þorsteinsdóttir.[62] Another similar

55 Ibid., p. 143.

56 See my further discussion in chapter 11 about the custom of adoption of illegitimate children of priests.

57 DI XI, pp. 379-80, and translation ibid., pp. 380-81, compare to *Lovsamling for Island,* I, pp. 58-59 See especially p. 59. An order of King Christian III, sent to Iceland in 1551, stated that the children of married priests could inherit, see *Lovsamling for Island* I, pp. 65-66, compare to DI XII, pp. 326-27, and in Icelandic translation from the year of 1600, ibid., pp. 327-28.

58 Compare to the translation of ibid., pp. 327-28.

59 DI XI, p. 557. See Figure 6.

60 Ibid., p. 786.

61 See DI III, pp. 501-502, from the year of 1394. Þórður Þórðarson, a priest, handed over a landed property to his housekeeper Valdís Helgadóttir, according to ibid., pp. 676-78, and in 1402 a statement of accounts was made between them, and in this statement it says that she had a child with the priest. See also another example in DI IX, pp. 658-59, which is a marriage contract of the priest Björn Jónsson and Steinunn Jónsdóttir from 1533.

62 Ibid., pp. 19-20: "Skýrsla um kaupmálabréf séra Guðbjarts flóka Asgrímssonar og Þorbjargar Þorsteinsdóttur."

contract was made just before the Reformation, on 25 April 1536. It was a contract that was drawn up by parents who gave their daughter a large amount of landed property. The priest with whom she was going to live also gave the same amount, as well as three pieces of land and thirty cows. In return, the woman was to take care of the priest for the rest of her life. Although this contract did not state that there would be a sexual dimension to their relationship, it was nonetheless similar to a marriage contract in many respects. It stated that "the wealth that this agreement concerns shall go to their children if they have any."[63] The agreement was made with the consent of Bishop Jón Arason of Hólar, who himself had a mistress and many children with her. After the Reformation the priests were allowed to get married, and they were making marriage contracts with specific reference to the new marriage rules.

This change, by which the housekeepers of priests became their legal wives, was perhaps the greatest alteration as a result of the Reformation. There was, however, also a need to "adapt" the new rules made by the Danish authorities into the custom of the Icelanders. The assembly at *Alþingi* gathered clerics together in order to make general statements about sexual matters. One such statement was issued at a clerical meeting in 1552. It states that priests should forbid all people from living together whose marriage banns had not been published in church three times before they married,[64] or if the woman had not been legally betrothed, or if the couple had not been married in church. Marriage would be allowed with the consent of both parents if they were alive or, if the parents had died, with the consent of other closely related persons. If a man had betrothed a woman without the necessary consent, then the priest marrying them would have to do penance.[65]

This agreement of 1552 was based in part on the continuation of older marriage regulations. Clandestine marriage was forbidden, as it had

63 Ibid., pp. 764-65: "þesser peningar fyrr sagder skylldu falla til þeirra barna eff þeim jrdi þeirra audid."

64 The rule that marriage banns need only be published in church once or twice instead of three times does not seem to have been followed here.

65 DI XII, pp. 438-41, see especially pp. 438-39.

been in the statute of Bishop Jón from the early fourteenth century.[66] The priests should announce the marriage banns publicly, as they had done before, and make sure that there were no objections to the match. But in this case there was a further development. The priest was now always an integral part of the wedding ceremony, because he was obliged to marry the couple.

After the Reformation the state could not have full jurisdiction over marriage, and that is why the law from 1542 made in Ribe, again established that the clerical courts should take care of matters related to marriage. No regulations were issued by the royal authority about how marriage could be controlled by secular courts until a later stage in Denmark. This was also the situation in Iceland. The officer representing the royal authority in Iceland lacked the expertise to suddenly take over the juridical work of the clerics. In practice this meant that clerics, and especially the bishops, continued their role in making judgements and collecting fines in matters relating to marriage. In the agreement from *Alþingi* of 1552 it was declared that both the secular authority and the clerics should share jurisdiction in matters concerning each other, but it was at the assembly at Þingvellir that such statements were made.[67] At the same time it is important to underline that this was just the continuation of earlier practice in Icelandic law courts where both clerics and members of the laity had served on the jury.[68] This development in Iceland was not very different from what we know from Thomas Max Safley's studies in Southwest Germany. He writes that the *status quo* of marital jurisprudence between 1550 and 1600 was based primarily on canon law. Despite some admittedly crucial alterations in marital law, especially the allowing of divorce among Protestants, the disciplinary and doctrinal teaching of the Catholic Church continued to receive attention and to be practiced in religious and civil courts regardless of confessional allegiance. He further assumes that the greatest consequence in legal practice regarding marriage was a strengthening of the established system

66 See here discussion on p. 118, compare to DI II, p. 803.

67 DI XII, p. 439.

68 Compare to the courts of Bishop Jón Vilhjálmsson, discussed here on pp. 134, 136 ff.

through the "clarification and reaffirmation of age-old status. Continuity outweighed change."[69]

There is, however, no doubt that after the Reformation a certain amount of confusion existed in Iceland concerning who should judge in matters involving sexuality and marriage.[70] This confusion was related to the fact that even if the Church ordinance of 1537 did not make great changes in relation to the definition of legal marriage, and that the jurisdiction of the Church was not any weaker after 1542, it did clearly indicate, however, that the punishment for sexual misconduct should be stronger, whilst previously sexual relationships outside marriage had been controlled by the less official penitence regulation of the Church.[71] The law of *Kaldangrsrecess* from 1558 was the first in which clear rules were incorporated about the types of penalty to be faced by those living in adultery: i.e. paragraph 60 deals with adultery and illegitimate sexual relationships.[72] This law was enforced force in Iceland through a letter sent by the king to Icelanders in 1563.[73] However, this order was last to be only two years, at which point the new judgement of *Stóridómur* of 1564-65 was instituted by the king. This was a statute passed in an assembly at Þingvellir on 30 June 1564, and ratified by the king the following year. It redefined the penal code for moral offence, especially in cases connected with adultery and sexual intercourse between persons related either through affinity or consanguinity, where the allotted punishment was the decapitation of men and the drowning of women. Confusion about which of these two laws – the one from *Kaldangrsrecess* of 1558 or *Stóridómur* of 1564-65 – one should follow, meant that the judgement of 1558 was used in some court cases after 1565, while the judgement of *Stóridómur* was used in others. Let us take a closer look at this new judgement.

69 Safley 1984, p. 38.

70 Compare to the forewords of the *Kaldangrsrecess*, in DI XIII, pp. 349-58, see especially p. 351. One of the publishers of this document in DI has written: "að með skiðskiptunum gerðist hér svo mikil óvissa á ýmsa lund um lög og rétt, sem lengi eimdi eftir af, að menn vissu ógerla, eftir hverju mátti fara örugglega."

71 These rules will be discussed in chapter 5.3.

72 DI XIII, pp. 349-58. In the first instance, a person found guilty of living in adultery should pay a monetary fine; for the second offence, the penalty was a monetary fine as well as being deemed an outlaw; and, in the event of a third offence, the man would be beheaded and the woman drowned.

73 DI XIV, pp. 72-75.

Great efforts had been made before the judgement known as *Stóridómur* was accepted at Þingvellir on 30 June 1564,[74] and later confirmed in 1565 in Lund by King Frederik II.[75] For example, the Icelandic bishops' wish to know how to deal with the problem of incest led the Danish king to seek the advice of experts at the University of Copenhagen.[76] In January 1561 the king consulted some professors concerning suitable punishment for incest and adultery.[77] The advice of the professors resulted in the new law of *Stóridómur,* and thus a new moral court was introduced into Iceland.[78] The idea was that it should be possible to appeal cases from the law council of *Alþingi* to this new moral court, at whose head was the royal officer of *höfuðsmaður*. The court as a body of appeal did not, however, start to function until 1593, because of the resistance against it in Iceland.[79] However, from a legal point of view it marked the starting of the end of a period that had begun with the introduction of the *New Christian Law* in the see of Skálholt in 1275, when the Church gained the jurisdiction over marriage. From 1564 and onwards it was established that only the secular authority, either the assembly of the *Alþingi* or the king's functionary in Iceland should declare whether a marriage was legal or not – and not also the bishops as before.[80] This was a direct consequence of the fact that the Church should no more have jurisdiction over marriage. Even if *Stóridómur* did not start to function fully as a court from the start, its existence can be explained as a part of the constitutional development of the sixteenth century. Secular royal authorities began to interfere more directly in matters hitherto regarded as religious.[81] This meant that royal authority

74 Ibid., pp. 271-76. See also *Lovsamling for Island* I, 84 ff, compare to also DI XIII, pp. 478-80, and DI XIII, pp. 499-500.

75 DI XIV, pp. 357-60. See also *Lovsamling for Island* I, 89 ff.

76 See letter from the professors of the University to the king, 2 February 1561. DI XIII, pp. 569-73.

77 Ibid., pp. 567-68. This demonstrates how new laws issued by the royal authorities were related to the way in which local Icelandic authorities were dealing with the problem.

78 This new moral court has been studied by Már Jónsson; see his doctoral thesis from 1993. It is not within the scope of my study to analyze the consequences of the Reformation on the sexual behavior of the Icelanders in the Early Modern period. The historical meaning of this court is only discussed here in relation to the juridical change that followed in the sixteenth century.

79 Eiríkur Tómasson 2001, p. 104.

80 Compare to DI XIII, pp. 746-48. But as mentioned before the practice was different, it was both the clerics and laymen who were judging in the council.

81 Ibid., p. 351.

was getting more and more involved in everyday life. A document from the highest royal functionary in Iceland, Páll Stígsson, of 2 July 1563 can be used as one example of this. The letter considers the behavior of people in church.[82] In another document, this time from 1565, the same functionary wrote that people should not be allowed to take babies and dogs to church.[83]

This increasing secular interference in Church matters was taken even further by the ordinance issued by King Frederik II concerning marriage in Iceland in 1587.[84] The ordinance marked the first radical change in marriage regulation since the marriage laws of the late thirteenth and early fourteenth century. According to the prologue of the regulation, the issuing of the marriage law of 1587 focused on the fact that the former marriage law of the country no longer constituted the valid law.[85] But according to its content, we can once again see that compromises were made between the old understanding of marriage and this new one.

The ordinance is divided into four main chapters. The form of engagement known as *trolovelse* replaced the old custom of betrothal, *festar*.[86] Once engaged, the couple was not allowed to share the same bed until they had been married in church. The priest was not allowed to bless couples from parishes other than his own, nor people he did not know well. People related within the third degree were not allowed to marry.[87]

Changes were introduced. A new rule was included which stated that a couple should not be married before getting to know each other quite well. Secondly, for the first time in an Icelandic legal regulation, the ordinance of 1587 highlights the importance of the virginity of the bride. If she was not a virgin the husband could divorce his wife, although

82 DI XIV, pp. 113-17.

83 This letter was written at Bessastaðir 21 July 1565, DI XIV, p. 403 ff.

84 *Lovsamling for Island* I, pp. 113-24: "Ordinants, hvorledes udi Ægteskabssager paa Island, dömmes skal. Kronborg 2 June 1587." In this Icelandic regulation the king quotes another Ordinance from 1582 for Denmark and Norway. The Icelandic one is similar to the Danish one in almost all parts.

85 Ibid., p. 114.

86 Ibid., p. 114.

87 Ibid., p. 115.

he could show compassion if he wished.[88] In addition, the ordinance of 1587 stated that a man who had *krænket*[89] (deflowered) a virgin could declare his intention to marry her, if the priest announced in church what had happened.[90] This must have been an efficient form of collective control over sexual behavior. The second chapter in the ordinance of 1587 concerns those men who took a woman's maidenhood, persons known as *jomfrukrenkere*.[91] If this happened to a virginal woman, she could not of course have been accused of adultery, but the man should offer to marry her. If the woman and her guardians would not accept marriage, the man would have to give her money and property in accordance with the advice and the consent of her friends.[92] The notion that such payment should go to the woman herself was a novelty. It was no longer a question of her family punishing the man, as had been the case under the earlier law. If a man was found guilty of having sex with many women without intending to marry them he would be punished by death.[93] This was related to the legal development, which in many aspects could be described as a development towards the criminalization of all sexual activities outside marriage.

The third chapter concerned separation or, rather, reasons why separation might come about. It should be remembered that according to canon law separation was only possible if the marriage had never been legally contracted, which gave the separation the form of an "annulment", a declaration that the relationship had never been valid.[94] The first reason for separation discussed in this chapter was adultery. The importance of proof in such cases was emphasized, since otherwise an allegation of adultery could easily be used by partners to harm each other. The second reason for separation was called *desertio*. This referred to situations

88 Ibid., p. 117-18. On how medieval people tested or verified virginity in general, see Kelly 2000, pp. 1-16, and especially p. 18.

89 Regarding this word, see the definition in *Ordbog til det ældre danske sprog* II, p. 444. The technical meaning of the word was to have had a sexual relationship in the meaning that the woman had lost her maidenhood. The Latin term was *defloratio* and did not have the same legal meaning as *raptus* for rape.

90 *Lovsamling for Island*, I, p. 117.

91 Ibid., pp. 118-19.

92 Ibid., p. 119.

93 Ibid.

94 Ibid., pp. 119-22. See also discussion in Einar Arnórsson 1955, and Ragnheiður Kristjánsdóttir 1994 (unpublished thesis).

in which one member left the other without reason and without the consent of the other.[95] The third reason for separation was if the couple could not have children because of the impotence of the husband, but in such instances separation was only allowed after attempts had been made to solve the problem.[96] The fourth chapter of the ordinance dealt with the lifestyle of couples after marriage.[97]

It is important to acknowledge that behind many of these measures the influence of the Christian understanding of marriage that had developed over the previous centuries is obvious. The changes are related to the consequences of the canon law definition of marriage: matrimony could not be deemed holy if one of the partners lived in adultery; a marriage could, according to canon law, also be annulled because of desertion; and, impotence was also a reason for the annulment of a marriage, because a marriage could never have been consummated if either partner was incapacitated. The new thing in the marriage regulation of 1587, however, was a determination to judge unacceptable sexual behavior as something criminal. This legislation marks the end of the process, which had started in the twelfth and thirteenth century. The basis was still canon law, but what was new about the legislation of 1587 was its promulgator: a king had replaced the pope. Thus, the Danish Church ordinance of 1537/39 issued as a result of the Reformation, and the marriage legislation of 1587, should be understood as parts of the process of establishing stronger royal interference in Icelandic matters: a process that had started in the previous century. The Church ordinance and the marriage legislation of 1587 had the backing of a stronger executive power than the earlier *réttarbætur* of the late thirteenth and early fourteenth centuries. This did not, however, necessarily affect the content of the legislation. The legal rules about marriage relating to the Reformation closely reflected themes from earlier statutes.

After the Reformation the Church ceremony became a legal means of marrying, but it was nonetheless the state authorities that controlled

95 *Lovsamling for Island* I, p. 120. This was a well-known phenomenon in the Middle Ages and therefore often mentioned in canon law.

96 Ibid., I, pp. 121-22.

97 Ibid., I, pp. 122-24: "tilfald udi Egteskab."

the legal recognition of marriage. The relatively substantial number of sources concerning marriage and sexual matters from the last part of the sixteenth century compared to the earlier centuries, are products of this system of control. In order to understand this process better we need to study what happened on the local level in the law courts.

4.3 The era of practical change

We have already considered how changes in the definition of what constituted a legal marriage are revealed in the royal and ecclesiastical laws and in other legal documents. By changing the focus to the local law courts, the issue now is going to be how the different bishops judged in marriage cases, and which role the member of the *Lögrétta,* (the law council of the assembly of Þingvellir), had in such matters.

4.3.1 The local courts

During the twelfth and thirteenth century a law council, called *Lögrétta,* was the most central part of the assembly of the *Alþingi* in Þingvellir. This council had legislative power in matters concerning the Church as well as in other matters.[98] The role of this law council changed though when Iceland came under Norwegian rule. The assembly continued to exist, but the law council became primarily a law court.[99] However, the role of the court in relation to the Church was not altered. In Iceland a special *ius particulare* evolved. It meant that the laws of the Church were closely related to regional custom, even though the *ius divinum* called *guðs lög* (canon law) had been accepted at the assembly in 1253.[100] This acceptance, however, did not have any practical meaning, and it was first in 1275 that the Church gained jurisdiction over its affairs under the *New Christian Law* of Bishop Árni Þorláksson.

98 Einar Arnórsson 1953-54, p. 5.

99 Gunnar Karlsson 2000a, p. 18.

100 Einar Arnórsson 1953-54, p. 6. Einar Laxness 1995 II, p. 64. In 1253 the agreement was made at the law council, but it seems that this agreement was only accepted this one time by the council. The existence of *ius divinum,* as a legal concept is, however, evidence for how canon law was a part of the legal thinking in Iceland.

Statements from the bishops, as well as the Church statutes more generally, had the status of Church law in Iceland.[101] Church law was not always easily determined and there were sometimes great disputes about what was the correct rule to follow.[102] Nonetheless, in theory if there was any discrepancy between the secular law of the country and the law of God, the law of God should always take precedence according to canon law.

After the law council became primarily a law court under the new rules of the late thirteenth century, new royal officials known as *lögmenn* (lawmen) and *sýslumenn* (district commissioners) presided over the court proceedings.[103] Clearly this change meant that the king began to receive an income from the payment of fines in Icelandic criminal cases, and in this way some landed property got into the hands of the authorities overseas. But because canon law started to have direct influence also on the secular proceeding in juridical matters, the royal officer often modified criminal cases according to the canonical methods of inquisition. This meant that the burden of proof began to have greater meaning than before. And written documents such as marriage contracts could be used as proof in both civil and ecclesiastical courts.[104]

What kind of courts dealt with marriage cases? Apart from the court at Þingvellir the most important were the courts of the bishops at the sees of Hólar and Skálholt, and a change in this regard only took place towards the end of the sixteenth century, as mentioned earlier, when the bishops increasingly held their jurisdictional meetings at the assembly of Þingvellir.

It is important to realize that even if the civil law codes contained no rules concerning Church law,[105] the distinction between legal matters to

101 Björn Þorsteinsson and Guðrún Ása Grímsdóttir 1990, pp. 42-43.

102 Compare DI VIII, pp. 429-52. There are two copies of *Leiðarhólmsskrá*, a list made by laymen concerning the Church laws that had the status of legal rules in Iceland. This document dates from 1513, and it rejects the growing power of clerics at that time.

103 Gunnar Karlsson 2000a, p. 18.

104 Eiríkur Tómasson 2001, p. 104.

105 Einar Laxness 1995 II, p. 64. The Norwegian law of 1271-4, as well as the Icelandic law books of *Járnsíða* and *Jónsbók*, do not include any law paragraphs about matters of the Church. The reason is that the Archbishop Jón rauði (1268-82) wanted to make the Church more independent from secular power. This was

be dealt with by the Church and matters to be dealt with by the secular authorities was never that clear at the level of the courts. Normally the bishops placed laymen and priests in their courts. About twenty to thirty statements and judgements have survived from such episcopal courts in the period 1350-1450. Most of them are to be found in the copybook of Bishop Jón Vilhjálmsson, thus covering especially the period 1425-35 when he was bishop at the see of Hólar. These judgements were issued as a result of the Church's right to have jurisdiction in its own affairs.[106] In a few cases only priests were included in the jury, but in judgements concerning sexual matters, as well as in those concerning marriage, both clerics and laymen acted as judges because these matters were seen as external,[107] while other rules covered internal matters, such as the question of confession. Only the bishop or one of his officials was able to hear confession and grant penance to women who had given birth to illegitimate children or who had lived in adultery.[108] Appeals against judgements of the bishops could be made to the archbishop or to the pope.[109] It is clear, however, that any direct involvement of the papacy in local matters, for instance by the issuing of marital dispensations, does not seem to have been accepted by the Icelandic elite.[110]

4.3.2 The late fourteenth and early fifteenth centuries

The law courts constituted the forum in which the definition of a legal marriage was established. Existing formulas used by the clergy reveal the variety of marital offences the Church was dealing with during the late medieval period. An example of these can be taken from a document dated to around 1490 and written by the dean Gunnar Jónsson in the

also the work of Bishop Árni Þorláksson in Skálholt (1269-98), but he succeeded where the Norwegian archbishop did not. The *New Christian Law* of Árni was acknowledged by secular authorities at the assembly at Þingvellir, while the clerics in Norway needed to wait a century before getting their *New Christian Law* accepted by the Norwegian authorities.

106 Björn Þorsteinsson and Guðrún Ása Grímsdóttir 1990, p. 61.

107 Ibid., p. 63.

108 Ibid., compare to DI IV, pp. 362-63, 403-404, 495.

109 Björn Þorsteinsson and Guðrún Ása Grímsdóttir 1990, p. 65.

110 Compare to DI XIII, p. 231, from *Spjaldhagadómur Eggert Hannessonar of 1557*: "hofum vier þar alldri logmal til fundit. ad pafvaligt valld hafi matt aftaka edr vid auka vorre landzlagabok". See also the discussion here in chapter 5.2.2 and in Agnes S. Arnórsdóttir 2003, pp. 159-69.

northern diocese of Iceland. It contains three legal formulas dictating some judicial ordinance for marriage.[111] The first formula considers the consummation of marriage. Another of the formulas considers a case of marriage within the forbidden degrees of kinship. And the third formula describes the pronouncement of a marriage as legally binding as long as bridal consent had been indicated by a handshake made in front of witnesses.[112] These formulas reveal common concerns about marriage that were raised in Icelandic courts at the end of the fifteenth century, and were, among other things, designed to ensure that a clandestine marriage could be pronounced as legally binding. Sexual union without any other ceremony or contract initiated such a marriage. Cases concerning couples that had been cohabitating for ten years, and declarations of marriage that had been made according to the law of God came before the courts.[113]

There are only few Church statutes or *réttarbætur* on marriage from the late fourteenth and early fifteenth centuries. This is partly explained by the fact that in this period the bishops in Iceland were appointed directly by the pope, thus often being foreigners without local knowledge. One of these foreigners was Bishop Michael, who according to *Flateyjarannáll,* was Danish and was elected bishop in Skálholt in 1383 without any consultation with the Church authorities in Niðarós.[114] This meant that the influence of the archbishop of Niðarós was dwindling, something which the Icelandic historian Jón Jóhannesson interpreted as the beginning of a dark period in the history of the Icelandic Church.[115] Michael had been in Rome, and according to Jón Jóhannesson his appointment was probably influenced by Queen Margrethe's active policy for putting Danish people in political positions also in Norway.[116] The

111 DI VI, pp. 731-32: "Skjalaforsagnir þrjár, er Gunnar prestr Jónsson í Goðdölum og prófastr (í Skagafirði) hefir haft fyrir sér."

112 Ibid., p. 732.

113 Compare to DI III, pp. 733-34. See also Figure 8.

114 Jón Jóhannesson 1958, p. 114.

115 This interpretation appears in ibid., p. 115.

116 Ibid., pp. 114-15. He states: "Miklar líkur eru til og raunar nálega víst, að Margrét drottning hafi staðið á bak við þetta, því að hún hafði hug á að koma dönskum mönnum í sem flest embætti í Noregi og skattlöndunum, en vita mátti hún, að dómklerkasamkundan í Niðarósi mundi ekki kjósa þá, og var þá tekinn sá kostur að ganga alveg fram hjá henni. Fáum árum áður (1380) hafði páfi neitað að vígja norskan mann, er samkundan hafði kosið til erkibiskups, og vígði í staðinn danskan mann af aðalsætt. Annar norskur biskup nývígður

period in which bishops were appointed directly by the pope lasted until 1442 in the see of Hólar, and until 1466 in the see of Skálholt from which point the Icelandic bishops were once more elected by the archbishop and the cathedral chapter in Niðarós.[117] This change was a consequence of the Concordat of Vienna in 1448, which re-established the right of the cathedral chapels to elect their bishops, and which was shortly afterwards recognized by King Christian I. The changes where reflected in King Christian I's *réttarbót* of 26 November 1450, also known as *Langarréttarbót*.[118] According to Jóhannesson this constituted a step forward in the process of improving the difficult situation.[119]

This interpretation is influenced by Jóhannesson's nationalistic historical view. He was also more interested in explaining the institutional organization of the Icelandic Church, rather than studying the religious culture. My point is, however, to underline that during the time when the local bishops were appointed directly by the papacy, both the Church organization as well as the Christian faith was strengthened. The bishops made a register concerning Church property, produced statutes (which have only been preserved in Icelandic translations), and issued ordinances for their clerics to follow.[120]

Some of the bishops were very active. The Danish Bishop Vilchin Henriksson (1394-1405) issued an order in Skálholt after a meeting of priests in 1396, which stated that priests should send away the women with whom they had begotten children, and their concubines as well.[121] He also underlined the importance of confessing clandestine marriage, and announced that the same penance should be used for clandestine marriages as for living in adultery.[122]

One of the bishops appointed directly by the pope was the above-mentioned Englishman Jón Vilhjálmsson Craxton.[123] He was consecrated

varð að hrökklast frá embætti, sökum þess að maður kom frá Róm með veitingu fyrir því." Recently this has been studied more in detail in Haug 1996, p. 180, and forward.

117 Jón Jóhannesson 1958 p. 115. See also Appendix IV.

118 DI V, pp. 62-69.

119 Jón Jóhannesson 1958, pp. 118-20.

120 Björn Þorsteinsson and Guðrún Ása Grímsdóttir 1990, p. 42.

121 DI III, p. 615.

122 Björn Þorsteinsson and Guðrún Ása Grímsdóttir 1990, p. 51.

123 See p. 134.

as bishop of the northern see of Hólar in 1425.[124] There had been no bishop in Hólar for two years when he arrived and there were many problems requiring his attention. He worked hard to change people's behavior and he succeeded in having a number of his claims accepted in the courts.

The reason for his success in this respect remains obscure but his achievements may possibly have been due to his background or to his close alliance and friendship with the powerful and rich Loftur Guttormsson. It is known that Loftur gave considerable assistance to the bishop in his tasks, though it is probable that Craxton's connections with local authorities, as well as with the papacy were also important.[125] As soon as he entered his see the bishop started a campaign to build up respect for Church law and had considerable success with regard to some issues.[126] But he was mostly acting against his own clerics.[127] In 1431 Craxton wrote a letter to the priests of his diocese which was to be read aloud in every church. In the letter, he forbade the priests to administer the Eucharist to those who had committed a variety of sins of adultery and fornication. Craxton says in his letter that his aim was to strengthen Christianity. The letter considers the sins of adultery and concubinage, as well as the sin of sexual relations between people related through god-parenthood.[128]

During Craxton's episcopacy, there was a special court at Hólar presided over by both secular and clerical authorities.[129] Owing to the survival of Craxton's copybook a wealth of information is available regarding his policy on family matters. It is a skin manuscript and the oldest copybook of an Icelandic bishop, dating back to the first part of the fifteenth century.

124 Craxton was to be in Hólar until 1435, but then he became bishop in the see of Skálholt and was officially bishop of Skálholt until 1438, although he never visited his see. It was said that he died in poverty in London in 1438. See Björn Þorsteinsson and Bergsteinn Jónsson 1991, p. 473, compare to Björn Þorsteinsson and Guðrún Ása Grímsdóttir 1990, p. 41.

125 Ibid., 1990, pp. 42, 56, 60.

126 We can find in the copybook of Jón Vilhjálmsson many examples of his efforts to influence the life of the community. He accused the lawman Rafn Guðmundsson of many things and threatened him with excommunication. See DI IV, pp. 487-88.

127 See for instance in ibid., pp. 489-90.

128 Ibid., pp. 441-42, see the original in AM 235 4, the copybook of Bishop Jón Vilhjálmsson.

129 Compare to DI IV, p. 448.

What kind of marriage cases was Craxton dealing with?[130] Some were concerned with adultery.[131] Others dealt with confession and penitence, of which the letter of confession by Ingibjörg Sturludóttir from 1430 is an example.[132] One dealt with clandestine marriage,[133] while another was directly involved with dissolving such a relationship, namely the case of Þorleifur Þórðarson and Þorgerður Böðvarsdóttir from 1429.[134] There is also a case about a nun who had given birth to children, and in one case the father of the child was a priest.[135] The priest had written a letter of confession in which he admitted that he had had a sexual relationship with the nun and that he was the father of her child. It is worth mentioning that the mother had only been a nun for a year when this happened. The priest lost his benefice, thus receiving the usual penalty for this kind of crime. He had, however, also to do penance and since he was not physically strong enough to undertake a pilgrimage to Rome, he instead had to walk barefoot from church to church in the diocese of Hólar. Having done that, he was told to enter a monastery and never again visit a convent of nuns. A passport in Latin for a penitent on his way to Rome has survived from one of the other cases involving nuns who bore children.[136]

When the bishops appointed by the pope arrived in Iceland they probably soon realized that the knowledge of canon law was not lacking amongst the Icelanders. In the register of the see of Hólar many legal books of the international Church are mentioned, including the *Corpus Juris Canonici*, as well as glossaries and works of leading canonists of that time.[137] The bishops realized, however, that it was necessary to change the actual habits of the people, so these bishops engaged themselves actively in efforts to change the sexual behavior of the Icelanders. The role of the foreign bishops thus became very much concerned with

130 In ibid., pp. 367-71 is a register over the content of his copybook.

131 Ibid., pp. 456, 733.

132 Ibid., pp. 403-404.

133 Ibid., p. 392.

134 Ibid., pp. 394, 395, 395-96. See also another example of separation in ibid., p. 430.

135 Ibid., pp. 456-58.

136 Ibid., pp. 733-34. Having sexual relations with a nun was, according to canon law, a kind of *sacrilegium*, a sin for which only the pope could give absolution.

137 Björn Þorsteinsson and Guðrún Ása Grímsdóttir 1990, p. 46.

strengthening the practical meaning of canon law in Iceland. In this way they managed to guarantee that the law courts were judging in accordance with the main principles of canon law, at the same time as it strengthened the authority of the clergy.[138]

After the period in which the bishops were appointed from Rome, the authority of the archbishop in Niðarós was re-established. For the next century, from 1450 until the Reformation around 1550, only Icelandic bishops were elected. They continued the work of the earlier bishops. It appears that the ecclesiastical authorities wanted to extend their involvement and wanted from this point onwards to intervene strongly in matters concerning sexual behavior before and during marriage. Such cases are related to the work of certain bishops and their clerics. We can mention especially Ólafur Rögnvaldsson, bishop of Hólar from 1460 to 1495, and his successor Gottskálkur Nikulásson, bishop from 1498 to 1520, both of whom received the support of the archbishop of Niðarós in many of the cases they were dealing with.[139] One was a case of incest known as the case of Hvassafell,[140] which was about intercourse between a father and his daughter, and the case of Jón Sigmundsson concerning his marriage to a woman related within the forbidden degrees of marriage.[141] Many judgements and documents dealing with marriage matters have also survived from the bishops of Skálholt, Stefán Jónsson (1491-1518), and Ögmundur Pálsson (1520-40).[142]

We can sum up by saying that even if the authorities during the late thirteenth and early fourteenth century were giving the Icelanders new marriage legislation, the local influence on forming the law was great from the beginning. When the law was introduced at the general assembly of Þingvellir in 1281, three groups of people protested. These were the clergy, the royal officers, and the farmers called *bændur*, which in this Icelandic context means householders who owned or rented

138 Ibid., pp. 65-66.

139 Ibid., pp. 126, 134, 136.

140 Ibid., pp. 132-34. Many people have written about this case. See for instance Einar Arnórsson 1932-35, 1936-39, Már Jónsson 1993, pp. 47-49. This case will be studied further in chapter 5, see pp. 211-212.

141 See DI VII, p. 778. Einar Arnórsson has written about this case in a paper from 1953-54 about the relationship between Bishop Gottskálkur and the lawman Jón Sigmundsson. See Einar Arnórsson 1953-54.

142 Björn Þorsteinsson and Guðrún Ása Grímsdóttir 1990, pp. 138, 150.

land.[143] The precise objections of the royal officers are unknown. The protest of the clergy was that kin-groups should not have any superior claims in land rights (*brigð*), while the farmers, *bændur*, emphasized that they would not accept any limitation of their rights to sell or purchase land freely.[144] The bishop and his clerics wrote a letter to King Eiríkur on the matter, objecting to *Jónsbók* and specifying the rules that were unacceptable to them.[145] For example, they could not agree with the regulation concerning the marriage of women[146] and demanded full jurisdiction over marriage.[147] Another letter sent by the *bændur* to King Eiríkur expresses the attitudes of this group towards other rules included in *Jónsbók*.[148] The *bændur* stressed that all agreements which were made with the knowledge of witnesses should be upheld, and this should include both the marrying of women and agreements about movable property.[149] The objection of the *bændur* was thus mainly concerned with cases of property ownership rights.[150]

This discussion concerning the acceptance of the new law shows how central the issue of property rights was for each different group. The bishop did not agree that relatives should have priority in buying their family's land. At the same time the *bændur* demanded that if a piece of land had been sold legally, this agreement should be adhered to, and every property owner should have the right to dispose of their property, as King Magnús had promised.[151]

This reaction against the new rules of *Jónsbók* shows how the landed aristocracy reacted to the new law. Later the authority of the Church was to be strengthened in Iceland, however. The early fifteenth century was a period characterized by a relative weakness in Iceland's royal administration, and especially during the period 1421-48 when there was very little contact between royal officials in Iceland and the administrative centre

143 Compare to Jón Jóhannesson 1958, pp. 22, 28. See also DI II, pp. 282-88.
144 Magnús Már Lárusson 1967, p. 501.
145 ÍF XVII, pp. 98-101.
146 This concerned the rules about *kvennagiptingar* in *Jónsbók*.
147 See this also in DI II, pp. 206-208.
148 ÍF XVII, p. 100.
149 DI II, pp. 208-209.
150 Magnús M. Lárusson 1962b, p. 615.
151 Magnús M. Lárusson 1967, p. 501, compare to *Árna saga biskups*, chapter 28.

of the royal power in Copenhagen.[152] During this period, the Icelandic bishops were the most influential official authority in Iceland. Royal authority in Iceland began to increase though around the middle of the fifteenth century, as the law of *Langarréttarbót* issued by King Christian I – a special ordinance created for Icelanders – indicates.[153] From that point both royal and ecclesiastical authority was strengthened.

4.3.3 *The role of the bishops after the Reformation*

Many documents exist which show how the central authority became stronger in Iceland in the sixteenth century. One of these is Bishop Gissur Einarsson's copybook.[154] It provides the opportunity to examine the policy followed by this first Lutheran bishop when judging different kinds of marriage issues. Gissur was bishop of Skálholt from 1540-48, and because his copybook is so rich in evidence it allows us at the same time to analyze how the legal regulation of sexuality was implemented at the law court level in the period immediately after the Reformation. Gissur was judging in accordance with the old marriage law of Iceland, as well as in accordance with the few changes that had been made by the Church ordinance of 1537-39, which he himself had translated from Latin to Icelandic.[155]

The first case to be mentioned here is related to the issue of the legality of a marriage. It is a *stefna*, a writ from the bishop to Kolbeinn Ólafsson to come to Skálholt because of his marriage to Sigríður Einarsdóttir.[156] According to another document of the following year, 1541, Bishop Gissur declared the couple to be separated because Kolbeinn had never managed to be a proper husband to his wife having failed to fulfill his

152 The explanation is partly that King Erik of Pommerania was at war with the Hanseatic League and the counts of Holstein. See Björn Þorsteinsson and Guðrún Ása Grímsdóttir 1990, pp. 31-32.

153 Björn Þorsteinsson and Guðrún Ása Grímsdóttir 1990, pp. 73-78. The first paragraph mentioned that royal officers should ensure that the law of the country was followed. In the third paragraph it was stated specifically that it was forbidden for wealth or property to be taken from other people illegally. The legislation aimed to change the situation in the decades after the plague of 1402-04.

154 This book exists both in a transcript of the mid-seventeenth century and as an original document. See AM. 266. fol, which is the copybook in transcription of Halldór in Reykholt from 1654-57, and the original document in AM. 232. 8vo.

155 See discussion here on pp. 122 ff.

156 DI X, pp. 567-68.

marital duty.[157] According to the declaration Sigríður had complained to the bishop that Kolbeinn was impotent.[158]

Impotence, according to canon law, was a valid reason for breaking a legally made marriage contract. Here it was used as a reason for formal separation.[159] The argument in favor of impotence as a reason for separation was probably taken from a canon law text known by Bishop Gissur.[160]

The other cases from the copybook of Bishop Gissur demonstrate his active involvement in matters relating to marriage. One such case concerned the legal marriage of Guðni and Ingibjörg. Guðni was ordered to relinquish another woman, Guðrún, with whom he had had children, and take his real wife, Ingibjörg back again.[161] This was in accordance with normal canon law practice.

Two documents concern the marriage of Þorleifur Þóroddsson. The question under consideration here was, according to the first document, whether his marriage was legal, because he had been having a sexual relationship with the sister of his wife. Six priests judged the marriage to be legal because the couple had been living together after the illicit relationship was revealed.[162] The second letter explained the case more fully. It contains the judgement which Bishop Gissur himself made in 1543 and is known as the letter about the criminal Þorleifur Þóroddsson. The marriage contract of Þorleifur and his wife was used to prove that Þorleifur had made a marriage agreement with his wife with the consent of her parents, and that the marriage banns had been published in the church according to the law. It was thus not possible to break this marriage. Another problem arose because his wife had continued to have a sexual relationship with Þorleifur after he had committed his crime. Here it was declared that Þorleifur had confessed his crime to a priest

157 Ibid., pp. 669-70. See his seal, Figure 10.

158 Ibid., p. 669. Compare to: "giæti ecki golldid sier þa hionaskylldu sem til bæri ad lijkamligu samrædi huar fyrir ad hun beiddi sig ad lata skilia vid greindan kolbein ef þad leyfdist eptir laugum."

159 Ibid., pp. 669-70.

160 Ibid., pp. 669-70, see especially p. 670. In the documents it reads: "Cum alter conjugatorum propter naturalem impotentiam ad matrimonium contractum fuit inutilis naturali conjugio non potest alligari. divortium ergo inter eos decernatur".

161 Ibid., pp. 647-48.

162 DI XI, p. 226.

and had received absolution for it. The case was judged according to the *New Christian Law* of Bishop Árni from 1275, and the arguments in the case were as follows:

> such criminals should be outlawed until they had paid a penalty and confessed to the bishop. We thought it necessary that he [the husband] help his poor children and wife and that is why from now on he must be free from his sins according to Church law.[163]

Thus it seems that Bishop Gissur was not very much in favour of separating or annulling marriages. A personal letter written by the bishop to Abbess Halldóra of the nunnery at Kirkjubæjarklaustur gives further information about his belief in the inviolability of marriage. He wrote:

> Dear sister, I have heard that the wife of Bergur Ingimundarson has stayed and still is there with you. But because, according to the law of God and the country, it is not allowed to be separated even if the husband made the life of his wife unbearable by hitting her, and by doing other bad things, it is therefore my full wish and advice that you do not keep her longer with you, rather that you take care that she comes back here to the south. Someone will try to give the husband good advice so this problem will not continue, otherwise the case will be a more serious matter.[164]

The bishop based his judgements on the *New Christian Law* of Bishop Árni of 1275 and *Jónsbók* from 1281. His attitude was affected by his desire to get the abbess to persuade the woman to return to her husband. Gissur believed that it would be possible to continue to monitor the situation, maybe having in mind that the parish priest should discuss the situation with the couple. This was in fact the duty of the priest according to the new reformed Church ordinance. Besides this, Gissur's decision was in full accordance with canon law, which said that neither

163 Ibid., p. 227: "at sliker sakamenn sieu fridlauser. þar til ad þeir taka lausn og skripter af biskupi. leizt oss naudsyn til uera þad hann hialpadi sinum fatækum baurnum og konu. og hann fridhelgr uera eptir kirkiunnar laugum."

164 Ibid., p. 271: "Kiæra systir. heyri ec ad kuinna bergs jngemundarsonar skuli dualizt hafa og enn uera þar hia ydur. Enn fyrir þann skulld ad þad er ecki skilnadar sauk uid hennar mann. epter gudz laugum og landz þott hann ueiti henni. ouistum. med slaugum og audru illu. þa er þad minn fullkomligur uilie og radlagning ad þier halldit hana ecki leingur hia ydur. helldur ad þier siaid til suo hun komizt aptur hingad aa sudursueitirnar. Verda þa einhuerier til ad leggia honum gott til. þess betra mal sem hun hefur til handa ad bera. annars (kann) hier uerda meira mal ut af."

a husband nor a wife could enter a monastical institution without the consent of the other.[165]

There is more information to be found in the copybook of Bishop Gissur concerning marriage. The dominant theme in many of these marriage cases is Gissur's efforts to send wives back to their husbands.[166] One, from 1547, is a letter to a man instructing him to send his mistress away and take his wife back.[167] From a judgement of 1547 concerning the marriage of Gils Gilsson and his wife, we know that the husband came to the bishop and complained that his wife had left him. Rumors had spread about the reason for her departure. The bishop said that she was obliged to return to her husband at least until a formal judgement was given in the case.[168] The bishop's active involvement in matters of marriage can perhaps reflect some of the intentions of the new Church ordinance, e.g. that clerics should offer guidance to spouses with regard to marriage problems. His judgements were, however, very much in accordance with the old marriage legislation and, as previously, it was canon law that provided the tenets to be followed, and it was the clergy who continued to have jurisdiction over marriage.

The various cases from the copybook of Bishop Gissur thus provide information about his important role in the law courts. And the bishops who came after him followed his work. A general judgement about marriage from 1559 gives a good insight into how the bishops continued to deal with marriage issues after the Reformation, (See Figure 7). The judgement is based on several marriage cases. It states that Bishop Gísli Jónsson of Skálholt had assembled some of the priests from the diocese of Skálholt as well as some of the members of the law council called *lögréttumenn*. It declares that marriage could only be made according to the King's ordinance (i.e. the Church ordinance of 1537/39), "and according to all the customs and habits of our old Icelandic law."[169] The judgement focused on the problems the clergy were having in controlling

165 Compare to Brundage 1990, pp. 202, 242, 288, 296 and 375.

166 His attitude is quite similar to what seems to be a common pattern in many litigation cases from late medieval England. See Helmholz 2004, p. 536.

167 DI XI, pp. 602-603.

168 Ibid., pp. 562-63.

169 DI XIII, pp. 430-33, see especially p. 433.

behavior in relation to marriage. The judgement discussed four general issues:

1) The marriage of men to women with whom they had previously been living in adultery.
2) Whether a marriage was legal if it was decided in the morning, with the betrothal ritual taking place on the same evening, and the consummation of the marriage the very same night.
3) The marriage of people who had done so in the knowledge that the marriage was not allowed due to problems of affinity or a relationship within the forbidden degrees.
4) The marriage of people in another parish that is not their own.[170]

Problems such as adultery and the marriage of those related within the forbidden degrees had been known before the Reformation. There were, however, new problems. Clerics no longer accepted that a couple should consummate the marriage on the same day that they made their agreement without any church ceremony. Also, the movement of people from one parish to another became a problem since it made it more difficult to control the legality of marriage contracts.

It is interesting that a number of law codes were cited to justify this judgement. The first such justification came in the form of a biblical reference. It is first after the Reformation that arguments drawn directly from the Bible begin to be used in court cases. At the same time, references to either the king or to his declaration became more common, as a case from 1568 shows.[171] At the same time the marriage legislation of the late thirteenth century continued to be cited. The issue of parental consent was highlighted by references to rules related to marriage contained in *Jónsbók*, the *New Christian Law* and the King's ordinances.[172]

By looking at the marriage regulations from the end of the sixteenth century, it becomes clear that the role of the bishops in law courts

170 Ibid., pp. 430-33.
171 DI XV, pp. 148-49.
172 DI XIII, p. 432.

continued to be great in relation to marriage regulation. By examining the efforts of Bishop Oddur Einarsson in Skálholt at the end of the century we can see that the Icelanders were following the 1587 ordinance of King Frederik II concerning marriage. In Bishop Oddur's clerical agreement, *Prestastefnusampykt* from *Alþingi* of 1589,[173] it is stated that no couple shall be married without the consent of the guardian.[174] Other agreements also exist from a meeting of priests with Bishop Oddur Einarson from the year 1592.[175] Some of the paragraphs should be seen as an attempt to pass on the message of King Frederik's marriage ordinance to the people. But it is interesting to note that some of the paragraphs dealt directly with special cases relating to Iceland.[176] These agreements made by the Icelandic bishops and clergy demonstrate how legal regulations issued by the central authorities were followed up by the local Church authority in Iceland.[177]

An agreement of 11 May 1592, known as a writ from the meeting of the priest at Stafholt, *Stafholtsprestastefna,* or as the writ of the priest Jón Guðmundsson concerning a range of issues that were presented as a series of questions and answers. It indicates the problems priests were dealing with, as well as possible solutions to them. One question given particular consideration was whether secular authorities could marry couples. The answer given to this question was no, particularly in situations where it was possible for a priest to perform this function.[178] This point was reiterated in the agreement of the Bishop Oddur and his

173 *Alþingisbækur Íslands* II, pp. 146-51.

174 Ibid., p. 147.

175 Ibid., pp. 254-70.

176 Ibid., p. 258. About separation it says in 1592: "Að hjónin skilji sig ekki sjálf ólöglega að neinum samvistum, þó þeim sé það báðum jafnviljugt, utan í hæstu tilfallandi nauðsyn, og sé héðan af fyrirboðið, að hjónin visti sig á sínum bæ hvort, eða setji hvort öðru nokkrar fjærvistir, því það kann að vera tilefni mikillra háskasemi um þeirra hjónaband."

177 Ibid. The texts of the clerical agreements from the end of the century give an interesting view of the meeting between the old Catholic culture, or the even older religious custom, and the spirit of the Protestant reformers. Compare this to text from the *Héraðs synodalia* by Oddur Einarsson: "Prestarnir fyrirbjóði héðan af hestaþing og smalabúsreiðar og vökunætur á helgum dögum og aðra slíka heiðinglega háttu, hvort það skeður nótt eður dag. En dirfist nokkur að fara í þvílíkar samkomur og finnist þar, sem ekki hefur [áður] hlýtt guðs orði á þeim degi, [hans nafn skal uppteiknast og klagast fyrir sýslumanni. Einkum skylldu og prestarnir [sjálfir] varast að gera nokkuð að slíkri gleði, [heldur hitt með röksamlegum áminningum að hepta slíkan ósóma, svo sem þeim er mögulegt."

178 Ibid., p. 262. The dialogue gives an interesting picture of the everyday problems the priests were dealing with.

clergy, *Prestastefnusamþykt Odds biskups Einarssonar og klerka hans,* at the assembly of the *Alþingi* 1592.[179] The distinction between what constituted the job of the clergy and of the secular authorities seems to have been quite clear from the clerical point of view. The secular authorities were not supposed to interfere in the church ceremony, even if they had jurisdiction over marriage more generally. This view was confusing as it was contrary to the former understanding of marriage.

However, the changes following the Reformation reinforced the need to make agreements in accordance with older customs, and the agreement of Bishop Oddur from 1592 can be interpreted as a sign that there were problems gaining acceptance of the new regulations. In 1595, Bishop Oddur again sends the proposal:

> That all priests in their own parishes shall forbid that any persons hereafter should live together, who have not let the relationship be published three times in church, betrothed their wives legally, and later on their wedding day they should be married by a priest. The marriage shall be made with the full consent of both sets of parents if they are alive, and the nearest relatives. But each man that betroths a woman and does not marry her legally shall pay the king 12 ounces of silver.[180]

Judgements from the same bishop from the year 1594 show us more about the problems the bishop had to deal with. For example, there were judgements concerning men who wanted to marry the women with whom they had been living out of wedlock; women that did not want to reveal the names of their childrens' fathers; a marriage for which the bishop did not have adequate documentation or proof; and a husband who complained about his wife's illness and was given permission to separate as a result. Other cases concerned men who lived with concubines, disregarding warnings from their priest about how sinful it was to live in that kind of relationship. These cases also highlight the problem

179 Ibid., p. 267.

180 *Alþingisbækur Íslands* III, p. 56, compare to DI XII, p. 439. Alþingissamþykkt from 1552 seems to be the same: "jtem að prestarnir allir í sinni þingá skulu fyrirbjóða, að nokkrir þeir séu hér eptir til samans, sem ekki hafa fest sínar konur löglega og látið lýsa áður þrisvar í kirkju, og gangi síðan á þeim giptingardegi og láti vígja sig til samans. og skal hjúskapurinn gerast með beggja foreldra ráði, ef til eru, eða hinna næstu frænda. En hver, sem festir konu og lætur sig ei saman vígja við hana löglega, gjaldi kongi.xij. aura."

of the farmers for whom these unmarried men were probably working, who did not dismiss the men from their farms.[181]

At the end of the century Guðbrandur Þorláksson became bishop of Hólar and in this post he continued the old fight against clandestine marriage. In an agreement from 1597 made by him and a lawman, clandestine marriage is discussed in one of the paragraphs:[182]

> Because many women and girls get tempted by promises of marriage, against the law and against the advice of their guardians, the priest shall hereafter make it clear for everyone, maidens and women, often and seldom, each in his parish, that such secret engagements are useless and not valid. So all female persons shall guard themselves after this day, and are not tempted by talk like that which has often taken place before now.[183]

The case of the priest Jón Loftsson in Vatnsfjörður[184] clearly shows how the court of *Alþingi* worked at the end of the sixteenth century. According to local witnesses the priest Jón Loftsson lost his wife in the winter of 1592. After her death he came to an agreement with another woman.[185] It was said that he brought this woman into his home shortly after the death of his first wife, and that he asked a third woman to marry him between these two events.

Two years later a judgement on the case was made in his home district of Vatnsfjörður. According to the judgement the marriage with Guðrún Sigmundsdóttir had been made with the consent of her guardian and in accordance with the rules about marriage formation stated by the law of the Church and the secular law. The problem was that no other priest than the bridegroom himself was involved in making the agreement and no priest published the marriage banns or blessed the couple. Jón was asked to apologize and to come to the court to explain himself,

181 *Alþingisbækur Íslands* II, p. 417: "frillulijfizmenn sem sig hallda til samanz ä moti ämijnnijngum prestsinz, og bændur þikiast Ecki skilldugir þä j burtu ad läta."

182 *Alþingisbækur Íslands* III, pp. 127-29.

183 Ibid., pp. 128-29: "Med þui ad margar konur og stulkur lata locka sig med lofunum og fyrirheitum Eiginordz. j moti logum og Radi sinna giftingarmanna. þa giori prestarner hier epter ollum viturligt. meyium og konum opt og osialldan. huer j sinne þingää. ad soddan heimugligar trulofaner eru onýtar. og ad aungud halldandi. so allar kuenmanz personur vakti sig epter þennan dag. og lati sig Ecki a talar draga so sem hier til hefur opt sked."

184 Ibid., pp. 19-26.

185 Ibid., p. 20: "Hann miste kuinnu sinnar … enn med annare og sier keiptti hann sialfur og drack handzalzøl".

but he failed to do so, later excusing himself by claiming bad weather as the reason for his absence. He also explained that other priests had been at such a great distance from his home that he could not have asked a priest to come and marry him. Finally, it became clear that he did not think he was doing anything wrong. Consequently the judgement made at the local level was forwarded for consideration by the bishop.[186]

The bishop asked for advice from a number of his clerics. Because there was no sign that the priest was going to change his living arrangements, the clerics decided that he should come to the next assembly "and follow the judgement, and the punishment that was determined by Bishop Oddur Einarsson with the advice of the secular authority."[187] If he did not come, he would lose his office.[188] The priest did not obey and the case finally went before the court at *Alþingi* in 1595. There, the priests decided the judgement, but the bishop had also presented the perspective of the highest royal officer in the country. The result was that Jón Loftsson was judged to be suspended *ab officio.* This was no longer simply a case about the legality of his marriage; it was now also a case about his lack of obedience to the authorities. The judgement therefore concluded with a general statement about how priests should obey their superiors in the Church.[189]

One of the changes made by the judgement of *Stóridómur* of 1564-65, was that while the secular authorities were supposed to judge on marriage cases, the role of clerics was supposed to be akin to that of moral guardians. According to Bishop Guðbrandur's agreement of 1597 the problem was related to the lifestyle of the priests themselves, since those who lived together out-of-wedlock could not continue in their priestly office. Another paragraph stated that those priests who had not been legally married to their own wives had neglected the Church ordinance and the laws of marriage of all honorable men.[190] These statements from the Icelandic bishops from the end of the sixteenth century were

186 Ibid., pp. 21-23.

187 "under þann urskurd. straff og hegning sem biskupinn herra Oddur Einarsson med hofudzmannsins raadi og samþycki vill aa hann leggia."

188 Ibid., p. 24.

189 Ibid., pp. 24-26.

190 Ibid., pp. 127-28.

related to the strengthening of the role of the clergy as examples of good behavior. The writings of Bishop Oddur Einarsson suggest that the role of Church leaders as guides in moral matters was becoming greater at the end of the century.

On the other hand, examples mentioned here show how the bishop worked through the courts to translate abstract laws to function in reality. We can see a gradual change in judicial practice by comparing cases from the copybook of Bishop Gissur Einarsson and the later judgements from the assembly of *Alþingi* from the end of the sixteenth century. Evidently clerics continued to have jurisdiction over marriage cases, but by the end of the sixteenth century the courts of *Alþingi*, with a combination of clerical and secular judges, became more prominent.[191]

4.4 *Conclusion*

This chapter has considered the regulation of the rules of marriage. Change in the legal regulation of marriage was largely uncontroversial because new rules normally were based on already-existing marriage traditions. Iceland was established as a special judicial territory within the Norwegian kingdom. This had direct consequences for the formation of the law. Old Icelandic customs continued to be respected at the same time as new rules were added to the older ones. Even though the Church gained full jurisdiction over marriage at the end of the thirteenth century the process of legal change was not finished. The question of what constituted a legal marriage was not solved by the marriage legislation of the late thirteenth century. In the *réttarbætur* of the late thirteenth and early fourteenth centuries marriage regulations continued to be included. These issues were still a real problem throughout the fourteenth century. Both the royal legislation of the *réttarbætur*, as well as the Church statutes, demonstrate the ongoing process of defining what constituted legal marriage.

It is interesting to discuss changes in the marriage regulations of the twelfth and thirteenth centuries together with the changes of the

191 Compare to the case of 1574 in the copybook of Bishop Guðbrandur Þorláksson, see *Bréfabók Guðbrands biskups*, pp. 70-71, and to *Alþingisbækur Íslands* I, p. 358, as well as pp. 403-404.

sixteenth century. Firstly, it is at the end of the sixteenth century that we first find strong enough authority to back up such regulations. Moves were being made at this time towards more fixed rules and regulations, as well as towards a more stable court system. Secondly, by comparing these two periods of change we can study the effects that these changes had on people's understanding of the regulation of marriage. After the Reformation we find documents that express some confusion about what constituted a legal marriage. Change in the marriage law at the end of the sixteenth century was, as before, very concerned with securing older principles. This was also the case in the fourteenth century, something that will be discussed further in the next chapter. The fourteenth century regulations were not about secular principles that needed to be clarified. Rather, what was presented was a statement giving clear directions about how individuals should live in Christian marriage and how this institution should be controlled by the authorities.

The change or "correction" of the law that occurred through the *réttarbætur* at the beginning of the fourteenth century, was also a step forward in defining the position of Iceland as a special judicial area within the Norwegian state. This process was not only the result of changes "from above",[192] but was also strongly influenced by the Icelanders themselves. The principles that are found in the *réttarbætur* can be viewed as an attempt by the Icelandic aristocracy to redefine their inheritance strategy in order to maintain their position. This strategy is most evident in the regulations affecting the transfer of property, and especially the making of marriage contracts.

Secondly, for many centuries after the correction of the law in the *réttarbætur* of the late thirteenth and early fourteenth century there were few formal changes in the law.[193] However, in the centuries that followed more changes occurred on the question of what constituted legal marriage. The fifteenth and sixteenth centuries provide rich information on how the meaning of marriage changed. This change will be discussed further in the next chapter, but it was only possible because of the active

192 For example special rules needed to be specified for Iceland, see for instance King Eiríkur Magnússon's open letter to Iceland in *Lovsamling for Island* I, pp. 22-23.

193 Magnús Már Lárusson 1962b, pp. 612-17.

role taken by the local authorities in placing new doctrine alongside established customs. At the end of the period we see that the local royal authorities gained stronger control. New legislation from the end of the sixteenth century reflects stronger central power, resulting in the judgements from the *Alþingi* becoming more forceful than before.

Change at the end of the sixteenth century was in many ways more gradual than sudden. The Reformation did not change the definition of what constituted a legal marriage. It continued to be marriage based on the consent of two individuals, who were not too closely related. The marriage banns should be published in church, and the consent of the parents was important to make the agreement valid. However, even if marriage lost its status as a sacrament and the Church – at least in theory – partly lost jurisdiction over marriage, the idea of what a Christian marriage meant was strengthened. The woman should be a virgin before marriage, and adultery became a crime to be punished by the civil courts. Therefore, to be able to control virginity, punish adultery, and deal with cases of separation and divorce, a more effective executive power was nessessary in Iceland. By the end of the sixteenth century the central power was getting stronger, and the new seal of the island of Iceland from 1592, (Figure 10), thus became a symbol of that change.

CHAPTER 5

The local knowledge of canon law and the internalization of new norms

The Church courts asserted their jurisdiction over marriage by defining its meaning. In addition, the Church's authority was extended to consider what constituted correct Christian behavior in married life. Over time, this authority made it possible both to collect penalties and to allow people to remake their marriage agreements. At the same time as the authority of the Church grew stronger in controlling sexual behavior, the existing documents about marriage litigation illustrate that it became common to question the legality of a marriage contract for local people. Frequently, this process began with just a rumor. This explains why a large quantity of documents was produced by the courts.

So far this study has focused on this legal change. Here I shall continue to deal with court cases in order to analyze how different actors used elements of the law code to argue in favor of their claims. The aim is to explain how members of the law courts and the people involved in bringing cases were active participants in marriage litigation. After a case was taken to the court, the documents produced were often retained in private possession. Those legal documents were often results from dispute-settlement of several cases. Collections of legal documents represent the important role of the law courts.[1]

The documents under consideration reveal common concerns about marriage, and the cases give information about how people involved in

1 See for instance AM 229, 4to. 175 bl, from the seventeenth century, written by Þorsteinn Magnússon. There are paragraphs number 6, about marriage contracts ("Kommentar til Ægteskabskontrakt"), number 9, about engagement ("Om straf for hævet trúlofun 1642 med en efterskrift 1646"), number 10, about patrimonial inheritance rights ("Om odels-salg").

such cases interpreted and applied the laws. The aim in this chapter is to give a clearer picture of this process. The discussion will be divided into three main sections. The first section treats the question of what was a legal marriage according to the judgement from the Icelandic law courts. One way of studying this problem is to analyze the structure of the narration in the court cases better. The second section will thus study how the knowledge of canon law shaped the inheritance disputes. The question is not only about how the authorities regulated sexuality, but also how control of sexuality was shaped by the knowledge and use of both canon law and local customs. Court proceedings will be used as evidence for the way in which people could use some of the arguments from canon law to make a marriage legal or illegal.[2] The questions under consideration will thus not only concern the control of legal marriage, but also how the written evidence reflects the way new Christian ideals were adopted. This will especially be studied in the section about how people used the possibility to get dispensation from the marriage rules.

The third section treats how internalizations of the new Christian norms limit the possible ways of using the courts for purely strategical purposes. To throw light on these cases, which give information about the penitential practice, rules about penance will be discussed, as well as the confessional culture and the criminalizing of non-marital sexual relations at the end of the sixteenth century.

5.1 Judgement of legal marriage

According to the *New Christian law* of 1275 every member of the community was obliged to ensure that only legal marriage contracts were made.[3] Other studies have shown how religious life in the Middle Ages normally became regulated by interactions between the authorities and

2 Compare to the discussion in Helmholz 2004, p. 531 and p. 534, about how knowledge of canon law can be studied through the court cases about marriage litigation. See also Pedersen 2000, pp. 59-84.

3 This can been seen in the statute of Bishop Árni Þorláksson in the paragraph about the publishing of weddings on three successive Sundays in front of the people of the parish, from DI II, pp. 26-27.

the local people.[4] This was also the case in Iceland. In the last chapter we have seen how a regulation of marriage in Iceland was shaped not only by the royal authorities and the Church, but also by the local customs. One of the greatest problems was to define what a legal marriage was. Studies from other parts of Western Christianity have shown that this was amongst other things related to the problem that many possible impediments could annul marriage. According to the rules of canon law all impediments were clearly defined, but the problem was that those rules were practiced differently on a regional court level.[5] In this chapter I shall discuss how Icelandic charters also demonstrate that a certain frustration existed about a similar marriage issue in Iceland.[6] Still at the end of the sixteenth century it was common in court cases to discuss the legality of marriages and the elements that established this validity. Many of these cases considered what was deemed to be correct and incorrect sexual behavior.[7] Adultery, bigamy and other sins became crimes that could make an otherwise legal contract invalid.[8] The legality of marriage was an issue which arose frequently, first and foremost in cases in which a relative challenged the inheritance of children because their parents had never been legally married.

We shall study closer these differences and see that while the earliest cases are very much shaped by the question of inheritance rights, they gradually became more and more concerned with the question of sin, which finally by the end of the sixteenth century became criminalized by the law courts.

4 On this process of change in religious culture see Swanson 1997, pp. 241-49.

5 Helmholz 2004, pp. 551-53. He mentions twelve known impediments from canon law but not all of these were used, for instance, in English court cases.

6 Magnús Már Lárusson 1959a, p. 240: compare to a case in DI IV, pp. 391- 92. It is from the copybook of Bishop Jón Vilhjálmsson, concerning a man who had been married for ten years, when it became clear that he secretly had promised to marry another woman. The question as to which of these women was his legal wife was not easy to answer.

7 See also here the register about the question of legal marriage and impediments to marriage in *Alþingisbækur Íslands* I, p. 514, with reference to pp. 41, 42, 43, 46, 80, 111, 132, 240, 263-64, 270, 271, 334, 340-41, 370.

8 Concerning this matter, see *brot* (hór, tvíkvæni, réttur manns á konu sinni), in ibid., p. 514, compare to pp. 154, 155, 272, 274, 337, 338, 357-59, 405.

5.1.1 Legitimacy and the question of inheritance

On 10 February 1450, the bishop of Hólar declared a certain marriage legal. It was the husband in this marriage, Víðnæmur Jónsson, who had asked for the bishop's judgement as to "whether Helga Einarsdóttir was his legal wife or not." A witness was produced who declared that he had been present when the bride gave her verbal consent and shook hands with the bridegroom, who also shook hands with her parents. The husband declared that they had consummated the marriage. The bishop declared the marriage to be legal and that Helga had been his wife ever since "they started to live together".[9]

What had prompted the husband to go to the bishop to acquire a declaration about his marriage? Another letter, dated three days later, reveals that his wife was living with another man.[10] Here the issues of consent to the marriage, as well as its consummation, were used to declare the marriage legal. Even though adultery was a sin, in this case it was not criminalized: thus, adultery alone was not a reason for this marriage to be "annulled". By looking further at the arguments used in this court case and many other similar cases, it is possible to see how the definition of what was a legal marriage was closely related to the involved partners' interest in the question of inheritance.

The oldest of the documents we shall take under consideration was produced in 1375. At that time it makes plain that the issue of adultery was more often considered in relation to the question of inheritance rather than being seen as a criminal act. The document of 1375 contains a judgement based on one particular case. Pétur Hálfdánarson, the legitimate nephew[11] of Gunnar Andrésson, was to inherit from Gunnar instead of Gunnar's grandson, because the grandson's mother (Gunnar's daughter) had been *hórgetin,* which means born in adultery.[12] Another case from the fifteenth century gives the impression that adultery was not seen as a great problem as long as the people involved paid a penalty

9 DI V, pp. 45-46.

10 Ibid., pp. 48-49, especially p. 49.

11 The son of Gunnar's brother.

12 DI III, pp. 299-300. From the year 1375, it is called *réttarbót.*

and confessed their sins.[13] There existed even a formula from ca. 1400 by which a husband could discard his concubine and take his wife back:

> That you will admit in front of God by this oath on the book, that you will take X your wife back home into holy matrimony and send away the mistress you have been keeping with you to this day.[14]

At issue was the possibility of losing the right to inheritance because of illegitimacy, not whether this status was considered sinful or criminal. Thus, what was typical for the late fourteenth and early fifteenth century's cases concerning the control of legal marriage was how closely related to the question of inheritance rights, the arguments were.

That is why it is impossible to understand why these cases were brought to the court without considering the significance of inheritance rights. The transfer of property through inheritance was a central focus in alliances arranged by marriage. Thus any change in what constituted a legal marriage affected the system of alliances as well as ownership rights. Accordingly, heirs used a variety of strategies to guarantee their inheritance. If relatives challenged certain children's rights to inherit on the ground that their parents had never been validly married, proof of the marriage could be difficult to produce.[15] This was emphasised in the rules of the late thirteenth century. In a letter that King Magnús wrote to the Icelanders when *Jónsbók* was issued, he stated:

> After the chapter of "mannhelgi" the next chapter is about inheritance, as well as other related matters, and it starts with the marriage of women, because it is important for heirs to be born in a legal marriage.[16]

13 DI IV, p. 442. This is a letter from Hólar 3 March 1431, in which Knútur Einarsson admits he had betrothed Ingiríður Þórisdóttir in front of some witnesses and that he "promised to take her back as a wife and make an agreement with the man Jón Dahl, who had been having an affair with his wife." "lofuadæ knutr (ath) taka greinda jng(i)ridæ þorirs (dottur) aftur til sin til æigenkono oc settizst med jon deel sæm hafdi lægit (med henne)."

14 DI II, p. 508: "[Þ]ath iatar þu gude med suornum bokareide ath þu skalt heim aptr taka x eiginkonu þina j heilagt hiuskaparband ok samuist ok brott reka fra þer horkonu þa sem þu hefir haft med þer til þessa dags."

15 Compare to Brundage 1995a, pp. 72-73, 74.

16 *Jónsbók*, pp. 1-4. The letter of King Magnús, was written before 9 March 1280. See p. 3: "Næst mannhelgi er erfðatal með því fleira, sem því heyrir, ok hefr þat með kvenna giptingum, því at miklu varðar þeim sem til arfanna kalla, at þeir sé í lögligum hjúskap getnir."

In this way, rules relating to the marriage of women and inheritance laws were tied into an established pattern of property distribution. Jack Goody has explained it as follows:

> If women are receivers of "male" property, either by inheritance or else by dowry, then the nature of the marriage they contract will be influenced by this fact. Such influence will be particularly strong when the basic means of production, i.e. land in an agricultural society, is included in this inheritance. Where property is transmitted to women in this way, then there will be a strong tendency to control their marriage. An heiress cannot marry just anyone; her partner is more likely to have been chosen for her.[17]

Another potential inheritance problem was related to remarriage. A case from 1427, also concerned with inheritance, produced a juridical statement that two girls could inherit from the brother of their father, even though their father had been married twice. The girls received their inheritance because, as the document states, the daughters of a brother were number six in the line of inheritance, after the sons of the brother.[18] If it had not been proved that both marriages of the father, Ólafur Marteinsson, had been legal, the daughters from the second marriage would have lost their rights. The doubts concerning the status of these girls as legally born are clearly related to the question of remarriage.

Remarriage was a popular theme among the canonists of the twelfth and thirteenth centuries, whose discussions could be rather technical, considering, for instance, the differences between the second and the third marriage.[19] The result of their deliberations was that remarriage was deemed legal, although considered sinful. Remarriage had not been a problem under the marriage rules of *Grágás*, and in practice it continued to be common to marry a widow in the Late Middle Ages. However, it was seen as important to maintain the property from a man's first marriage as separate to that from his second marriage. In 1491, Vigfús Bjarnason and Steinunn Gunnarsdóttir married. He was a widower, having previously been married to Kristrún Ormsdóttir. It was declared that he did not own anything but the land at Meðaldallur í Dýrafirði and an

17 Goody 1988b, p. 13.
18 DI IV, pp. 346-47.
19 Brundage 1990, pp. 199-205, 242-45.

amount to the value of four cows. All possessions associated with the first marriage were the property of the children from that marriage.[20]

The issue of remarriage, and its discussion in law courts, is also evident in documents emanating from other parts of Europe during the Later Middle Ages.[21] The main task of the courts in Iceland, as in other places, was to declare whether children were legitimately born or not, and in so doing to decide on their legal status as heirs. What is also important to mention, is that the arguments used to declare a marriage legal came from canon law, and that these continued to be used in the courts after the Reformation, as mentioned before.[22] In 1578, the marriage of Benedikt Pétursson (who had died before 1578) and Birgit Gísladóttir was judged legal at the court of the assembly at Þingvellir, whereas Benedikt's second marriage to Álfheiður Arnardóttir was judged illegal. According to the record of this case he had separated himself illegally from his first wife in order to get married to the second. The first marriage had been made according to the law of the country and with the consent of Benedikt's father. He had taken part in a *festaröl* (see Figure 11), a drinking feast to mark the betrothal, and had lived together with Birgit for fifteen years. They had had six children. A contract had also been written at the time of this marriage, in clear accordance with the rules set out for entering into marriage. Since the case came before the court after Benedikt's death, it was probably raised in order to settle the inheritance rights of the children involved.[23]

To sum up, we can thus say: firstly, that many of the judgements on legal marriage from the Icelandic law courts dealt with the question of inheritance. And secondly, the examination of judgements on the legality of marriages made by the courts in the Late Middle Ages underlines the fact that many of the law court cases concentrated on the legitimacy of the marriage contract shown through the knowledge of the correct

20 DI VI, p. 746, see also Appendix I, the period 1451-1500, year 1491.

21 Calvi 1998, pp. 275-96.

22 This was also the main pattern in Germany see Safley 1984.

23 *Alþingisbækur Íslands* I, pp. 357-59. That the case was a matter of inheritance and payments of fines to the royal authority becomes clear by looking at the arguments on p. 359 where the inheritance rules are referred to, as well as pp. 359-60, which is a document about the wealth of Benedikt.

conduct of the acts which marked such a marriage.[24] This leads us to the second aspect of this section, namely, to discuss how the legal arguments for justifying the cases slowly changed.

5.1.2 *Control of illegitimacy and the question of sin*

Although the Church gained formal control of marriage and imposed its rule of monogamy, marriage continued to be an unstable legal institution. The simple reason was that even if marriage had been correctly made in the view of the spouses, it could be declared illegal by the local courts if it had not been contracted according to canon law rules. A judgement which stated whether a certain marriage was legal or not, had the effect that, if the marriage was ruled invalid, the relationship was annulled and the couple concerned separated. One of the consequences of the change in marriage rules at the end of the thirteenth century was that divorce, as mentioned before, became impossible.[25] However, separation based on the suspected illegality of marriage was common.[26] Because divorce was impossible in the modern sense of the word, an alternative strategy was to claim that the marriage had not been legally made, or was no longer valid due to unacceptable behavior by the couple. Divorce in the medieval meaning was thus most commonly used for what would be called "annulment", a declaration that a marriage had been invalid from the beginning.[27] It was not difficult to get separated according to a charter from 1470.[28] To do so, a valid reason had just to be found. The consent of the woman[29] followed by the consummation of the marriage[30] were the two criteria for making a legal marriage. If the marriage had not been made with mutual consent, or it had not been consummated, then it had never happened. This created considerable confusion and

24 These cases provide specific information about marriages judged legal during this period. It is also possible to find other cases in charters that give less direct information about marriage.

25 See here discussion in chapter 3.2.2.

26 DI V, p. 609. Compare to DI VI, p. 729.

27 Helmholz 2004, p. 540.

28 DI V, p. 585.

29 See marriage cases of 1429-1431 in the copybook of Bishop Jón Vilhjálmsson, DI IV, pp. 394-96, 430, 448-50. See also Páll Eggert Ólason II, 1949, p. 8.

30 DI IV, pp. 495-96. Compare to Ngl V, pp. 38-39.

it is understandable that clerics kept transcripts of court records about the matter. These judgements could be used as an example in future cases. Accordingly, court records were kept in record books, among other documents.[31]

Further studies of court cases concerning marriage in the sixteenth century clearly indicate that change occurred over time. Instead of the emphasis being placed principally on declaring a marriage legal, it became increasingly important to collect a penalty for incorrect behavior as well. This change requires closer examination.

In 1509 a priest, Jón Arason (who was later to become bishop of Hólar), declared that Tómas Hjálmarson had not been legally married to Helga Þorvarðardóttir, although he had assumed that she had been his wife for more than twenty years. I discussed previously the rule from the *réttarbót* of King Hákon of 1305,[32] stating that a couple who had lived together for more than ten years should be considered married, and their children considered legitimate.[33] This argument, which also can be found in *Jónsbók* is to be found in many cases, as, for instance, one from 1429 concerning the couple Ingveldur Erlendsdóttir and Sigurður Oblandsson.[34] And in another document from the late sixteenth century, the same argument was used for proving the validity of a contract.[35] In this case from 1509, the 1305 *réttarbót* of King Hákon was, however, not used. The outcome of the case was that the priest sentenced Tómas to pay 12 ounces of silver for each year he had been living with Helga, unless he could prove that he had in fact made a legal contract with her.[36]

31 DI X, p. 44. Some judgements about divorce cases were, for instance, preserved together with other documents, like the votive letter from the people of Eyjafjörður from 1477.

32 DI VIII, pp. 270-72, compare to *Lovsamling for Island* I, pp. 24-26.

33 See the discussion here in chapter 4.1.1, p. 117, where the whole rule is cited.

34 DI IV, pp. 391-92.

35 *Bréfabók Guðbrands biskups Þorlákssonar*, p. 436. In this case two brothers sought to establish their legal birth status, because the brother of their father had declared himself as the legal heir. In that case it was stated that the parents had always seen themselves as legally married "and it had never been said that she had been his concubine." Also, the marriage contract of the parents was used to prove the statements of the brothers, as well as the witness of another man that he had been present when the parents had legally become betrothed.

36 DI VIII, p. 271.

The motive for bringing the case to court had probably nothing to do with the children's inheritance, but rather with the collection of the fine imposed. It is important to read the document dealing with this case with an awareness of its context. Tómas Hjálmarsson was also accused of not paying his tithe to the Church. It is apparent that clerics were not only judging whether a marriage contract was legal or not, but also had authority to collect fines. The couple in question had to do penance for the twenty years in which they had been living together improperly, and after making their payment had to be remarried. A case from 1517 involving Ingilbrikt Jónsson and Halla Vilhjálmsdóttir also provides information about how adultery was used as a argument for remaking marriage. According to a witness's letter, the prior of the monastery of Möðruvellir testified that Ingilbrikt had paid a penalty for his adultery, confessed, and received absolution, whereafter he received a document confirming this. Another witness declared also that he had seen and read a written testimony from the deceased priest Jón Pétursson, declaring that Ingilbrikt had earlier been legally betrothed to his wife in accordance with the law of the Church. The marriage was thus judged legal, but due to the husband's adulterous lifestyle it was stated that he was obliged to hold a wedding ceremony (*brudlaup*) again within twelve months.[37]

The conclusion of this case was very different from the verdict in the case concerning Víðnæmur Jónsson and Helga Einarsdóttir from 1450 mentioned before.[38] In this case it was alleged that although Helga had been unfaithful, her husband had not sought to have her marriage contract declared illegal. Víðnæmur and Helga did not need to make a new agreement or to remarry. During the sixteenth century it became, however, more common to declare marriage illegal when the spouses were not respecting the marriage bond. Adultery thus started to become a successful argument also for the heirs who wanted to claim property

37 Ibid., pp. 619-20.
38 See p. 156.

from the married couple. We find many cases, which illustrate how adultery could be used for exactly that purpose.[39]

This means that by the end of the sixteenth century inheritance cases thus began to be more concerned with seeing adultery as a crime. At the same time it became more and more common to get a declaration from the law courts stating that one was born in a legal marriage.[40] This is the same trend as we can find elsewhere in Europe where legal control of sexual behavior became stronger during the Late Middle Age.[41] We have examined how the local bishops in Iceland from the fourteenth century onwards had strengthened their control through the court system.[42] The judgements in the before-mentioned copybook of Bishop Guðbrandur Þorláksson illustrate this quite clear. One is about the marriage of Jón and Halldóra.[43] The brother of the husband claimed this marriage was not legal. The judgement referred to the contract between them as well as to a statement from another person who had been present on the day of the marriage, and to the fact that the spouses had regarded themselves as being married. A testimony dating from 1584 also states that the couple had been married.[44] The accumulation of evidence meant that the brother did not win the case. That can be explained by the development of a stronger control of the court system at the end of the sixteenth century, at which time the authorities could not only define

39 See for instance DI VIII, pp. 154-55. The document is from the 5 July 1507. Þorbjörg Brandsdóttir was supposed to have given her husband a gift of *fjórðungsgjöf*. Such a gift could be presented by the giver to whomever he or she wished, but it was not allowed to consist of more than one quarter of one's own possessions, in contrast to the wealth that was inherited. The issue was first raised in court after the husband's death, when a ruling was sought on the question of how much his heirs and his widow should receive from the couple's possessions. The problem in this case was that the person who claimed that a gift had been made was not deemed a trustworthy witness because she had been living in adultery with Þorbjörg's husband. See more about *fjórðungsgjöf* pp. 366 ff.

40 DI XIII, pp. 360-61. This case from 1558 concerning the marriage of Jón Pálsson and Ásdís Fúsadóttir, and whether their son Vigfús was legitimately born, gives us an idea of how legality became such an important issue. This time, however, the passing of a judgement alone seems not to have had sufficient impact. Four years later, another man witnessed that he had been at the farm Mýrdalur in Kjós and heard Jón Pálsson declare that he was the father of their child Vigfús. It was the son himself who had asked the father to declare whether he was the son of a mistress or a wife. The father had answered that, to the best of his knowledge, Fúsi was his legitimate son. Another man who had been at the farm gave similar testimony a year later, in 1559.

41 See discussion here in chapter 3.2.1, p. 85, with a reference to Brundage 1990, pp. 546-47.

42 See discussion here in chapter 4.3.2.

43 *Bréfabók Guðbrands biskups Þorlákssonar*, pp. 435-36.

44 AM dipl.isl.fasc. LXIX, 4.

what a legal marriage was, but could also give those couples who were legally married better assurance of the fact that their relationships could not be declared illegal.

During the early fourteenth century cases tended to be directly related to relative's questions of inheritance, in such a way that those who wanted to get a marriage declared illegal could file a lawsuit against the couple, using different types of arguments for the marriage not being legal.[45] Later cases also became more associated with the clergy's efforts to control sexual behavior.[46] A case illustrating this is one from 1580 concerning Guðmundur Þorsteinsson and Helga Fúsadóttir.[47] While their marriage was declared to have been legally made, it was nevertheless considered in court because Guðmundur, during his married life, had also committed the sin of adultery and his wife had also been found guilty of double adultery.[48] Both Guðmundur and Helga accepted this judgement, and it seems that they made a new statement about their marriage agreement at the same time.[49]

The definition, interpretation and use of marriage law thus changed over time. The key to understanding this change is partly related to the stronger control of the authorities. Another important explanation is that this new legal control was established on the basis of the old understanding of the marriage rules. It is through cases in which marriages were declared illegal that it becomes most apparent on which elements of the law these judgements were based. It is also evident that what we find here is a mixture of older and newer elements of the law combined in these documents. Let us finally take an example from the

45 In this regard it can be mentioned that Richard Helmholz has underlined that the question of whether marriage was valid or not, became less important as time passed in late medieval English courts. He does not give any simple reason for why this happened. See Helmholz 2004, pp. 563-64. By comparing my results from Iceland to his results, however, one can point out that both stronger legal control, as well as the more general acceptance and use of canon law must have influenced which arguments were used in the court.

46 On this topic see also Dean 1998, p. 86. He says that generally the thirteenth century statutes were silent on adultery, but that in the early fourteenth century it became common to impose financial penalties on the man and then also on the woman, especially in the form of a fine or loss of dowry. The rule stating that the woman should lose her dowry if she lived in adultery was also known from *Jónsbók*.

47 *Alþingisbækur Íslands* I, pp. 403-05. In the title of the document, Guðmundur is named Sigmundur.

48 Ibid., pp. 404-405. The case was that Gudmundur: "hefdi nockud Raskad adur sijnu hiuskaparbandi. j þui ad hann hefdi tekid adra kuinnu. fram hiä sinni kuinnu Helgu. þui þötti oss sem Gudmundur mundi Ecki meiga taka fullan Rett a henni."

49 Ibid., pp. 404, 407. This new agreement was about their property agreement, see especially paragraph two.

case of Guðmundur Ingimundarson and Guðrún Magnúsdóttir, whose marriage was declared illegal in 1559.[50] This judgement was made at the local assembly at Vatnsdalur and priests from the see of Hólar as well as the secular judges were called into the law court by the dean and the representative of the royal authority. The husband had asked the court to judge whether his marriage to Guðrún Magnúsdóttir had been made according to the laws of "God and the country". He had become betrothed to Guðrún without the consent of her brother, who was her guardian. The arguments on which the conclusion was based were first taken from the marriage law of *Jónsbók*, which stated that the father and the mother should decide the marriage. Secondly, her brother had at an earlier stage given his sister over to another man with her full consent.[51] The document continued with arguments that because of this her later marriage was illegal. The *réttarbót* of King Hákon is cited, along with paragraph 13 of the *New Christian Law*, and paragraph 15 of the church ordinance.[52] Using these references, the importance of the woman's consent to the first marriage and the lack of the consent of her relatives to the second marriage were emphasized in the final judgement. This second marriage agreement of Guðmundur and Guðrún was thus judged illegal because it was "against the law of the king and the Church."[53] This demonstrates that it was no longer enough to have witnesses to the fact that the spouses had been living together for more than ten years or that she had given her consent to the agreement. If a marriage should be judged legal in the courts, some kind of proof from the official authorities was needed.

The authorities at the time used different law codes to justify their judgements. New law codes seem not to have denied the value of existing

50 DI XIII, pp. 382-86.

51 Ibid., p. 383.

52 Ibid., p. 385.

53 Ibid., p. 386: "j mote kongssins logum og kyrkiunnar." Another example can be taken from a judgement of 1562 concerning the marriage of Hans Eylertsson and Oddný Jónsdóttir, which declared the couple divorced because of her adultery. DI XIV, pp. 16-18. This seems to be the first case in which a woman was judged for adultery. Paragraphs from the Gospel of Matthew, as well as the *New Christian Law* and *Jónsbók*, were used to provide arguments in this case. It referred to a rule from the *New Christian Law* which stated that nothing except adultery could separate spouses who were living together and having a sexual relationship. According to another rule in *Jónsbók*, an unfaithful wife should lose the marriage gift of *tilgjöf*.

law codes, but simply added new elements to established tradition. Thus, by the end of the sixteenth century a variety of judgements have survived which make references to: the King's ordinance of 1587 concerning marriage; the Church ordinance of 1537/39; the *réttarbætur* of the early fourteenth century; *Jónsbók* of 1281; and the *New Christian Law* of Bishop Árni from 1275. A sentence was also often added to the final judgement, stating that it had been made "according to the custom of God and the country". At a later stage the king was added to this formula.

The force of these judgements can only be fully understood if the audience for which they were intended is considered, because even if the control of married life was increasingly becoming a matter for the courts in the sixteenth century, exercising this control was never an easy task. In 1567 a farmer was judged guilty of allowing a married man to stay with him after the man had run away from his wife and two children.[54] This case was partly concerned with the exercise of jurisdiction between different regions because, as referred to before, the law codes emphasized that nobody could marry outside their own region without providing proper proof that they had not been married before. The community of the parish, the priest and other witnesses, would ensure that only legal marriages were performed.

The common use and knowledge of canon law was related to the work of the Church in the fifteenth century. The cases which we have studied from the end of the sixteenth century further illustrate this great concern among the bishops to judge people for illegitimate sexual relationships. This awareness was already apparent in cases from the early sixteenth century, and was therefore not only a result of the change after the Reformation.

5.2 Drawing the lines: Local people's use of the law

Many judicial cases gained the status of law codes, or they were at least referred to as authoritative in marriage and inheritance matters. One

54 DI XV, p. 45.

example is a case from 1375.[55] This was an inheritance dispute involving the legitimately-born sons of a brother and their right to inherit in preference to the legitimately-born sons of a daughter, who was herself illegitimate. The result of the case was that the king demanded that this rule should be included in *Jónsbók*, giving it the status of a *réttarbót*. It has survived in many copies and has been called *Helgafellsréttarbót* because many copies of this document were made at the farm in Helgafell.[56] This case illustrates how new legal rules could be made as a result of individual cases. Here we shall further use some examples, firstly to show how knowledge of canon law actually shaped the arguments and the presentation of legal cases. Secondly, we shall see how many legal rules about marriage issues became shaped in the interaction between the authorities and the local customs.

5.2.1 *The narrative use of canon law*

We have been using the legal documents from the Late Middle Ages as evidence for the development of legal regulation. Here we shall continue to study similar documents, although not as evidence for legal changes, but more as texts, which can give information of the knowledge and use of canon law. This approach is based on the fact that knowledge of canon law is not only evident by the content of the court cases, but also lies behind the construction of the cases. This means that the narration of the cases, that is to say the way they are presented, is of essential importance. This can best be seen in some law cases from the fifteenth century, which show how the presentation of the cases was closely related to the question of consent. The marriage case of Þorleifur Þórðarson and Þorgerður Böðvarsdóttir can be mentioned as an example of this. Þorgerður in 1429 told the bishop, an abbot, and a priest that she had never been bound to the marriage by her own free choice.[57] Her

55 Another *réttarbót* that can be named in this context is the one called *Möðruvallaréttarbót*, see the discussion in the third part of this study pp. 417-18.

56 DI III, pp. 299-300, compares to "AM 128. 4to bls. 160-161, skb. from c.1490, eptir transskripti frá 28. Apr. 1389." The original is from the end of the fourteenth century, written in Niðarnesi on 10 June 1375 and given as a *réttarbót* by King Hákon. It deals with the inheritance of Gunnar Andrésson.

57 DI IV, p. 394.

husband Þorleifur verified her version of the story. He said that he had first asked her father and later spoke to her

and when he spoke to her, she said neither yes nor no. And then later when he talked to her about the agreement, she said yes that her father should decide. Even knowing this, the bishop asked him if he had betrothed her, but Þorleifur said he had not done so.[58]

This account of the case is largely built up to verify that she had not given her consent, in which case the marriage could be annulled. However, the marriage was not declared illegal because another document testified that they actually had made the agreement of betrothal with their mutual consent.[59]

This case clearly demonstrates how knowledge of the consent theory shaped the marriage litigation, but the outfall of the marriage cases was normally based on many different testimonies. This becomes even clearer by studying cases where consent to marriage was absent, as in a case for instance, from 1431 concerning a woman who declared that she had been given in marriage without her consent.[60] The case provides information on the possibility of an annulment of the marriage. The woman involved had run away from her husband and after that she took the case to her bishop's court.

[They] came to us in the corridor in front of the living room at Hólar in Hjaltadal, Skeggi Allason and Þórdís Magnúsdóttir, but she claimed that she had not been legally married to this man Skeggi, and she said she had never wanted to have him as a husband.[61]

58 Ibid., p. 394: "Ok þa han taladi med hana þa sagdæ hon huorcki næi næ ia. Ok þar æfter er han taladæ sidar med hana þa kaupit for fram þa sagdi hon jaa ath fader hennar skuldæ rada. æi sidr spurdi herra biscupenn hann huortt han hafdæ hana (fæst) ædr æi. en þorleifr sagdizst ecki hafua fæst hana."

59 Another document gives the testimony of two men about this marriage, and according to them they made the *festa* contract which concerned the handshake of Böðvar Arason and his daughter Þorgerður and the husband to be Þorleifur Þórðarson. Böðvar married his daughter to Þorleifur as a legal wife, and they heard her say 'yes' to this marriage. They also said that Böðvar had talked to his daughter before the handshake, and told her she should not go into it if she did not agree, but she had said she would. This case is printed in ibid., p. 395.

60 Ibid., pp. 448-49.

61 Ibid., p. 449: "komo firir oss j forstofuona firir timbrstofuonnæ a holum j hialtadaal skæggi alla(son) oc þordis magnusdotter huer ær æigi þottizst med logum æiga græindan skæggia oc sagdizst aldræ hafua viliat hann æiga til æigænbonda."

Þórdís had never wanted to marry Skeggi, although she had been living with him for ten years[62]

and she was then fifteen years old when Skeggi made the agreement with her in the church at Felli in Sléttuhlíð, her mother Guðrún Eiríksdóttir was there too and gave her consent to the agreement and Erlendur Þórisson said how the agreement should be.[63]

The testimony of Erlendur became stronger than the one from the wife Þórdís Magnúsdóttir. Erlendur admitted: "that they had shaken hands and he had made the contract between them according to the custom of the country, and the law of God was also followed."[64] So the marriage was not annulled.

The cases could indicate that during the fifteenth century it was rather difficult for women to use the rules about the consent of marriage in their own favor. Whether the gender issues were the most important factor here is uncertain, but only a study of the context of the cases can actually give information about the interest behind it. What is of the greatest importance here is that when studying the narrations, it becomes quite clear that consent – or the opposite – to marriage was used as a criteria for determining whether a marriage was legal or not. It was, however, not always easy to confirm, but it could be even more difficult to prove consummation of marriage. Some documents have survived concerning this issue. One concerns the promise of marriage which Kolbeinn Böðvarsson had made with Kristín Jónsdóttir.[65] By saying that their marriage had never been consummated he tried to extricate himself from his promise to her. He declared that he had never made love to her, nor had she lived with him as his concubine. The case also tells us why he wanted to get rid of Kristín. He admits that he had *keypt,* that is, made

62 This rule, under which couples who have been living together for 10 years or more are considered married, and their children thus legitimate, is also mentioned in *Jónsbók* and in *réttarbót* from 1305, as mentioned previously. See discussion in chapter 3.2.2 and pp. 117 and 161.

63 DI IV, p. 449: "oc war hon þa fimtan wætra ær skæggi kæypti hana j kirkonæ a fælli j slættuhlid gudruno Eiriksdottur modur hennar nerverandæ oc samþyckiandæ þeirra kaup ok ærllendi þorissyni segiandi firir þeirra kaupi."

64 Ibid., p. 449: "þau hæfdi hondum saman tækit oc ath hann kæypti med þeim suo sæm her j landet ær plaghr oc sidr til og gudz logh æigi j motæ tala."

65 Ibid., pp. 462-63. The letter has been dated to the period c.1431-49.

an agreement with another woman, Helga Snorradóttir, and by doing so made her his legal wife.[66] Once again the case is in favor of the man not the woman.

The question of legality continued to prompt the need for documentation of marriage after the Reformation as well as before.[67] The focus in the narration continued to be constructed according to the rules of canon law, but there is some indication of change in that women also could now begin to use the courts to their own advantage. A judgement of three clerics and three laymen from 1545 concerning the relationship between Einar Salomonson and Guðrún Jónsdóttir is an example of this.[68] The narration of the case is actually built up in favor of the woman. Einar had made a marriage agreement with Guðrún, and her parents had given their consent. The marriage banns had been published in church. Guðrún said that she had been forced to make this agreement, in accordance with the wishes of her parents. Witnesses backed up her story, saying that the same account of the situation had been heard by almost everyone. Secondly, Guðrún claimed that it was not possible for her to live with her husband since he did not take good care of her, providing her neither with food nor with clothing. She said that his behavior was so bad that she was actually uncertain whether she would live or die. Her testimony even alleged that he had tried to kill her more than once. However, the bad behavior of husbands was not always enough to get separated. This is illustrated in the case from the copybook of Bishop Gissur Einarson, about the wife who fled to the Monastery of Kirkjubæjarklaustur.[69] The judgement given in the case of

66 Ibid., pp. 462-63. We have more cases of the lack of consummation, which were taken to courts. On 7 February 1432 Árni Steingrímsson betrothed Ingunn Ólafsdóttur to be his wife. The marriage was made in accordance with the law of God, but twenty-one days later they annulled the marriage "because they had not consummated the marriage as the men present could witness." The couple promised to obey the judgement of the bishop, but the result of the case is unknown. See DI IV, pp. 494-95, 496-97.

67 A statement from 1555 survives concerning another marriage made in 1547. In it, a brother of the bride says that he had given his full consent to this marriage. See DI XII, p. 103. This is the first time the word *ekteskap* was used in an Icelandic contract. It can probably be explained as an influence from Denmark, reaching Iceland through the Church ordinance of 1541. Another document also confirms this marriage contract. See Ibid., p. 104. There must have been some kind of confusion about the legality of the marriage related to inheritance rights. A third letter, from 1562, also states that this was a legal contract, but by this time both partners, the husband and the wife concerned, were dead. See ibid., pp. 104-105.

68 DI XI, pp. 407-08, 419-20.

69 See discussion here on p. 143-44.

Guðrún is different. She was allowed to separate from her husband since he could not deny the charges made against him. One other case exists from 1524, which also gives the impression that a woman could get her marriage annulled by claiming that she had not consented to it.[70]

The point here is that these cases must not only be understood as evidence of the significance of parental consent in Iceland during the sixteenth century, resulting in some women being forced to contract marriages against their will. Perhaps more, they are also an example of how it was possible to get a separation. Forcing women into marriage contravened Church law, and when there were also testimonies that the husband had tried to kill his wife, as was the case in 1545, there was no doubt that the marriage should be annulled.[71]

Even if there was always the possibility of using the law to one's advantage, this was never a simple process. This section will further study how rules other than the principle of consent and consummation were used to declare marriages valid or invalid. It concerns both the question of impotence, adultery and the legal concept of *desertio*. We have no medieval cases illustrating this so well, but many examples from the sixteenth century show that canon law rules still determined how marriage cases were presented and judged.

One reason for divorce, besides adultery, was impotence. Bergur Jónsson and Salvör Nikulásdóttir both wanted to separate and according to the documents related to their case the reason was Bergur's impotence.[72] They were permitted to separate, and this was allowed according to the law of King Frederik II from 1587. They were thus separated according to the law.[73] As mentioned before, impotence was a reason for separation

70 The judgement made in 1524 by twelve clerics and Bishop Ögmundur dealt with the marriage of Sigríður Björnsdóttir and "her second husband", Finnur Arnórsson. The spouses were both at the court, and Finnur had nothing to complain about, while Sigríður said that she had been married against her will. See DI IX, pp. 201-202. This was against the rules of the holy Church. The clerics believed her, and she was asked to swear an oath that she was telling the truth, after which the marriage was annulled.

71 Compare to the discussion in chapter 3.3.

72 "hann hafi hafft sama vanmatt".

73 *Alþingisbækur Íslands* III, p. 121. See also the case of Tómas Arnarson and Ingibjörg Ólafsdóttir from 1597. Ibid., p. 117. They both came to the bishop and wanted a separation because "þess vanmegnis sem Tomas a sig medkendis." Before Tómas began to have this problem of impotence, he had been living an adulterous life with more than one woman, and it was decided to try to get these women to testify about his earlier lifestyle.

according to canon law, and was included in the Icelandic law codes of the late thirteenth century. However, it was not used commonly as a reason for separation until the end of the sixteenth century.[74] One of the reasons why impotence was not so often used as an argument for annulling marriage can be that it was not easy to prove. Richard Helmholz says that canon law regarded impotence cases with a certain amount of suspicion. One problem was, for instance, stories about men who were "cured" of impotency after having secured a divorce and married someone else.[75] According to canon law, impotence should be proved: a) by the parties concerned taking an oath, and b) an inspection to check the woman's virginity, to be carried out by "faithful matrons of good reputation [who are] experts in the nuptial art."[76]

Adultery was another reason at the end of the sixteenth century for claiming divorce, as discussed before.[77] A case dated 8 July 1594 deals with the marriage of Jón Jónsson and Grafar-Gunna and their subsequent separation.[78] The case came from priests and laymen and was addressed to Bishop Oddur Einarsson and the king's district commissioner, Árni Oddsson. The background to the case was that in 1590 Grafar-Gunna had claimed that Jón Jónsson had not been a proper husband to her.[79] Another document from 1591 tells us that her husband accused another man, also called Jón, of having a sexual relationship with her and then running away with her. Bishop Oddur Einarsson and the lawman made a judgement in 1592 at the assembly at *Alþingi*. It considers whether this couple should be allowed to separate: "because they wanted so seriously and desperately to separate, as she would by no means live any longer with him."[80] At an assembly again in 1594 it was ruled that the case should be sent back to the local authorities to be judged by the bishop.[81]

74 A single exception is to be found though in Gissur Einarsson's copybook, where he uses impotence as a reason for separation, see DI X, p. 664. This was also the case when Sigríður Einarsdóttir complained to Bishop Gissur Einarsson about her husband's impotence.

75 Helmholz 2004, p. 548.

76 Ibid., p. 549. He also refers to such inquests from English courts to test a man's sexual abilities.

77 See discussion here in chapter 5.1.

78 *Alþingisbækur* Íslands III, pp. 46-49. On this case, also see Agnes S. Arnórsdóttir 2001b.

79 *Alþingisbækur* Íslands III, p. 46: "hann hefði sér ekki að karlmanni orðið".

80 Ibid., p. 47: "þar sem þau leituðu svo þrásamlega og alvarlega þar eptir, að þau mætti aðskiljast, því hún vildi i aungvan máta leingur við hann halda."

81 Ibid.

The view of the local authority was clearly reflected in one final document, dating from 1595. The couple was supposed to come to court. Jón came but Grafar-Gunna did not because she had run away with another married man, to an unknown place in the most distant region of the country.[82] The judgement was based on biblical texts and the law codes of *réttarbætur* and *Jónsbók*.

The following biblical arguments were made: Marriage should be honored, and the bed of a couple should never be defiled. Men should love women and be kind to them, and in the same way women should be kind to their men.[83] A woman had no authority over her own body; her body was to be at the disposal of her husband. Likewise, the man's body was to be at the disposal of his wife. Consequently, neither of the sexes should tempt each other. God had ordered that a woman could not separate herself from her man and, if she did, she should be excluded from marriage and from later attempts to make a marriage agreement with her husband. The woman should be humble towards her husband, showing her subjection to him in the same way as she did to God.

After these arguments, taken from the *Bible*, the judgement cites arguments from the *réttarbætur* as well as certain rules about marriage and divorce emanating from the king. These were taken from the ordinance of 1587 of King Frederik II concerning marriage.[84] Adultery was given as the first reason for separation, but if the two individuals wanted to be joined again, they would be allowed to do so.

Jón Jónsson had given Grafar-Gunna the chance to return, but she instead ran away with another man. The judges concluded that they should free the couple from their marriage bond, which had been made by the law of God and the country.[85] Jón Jónsson could get married again, though not to Grafar-Gunna. The authorities wanted to punish her for her bad behavior, and punished the man as well for his unchristian life.

82 Ibid., "í burt hlaupin með öðrum giptum manni, Birni Þorleifssyni, í óvísa staði og fjarlæga landsfjórðunga."

83 Compare to 1 Cor. 7.4. This idea is related to the "conjugal debt" that unless by mutual consent, neither husband nor wife could deny the other the right to sexual access. See Helmholz 2004, p. 547. He refers to Makowski 1977, pp. 99-114 and Elliott 1993, pp. 142-55.

84 *Lovsamling for Island* I, pp. 113-24.

85 *Alþingisbækur Íslands* III, p. 48: "sundurskilin frá sínu hjúskaparbandi að guðs lögum og manna."

The case of Grafar-Gunna and Jón Jónsson can be used not only as an example of the way the authorities wanted to punish them,[86] but also as a way of saying something about their own wishes. According to the agreement of the lawman and twelve other persons in 1595, a penalty of one mark should be paid by any person running away to a distant place to get married.[87] This problem of *desertio* had gained new meaning after the marriage legislation of 1587, because it was named there as one of the reasons for obtaining a separation. The problem had been known before,[88] but it had not been referred to in Icelandic legislation. As soon as it became a legal phenomenon that could be described in general legal terms, it gave new significance to those situations in which people ran away from their home districts to other places. The case of Grafar-Gunna and Jón can be explained in relation to this. The story of Grafar-Gunna indicates that women did not play their role unwittingly. They seem to have been perfectly aware of the variety of strategies they could use to achieve their intentions, just as men did.

There is indeed a complex relationship between the role of the law's connection to collective cultural values, and the way the law could determine behavior.[89] But as this case illustrates, change in the judicial culture must have affected the participants in the courtroom.[90] The case of Grafar-Gunna could indicate change in the position of women in the court: by refusing to come to the court, running away with another man, and using the legal concept of *deserito*, Grafar-Gunna made it clear that she wanted a separation and had no intention of being reunited with her husband. Another possible way to understand the case is to look at it from the husband's point of view: Perhaps he just used the story of her

86 Compare to the discussion here on pp. 144 ff. about stronger control by the authorities of marriage matters at the end of the sixteenth century.

87 *Alþingisbækur Íslands* III, pp. 39-40.

88 Compare to a case from the copybook of Bishop Gissur Einarsson, see DI XI, pp. 306-08.

89 Bonfield and Poos 1986, p. 289.

90 This analysis of the Icelandic court cases has been inspired by a lecture which L. R. Poos gave in Copenhagen 1999, but was first published recently. See Poos 2009, pp. 181-207. See especially p. 202. "Legal scholars writing in this tradition emphasize law as a normative system of power enshrined in words. They thus depict legal disputes as competing narratives in which contestants and the courts themselves (with implicit and explicit legal and jurisprudential assumptions embedded within them, and shaping but not always dictating the direction of resolution) seek to impose retrospective meaning upon complex circumstances, and the position of respective sides in disputes as texts to be read by hidden codes".

running away (*desertio*) with another man (adultery) as an argument for getting divorce.

As this case indicates, the individuals directly involved in a potentially problematic situation could take their case to court. These individuals could include the clergy, the spouses themselves or their possible heirs. The cases studied here reflect just as much the internal local conflicts of lay folk as the efforts of the authorities to control the legality of marriage. A judgement from 1599 should be mentioned here as the last evidence to underline how knowledge of the consent theory as the main principle of what constituted a legal marriage, could be used for the instigators of a case for their own benefit. The case is a judgement from the end of June 1599 from the assembly at Þingvellir. It describes a criminal act of which Björn Magnússon and his friends had been accused.[91] In the course of the trial it became evident that Björn took a girl called Oddný Jónsdóttir from her parents' home. He was sentenced for this crime although not as an outlaw because the girl had not been taken by force but by her own free will. The norm was that women could not be taken from their husbands or guardians,[92] but because it could be proved that she had freely chosen to join Björn the case was no longer considered a criminal issue. Here the woman's own consent was used as an argument against the argument that her parents should give consent to her marriage.

It is through the discussions of the lawmen – using different legal principles as the basis for their arguments – that the conflict between Björn and the girl's parents, her capture, and the acceptance of the capture, are presented to us. As mentioned previously consent cases could be understood as reflecting a conflict between the parents' authority and the girl's own will. But in this case not all the involved parties were represented, since the parents and the young girl did not actively participate in the case. It was the man, Björn Magnússon, who was the instigator of the case; he had written to the king on the subject, claiming

91 *Alþingisbækur Íslands* III, pp. 156-57.

92 Ibid., p. 157: "Enn suo stendur liöslega j lögunum ad þeir sieu obötamenn sem taka konur naudugar. med Räni Edur herfange. huort sem þeir taka frændkonur manna Edur dætur fyrer vtan vilia þeirra manna. Er forrædi Eiga a þeim ad lögum."

his right on the basis of the fact that the consent of the woman became a requirement, which took precedence over the consent of her parents. This legal case emphasizes therefore an important change in the legal practice concerning the woman's position in relation to her parent's wishes and her own right to choose her partner.

Therefore, from the focus in the narration of these court cases we can see how the different legal principles were used. The stories, which lay behind many of the court cases, were translated into the legal language of the courtroom in a way that could affect the outcome of the case.[93] Court cases involving the question of consent and consummation clearly show how canon law was used to try to declare a marriage legal or not. Many more examples exist which illustrate how knowledge of canon law shaped court cases and, in particular, the way in which such cases were presented. Let us take a look now at the use of the canon law concept of "rumor" and its role in these legal cases.

5.2.2 *Rumor*

Several cases about how "rumor" existed as a legal phenomenon are to be found in the Icelandic documents. Often a case started with the spreading of rumors about the people involved, which could ultimately result in a marriage being deemed illegal, even if it was both consummated and made with the mutual consent of the spouses. One reason for this is already given in the old provincial law of *Gulathing*: i.e. if an impediment became apparent, the spouses could be separated.[94] According to the *New Christian Law* children could be judged legitimately born if their parents did not know there was a hindrance to their marriage.[95] This did not, however, necessarily refer to the fact that the spouses were too closely related. For example, a *mein* (impediment) could also refer to the husband having had a relationship before the wedding with a woman

93 On the translation of oral culture into formal legal proceedings, see Granquist 2001. See also her study in full length in Granquist 2004, especially her comments on pp. 99-100 about the court documents as a text have great value for understanding how it is possible for the historian to use the court material more as a narrative construction.

94 NgL I, pp. 27-28.

95 Einar Arnórsson 1953-57, p. 105 compare to chapter 23 in the *New Christian Law*.

PART I

Fig. 1. A drawing of a newly slaughtered cow. Animal husbandry was the foundation of the Icelandic economy during medieval times. This picture is from a late fifteenth-century manuscript of *Jónsbók, Heynesbók AM 147 4to, Arnamagnæanske Institut*, Reykjavík.

REYKNESINGAR | **VATNSFIRÐINGAR** | **SKARÐVERJAR** | **LEPPSÆTT**

EIRÍKUR SVEINBJARNARSON

1300

EINAR —— GRUNDAR-HELGA

1350 ÞÓRÐUR SIGMUNDSSON

BJÖRN JÓRSALAFARI —— SOLVEIG ÞORST. GUTTORMUR ORMSSON

ODDUR LEPPUR

Concubine

1400 ÓLÖF —— ARI ÞÓRLEIFUR ÁRNASON —— VATNSFJARÐAR-KRISTÍN —— JÓN LOFTUR —— KRISTÍN GUÐNI

GUÐMUNDUR RÍKI —— HELGA EINAR ÁRNI BJÖRN RÍKI —— ÓLÖF RÍKA KRISTÍN —— JÓN ÁSGEIRSSON

1450

GUÐNI

BJÖRN IN ÖGUR D. 1518

ERLENDUNGAR | **URÐAMENN** | **ÁSVERJAR**

ERLENDUR STERKI ÓLAFSSON LÖGMAÐUR

1300 HAUKUR JÓN Á FERJUBAKKA Í BORGARFIRÐI

SR. FLOSI Á STAÐASTAÐ

1350

ÞÓRÐUR VIGFÚS

1400 ODDUR LEPPUR ÞORSTEINN EYJÓLFSSON

KOLBEINSSTAÐAMENN

1450 ARNFINNUR HIRÐSTJÓRI FINNBOGI GAMLI JÓNSSON

EYJÓLFUR RIDDARI STEINUNN —— JÓN ÞÓRUNN —— SR. JÓN PÁLSSON MARÍUSKÁLD

FINNBOGI

Fig. 3. *Kaupbréf*, documents about property agreements. According to a legal rule in *Jónsbók*, it was obligatory to make a written agreement if one bought property to the value of six *hundrað* or more. This image of written documents being handed over to the judges is from a late sixteenth-century manuscript of *Jónsbók. Reykjabók AM 354 folio, Arnamagnæanske Institut*, Reykjavík. *Íslenskur söguatlas*, p. 122.

← Fig. 2. Map showing the land owned by the most powerful families in Iceland in the fourteenth and fifteenth centuries. Their family trees are shown below, (see also Figure 14).

Fig. 4. This Roman church bell from Háls in Fnjóskadalur in the North of Iceland is evidence of the early influence of Christianity in Iceland. The bell was made in the late twelfth century and is among the oldest existing church bells in the Nordic countries. *National Museum of Iceland.* Þjms. 6743, *Hlutavelta tímans,* p. 248.

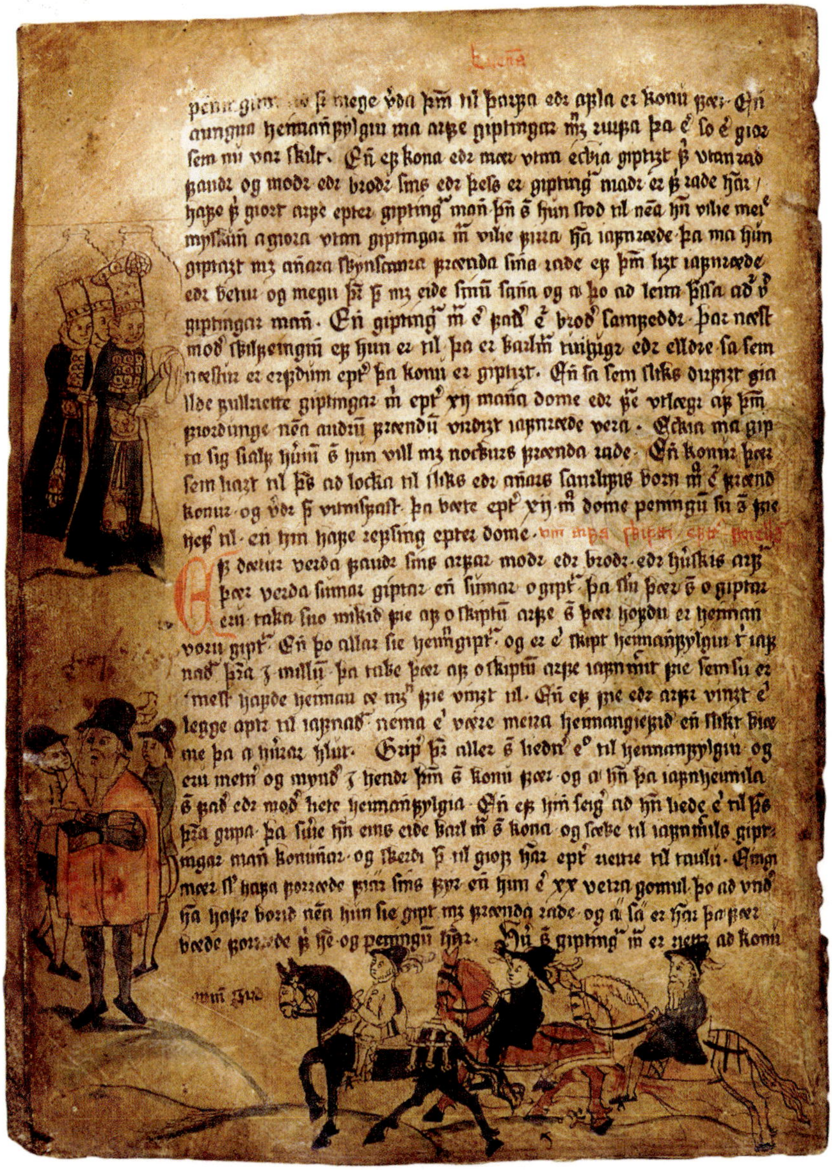

Fig. 5. Wedding celebration from a late sixteenth-century manuscript of *Jónsbók*. On the left, the bride and two other women. Below them the bridegroom is seen together with other men waiting for the guests. And finally, the picture at the bottom shows the wedding guests riding to the banquet. *Reykjabók AM 354 folio, Arnamagnæanske Institut,* Reykjavík. *Hlutavelta tímans,* p. 239.

Fig. 6. Royal document from 1545, giving priests permission to marry, with the seal of King Christian III, "Konungsbréf um hjúskap presta 1545". *National Archives of Iceland*, Bps. A. I. fasc. I, 1.

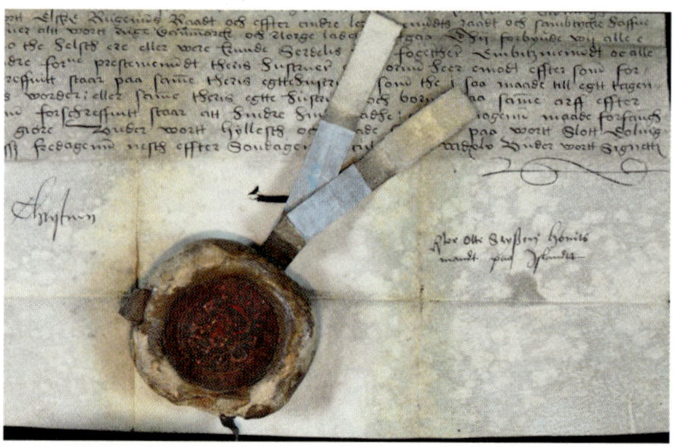

Fig. 7. Judgement from 1559 on a marriage. From the mid-sixteenth century till 1600 it became more and more common for the authorities to hold meetings at the Assembly at Þingvellir to make general judgements concerning marriage. "Tylftardómur 15. júlí 1559 um hjónabönd", *National Archives of Iceland,* Bps. A. I. fasc. I, 5.

Fig. 8. Early fifteenth-century crucifix from the church in Húsavík in the North of Iceland. As the bishops were making statutes of legal importance, the local church was contemporaneously becoming a place for Christian icons and symbols, as this Icelandic gothic crucifix shows. *National Museum of Iceland*. Þjms. 2397.

Fig. 9. The seal of Bishop Gissur Einarson. *Íslenskur söguatlas,* p. 151.

Fig. 10. The seal of the island of Iceland from 1592. The Icelanders had asked the royal administration for their own seal in 1592. This was granted. The seal shows a cod fish, encircled by the words SIGILLVM INSVLÆ ISLANDIÆ, *Íslenskur söguatlas,* p. 177.

Fig. 11. The old tradition of *festaröl,* drinking feast to mark a betrothal, continued to exist through the centuries, as the many surviving drinking horns are proof of. This special drinking horn from the late sixteenth century has many Biblical motifs, e.g. images of both St. Anne and the Virgin Mary with the child Jesus. *National Museum of Iceland.* Þjms. 261

Fig. 12. Marriage dispensation from 1535 given by Bishop Ögmundur to Þórður Ketilsson and Sigríður Jónsdóttir. *National Archives of Iceland,* Bps. A. I. XX, fasc. 66.

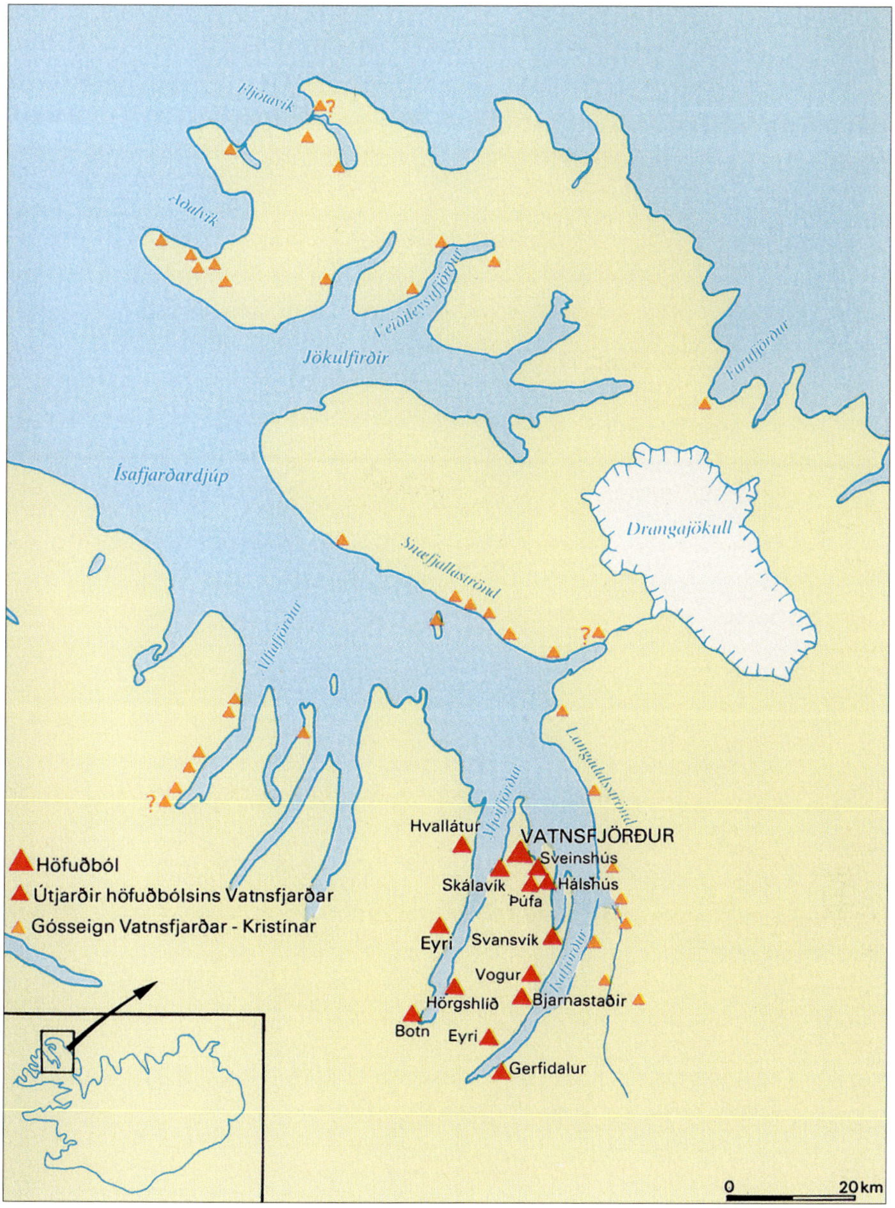

Fig. 13. Map of the property belonging to Vatnsfjarðar-Kristín from the early fourteenth century. *Íslenskur söguatlas*, p. 123.

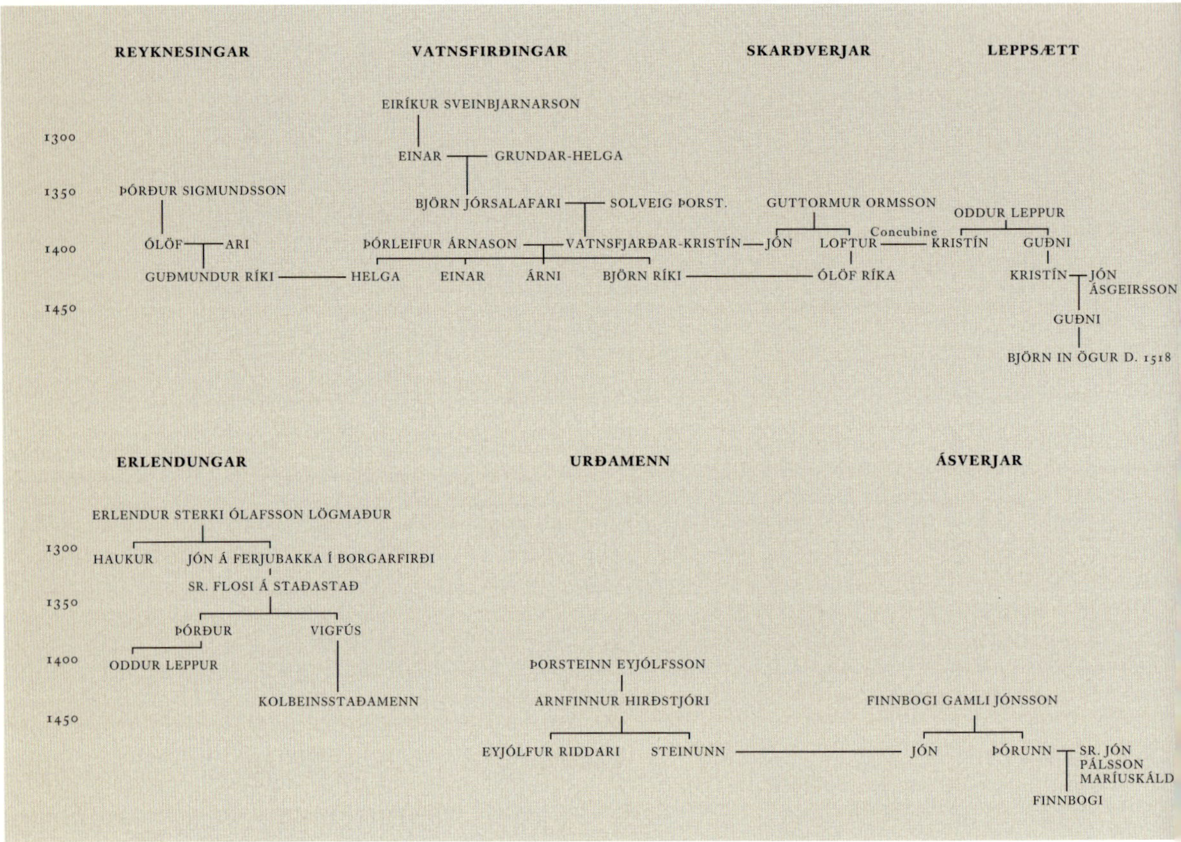

Fig. 14. Family tree of the most powerful families in Iceland in the fourteenth and fifteenth centuries. *Íslenskur söguatlas*, p. 123-124.

who was related to his future wife, as court cases which deal with the problem of impediments to marriage indicate.

Many of the existing cases, for instance one from 1483, arose because of a rumor, *byggðarrymt*. A person complained to the officials of the church of Hólar that Guðni Eyjólfsson had had sexual intercourse with a woman called Steinunn Bjarnadóttir before his marriage to Guðrún Gunnlaugsdóttir. Steinunn and Guðrún were related within the third degree, so the marriage was declared illegal.[96] The case had been taken to the court after Guðni had died. Inheritance rights lay behind this case. The procedure in court was as follows: Two persons witnessed concerning a rumor that Guðni Eyjólfsson had had sex with Steinunn before his wedding to Guðrún. The official then asked Steinunn if she denied this. Her answer was that "she could not do so, and she admitted in front of all these honest men that Guðni had made love with her."[97] Steinunn was obliged to prove this by an oath on the *Bible* and afterwards she swore with the oath of *lýrit*,[98] that at the time of the wedding she did not know that Guðrún was her kin. Later she realized that they were related in the third degree. When these rumors emerged, Guðrún asked Steinunn never to speak about this to anyone, but the significance of rumors was related to the obligation of the members of a parish to testify in marriage cases.[99] After Steinunn's testimony had been heard, another woman swore by an oath on the *Bible* that she had seen Guðni and Steinunn "totally naked lying in a bed, under one blanket, and this happened before the wedding of Guðni and Guðrún".[100]

Another case, from 1499, dealt with a similar problem, although in this case the outcome was different. The man concerned, Sturla, went to Bishop Stefán of Skálholt and asked him if he could marry Guðrún Finnbogadóttir or if the marriage would be against the rule of God.[101] The problem was, again, a rumor that Sturla had had a sexual relationship

96 DI VI, pp. 497-98.
97 Ibid., p. 498: "enn hun sagdist þad ei giora meiga og medkendist þar firir aullum dandimonnum þeim þar voru ad g(udni) hefdi l(eigit) hana."
98 The oath of *lýrit* was a veto against illegal judicial matters.
99 See discussion here on pp. 93-94.
100 DI VI, p. 499: "alnakin j einni sæng vnder einum klædum. adur enn brudkaup þeirra gudrunar gunnlaugsd(ottur) var og gudna."
101 DI VII, p. 414.

with a woman to whom his intended wife was related. This woman was related to the lawman Finnbogi Jónsson, the father of the bride. The difference is that in this case the bishop managed to *hrinda þeirri hindran*, or takes away the hindrance, and afterwards gave his dispensation for the marriage. Sturla Þórðarson knew of this impediment and therefore went to the bishop and received permission to marry. This knowledge can easily be related to the influence of Sturla's later father in-law, as he was a powerful lawman. His own marriage contract shows that he clearly knew how to make a legal contract.

The third case to be considered in relation to this issue dates from 1502. It was also dealt with by Bishop Stefán, but this time he was required to judge whether a marriage and a betrothal had been legally made. The marriage was judged invalid, and the records of the case provide a list of reasons for this decision. It stated that the couple concerned came to be related within the third and fourth degrees, because the man involved had had intercourse with a woman related to his future wife. This was a serious charge as the husband knew this before he married the other woman. He aggravated his crime by having had eight children with a concubine, who later became his wife. In addition, he had not sought absolution except after the birth of his seventh child.[102] Another element of this case was that the marriage banns had never been published in church. In this case it was the husband, Daði, who was blamed for all these deficiencies. Neither his wife nor the priest in the parish, where the marriage banns should have been published, faced any charges. This judgement clearly indicates the powerful jurisdiction of the bishop in marriage matters. All seven children were judged illegitimate and without the right to inherit from their parents.[103]

Cases, which often had their origin in rumors, could be judged at courts and further be a basis for statements or general rules about behavior,[104] and many of these cases concerned men who had had sex

102 Ibid., p. 605.

103 Ibid., p. 606.

104 The marriage of Sigmundur Oddson and Guðrún Guðmundsdóttir was also deemed illegal because he had been having a sexual relationship with a woman related to Guðrún within the third degree, see DI XIII, p.

with a woman related to their wives before they got married.[105] A case from 1521 also concerned a rumor that a man had been having a sexual relationship with a woman before his wedding. However, in this instance the woman concerned was actually the intended bride. For this reason, the parents destroyed the agreement they had arranged concerning the financial gifts to her, especially those concerning the farm at Grafargil in Valþjólfsdalur.[106] This case demonstrates strong parental authority related to the transfer of property.

Church courts on the Continent did not attempt to solve disputes over the division of marital property, because these matters lay within the competence of civil courts,[107] and this was the reality in Iceland as well. A man who had a sexual relationship with his future wife did not receive her property after he had broken the marriage agreement made with her parents. This case is therefore not only based on canon law, but also the secular law of *Jónsbók*, and is based both on using the law of the country as well as the law of God.

To be able to study further the suitors behind these cases, we need to analyze the legal texts in relation to other source material about the persons involved. The motive behind the cases cannot be explained by the court material alone, therefore we shall further study examples of marriage dispensations from a broader point of view.

5.2.3 *The forbidden degrees of marriage*

Change can reflect central authority's interventions in local society as discussed in chapter 4. But as the arguments in chapter 5.2.1 clearly illustrate the local communities could also use the decisions of the secular and

399; compare to Ibid., pp. 430-31. It was Bishop Gísli Jónsson who was responsible for this judgement, and later in the same year he called together *tylftardómur* to make a more general ruling. From this point on no marriage that was not made according to the King's ordinance should be legal.

105 The marriage of Jón Þorvaldsson and Vilborg Sigurðardóttir was declared illegal because Jón had been found guilty of having had sexual intercourse with a woman related to Vilborg before their wedding. It stated that: "Jón had sexual intercourse with her, as many people could testify". See DI VIII, pp. 96-97, particularly p. 96: "er jon hafdi samrædi med hafft ad margra mana vitorde."

106 Ibid., pp. 775-77.

107 Brundage 1995a, pp. 74-75.

ecclesiastical rulers to their own ends.[108] This aspect will be examined in more detail here through a study of all known cases concerning dispensation from the forbidden degrees of marriage in late medieval Iceland. This also includes information regarding previously unknown dispensations recently discovered in the archives of the Papal Penitentiary in Rome.[109] It is important to make clear that the need for dispensations from the forbidden degrees of marriage was great among the higher echelons of Icelandic society.[110] The sources we have been studying reflect the way in which these late medieval cases were related to inheritance disputes among the richest and most powerful families in the country.

When studying the existing cases about marriage dispensation it is important to remember that the clergy actually tried to prevent marriage between people who were related within the forbidden degrees. For instance Bishop Ólafur Rögnvaldsson and his clergy at the see of Hólar made an announcement in 1490-92 that those who wanted to marry, but had heard rumors about hindrances to the marriage, were obliged to prove that there were no such impediments if they wanted the marriage to be legal.[111] At the same time it was possible according to canon law to give dispensation from the rules relating to marriage, in a development which was connected to the broader culture of papal policy. After the Fourth Lateran Council of 1215 marriage was not permitted within four degrees. A papal dispensation was thus necessary for cousins related within the fourth degree to marry.[112] Persons related by legal ties were also forbidden to marry each other, meaning that in-laws could not marry one another, and neither could godparents marry one another or any close relative of their godchild. This rule applied to direct relatedness (*consanguinitas*), to relatedness through marriage

108 Compare to the study of Benadusi 1995, p. 165.

109 Compare to the study on the Swedish and the Finnish cases in Salonen 2001, pp. 103-19, and pp. 250-77.

110 Compare to the discussion in chapter 3, 3.2.1 about the correspondence between Pope Alexander III and Archbishop Eystein about marriage between relatives up to the seventh degree.

111 DI VI, pp. 729-30. We have also discussed more of these cases in chapter 4, 4.3.2, as well as in chapter 5, 5.2.2 about the role of Bishop Stefán.

112 This rule was widely accepted. Giovanna Benadusi has shown how a papal dispensation for fourth-degree cousins was a possible family strategy in Tuscany in the late sixteenth century. See Benadusi 1995, p. 163. See also the papal dispensation practice related to the Scandinavian countries during medieval times in Ingesman 1998, pp. 3-6, compare to Ingesman 1997, pp. 193-99, especially p. 196.

(*affinitas*) and to the so-called spiritual relatedness (*cognatio spiritualis*), which baptism and confirmation created. The Icelandic terms for these concepts are *sifjar* or *frændemi* for "consanguinitas", *mægðir* for "affinitas", and *guðsifjar* for "cognatio spiritualis".[113]

As mentioned before, couples who were related within the fourth degree or closer were not allowed to get married according to an amendment to *Grágás* from 1217. The rules about the forbidden degrees of marriage were repeated in *Jónsbók* from 1281, as well as in the Church statutes of the early fourteenth century.[114] We do not, however, have any written evidence of petitions for dispensations in the charters before the year 1471.

Several dispensation cases are known from the late fifteenth and early sixteenth centuries (see Table II).

Table II	*Marriage dispensations and cases about the forbidden degrees of marriage*
1471	Einar Ormson and Cecile Þorsteinsdóttir[115]
1472	Þorleifur Björnsson and Ingveldur Helgadóttir[116]
1476	Ormur Jónsson and Ingibjörg Eiríksdóttir[117]
1476	Páll Jónsson and Solveig Björnsdóttir[118]
1477	Þorleifur Björnsson and Ingveldur Helgadóttir[119]
1479	Páll Jónsson and Solveig Björnsdóttir[120]

Continued →

113 Páll Vídalín 1854, p. 489, Magnús Már Lárusson 1962a, pp. 374-75.

114 *Jónsbók*, p. 77. Here it is only stated according to the law of God, which also includes the general rules of the fourth degree relation. See also DI II, pp. 590-91.

115 DI V, pp. 608-609. In 1471 the case of the marriage of Einar Ormsson and Cecile Þorsteinsdóttir was brought to the court, but it had been made in "fjórmennings meinum". See Einar Bjarnason 1969, p. 142 ff; compare to AM Apogr. 2487 where it says it is not an original judgement, but a draft of the case.

116 *Diplomatarium Poenitentiariae Norvegicum*, pp. 105-06, with a reference to Archivio Segreto Vaticano, Penitenzieria. Registri delle Suppliche, vol. 20, fol. 67r.

117 Ibid., p. 106, with a reference to Archivio Segreto Vaticano, Penitenzieria. Registri delle Suppliche, vol. 25, fol. 13v.

118 Ingesman 2001, pp. 140-41, which cites Archivio Segreto Vaticano, Penitenzieria. Registri delle Suppliche, vol. 25, fol. 13v. This is the first dispensation to Páll and Solveig.

119 DI VI, pp. 102-03.

120 Ibid., pp. 234-35. This is the second dispensation.

Table II. continued	*Marriage dispensation and cases about the forbidden degrees of marriage*
1480	Páll Jónsson and Solveig Björnsdóttir[121]
1480	Ormur Jónsson and Ingibjörg Eiríksdóttir[122]
1493	Vigfús Erlendsson and Cecilia Eyjólfsdóttir[123]
1493	Einar Eyjólfsson and Hólmfríður Erlendsdóttir[124]
1499	Sturla Þórðarson and Guðlaug Finnbogadóttir[125]
1502	Daði Arason and Þóra Þórarinsdóttir[126]
1506	Jón Þorvaldsson and Vilborg Sigurðardóttir[127]
1507	Jón Sigmundsson and Björg Þorvaldsdóttir[128]
1508	Björn Þorleifsson and Ingibjörg Pálsdóttir[129]
1508	Jón Narfason and Dýrunn Þórðardóttir[130]
1535	Þórður Ketilsson and Sigríður Jónsdóttir[131]
1544	Þorsteinn Arviðsson and Vilborg Sigurðardóttir[132]
1545	Finnbogi Einarsson and Þuríður Þorgrímsdóttir[133]
1556	Vigfús Þorsteinsson and Anna Eyjólfsdóttir[134]
1563	Þorleifur Grímsson and Sigríður Jónsdóttir[135]
1563	Eggert Hannesson and Steinunn Jónsdóttir[136]
1564	Þorleifur Björnsson and Ragnhildur Jónsdóttir[137]
1565	Magnús Magnússon and Guðrún Þorleifsdóttir[138]

121 Ibid., pp. 418-21. This is the third dispensation.

122 Ibid., pp. 418-21. This dispensation is in the same letter as the third dispensation of Páll Jónsson and Solveig Björnsdóttir.

123 *Diplomatarium Poenitentiariae Norvegicum*, p. 108, with a reference to Archivio Segreto Vaticano, Penitenzieria. Registri delle Suppliche, vol. 42, fol. 47v.

124 Ibid., p. 108, with a reference to Archivio Segreto Vaticano, Penitenzieria. Registri delle Suppliche, vol. 42, fol. 48r.

125 DI VII, pp. 414-15.

126 Ibid., pp. 603-06.

127 DI VIII, pp. 96-97. Declaration about separation.

128 DI VII, pp. 325-26; compare DI VIII, pp. 133-35. This is a marriage contract and a judgement about their relationship. They married in 1497, and the judgement is from 1507.

129 Ibid., pp. 250-51. This is a marriage dispensation.

130 Ibid., pp. 205-206. Absolution for having relationship in the forbidden degrees of marriage.

131 DI IX, pp. 735-36. This is a marriage dispensation. See Figure 12.

132 DI XI, p. 335. This is a marriage dispensation.

133 Ibid., pp. 415-16. Absolution and a marriage dispensation.

134 DI XIII, pp. 226-33, especially p. 228.

135 DI XIV, pp. 57-58. Compare also to DI XV, pp. 237-39 and to ibid., pp. 286-88, 288-89, 289-09.

136 DI XIV, p. 76.

137 Ibid., p. 277.

138 Ibid., pp. 363-64.

As we can see in Table II our source material provides an insight into the granting of dispensations in Iceland from the pope in Rome as well as from the local ecclesiastical authorities. Both the archbishops in Niðarós and the Icelandic bishops could give dispensations, but after the Reformation the authority to do so in Iceland was also given to the rural deans.[139]

Many of the dispensations were related to matters of inheritance. The case of Einar Ormson and Cecile Þorsteinsdóttir, which was judged in 1471 in Skálholt, is one of these.[140] The dispute was between the widow Cecilia Þorsteinsdóttir, and her husband's brother, Loftur Ormsson. The issue at stake was whether the children of Cecilia and her husband, Einar Ormsson, were their legitimate heirs. The couple was related within the fourth degree. The bishop judged the marriage to be illegal. Thus, the brother of Einar, Loftur, was granted the first right to the inheritance.[141] Making a will was one strategy for transferring property through channels other than legal marriage. Einar Ormsson had made a will in 1470 which gave property to eight of his children. Six of them were the children of Einar and Cecilia.[142] His also gave alms to the Church and clerics, which has been interpreted as evidence of his piety. This may also be seen as a result of the culture of will-making, according to which a person would always donate some of his or her property to the Church. Because of Einar Ormsson's need for a marriage dispensation, a donation to the Church must be seen as one element of his efforts in this respect. However, his brothers did not respect the wishes expressed in this will, and managed to get the marriage declared illegal at the bishop's court.[143]

Of course, this case was concerned with acquiring great wealth. Einar and Loftur were the sons of Solveig Þorleifsdóttir and Ormur Loftsson, who had been married in 1434.[144] Solveig was the daughter of Þorleifur Árnason and Kristín Björnsdóttir, who lived at the manor Vatnsfjörður. Ormur was son of Loftur Guttormsson, owner of the manor at Skarð

139 In relation to the practice after the Reformation see DI, XIII, pp. 226-33.

140 See Arnór Sigurjónsson 1975, p. 153, compare to Einar Bjarnason 1969.

141 DI V, pp. 608-09. There was also a question as to whether Loftur's brother, Halldór Ormsson, who is named in the document as sitting in the court as the bishop's official, should also receive inheritance.

142 Ibid., pp. 608-09, see also Arnór Sigurjónsson 1975, pp. 153-54.

143 Ibid., pp. 157-58.

144 Ibid., p. 144. Their wedding had been held at the manor of Reykhólar.

in Skarðsströnd. By the marriage of Solveig and Ormur the wealth of these two great families, the Skarðsverjar and Vatnsfirðingar, was united. The property strategy of these leading families during the fifteenth and sixteenth centuries will be considered later in this study when marital property and marriage strategy are analyzed.[145] Here it is important to use these cases to illustrate both how the legal knowledge of the persons involved in the cases of application for dispensation, as well as the legal disputes at the courts themselves, can be understood as disputes reflecting both the old and the new understanding of marriage.

The application for dispensation from the forbidden degrees of marriage had started to be practiced by the end of the fifteenth century. Before this time members of the aristocracy who had married within the forbidden degrees risked losing their children's right to inherit. This risk, however, did not deter people related within the fourth degree from having children. The father of Grundar-Helga's son, Björn Jórsalafari, was Einar Eiríksson of Vatnsfjörður, to whom she was related within the fourth degree. Even though Björn was illegitimately born, he managed to inherit the family estate at Vatnsfjörður.[146] (See Figures 13 and 14)

Illegitimacy was not necessarily a hindrance in rising to a powerful position in the fourteenth century, although awareness of the sinfulness of this situation may be one explanation for the many pilgrimages to Rome undertaken at that time. In other words, a tradition was utilized that secured the rights of those who had been born illegitimate.[147]

But it is clear that in the late fifteenth century the possibility of obtaining marriage dispensations could have given the aristocracy a new strategy for marrying inside the fourth degree. To get a better understanding of the dispensation practice three examples of dispensation cases from late fifteenth- and early-sixteenth century Iceland will be studied further here.[148] All three cases were debated over many years. Two of them involved the same family and concerned the couples Þorleifur Björnsson and Ingveldur Helgadóttir, and Solveig Björnsdóttir (Þorleifur

145 See her chapter 9.3.
146 That is, a half part of the estate, which was not the local church property.
147 See more on this matter in Agnes S. Arnórsdóttir 2005, pp. 207-19.
148 This part of the study has also been published in Agnes S. Arnórsdóttir 2003.

Björnsson's sister) and Páll Jónsson. The parents of Þorleifur and Solveig were Björn Þorleifsson and Ólöf Loftsdóttir.

Over twenty documents survive concerning the case of Þorleifur and Ingveldur. They were members of the Icelandic elite, both coming from rich and powerful families. Because they were related within the fourth degree, they could not have expected to be married without complications arising. Giovanna Benadusi has described how the gaining of dispensations for this sort of union was the means by which the Tuscan ruling elite during the Early Modern period managed to ensure that both wealth and offices stayed within the same families.[149] Similar forces were clearly at work in late medieval Iceland. Ingveldur and Þorleifur lived together and had children.[150] In 1471, when they had seven children, they received absolution for their sins after paying a penalty and confessing their sins to a priest. In 1474, they must have broken their promise to sin no more, because they had an eighth child. They must have returned to the priest to confess again.

Þorleifur and Ingveldur gained a dispensation for their marriage. In a royal letter of 25 February 1477 it is stated that "our Holy Father the Pope" had given them dispensation.[151] However, Bishop Magnús Eyjólfsson in Skálholt would not accept this. This obstacle was overcome by a compromise between the Bishop and Þorleifur. These were two of the country's highest-ranking men. Þorleifur later became a *hirðstjóri*, the highest official of the royal administration. It was agreed that if Þorleifur received another dispensation from both the archbishop and the pope,[152] Bishop Magnús would accept it. The dispensation was granted and their marriage was declared legal.[153]

Once Ingveldur and Þorleifur had received the papal dispensation for their marriage, their children could be proclaimed legitimate, including those born before the marriage.[154] Eventually the dispensation was issued

149 Benadusi 1995, pp. 163-64.

150 DI V, pp. 622, 733-35. See also Einar Arnórsson 1949-53, p. 127.

151 DI VI, pp. 102-03.They had received the dispensation from a papal legate: "Thaa effir thii at the haffve loff aff wor helgeste ffather paven. som hans legatis breff the ther vppa haffve ydermer vtviise".

152 Ibid., pp. 150-51.

153 See judgement from 1 July 1500 in DI VII, pp. 492-95, especially p. 494 where there is reference to the accept of Bishop Magnús.

154 See Arnór Sigurjónsson 1967, pp. 99, 119-21, 123-26, 128, 134, 206.

by all the relevant authorities: an Icelandic bishop, the royal authorities,[155] the archbishops of Niðarós[156] and finally the pope.[157] The granting of the dispensation was aided by Þorleifur's network of affinities.[158] However, after Þorleifur's death his relatives initiated proceedings to have the marriage declared illegal, and the dispensations void. This lawsuit continued for years but eventually led to victory for Þorleifur's relatives, who had never accepted the dispensation. After Þorleifur's death these relatives became his heirs by having his marriage to Ingveldur declared invalid.[159] The case produced a wealth of documentation which still survives. The case was recorded in many copies, which underlines how important it was. In a clerical judgement concerning the case made in Skálholt in 1500, Bishop Stefán was in favor of the dispensation, and declared the marriage legal.[160] However, Björn Guðnason from Ögur, the leading figure in getting the marriage declared illegal, wrote to both the clerical and royal authorities concerning the matter. In a letter to a lawman he referred to the customary law, stating that according to both *Jónsbók* and the *New Christian Law* of Bishop Árni Þorláksson, the marriage of people related within the fourth degree was illegal. The case continued and Björn Guðnason did not give up fighting against what he called the Roman dispensation, which was contrary to the accepted law of Iceland. The clerical judgement of 1500 on this matter was never overturned, although Björn Guðnason and his co-litigants never accepted this. The dispute between Björn Guðnason and Björn Þorleifsson (Þorleifur and Ingveldur's son) continued over two decades.[161] Þorleifur's heirs used every opportunity to state their objections to the dispensation.

This case was not only concerned with the risk to Þorleifur and Ingveldur's salvation because their marriage was a forbidden relationship, it was primarily a question of control over considerable wealth. It is thus too simple to explain the motivation for the campaign against the

155 DI VI, pp. 102-03. A dispensation from King Christian I, from 28 February 1477.
156 Ibid., pp. 162-63. A dispensation from Archbishop Gauti from 26 September 1478.
157 Ibid., p. 103.
158 See Arnór Sigurjónsson 1975, p. 206.
159 Ibid., p. 128, and forward. He states that Björn í Ögri and his followers never accepted the dispensation.
160 DI VII, pp. 530-31.
161 Arnór Sigurjónsson 1975, p. 128.

dispensation as a lack of respect for the ecclesiastical model of marriage, or even as a lack of respect for the papacy. It was rather an internal conflict between leading families in Iceland. Þorleifur became connected with the royal administration of King Christian I,[162] and in 1480 he became a *hirðstjóri*.[163] At this time Hrafn Brandsson and Einar Ejólfsson were lawmen. There was enmity between them and Þorleifur Björnsson, with whom they were probably engaged in a conflict.[164]

It is important to see these dispensations in relation to the strategies employed by the ruling families of the late fifteenth century. The efforts of getting dispensation for marriages within the forbidden degrees were related to the marriage strategy of the families involved. The historian Einar Bjarnason has assumed that the policy used by both Þorleifur Björnsson and Einar Ormsson, which was to marry women to whom they were related, was a tactical move. In this they were manipulating the local Church authorities by using the dispensation from the forbidden degree as a tool for their own purposes. Furthermore, he suggests that even if such dispensations had been heard of, they had not been used in Iceland before this time.[165] Einar Bjarnason assumes that the Icelanders who knew about this possibility of gaining a dispensation had not been able to do so because the Icelandic bishops were resistant. Certainly no dispensations were granted during the episcopacies of Sveinn Pétursson who was bishop in Skálholt from 1466-75, and of Ólafur Rögnvaldsson bishop in Hólar from 1460-95. In 1476 Magnús Eyjólfsson became bishop of Skálholt, and it seems that he also refused to follow the instruction from the papacy.[166] Three letters from the pope survive with regard to the case of Páll and Solveig Björnsdóttir (Þorleifur's sister), all of these letters having been prompted by the bishops' resistance to the authority of the pope.[167] Bishop Magnús Eyjólfsson of Skálholt was not willing to

162 DI VI, pp. 281-85.

163 Ibid., pp. 397- 99. He was appointed to the office from Bergen, as Iceland continued to be a province under the Norwegian monarchy, also after the establishment of the personal union between Norway and Denmark.

164 DI VI, p. 282.

165 Einar Bjarnason 1969, pp. 147-48.

166 Ibid., pp. 148-49.

167 It was assumed by Einar Bjarnason 1969, that the dispensation documents concerning Solveig and Páll were fewer in number and that the letters which have survived from 1479 are two copies of the original letter from 1476. Einar Bjarnason was wrong, however, as the arguments later in this section will show.

give a dispensation for this marriage, which was crucial in determining the rights to control the main manors in the Vestfjörður district.

Solveig lived on the farm of Hóll in Bolungarvík, which she had inherited. She had eight children with Jón Þorláksson who managed the affairs of the farm.[168] They were not married, probably because he was not from a suitable family. In 1479 another man, Páll Jónsson, wanted to marry Solveig although they were related within the fourth degree.[169] In a letter related to Solveig's marriage, her mother Ólöf ríka, agreed to accept the match as long as the couple received dispensation from the holy Church.[170]

Two letters from the pope concerning this case are published in the *Diplomatarium Islandicum.* These are not the original documents but later Icelandic translations. According to these documents, the pope had under the threat of interdict ordered Bishop Magnús of Skálholt to give dispensation to Solveig and Páll. The letter from 1479 refers to an older dispensation.[171] In 1481 Bishop Magnús Eyjólfsson was again ordered by the pope's to give the couple dispensation.[172] The oldest dispensation in this case, that from 1476, is probably the one to which a reference was recently found in the archives of the Papal Penitentiary. This is a short reference stating that the couple had gained dispensation to marry.[173] This information regarding the dispensation reinforces the interpretation of the publishers of the *Diplomataricum Islandicum* that there were actually three letters of dispensation in this case, and not only one as Einar Bjarnason assumed.

Having received all those dispensations, it would be reasonable to assume that Páll and Solveig could consider themselves legally married. It seems, however, that the bishop never accepted the dispensation to

168 Einar Arnórsson 1955, p. 130. Compare to *Sýslumannsævir* II, pp. 491-98.

169 Einar Arnórsson 1955, pp. 131-32.

170 The letter was made at the farm of Skarð, where Ólöf then lived. It was made by her, using her own seal. See more about Ólöf Loftsdóttir in Agnes S. Arnórsdóttir 2009.

171 DI VI, pp. 234-35.

172 Ibid., pp. 418-21.

173 See Agnes S. Arnórsdóttir 2003, compare to Ingesman 2001 who has found these cases in *Archivio Segreto Vaticano, Penitenzieria. Registri delle Suppliche*, vol. 25, fol. 13v: Now this information is published in *Diplomatarium Poenitentiariae Norvegicum* 2004, p. 106.

the couple,[174] and this explains why Solveig realized that there would be problems with inheritance after her death. She swore that she had never had a sexual relationship with anybody except the two men, Jón and Páll.[175] In an effort to ensure that her children received a portion of her property Solveig wrote a will,[176] on 17 January 1495. She died later that year.[177]

Solveig had been the heir to her brothers Þorleifur and Einar Björnsson. This meant that she controlled all the manors and wealth of her parents, Björn and Ólöf ríka, including the property of her brothers. It had never been possible to enforce the claim that the children of Þorleifur and Ingveldur were legitimately born, so they did not inherit a share of the property of their parents.[178] When Solveig passed away, her husband Páll was abroad. Thus Björn Guðnason at Ögur, Páll's nephew, claimed the right to inherit from Solveig unless the children she had had with Páll were declared their legitimate heirs.[179] When Páll returned to Iceland, he and his son took control of Solveig's wealth.[180] This case will not be described further, except to say that Páll was killed by a group including Björn Þorleifsson, the son of Þorleifur and Ingveldur. Björn lived for many years after this murder and did not have to pay a large penance for his involvement in this crime. He became the main protagonist in the dispute concerning his parent's inheritance against Björn Guðnason at Ögur, until his death in 1518, whereafter the dispute continued with Björn Guðnason's heirs,[181] (see Figure 14).

The third marriage dispensation to be discussed is that of Jón Sigmundsson and Björg Þorvaldsdóttir.[182] Jón was a lawman, and therefore

174 Einar Bjarnason 1969, p. 153.

175 Einar Arnórsson 1955, p. 133 compare to DI, VI, pp. 511-12.

176 DI VII, pp. 242-47.

177 See ibid., p. 238 where it is assumed that she had died before 28 March, because it was then that Björn Guðnason got the news about her death. See ibid., pp. 256-57.

178 Einar Arnórsson 1955, pp. 134-35, compare to DI VII, p. 256.

179 He probably did this so that no other heirs could get the inheritance, for instance the children of Þorleifur and Ingveldur.

180 Einar Arnórsson 1955, pp. 134-35.

181 DI VII, pp. 358-64. A judgement made after the death of Páll, seems to be constructed very much in a saga style narration. It says that Páll was in bed asleep when his enemies came. They threw stones at him from the roof of the house. Páll jumped out of his bed, naked, carrying a sword to defend himself. He managed, however, to put his trousers on during a break in the stone-throwing attack.

182 The case has also been discussed in Agnes S. Arnórsdóttir 2003.

a member of the group that had the best knowledge of the law. Their marriage contract was concerned with the problem of getting dispensation from the forbidden degrees of marriage. The agreement was made between the couple, and was announced and confirmed with a written contract dated 2 February 1497.[183]

The second part of the agreement describes the publishing of the marriage banns in church, and the question of whether anyone knew there was an impediment to this marriage. It specifically states that the officials of the priest of the church of Hólar, Jón Þorvaldsson, had asked this question and there had not been ant objection to the marriage. The priest, who was Björg's brother, had subsequently declared that Björg was married.

Another document concerning this contract was made on 5 February 1497.[184] According to this document the marriage had been published in the church for three Sundays, and this meant that:

> no one could find any hindrance and at the right time after the publication of marriage banns, then this property agreement and this condition were declared at Höskuldsstaðir in Skagaströnd in public, with many people in attendance. Then the priest again asked if any people were present in this living room or at the farm who knew of any hindrance to this marriage, whether there were any affinities or any blood relation inside the forbidden degrees between Jón and Björg. All those that were together there said no, they did not know or had known that Jón and Björg were related. This publication between these persons was later published in the holy Church and heard by all those that were nearby.[185]

After this declaration the contract continues:

> And after this with the consent of Björg and the consent of the priest, Jón, who was the guardian of Björg, took her hand and betrothed her to be his legal wife after all the

183 DI VII, pp. 325-26.

184 Ibid., pp. 327-29.

185 Ibid., p. 328: "gatu aunguer neinna meinbuga ok at wmlidnum lysingum at tilsettum tima þa war þessi maldagi ok skildagar fram sagder æ hoskolldzstodum æ Skagastrond oppinberliga j fiolmenne. war þar þæ enn opinberliga epter lýst af fyrgreindum officialis sira jone ef nockurer menn væri þeir þar jnan stofu eda stadar ath nockura meinbugi uenzl edr skulldugleicka uissu æ fyrgeindra mana æ millum jons ok biargr en aller þar samankomner men sogdu þuert nei til at þeir uissu eigi ne uitat hefdi nein skulldugleika æ greindra mana æ millum jons ok biargar. war þessi lysing greindra mana æ mille en sidazta j heilagri kirkiu ollum monnum æ heyronndum."

words of the Christian law which are supposed to be said with legal engagement, in the presence of the witnesses.[186]

This case can be followed over time in many documents.[187] All the documents produced before 1506 provided proof that the spouses were not related, however. A letter written in 1506 suddenly presented a different picture. It testifies that they were actually related in the fourth degree.[188] This was the testimony of a woman who had heard a rumor that Jón and Björg were blood relations. The next document in this case is a judgement of eight priests from 1507. It stated first that Björg Þorvaldsdóttir had intentionally married Jón Sigmundsson, knowing that he was related to her within the fourth degree. She was ordered to pay a *penalty and to confess*. Secondly, she was found to have been living with him in a sexual relationship after they had been ordered to separate, and because of this she was excommunicated and ordered to confess and pay fines to the Church. Thirdly, she had continued to be with him after he was placed under interdict and excommunicated. Fourthly, she had not come to Hólar, as the bishop had ordered, to confess and receive absolution for this illegal relationship with Jón.[189]

According to *Skarðsárannáll* in the year of 1509, Bishop Gottskálkur had taken steps to separate the couple.[190] The bishop's imposition of a separation must have been the reason why Jón Sigmundsson tried to get help from the archbishop, who issued statements on this matter in 1509.[191] Thus, it became evident that the couple was related within the forbidden degree of fourth.[192]

186 Ibid, p. 328: "Og hier epter med jayrdi biargar ok samþycki greinz officialis sira jons sem war giftingarmadur sagdar biargar þa tok jon hond henar ok festi hana sier til logligrar eiginkonu epter ollum þeim laga ordum. sem kristinrettur vttvisar ok logligri festing tilheyrer þessum festingarwottum herverondum."

187 See for instance ibid., pp. 329, 412-13, DI VIII, pp. 87-88.

188 Ibid., pp. 92-93.

189 Ibid., pp. 133-35.

190 *Annálar 1400-1600*, I, pp. 78-79, compare to DI VIII, pp. 272-73. See also a document from 1505, ibid., pp. 767-69. The role of the bishop is interesting, because he himself had not been following the rules of living in celibacy. He had himself had children, as is known from a document from 1505, where he gave a dowry to his daughter who was going to get married. See DI VIII, pp. 230-31.

191 DI VIII, pp. 272-73.

192 Ibid., pp. 312-14, see also DI VII, pp. 775-77, 782-85.

A testimony concerning this matter was made by the priest Jón Jónsson in 1510, who had heard a statement from the abbess Agnes from the nunnery of Staður (the sister of Þorvaldur, father of Björg) about the matter.[193] Another document exists, which is a testimony from the nunnery at Staður in Reynisnes, given by the nuns and their abbess.[194] They testified to have heard a conversation between Agnes and her brother Þorvaldur, the father of Björg, in one of the living rooms at the nunnery. Agnes had asked her brother whether he had married and given away his daughter to Jón Sigmundsson. He said that he had never given her away, and he said that he had told his daughter that she and Jón were related. He had forbidden her to make any agreement with Jón. Then Jón and Agnes continued the discussion and Agnes repeated a story that her father Jón at Móberg had told her, that the couple Björg and Jón were related.[195] Maybe this testimony provides the missing information as to why it was Björg's brother and not her father that gave her to Jón Sigmundsson.

The marriage of Björg and Jón was probably never declared legal. Even if Jón Sigmundsson was a lawman and knew that he could use different types of methods to try to win the case, he never received any dispensation from Bishop Gottskálkur for this relationship. Bearing in mind the dispensation cases of Þorleifur and his sister Solveig, seeking dispensation may not have been the best strategy in this situation. Jón was probably aware of that when he wrote letters transferring legal gifts to his daughters and his wife, at the same time asking his son from the first marriage to accept his legal gifts.[196]

The possibility of obtaining a dispensation was also related to the policy of each bishop. It was clear that Bishop Magnús in Skálholt was not very positive towards the practice, while later some of his successors in Skálholt had another policy. According to the letter of dispensation given by Bishop Stefán of Skálholt in 1508, the bishop had cleansed the

193 DI VIII, pp. 309-10. See also ibid., pp. 92-93.

194 Ibid., pp. 312-14.

195 Ibid., p. 314.

196 DI VII, pp. 756-58. Legal gifts will be discussed more in the last part of this book, see especially chapter 10.3. See also Agnes S. Arnórsdóttir 2005 for a discussion about how it was possible to use a will to give illegitimate children a share in one's belongings.

couple Björn and Ingibjörg and removed impediments to their marriage by granting them dispensation, which of course also meant that they received absolution of their sins through a payment.[197] Afterwards they could once more be married legally. There were a range of possibilities for receiving dispensation in this manner, but even if the bishops of the early sixteenth century began to be more positive towards the dispensation practice, not everyone could get one.[198]

In this context it is interesting to look at a later judgement of Spjaldhagi from 1557 concerning marriage within the forbidden degrees. According to this document, the country became more peaceful after the Reformation, when the forbidden degree of marriage was changed from the fourth to the third degree. This was explained by reference to the custom of receiving dispensation from the forbidden degrees of marriage from the pope, which was seen as against the former custom of the country. After the Reformation, the Church authorities in Rome could no longer interfere in Icelandic affairs, which had the effect that the relatives of couples stopped questioning the legality of marriage.[199]

The judgement declares that dispensation from the pope had never been fully accepted in Iceland. This understanding can be found in earlier sources. One of the arguments used by Þorleifur Björnsson's relative, Björn Guðnason, in 1501 is found in his letter to the lawman, Finnbogi Jónsson. There it was stated that everybody knew that the old law of the country and the Christian law had not been followed in the case of Þorleifur and Ingveldur. It was well known that their children were illegitimate and born within the forbidden degrees of marriage.[200] The

197 DI VIII, pp. 250-51.

198 See for instance DI IX, pp. 130-31. Bjarni Narfason, who had had a sexual relationship with a married woman within the forbidden degree, was accused of double adultery. He claimed to Bishop Ögmundur that he had made an agreement with this woman, with the consent of her parents, but that she had then married another man. The bishop did not believe him, and Bjarni was then also charged with planning a clandestine marriage, as well as with having sexual intercourse with this woman against the law of God. This could not be forgiven. But this should not be understood as if the bishop was against giving marriage dispensations. For instance, see ibid., pp. 735-36, when Þórður Ketilsson and Sigríður Jónsdóttir on 27 June 1535 got a dispensation in Skálholt. In that dispensation letter the bishop refers to both the pope and to the archbishop of Niðarós, who by their kindness had also given their dispensation in this case.

199 This was related to the marriage of Vigfús Þorsteinsson og Anna Eyjólfsdóttir, compare to the *samþykktarbréf Ólafs Hjaltasonar um fjórmenninga, Bólstaðarhlíð* from 27 August 1556. See DI XIII, p. 228, and the whole judgement of Eggert Hannesson in ibid., pp. 226-33.

200 DI VII, pp. 561-67, see especially p. 566.

rules referred to in this letter are the rules governing marriage from the end of the thirteenth and the beginning of the fourteenth centuries. According to this letter, the right of the authorities to give dispensation from these rules had not been accepted, and therefore it did not help in the case of children trying to obtain inheritance after parents who had married in the fourth degree.

This would explain the resistance of Bishop Magnús Eyjólfsson. It was a resistance against the new marriage strategy of some of the wealthiest families in the country. Both Þorleifur Björnsson and his sister Solveig Björnsdóttir used the possibility of receiving papal dispensation as a means by which to keep their wealth inside their own families. By doing this they were using new inheritance strategies that were not accepted as part of the law of the country. Björn Guðnason and Bishop Magnús Eyjólfsson appear to have referred to the old custom of the country, i.e. the marriage legislation of the thirteenth and fourteenth centuries. At the same time the king's official, Þorleifur Björnsson, sought dispensation from the pope. In the Icelandic context this was a much newer marriage practice. At this point we can conclude that those dispensations that were awarded were granted by the archbishops; while in those cases in which an application had been made directly to the pope, the resulting dispensations were never fully accepted in Iceland by the authorities or by the relatives of the couples involved.[201] Dispensations seem to have been most common in the late fifteenth and early sixteenth centuries. This is a result of the well-established tradition of the papacy granting marriage dispensations. A study of the Icelandic sources indicates, however, that such dispensations were not sought by Icelanders before 1470.

After the Reformation the papacy could no longer interfere in Icelandic affairs. No more great disputes existed, because the marriage dispensation given by the king was widely accepted. It seems that the relatives of couples stopped questioning the legality of marriage between people related in the third and fourth degree.[202] This was also related to

201 Compare to the discussion in Einar Bjarnason 1969, p. 158.

202 Compare also to a judgement from 1557 where it is stated that the relatives of the couples stopped questioning the legality of those marriages. See DI XIII, pp. 226-33.

the development of the royal political and constitutional institutions in the sixteenth century. Even though at the end of the sixteenth century the courts of *Alþingi* were still a combination of clerical and secular judges, there was only one authority to obey in such cases and that was the king. This was not the case in the fourteenth and fifteenth century. To conclude, let us now take a closer look at the penitential practice and control of sexual offenses.

5.3 *Penance, confession and sexual crimes*

Many of the court cases that have been discussed here were concerned with questions of inheritance rights. The oldest cases were judged as matters of inheritance, and the question of legality was related to whether the marriage could be seen as having been correctly performed. As we have seen, these cases also demonstrate change over time. From the end of the fifteenth century onwards the cases started to be treated as a discreet category which displayed incorrect sexual behavior, and they were judged as such. The people involved in these offences needed to pay penance, confess their sins and remake their marriage contract if they wanted their children to be declared legitimate. Legal control of sexual behavior became thus more and more related to the question of sin. Elements of this control were also carried out in church, something which will be discussed here in this last section of chapter 5. The aim is to show that the influence of the central authority, clerics and royal offices working together at the central court at Þingvellir had grown stronger in Iceland at the end of the sixteenth century. Previously, the questions concerning penance were more of a clerical matter, which should be dealt with privately. It is for this reason that we do not have the same quantity of documents relating to incorrect sexual behavior from the fifteenth century as from the sixteenth.[203]

203 About change in jurisdiction after the Reformation, see Gísli Ágúst Gunnlaugsson 1997, pp. 68-69, compare to Hjalti Hugason 1998, p. 269 saying that the change towards sin is not primarily a result of the Lutheran doctrine. It is also connected to the fact that there was no secular court that took over the cases, and as such they were criminal cases. What is of importance here is that more central control over moral matters and private affairs was established.

Changes that had come in the wake of the Reformation resulted in harsher penalties for forbidden forms of sexual behavior. Whereas confession and other penalties had been acceptable before, the idea of a death penalty started to become more actual as a punishment. Thus the issues under consideration were not only those concerning changes in what was accepted as normal behavior. Another issue at stake was change in the attitudes to the penalties imposed. Development in this area was gradual, starting long before the Reformation and not fully developed until after this period. Here I shall discuss which forms of penance existed before and after the Reformation, as well as study what role the practice of penance had for the internalization of new marriage norms.

5.3.1 The rules about penance for different sins

Salvation was possible, no matter how great the sins committed, as long as the individual made confession, professed his remorse, and thereafter paid a penalty and submitted to some kind of punishment. Several penitentials exist from the Icelandic Middle Ages. One of the oldest is the penitential of Bishop Þorlákur Þórhallson (1178-93). The penance for sexual crimes[204] varied according to later editions of his penitential. For example, fifty days of fasting should be the consequence for having sex with a woman to whom one was not married.[205] Whether people followed these rules is unclear, as indeed is the extent to which clerics intervened in people's behavior.[206] The precepts drawn up by the Bishop of Hólar in 1341 have survived. These drew on the works of Bishop Jörundur Þorsteinsson (1267-1313), Bishop Lárentíus Kálfsson (1323-31), and Bishop Egill Eyjólfsson (1331-41).[207] According to these precepts the penance for those who sinned by having a relationship within the fourth degree of consanguinity or of affinity, or through a similar offence, was:

204 On the regulation of sexuality in the earliest Christian penitential literature, see Payer 1983, in three main chapters he discussed the penitential rules before 813, during the ninth century and in the later canonical collections, whereas on pp. 88-114 there is a list over the known penitential texts from those later collections.

205 *Medieval handbooks of penance* 1990, p. 355. See also on the penitential of Bishop Þorlákur, Sveinbjörn Rafnsson 1982.

206 Lára Magnúsardóttir 1998, p. 211.

207 *Medieval handbooks,* p. 359 See also DI II, pp. 130-38: "Skriftarboð Jörundar biskups Þorsteinssonar, Laurentíusar biskups Kálfssonar og Egils biskups Eyjólfssonar 1276-1323/41."

a fast of water during twenty nights on water and bread or other fruits of the earth, or if these are lacking, on half a pound of dried fish; and every fasting night let them recite the paternoster and the psalter, falling on their knees at every paternoster. They shall stand without the church during the time of Lent, in Advent, and in the thorough fasts; but on festival days they shall have access to the church. They shall observe the minor thorough fasts through the next year, that is, they shall eat milk foods once a day on Mondays and Wednesdays and recite the paternoster seven times, falling on their knees each time, and the Ave Marie nine times. In the year following this, they shall keep the thorough fasts, taking food only once on Wednesdays, and at the same time reciting the paternoster, falling on their knees, five times. In the third year they shall observe the thorough fasts by recitation of prayers, and by reciting the paternoster five times, with one Ave Marie. A fine of twelve ounces of silver ...[208]

Penance was also indicated for spiritual consanguinity, contracted in baptism or confirmation. The basis for some of these prescriptions is references to the new ecclesiastical law, *ius ecclesiasticum recentius*.[209] Several fragments of formula about penitential practice also give some information about the possibility to get absolution for a sinful live. A formula by which a priest could gain absolution after living with a concubine also survives, and so does a second formula by which a woman who had been living as a priest's concubine could seek absolution.[210]

A penitential of Bishop Jón Halldórsson in Skálholt from 1326 discusses sinful lifestyles and the various penances due for different sins.[211] This was a reworking of the penitential of Bishop Þorlákur Þórhallson from the late twelfth century.[212] Homosexuality is named as one of the greatest sins. It says that if two women have sexual relations and they reach orgasm, then they shall receive the same penance as men that make the most sinful adultery with each other.[213] This text also deals with bestiality and the torture of women.[214]

208 *Medieval handbooks*, pp. 359-60.

209 Ibid., p. 360.

210 DI II, pp. 134-35. This is a formula written in Latin ca. 1500 by a man who had little knowledge of Latin. See ibid., p. 131. See the original copy AM 350 Fol bl 151b.

211 DI II, pp. 596-606. Those are to be found in two copies, printed in ibid., pp. 596-601, version A from AM 42A 8vo bls. 228b-234 skinnb. c. 1480, and printed in DI II, pp. 601-606 as B from AM 625 4to bls 154-159 skinnb. c. 1480.

212 Compare to DI I, pp. 237-34. The penitential of Bishop Þorlákur is assumed to be originally from the year 1178.

213 DI II, p. 598.

214 Ibid., pp. 598, 604.

Other sins mentioned included intentional homicide. The court needed to deal with this issue. Forced marriage could end in tragedy as we find in cases where violence occurred between the spouses. In 1461 Þorsteinn Guðleiksson was accused of beating his wife Guðfinna Jónsdóttir[215]

> 10 times in the head with his hands, 15 times on the body and once throwing her to the ground, he beat her four times under the knees, and had once kicked her breast with his feet.[216]

He was ordered to pay a penalty to her and to the king unless he could prove that this was not truth.[217] We do find several cases about violence and even murder related to married couples. One of those is a judgement from 1511 which concerns Jón Halldórsson, who was accused of having killed his wife.[218] Another case from 1540 concerned rumours that Steingrímur Böðvarsson had been killed by his wife Cecilia Loftsdóttir (Hamra-Setta). This case not only involved the wife but also her servant Bjarni Skeggjason.[219] In an effort to find evidence, the dead body was exhumed and was deemed to exhibit marks that were more likely to have resulted from human mishandling than from decomposition.[220] The case ended by a judgement in 1543 where Cecilia Loftsdóttir was judged to have intentionally murdered her husband.[221] In the sentence it was noted that no other members of the household could have killed him, as "on this farm there was only herself, Cecilia, and the servant with whom she had been having an affair while her husband was still alive".[222]

215 DI V, pp. 229-30.

216 Ibid., p. 229: "hefdi sleigit sig x haufuthaugg með hnefanum og xv á bukinn og j jarduarp., iiij knieskot og sleigit eitt sinn firir briozit sier med fætinum".

217 Ibid., p. 230. This case was not judged at the court of the bishop, but was judged by the district officer Egill Grímsson.

218 DI VIII, pp. 343-45. Just as the case from 1511, this case was also judged by the civil authorities.

219 DI X, pp. 527-28, and, pp. 528-29.

220 Ibid., p. 528.

221 DI XI, pp. 253-54.

222 Ibid., p. 254: "En þar vorv ecki adrer aa þessvm bæ en hvn cecilia oc sa dreingur sem med henne hafdi legit [fram hia] bonda hennar lifanda."

Here adultery and homicide were the subjects of one and the same court case, but the case was judged by civil authority, and a fine should be paid to the royal authority. Criminal behavior in the courts was, however, not always judged alone by the civil courts. If the case was about adultery for instance, it normally was a subject under the jurisdiction of the Church, even if the outfall of such cases could be the threat of the death penalty.[223]

Before the Reformation and the judgement of *Stóridómur* from 1564-65, this control was very much in the hands of the clergy. The legal role of the priest was both to judge in court and to give absolution once people had confessed their sins. It was, however, not only the Church that collected fines for adultery. The old tradition of paying a fine to the relatives of the fallen woman and her assaulted husband also continued.[224] In this way Christian norms controlled sexual life, though older traditions continued to hold sway. An awareness of a woman's own sexual pride was added to the age-old respect for the honor of her family.

By the time of the Reformation it seems, however, that the distinction between the ecclesiastical jurisdiction and civil matters, as well as the private penance and the rules about official punishment was getting clearer. A penalty for a sinful life should be dealt with by the Church, while criminal cases, such as violence between husbands and wives, should be dealt with by civil courts. To be able to understand this process better, we need to study the development of confessional practice as well as the change in the approach to punishment which occurred in the last decades of the sixteenth century.

223 Compare to a case from the end of the sixteenth century, DI XI, pp. 328-29: "lijflaus fyrir dæmd ef hun fielli a þeim eidi sem henne war dæmdur."

224 A case from 1478 is proof of this, see DI VI, pp. 138-40.

5.3.2 *Sin no more and the letters of confession*

"It is human to sin, but it is a Christian life to stop sinning and change to the better".[225] The Church managed to collect penalties[226] for improper sexual behavior,[227] and by doing so was able to have some influence on moral values. At the same time, though, some of the cases in which penalties were paid seem to indicate that people could behave against the principles of the Church as long as they paid for receiving forgiveness.[228] Interestingly, the most extreme cases were often those related to the sexual behavior of the clerics. In these cases we can examine the discrepancy between moralizing words and everyday deeds.

In the early fourteenth century Lárentíus, a priest who later became a bishop, did not find anything sinful in one of his colleagues having a mistress. According to the Saga of Bishop Lárentíus, the woman in question was very dull, and it would have been difficult to find an uglier woman. Lárentíus asked how it happened that his colleague wanted to have such an ugly woman with him. He received the following answer:

> I am a man of big temper, and I would not like it if any other man tried to tempt my woman away from me, and that is the reason I chose this woman, because I know that no man would have desire for her.[229]

225 "Thvi at mannlegt er ad falla en thad er kristilegt ad lata af og betra sig." From the *Bréfabók Guðbrands biskups Þorlákssonar*, p. 525. Compare to John 8, 2-11. "They all went home, and Jesus went to the Mount of Olives. At daybreak he appeared in the Temple again; and as all the people came to him, he sat down and began to teach them. The scribes and Pharisees brought a woman along who had been caught committing adultery; and making her stand there in the middle they said to Jesus, "Master, this woman was caught in the very act of committing adultery and in the law Moses has ordered us to stone women of this kind. What have you got to say?" They asked him this as a test looking for an accusation to use against him. But Jesus bent down and started writing on the ground with his finger. As they persisted with their question, he straightened up and said. "Let the one among you who is without guilt be the first to throw a stone at her." Then he bent down and continued writing on the ground. When they heard this they went away one by one, beginning with the eldest, until the last one has gone and Jesus was left alone with the woman, who remained in the middle. Jesus again straightened up and said, "Woman, where are they? Has no one condemned you?" "No one, sir" she replies. "Neither do I condemn you," said Jesus. "Go away you", said Jesus. "Go away, and from this moment sin no more."

226 DI VI, pp. 444-45. 21 July 1482. Because a priest had fathered children and had committed other transgressions, he gave the bishop a landed property.

227 Ibid., pp. 633-34. 31 July 1488. In order to be consecrated, an abbot asked for absolution for having a child. The bishop did not think that these two things were compatible.

228 Ibid., pp. 638-39. In 1488 Páll Þorsteinsson sold to Bishop Magnús of Skálholt ten hundred of the land of Hof in Öræfim, while Páll and Þórdís received absolution for having had six children.

229 ÍF XVII, p. 245: "Ek er bráðlyndr maðr, ok þyldi ek ekki vel ef nokkorr sinnti mína þjónustukonu frá mér, ok því tók ek þessa at ek veit hennar girniz enginn."

This story exemplifies in a rather humorous way the problem that confronted men who desired a woman already allied to another man. In this particular case, it is interesting to observe Lárentíus' role. According to the narration his dilemma was not a moral one, rather his problem lay in understanding how a man could choose to live with a woman who was not desirable. When Lárentíus later became bishop, he was a spokesperson in favor of change in sexual habits. He had drawn up a precept of a penitential as mentioned above.[230] And later in the account of his career, the saga says that he presided over many courts which dealt with marriage issues.[231] The purpose of the account from his earlier life was probably to emphasize his pious work later. The policy of the bishop at this stage was in contrast to his own earlier life. He himself had not lived in celibacy when he was young, so there is a clear message in this story.[232] Christian morality was gradually introduced to the Icelandic society, and as all the court cases from the Late Middle Ages show, this message gradually was being accepted and the idea of sin became more powerful. The internalization of new norms meant that people should repent their sins. An example can be taken from 1440. An abbot testified that he had had an affair with a married woman. The abbot showed his remorse, agreed to pay the fine for his sins and made himself ready to receive instructions for penitence.[233]

People continued though to sin and break the moral codes set by the Church even if they knew their actions were wrong. In the autumn of 1471, a priest presiding over an ecclesiastical court in Hólar found a man guilty of not having confessed adultery and for continuing his sinful life. The man had been found guilty of lying naked under a sheet with a woman, who was not his wife, inside a church.[234] His sin was compounded by the fact that this was not the first time he had been

230 *Laurentius saga biskups*, pp. 44-45. See also here on p. 196.

231 *Laurentius saga biskups*, p. 46.

232 While he was in Norway he was taken prisoner by the *kórsbræður* and while in captivity a woman, Þuríður Arnardóttir, had often come to him, giving him food and helping him. She gave him what he needed through the window of the cell where he was held prisoner. It also says in the account that she was the mother of his son, Árni. See *Laurentius saga biskups*, pp. 52-53.

233 DI V, pp. 13-14.

234 Ibid., p. 644.

unfaithful. The year before his wife had written to the bishop asking permission to separate from her husband because of his adultery.[235]

The high number of cases coming to court at the end of the sixteenth century suggests that sexual control was getting more public, and there were no limits on the sorts of cases that could be considered by the courts. Thomas Jónsson was charged for drinking milk from his wife's breast in 1590. The case was dealt with by the local court, but the spouses were also both accused of adultery after the wife had claimed that her husband had permitted another man to make love to her. Thomas denied these charges, but if he should be found guilty for accepting this adulterous life, he should be punished with twelve strokes and he should be branded between the eyes with a burning iron. She should on the other hand only be punished by a stroke, but the lawman did not know any legal rule for punishment for drinking milk from a woman's breast. So he decided that it was up to the law council of Alþingi to decide how to deal with that problem.[236] No more information exists about the case.

When discussing legal control of sexuality, it is also important to remember that such control was not only dealt with at the clerical courts or at the assembly at Þingvellir, but also in the privacy of the confessional.[237] Sins, like adultery, should be admitted at confession, but according to the *New Christian Law* of Bishop Árni, the only penalty for sin was paying fines to the Church. Penitent sinners should also, according to canon law, give the impression of regret through so-called *satisfactio*, which could be done by giving alms to the poor, as well as through praying or going on pilgrimage to holy places.[238] According to the 1275 *New Christian Law* of Bishop Árni Þorláksson, every person was obliged to confess once a year.[239] In the statute of Archbishops Eilífur, which was published in Iceland in 1323, it says that a person should confess every seven months.[240]

235 Ibid., pp. 584-85.

236 *Alþingbækur Íslands* II, p. 197.

237 On this practice of confession and penance, as well as paying fines to the Church in Iceland during the medieval time, see Gunner F. Guðmundsson 2001, pp. 213-27.

238 Ibid., p. 223.

239 NgL V, p. 50. This was in accordance with a decision of the Fourth Lateran Council from 1215.

240 DI II, p. 519.

Four texts of confessions have survived from Iceland in the Middle Ages.[241] Two of these confessions were according to the editor of *Diplomatarium Islandicum,* assumed to be real confessions of Solveig Björnsdóttir and Ólöf ríka, although no evidence can be found in the contemporary sources to confirm this.[242] Later the historian Magnús Stefánsson and especially the scholar Stefán Karlsson have stated that the confession of Ólöf ríka should be interpreted as representing the attitudes of the Church with regard to what constituted sinful lifestyles, rather than as a truly personal statement.[243]

Because of the rules about secrecy, the written confessions have been understood as examples of confessions drawn from Church records. There is reason, however, to believe that the written confessions can be true statements. Other evidence exists of written confessions from other European countries in the Middle Ages, which are authentically personal statements and not just records. These confessions were not public but private, however, because they were read aloud privately for a priest.[244] Rules on confession were issued at the Fourth Lateran Council of 1215, and some of them were repeated in the Icelandic statute of Bishop Magnús Gizurarson of 1224.[245] It is important also to underline that there was a difference between the confessions which should be an act of penitence revealing a person's sinfulness before a priest secretly, and the other type of confessions which were defined as public acts.

According to the statute of Archbishop Eilífur and Bishop Jón Halldórsson in Skálholt from 1323, which was following the main instructions of the Lateran council, a priest should teach people how to confess. There were, however, some important principles always to have in mind: an individual should confess only his or her own sins, and not, for instance, the sins of his or her sister. Secondly, one should deeply

241 Stefán Karlsson 1988.

242 DI VI, pp. 236-47, DI VII, pp. 238-41. See also Stefán Karlsson 1988.

243 DI VI, pp. 236-47. See also Magnús Stefánsson 1991, pp. 49-60, and Stefán Karlsson 1988. I have recently written an article about which role the image of Ólöf has had in Icelandic history, and pointed out that this written confession existed amongst other manuscripts and charters at her manor in Skarð during her lifetime. See Agnes S. Arnórsdóttir 2009, pp. 30-31.

244 See Tentler 1977, p. 86.

245 DI I, pp. 423-66: "Um saung og þjónustugjörð i kirkjum, sömuleiðis um innleiðslu kvenna í kirkju."

regret and confess all one's sins and bad deeds without hiding anything.[246] If we do not believe that the written confessions of the Icelandic woman were actually private statements, it should be emphasized that privacy was also maintained in the written document because the names of the people involved in these confessions are not given. Thirdly, according to the statute from 1323, it is against the rules to admit sins on behalf of another person. If the written confessions were just instructional manuals, it would have been very wrong of the confessor to give such information about what another person should admit. So there is good reason to believe that the confessions are actually based on real statements. What is special about the Icelandic confessions is perhaps not only that they were written down, but that they were kept for centuries in Iceland, among other private documents, and later copied in the eighteenth and nineteenth century.[247]

I would suggest that we view the confessions both as having some elements of a "guidebook" character for those people *who kept them*, as well as being real statements. As such, the "confession of Ólöf" is an interesting source for how women in the fifteenth century actually could confess their sins. The fact that they had been kept, copied and preserved could mean that they served as a testimony of a contrite heart and as such they could also provide moral guidance for them who kept them, in the form of a statement of unacceptable and sinful behavior.

"Ólöf's confession" which was kept in written form at her manor at Skarð during her lifetime, provides an excellent focus for an examination of the conflicting attitudes that could be demonstrated by a penitent woman. The confession is an interesting example of self-reflection. In her relationship with her husband she had committed endless sins. "I never loved my husband according to the law of God," she said, probably meaning that they had made love on forbidden days, and that she

246 DI II, pp. 520-21.

247 DI VI, pp. 236-38. In this introduction to the confession of "Ólöf" the editor of the DI, Jón Þorláksson, argues that the confession is hers, because of the fifteenth century's language of the documents, as well as the facts about this woman which match to her. The confession exists in a copy by the priest Ásgeir Bjarnason (d. 1773), that is copied from the original skin manuscript. It became known in 1898 that the original document was lost. The other confession of "Solveig" is printed in DI VII, p. 238 and forward. It is found in the Advocates Library in Edinburgh, in the collection of FMagn. 64. 4to (21, 7, 14). It is a copy written in 1770 by Björn Halldórsson in Sauðlauksdal after the original manuscript.

had had a desire for her husband that was greater than that required for procreation. She had made love to her husband while she was menstruating, as well as during pregnancy, after childbirth and before she was made clean again in the Church. She also confessed to using a position during intercourse other than that of lying under the man. Sometimes they both lay on their sides, and sometimes she was face down with him on top. In all this, she enjoyed the sweetness of the flesh, with her blood streaming warmly. She enjoyed the movement of their bodies, which were joined in the sweetest kisses, gentlest of words and the touch of their hands.

In addition, she had been kind towards other men. She had even kissed them and embraced them, spoken soft words to them, looked at them, and touched them and given them many clear signs of her affection.

The confession is full of remorse. She had been wicked to her husband, and to the poor, and to others who served on her estates. She had been jealous because she had suspected her husband of having an affair with another woman (although this is not surprising if we consider her account of her own dealings with men), and she had not been fair in business transactions, to name but a few of her confessed sins.[248]

Whether this confession is interpreted as a personal account or as being formulaic, it gives a picture of "Ólöf" as a strong and independent woman. If the motive for its publication was to give a moral lesson, there is no sign that this resulted in her having an inferior status in society. The woman who made this confession was an influential and active person.

"Ólöf's confession" is like a mirror reflecting the two models of marriage in medieval Iceland. It was good that a woman was able to make her own decisions and that her sexuality was accepted. She was an object of desire, but as such also a potential threat. However, it was not only their sexuality that gave women freedom to act. They had real influence as owners of property, ladies of their manors, which they either could own independently or together with their husbands.

248 DI VI, p. 245.

The letters of confession express remorse, and that was enough for the Church to grant absolution to the individual involved. The Church was thus able to collect fines for improper sexual behavior, and as time passed the moral judgements inherent in such rulings changed the perceptions of acceptable behavior.

The confessions of "Solveig" and "Ólöf" have been dated to the end of the fifteenth century although Magnús Stefánsson believes that they are actually from the early fifteenth century.[249] I would agree with Stefánsson on this issue, and suggest that it is likely that they relate to the period of Jón Vilhjálmsson's episcopacy.[250] Other written confessions have survived from this time. They are the confession of a priest to the bishop, and a confession letter to Ingibjörg Sturludóttir, which gives her absolution for the sin of adultery. The letter contains a list covering the penance she should do to obtain absolution. These letters may have been written down because the English bishop had problems understanding Icelandic.[251] Another explanation for the existence of these written confessions could be that they were kept privately as written evidence of the pious life of those persons who had confessed their sins.[252] No matter how we interpret the confessions, they remain interesting documents from the fifteenth century about the existence of penitential life.[253]

5.3.3 From sin to crime

The campaign against a sinful life had already started in the twelfth century, but there is little evidence to support that sins like adultery, for instance, became a subject for the Icelandic courts at that time. This did

249 Magnús Stefánsson 1991, pp. 50-51.

250 See the discussion here about his great influence on marriage liturgy in the fourteenth and fifteenth century: pp. 134 ff.

251 We have these two letters of confession in the copybook of Bishop Jón Vilhjálmsson. These letters of confession did not concern the sins of the confessing people, but the penalties they received. See Björn Þorsteinsson and Guðrún Ása Grímsdóttir 1990, pp. 158-59 on the letter of the priest Þórður Roðbjarnsson, which the bishop gave to him in 1431. The other letter is the "skriptabref" of Ingibjörg Sturludóttir, see DI IV, pp. 403-404.

252 See discussion about death culture in Agnes S. Arnórsdóttir 2005, and 2007.

253 It is not possible within the scope of this thesis to study all the documents that are to be found in relation to confessions in Iceland. See for instance in AM 186 4to, 1-4v, about how to confess and repent.

not happen before the late fifteenth century, and it was not until the late sixteenth century that adultery was criminalized by the courts.[254] This development can be understood in the light of what I have discussed about canon law rules, i.e. that during the fourteenth century they were mostly referred to in disputes about inheritance cases, while during the fifteenth, and especially the sixteenth century, the focus on adultery was not only the result of the efforts of lay people to have their marriage annulled, but it was also a result of the clerical demand to judge adultery as a sin. Adultery should be regretted and a penalty paid.

By the late fourteenth and early fifteenth centuries marriage cases were frequently taken to the courts. Thus it was important to have solid proof of the legality of a marriage, such as a written contract. If, however, some doubts were raised about the legality of a marriage, and the persons involved had been living a sinful life, they needed to pay some fines. A person, after the payment of a fine, confession and the demonstration of remorse could be granted absolution for committing a sexual sin. By the end of the sixteenth century, the authorities, however, stressed that punishment for a sexual offence through penance alone was not sufficient. Instead, the law should punish the offender.[255]

This development was closely related to changes in the royal administration in Iceland in the late sixteenth century, already discussed above.[256] By the end of the sixteenth century this meant that jurisdiction over marriage was concentrated in the hands of the members of the court at Þingvellir. The members of this court were drawn from both the secular authorities and the clerics. The change resulted in a greater professionalism. It was no longer only a question of the personal style of each bishop that determined how cases were judged. We begin to find a clearer pattern in the court cases, a pattern that is strongly based

254 At this time it first became a valid argument for claiming inheritance, and a judgement from 1580 shows that this could be a complicated issue. *Alþingisbækur Íslands* I, p. 405: "Ef laus madur lægi med þeirri konu. sem fallid hefur adur j hördom., og væri fra manni skilin. leist oss þar Ecki meiri sok a Enn frillulijfs sök. [Er hun þa sek vj örum enn hann] 3 aurum."

255 *Lovsamling for Island* I, pp. 111-12: "Aabent Brev til Island, ang. at Horsager og Blodskam, ikke skal straffes med Böder, men straffes efter Loven." Frederiksborg 29 April 1585.

256 Compare to the discussion earlier concerning *Stóridómur* and other changes from the middle to the end of the sixteenth century. See also Hjalti Hugason 1998, p. 269.

on the new rules formulated at the end of the century. I shall now study this development closer.

The restrictive rules of sexual behavior described in the penitential of the bishops from the twelfth and thirteenth centuries cannot be used directly as evidence of how the Church actually managed to control sexual matter. They do, however, indicate the intension or the wish of the clergy to do so. Furthermore, when we study the court material of the fifteenth and sixteenth centuries, it becomes clear that the authorities actually interfered actively on a daily basis with the ordinary and frequently sinful lives of common people. Thus the transformation towards more external punishment did not mean that the idea of sin was dismissed, and the bishops continued to have a central role in the process of finding evidence.[257]

A judgement made just after the Reformation on 20 May 1544 shows how the clergy were dealing with the problem of controlling sexual matters. It is recorded in the copybook of Bishop Gissur Einarsson, but made by six clerics, and is about the punishment of those:

> that had married and made an agreement with a woman that they were to marry under the law of God, but then after having had sexual relations with her, they do not behave better than to leave her again.[258]

The judgement further stated that men who were correctly married behaved badly if they separated themselves from their wives. After their departure they would just take another woman and have children with

257 Information about adultery cases was often given under oath. Details of an oath made by Margrét Erlendsdóttir at her own farm in 1556 show how she swore in front of Bishop Ólafur Hjaltason that she had not been sexual involved with any man other than her husband, Páll. The bishop confirmed that the spouses had made a marriage contract. Hearsay continued to provide a basis for evidence in adultery cases. It is impossible to find additional information about the woman who had spread these rumors, but Margrét's testimony was further strengthened by the statement of the priest about the marriage contract. The priest had been at the farm Einarsstaðir in Reykjadalur, one year after the couple married. Her brother was also there and they discussed how the marriage agreement had been concluded between the couple on their wedding day. The reason for the meeting was that Páll had sold farm property to his wife, and in exchange received her *málajarðir*, which was the land named as hers according to the marriage contract. See DI XIII, p. 154.

258 DI XI, pp. 306-308. See especially p. 307: "sem sig hafa bundit i hiuskap og keypt sier meinalausa konu epter riettum gudz laugum og leigit hana þar uppaa enn sidan breyta þeir ecki betur enn swo at þeir skilia sig vid þær."

them. According to the judgement wives of these men are no better. They had the same unchristian way of living as the men. There are arguments from the *New Christian Law*, and from the *Bible* with reference to the instruction 'what God has joined together, let no man put asunder.' Thus men who "run away from their wives, to whom they have been legally married, are to be judged for adultery and are guilty against the Church authorities".[259] The problem is obvious. Men and women "run away" from their holy marriage to stay with their lovers, as happened in the case discussed above about Grafar-Gunna.[260]

Bearing in mind how difficult it was to control issues of sexuality, the authorities also considered how this could best be achieved in practice. An open letter of 1578 from King Frederik II to the Icelanders describes how absolution could be gained if the crime of adultery had been committed.[261] The letter makes reference to the custom of the country, that men and women who had been living in adultery should publicly confess to the right authority, i.e. "the superintendent here in the country, in the cathedral." But because the country was large and because of the long distances involved, it could be difficult to make confession. Thus the people who committed the crime of adultery were allowed to confess to the local dean, who lived closest to their home.[262]

To sum up, we can say that adultery, which was already established as a reason for separation by the *New Christian Law* of Bishop Árni of 1275, was not commonly used in court cases concerning separation until almost three centuries later. The few adultery cases which came to court in the fourteenth and early fifteenth centuries were all cases of inheritance disputes. One of the reasons for this can be related to the slow internalization of the understanding of adultery as a crime that ought to be judged by the courts. My argument, however, is that rather than being considered by the civil courts, adultery cases were usually dealt with by

259 Ibid., p. 307: "ad þeir hlaupa a burt fra sinum kuinnum sem þeir hafa sier laugliga keypt seka fullre hordoms sauk uid kirkiunnar walldzmann."

260 See pp. 172-74, compare to *Alþingisbækur Íslands* III, pp. 46-49.

261 *Lovsamling for Island* I, p. 106.

262 Ibid.

clerics before, and this meant that people who lived in adultery or who had children outside marriage confessed their sins, paid a penalty and received absolution from churchmen.[263] Many documents from the early sixteenth century concern absolution in such circumstances.[264] Later, after the Reformation, and especially after the judgement of *Stóridómur* in 1564 became a rule, adultery began to be treated more as a crime and cases of this sort were judged as criminal cases by royal officials.[265] By the end of the sixteenth century it became usual for these cases to be judged at the assembly at Þingvellir, even if they could also be judged in the local districts.[266] The Reformation confirmed and reinforced the developments of the fifteenth century. Marriage became more and more regulated both by the royal and clerical authority. By the end of the sixteenth century the family involved in a marriage agreement could not, for instance, make it legal, without clerical interference as they could in the thirteenth century.[267]

At the same time we can see a development aimed at stronger sexual control. When adultery became a crime which could be judged by the

263 Compare to DI VIII, p. 351. In 1511 Bishop Gottskálkur gave absolution to men for having four and five children. It was important that even if these children were not legitimate there were no serious repercussions in those cases. The women were *meinlausar konur*. See also DI VIII, pp. 685-86 for the year 1519 when the priest Jón Arason and Helga Sigurðardóttir got absolution for having their ninth child as well as DI XII, p. 698, from the year 1554. Jón Björnsson and Guðný Þorleifsdóttir got absolution for having their fifth child, born in a *einföldu frillulífi*.

264 The clerics normally dealt with the adultery cases at their own courts. See cases from 1514 in DI VIII, pp. 521-22, and for the period 1524 to 1536 see DI IX, pp. 244-45, 277, 417-18, 508-09, 559-60, 616, 709-10, 763-64. And DI X, pp. 91-92, 101-102, 103-104, 703-704, DI XI, pp. 476-77, DI XII, pp. 743-44. These describe *kvittanir*, absolution for adultery and in most of the cases also absolution for having had illegitimate children.

265 This can be seen by comparing who judged the cases from 1552-69, and by looking at the penitence practice. See case from 1552 in DI XII, pp. 375-76, from 1554 in ibid., pp. 750-52, from 1555 in DI XIII, pp. 32-34, and from 1561 in ibid., pp. 604-605, and from 1562 in ibid., pp. 765-67, from 1568 in DI XV, pp. 113-14, from 1569 in ibid., pp. 271-74, 281.

266 See cases from *Alþingisbækur Íslands* I, from 1573, pp. 154-55, from 1578, p. 363, *Alþingisbækur Íslands* II from 1588, pp. 118-20, from *Alþingisbækur Íslands* III, from 1598, pp. 151-53. These cases were judged by the court at the assembly at Þingvellir, but in some of the cases the *þingaprestur*, the priest of the assembly, also took part in the examination of the case. However, change after the Reformation was not sudden. Few cases survive from the period after the Reformation which were judged only by clerics. See from 1554 DI XII, pp. 743-44, from 1556, DI XIII, pp. 128-29, from 1562, ibid., pp. 710-12.

267 An example of a stronger public control of marriage is the marriage case of Helgi Þórólfsson and Katla Þorláksdóttir from 1577. She had become his wife with the consent of her mother, but not her brother. One man had pronounced an agreement, but no legal marriage agreement had been made according to the law. After that she was taken as a concubine by another man, but even if her brother took her back home to Helgi, the relationship of Helgi and Katla was never regarded as legal because no authority could prove that the marriage had been made. See *Alþingisbækur Íslands* I, pp. 340-41.

courts, it could also be used as an argument for declaring a marriage illegal. Thus, while adultery, as an example of incorrect sexual behavior, had previously been an issue dealt with by clerics alone, it had now become a focus for the courts because of the question of inheritance. In this way cases concerning sexual behavior could be examined differently depending on the purpose behind bringing the case to court. As the story from the *Bible* – "stop sinning" – referred to at the start of the last section implies, extreme cases could be used to demonstrate how a person could be forgiven. The case of Bjarni Ólason and his daughter Randíður was perhaps such a case.[268]

This was not only a case of incest between a father and daughter, but also a dispute between the secular and ecclesiastical authorities. Bjarni was a rich man and had many farms. His main property was Hvassafell, but rumors said that it was at one of his other farms, Þórsá, that he had had sex with his daughter.[269]

On 18 October 1480 two priests gave witness in Mörðuvellir, stating that Bjarni had often lain naked in the same bed as his daughter, and that this had happened at the farm Þverá in Fnjóskadalur. At that time the daughter had only been thirteen years old. They had lain together under one blanket.[270] Another man gave the same testimony as the priests and said he had seen them during the previous autumn.[271]

Bjarni's confessions have also survived. He stated that he had been "lying bodily with his daughter" on so many occasions that he could not count them. He said he had not wanted her to be pregnant and felt bad and shameful about the fact that he had ejaculated his own semen in his hand or in other places each time he had been with her.[272] The case came to court on 30 June 1481.[273] The bishop pronounced a judgement stating that Bjarni must leave Iceland and visit certain holy places, as well

268 Many documents have survived in relation to this case. See DI VI, pp. 297, 298, 302-304, 309, 369, 371-73, 376-79, 384, 385, 404-407. This case has later been called the case of Hvassafell, and has been analyzed both by Einar Arnórsson and Már Jónsson.

269 See Einar Arnórsson 1932-35, pp. 343-87, and 1936-39, pp. 37-49.

270 DI VI, p. 297.

271 Ibid., p. 298.

272 Ibid., p. 301.

273 Ibid., pp. 376-79.

as pay a fine, whilst his daughter Randíður was to make her confession in Iceland.

The court material gives additional information about this case. It is nonetheless difficult to determine whether Bjarni and his daughter were in fact guilty of the crime of incest.[274] The sources say that the bishop had tortured Bjarni to make him confess. Witnesses from 1575 testified that after Bjarni had been free again, he himself had said that he had been tortured.[275] Certain aspects of this case continue to be puzzling. If it was true that Bjarni had had a sexual relationship with his daughter, why did she not go to the bishop instead of the secular authority? The lawman Hrafn Brandsson was not willing to hand her over to the bishop. This, and the fact that the subsequent confession of her father may have been made under torture, give reason to suspect that they may not have been having a sexual relationship.

Local customs and the ideas of the clergy were often incompatible. It may have been common practice among people in this region to lie naked in bed without any sexual activity taking place. The clerics may have come to interpret this local custom as being in contravention of their rules. Another more reasonable explanation can be that because of the change in the penitential practice at the end of the sixteenth century, the authority was able to exert stronger control of sexual matters. This stronger control was, however, not only a legal procedure, it was also very much related to the development of the internalization of the Christian idea of sin and the practice of penance.

5.4 *Conclusion*

What is clear after having studied cases of marriage judgement from the law courts of the Late Middle Ages, is that the question of legality was something which came to be dealt with in a dialogue between the Church's definition of marriage and the local understanding of what marriage was about. This chapter has underlined further how authorities

274 Már Jónsson 1993, pp. 47-49.

275 Ibid., pp. 48-49, compare to *Alþingisbækur* I, pp. 364-65.

defined their rules in this area, and how they became used by the Icelandic elite (which of course included officials of the Church as well as the royal power). This chapter has thus given us an idea of the flexibility of legal culture at this time. The rules described above were not fixed but to a certain degree were open to change by the parties involved. Many cases had a great deal to do with securing existing principles of the secular marriage contract. The issues at stake were economic ones, as well as determining what constituted a legal marriage. The question of legality was in this context mainly related to issues of inheritance. It was important to know what made a marriage valid in order to determine whether the legal heirs of a couple were the couple's children or the relatives of the man and woman involved.

This chapter has demonstrated how legal knowledge and alliance with the right authorities could be a key to the successful pursuit of a law case. There was, for instance, great difficulty in gaining acceptance of the principle that the pope could directly interfere in legal affairs in Iceland. Although it says in the *New Christian Law* of Bishop Árni that "everyone should obey the pope in Rome", there was no strong tradition of obedience of this kind. Some legal rules were widely used and accepted, while others were ignored. In this way certain channels through which the law could be used became firmly established, while others were never pursued. The legal rules where shaped in a dialogue between the Icelanders and their rulers. It was possible to get dispensation from the rules so the lines drawn between what was a legal or illegal transfer of property were thus not very clear. That is why the process of dispute-settlement of the court system was so important. The discourse of the courts was that of canon law, as well as the custom of the country. The actors could be related both to the clerical as well as the royal authorities, or could just be members of the richest landowners group, which considered themselves very much as the ruling elite of the country.

We have been considering how local people were approaching and using the courts to resolve problems concerning marriage and sexual matters. Interest in property rights rather than concern about Christian sexual morality, was the main reason why someone needed to know whether a marriage was legal or not. However, change in the institution of marriage also took place through this process, a process which also influenced the internalization of Christian norms. This transformation took a much longer time than the acceptance of Christian marriage legislation.

One example of this process of the internalization of new norms concerned the issue of getting dispensation for marriage within the fourth degree. A study of rules concerning the forbidden degrees of marriage offers an opportunity to analyze changes in the growing tendency of the authorities to interfere in marriage cases. It is also possible to study how members of aristocratic families used the different authorities tactically. These dispensations were not judged in courts until the end of the fifteenth century. The group of aristocratic families in Iceland during the Late Middle Ages was small, so the perceived need for dispensation was strong. Obtaining a dispensation meant that previously unacceptable relationships were made legal, making it easier to keep property within this group of aristocratic families. This could favor endogamy and the concentration of property.

Secondly the practice of marriage dispensation illustrates how some of the mechanisms behind changes in the law were political: Marriage cases that came to court were often concerned with identifying legal heirs. Disputes concerning inheritance were using different understandings of marriage to make and enforce decisions in this area. Should inheritance be determined by contracts between families, so that relatives could have their property returned if a couple did not have legitimate children? Or was this a sacred matter, determined by the mutual consent of the couple, and in which the pope had full authority to make exceptions to the rules? These two models existed simultaneously, and both were used in court cases. However, serious conflicts first occurred when political struggles over rights to the wealthiest manors emerged. This conflict intensified when members of the elite began to ask for dispensations from the pope from rules that for centuries had been understood as the rules of God and the country. There were, however, differences concerning what channels of authority were accepted. A tradition existed, dating back to the thirteenth century, in accordance with which it was accepted that advice and help could be sought from the royal authorities, while at the same time it was expected that the archbishops of Niðarós would be obeyed. But it seems that the Icelandic bishops in the Late Middle Ages did not so readily accept that papal authority could change marriage rules among the local people.

In the courts, arguments from different law codes were combined. Gradual change in the legal regulation of marriage from the late thirteenth century to the end of the sixteenth century had fundamental concerns in the connection between inheritance and property. Rightful inheritance was dependent on legitimate birth in marriage. At stake was property transferred through marriage. There were, however, many ways in which a marriage could be judged illegal, with the possibility of doing penance for unacceptable behaviour so that it could be ruled valid again. Over time this process did change the understanding of the relationship between legality and virginity. Intercourse outside marriage according to the law of God and the country became a crime. This is why chastity for both women and men was expected before people entered marriage. This was also related to change following the Reformation. Previously, illegitimate sexual relationships had sometimes been judged "secretly" in the bishops' courts, or had been private matters to be dealt with by confessors and their clients. At the end of the sixteenth century these cases became public criminal cases.

Part II
Ritual aspects of marriage

One of the more useful ways – but far from the only one – of distinguishing between culture and social system is to see the former as an ordered system of meaning and of symbols, in terms of which social interaction takes place; and to see the latter as the pattern of social interaction itself. On the one level there is the framework of beliefs, expressive symbols, and values in terms of which individuals define their world, express their feelings, and make their judgements; on the other level there is the ongoing process of interactive behaviour, whose persistent form we call social structure. (Geertz 1993, pp. 144-45.)

Marriage can be regarded as a cultural phenomenon, as well as a social reality. The two models of marriage presented by Georges Duby can be understood as an example of a cultural system. Here in particular, the marriage doctrine of the Church can be understood as a framework of beliefs, expressive symbols and values, while at the core of the secular model of marriage was the social interaction itself. Later Christian beliefs also affected this interaction. When attempting to understand the formation of Christian marriage rites during the Middle Ages it is important to examine what happened when the new regulations were put into practice. So far this change has been explained from a normative point of view – how canon law was incorporated in legislation – and from the practical point of view – how people understood and implemented this legislation. The first part of this book has thus considered the way in which changes were made by lawmakers and how the wider population accommodated to them. In this second part of the book a focus on changes in the wedding rite will be of primary importance, especially in relation to the ways in which marriage got a new meaning.

Wedding rituals differed from place to place because the medieval Church did not form a single, uniform, monolithic institution. Circumstances varied enormously from region to region. That is why a focus on how Christian ideas and beliefs more generally became a part of marriage ritual can give us new insights into the way in which the local community also actively formed the Christian ritual. This part of the book is thus a study of communication. It is concerned with the way in which the Church came to be involved in the rituals of wedding ceremonies and marriage contracts and by this changed the meaning of these rituals. At the same time marriage also continued to be a contract concerned with property transfer and therefore many of the old rites continued to exist after the Christianization of marriage. The way these developments were reflected in rituals will be the main topic of this second part. The first chapter will focus on the character of marriage rituals in order to study the entry into marriage. The second chapter, which is based on analyses of all the marriage contracts from the late fourteenth century till 1600, focuses especially on how the contracts changed in character due to the Christian influence. The third chapter about holy bonds and human bonds is related to the question of how change in social relations occurred over an extended period, also asking which meaning the change had for gender identity and gender relations.

CHAPTER 6

The marriage ritual: The entry into marriage

The main aim of this chapter is not to explain the driving forces behind the changes that we have seen in the Icelandic marital law but rather to ask how change happened. Here the study of rituals is of central importance. According to Durkheim, it was through rituals that the transformation of everyday ideas into the sacred took place. Ceremonies and rituals are "essential to binding the members of groups together … collective ceremonials reaffirm group solidarity."[1] The function of ritual is not to inform people, to report facts to them, but to influence them, according to Maurice Bloch.[2] In the communication of religious ideas there are no tools of explanation.[3] Rituals are thus often characterized by repetition, without any hidden meaning, "only the examination of the given code in which communication takes place."[4]

Here we shall first deal with rituals accompanying entrance into marriage. The change in the language of ritual is of special importance.[5] We shall thus focus on the linguistic change in relation to the process by which language was transformed from secular to religious in formulae associated with marriage. This change reflects how secular rituals slowly became more sacred in character. Secondly, we shall examine the change from the ritual of making oral contracts to writing them down. And, thirdly, we shall show how ritual change was not only related to change

1 Here after Giddens 1993, p. 465.
2 Bloch 1989, p. 32.
3 Ibid., p. 37.
4 Ibid., p. 42.
5 Ibid., pp. 22 ff.

in the entrance into marriage but also included change in the content of the marriage contract. In this instance surviving marriage contracts from the fourteenth and fifteenth century will be examined.

6.1 Linguistic change in the marriage contract

Icelandic and Norwegian law codes from the twelfth and early thirteenth centuries are the oldest documents available, which give information about the terminology concerning entry into marriage. In these sources it is said that the woman was given, *gift*, *gefin*, or betrothed, *föstnuð*, to the man, and that he received a woman, became *kvángaður*, or *kvæntur*. The word *kvánfang – quanfang – kuænfang* effectively means to capture a woman. *Kván*, *kvón* or *kvæn* means wife, and it is related to the words *kona*, woman, and *fang*, to hunt or to capture.[6] The custom of *konurán*, the capture of a woman, is believed to have been practised in the early Germanic era on the Continent. At a later stage the terminology changed so that it was said that a woman was acquired through the payment called *mundur*.[7] The *mundur* was an amount that the bridegroom paid, originally to her father, later to herself, in return for the right to become the woman's guardian.[8] This meant that he had the right to control her property. It is very important to underline that this "buying" did not mean that the man owned the woman in the modern sense of the word, only that he had the right of guardianship over her and her property.

6 Bjarni Einarsson 1974, p. 52.

7 According to Reynolds 1994, p. 93 the earlier Lombardic law treats a man's acquisition of a wife as transference of a power or control known as *mundium* (the Latinized version of *munt* or *mund*). He says that this conception is very similar to that of the Roman *manus* – marriage, and the word *munt* itself, like *manus*, means hand.

8 Magnús Már Lárusson 1959a, p. 237. On the discussion of the name of this gift see Goody 1988, pp. 240-61, especially pp. 242-43. This gift was traditionally often called "brideprice" in the nineteenth century, but Goody prefers to call it "indirect dowry". That is a payment or gift from the husband to the wife or her family. There are, however, according to Goody two types of indirect dowry. The first one is the morning gift, a gift given in the morning after the consummation of the marriage. The second is payment for the bride, originally to her father, but later it became a part of the *dotal* agreement of the couple. Because of the very different historical character and meaning in the Icelandic sources of the payment of *mundur*, and the morning gift, I do not find it meaningful to use the term indirect dowry, for the payment of *mundur*, as it is described in *Grágás*. Instead I use the term brideprice, or just payment of *mundur*. There is no evidence in Icelandic documents that this sum went to the parents of the bride. On the contrary it was always paid to the bride.

The word *kvánfang* was frequently used in the Icelandic law codes and in Icelandic and Norwegian charters. In the Norwegian charters it was used when someone was given a landed property because he wanted to marry, *gefuet till kuanfangz/kuænfanghs*.[9] In order to marry one needed to give land, silver or gold in exchange for the wife. A Norwegian contract stated that the man could receive a certain amount of wealth for marrying.[10] A man could not marry without making a proposal to the woman, *biðja sér konu*. If a man wanted a particular woman, it was often said that "he had *hug* to her", indicating that he thought about this woman.[11]

Expressing *hug* towards a woman initiated the process that could lead to marriage. This was completed by a proposal which, if accepted, would result in either land or money being exchanged according to so-called *festarmál*, which is probably the same as what is called a dotal agreement in the European context.[12] The payment of *mundur* either formed part of the jointly-owned property of the couple or became the woman's personal property.[13]

The gifts made by the bridegroom were different from those brought by the woman to a marriage. The woman herself was given away, *gifta* to the husband, as was her dowry *heimanfylgja*, which was supposed to come under the guardianship of her future husband.[14]

By the end of the thirteenth century changes had begun to take place in the use of this terminology in Norway. The linguistic change can be related to the influence of French literature. The verb *púsan* was introduced to describe the act of marrying a woman. This word was

9 *Grágás* II, p. 152 law concerning "q*u*anfa*n*gs eið. oc lögrétto fe"; see also a similar law in NgL V, p. 36. The terms can be found also in the Norwegian charters; DN II, p. 215, from the year 1343; DN, I, p. 140, from the year 1320; DN IV, p. 197 from the year 1336.

10 DN V, p. 167 from the year 1349.

11 *Ketils saga Høings*, p. 123.

12 Goody 1988, pp. 241-43.

13 Other gifts given by the bridegroom or his family were in the old legislation of *Grágás* called *gagngjald* and *viðgjöld*. Those gifts literally meant payment added to agreement about the bride and the wealth she brought into marriage. See my further discussion in chapter 9, about the different gifts and payments, which were exchanged through marriage.

14 In the old marriage legislation of *Grágás*, dowry was not a requirement for legal marriage as the payment of *mundur* was. However, the law indicates it was a custom, and my own study in other sources from twelfth and thirteenth century Iceland, indicate that it was a common practice to give the women dowry when they entered into marriage. See Agnes S. Arnórsdóttir 1995, pp. 149-50.

taken from the French word *éspouser* and it began to be used to describe instances in which a couple was married by a priest.[15] The original Latin meaning of the word is more related to the promise of marriage, than the marriage act itself.[16] It is to be found as mentioned previously in the bishops' statutes of the fourteenth century.[17]

Another change was that the verb to give, *gifta*, began also to mean to marry. The first example of this change came with the 1226 translation by brother Robert of the history of 'Tristan and Isolde' which was made for King Hákon.[18] By the end of the sixteenth century this meaning of the word *gifta* was used frequently[19] and the change is evident in documents from Iceland concerning entry into marriage in the Late Middle Ages.[20] This change calls for closer attention.

The word *festa* means binding a woman by a contract before entering into marriage.[21] The old marriage contract was an agreement made without any interference from external authorities.[22] It was a contract between two families, usually from the same social level.[23] The betrothed woman was called *festarkona*, and the name given to the bridegroom was *festarmaður*. During the late eleventh and early twelfth centuries, the reformers of the Church on the Continent did not want the custom of betrothal to constitute the formal criteria for a legal marriage, but they accepted it as one element in the making of marriage as a public contract.[24] This was a result of an earlier development. As Philip Reynolds has underlined, the Church from an early date had good reason for wanting marriages to be celebrated at least in a formal and documented manner, and preferably in church. He also assumes that the Germanic

15 Bjarni Einarsson 1974, pp. 47-48.

16 Reynolds 1994, p. 315, note 1. In English married persons are called spouses, and the word *spouse* comes from the French *épouse,* which likewise means "married woman", but the word *épouse* comes from the Latin *sponsa*, and this in turn is derived from *spondere* "to promise".

17 See chapter 4.1.2, p. 119.

18 Bjarni Einarsson 1974, p. 48. Compare to *Trístrams saga ok Ísöndar* 1878, p. 128.

19 Ibid., p. 51 and forward.

20 See for instance DI XI, p. 113. This case is also discussed here on p. 265.

21 *Fritzner ordbok*, I, p. 409. Compare to Reynolds 1994, p. 108 stating that the custom of German betrothal was a formal contract.

22 Vilhjámur Finsen 1849, p. 225.

23 Compare to the importance of *jafnræði* Agnes S. Arnórsdóttir 1995, pp. 147-48.

24 Brundage 1990, p. 190.

betrothal, which was in effect a formality substantiated by witnesses, recommended itself to Christian bishops and reformers as something that could be adopted and Christianized. The meeting of families became a public inquiry supervised by the Church.[25]

In the Norwegian law,[26] and in *Jónsbók*, *festar* continued to be central in the ritual associated with the start of marriage.[27] By the late thirteenth century *festar* was still seen as the most important legal act in creating a marriage and it continued also to be important later on.[28] Thus, the Church accepted the institution of *festar* probably because it made the marriage contract public. This incorporation of *festar* within the new understanding of marriage was also important for getting the new meaning of marriage accepted. *Bryllup*, the wedding ceremony, should be held no later than twelve months after the *festar* according to *Grágás*. In the statutes of Bishop Magnús Eyjólfsson of 1479, the old rules from *Grágás* are repeated.[29] However, women could be bound by the betrothal contract, called at *sitja i festum* for a longer time.[30] This required that the promise had been made before.[31]

This did not, however, mean that the old institution of *festar* continued to exist without any ritual change.[32] After the Reformation the engagement, or *trúlofun*, became introduced and in the marriage ordinance of King Frederik II from 1582, which was accepted in Iceland in 1587, it is stated that:

25 Reynolds 1994, p. 117.

26 See for instance *Gulathings-Christenret* in NgL II, p. 33.

27 Compare with *Jónsbók* p. 80: "þá eru þau börn, er hann á með þeiri konu, öll lögliga til arfs komin, hvárt sem þau eru getin fyrir festing eða eptir."

28 See NgL V, p. 39 compare to DI VII, p. 563: "hvarvetna þar er madur fester sier may eda konv ad guds lvgom og samþykt beggia þeirra þa erv þeirra barn lavligha til arfs komen hvort þaue ru geten firir festing, eða epter." See also DI II, p. 364: "þa ero þau born .... öll löghligha til arfs komen huart sem þau ero getin firir festing eða eptir", and DI VII, p. 492: "og þeirra bornn geten fyrir festing."

29 DI VI, pp. 209-10, see particularly p. 210, compare to *Grágás* II, p. 204.

30 There are references both in *Njálssaga* and *Þórðarsaga* about the matter. See ÍF XII, p. 10, where it is said that a woman waited three winters in *festar*. And in *Þórðarsaga hreðu*, see ÍF XIV, p. 18, nr. 23, also about three winter's betrothal.

31 See *Þorsteins saga Víkingasonar*, p. 394, where it was discussed that the wedding should now be prepared but Víkingur said he did not want that. She should *sitja í festum þrjá vetr*, but he should go to a war, *hernað*.

32 It is for this reason that it is not possible to classify the terminology of marriage according to what was a Christian term and what was non-Christian. The meaning of the same term changed over time.

> No engagement shall take place … without a priest in attendance and at least five other witnesses. Those correctly engaged shall not be allowed to go to bed together until they have been blessed and married in church.[33]

Even if *trúlofun* was first made as a legal requirement by the marriage law of 1587, the idea had been introduced earlier. In the statute of Archbishop Árni of 1346/49, we find the expression *trulofuan oc festing*. The concept of *trulofun*, a promise to be faithful, also had the meaning of confirming or promising to follow one's decision.[34] In a document from 1505, the expression "handshake and trustful engagement", *handabands og traustrar trúlofunar*, is used.[35] The idea of *trúlofun*, engagement, thus had started to have meaning long before the Reformation, and from the saga literature we find evidence of how the idea of being faithful through the promise of engagement became slowly introduced. In these sources the entry into marriage is closely related to the meaning of the word *heit*, or promise. The word *heitkona* is found in *Gunnlaugs saga Ormstungu*. It was used when Illugi, a relative of Gunnlaugur Ormstunga, wanted to propose marriage to Helga Þorsteinsdóttir. Her father would not agree because Gunnlaugur was going abroad. But he said: "Helga shall be Gunnlaugur's *heitkona*, but not his *festarkona*, and wait for him for three winters, but Gunnlaugur shall go abroad and behave well."[36] The difference here is that *festar* was a formal contract, while *heit* was just a promise to make that contract. The promise between Þorsteinn and Illugi was not a betrothal, only a promise that Þorsteinn would not give his daughter to any other man for three winters. If Gunnlaugur came back to Iceland and Þorsteinn accepted Gunnlaugur they could marry. Promises of marriage of this sort can be associated with the Christian

33 Loftur Guttormsson 1992, pp. 173-74, compare to *Lovsamling for Island* I, pp. 113-24: "engin trúlofun skal ske … utan presturinn sé þar viðstaddur og að minnsta kosti fimm önnur vitni. Eigi skal þeim heldur leyfast sem réttilega hafa trúlofast til samans að samrekkja hvort með öðru fyrr en þau eru saman vígð gefin tilsamans í kristilegri kirkju."

34 Compare DI XV, p. 151: "Hannes og Gudrun i allann mata medkiendust þau hefdi giort og trulofad. Eptter þvi sem greint bref vtuijsar og nu enn ad nyiu trulofudu med handsolum…"

35 DI VII, pp. 797-99.

36 ÍF III, pp. 67-68: "skal Helga vera heitkona Gunnlaugs, en eigi festarkona, ok bíða þrjá vetr; en Gunnlaugr skal fara útan ok skapa sik eptir góðra manna siðum."

understanding of the *sponsalia per verba de futuro*.[37] This understanding in the meaning of the ritual of entry into marriage must be related to the time in which these sagas were written. Sigurður Nordal assumes that *Gunnlaugs saga Ormstungu* is from the period 1270-80.[38]

There are also examples from the saga literature which demonstrate the way in which a woman should be a *festarkona*. In both *Njáls saga* and *Grettis saga* the women are bound by the agreement of betrothal, *sitja í festum*.[39] Hrútur had made a *festar* agreement with Mörður concerning Mörður's daughter Unnur. He needed to go to Norway, and was worried about his arrangement with Mörður. His brother Höskuldur said: "You shall ride south to meet Mörður, and ask him to make another agreement, *máldaga,*[40] and then she shall wait for three years *í festum*."[41] Höskuldur wanted the bride of his brother to *sitja í festum*, as a *festarkona,* until Hrútur came back to Iceland. This meant that he was bound to the promise of the contract of betrothal. However, a *heit* was just a promise to remain faithful, not an economic commitment.

Two levels are thus apparent: the first is to be *heitkona*, the second one is to *sitja í festum*. For many centuries we find these two customs side by side. We can thus sum up by saying that the existing marriage contracts show that the institution of *festar* continued to be strong during the Late Middle Ages. But the written contract gives no standardized information about the ritual. One of the oldest surviving marriage contracts in *Diplomatarium Islandicum,* from 1381, provides evidence of *festaröl*, or a beer drinking feast, after the *festa* contract had been made.[42] With this, certain customs had to be followed. The beer should be drunk after the agreement had been completed.[43] This may have taken place on the

37 See the discussion in chapter 3, pp. 70 ff.

38 Magnús Már Lárusson 1959a, p. 240, see also Sigurður Nordal in ÍF III, p. lx.

39 ÍF VII, p. 10; ÍF XII, p. 10.

40 *Máldagi* means agreement, usually concerning the property of the Church, but it was also used, as here, in connection with marriage agreements. See footnote no. 6 in ÍF XII, p. 10.

41 ÍF XII, p. 10: "Þú skalt ríða suðr til fundar við Mörð, ok bið hann, at þit skipið máldaga annan, ok siti hon þrjá vetr í festum."

42 DI IV, pp. 13-14, year 1381. This is a copy of the contract made ca. 1730. *Festaröl* is also named in DI IX, p. 436. This is an original document from 1527, which refers to the "festaravl" held for Björn Þorleifsson and Ingibjörg Pálsdóttir. According to both the AM ordbog, as well as Magnús Már Lárusson 1959a, these are the only times this is mentioned in DI.

43 Fritzner I, p. 409. See *festaröl*.

same day as *festar* had been made (compare to the word *festingardagur*)[44] or later. But according to the saga literature, it should occur before the wedding feast, and the beer could even be drunk before *festar*. Beer was often referred to as *festaröl* in relation to the marriage of kings. The beer was drunk to do honour to the woman, and according to the sagas it was important that the beer was strong, (see Figures 15 and 16).[45]

It is important to underline, however, that no fixed rules existed, before the marriage ordinance of Frederik II in 1587 that dictated the ritual of entry into marriage. This may explain why the information about the ritual shown in the marriage contracts from before this time varies as much as it does.[46] In some instances the engagement undertaking called *trúlofunarhandsöl*[47] was made to initiate the marriage, and then the act of making the engagement by handshaking, *handsöl,* was made again on the wedding day, such as in the case between Árni Einarsson and Vilborg Eiríksdóttir in 1554.[48] At the same time some documents known as a *festingarbréf* continued to include the dotal agreement of property transfer, for instance one contract from 1561-62.[49]

Literature and marriage contracts thus reflect linguistic change in the terms used for entry into marriage, but there was no sudden change. Marriage documents from the fourteenth and fifteenth centuries indicate that the rules of entry into marriage became a mixture of old and new rituals. But even if the contracts seem to give us rather confusing information about changes in these rituals, there is reason to believe that there was real change in their meaning. When *trúlofan* was added to the pre-existing traditions of betrothal, it signified that marriage was not only about the transfer of property and women, but was also concerned with fidelity between man and wife. This emphasis was

44 See DI V, p. 372 year 1462, p. 415, year 1464, DI VIII, p. 324, year 1510.

45 See AM ordbog: *festaröl*, with a reference to *Æfintýr* lxxx vb, p. 34: "skalltu kalla vini þína ok drekka til mín festaröl en brúðkaup máttu síðarr hugsa." Compare to: *Æfintýr*, lxxx v, p. 6: "gjörir hann þegar festaröl til hennar, ok litlu síðar festir hana." An example of a beer drunk to the honour of the woman is to be found in *Hrólfs saga Gautrekssonar*, p. 62, gr. 20: "drekkr hann enn hit sterkasta festaröl til Íngibjargar."

46 DI IX, p. 279. An example can be taken from this document from 1512 where it is said that a *festarkona* was taken to the church, to participate in the ritual of "cleaning" the woman after childbirth. It indicates that the term *festarkona* was used here as a synonym to the term wife.

47 We have an example of *trúlofunarhandsöl* from 1554. See DI XII, pp. 711-12.

48 DI XII, pp. 711-12.

49 DI XIII, pp. 628-29.

related to an awareness of the Christian meaning of marriage. Several sources indicate this change in people's attitudes, a change which was related to the idea of fidelity or even care for each other. In 1429, a woman stated that she had not given her *trw*, or promises to marry anyone.[50] A similar situation is described in a judgement concerning the engagement and marriage contract, called *Trwlofaner* and *kaup* from 1565-70. The future husband and the father of the bride had put everything in place for the marriage to go ahead. The bridegroom had made an agreement with the bride and the marriage banns had been published in the church, as it should be according to the law. But the judgement states that after these preparations had been made the prospective husband did not want to *festa* the prospective bride. And when he was challenged as to why he had not fulfilled his promise of marriage, he claimed that he did not desire or wish to make this marriage.[51] It is tempting to use this evidence not only as an example of how a man used special legal arguments for not marrying a woman. Many other legal arguments could have been more powerful for that purpose. The argument, which is used, is related to the man's feelings. It indicates that at least some kind of awareness existed that the feelings between the man and the woman started to matter in relation to the entry into marriage.

Trúlofun was related to a couple's promises of marriage to each other.[52] Marriage was thus no more only a contract between the families rightfully made according to the rules of "God and human beings". It was also about something more. By the end of the sixteenth century, *trúlofun* marked the promise to entry into marriage, while *festar* continued to be concerned with the financial agreements that were made by marriage.[53] However, until the early seventeenth century *trúlofun* was

50 DI IV, p. 394.

51 DI XIV, pp. 453-54. The reason was his own strong mind: *þverbrotenn vilia*.

52 In a judgement from 1591 it was mentioned that if a man made an agreement with a woman, he should not break his *trúlofun* to her. See *Alþingisbækur Íslands* II, p. 235. Compare this to the rules of the marriage ordinance of 1587.

53 An example can be taken from a judgement of 1599 which give the impression that *trúlofun* and *festar* were two different rituals. *Alþingisbækur Íslands*, III, p. 156: "Suo birtist oss og su suplicatia sem þeir brædur höfdu fyrer kongl Maiest. borid. huor oss virdtist Ecki riett biuijsast j þeirre grein. ad Oddný Jónsdóttir hefdi verid trulofud sögdum Birni. Enn sijdur hun væri hanz festarmej."

also often understood to constitute marriage itself as the old institution of *festar* had done.[54]

We can conclude by saying that the Christian influence on the customary marriage ritual of *festar* gave it a new meaning without the traditional meaning being lost. At the same time the Church introduced new terms and an institution concerning marriage, of which the institution of *trúlofun* is an example. *Trúlofun* refers to the promise to marry, in which the priest was supposed to marry the couple after they had promised to remain faithful to each other. This was a new dimension to marriage, which had never been a part of the old institution of *festar*.

6.2 The spoken and written words of marriage

In oral societies an open and public announcement is usually at the centre of the rites accompanying birth, marriage and death. Dancing, beer-drinking or singing often follow the performance of these rituals.[55] Some of the old rituals of the oral society are described in *Grágás*. At later stages *Jónsbók*, the *New Christian Law*, as well as certain Church statutes and the written contracts of the Late Middle Ages document the Christian influence of the Church on the marriage ritual.

Some of the sources indicate a shift from oral to written forms of making contracts. This was sometimes expressed with reference to the memory of the oldest people.[56] The marriage contract was made by *festar*.[57] Word with the same meaning are: *festarmál*; the agreement of betrothal. *Máli* was the marriage contract covering the separate belongings of the wife, but the word *kaupmáli*, mean the marriage contract, and *mundarmál* the agreement about the brideprice.[58] The words for *festar* are quoted in *Grágás*, and were also included in the *New Christian Law*.[59] The oral

54 Because the old tradition of writing contracts and making *trúlofunargjörningar* between a couple continued to be followed, priests did not register the marriage, compare to Loftur Guttormsson 1992, p. 175. *Þjsks: Prestþjónustubækur. Prestþjónustubók Reykholts, Borg, 1664-1788*, is the oldest surviving register of marriages in Iceland.

55 Goody 1992, p. 42.

56 See for instance DI III, pp. 54-55, from the year of 1351.

57 *Grágás*, Ib, pp. 29-75, II, pp. 152-209.

58 Magnús Már Lárusson 1959a, p. 237.

59 Ibid., pp. 236-40.

character of the written marriage contracts is also quite clear. *Festarorð*, the word of betrothal, was the last word to be said in the ceremony of betrothal, *festar*.[60] According to *Grágás*, the text is as follows:

> A woman is legally betrothed if the bridegroom shows the economic contract (*mundarmál*). And then the guardian and the man to whom the woman is betrothed should name the witnesses. "We name witnesses to this", the man shall say who is betrothed to the woman, "that you N betroth N to me by a legal betrothal and you give me (*handsalar*) the dowry."[61]

After written marriage contracts became common these words of betrothal were often recited, but sometimes only by referring to the fact that the right words of the betrothal ritual had been spoken, as in a judgement about the betrothal of Jón Hallgrímsson and Helena Þórarinsdóttir in 1521.[62] The written contracts of the Late Middle Ages were thus partly shaped by the older oral tradition. The witnesses played a central role in making the contract valid, and the start of the marriage could not be confirmed without following the rules of the betrothal formula. However, the role of the witnesses as well as the character of the formula changed. These changes in the making of marriage will be examined closer in this section.

6.1.1 Formulae

The formulae were standardized rules which dictated how the judicial act of marriage should be performed.[63] The use of standardized formulae facilitated the change from the oral contract to the written contract. It was the use of correct forms that guaranteed a legal contract. No books of formulae are known from the Icelandic Middle Ages, but many manu-

60 *Fritzner ordbok* I, p. 409.

61 *Grágás*, II, p. 162: "Þa e*r* kona föstnoð at lögo*m*. ef m*aðr* tín*ir* mu*n*dar mál. En siþ*an* a lögraðande oc sa m*aðr* e*r* konan e*r* fest. at n*efn*a v*att*a. At þ*v*i ve*tt*i. nefno*m* vit s*ca*l h*ann* segia sa e*r* kono eignaz. at þu. N. fastn*ar* me*r*. N. lögföstnon. oc þu handsalar m*er* hei*m*an fylgio."

62 DI VIII, pp. 783-84. See especially on p. 784 a reference to the correct words of betrothal as well as a reference to the rule of the *New Christian Law*.

63 Berulfsen 1959, pp. 491-92. Magnús Már Lárusson 1959b, p. 492.

scripts of the law codes include different kinds of formulae.[64] Not many of those are about betrothal.[65]

The old Norwegian laws had several kinds of betrothal formulae.[66] The formula in *Grágás* suggests that the bridegroom spoke the words of betrothal to the guardian of the bride,[67] while several of the Norwegian formulae give a more personal picture of the betrothal between the man and the bride: the man himself spoke to establish his bond to the woman.[68]

It is assumed that many of the known marriage formulae came from the papal curia.[69] The Christian formula from around 1300, *formáli fyrir hjónavígslu*, probably had this origin. It is found in a handbook for priests in the Diocese of Niðarós:

> But now the free consent should be witnessed in the audience of God and the holy Church and for me. Do you X wish to take this woman to your wife, to keep her whether sick or healthy? Do you take this man to your husband, to keep him, and take care of him when he is sick as well as in good health? And no matter what happens to you while you live together, you should both keep this holy law and not disturb this bond. By the aforementioned contract I give you this woman in the name of God. [Then the bridegroom says:] And with this golden ring I engage you, and this silver I give you, and with my self I will honor you, and as long as we live keep you with God's help and mercy.[70]

64 Magnús Már Lárusson 1959b, p. 492. In the DI there are many formulae. See for instance in DI II, pp. 328f, 506 ff, 653 ff, 701 as well as Gissur Einarsson's copybook, DI X, pp. 575, 586 ff and DI XI, pp. 132, 452, 520.

65 An exception is DI II, p. 328, which is probably of Norwegian origin, and DI IV, p. 495. See also the register in the AM collection, AM 241b, fol, vii, c. 1490, *Brudstykker af formularer til brug ved brudevielse.*

66 Magnús Már Lárusson 1959b, p. 492, Boyle 1976, p. 86.

67 *Grágás* II, p. 162.

68 NgL II, p. 319 in *Gulathings-Christenret*: "Ek festir þic mer till eignar konno." Ngl II, p. 300 in *Borgarthings-Christenret*: "Ek fæsti þik mer ok næfni hana a nafn.", NgL II, p. 333 in *Gulathings-Christenret*: "Ek festir þik.N. mér til æiginnar. kono."

69 Ljungfors 1959, pp. 484-86.

70 DI II, pp. 328-29. From a marriage formula c. 1300. Thott. No. 110, 8vo, pp. 136-146. The manuscript is from a manual for priests in the archdiocese of Niðarós: "En nv æigi iatta i høyrn guði ok hæillag /rar kyrkiu ok firir mer at vilia yckrum /þesso sambande. villt þu X þessa ko/no taka þer till æignar kono. at gøy/ma hennar sva sivkrar sem hæillar/ vill tu taka þenna man þer till æig/nar manns at gæta ok varðvæita sva / sivkan sem hæillan. at hvat er yckr / kann till handa at bera mæðan þit /bvið bæðe skolu þit hallda þessor guðs / logh ok æigi raska þessare samteng /ging. Mæðr þessom firr sagðum ka/upmala far ek þer kono i guðs / namfni. Mæðr þæsso fingr gulli / festi ek þic. ok þætta sýllfr gef ek / þer ok með mer siallfum søme ek þic / ok sva længgi sem mit lifum skal /ek þic hallda med guðs hiolpp ok miskun."

This example clearly shows how the Christian formula was added to the traditional formula for making the economic contract. The priest gave the man the bride and she was bound to him by the exchange of gold and silver. It is assumed that this formula from around 1300 could have been used in Iceland, although the linguistic style of the text is more Norwegian than Icelandic.[71] In any case, if the formula could be used in Iceland it was not obligatory to do so.

The Icelandic historian Magnús Már Lárusson has argued that this text was not related to a priest's blessing of the couple in the traditional meaning of a wedding, although the editors of the *Diplomatarium Islandicum* assumed this. Lárussons interpretation is in accordance with the general medieval marriage practice. The medieval marriage liturgy does not mention a blessing. Instead the couple simply participates in a mass standing before the congregation. The formula from the archdiocese of Niðarós was, according to Lárusson, employed after a contract had been concluded and the contract often took the form of a written document outlining the financial obligations of the two families towards the couple. In the quotation above, the speaker is the priest standing in front of the church door. The financial contract had already been made, and it was part of the priest's role to refer to the completed property transfer. Yet in doing so, the priest gave the agreement a new meaning, because he was also the person who could give the woman to the bridegroom.[72] This is how the word *gifta* did not only mean the parents giving the bride to her future husband, but also meant the priest was a central figure in the ritual. In the name of God, he, as well as her parents, could give a woman to her husband-to-be.

All the formulae demonstrate the importance of speech in these rituals, but the Norwegian formula emphasizes the commitment of the bridegroom to the bride, while the formula in *Grágás* focuses on the contract between the men of the two families. This changed in Iceland with the formula that followed the *New Christian Law* of 1275. The

71 DI II, p. 328.

72 On this Magnús Már Lárusson has written: "Det drejer sig ikke om selve brudevielsen, således som udg. af DI II tænkte sig, men om fæster som skete uten for kirkedøren, når alle formkrav skulle opfyldes." See Magnús Már Lárusson 1959a, p. 239.

procedure was that the man would go directly to the woman he wanted to marry, he would take her hand in the presence of witnesses, say her name, and declare that he was betrothed to her according to the law of God. The witnesses would hear the woman pronounce an audible "yes".[73] The law stated:

> The one who shall become betrothed to the girl or the woman shall hold her hand, name two witnesses or more, and say these words.
>
> "I betroth you to me as my proper wife by the law of God and after the holy writ and you are my legal, proper wife."[74]

Contracts are evidence of betrothal agreements, as well as contractual agreements. The woman's "yes", or her consent, had to be heard clearly and the right formula of betrothal had to be used, and only after the marriage banns had been publicly announced three times in the church.[75]

Many other copies of formulae exist from the Late Middle Ages. One formula from 1490 refers to the blessing of the bride.[76] Another formula from 1432 was part of a marriage contract and contained the words of the bridegroom at the betrothal, spoken in front of witnesses.[77] Yet another formula, contained in a marriage contract from 1537, was similar to the one from 1432, but with an interesting change, in that the husband should say the words to the bride, and not only to the witnesses.[78]

It is not possible to reconstruct fully the relationship between the formulae and the way in which they were used. A document from 1521

73 Jochens 1986b, p. 144. See NgL II, pp. 299-300, NgL III, p. 368, NgL V, p. 37.

74 See chapter 16, NgL V, p. 37: "Scal sa hallda i hönd meyju eða kono sem ser scal hana festa. oc nefna vatta tva eða fleiri. oc mæla þessor orð. eg festi þic mer til eiginnar kono eptir guds logom og helagra feðra setning oc ertu min loglig eigin kona heþan af."

75 Magnús Már Lárusson 1959a, p. 239. Compare to DI VII, pp. 413, 425.

76 See Kålund 1889, vol. 1, p. 212, who refers to: AM 241b, vii, from ca. 1490 which contains fragments of marriage formulae.

77 DI IV, p. 495, from the original document of AM 235 4to, p. 42, copybook of Bishop Jón Vilhjálmsson. This formula from 1432 is in the contract of Árni Steingrímsson and Ingunn Ólafsdóttir: "Gudh sæ wattr okar oc þeir goder mænn sæm hia ero ath ek arnæ stæingrimsson fester mær jngunnæ olafsdottor mær til æigenkono med gudz logum ok landz ok æfter hæilgra fedra settningh. gud være med oss."

78 DI X, p. 116. This formula from 1537 is in the contract of Jón Narfason and Sesselíu Bassadóttir. The witnesses heard this "ord fyrir ord talandi sem hier seiger: Ec jon narfason festi þig settseliu bassadotter mier til eiginkonv epter gvds laugvm ok heilagra fedra setningv ok er þu min lauglig eiginkona hiedan af þessum uottum hia verendvm fyrr skrifudum ok fleirum audrvm."

refers to a betrothal, *festar*, made in accordance with the *New Christian Law* of 1275.[79] Some marriages were made using formulae many centuries old. Elements from more than one formula could also be used together in order to make a marriage. This makes it difficult to use formulae as historical documents. It can be stated, however, that evidence of the use of an old formula can be used to demonstrate the longevity of a particular custom. On the other hand, the introduction of new formulae can be interpreted as evidence of changing customs.

The formula dating from 1300 was probably an example of the latter, while the formula in the *Íslandslýsing* from the end of the sixteenth century is an example of the former. The sixteenth century formula indicates the continuation of the old custom of *festar* from *Grágás*, which had been combined with elements of the Christian formula:

> God shall be my witness and those kind men present. I NN-son betroth you NN-daughter following the law of God, the country, and the Holy Fathers' scripts, with your witnesses NN-son and you NN-son and all those who hear my words. And now you are my legal wife.[80]

When this was said, the bridegroom would kiss the bride, and this kiss would be the symbol of "the love and duty of their joined minds."[81] This formula, more than any evidence already referred to, expresses the way in which the Church had managed to give marriage a new meaning by changing the old rituals of entering it. Another formula from the end of the sixteenth century gives an even clearer picture of this new situation. This formula is to be found in the work of the humanist and rector at Glaumbær, Gottskálkur Jónsson (d. 1593), and is called "formula for a certain couple."[82]

79 DI VIII, p. 784.

80 *Íslandslýsing* 1971, p. 84: "Guð sé vottur minn og þeir góðir menn, sem hjá eru. Ég NN-son fastna þig NN-dóttir eftir guðs lögum og landsins og heilagra forfeðra setningu, með vitni þínu NN-son og þínu NN-son og allra þeirra, er orð mín heyra. Og nú ertu mín lögleg eiginkona."

81 Ibid., 1971, p. 84: "skyldusamrar ástar eða nánari og innilegri sameiningar huganna".

82 In Icelandic called: *Formali yfer hionum nockr.* The formula is found in an Icelandic manuscript at the British Library number 11242, 4o, but it has been described by Jón Þorkelsson 1892, pp. 217-35; concerning this formula see especially, p. 225.

God, you who with the power and strength of your blessed son, created all things from nothing, and so wonderfully made marriage as a holy agreement, by which the Holy Ghost joined a man and a woman, and by so doing made the world to be rich in people. Bless thou this couple by your holy hand and give them mercy, so they will love you day and night … and may they live so long that they could see their grandchildren and great-grandchildren be born…[83]

6.2.2 The witnesses and the role of the priest

According to *Grágás*, a marriage contract was valid as long as the witnesses were alive and no other agreement was made.[84] It did, however, not mean that the contract became invalid if the witnesses died, but it could certainly be a problem if the marriage became questioned at court, and no one could testify that it had been made. A judicial change occurred in the late thirteenth century concerning witnesses. In some ways, the written contract was partly to take over the role of those who testified the contract. This meant, from a juridical point of view, that the marriage contract did not only last as the persons involved could remember, as had been the case according to the rules contained in *Grágás*.

However, witnesses continued to play an important role in the making of all marriage contracts during the Middle Ages. During this period the written marriage contract had to be witnessed by at least two people.[85] *Festaváttur* refers to a person who was present when a marriage agreement was concluded, and who would be able to testify that the marriage had been legally performed.[86]

The role of the witnesses to a marriage was important. The witnesses to the marriage of Ólöf Arnardóttir and Þorlákur Eyjólfsson in 1595 could testify that this marriage was valid.[87] It seems that only men witnessed marriage contracts. One exception is the contract of 1545, made in Hólar between Bessi Þorsteinsson and Guðrún Tumadóttir. In

83 Gjerløw 1980, pp. 68-69: "Formali yfer hionum nockr. Þw gvd er med valldi og krapti þinz blezada sonar skapader alla hlvti af engu efni hver er med hafv stormerki hivskapligt samband helgadi[r]. Svo at kriz heilagr andi skyllsi samteingaz mille kallmanz og konu svo at þar af skylldi mannkynit avkaz j verolldine. Bleza þv nv þessi hion med þine blezadri hendi og myskunn svo þav elski þig nott og dag … Enn lifi svo leingi at þau megi sia sonv sina og dætvr allt til þridia og fiorda ættkvistar…"

84 Compare to Agnes S. Arnórsdóttir 1986, p. 26.

85 Hamre 1997, pp. 126-37, see especially p. 137.

86 Compare to Magnús Már Lárusson 1959a, p. 238.

87 *Alþingisbækur Íslands* III, p. 5.

this case the female housekeeper was mentioned as one of the witnesses as well as other women.[88]

One important change in the making of marriage contracts related to the culture of testimony is that the role of the priest became more important as time passed. As mentioned before, according to canon law it was not necessary that a priest blessed the couple to make a marriage valid. The blessing of the couple by a priest was first mentioned in Iceland in the *New Christian Law* of 1275. This blessing should be performed after the *festar*.[89] However, Icelandic and Norwegian provincial law codes of the later thirteenth century reflect the principle that it is consummation[90] and consent which matter, not the blessing of the priest.[91]

Thus, even if blessing is first mentioned in the *New Christian Law*, it was not legally necessary until 1587, according to the marriage law of King Frederik II. There is, however, some evidence of interference from priests before that. An illustration has survived in a manuscript of *Jónsbók* from the late fourteenth century, which shows a priest blessing a couple.[92] It is possible that the illustration has been copied from other manuscripts concerned with marriage, but it is tempting to believe that this custom was in some instances actually practiced in Iceland at the time from which the manuscript of *Jónsbók* dates. It is known that from at least the early thirteenth century priests were present at wedding feasts.[93] Of course, the reason for their presence may not have been religious, but because priests were so often mentioned there is reason to believe that they performed some kind of sacred function.

Priests were used as witnesses to marriages in fourteenth century France, before blessings or weddings became the rule.[94] We find the same development elsewhere in Europe during the Middle Ages, al-

88 DI XI, p. 435. Occasionally women acted as witnesses to other types of declaration, for example, the declaration that a certain dying man did not have any debts, see DI IV, p. 492.

89 Compare to Jón Jóhannesson 1956, p. 221. See also the discussion here on pp. 118 ff.

90 Compare to *Jónsbók*, p. 77: "ef síðan er lagz með henni er hann handseldi sér eða festi, ok fær hann hennar, þá á hann bæði rétt ok ráðspell."

91 Compare to NgL II, p. 319.

92 Gunnar F. Guðmundsson 2000, p. 259.

93 Agnes S. Arnórsdóttir 1995, p. 112, compare to Sts. I, pp. 66, 223, 304, 474, 505.

94 Ariès and Duby 1988, p. 126.

though the practice differed from place to place.[95] This was clearly also put into practice in the Late Middle Ages in Iceland.[96] The role of the priest was to announce the marriage publicly and to act as a witness of the contract. In Iceland it seems though that the priest did become one of the witnesses until the early fifteenth century.[97]

In statutes or in other prescriptive clerical documents the blessing was undoubtedly a well-established tradition by the fourteenth century.[98] But in the wake of the Reformation the priest's blessing of the marriage ceremony gained a more important role as one can see from court material from the late sixteenth century.[99] In the Church ordinance of King Christian III of Denmark from 1537/39, translated into Icelandic by Bishop Gissur Einarsson, it is stated that priests should be paid as much for *hjónavígslur* (the marrying of a couple), as they had before.[100] This also suggests that priests were paid for their involvement in weddings before the Reformation, but the Church ordinance may refer only to the practice in Denmark rather than in Iceland. However, information obtained from the registers of charters detailing debts owed to the Church, called *máldagar*, also indicates that priests married couples before the Reformation. Once again this information suggests that in some churches or chapels, priests were permitted to perform marriages. This is apparent from the charter *máldagar* by Bishop Stefán from the end of the fifteenth century and the beginning of the sixteenth century. Vilchin's copybook from 1397 also indicates this.[101] A judgement from 1431 also confirms that marriage contracts actually were made nearby in the church. According to this document a man made a marriage agreement in the church at Fell in Sléttuhlíð.[102]

95 Brundage 1990, p. 502.

96 In most of the marriage contracts after 1450 in DI that refer to witnesses, these people are from two groups: the clergy and lay people.

97 See Appendix I, the contracts from 1433, 1434 and onwards.

98 DI II, p. 804. Compare to the ordinance of Bishop Jóns Sigurðsson from 1345: "Suo er oc fyrirbodit sub pena suspensionis at syngia pvsvnarmessu yfir konum er þær giptaz oc yfir einvm nema iungfrvm einvm."

99 See above the example concerning *trúlofun* and *festar*, *Alþingisbækur Íslands*, III, p. 44: "fyrst ad hion skyllde Ecke saman vijg(i)ast fyrr Enn iij sunnudaga hefdi verid adur lyst j kirkiunni."

100 DI X, p. 156; see also DI X, p. 288 in Latin.

101 DI IV, p. 129; compare to ibid., pp. 596, 592, and DI V, pp. 493-99.

102 DI IV, p. 449.

Thus it is possible to conclude that priests had married couples in Iceland before the Reformation, but that this was not necessary for the legality of the marriage, as according to canon law, a marriage was valid without a priest having blessed the spouses.

6.3 The form of the written contract

Written marriage contracts were legal documents concerning property transactions that not only had significance for the persons involved, but were also documents that could be used many years later as evidence in court cases. These contracts were called *festingarbréf* or *kaupmálabréf*[103] and all such agreements should be written and testified with seals.[104] They were preserved privately and people soon learned to use the contracts in court cases.[105] They could be used to prove that a marriage was legally made, as well as a person's property rights.

In contrast to what Georges Duby found in France, i.e. that the numbers of written agreements sealed by large family groups were increasingly replaced by documents sealed by the contracting couples,[106] medieval Icelandic marriage contracts were not sealed by the couple, but by the witnesses to the contract. In Iceland the names of the witnesses were recorded as part of the marriage contract.[107] The priest was first on the list of witnesses and his seal gave the document more value because it proved that the marriage had been contracted in accordance with the rules of the Church. Secondly, some laymen could witness the contract, and often some of them were members of the royal administration in Iceland. The third group participating in the contract could be the couple's close relatives.

It was common for contracts to be written down and witnessed at some unspecified time after the wedding ceremony. This interval could

103 Magnús Már Lárusson 1959a, pp. 238-39.

104 *Jónsbók*, p. 222.

105 DI VII, pp. 314-15, see especially p. 315: "kom fyrir oss j fystu festingarbref olafs filippussonar at hann hefde fest vigdisi jonsdottur konu sina at laugum og hun hefde at laugum gipt verit."

106 See Duby 1994, p. 110.

107 See for instance DI IV, p. 278. This is a marriage contract from 1420: "voru þessir festingarvottar a brullavpsdegi."

sometimes be very long. For example, Bjarni Ólason and Margrét Ólafsdóttir started their married life in 1461, but their marriage contract was not written down until 1471.[108] This delay may have been associated with the process of change from oral to written documentation. But it was not an exclusive trend: the contract of Andrés Guðmundsson and Þorbjörg Ólafsdóttir was published in 1462 and confirmed on the day of their betrothal.[109]

Two types of written marriage contracts survive. One type started with a sentence stating that the contract was made publicly and was confirmed (*lýstist og staðfestis*). The second type started with an announcement "we make it known" (*við gerum kunnugt*). The significance of these two types of documents relates in part to the document's function: whether the document witnessed the event or instead whether it was a confirmation that the contract had already been made. In the first type of contract, the names of the witnesses appeared at the end of the document,[110] while in the second type the names of the witnesses appeared at the beginning. A marriage contract from 1465 between Eyjólfur Böðvarsson and Guðrún Þorkelsdóttir, the daughter of a priest, is an example of this second type. After the announcement "we make it known", done by two priests and four laymen, it starts with declaring that:

> The priest Þorkell Guðbjartsson [the father of the bride] had heard and saw the handshake of the couple, and Eyjólfur Böðvarsson on behalf of the other family, with the condition that Þorkell gave (*gipti*) his daughter Guðrún to Eyjólfur, with the consent of her mother Valgerðue Magnúsdóttir.[111]

108 See DI V, pp. 610-11. See also in DI VII, pp. 223-34, another example that the contract was not written down until many years after the marriage had been made. The contract is from 1494 when Finnbogi Jónsson betrothed Málfríður Torfadóttir, but the mother of Málfríður, Kristín Þorsteinsdóttir had already given her daughter to be married to Finnbogi in 1467. It is hard to identify why this contract of *festar* was made so late in this relationship. There must have been doubts about the legality of the initial contract. By making a new marriage contract with his wife, Finnbogi secured its legality.

109 DI V, pp. 372-73.

110 Ibid., pp. 415-16, compare to ibid., pp. 87-88.

111 Ibid., p. 454: "vórum vær j hia saam oc heyrdum vpp aa ord oc handaband þeirra sira þorkels gudbiartzsonar af einne aalfuo enn eyiolfs bauduarssonar af annarri aalfuo Med suo felldum skildaga at fyrr nefndur sira þorkell gipti aadur greindum eyiolfui gudruno dottur sina med samþycki valgerðar magnusdottur modur hennar."

Then the description of the financial agreement came. At the end of the document, the following statement appears: "and hereafter Eyjólfur betrothed Guðrún Þorkelsdóttir to be his legal wife according to the law of God, with the words that belong to that agreement."[112] At the end of this contract it is stated that the before-mentioned men (those who made the announcement) put their seal on the document.

This type of contract began with the words, *við gerum kunnugt* ("we make it known") and in this type the names of the witnesses appear at the beginning of the document. A contract from 1467 exemplifies this kind of announcement, here made between the *ærligra manna* ("honest men")[113] Magnús Magnússon and Sigríður Jónsdóttir. The contract does not include any spiritual information, and it was testified by five men, where no one is called a priest. At the end of the document it is stated that to further confirm this agreement, Magnús himself, as well as the father of the bride, put their seal at the bottom of the document.[114] A letter of betrothal (*festingarbréf*) between Sumarliði Eiríksson and Guðrún Árnadóttir from 1468 provides another example of this type of contract. The priest and secular witnesses at a farm in Kalmanstunga announced that Sumarliði had

> [betrothed Guðrún] herself to be his legal wife and documented as we have before heard how the most honorable men betroth their decent wives, and we cannot find any hindrance to this according to our best knowledge.[115]

This statement indicates one way in which clerics made their statements when a legal marriage took place. It also shows that the laity was concerned about the reading of banns, as the sentence: "we cannot find any hindrance to this according to our best knowledge," indicates.

112 Ibid., p. 454: "enn her epter festi eyiolfur bauduarson gudruno þorkelsdottur sier til laugligrar eiginkono at gudz laugum med þeim ordum er þar til heyrer."

113 This phrasing agrees with the standard Latin across Europe: *[bonis et] honestis viris*, but all the Icelandic contracts where written in the vernacular language.

114 DI V, pp. 506-507. There were thus originally seven seals to this document.

115 Ibid., pp. 532-33: "ser til logligrar eiginkonu suo skialliga sem uær hofum adur heyrt ena ærliguztu menn festa sinar dandi konur ok eigi kunnum uær þar at finna epter uorum uiztmunum."

The other type of contract was the same as this one from 1467. The agreement started with a declaration that the "contract was announced and confirmed that marriage *gipting* between Rafn Brandsson on the one hand and Margrét Eyjólfsdóttir on the other hand … on their wedding day."[116] Again it was the priests and laymen that were named as witnesses, but here, at the end of the document. This form of contract often started with the publication of marriage banns. A document from a priest in 1499 can be cited in order to explain this procedure better. The priest witnessed that he had published the banns three times in the holy church for the marriage agreement between Bárður Jónsson and Sigríður Jónsdóttir, and later made a betrothal contract between Bárður and Sigríður according to Church law.[117] Another example of this type of contract is one made in 1480, on the wedding day of the couple named at the beginning of the contract. After this, the financial agreement is outlined, and at the end of the contract it says that this agreement was achieved by a legal betrothal, *festing*. Thereafter the names of the witnesses are given, including the priest as well as laymen.[118]

In summary, several points are worth highlighting. First, although the marriage customs outlined in *Grágás* were based on contractual arrangements, they were confirmed by an oral agreement. Second, we can say that after 1281 when the *Jónsbók* demanded a mandatory written contract concerning financial arrangements for marriage[119] the process of changing the contract from oral to written agreements started. Oral and written contracts were based on much the same formulae. Thus, third, the main change unfolding in the way marriage was practiced concerned the people involved in the contracts. As a new thing, both women and priests became active participants in the formal drawing up of written contracts. It is noteworthy also that although some elements, such as the requirement in *Grágás* that the parties should have a certain minimum level of wealth before they married, were *removed* from the

116 Ibid., pp. 504-506: "Lystizt oc stadfestizt suo felldr kaupmæli j gipting Milli þeirra Rafns branzsonar af einni ælfuo en margretar eyiolfsdottur af annarri … aa þeirra brullaupsdegi."

117 DI VII, p. 425.

118 DI VI, pp. 295-96.

119 *Jónsbók*, p. 222.

standard contract,[120] new elements were *added* to it, most notably the emphasis on the mutual consent of the partners themselves, including the bride.

Finally, it is worth noting that even after the production of written contracts had become commonplace, oral customs persisted. A written testimony from 1600 confirms that the written contract was read aloud after it was made.[121] Indeed, to this day the spoken word continues to have legal significance. In the modern wedding ceremony, the bride and the bridegroom are requested to say clearly whether they want to be together as a loving wife and husband. The anticipated response, needless to say, is "I do."

6.4 Conclusion

This chapter has examined changes in ritual in order to explain how the new Christian meaning of marriage was communicated to people. One of the aspects of this change was a change in the language of marriage rituals, and it has been important to ask whether changes in the practice of marriage rituals followed. Changes in the making of marriage bonds was achieved by introducing a new message into the established rituals associated with the start of marriage. The new message had a strong religious meaning, and because Christian doctrine became so prominent it is possible that ritual played a key role in changing the meaning of the bond. It is hard to identify any change in this meaning during the period in which the old ritual was used. But words were not without significance. As the new meaning of marriage was slowly introduced into a known ritual context, people's own perception of marriage probably also underwent gradual change.

One example of this is the strengthening of parental consent in the legislation of *Jónsbók*, discussed here in the first part of this book. This can be seen as a response to the Christian doctrine of the mutual consent of the couple. It is on this second level that the ongoing process

120 However, the ritual of *festar* continued to exist.

121 AM dipl. isl. fasc. lxix, 8: "og að þeirra Kaupmálabréf þar upplesnu".

of interactive behaviour occurred. The written marriage contracts are direct evidence of this change in behaviour. The old marriage contracts had only been orally made. From the late fourteenth century it became common to make written contracts. Thus the communicative function of rituals in providing frameworks for Christian beliefs became part of everyday life.

According to Clifford Geertz, we can expect to find radical discontinuities between these two levels during periods of change. Some of the driving forces behind change can even be found in this discontinuity.[122] On the basis of the sources that have been analysed in this chapter we find differences between the framework of Christian beliefs and ritual practice. It is not possible to identify the change in the making of marriage as a sudden change from a secular towards a more ecclesiastical model of marriage. The marriage formula could be spoken at a farm when the financial contract was made, or it could be spoken in front of the church door. However, the formula, which originally was only concerned with the woman and the financial agreement, changed over time. The symbols that came to be used were related to the sacred meaning of marriage, and the role of the priests in making marriage contracts became greater. However, before the Reformation it did not alter the legal value of the contract if a priest did not perform the marriage ceremony. The important thing was that it could be testified that a marriage was made according to the law of God. No standardized form existed on which contracts should be made. They could take the form: a) of a letter of witness stating that marriage had been made according to the law of God; b) of outlining how the financial contract was made; c) of a proper contract detailing the property transfer; or, d) of a declaration that a given marriage had been legally made.

There are two main types of contracts that have survived: those that started with a declaration that a marriage had been made, and those that took the form of a testimony concerning the contract. As the discussion has indicated, the religious formula was a spoken one, and continued to be so until the fifteenth century. In practice a couple could first become

122 Geertz 1993, p. 144.

married either by uttering the formula of marriage, (or having a priest do so), and then make a written contract to record their property agreement. Alternatively, the contract could be made first, with the words of betrothal spoken afterwards.

CHAPTER 7

Christian influence and change in the form of the written contract

The new meaning of marriage was communicated to people, not only through the rituals, but also by the introduction of the new rules of the written contracts. Furthermore, changes which occurred in the making of the contracts show how slowly the Christian elements were added to the older forms of making oral marriage contracts. In this chapter all the preserved marriage contracts from the fourteenth to the sixteenth century will be discussed in relation to the question of how the contracts continued to be a mixture of both old and new elements. These contracts indicate that certain formalities were followed. The settlement was made in accordance with the rules governing how to make a legal marriage contract. Marriage should be made with the consent of the spouses and produce an agreement about their financial affairs, a *fékaup*, which was confirmed in a document called a *kaupmálabréf,* or letter of marriage contract.[1] These refer to the financial arrangements of the spouses concerning the agreement.[2]

First, the earliest contracts will be studied in details. Only five contracts are preserved from the fourteenth century, and they will be used as evidence for the oldest known form of the written marriage agreement. Secondly, the evidence from the marriage contracts of the fifteenth century about the property agreement, and the Christian influence, will be discussed. Thirdly, the last part aims at discussing the financial and

1 Magnús Már Lárusson 1959a, pp. 236-40.

2 One good legal example can be mentioned from DI VI, pp. 547-49, which is an original contract written on parchment. This was a marriage contract from 1485-86, written by the father of the bride who was also a lawman.

religious aspects of the contracts in the fifteenth and sixteenth century. This last section will include a discussion about the role of the priests in the making of the marriage contract, the change in the rules about the celibacy of the clergy after the Reformations, and – finally – how the Christian influence actually strengthened the parental consent in marriage.

7.1 The earliest evidence of written contracts

The oldest existing written marriage contracts are from the late fourteenth century. No contracts are preserved from the period 1300-50 even if many documents concerning the transfer of property have survived from this period. Thus, it was not property transfer resulting from marriage that was first recorded in written form. That no written marriage contracts have survived does not mean that the written form had no legal significance in relation to marriage. A document from the period c.1330-40 suggests there was a phase of transition from the old oral contract to the written *kaupmáli*. It is a list of the debts to various people of an un-named man in Húnavatnsþing. According to this list a woman called Ragnhildur should own part of his *garður*, both land and other wealth. This expression *að eiga í garði* was common in marriage contracts, and means that a wife owned a separate part of her husband's property.[3] Another document from 1332 concerning a property transaction deals with the transfer of landed property from a married couple to a bishop. This letter of witness confirms that the husband could not make any financial commitment without his wife.[4] Another letter of witness concerning this transfer records the wife's clear consent to this sale.[5]

All the marriage contracts from the late fourteenth century concern only the property agreement. The oldest document published in *Diplomatarium Islandicum*, a marriage contract from 1366, is not Icelandic, but

3 DI V, p. 1.
4 DI II, pp. 673-74.
5 Ibid., p. 675.

Norwegian.[6] The reason why this contract has relevance for Iceland is that the daughter of the couple later married an Icelandic man.[7] The marriage of this Norwegian couple was witnessed by six men. The contract concerned both their marriage and the division of property between the bride and the bride's brother, who was at that time very young.[8]

The oldest document witnessing an Icelandic marriage contract is from 1380. Two fathers made a legal marriage agreement, *keyptu löglega hjúskaparkaupi*, between their children Þórður and Járngerður, (see Figure 17). This was a contract made between the two families, a similar type of contract to that which the formula of *Grágás* refers to, i.e. is the father of the bride giving her away. It did not contain any Christian expressions and was primarily a financial agreement.[9] A year later a contract was made between Jórunn Brynjólfsdóttir and Ólafur Sigurðsson. It was Björn Brynjólfsson, Jórunn's brother, who was her guardian, *giftingarmaður*, because her father was dead. The agreement called *fékaup* was made between Jórunn's brother and Ólafur's father. It is the same type of contract as the one from 1380 and was primarily financial in nature. But in addition it says that this agreement was confirmed by the couple.[10] This was then a contract outlining the double consent to the marriage, by both the male relatives and the couple itself. Ólafur's father paid for the wedding from his own wealth. However, both the brother of the bride and the father of the bridegroom were to share the cost for her betrothal feast. It was also his father and her brother who made the agreement.

A short summary or report has survived concerning a contract made in 1383 between a priest, Gudbjartur flóki, and his concubine, *fylgikona*. This was a document of a private character, kept amongst other

6 Written marriage contracts exist from Norway from the early fourteenth century. About marriage contracts in DN see: Græsdal 2000, pp. 81-97. From the Norwegian DN we find information about making marriage contracts. See, for instance, from 1325 concerning a marriage contract: DN IV, p. 151. And a document from 1339 gives information about another contract, see: DN V, p. 107. See also unpublished thesis, Aronsen 1999.

7 Compare this daughter's marriage contract from 1397: DI III, pp. 616-17.

8 DI V, p. 3.

9 DI III, pp. 351-52.

10 DI IV, p. 13.

documents by the priest Oddur Þorleifsson at Borg.[11] It provides no information about the contract, but the summary is interesting because it indicates that in 1383 a priest made a formal contract with his concubine.

The reverse of a document from 1397 bears the words: this is the marriage contract of Guðríður Ingimundardóttir. Guðríður was the daughter of Hólmfríður and Ingimundur, who were mentioned in the Norwegian contract from 1366. The document concerns the financial agreement for her marriage. There is no evidence of the use of a Christian formula in this contract.[12]

While the acceptance of the Christian marriage did not exclude the old property-based agreement, these earliest contracts (mainly based on financial agreement) may still have been made in accordance with the law of God, even if this was not documented. The reason why no Christian formula was included in these contracts could be that the agreement of property, called *kaup,* and the publication of marriage banns, called *lýsing,* which was a declaration that the marriage had been made by the law of God, existed separately. The publication of marriage banns and the mutual consent of the couple were first made orally, but from the early fifteenth century we start to get information which shows that it was also written in the contract that the publication of the marriage banns had taken place.[13] This evidence from the early fourteenth century indicates thus that the custom of making written marriage contracts was probably not a sudden development. It may have begun with the production of documents, which were more like notes recording the marriage than formal contracts.

It is difficult to give any straightforward interpretation of developments in the making of marriage contracts during the fourteenth century, because the documents are few and varied in form and content. The contents of fifteenth-century marriage contracts produce a very different picture.

11 He held the parish of Laufáss and Grenjaðarstaðir at the time of Bishop Ólafur Rögnvaldsson, although Oddur had studied in "Paris in Germany" as it says in this document. DI IX, pp. 19-20.

12 DI III, pp. 616-17.

13 Compare to DI III, pp. 720-21, 756, where you can see, that the letter about the publication of marriage banns is separated from the letter of witnesses.

7.2 Property agreements and marriage according to the law of God. The evidence from the marriage contracts in the fifteenth century

From the period 1401-50 we have preserved 18 marriage contracts. The contracts reveal changes when compared to those of the fourteenth century. The contracts of the early fifteenth century were not only concerned with property, but also contained elements of the Christian formula for marriage. An example of this can be taken from a document from 1428, which was a declaration made by a husband that he had betrothed, *fastnað*, his wife in accordance with the law of God and the holy scripts. As a consequence of this all their children were declared to be legitimately born and the rightful heirs of the couple.[14]

A clearer example of this can be seen in the marriage contract made between Sigríður Björnsdóttir and Þorsteinn Ólafsson in Hvalsey in Greenland. They appear to have been married in 1408.[15] The need for a declaration about the marriage of Þorsteinn and Sigríður was probably greater because they were not living amongst their relatives in Skagafjörður. One of the documents that witness this marriage is a letter from one of the women's relatives, Sæmundur Oddson. In 1429, he testified that Þorsteinn took Sigríður to be his wife with the advice and the consent of himself, both by saying yes and performing a handshake to confirm the financial agreement.[16]

There are two points to notice with regard to this contract. First, the man married the woman with her consent as well as with the consent of her guardian. Secondly, the husband became betrothed to her according to the law of God and the holy Church and after the publication of the marriage banns. The first part is concerned with the agreement of the woman and her guardian, and the commitment of the man that was related to the ritual of *festar*. The second part, the publication of banns, was closely related to the ritual of the Church.

14 DI IV, p. 358.

15 Ibid., pp. 316-17. This is a copy from the original document from 1625, compare to other documents about this case in DI III, pp. 720-21, 756.

16 Ibid., p. 756. This contract was found in 1625 in the belongings of the male householder Árni Oddsson at Skálholt.

This illustrates how the marriage rituals came to be a mixture of both old and new customs.

Another change is found in the formula for making a marriage in a contract dating from 1434. The contract was publicised, *lýstur,* and confirmed, *staðfestur,* by two honourable men, *tueggia velborinna manna.* The persons involved were Ormur Loftsson and his wife, *eiginkuinnu hustru,* Solveig Þorleifsdóttir.[17] From this time onward it became more common for couples to make their own contracts, in the meaning to confirm it personally.[18] The focus is on the couple at the start of the contract, as can be seen in a contract from 1449, even if the rest of the contract is made according to the older form of making marriage contracts between two families.[19]

The statement that a marriage was made according to the law of God is normally found in almost all the contracts from this period. As an example we could mention a short contract from 1428 in which a husband declared that his wife had separate belongings. The betrothal had been made after the law of God and in accordance with the scripts of the Holy Fathers, and as a result all the children that would be born to this marriage should be legal heirs of the married couple.[20] No witnesses were named in the document, a fact which probably made the statement about the marriage having been made according to the law of God even more important. If there were witnesses to the contract, especially a priest as in contracts of 1433 and 1449,[21] they should guarantee that the contract was legally made. The ceremony of marriage, which was related to the law of God, did not need to be recorded in writing if there were enough witnesses to testify to the contract.

Another document, from 1429, gives the information that a man had got married with the consent of the parents of the bride, and with the publication of the marriage banns in church. It stated that the couple

17 DI IV, pp. 548-49.

18 See, for example, DI VI, pp. 92-93 a contract between Guðni Eyjólfsson and Guðrún Þorkelsdóttir.

19 DI V, p. 30. In this case the man had wealth with which to make an agreement with his wife, but it says only that her parents gave her property. It is her parents that decided what kind of agreement should be made.

20 DI IV, p. 358.

21 Ibid., p. 525, DI V, p. 30.

involved had been living together for ten years,[22] thus demonstrating the awareness among those involved of what made a marriage legal according to canon law and the law of the country. Consent in marriage was discussed in chapter 3, which concluded that the introduction of the need for the mutual consent of the couple meant that the consent of the couple as well as the parents became the norm. The evidence from preserved contracts confirms this very well. The need for the consent of the parents did not preclude young people from making their own marriage: thus it was with the consent of her mother that Oddfríður Aradóttir in 1433 chose to contract a marriage whereby she would have her own belongings, *málakona*.[23] As this example shows it was not always the case that women took a passive role in the making of contracts, although it was more common for the parents of the woman to decide whether she should have separate possessions or jointly-owned property.[24]

In 1434 Kristín Björnsdóttir arranged a marriage for her daughter and made a property agreement on her behalf. Three priests acted as witnesses to this contract as well as three laymen.[25] From this time onwards the group of witnesses almost always included one or more priests. In 1436 three priests and three laymen were witnesses at the marriage of Þorvarður Loftsson and Margrét Vigfúsdóttir.[26] The mother of the bride decided whether she should have separate belongings or not, and both the mother and her relatives retained the right to retrieve the lands that were involved in the agreement if the couple did not have children. The couple themselves had the central place in the contract, which was a document drawn up to describe an arrangement made between the two individuals. The same pattern can be found in a contract from 1446,[27]

22 DI IV, pp. 391-92. The problem in this case was that the man had been having affairs with other women. This document was a writ from the Bishop Jón Vilhjálmsson to two women, to come to the see of Hólar, because one had been living in adultery with this married man, while the other had been living with him secretly, before the marriage.

23 Ibid., p. 525.

24 As in the contract of 1449, when the parent chose that their daughter made a contract of joint possession to her husband to be. DI V, p. 30.

25 DI IV, pp. 548-49.

26 See ibid., pp. 562-63. The later chronicle of *Skarðsárannáll* tells that this marriage was made in 1433. *Annálar 1400-1800* bind I, pp. 57-58.

27 DI IV, pp. 673-74.

and in this instance too it was the mother of the bride that decided that her daughter should be a wife with her own possessions.

Thus the contracts of the early fifteenth century were not only concerned with financial arrangements. Elements of the sacred contract were also written down, and this was also the case in the contracts of the late fifteenth century. From the period 1451-1500 we have information about 39 marriages, coming mainly from two types of documents: marriage contracts and witnesses' letters stating that a legal marriage contract had been made. The custom of making a written marriage contract had been well established by this time, and when looking at the documents surviving from the whole fifteenth century the evidence for changes becomes even clearer. The changes are connected to a shift from the making of marriage as a property contract sealed by the handshake of two families to incorporate the handshake of the spouses as well. A contract from 1485 demonstrates this procedure for making a marriage. The contract starts by mentioning that the priest and other witnesses send their greetings and announce this event. It was the fathers of the bride and the bridegroom that made the contract, but the handshake, *handaband*, was made between all of the parties involved. The seals of those witnesses that made the document were added.[28] A contract from 1489 was also made in the same form, but in this instance the fathers are not partners in the arrangement. It was the bridegroom that bonds the bride "to be his legal wife with her consent according to the legal rule."[29]

Til kaups ok kuonarmundar is named in a contract from 1458,[30] which literally means to make an agreement and buy the wife with the brideprice. This sentence is again found in a contract from 1460.[31] This is evidence of the continuation of the old custom of marriage-making. This custom was primarily concerned with the property agreement, and even if the tradition of paying the *mundur* was no longer a legal requirement, the term continued to be used in the contracts. It is, however, very important to underline that in the written marriage contracts the

28 DI VI, pp. 547-49.

29 Ibid., pp. 648-49: "til logligrar eigenkonu med hennar iayrde ok lavgbokarenar ordvm sem þar til heyra."

30 DI V, pp. 171-72.

31 Ibid., pp. 205-206.

term did not have the same legal meaning as it had before, according to *Grágás*. In the contracts of the fifteenth century it was not the payment of *mundur*, but other formal criteria from canon law, which made the contracts legal.[32]

The documents related to marriage confirm that sometimes there were references to canon law.[33] These contracts were normally performed in the name of the law of God and the country.[34] This implied that the main criteria for a legal marriage had become compliance with the law of God, which included the mutual consent of the spouses as well as the parents, publication of the banns and the production of a written marriage contract. Marriage contracts thus became contracts made between husbands and wives, rather than between the couple's parents. This is the reason why it became essential to say that such a contract was consented to by the bride's parents as a guarantee that the closest kin favored the arrangement. The form of the contracts as well as the role of the priest in the making of the contracts, therefore, slowly changed the ritual.

At the end of the fifteenth century the making of marriage contracts had become more standardized than before, especially in the case of contracts for jointly-owned property.[35] It seems that during the late fifteenth century written contracts had become the norm, since less evidence has survived, than from the fourteenth century to indicate that oral contracts were made. The growing number of contracts from the sixteenth century also indicates this.[36] The number of surviving contracts from the first fifty years of that century is 66, while 65 contracts have survived from

32 Compare to the discussion her in chapter 3.2.1, especially p. 85. The discussion of the development of the exchange of marriage gifts will be discussed more in detail in chapter 10.

33 See for instance DI VII, p. 425. In 1499 the priest Böðvar Jónsson testified that the marriage of Bárður Jónsson and Sigríður Jónsdóttir had been legally made, and in this document he mentioned that the marriage had been made according to canon law.

34 See for intance DI IV, p. 495 from the year 1432: "fester ... med gudz logum ok landz ok æfter hæilagra fedra settningh". And DI V, p. 505, for the year 1467: "festi ... ad guds laugum med þeim ordum sem þar til heyrer."

35 An example can be taken from one contract from 1476. It is an agreement between a couple, recording the gift made by the father of the bride and with the acceptance of her mother. After this betrothal the man confirmed that the woman was to be his wife according to the law of God, using the words that were appropriate for betrothal. See DI, VI, pp. 92-93, especially p. 93.

36 See overview of all contracts in Appendix I.

the following fifty years.[37] Because of their high numbers it is possible to study contracts from the sixteenth century in a more thematic way.

7.3 *Financial and religious aspects in the fifteenth and sixteenth century*

As discussed in chapter 7.1 the oldest surviving marriage contracts from the fourteenth century were concerned exclusively with financial arrangements. The contracts of the fifteenth and sixteenth century continue to be very much concerned with the property agreement. An example can be taken from the contract of Finnbogi and Málfríður made in 1467. Málfríður's mother gave her to her future husband by way of a handshake, with her daughter Málfríður's consent. On the property agreement the contract states the following:

> This financial agreement, *fěkaup*, was made between the named persons. Finnbogi had all his wealth, which he had in both landed property and movable property, to make the agreement with Málfríður. He accounted this to be 400 hundred. Against this Málfríður had 200 hundred of her inheritance from her father to make the agreement. Finnbogi gave Málfríður 60 hundred in a countergift, and another 60 hundred in the gift of the bench, and those other gifts he wanted to give to her honor.[38]

No great change seems thus to have taken place on the economic level, called *fěkaup,* in the contracts of the fifteenth and sixteenth century. The contract from 1467 shows how both the old financial aspects and the new Christian values coexisted. The gifts given to do "honor" to the woman were related to the new definition of the role of the wife in marriage.

By the sixteenth century the idea of marriage as a Christian contract had started to be more central in the contracts. This becomes clear by studying the contracts from this period. Very soon after the Reformation

37 As already mentioned the relevant unpublished documents which have been identified within the AM collection have been examined, as well as the published documents from the *Alþingisbækur Íslands*, and some of the unpublished charters from the *Þjóðskjalasafn Íslands*. DI goes only as far as 1570.

38 DI V, pp. 509-10: "uar þetta fekaup greindra manna j milli. ath finboge hafde til kaups uid malfride alla þa peninga er hann atte j faustu ok lausu. fridu ok ofridu. reiknade hann þad fiogur hundrud hundrada. hier j mote hafde malfridur til (kaups) med finnboga tuau hundrud hundrada af sinum faudur arfi. gaf finboge malfride sextige hundrada j tilgiof ok annat sextige hundrada j beckiargiof ok þer adrar giafer sem hann uillde henne til heidurs giora."

PART 2

Fig. 15. *Festaröl* was an important drinking ritual which happened after a betrothal contract had been made. This picture shows a woman lying down with closed eyes, and another comes to her with a pitcher of beer. The text below the resting woman says, "I cannot drink any more". From late fifteenth century manuscript of *Jónsbók, Heynesbók AM 147 4to, Arnamagnæanske Institut,* Reykjavík.

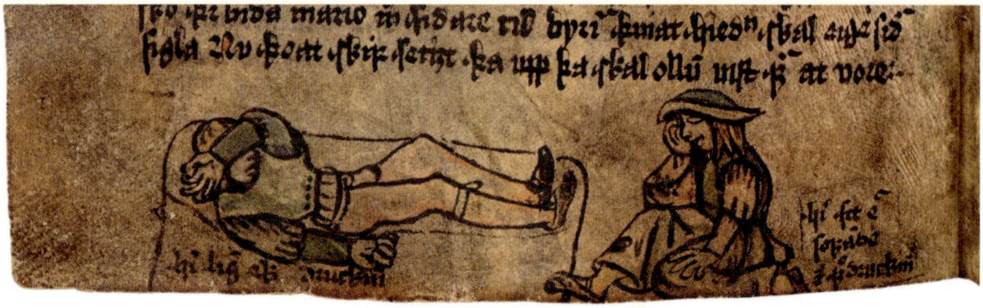

Fig. 16. This image shows two drunken men. The texts beside them say: "Here I am lying drunk", and "here I am sitting, asleep and dead drunk". From late fifteenth-century manuscript of *Jónsbók, Heynesbók AM 147 4to, Arnamagnæanske Institut*, Reykjavík.

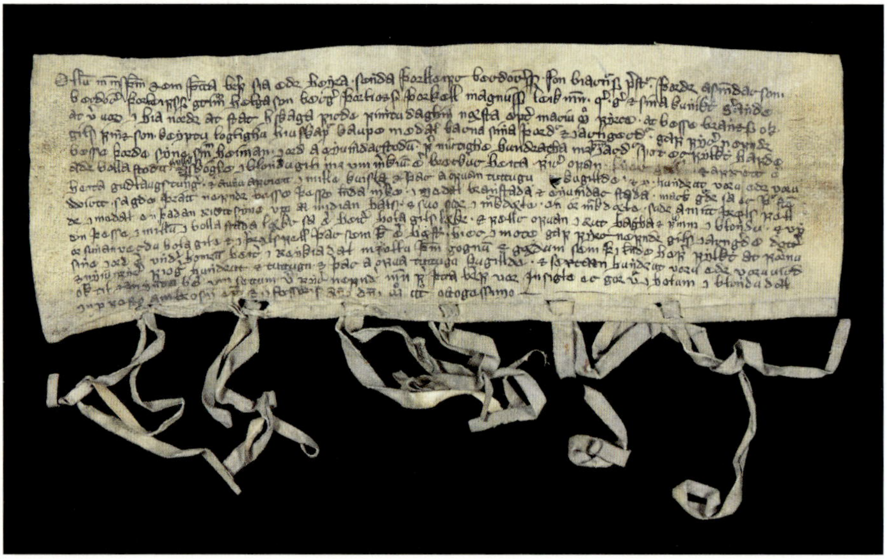

Fig. 17. Marriage contract of Þórður Bessason and Járngerður Gilsdóttir from 1380, shown here in the original version written on skin. *National Archives of Iceland,* Bps. B. 1. fasc. II, 1.

Fig. 18. Ring-shaped buckle from fifteenth- or sixteenth-century Iceland. This buckle is made of bronze and has the prayer Ave Maria written on the back. *National Museum of Iceland*. Þjms. 3464.

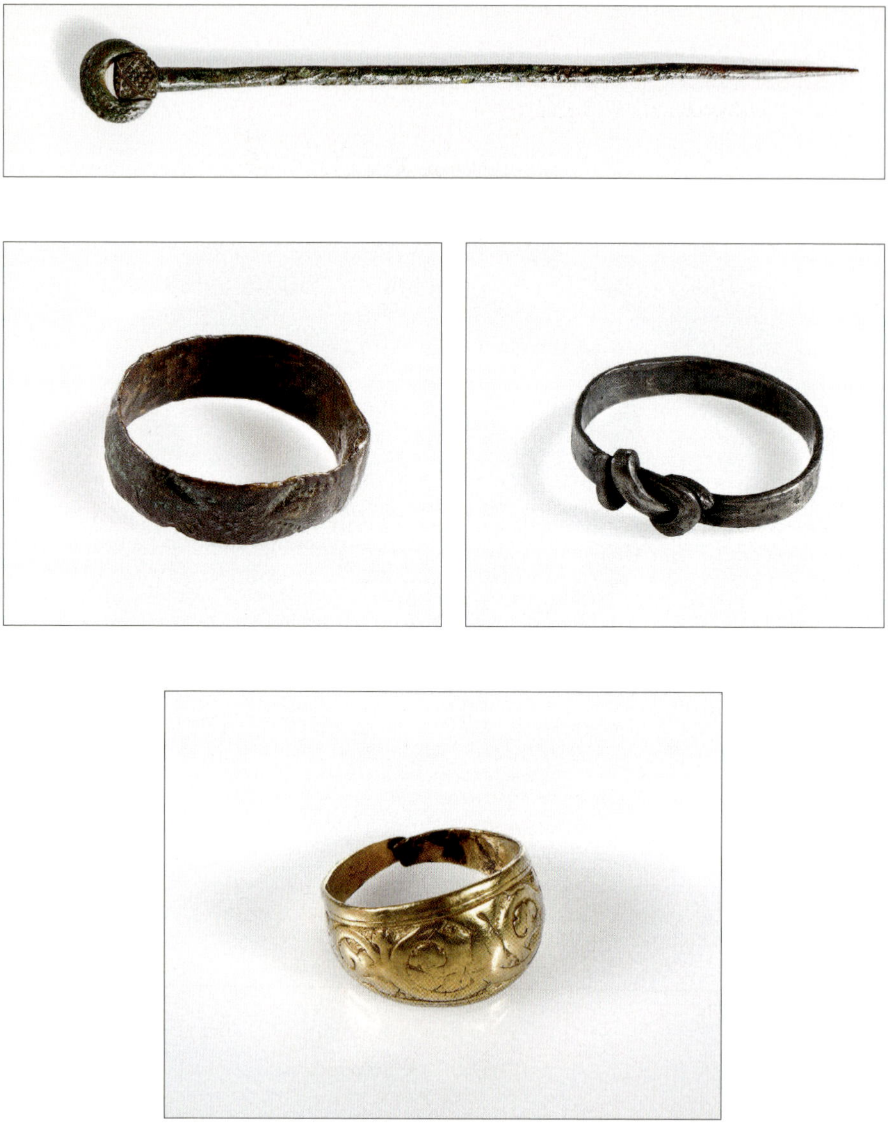

Fig. 19. Silver and gold rings found in Iceland from the tenth to the fifteenth century, and a bronze ringed pin with Celtic ornamentation. Bronze ringed pins were used as fasteners for clothes. The golden ring has recently been found in Reykholt, and it is a female ring from the fifteenth century. *National Museum of Iceland.* Þjms. 4144, 6720, 13098 C, 13681.

Fig. 20. This golden ring of medieval type was unearthed recently from a grave inside the cloister at Skriðuklaustur. *National Museum of Iceland.* Þjms. SKR 2008-36-895-4.

Fig. 21. Drinking horn from the fourteenth and fifteenth centuries, used to drink the toast of St. Martin. *National Museum of Iceland.* Þjms. 11007.

Fig. 22. The tapestry from Draflastaðir is an example of one of many outstanding tapestries with religious motifs from early sixteenth-century Iceland. *National Museum of Iceland*. Þjms. 3924, *Hlutavelta tímans,* p. 272.

Fig. 23. Embroidery, silk on linen, said to have belonged to Páll Jónsson. The embroidery, with a dense floral and foliage pattern, depicts animal and human figures in sixteenth-century costume. Close to one end is a shield, probably intended for embroidering a coat of arms. Not of Icelandic origin. *National Museum of Iceland.* Þjms. 5028.

Fig. 24. Renaissance-style chest from 1578 belonging to Páll Jónsson. The chest is decorated with the three principal virtues, Faith, Love and Justice. *National Museum of Iceland*. Þjms. 2461.

people became aware that changes had occurred in the making of marriage bonds. The marriage contract of the lawman Erlendur Þorvarðsson and Guðrún Jónsdóttir from 1541 can be used to illustrate this awareness. The contract ended with the words "then the lawman Erlendur made wedding feast and betrothed the mentioned Guðrún, according to the law and the old custom."[39] The "old custom" refers to the rules concerning marriage that had been followed ever since *Jónsbók* and the *réttarbætur* of the thirteenth and fourteenth centuries. But it was first after the changes of the Reformation that it became necessary to refer to this as an old custom.

Other documents reflect this knowledge of change as in a case about a marriage dispensation from 1542 in which the bishop declared that:

> because Jón Grímsson wants to seal his marriage with Þórunn Helgadóttir according to the law, and because they are related in the fourth degree, which is not any more a legal hindrance according to the law of God, or the acknowledged ordinances of the Church. Therefore I give the dispensation to this marriage to be made and confirm that it in all ways is legally declared.[40]

This case indicates knowledge of the change in marriage rules relating to the forbidden degrees of marriage. In the next part of the chapter the examination will further consider how the economic as well as the religious aspects of marriage contracts changed, by focusing especially on the role of the priests and the parents of the spouses.

7.3.1 The role of the priest

In order to demonstrate the role clerics could play in the making of marriage, the marriage of Ólafur and Vigdís from the late fifteenth century can be cited. First, we have a letter from the priest Gunnsteinn Ásgrímsson who testified to have been in the small sitting room on the

39 DI X, pp. 667-68, see especially: "giorde Ellendvr logman brvdlop. og festing til optt nefnd(r)ar gvdrvnar epter logvm og gomlvm vana."

40 Ibid., p. 703: "Sakir þess ad jon Grimsson vill binda sitt hionaband uid þorvni helgadottur epter laugum og af þui ad þar ero j mille fiormennings mægdir sem þo ero ecki lauglig hindran epter Gudz laugum ne laugtekinne kirkiunnar ordu. þa leyfi ec og tillæt ad þetta hionaband bindizt til samans og þad j allan mata lavgligt og fullmyndugt urskurda."

farm Skarð in Skarðsströnd during the visitation of Bishop Stefán. The priest asked what kind of advice the bishop would give about this marriage.[41] The problem was that Ólafur had not been completely obedient to the bishop. Therefore, the priest wanted the couple not to make their marriage agreement until after the visitation of the bishop.[42] Five days after the visitation, the marriage agreement of Ólafur and Vigdís was made at the farm in Ögur in Ísafjörður. The priest Gunnsteinn was one of the witnesses, but the agreement was not written down until 1496.[43]

As this case demonstrates the role of priests in controlling that marriage was made according to the rule of canon law was already getting stronger before the Reformation. They were no longer present merely to witness contracts as in the earlier agreements. There is evidence that the priest could be one of the main actors in the making of documents concerning marriage – such as, for example, a letter of witness from a priest concerning the publication of marriage banns from 1510 would indicate.[44] A document from 1540 is another example of this practice. It is a declaration from a priest who states that a man had betrothed a woman to be his legal wife "after my best knowledge according to the words of the book."[45] This was a role the priest could take as one of the witnesses, and it could mean that he was the one who should also "pronounce their property contract"[46] such as was the case in the marriage of Jón Sigurðsson and Margrét Eiríksdóttir in 1549. The letter that witnessed this marriage dates from 1564.[47]

One contract that provides good information about the role of the priests in the making of marriage contracts after the Reformation dates from 1548. It states:

41 DI VII, pp. 138-39.

42 Ibid., pp. 136-37. The marriage contract of the couple is printed in ibid., pp. 138-39.

43 The reason for this is probably that it had taken time to reach peace between Ólafur and the bishop. A declaration has survived from 1498 from the Bishop Stefán concerning the matter, see ibid., pp. 385-86, and also pp. 313-14. An oath from Vigdís has also survived concerning that no impediments existed between herself and Ólafur: DI VIII, p. 544. She also made an oath that she had not been having a sexual relationship with any other man than her husband: ibid., p. 545. Also a clerical judgement concerning this marriage exists, see ibid., pp. 506-09.

44 Ibid., p. 331.

45 DI X, pp. 546-47: "ad minv vite rett epter bockarenar ordvm."

46 DI XI, p. 720: "sagdi firir kaupi þeirra."

47 Ibid., pp. 719-20.

the priest Þorsteinn Hallsson made with them the whole legal agreement according to which legal marriage should be made by the law. [Then the husband] made the agreement with his wife and betrothed her with these words of legal betrothal: "I, Pétur Vigfússon, betroth you, Þóra Jónsdóttir, to be my legal wife, according to the law of God and the Holy Fathers' scripts, you are now my legal wife."[48]

The document says that after this the couple would make a contract of joint possessions, *helmingarfélag*. It is a testimony where the role of the priest seems to have shifted from being one of the witnesses, to being the person who made the contract. It says that the priest "made the whole contract."[49]

The first direct evidence of a priest marrying a couple after the Reformation can be found in the contract made between Þorvarður Björnsson and Guðrún Halldórsdóttir in 1552.[50] Another contract from 1553, between Torfi Þorsteinsson and Guðný Magnúsdóttir, is said to have been made on their wedding day, *giptingardeigi*, with a legal betrothal and the marrying of the couple, *festingu og hionavixlu*.[51]

Even if the role of the clerics in marrying couples became more prominent after the Reformation they could also continue to be members of the group of witnesses as well.[52] Thus, their role in marrying a couple did not exclude them from playing the role as a primary witness, *forsagnarvottur*.[53] A letter written by a priest from 1567 concerning the marriage of Eiríkur Böðvarsson and Guðrún Þórðardóttir is interesting in this context. It is a testimony from the priest who states that:

I made the legal contract between Eiríkur Böðvarsson and Guðrún Þórðardóttir, as I should do according to the law concerning marriage, which means that I made the agreement with them, and I married them to each other on their wedding day. But I was not

48 DI XII, pp. 119-20: "Siera Þorstein(n) Hallsson giordi med (þeim) allan lagagiorning epter þui sem riettum hionvm ber at hallda med logum. keypti hann sina konv og festi epter þui sem log utvisa med þessum logfestingarordum sem hier inne standa. Eg Petur Vigfusson festi þic Þora Jonsdotter mier til eiginkonv epter Gudz logum og heilagra fedra. setninge. nv ertu min loglig eiginkona."

49 Ibid., pp. 119-20: "giorde med (þeim) allan lagagiorning."

50 Ibid., pp. 467-68. See especially p. 468. He *festi*, betrothed, her to be "eiginkono epter laugbokarenar ordum sem þar til heyrer. Var þetta æ þeirra samuixludegi."

51 Ibid., p. 627.

52 An example can also be taken from a contract of 1567, see DI XIV. p. 575: One priest and two other men put their seal on the contract.

53 In a letter from 1554 the bishop is *forsagnarmadur*. See DI XII, p. 775.

nearby when they made the property agreement, and I do not know how it was made, but I have heard that it was *helmingarfélag*, but I never made it and neither have I given a testimony about their jointly-owned property, as far as I know or can remember.[54]

This testimony documents that there was a continuing need for written marriage contracts at the end of the sixteenth century, even if the priest had started to bless the couple.

7.3.2 The clerical entrance into holy matrimony

Many documents of the late sixteenth century concern priests who married the women they had been living with for a long time.[55] In some of these contracts it is stated that if it did not become acceptable for priests to get married, then they should have their children adopted, as had frequently been done before the Reformation.[56] The oldest document that has survived concerning the marriage of priests after the Reformation is from 1541. Bishop Gissur had given the priest Einar Árnason permission to marry Arndís Snorradóttir, in accordance with the Church ordinance of 1537/39 and the holy scripts.[57] This is recorded in a document written in Latin, which is not very common for Icelandic documents from the Late Middle Ages. It does not reflect any change in the religious content of the contract. The marriage contract of the Reformation Bishop, Gissur Einarsson, also exists and it has survived in two documents: a

54 DI XV, pp. 46-47. See especially p. 47: "ad jeg giordi þann lagagiorning med Eiriki Bodvarssyne og Gudruno Þordardotter som mier bar med løgum um þeirra hiönaband. sem er ad jeg keypti med þeim. og jeg vigde þau samann j þeirra brudlaupi. Enn um þeirra fielag var jeg hvørki hia. og Eige veit jeg hvørnin þad var lagt med fullum sannindum ad minu viti og minne. Enn heyrtt hefi jeg sagtt ad helmingafielag hafi verit lagtt med þeim. Enn það hefi jeg alldri giortt. og alldri hefi jeg frekar vitni um þeirra fielag borit ad minu viti og minni."

55 To mention just one example: *Festingar og kaupmálabréf* of the priest Þorleifur Björnsson and Ragnhildur Jónsdóttir has survived from 1543. See DI XI, pp. 193-94. The contract was made between them, with the consent of her parents.

56 DI XI, pp. 193-94. But as was discussed earlier the clerics had concubines, with whom they made financial agreements. In 1533 the son of Bishop Magnús Jónsson, who was a priest, gave Kristín Vigfúsdóttir til *fylgjulags*, "hundrað hundraða í sína fjórðungsgjöf og þær löggjafir sem hann mætti framast." See DI IX, pp. 682-84.

57 DI X., pp. 652-54.

kaupmálabréf[58] and a later *festingarbréf*.[59] The first deals with the land transferred, whereas the latter concern the consent to this marriage. This division between the religious and the financial elements of the contract seems to go back to the tradition of the fourteenth century mentioned earlier in this chapter. The difference here is that what before had only been orally declared was now also written down. This way of making written evidence for the whole religious and financial part of the marriage agreement was, however, not very common. Maybe this exception can be explained by the special awareness of the Reformation bishop, Gissur Einarsson, about the importance of written evidence.

In 1553 at Urðir in Svarfaðardalur the priest Steinn Ólafsson and Arnbjörg Brandsdóttir made their marriage contract. This was later testified in a document by Bishop Ólafur Hjaltason of Hólar in 1556.[60] This contract was made in accordance with:

> The law of God, the ordinance of the king and by the duty of the bishops between the priest Steinn Ólafsson and Arnbjörg Brandsdóttir who before had been his concubine and mother to his children against all the laws of God. He should get married to her, and by so doing make their children legitimate.[61]

It is interesting to look more closely at the formulae used in the cases in which priests got married. In a contract from 1555, *festingarbréf*, it says that the agreement was made at the farm called Hof in Vopnafjörður, and the witnesses were standing by, so that they saw and heard:

> with all the people from the household there, that the priest Finnbogi Tumason betrothed Þórunn Þórðardóttir with her consent and free will, holding her by the hand, speaking these words: I Finnbogi Tumason betroth you Þórunn Þórðardóttir to be my

58 DI XI, p. 257, from 9 September, 1543.

59 Ibid., pp. 259-60, from 7 October, 1543.

60 DI XII, pp. 619-21. See also, in general on the wives of the priests after the Reformation: Guðrún Ása Grímsdóttir 1996.

61 DI XII, p. 620: "guds logum. konglig maiestets ordinancio og uorre biskupligre skylldu j millvm sira Steins Olafssonar og Arnbiargar Brandzdottur sem adur hafdi verit hans frilla og barnamoder j moti ollum guds retti. skylldi hann giora eiginord til greindrar kuinnu. og giora þeirra born skilgetin." Another priest was married in 1554, see Ibid., p. 699. It was Gísli Jónsson who betrothed Kristín Eyjólfsdóttir to be his legal wife, after the law of God and by the permission of the "merciful king".

wife in accordance with the law of God and the Holy Fathers' scripts, and you are my legal wife after this.[62]

Another priest's marriage contract from 1555 was a contract concerning the financial transaction and stating that this had been done according to the law.[63]

Interesting material concerning the marriage of a priest and his concubine has survived in another document from 1555.[64] It is the *festingarbréf* of Þorlákur Hallgrímsson and Helga Jónsdóttir. The author of the document was Bishop Ólafur Hjaltason. He attended the visitation in Staður in Hrútafjörður, because:

after the command of the king and because of my poor priesthood, I ordered that the honorable person the priest Þorlákur Hallgrímsson should make the final betrothal and agreement with the honorable and humble woman Helga Jónsdóttir, so that the words of God would not suffer anything by his behavior and way of life as had been the case previously in the time of the popes. Rather he should follow the rules and orders which were given by our all merciful lord and king of this country and in accordance with the words from the order of God and the holy Gospels, that every cleric should be married.[65]

After this they were betrothed in accordance with the law and the holy scripts. This indicates that living with a concubine after the Reformation was suspected to indicate some kind of papal or Catholic heresy.[66]

Some of the marriage contracts made after the Reformation give information on the way in which priests had been living with women

62 DI XIII, pp. 89-90: "med ollu odru heimafolki Þar. Ath Sira Finbogi Tumason festi Þorunni Þordardottur, med hennar jayrdi og godan vilia. Haææedandi j hennar haund. Talandi Þessum ordum. Eg Finbogi Tumason festi Þig Þorun Þordardotter mier til eiginkono epter gudz lögum og heilagra fedra setningi. Og ertu min loglig eiginkona hiedan af."

63 Ibid., pp. 72-73.

64 Ibid., p. 81.

65 Ibid., p. 81: "epter konglig maiestets bijfalning og skipun oc mijns fatæka kalls og embættis vegna. skipadi ec og tilskylldadi ec þa heidarligu personu sera Þorlak Hallgrimson at giora sijna fullnadar festing og kaup vid þa heidurs fromu dandi kuinno Helgu Jonsdottur so at güdz ord hefdi ongua hneykning af hans framferdi og lijferni epter pauadomsins fornum hætti. helldur epter þui sem þa var innsett og skipad af vorum nadugasta herra og kongi j landit oc gudz orda skipun og heilagra gudzspialla. at huer eirn gudz orda þienari skylldi eigingijptar vera."

66 Another contract of marriage of a priest survives that was made on his wedding day in 1564. The Bishop Ólafur Hjaltason was the primary witness, *forsagnarvottur*, but also other persons witnessed the contract, both priests and laymen. See DI XIV, pp. 256-57.

before, especially that it was with the full acceptance of the parents of the women involved. In 1564 Páll Stígsson, the highest royal officer in Iceland, issued a judgement about the marriage of the priest Þorleifur Björnsson to Ragnhildur Jónsdóttir. According to the document Þorleifur Björnsson came to Páll and told him about the relationship between him and Ragnhildur Jónsdóttir, who had been taking care of him for many years. Then it continued:

> This woman was first given by her father and her mother into the power of the named priest, on the understanding that he promised that he would always keep her as if she had been his wife, and then later make a marriage with her once it was accepted in the country that priests were allowed to get married. But, for some years this woman committed the crime of having an affair with another man who was related to Þorleifur within the third degree.[67]

It was her parents who had placed her in the "power of Þorleifur if he promised always to keep her as his own wife."[68] This had taken place before the Reformation and it is said that she had served him during all the intervening years. After the Reformation the couple was finally able to get married.

The *festingarbréf* of Þorleifur and Ragnhildur made in 1565 says that he *festi hana epter laugbokarinnar ordum*, "he bonded her according to the words of the lawbook", in front of the church door at Reykhólar in Reykjanes. On this occasion the judgement of Páll Stígsson about the marriage permission was read aloud.[69] This indicates that the act of entering marriage was moving more away from the farms to the church. At the same time the priest should bless the couple in front of the church door.[70]

We can thus sum up by saying that there was some change in the social bonding through marriage because of the Reformation. Another

67 Ibid., pp. 277-78, "var þessi kona fyrst gefinn bædi af hennar faudur og modur j valld fyrr nefndz Sijra Þolleifs. þo med suoddann motj. ad hann skylldi ætijd j sijna daga vid hana hallda sou sem vid sijna eckttakonu og suo lika hionaband med hana binda. þa þad j landinu stadfest væri ad prestmenn sig giptta mættu. enn nockrum ärum forlidnum vard þessi kona brotlig vid þann mann sem ad var þrimininingur Sijra Þolleifs."

68 "i valld Sijra þolleifs. þo med suoddann motj ad hann skylldi ætijd j sijna daga vid hana hallda suo sem vid sijna eckttakonu."

69 Ibid., pp. 323-24, see especially p. 324.

70 DI XII, p. 439.

change was that these changes brought about by the Reformation were in many respects matters of formality rather than an actual change in their sexual life.[71] This formality did, however, change the status of women living with clerics, as well as the status of their children. They received permission to marry, even though the woman had previously lived with the priest. People related in the third degree were also permitted to marry. At the same time the marriage ceremony moved closer to the church building itself, and the couple to be married seem even to have taken their written property contract with them to the church.

7.3.3 *Parental control*

By the end of the sixteenth century the couple had come to take a more central place in the marriage contract, although at the same time the importance of parental consent was strongly underlined.[72] The marriage contracts of the first part of the sixteenth century are very different from those of the late fourteenth century. It is more common to find contracts from the sixteenth century that were made by the couple themselves.[73] An example can be taken from the *Festingarbréf* of the lawman Eggert Hannesson and Sesselía Jónsdóttir from 1559.[74] Two men, a priest and another witness, testified that they did not have any objection to the relationship. Then Eggert asked

> the named Sesselía, whether she would like to marry him, and she said yes, and so they shook hands and Eggert betrothed Sesselía with the words: I Eggert Hannesson

71 See discussion here on p. 125.

72 An example of parental consent is to be found in an agreement from 1552, which stressed the importance of the consent of both parents, see: DI XII, p. 439. Another *kaupmálabréf* from the early 17th century (1620) illustrates how strong the parental consensus was. It is a contract between Sveinn Símonarson on behalf of Magnús Gissurarson, and Þóra Bjarnadóttir on behalf of her daughter Þórkatla Bjarnadóttir. See AM. dipl. isl.fasc. LXI, 9.

73 Compare to the contract from 1529 between Þorsteinn Einarsson and Guðrún Bessadóttir. He betrothed himself to her, *festir sér til eiginkonu,* after they had had three children. DI IX, p. 499. Another contract from 1535 between Ormur Sturlason lögmaður and Þorbjörg Þorleifsdóttir is also an example of this, see ibid., pp. 739-40.

74 DI XIII, pp. 440-41. It seems that he was either marrying for the second time or that there was some concern about the woman's name, because a dispensation from the king has also survived by which Eggert gained permission to marry Steinunn Jónsdóttir, even if she had been found 'brotleg' because she had been living with Eggert's relative, Guðni Þormóðsson. See DI XIV, p. 76.

betroth you Sesselía Jónsdóttir to be my legal wife according to the law of God, and the country and the Holy Fathers' scriptss, and by this you are my legal wife as the priest Árni Steinólfsson, and you Arngrímur Björnsson will witness.[75]

In this case we see the continuing use of the old Christian formula, at the same time as the contract was also concerned with the financial arrangements. These two elements were combined in a contract from 1560 according to which a man made a legal marriage to his future wife after the old and good custom of the country and in accordance with the law.[76] By this time the word *gifta* meant to get married, rather than meaning that a woman was given away.[77] This new meaning of the word was related not only to the changing understanding of marriage as mentioned before, but also to changes in social bonding.

The parents continued to give consent to the marriage of their children.[78] When marriage became a contract between a future husband and wife, the consent of the parents gained even greater importance than before as a guarantee of the elements of the agreement that were concerned with property.[79] The need for the consent of the parents was greater for the parents of the bride than for the parents of the groom. This was related to the fact that the husband's role in the making of the marital contract was generally more active than the wife's,[80] and the bride continued to be more dependent on her relatives than the bridegroom was.

75 DI XIII, pp. 440-41. See especially page 441: "greinda Sesseliu huortt ad henne være vilugtt ad eiga sig. en hun ja sagdi. med þad toku þau þa hondum saman. og feste þratt nefndur Eggertt … Sesseliu … med suo felldum ordum sem hier epp er seiger. Eg Eggertt Hannesson feste þig Sesseliu Jonsdotter meir til loglegrar eiginkonu. eppter gudz logum og landz og heilagra fedra settningi og erttu min logleg eiginkona hiedan aff ad vittne þinu sera Are Steinolbsson og þinu Arngrimur Biornsson."

76 Ibid., pp. 530-31.

77 DI XI, p. 113, in a copy from 1666 of a short *ágrip af kaupmáli* from 1533. It was Jón Ólafsson that *giftist* Þóra Björnsdóttir. It is possible that this has more to do with the more common use of the word in 1666 than in 1533, but at least it indicates a change in the use of the word.

78 Ibid., p. 305. In 1505 an agreement was made between a woman's parents on the one hand, and the couple on the other. It says that the future husband made an agreement with her parents with regard to the dowry. See DI VII, p. 755. This document was not made until 19 years later, in 1524. There exists more written evidence about parents giving their daughters' property before marriage. See for instance DI X, p. 497. This is a document that states that in 1539 a father gave his daughter property to *giftumála*.

79 Ibid., pp. 421-22: In 1539 a future husband went to make a marriage agreement with the future bride with the parents' consent.

80 See for instance DI X, pp. 331-32. In 1537 another contract, also made between the couple themselves, stated that the man contributed property both to *kaups* and *kuonarmundar*, to the financial agreement and the brideprice, while the father of the bride gave her to the husband. And in DI XI, p. 739 it is stated that

Documents related to the marriage of Helga Aradóttir and Páll Jónsson in 1558 show, however, that it was possible to seek permission to marry from other relatives even if one's guardian did not approve the marriage.[81] Þorleifur Grímsson, the grandfather of the bride on her mother's side and her rightful guardian, had given his acceptance in a written document, "even if he did not now want to have anything to do with the case."[82] But men of honor and the priest said that the woman could get married because she had the consent of other relatives.

This is why Helga Aradóttir had asked her grandmother, Helga Sigurðardóttir, and the sister of her father, Þórunn Jónsdóttir, as well as the brother of her father, the priest Sigurður Jónsson, to consent that Helga Aradóttir really wanted to be the wife of Páll Jónsson.[83]

It seems as if her grandfather Þorleifur had changed his mind about this marriage. The marriage is documented in another letter from January 1558. This was a letter of witness from four priests and five laymen who declared that the priest Sigurður Jónsson (the brother of Helga's father) was her guardian, since Þorleifur had previously accepted the marriage, even if he had not been present at the right place at the appropriate time to complete the contract.

This document contains valuable information concerning the general nature of marriage. It was the guardian who asked for advice from the witnesses:

He said that he thought this marriage was not as optimal as he wished and it was therefore necessary to be certain that the woman would not lose her honor by marrying a

in 1549 Örnólfur Jónsson and Steinunn Ólafsdóttir made a marriage contract in which it was said that he had *til kaups og kvonarmundar*, a quantity of wealth to get her.

81 DI XIII, pp. 127-28, 270-73, 278-81.

82 Ibid., p. 271: "þö ad Þorleifur vilie nu ei nærri vera."

83 Ibid.: "þui hefdi hun Helga Aradotter nu um bedit sijna faudurmodur. Helgu Sigurðardotter. og sijna faudursystur Þorunni Jönzdottir. og suo sinn faudir Brödur Sira Sigurd Jonsson. at samþyckiast sijnum wilia. og ad optnefndri Helgu Aradottir væri þad til fullkomligs wilia. ad eiga Päl Jonsson."

man of lower rank. He told us that the man who wanted to marry her was from a high ranking family, and that he was wealthy and a gentleman.[84]

The consent of the woman to this match was also emphasized to make it clear that the marriage was without any hindrance and would be between two equal partners.[85] This couple was judged to have been legally married, but the case also shows that women could rely on different relatives, something which is characteristic of the bilateral family structure.

In a marriage contract from 1562 the bride's guardian, *giftingarmaður*, was her mother.[86] Both parents could perform the handshake to confirm the marriage agreements of their children. This was related to a strengthening of the wife's position in consenting to all kinds of property agreement, although the emphasis placed on paternal consent remained stronger than on maternal consent.[87] When we do find both the man's and the woman's parents consenting to marriage it was often in cases in which both of them had given property to their children. If this was the case it usually had to do with the kind of contract which had been made concerning the parents' marriage.

The control of marriage in the Late Middle Ages should thus be viewed in terms of parental control rather than paternal control. This was true of the control of both sons and daughters. The practice of parental control is widely evident in the earlier documents. A document from 1281 lists the reasons that a father could use to disinherit his son.[88] A document from 1479 describes how a mother agreed to her daughter marrying a man to whom she was related in the fourth degree, as long as she received a dispensation from the clerical authorities.[89] Another example, from 1483, involved parents who did not agree to their daughter getting married because she had chosen a potential husband without their consent. In this case the parents forgave their daughter and accepted her

84 DI XIII, p. 279: "ad honum þætti hennar räd med spiöllum fara. og þui naudsyn vera ad hun væri ej fijrd sijnu jafnrædi og sæmd. sagdi hann oss ad hennar villdi fa til ektaskapar [og eigenordz] eirn velborenn. fiadur og forsöktur heidarlegur dandess sveirn."

85 Ibid., p. 280.

86 DI XIV, p. 15.

87 See the discussion in chapter 4 of the *réttarbót* of 1294 and further discussion in chapter 10 about practice.

88 DI II, pp. 234-35.

89 DI VI, p. 182. Ólöf Loftsdóttir to Solveig and Páll, compare to the discussion on p. 188.

into their family again, which probably meant that she was confirmed as their heir once more.[90]

A further example can be taken from 1487, when Bishop Magnús of Skálholt gave his sister landed property and agreed that she could give it to her son as long as he got married with the consent of his mother and the bishop, as well as his father.[91] It is clear that this parental authority or, seen more generally, the right of family members to control the transfer of property through marriage was not perceived to be in conflict with the ecclesiastical authority.

A personal letter from Bishop Gissur Einarsson to Guðrún Björnsdóttir in the autumn of 1544 will be mentioned here at the end, as final evidence of the strong parental control over marriage. The bishop had sent his nephew Þorlákur to the farm at Núpur in the district of Vestfirðir to his newly wedded wife, Guðrún Hannesdóttir, a daughter of Guðrún Björnsdóttir. The letter written by Gissur himself was sent with his nephew and his follower. It is evidence of the strong ties between the guardian of the bridegroom and the mother of the bride.

> A letter written to be taken along with Þorlákur. I send you my friendly and loving greetings, great thanks for all the goods things you have done for me, both in words and in deeds. I will hereby make it known to you, my dear friend, that I now send to you westward in the country, my nephew Þorlákur Einarsson, in accordance with the marriage contract that has been made between him and your daughter, and you has written to me about.[92]

The letter continues by saying that he hoped the bridegroom would reach her farm in time. Then Gissur continues: "I should myself personally have gone with him, according to your wishes,"[93] but the bishop had unfortunately not been able to do so, and instead wrote her a letter,

90 Ibid., p. 475.

91 Ibid., pp. 604-605. See also DI X, pp. 68-69 a case about a person who received a gift from his grandfather, but his grandmother did not give her consent to it.

92 DI XI, pp. 364-65: "Sendibref uestur skrifat med Þorlake. Vinsamlig og kærlig heilsan sie ydur allan tid af mier til send. Þackar eg ydur mikilliga fyrir allt hid goda, sem þier hafit mier sýnt. med ord oj uverk. Kunngiori eg ydur kiæra uinkona ad ec sendi nu uestur til yduar Þorlak Einarsson frænda minn. epter þui sem at kaupmali hefu j mille hans og dottur yduar giordur uerit. og þier hafit mier til skrifat."

93 Ibid., p. 365: "skylldi eg sialfur personuliga þessa ferd farid hafa epter yðuari bon."

which symbolized very well the personal relationship and commitments between the mother of the bride and the guardian of the bridegroom.

7.4 *Conclusion*

The evidence of marriage contracts from the fourteenth century is too sparse to allow us to say anything about general patterns in marriage contract making during this period. The sources indicate, though, that contracts were not made by the couple themselves, but rather that the agreement was made between the fathers. However, this cannot be used as evidence that the Christian element in marriage agreements was not accepted. All the contracts from the fourteenth century deal with the property agreement, but not with the personal commitment established between the couple according to the law of God. There is no evidence that commitments of this sort were recorded in writing in this century. As the contracts from 1380 and 1381 show, it was the fathers of future couples, or their fathers and brothers, who made the agreement. The contracts were made by the relatives of the couple rather than the couple themselves. Thus, these contracts represent the former understanding of marriage agreements as property arrangements made between two families.

Whereas the marriage contracts from the fourteenth century still reflected the old tradition of marriage-making, the sources from the next century indicate significant changes in the making of these contracts. The couple took the central place in the contracts of the fifteenth century, even if parental control was also strong. The mutual consent of the spouses symbolized their personal commitments to each other and to God. The change in the contracts from the early fifteenth century which becomes evident when they are compared to those from the fourteenth century is also interesting in relation to the developments in marriage regulation and the law courts' treatment of marriage cases which were described in chapters 4 and 5. It is in the fifteenth century that the first written evidence can be found of a greater understanding and acceptance of Christian norms related to marriage matters.

In conclusion it can be said that there were different ways of making marriage contracts during the sixteenth century, but that all contracts contained financial commitments. Sometimes elements from the Christian liturgy are evident within financial contracts, and in other instances two separate agreements were made, although the one stating that the marriage had been made according to the rules of God was not always written down. In some cases it was merely stated that a contract had been made according to the law of God, or that the marriage banns had been published. This should have been enough to provide a guarantee that the marriage was legally made. Also in this century written contracts were, however, more concerned with financial arrangements than with the religious aspects of marriage. After the Reformation it became more common for the Christian part of the ritual to be recorded first, followed by the property contract, although the praxis continued that the religious element eventually could just be oral. The role of priests became more prominent and after the Reformation they were allowed to marry, although before this time many of them had *fylgikonur*, concubines, and had even made written contracts with them.

To be able to reach a better understanding of some of the elements of the role of the Church in changing the marriage bonds to include not only the social element, but also the religious bonds, I shall further examine in the last chapter of this second part of the book, how some aspects of the sacred contract became realized.

CHAPTER 8

The making of holy bonds and human bonds

During the medieval period the Christian liturgy had been added to the old kin-based family contract in Iceland. In an order from Bishop Árni in 1281 it was implied that there were two types of marital bond, one called "the holy bond" and the other "the human bond." The bishop explained it as follows: because holy matrimony is made by God himself, but other agreements and bonds are made by human beings, it is important to be sure that a marriage is legally made, for instance that the couple are not related. Although the rules about getting married are made by human beings, God creates the marriage itself.[1]

This chapter will analyse more closely how changes in the content of the marriage contract can be understood in relation to changes in social binding. A court case from 1574 dealing with the marriage of Þorkell and Halldóra illustrates this problem. The couple said that they had made an agreement and had shaken hands in the presence of witnesses.[2] But it was questioned whether this was a legal marriage or not. The conclusion was:

> It is written in our law book: All cases settled by handshaking shall be held, as the witnesses know them to have been agreed on. It thus appears to us that this engagement cannot be broken by anybody but the guardian of Halldóra.[3]

1 DI II, pp. 210-11. See especially p. 210: "Nv af því at heilagr hiuskapr bindz saman af guði sialfum en önnur kaup ok bönd sem menn gera sin j millum bindaz af þeim sialfum."

2 *Bréfabók Guðbrands byskups Þorlákssonar*, p. 71: "giort sijn ää milli med handsolum. vottum hiaverondum."

3 Ibid., "Nu stendur suo j vorri landslagarbok. aull handsaulud maal skulu halldast sem vottar vito eda vid er geingid etc. þuj virtist oss þessa þeirra trulofun einginn riufa mega. vtan giptingarmadur nefndrar Halldoru."

The old traditions for making marriage contracts were kept alive, but by the end of the sixteenth century *handsöl* (making the agreement by handshake) could not by itself make a marriage valid. As this case from 1574 indicates, Þorkell was obliged to *fullgjöra sitt lögliga hionaband*, make a fully legal marriage with that woman, in accordance with the wishes of the bride's family.[4] As was discussed in the first part of this book in the thirteenth and fourteenth centuries people could make a marriage contract without much clerical interference, although they could not declare themselves married without the publication of the marriage banns in church. By the end of the sixteenth century, marriage was no longer a contract that people could simply make on their own without the interference of the clerics.[5]

This change, that can also be explained on the level of change in social bonding, probably reflects the shift away from the older idea of marriage as a family contract sealed by *handaband*, a handshake between members of the two families, towards the concept of marriage as the joining of two individuals, *hjónaband*, in a sacramental union. The spouses came to be joined in a personal union, and not by a contract that had its main roots in the transfer of wealth and property rights between two families.

To begin with, this chapter will take a closer look at the bonds made by marriage. It will show that Christian symbols came to have a central role in the marriage ceremony. These sacred rituals acted as a medium for communicating the religions aspect of marriage. The second part of the chapter will study this communication as well as explain the consequences it had for the understanding of the relation between the couple. The third part of the chapter treats more specifically how the late medieval marriage agreement, compared to the older marriage agreement, was based more on the personal relationship between husband and wife. This section also adresses the question of whether this new form of gender relations also resulted in a new gender identity.

4 Ibid., pp. 70-71.

5 Compare also to *Alþingisbækur Íslands* I, p. 341. In this judgement from 1577, a marriage was judged illegal because no legal agreement had been made. One of the problems was that only one layman had witnessed the agreement, but no priest.

8.1 Change in terminology – change in bonding agreements?

According to the oldest law in *Grágás* the contract of *festar* was made between male members of the two families involved.[6] On this formal level, men dominated the making of such a contract. The marriage contracts and related source material from the Late Middle Ages imply that it was the man who proposed to the woman or discussed the prospects for marriage with her parents.[7] This was related to the practice of making general agreements or transactions relating to wealth through the ritual of *handaband*.[8] Normally this *handaband* was made by the woman's guardian and by either the future husband himself or his father.[9]

As mentioned previously, another name for *handaband* was *handsöl*, which means to sell by handshake. This term could also be used for making marriage contracts. A man promised to marry a woman in 1595 *med handsölum*.[10] The expression *handzalzöl* is also found in a document from 1592.[11] This agreement combined two rituals, the handshake and the drinking of beer after making an agreement.[12] The word *handaband* also appears in Norwegian marriage contracts from the Late Middle Ages,[13] and Icelandic sources also use the term *hiuskapar handsal*, literary meaning handshaking the agreement of marriage.[14]

6 *Grágás* II, p. 162.

7 DI VI, p. 746: A witness letter from 24 April 1491 gives information about a man who "reid til at bidia Steinunar gunarsdottur." See also Agnes S. Arnórsdóttir 1995, pp. 130-39 concerning the tradition in the twelfth and thirteenth centuries.

8 See *Jónsbók*, p. 281: "Með handsölum skal jarðir byggja ok svá í borgan ganga." Compare to DI II, pp. 282-88, *Réttarbót* from King Eiríkur 1294, see especially p. 283: "Meðr handsolum skal iarðir byggia oc i börgan ganga." See also this same law printed in *Lovsamling for Island* I, p. 17. More generally about making a formal contract, see also Iuul 1959a, pp. 487-91.

9 In the *réttarbót* of 1294 the custom of the handshake is referred to. This is a statement that the custom of the handshake should be performed when people bought or sold landed property. The *réttarbót* as a whole is mostly concerned with agriculture and farming matters, but matters dealing with the transfer of property and marriage regulation are also mentioned.

10 *Alþingisbækur Íslands* III, year 1595, p. 5. The couple in this case was Björn Björnsson and Valgerður Jónsdóttir, but then he did not want to keep his promise.

11 Ibid., p. 20.

12 Ibid. This agreement, which is discussed in chapter 4, was made by the priest Jón Loptsson in Vatnsfjörður. According to a local witness the priest had lost his wife in the winter of 1592. Afterwards he made an agreement of his own with another woman, and drank *handzalzøl* with her.

13 DN XII, p. 38: "er þetta kaupmale … oc handaband þeirra at Ellendir seldi Vigdisi xj mata boll." See also Fritzner I, *handaband* references to DN concerning the more general use of the ritual of making agreements.

14 DI IX, p. 131, from the year 1523. Here this term *hiuskap* is used with a reference to a statute from the archbishop. Normally this term is not used in the sixteenth century for marriage. The term *hjónaband* had become the common one.

Thus, the old terms taken from the oral tradition continued to be used for legitimating the late medieval marriage contracts.[15] The old practice was used as a basis for the new Christian contract, but the handshake between the men no longer continued, as this was replaced by the handshake between the bride and the bridegroom. The *New Christian Law* states: "The one who will become betrothed to a virgin or a woman shall hold her by the hand, name two witnesses or more, and say these words [of betrothal]."[16] This picture is beautifully symbolised in ring-shaped buckles from both Norway and Denmark made in the fourteenth century and in a Danish engagement ring from the sixteenth century.[17] The ring-shaped buckle was used by both men and women to close a neck opening or to fasten a belt. A pair of joined hands was a popular motif during the Middle Ages, symbolizing the handshake of betrothal and marriage. The words 'Ave Maria' often accompanied the motif (see Figures 18 and 32). The same ornamentation is found on the Danish engagement ring from the sixteenth century. The hands are joined around a heart. This ring symbolised both the everlasting contract, and that the husband and the wife were bound together forever by their *handaband*.

A wedding ring was a symbol (*signum*) of the marriage, a symbol of the union of two individuals. According to Lisa M. Bitel's study, one late Irish *vita* refers to a wedding ring worn by a wife.[18] In the ninth century, Pope Nicholas I referred to the wedding ring, given by the groom to his bride and accepted by her, as a pledge of their fidelity.[19] And a wedding

15 *Handaband* was also used when women either gave or sold property. An example of this was when Solveig Þorsteinsdóttir gave half of Vatnsfjörður to her daughter, and the daughter's son with the consent of her mother Kristín Björnsdóttir, and her consent was confirmed by the handshake. DI IV, pp. 529-30.

16 NgL V, p. 37: "þa scal sa hallda i hönd meyiu eða kono sem ser scal hana festa. oc nefna vatta tva eða fleiri. oc mæla þessor orð."

17 See *Margrete I. Regent of the North* 1997, p. 339, ring-shaped buckle no. 151, and p. 397, ring brooch, no. 295. These are from The National Museum of Copenhagen and the Museum in Bergen. The ring is also to be found in the National Museum of Copenhagen: "Trolovelsesring med hænder foldet omkring et hjerte". Dated to the sixteenth century and found in 1894 in Aalborg. See also the front cover of this book.

18 Bitel 1996, p. 44. She referred to Plummer, *Vitae* 2:78, and Máirín O. Daly, translation of *Cath Maige Mucrama,* (Dublin 1975), p. 66-67 for the exchange between Art Mac Cuinn and the daugther of Olc Aiche.

19 Michael Sheehan has written an article about the ritual of marriage, which analyses the letter of Pope Nicholas in detail. This article is reprinted in Sheehan 1991, pp. 278-291. See here, of particular importance, note 32 on p. 287. "As the ritual of marriage assumed form in northwest Europe during the eleventh century, the ceremonies of ring and endowment ceased to be associated with betrothal and became part of the marriage ceremonies at the door of and in the Church."

ring is also known from a law in the Visigothic law code under the rubric *De non revocandis datis arias,* which determines that once a couple has become betrothed and a ring has been conferred, the promise of marriage was binding unless it was dissolved by mutual consent.[20] According to Isidore of Sevilla, a ring was given from the husband to his wife as a sign of faith and as a token that their hearts were joined together. This ring was placed on the fourth finger, because a vein from there runs directly to the heart.[21]

Marriage rings were not in common use in medieval Iceland, judging from how seldom the documents mention them. *Fingurgull* is mentioned though in literary sources from Iceland.[22] The word *festargull* occurs seldom in the *Diplomatarium Islandicum.* A document from 1481 mentions that Loftur Ormsson had given his wife Gunnhildur the morning gift and the *bekkjargjöf,* gift of the bench, as her *festargull.*[23] It does not necessarily mean a golden ring, and could also refer to gold in other forms.[24] There is thus little evidence in Icelandic written sources that rings were given as marriage gifts except that a ring is mentioned in the Christian formula of marriage from 1300.[25] Recent excavations in Iceland have resulted in new finds of both engagement and other golden rings for females, (see Figures 19 and 20) and some information concerning *fingrgull* can also be found in written sources from Norway. The first such evidence dates from a charter from 1341.[26] Gold or a golden ring given as *festarfé* is also mentioned in Norwegian charters, as one from 1355 demonstrates.[27] Even if engagement rings were not commonly used in Iceland, they did exist, and rings were given in Norway, which allows us to use the symbolic

20 Reynolds 1994, p. 79.

21 Here, after ibid., p. 92.

22 AM ordbog: with a reference to *Ólafs saga Tryggvasonar,* p. 108, no. 18. In the story of King Ólafur Tryggvason it says: "small gold for your finger will I give you, Appollanius, that my father gave to my mother as *festarfě."* He sent the queen a ring that looked like gold, and it was called *festarfě.*

23 DI VI, pp. 347-48.

24 Magnús Már Lárusson 1959a, p. 240.

25 DI II, pp. 328-29, see especially p. 329: "Mæðr þæsso fingr gulli festi ek þic. ok þætta sýllfr gef ek þer ok með mer siallfum söme ek þic ok sva længgi sem mit lifum skal ek þic hallda með guðs hiolpp ok miskun."

26 DN I, p. 220. This is a testimony about a betrothal from the priest Arne in the church of Mary in Bergen. According to the document the bridegroom gave the bride the gold and thereafter he kissed her. Then it is said that the priest saw the bride leave this meeting "as happy as when she came", which should probably be the guarantee for her free consent to the contract. See also *Regesta Norvegica* V, 1979, p. 187.

27 DN XI, p. 46.

meaning of that gift to obtain a better understanding of the context of the sacred contract. The ring signifies something that cannot be broken. The new rule of marriage described in the *New Christian Law* did the same. It was the handshake of the bride and the bridegroom that mattered, a handshake symbolizing the entry into lifelong matrimony.

The term *hjúskapur*, the old term of marriage, was very much related to the kind of marriage we know from *Grágás*, which could be broken.[28] The contracts from the sixteenth century indicate that the word *hjónaband* instead of the older *hjúskapur*, was by this stage used more commonly.[29] It can be used as evidence that some terminological change occurred over time. The changes can be related to the idea of engagement, *trúlofun*, the promise of a bond between the couple, *hjón*. The bond received the name *hjónaband*, based on the promise of being faithful to each other and to God.

This change both in the terminology as well as in the meaning of marriage can also be found in regard to which persons made the contract. In the written marriage contracts of the Late Middle Ages, the woman was much more prominent than in the older formulae.[30] This was in part a consequence of the changes involved in making the agreement. The agreement was now a contract between the husband, the wife, and God, whereas before – according to the oral contract – the agreement had usually been between the husband and the father of the bride.

In all the Nordic law codes, except the Danish, the rituals associated with entering marriage were important, and one element of the custom related to the handshake as it is found in *Grágás* was the payment of *mundur* by the man.[31] As discussed in the last chapter, the contract continued to be made according to this rule during the fourteenth century,

28 *Grágás* 1992, *atriðisorðaskrá*, p. 535. *Hjúskapr* was another word for marriage in addition to the word *hjónaband*. But the word *hjón* or *hjú* could also mean servant, or all the members of the household. In *Grágás* we find the expression *hjú tvö*, referring only to a couple. The term *hjónaband* was never used to describe a wider group or the household.

29 For instance DI XII, pp. 103, 439, 535. Compare to Fritzner I, p. 834, *hjúskapr*, see also *hjúskaparband*, p. 833 which are found in the *New Christian Law* of Bishop Árni.

30 Many of the marriage contracts of the Late Middle Ages show that the bride took part in the making of the agreement. This was a new role; compare to the older marriage tradition in *Grágás*. See here *Grágás* II, p. 156, where only the widow has a special juridical position. Again, in the marriage contracts from the Late Middle Ages the wife has a similar, clearly legally defined position.

31 Iuul 1959a, pp. 486-87.

even if the payment of *mundur* had been removed from the formula. This illustrates well how closely people in the fourteenth century related marriage agreements to other kinds of agreements concerning property transfer, rather than interpreting marriage as a sacrament.[32] Another example showing how closely people of the fourteenth century generally related marriage agreements to agreements about property transmission is that at the beginning of the fourteenth century, the word *kaupmála-bréf* was used for marriage contracts as well as for ordinary contracts of property transfer called *kaupbréf*.[33] By the end of the sixteenth century, however, the word *kaupmáli* does not appear to have been used to describe the general transmission of landed property. This indicates that by the end of the sixteenth century property transmission through marriage was seen as something different from other types of property transfer. It must be related to the fact that marriage agreements were no longer only concerned with property and alliances between families. The contract of *hjónaband* between wife and husband, by which she put her hand in his and they were joined together had become a reality.[34]

8.2 The sacred marriage

It has been indicated above that even if all the marriage documents from the fourteenth century were concerned only with property agreements, this does not mean that marriage had no sacred meaning.[35] The religious meaning of marriage was not necessarily something that would be documented in marriage contracts. In David D'Avray's introduction to his work on *Medieval Marriage Sermons,* it is underlined how marriage sermons were often delivered by notaries rather than priests. In

32 Compare to the ancient tradtion of understanding *familia* in relation to property, see Herlihy 1995, pp. 117-18.

33 Compare to DI III, pp. 65-66 in 1352, which is an agreement made between two men about the transfer of landed property. This agreement is called *kaupmalabref.* Other examples of this meaning of the word from the fourteenth century are: from the year 1332, DI II, pp. 673-74, from the year 1360, DI III, pp. 142-44, compare also to the year 1372, ibid., pp. 274-75, the year 1377, ibid., pp. 315-16, and the year 1378, ibid., pp. 331-32.

34 DI VIII, p. 813.

35 On the development and the meaning of the term "sacred marriage" especially during the Early Middle Ages, see Reynolds 1994, p. 413. First in the High Middle Ages it became one of the seven sacraments. Earlier theologians used the word *sacramentum* to express the especially holy nature of marriage.

addition, it was very common for friars to preach marriage sermons. These sermons were often more concerned with marriage as a metaphor or symbol, although such preaching could also be related to marriage practice.[36] Little is known or written about preaching in Iceland during the fourteenth century. But, as mentioned in earlier chapters, Icelandic clerics actively tried to change the sexual behavior of the Icelanders, and preaching with this purpose in mind was used as early as the late twelfth century.[37] Even if we do not have many written sources about clerical preaching, there exist some other sources that can give information about the sacred rituals of marriage. Here we shall study these rituals closer.

8.2.1 The bed and the bride

One of the conditions for a valid marriage in *Grágás* was that the couple went to bed in the daylight and with six witnesses present.[38] This custom was also practiced in other regions of Europe. One example can be taken from the sixth century Gaul, where a priest imparted a nuptial blessing while the newly-wed couple lay in the marriage bed.[39] Wedding rituals differed from place to place, but the blessing of the bedchamber also took place in England in the High Middle Ages. On the wedding night, when the bridegroom and bride had gone to bed, the priest was supposed to approach and bless the bedchamber and the couple.[40] The custom of couples going to bed in the presence of witnesses was thus not uncommon in different regions of Europe during the Middle Ages.[41] Whether the priest became part of this ritual in Iceland is uncertain.[42] However, we do have more evidence concerning the bedding ritual from late medieval Icelandic wedding speeches.

36 D'Avray 2001, pp. 4-5.

37 Compare to chapter 3 above.

38 *Grágás*, Ia, p. 222; Ib, p. 241; II, pp. 66, 204; III, p. 30.

39 Brundage 1990, p. 88.

40 *Women's lives in Medieval Europe*, 1993, pp. 83, 88-89.

41 The origin of this rule in *Grágás* and other legal codes could be traced to the influence of the consummation theory. But as Reynolds underlines, there is little if any indication in the earlier Latin codes of Early Medieval Europe, that consummation had any legal significance. See Reynolds 1994, pp. 350-51.

42 It is known from Norway in the early fourteenth century. See DN, IV, p. 132: in a letter from Bishop Audfinnur in Bergen it is mentioned that a priest "brudar sengh vighia."

These speeches are supposed to have been delivered during the wedding celebration. They are examples of the way in which Christian doctrine was incorporated into the old rites for celebrating marriage. Jón Helgason argues that these speeches date from the period before 1550, because of both the style and content of the texts.[43] These speeches were spoken or sung at the wedding feast, as a toast to the different saints. The first speech was to Saint Martin,[44] the second was supposed to welcome the guests,[45] the third was to Christ, the fourth to the Holy Olav, the fifth was for the Holy Mary, the sixth was for the Holy Spirit, the seventh was to the bride (when the wedding gifts from the bridegroom were given to her) and the eighth speech was a farewell to the guests.[46]

The seventh speech, addressed to the bride, has special relevance to this study.[47] This speech illustrates how Christian doctrine became part of the ritual of uniting the bride and bridegroom. It was less generalized than the other speeches, and thus was possibly related to a specific Icelandic marriage ceremony. The speech was made by the guardians of the bride, and commented on the bridegroom's gifts to the bride. There were four gifts: a special cloth called *mötull*, a silver cross, gold, and a blanket. It is obvious from the content of the speech that the counter-gift was the bride herself, and probably also her maidenhood.

The speech describes the "playing that could happen under the blanket", and how the bride should behave. The gifts given with a "clear mind and true love" symbolized the different acts in the bedding ceremony. The bride waited for her bridegroom, and provided space for him in her bed. This was her first countergift. Then the bride warmly invited her bridegroom into bed, hopefully to discover something she had never seen before. The speech continued with references to what she would be shown. She must not be scared; because she would enjoy this gift more than all the others she had been given.[48]

43 Jón Helgason 1960, p. 151.
44 This speech was probably related to rituals used by the guilds, especially one known from the Faroe islands. See also Figure 21.
45 This speech included *griðarsetning* compare to *griðarmál* (*trygðarmál*) in *Grágás*, *Heiðarvíga saga* and *Grettis saga*.
46 Jón Helgason 1960, p. 153.
47 Ibid., pp. 170-74.
48 Ibid., pp. 173-74.

In the *Saga of King Ólafur Tryggvasson* a distinction is made as to what gift should be included amongst the gifts the bridegroom gave to his bride, depending on whether the woman to be married was a maiden or a widow.[49] This gift could be called *bekkjargjöf* or *línfé*, both given by the bridegroom to his wife on their wedding day.[50] There is reason to believe that the wedding speech that has survived from late medieval Iceland was one that had been made when this gift was delivered by the bridegroom to his bride. The bridegroom should sit on a bench among the men, and the bride on another among the women, and then he should walk across the floor and give her the *línfé*. This could be a *möttull* for instance, which was a special cloth for women.[51] It seems that this gift of *bekkjargjöf* often included some cloth. The *Saga of Egill einhenti* contains information about what this could include, namely some cloth, a chess game, and a ring.[52]

The text of the wedding speeches demonstrates a totally different understanding of sexuality to that presented by the earlier literature of the sagas. The sexual innocence of the maiden is underlined, which was not common in descriptions of women in the earlier literature. Documents of the late twelfth and early thirteenth centuries suggest that maidenhood mattered less.[53] However, in the Christian literature women's virginity came to be more important than her property.[54] A woman, who was portrayed in the literature as strong and of high status because she owned great estates or was the daughter of a powerful man, was not the ideal type of woman in the Christian literature of the Late Middle Ages. From this time onwards, there was a stronger emphasis on the innocence of women who had not experienced sexual pleasure before marriage.

Although marriage had come to be Christianized it continued to function as it had done in the twelfth and thirteenth centuries as an

49 AM ordbog: with a reference to *Ólafs saga Tryggvasonar*.

50 See for instance NgL II, p. 305.

51 AM ordbog: *línfé* with a reference to: *Flateyjarbók* I, pp. 435, 454.

52 AM ordbog: *bekkjargjöf* with a reference to: *Drei lygisögur: Egils saga einhenta ok Ásmundar berserkjabana*, p. 73.

53 Agnes S. Arnórsdóttir 1995, pp. 122-24.

54 On the importance of testing virginity and chastity in the Middle Ages, see Kelly 2000, pp. 62-90. There is evidence of virginity tests, to be found in vernacular stories.

agreement between two families. An elaborate marriage was celebrated at the monastery of Viðey in the south of Iceland in 1405. The arrangements for the wedding were very expensive, and the highest-ranking officer of the country, Vigfús bóndi Ívarsson, *hirðstjóri*, sponsored the feast. This was one of the great aristocratic wedding feasts and it served an important political function. A wedding of this type had many participants, and often lasted for days.[55] Thus the Christianization of marriage rituals did not dismiss the old forms of marriage celebration. This interaction between the secular and the more sacred parts of the marriage ritual can be found not only on the practical level, but also on the symbolic.

Christian marriage was a symbol of the relationship between Christ and the Church. Similarities between the rituals for entering a nunnery and entering marriage in the Late Middle Ages indicate the Christianization of the image of the bride. The rites in both situations were similar. The designation of the Christian virgin as a bride of Christ can be traced to Tertullian in the third century and was in common usage by the fourth century. Ambrose of Milan also reported similarities between the rite for the consecration of virgins and the nuptial ceremony.[56]

The connection of the bride of Christ to the secular bride was a prevalent perception much commented upon during the Renaissance and Counter-Reformation in Italy. Kate Lowe has stated that the secular and the religious "marriage" can be considered as different versions of the same act at the level of perception.[57] The same emotional and financial terms were used to describe entry into a nunnery and entry into marriage. One of Lowe's conclusions is that the "decision about what the women should do was taken by their relatives, in practice mainly by their fathers."[58]

The picture presented by Kate Lowe concerns the conceptualization of brides. By studying the language in a woman's prayer book, it is possible to gain an insight into women's own perception of their role as the brides of Christ.

55 Loftur Guttormsson 1992, pp. 188-89.
56 Lowe 1998, pp. 41-65.
57 Ibid., p. 44.
58 Ibid., p. 65.

In a Danish prayer book from 1497, the last prayer was addressed to the bridegroom.[59] This prayer book belonged to a nun of noble origin, Anna Brahe, and was written in the Bridgettine Abbey of Maribo in Denmark. The prayer to the bridegroom was the nun's declaration of love to Christ:

> My very dearest God, my loving bridegroom, … because of your long time away my soul does suffer … I remember your beautiful mouth, may your sweet lips touch mine, then brush my chin.[60]

And later in the prayer it says:

> You have said that the marriage that God has joined together, nobody must separate, I wait, I attend, I shout, I call, and do not hold back my crying tears, to tempt you, till you come to me.[61]

This prayer book was written in a nunnery, but the nunnery was not only a place for the brides of Christ. The nunnery was also a place where girls from well-to-do families spent part of their youth receiving education.[62] After their stay in the nunnery they could of course become secular brides. Bridal status in both the secular and the ecclesiastical worlds therefore, was not two entirely separate spheres. This made it possible to use the same rituals and language for the ceremonies each type of bride would follow. For instance, a dowry was given to both the brides of Christ in a nunnery and to brides in the secular realm.[63]

59 *Middelalderens danske bønnebøger* II, pp. 282-83.

60 Ibid., p. 282: "Myn sødhe gudh/myn aldrekæristæ herre/myn ælskeligste brudgo*m*me … my*m*es thin faghre mwnd/thine søde læbe vet mek/tha rødmæ myne kynder/".

61 Ibid., pp. 282-83: "tw haffuer sagt ath th*et* æchteskap so*m* gudh haff*uer* sa*m*men føwet/maa enghen atskilliæ// iek vænther/iek biidh*er*/iek rober/ iek kallær/ og æy aff lader iek m*et*h grædendæ taare/ath locke tek/til thess thw ko*m*mer".

62 Jexlev 1991, p. 328.

63 Another example of the way in which the secular and ecclesiastical worlds were linguistically bound is that the terms used to describe the financial aspects of worldly marriage were also used to describe the transmission of wealth to the church. The word *máli*, or *kaupmáli*, was applied to a woman's property, while the word *máldagi* was applied to the possessions of the church. See further discussion about this in chapter 9.

8.2.2 Virginity and the legal consequences of the "joining of minds"

In the description of Iceland from the end of the sixteenth century, there is a discussion about a specific case concerning the inheritance rights of a woman who had lost her virginity. To be able to get inheritance from her father or relatives she had to be forgiven and her honor had to be restored. Those involved in the offence were instructed to pay a penalty to the secular authorities before they received forgiveness and an indulgence from the Church. The account of the case reads:

> This custom and this strict law preserves the chastity of both sexes and their beautiful youth without any dirtiness, until the fire of the pure love is lighted in them both, and they can legally be together according to the customary rules for living a married life.[64]

According to the author of this description the 'pure love' between a man and a woman, together with parental consent, were preconditions for a happy marriage. But use of customary law continued. The wealth of the bridegroom should be double that of his bride.[65] The formula that the agreement had been done "according to the law of God and the country, and other wise men" had been used for centuries.[66] After the formula had been read the bridegroom was to kiss the bride as a symbol of their love, closeness and the joining of their minds.[67]

The former understanding of marriage as a contract concerning the transfer of wealth between families is here melted together with the Christian understanding of marriage. This understanding was further symbolized by the image of youth, innocence and love. Furthermore,

64 *Íslandslýsing* 1971, p. 83: "Með þessari venju og strangleik laganna er vel hugsað fyrir skírlífi beggja kynja, svo að æskublóminn haldist ómengaður og óskertur, þar til í báðum kviknar eldur hinnar hreinu ástar og þau geta haft lögmæt samskipti, eftir tíðkaða viðhafnarsiði, við háttbundinn framgang hjónabandsins."

65 Ibid., p. 84. This picture is a clear one but it does not exclude the more practical side. It says that the bridegroom and his father should write to the guardian of the girl and inform him of their wishes. And in most cases the guardian responded positively: "svo fremi að biðillinn eigi svo mikið undir sér, að eigur hans jafnist á við tvöföld efni meyjarinnar."

66 Ibid., p. 84. After the ritual of *festar* the *hjónavígsla* takes over. But the author underlines that the old custom of the country was to be kept alive. In public the *festarmaður* takes the hand of the *festarmeyja* and says: "Guð sé vottur minn og þeir góðir menn, sem hjá eru. Ég NN-son fastna þig NN-dóttir eftir guðs lögum og landsins og heilagra forfeðra setningu, með vitni þínu NN-son og þínu NN-son og allra þeirra, er orð mín heyra. Og nú ertu mín löglega eiginkona."

67 Ibid., p, 84. After he says this he should kiss his "festarmey heiðarlegum og ósviknum kossi, svo að koss þessi, ... megi vera tákn skyldusamlegrasta ástar eða nánari og innilegri sameiningar huganna."

marriage thus understood the interests of the couple's parents, since only this situation could ensure the safety of both the honor of their family and its property. Only the fruits of pure and mutual love would secure the continuation of the family line.

Several documents have survived from the end of the sixteenth century, which record instances in which women swore an oath stating who was the father of their children, or in which other people testified in cases about paternity.[68] These oaths reflect a change in the definition of what the honor of the women was about. Such cases had begun to emerge from the privacy of the confessional to enter the public sphere of the courts. These oaths concerning paternity also reflect women's new status in court. Previously, the head of the household had most often represented women in law courts.[69] But from the late sixteenth century onwards a woman's honor was no longer merely an element of family honour, but also a personal issue, relating to her own virginity.

A new understanding of womanhood, which related unmarried women to the image of innocent virgins, can be traced in the court cases. In 1543, a woman claimed at a court that a foreigner had raped her, and the case came to a judicial hearing.[70] Rape had become a matter of the woman's own honour, not only a matter of the honour of her kin-group as had previously been the case under the law of *Grágás*.[71] This change can also be related to the influence of canon law. Under old Roman law, no distinctions were made between cases of violence against property and violence against women. The term *raptus* was used to describe all kinds of loss that a household could suffer.[72] It was in Gratian's *Decretum* of c. 1140 that rape was first defined as a crime not only against a woman's family but also against herself.[73]

One significant element of the changes in this judicial process, which did not take place in Iceland until in the sixteenth century, was

68 DI XIII, pp. 318-19, 633-35, 636-38, 663-64, DI XIV, pp. 100-103, DI XV, pp. 447-48.

69 Concerning the earlier situation, see the judgement regarding "rétt of ráðspjöll kvenna" from 1360, in DI III, p. 142.

70 DI XI, pp. 250-52.

71 Compare to Agnes S. Arnórsdóttir 1986, pp. 23-30.

72 Brundage 1990, p. 48.

73 Brundage 1993, pp. 64-65. See also Brundage 1990, pp. 249-50.

probably that in adultery or separation cases it was no longer sufficient for evidence to be given only by male witnesses. By 1594, the testimony of both the wife and the husband was necessary in divorce cases.[74] According to another judgement from 1565 about the marriage of Halldór Benediktsson and Helga Illugadóttir, she received permission to stay with her father instead of her husband, who was a priest. The reason given for this decision was the adulterous lifestyle of the husband. It is possible that adultery committed by a woman was not understood as a crime on the same level as adultery committed by a man. In the case under consideration here, this would appear to be connected to the old tradition of disregarding the woman as an actor in adultery cases brought to the courts. This is related to the older understanding of a woman as a passive object to be dealt with by the courts, rather than an active participant in their work. The judgement partly included this image – at least it contains a reference to the *Bible* describing how women should be subordinated. But this case shows that Helga knew that she could not be forced to stay with her husband if she could prove his adultery. She made a written confession on the matter which gives the clear impression that she did not love her husband, and that she preferred to go back to her parents.[75]

The impression of women given by documents from the courts at the end of the sixteenth century is, however, very different from the one provided by the description of Iceland from the end of the sixteenth century. This disparity between the idealized image of woman and the actual female involvement in court cases is not surprising. It does not necessarily mean that one of these pictures was false, but that they co-existed. At the same time as stronger control of sexual behavior was emerging, the romantic notion of pure and innocent love between the virgin and her bridegroom was reinforced. Cases like that of Grafar-Gunna, mentioned in chapter 5, came to court because the control of sexual behavior was now sanctioned by the authorities.

74 *Alþingisbækur Íslands* II, pp. 426-28.
75 DI XIV, pp. 365-68.

8.3 *New gender relations – freedom not force?*

> [It] is hard to believe that the dull and public business of marriage contracts should have no connection with the mad fusion of hearts and bodies that occurs in the secular narratives. Yet, on the surface, nothing but very basic resemblance linked the sensible exchange of property and persons that appeared in the laws and canons with the wild coupling found in romances and other stories. True, both representations followed strict, if quite different, guidelines with the aim of joining a man and woman in some sort of long-term relationship … To grasp the significance of the jurists' very consciously limited depiction of coupling, we need to look at the stories they did not tell, found in other extant sources concerned with the mingling of men and women.[76]

At the same time as canon law was beginning to influence the regulation of marriage, the courtly literature of continental Europe was blossoming also in the Icelandic and Norwegian world.[77] The functional and dry documents of the jurists and canonists can partly be understood in the light of the literary sources, which describe the "mad fusion of hearts and bodies." New gender relations were formed in the High and Late Middle Ages based on the new marriage policies of the Church. The classical canon law affirmed that freedom was an essential part of marriage. The canonists even tried to restrict the role that force and fear would play in litigation. Richard Helmholz has given us examples from English court cases that set forth the idea of how even a mother could treat her daughter by breaking her bones and throw her out of the house if she did not marry the person her mother wanted her to. This was an example of a case where the lack of consent and the use of force could be used as proof of impediment for the marriage and as such the daughter could be freed from her marriage.[78] We have been using similar cases from the Icelandic court material, but the saga literature also reflects the same theme.

Jenny Jochens has suggested that many of the authors of Old Norse literature emphasize the issue of consent because of their clerical training.[79] Sveinbjörn Rafnsson has further underlined that the sagas actually can be used as evidence for radical change in the gender relations in

76 Bitel 1996, p. 44

77 See here pp. 287 ff.

78 Helmholz 2004, p. 545.

79 Jochens 1986b, p. 170.

Iceland during the time where the sagas were written, mostly the thirteenth century.[80] At least the issue was raised in the saga literature at an early stage. The famous *Saga of Njáll*, one of the youngest sagas in the group of *Íslendingasögur*, probably written about 1280, provides a good example of this.[81] The author must have known about the rules demanding women's consent to marriage. The story of Hallgerður Höskuldsdóttir and Unnur Marðardóttir's marriage demonstrates this. They both became engaged by free consent.[82]

We can see how the literature of the High Middle Ages, both the Icelandic and translated stories, focused on changes in matters of marriage and love between the sexes. *Strengleikar*, an Old Norse text,[83] was translated from French to Old Norse at the end of the thirteenth century.[84] The text has been dated to 1270 or some years later, and is believed to have originated in Bergen or some other cultural centre in the south-western part of Norway. In its complete form it was a collection of twenty-one short stories, so-called *lais,* translated from Old French. It was Hákon Hákonarson, king of Norway from 1217 to 1263, who asked for the translation of this text during his reign. But it was probably not written until 1270 or some time during the reign of Hákon's son, King Magnús, "the Law-Reformer." Literary historians have dated the Old French version of the poems to the second half of the twelfth century, and they appear to have been composed for a certain lady known as Marie "de France."[85] A copy of a part of the Norwegian translation is also known to have reached Iceland.[86]

80 Sveinbjörn Rafnsson 1982, pp. 114-29. He discusses the influence of canon law on writing the Icelandic Sagas, especially on pp. 118-119; compare to note 13 on pp. 125-27.

81 Einar Ól. Sveinsson, ÍF XII, p. lxxxiv.

82 Einar Ól. Sveinsson, ibid., p. lxxx. He cites Lehmann: Die Njálssaga pp. 38-42 and pp. 80-81. This was possible according to the law of *Járnsíða* (1271-1280), but not according to *Grágás*. About the betrothal of Hallgerður and Gunnar, see ÍF XII, pp. 85-87. There it is stated that she betrothed herself. This had not happened in her first marriage, which did not have a happy ending, see ibid., p. 31 and forward. The narrative of *Sturlunga saga* does not mention consent as a necessary thing for a valid marriage, compare to Jochens 1986.

83 *Strengleikar*. An Old Norse Translation of Twenty-one Old French Lais, 1979.

84 Four fragments in the Arnamagnæan Collection, Copenhagen were discovered by Árni Magnússon in 1703, in the lining of a bishop's mitre from Skálholt in Iceland. The text is also known from fragments of the Icelandic manuscript *Ormsbók* a lost fourteenth century Icelandic manuscript by Ormr Snorrason.

85 *Strengleikar,* Introduction, pp. xv-xvi.

86 Ibid., with referance to AM 666b, 4.

Information concerning courtship in the late thirteenth century can be found in this kind of literature as well as in the law codes. Love stories were as popular in Northern Europe as they were in the south. The stories described the world of the knights and their love and longing. "Now the knight stays there alone, full of the unrest of longing and love, and yet he does not know in truth how his unrest arises."[87] In the love stories of *Strengleikar* there is a pattern that is echoed in the canon law concerning marriage. These stories of "true love" stressed the idea of monogamy; polygamy was not compatible with this worldview. This theme actually was in harmony with the ideology of the Church.

Canon law only tolerated marital affection between the sexes. This concept was derived from Roman law: the Code of Justinian stated that marital affection was the sole requirement for constituting a marriage. The dowry and ceremony were mere adjuncts to the creation of a marital union.[88] Marriage was often seen as a life-long union based on emotional ties of affection and dependence between the couple. At the heart of the Christian understanding of a sacred marriage was thus the idea that the couple loved each other. This understanding of marriage can be traced back to Paul's theory of the union between man and woman: "they shall be two in one flesh." According to Philip Reynolds' analysis, Paul did not understand the union into one flesh as only related to sexual intercourse. "It was Paul who added coitus to the conjugal debt that each partner owes the other."[89] This understanding of the conjugal debt must have influenced the idea of freedom in choosing a partner. At least we can conclude that a process began that did not end until much later in early modern or modern Europe.

The narratives seem to express the notion that love became the ideal basis for relationships between the sexes. Imagined dialogues between lovers became a popular topic in the sagas of chivalry, and many copies exist which reflect the interest in the topic.[90] And in the words of

87 See *Strengleikar*, p. 25, with the original text on pp. 24-25: "Nv duælsk þar riddaren æin*n* saman full*er* angrs ok astar uroar. en þo væit h*ann* æigi en*n* at son*n*u mæð hu*er*iom hætte uro h*ans* stendr."

88 Brundage 1975, p. 5.

89 Reynolds 1994, p. 333, compare to 1 Cor. 7:3 and see also Exod. 21:10.

90 AM 391, fol. pap. 36, pp. 7-12, *Dialog mellem tvende Elskende.*

the author of the *Íslandslýsing* from the end of the sixteenth century, the notion of love between husbands and wives is clearly underlined: "I also think that nowhere is the natural love between husband and wife warmer and deeper than in Iceland."[91] How far people identified with these new ideals is unclear. In practice, marriage involved many issues besides morality and love. The new rules concerning marriage were easy to understand and follow and they allowed marriage to continue to function as an instrument for alliances and the transfer of wealth, obligations and duties. A closer reading of the existing marriage contracts and related court material can, however, give some indications that the notion of marital love actually did matter.

A testimony concerning the marriage agreement made in 1397 between Vigfús Ívarsson and Guðríður Ingimundardóttir, use the word honorable, *ærleghr,* to describe him, and lovely, *kærligh,* to describe her.[92] This indicates that the moral codes applied to women and men were different. The word used to describe the man was concerned with honor, while the word describing the woman emphasized love and care. The case of the district commissioner Páll Jónsson and his wife Helga Aradóttir further illustrates this point.[93] In 1594 a judgement concerning their marriage could not be given because she had not testified. It was not enough to hear the testimony of the husband.[94] The case had first been taken to court in 1591, when the husband had accused his wife of leaving him many years before, without following the law of God and the country. In 1591, the husband wanted his wife to come to the court because she had given away landed property of 60 *hundrað,* before he had made the marriage agreement with her. Secondly, she had been separated from him for thirteen years by "table and bed." Thirdly, she had fought with him every time he tried to go into her bed. And finally, she had also given away or lost his wealth. She had gone to live with another man while her husband was in Denmark.[95]

91 *Íslandslýsing,* p. 85: "hygg ég líka, að hvergi sé hin lögmæta ást millum hjóna heitari og innilegri en á Íslandi."
92 DI III, pp. 616-17.
93 *Alþingisbækur Íslands* II, pp. 426-28.
94 Ibid., p. 428. Many cases from the end of the sixteenth century show that it was not seen as formally correct to judge in such cases after only hearing evidence presented by men. See my discussion above in chapter 4.
95 Ibid., pp. 427-28. See also Figure 23 and 24.

Luckily, we have more information about the persons involved in this case. Páll Jónsson was born in 1535, and when he was sixteen or seventeen years old he fell deeply in love with this woman Helga who was the daughter of the lawman Ari Jónsson.[96] She was reputed to have been a strong woman, as well as one of the most attractive women in the whole country. It was thought both by Helga and her relatives that her status was too high for her to marry Páll. But he persisted, writing many love poems to her, and they were finally married in 1558, albeit only after he had gained confirmation from the court that his status was as high as hers. They lived first at Eyrarland in Eyjafjörður, but later moved to Helgastaðir or Einarstaðir in Reykjadal. In 1553 Páll became a district commissioner, *sýslumaður*, of Þingeyjarsýsla. He died in 1598.[97]

Helga and Páll had children, but their marriage was not a happy one. As soon as they married, his love poems became negative in tone. One poem has survived from the time at which Helga wanted to separate from him. Páll claimed among other things that "all men" now laughed at him at the assembly.[98]

Páll and Helga were never formally separated. Instead Páll fell in love with another woman, Halldóra, the daughter of Bishop Guðbrandur. He did not marry her, but he wrote many love poems to her that has been preserved.[99] One of these poems dates from 1593.[100]

The story of Páll and Helga indicates that affection and love became one of the key criteria for a successful marriage.[101] At the same time, the case illustrates quite well how the honor of Páll was strongly related to having a loving wife. Conversely, a lack of love could become a reason for separation. In 1565, the marriage of the priest Halldór Benedikts-son and his wife Helga Illugadóttir was considered by the court.[102] The issue in this instance concerned separation. Helga asked the district

96 Páll Eggert Ólason 1951, IV, pp. 123-24.

97 Jón Þorkelsson 1888, pp. 381-82.

98 Ibid., pp. 383-84.

99 Ibid., p. 383.

100 Ibid., p. 388.

101 Evidence from other studies gives the same impression. See for instance Helmholz 2004, p. 528, about a case from London from the year of 1576. A man refused to take up residence with the woman with whom he had contracted orally, "because he thinketh she dith not love him."

102 DI XIV, pp. 365-69.

commissioner, *sýslumaður*, in the name of God to take this case into his hands because of her suffering. She gave him a written explanation of the situation.[103]

During the winter the couple's relationship had been in great trouble. She detested her husband and could not bear the thought of having him touching her. She had grown mentally sick because of the strength of this feeling and she could not control her emotions. The thought of continuing to live with him had almost killed her. However, even though she was ill, she had never denied him his wishes if he wanted to be with her. The reason for her torment was the infidelity of her husband, who insisted that the other woman with whom he had a relationship should live under the same roof, and refused to send this woman away. Helga separated from her husband because of his adultery, and texts from both the Bible and from the Church ordinance of 1537/39 were used to legitimate this separation.[104]

This case illustrates how a woman could take a complaint to court and get a judgement in her favor. It illustrates also, perhaps, how the husband, in this case a priest, could get rid of his wife and continue to live with his mistress.

Other letters attest this double standard in morality. A letter from 1596 describes how a mother and daughter made oaths concerning their fidelity to their husbands.[105] This should not be seen as an indication that women were always virtuous and faithful. What is interesting is that by this time women had a central place in the discussion of sexual issues. The possibility of a woman being unfaithful was perceived negatively by society. In earlier times such unacceptable sexual relationships had been dangerous to the honour of a woman's family. Shame had previously not been connected to the loss of virginity, but rather to the family's loss of guardianship over her. That is how the rules of courtship were related to issues of marriage. This was reflected in legal regulations as well as in much of the court material, although literature and the poems reflect a more emotional view of this change. The couple itself, who had become

103 Ibid., p. 366.

104 Ibid., p. 367.

105 AM dipl. isl. fasc. lix, 14: "um tryggð þeirra við menn sína."

the main focus of marriage rituals in the twelfth century, should love each other.[106] The meaning of marriage, thus, became a personal matter, not only a contract concerning wealth and social alliances within the wider kin-group.

8.4 Conclusion

The different surviving marriage rituals represent the Church's ideas concerning the way in which a marriage should be solemnized, rather than reflect the way marriage was actually performed. An analysis of changes in the rituals that accompanied the entry into marriage gives the impression that the Church gradually succeeded in giving the secular marriage ceremony a religious character. The earliest known marriage customs were those of *Grágás.* Men shook hands and discussed the financial aspects of the contract in front of witnesses. In the late thirteenth century, the woman to be married entered into this ritual, giving her consent in front of witnesses, *já í heyranda hljóði,* signifying the new nature of marriage. Finally, by the Late Middle Ages a written contract was produced and formally sealed, the legal impact of which could last for centuries. This marriage contract retained its original meaning while at the same time developing new elements. So, for example, the emphasis on fidelity, which had previously been motivated by financial considerations, came also to be motivated by a desire for personal commitment.

The twelfth and thirteenth centuries were thus important in the formation of marriage customs. This resulted in a stronger emphasis on making marriage a personal contract between a woman and a man which had meaning for the couple, their families and the Christian community as a whole.[107] Marriage continued to be a secular contract, based on the idea of *consensus,* but it was increasingly accepted that God had created the institution of marriage and that it was therefore holy, and as such indissoluble.

106 This meaning of the term love is juridically connected to the canon law understanding of *Maritalis Affectio.* Compare to Pedersen 1995, pp. 1-31, as well as Pedersen 1998, pp. 175-209.

107 Bear in mind that it is when a symbol first gains meaning both to individuals and to groups that it has an effect. See Keesing 1981, p. 346, compare to pp. 106-107.

This chapter has demonstrated how the ideology about the union of the married spouses became stronger. They should love each other, although it was only with full parental control that the beauty and the pureness of virginity could be maintained. This chapter has also discussed how a new gender identity was created. An analysis of the marriage contracts has shown that there were changes in the use of language, which were not only associated with the shift from oral to written contracts, but were also connected to who it was who spoke the words of the agreement. In particular, the future bride gained a role in this process. This was the main change in the way the agreement was performed. It was no longer only a *handaband* between two groups of people, but a *hjónaband* confirmed, as before, with a handshake, but this was not a handshake by two men, but by husband and wife. This change can also be traced through the study of the written contracts.

The marriage contract changed from being a contract made between two families to a public contract made between the spouses and God. This change was gradual and first took place through the language used and later through the understanding of the role of the bride and the bridegroom in this reciprocal binding. A new social bond was made by this contract. On the general symbolic level, the ring, showing the joining of hands around a heart,[108] was the symbol of a different type of commitment than that of the old *festa* contract in *Grágás*. However, it was only because of the continuity of the old contract that it was possible to introduce new Christian symbols.

By incorporating old rituals into its practices the Church invested these rituals with new meaning. Dumont's theory about the development of the individual during the Middle Ages explains how the consent of the couple and the parents could exist side by side.[109] Over time, the strengthening of the individual's relationship with God also affected the individual's position in the secular world. This was related to the idea that finding a marriage partner and making a marriage contract was a personal matter, which may have its roots in this process of individualization.

108 Compare to the engagement ring on the front cover of this book.

109 Compare to Dumont 1992, especially pp. 23-60.

To be able to conclude any further about how change in the making of the marriage contract affected the wider social structure, we need to compare the information included here in the second part of this study, with that of chapters 4 and 5. The analysis of contracts in chapter 7 suggests that after the marriage contract had gained meaning as a contract between the couple itself, rather than just between the parents of the couple, there was no need to state that the contract was made with the consent of the woman. However, it became necessary to say that the contract did have the consent of the parents of the bride. This shows that even if there was a shift towards contracts being more individual-orientated, the established social ties of the family that had a role in marriage formation continued to exist and may even have been strengthened.

At the same time, the position of the spouses as a unit in its own right was strengthened. By adding elements to existing rituals the Church made long-term changes in the meaning of rituals. Change occurred on two levels: one concerned the perception of the role of God in making a marriage, and it was in this context that the couple made their personal commitment. The other level on which change could occur was the secular one, in which the decisions of the family as a group were more important than individual choice. By adapting some of the established rituals, the Church gave them a new meaning and an extended life span. On the one hand marriage had become a contract involving the personal commitment of husband and wife to God, while on the other it remained an important tool in the operation of kin-group politics, in which individual choice counted for little. This development can be connected to another process described by Dumont. This is the change by which property – or, more generally, matters in the financial sphere – from being a medium for social relations,[110] becomes an end in itself. The last part of this book will examine the transfer of property in marriage contracts.

110 Compare to the reciprocity of the gift in Mauss 1990, foreword by Mary Douglas p. vii, and chapter 1, pp. 8-18.

Part III

Property aspects of marriage

Wealth was passed to future generations through marriage and inheritance. Written marriage contracts were based on the earlier forms of oral contract mentioned in part II, and thus the written word replaced the spoken word. Many of the Icelandic marriage contracts were kept to prove property rights in the event that these rights became the subject of dispute at any future date. The contracts and related material cannot, however, be understood in isolation from the intentions that lay behind their production. These documents not only provided proof of legally made marriages and the transfer of property, they were also tools with which to demand right over resources. In this last part of the book we shall study marriage contracts as a part of the property strategy of the Icelandic ruling elite.

James Brundage has underlined that canon law, as well as the changes in the social structure that it produced, gradually influenced people towards using more individual methods in dividing the property of deceased family members, and the property strategy of the Icelandic elite will be studied in the light of his work. The focus here will particularly be on how different kinds of marriage contracts were used for different purposes: for instance, with regard to wedding gifts, why were the preferences of the fifteenth century different from those that became common in the sixteenth century? As pointed out in the first two parts of this book, from the thirteenth century onwards the new Christian marriage doctrine had a great influence on marriage agreements, and in the following I shall further examine how this affected both the transfer of property through marriage (through the use of different types of marriage contracts and marriage gifts), and the use of legitimate and illegitimate channels of property transfer (such as the use of legal gifts and the custom of adoption). The last chapter deals with the effect that the Christianization of marriage had on the question of property rights.

CHAPTER 9

Marital property and marriage strategy

It is important to bear in mind that variations were great in the use of marital property[1] division in different regions of Europe, according to marriage contracts from the High and Late Middle Ages which have survived.[2] These contracts in addition to the marital property laws were not fixed or institutionalized but, rather, they were liable to change[3] and this is one reason why a comparative study of the different regions of Europe is interesting. Therefore the first part of this chapter will examine these regional differences.

The financial marriage arrangements that accompanied marriage will be studied in the second part of the chapter, as well as the different contracts of *máli* and *helmingarfélag*. The discussion here will concern the purpose of these contracts and the way in which they functioned in practice, especially in relation to the property strategy of the ruling elite. Disputes often arose between the children of a couple on the one hand, and the close relatives of the couple on the other. If the relatives could prove that the couples were not legally married according to canon law, the children of that couple risked losing their inheritance, as the cases discussed in chapter 5 concerning dispensation clearly showed. In this way the siblings of a married couple could retrieve landed property. If, however, the couple's children could prove they were born in wedlock,

1 Instead of the concept "household economy" the concept "marital economy" and "marital property" is used here to better underline the role of the spouses and their families and closest kin as the main actors behind the fundamental level of the economic activity of a household. Compare to Erickson 2005, p. 3.

2 This material is the subject of ongoing study. See for instance the studies of Howell 1998, Napran 2000, and Reynolds 2007.

3 An example of this can be taken from Charles Donahue's study from 1992, pp. 339-66.

the property could continue to be used either by the widow or widower if they were alive, or by the children. This meant that the household established by the parents could continue in its own right, instead of being broken up and dispersed among the wider kin-group.

In the third part of this chapter we shall take a closer look at the property strategy of the Icelandic aristocracy of the fifteenth and sixteenth century.

9.1 Regional differences in forming marriage practice

Germanic inheritance practices persisted through the Early Middle Ages, but both canon law and changes in social structure gradually shifted the Northern Europeans towards flexible and voluntary (rather than fixed and automatic) methods of dividing the property of deceased family members.[4] Charles Donahue's studies of the differences between English and French marriage cases in the Late Middle Ages, give us an idea how the marriage practices could develop differently.[5] He states that the differences between the English and Northern French records do not only concern a contrast in litigation patterns and legal institutions; they also reflect differences in the way the English and Northern French married. This difference was evident in the customary understanding of the nature of marriage, which was closely related to variations in social structure.

In England, most people married according to the rules for 'informal' marriage, while in Northern France most people made contracts to marry. In this context Charles Donahue asks if these differences were related to differences in property systems. The informal marriage seems to lie at the heart of the English cases, in which the spouses usually had separate possessions although it was possible for them to create joint possession of their belongings. In this system a woman would receive one-third of her husband's property as a dower if she became a widow. During the marriage the husband could take the rents and profits from his wife's property, which he managed. According to the Northern French

4 Brundage 1995a, p. 88.
5 Donahue 1992, pp. 339-66.

cases, marriage was for the most part viewed as a formal contract creating joint ownership for the spouses, except for the main estate which was the separate property of his or her family. There are quite a few separation cases in the Northern French records, but very few among the English. Donahue states: "my suspicion is that the English separated themselves and never went to court".[6] A couple that separated in England did not have to worry about breaking up jointly-owned property, because no such property existed. In Northern France, however, because of the jointly-owned possessions shared by husband and wife, a judicial pronouncement was necessary to achieve a separation.[7] Donahue's study reminds us not only of the close links between marriage patterns and different property systems, but also leads us to consider how the interpretation of the sources relates to the different marriage strategies in accordance with the different property settlements.

We can take another example from Denmark. According to the Danish *fællig*, the family land (passed on by inheritance) was excluded from the jointly-owned property, as in France.[8] The Danish *fællig* was however a different type of jointly-owned property than the *hjónafélag* and *helmingarfélag* in Iceland or Norway. *Fællig* took place automatically at the start of a marriage, and was concerned not only with the possessions of the couple, but also those of their children.[9] The Danes, on the other hand, seem to have been like the English in not having been keen on making written contracts.[10] This reverses what Donahue saw in the differences between France and England. Denmark can be added to his comparison as illustrating a third type of area. So even if we find a pattern in marriage which reminds us of the joint principle of transferring property this cannot be cited directly as evidence of one "northern" pattern.[11]

6 Ibid., p. 355.

7 Donahue 1992, p. 353.

8 Dübeck 2003, p. 93. Both in Northern France, as well as in the German and Danish area, the family property was excluded from the joint possession.

9 Iuul 1959b, pp. 487-88. See also Pederesen 1992, and Dübeck 2003, pp. 77-87, 121-28. On p. 85 she argues that in Denmark three types of *fællig* could exist: 1) Between married couple; 2) between family members; and 3) a more general agreement between non-relatives.

10 Iuul 1966, p. 523, based on his study from 1940.

11 Dübeck 2003, p. 84. On p. 93 she also underlines the variation in making marriage agreements both in Northern French, German and Danish families. See also on pp. 81-82 the discussion on the many possible variations of making marriage arrangements in Europe during the Middle Ages.

Few comparative studies have examined marriage practice in the Nordic countries during the Middle Ages.[12] This is in part a result of the available source material. Although many marriage contracts have survived from Iceland, hardly any such material has survived from Denmark, for example. This can be explained by the special Danish way of making joint ownership. Some documents have survived from Sweden which relate to the morning gift, but apart from Iceland, Norway is the only Nordic country from which medieval marriage contracts are extant, although they have not survived in the same quantity as those from Iceland.[13] The material that has survived may reflect the different character of these regions, but these contrasts may also be explained by the varying need for the retention of documents in private hands. In societies with a more advanced administration, and more firmly established rules about property transfer, there was probably less need for the private retention of documents than was the case in Iceland at the end of the Middle Ages. This may be one of the reasons why so many marriage contracts have survived from this period in Iceland.

We do not, however, only find regional differences in forming marriage contracts during the Middle Ages, but also great changes over time. By examining the development of marriage settlements in Iceland from the time of the earliest rules during the twelfth and thirteenth centuries, until the end of eighteenth century, one can identify a change in the position of a wife owning property separately[14] in the earliest time, to that of the joint possession of property by a couple which became the norm by the end of this period. Under this scheme each partner in the marriage owned half of their common belongings. The historian Inga Huld Hákonardóttir has argued that by the end of the eighteenth century the finances of a couple had come to be as melted together as their souls.[15] It would, however, be too simplistic to depict this as a shift from

12 See my discussion in the Introduction p.27, note 30. Lately a growing interest is evident about the better use of the existing material for each region. See for instance in the case of Sweden, Korpiola 2004, and in the case of Danmark, Dübeck 2003, and Vogt 2005.

13 There are ongoing studies of this material. See an overview in: Agnes S. Arnórsdóttir 2001a, pp. 175, 194-95.

14 This was the most common form of making an oral marriage contract during the twelfth and thirteenth centuries: compare to Agnes S. Arnórsdóttir 1995, pp. 156-58.

15 Inga Huld Hákonardóttir 1992, pp. 104-105.

one system to another. The joint possessions of *félag* was a term already known in the twelfth and thirteenth centuries from the marriage law of *Grágás*, and *helmingarfélag* was known from the thirteenth century literature of the sagas.[16] It is named both in *Sturlunga saga*, and the sagas of the Icelanders. The principle behind helmingarfélag is thus well known by the authors of the sagas,[17] at least by the author of the *Njáls saga*, which was probably written around 1280.[18] Thus, it existed in practice before this type of jointly-owned property was first introduced into the Icelandic law codes in the early fourteenth century.

If change in the making of marriage contracts was not evolutionary in character, meaning that one type of marriage arrangement replaced an older one, how can these different methods of making contracts be explained? We are going to explore this further in the following part of the chapter.

9.2 Two types of Icelandic marriage contracts: máli *and* helmingarfélag

According to the oldest marriage law of *Grágás*, there were two possible ways of making a financial agreement about marriage. First, the woman's dowry and the marriage gift of her husband could be kept as her possessions within the husband's property. This form of property agreement was later, in the written contracts of the Late Middle Ages called *máli*. Secondly, a financial agreement could be made whereby the woman owned one-third of the property, and the husband two-thirds. This was called *hjónafélag*, or *þriðjungafélag*, in the legislation of *Jónsbók*. The third type of agreement existed during the Commonwealth period. This was called *helmingarfélag*, according to which the couple each owned a half share of all their belongings. This type of jointly-owned property was first defined in the law codes of the early fourteenth-century, *réttarbætur*.[19]

16 On *helmingarfélag* in *Sturlunga saga* see Agnes S. Arnórsdóttir 1995, pp. 115-16, 160-62.

17 See Sigurður Líndal 1976a, pp. 496-97.

18 See also ÍF XII, p. 45.

19 Agnes S. Arnórsdóttir 1995, pp. 155-63.

According to law the couples could thus make marriage contracts establishing separate ownership, called *máli*, as well as contracts for jointly-owned property called either *hjónafélag*[20] or *helmingarfélag*. The written marriage contracts that have survived from the Late Middle Ages demonstrate on the contrary only the use of two main types of contracts: the so-called *helmingarfélag*,[21] which meant joint ownership by the couple, and *máli*, which meant a woman's separate ownership of a specific portion of possessions within her husband's property. *Hjónafélag* was never cited as a special form of agreement within the written marriage contracts. The word *þridiunga goze* was used in one contract of *máli* from 1550.[22] This is the only direct evidence for the possible creation of jointly-owned property of the type known as *hjónafélag*.[23] It seems that after the rules establishing *helmingarfélag* were introduced, this came to be the only type of *félag* made when marriages were concluded. This revision was made at the beginning of the fourteenth century, meaning that the rules concerning *hjónafélag* contained in the earlier *Jónsbók* were no longer needed.[24]

The woman's *máli* is referred to in both the charters and the law codes.[25] The principles behind the separate property of *máli* was that a woman's property was usually made up of her dowry from her parents as well as the husband's *tilgjöf*, countergift, so that *máli* was sometimes

20 See Hrefna Róbertsdóttir 1986, p. 32. On the situation in other Nordic countries see: Sawyer 1993, p. 174. This kind of jointly owned property gave the woman right to share in the uninherited property of the couple, usually a one-third part of the property. This type of *félag* was also known in Sweden. Compare to Iuul 1959b, p. 490.

21 Hrefna Róbertsdóttir 1986, pp. 31-40. She mentions in her study the following *helmingarfélags* contracts: DI: III, pp. 678-79, 679-80; IV, pp. 277-78, 312; V, pp. 30, 130-31, 205-06, 646-47; VI, pp. 92-93, 392, 547-49, 660-61, 738; VII, pp. 250-51, 406; VIII, pp. 136-38, 165-66, 230-32; IX, pp. 288-89, 476-77; XI, pp. 414-15; XII, pp. 88, 119-20; XIV, pp. 18-19. Information about following contracts are also printed in DI: DI IV, pp. 588-89, 667-68, V, pp. 560-61, VI, pp. 118-19, 683, XII, pp. 481, XIII, pp. 543-44, 687, XIV, pp. 14-15, XV, pp. 46-47.

22 DI XI, pp. 822-23.

23 Although it would have been possible to examine further all the contracts which are neither contracts of *máli* nor *helmingafélag* in relation to inheritance division – see for instance an agreement between brothers in DI VI, pp. 132-33 for the year 1478, concerning the inheritance of their parents, for which a marriage contract is also known, and compare to another case in DI VI, pp. 135-36 about the inheritance of persons for whom the marriage contracts have survived – the latter has not been done in this study as it would have involved the examination of a great amount of documents related to all transfers of property from the fourteenth to the sixteenth centuries.

24 Compare the discussion in chapter 3, see especially pp. 102-104.

25 In the law books, see for instance *Jónsbók*, p. 86.

Table III	Máli *and* helmingarfélag *in the Diplomatarium Islandicum*		
Year	**Uncertain**	**Máli**	**Helmingarfélag**
1351-1400	5 = 100%	0	0
1401-1450	4 = 22,2%	7 = 38.9%	7 = 38.9%
1451-1500	14 = 35,9%	12 = 30.8%	13 = 33.3%
1501-1550	25 = 37,9%	32 = 48.5%	9 = 13.6%
1551-1600	30 = 46,1%	30 = 46.1%	5 = 7.6%
Total = 193	78 = 40,4%	81 = 44.0%	34 = 17.6%

Sources: See Appendix I.

characterized as the contract made by *tilgjöf*. The joint ownership of *helmingarfélag* was sometimes also referred to as *lagsmæli* or *félagsmæli*, which literally means the oral ways of making a contract concerning joint ownership.[26] Table III shows how many of the surviving contracts of the Late Middle Ages were either *máli* or *helmingarfélag*. Judging from this list of contracts, *máli* was the more common type of contract.

Helmingarfélag, like *máli*, is better understood if the meaning of the word itself is considered. The term *félag*[27] meant to *leggja fé í lag*, that is, to join possessions together. *Helmingarfélag* could be made between a couple through a marriage contract, or could be made between two persons as a financial contract of a more general kind.[28]

No *helmingarfélag* contract has survived from fourteenth century Iceland,[29] although *helmingarfélag* was named as a possible agreement in

26 DI III, p. 296.

27 Compare to *fælaagh* in DN I, p. 524. See the term *félag* and *félagi* in the Icelandic law codes, in *Grágás* Ia, p. 228; II, p. 338; III, pp. 51, 448. In *Jónsbók*, p. 253. See also Dübeck 2003, p. 35 about the Danish meaning of the concept of *fællig*.

28 Magnús Már Lárusson 1959c, p. 212. A man and a woman could make *félag* without being married, just as other members of society could. See for instance *Lovsamling for Island*, pp. 6-7 *Tíundarlög* from 1096: "Ef karlmaðr ok kona eigu fé saman, þótt þau sé eigi hjóna, ok skal karlmaðr vinna þar eið." *Sturlunga saga* provides evidence of *félag* being made between a man and a woman in the early twelfth century. The widow Yngvildur Þórðardóttir made *félag* with the priest Ingimundur Einarsson. See Sts, I, p. 23. The term *félagi* could thus have the meaning of companionship.

29 This was not the case in Norway. Information can be found from Norway concerning marriage contracts from the early fourteenth century. In the Norwegian DN we can find information such as this from 1325, see DN IV, p. 151: "warom ver …thar i hia ok till kallader i communs stofuonne i felaghe ok hæyrdom upp

one document from 1393.[30] The oldest surviving marriage contracts of *helmingarfélag* date from the early fifteenth century. *Helmingarfélag* was recorded in the *Diplomatarium Norvegicum* from the year 1388. In 1398 the word *helminghar goz* was used in a Norwegian charter. This type of jointly-owned property seems to have been quite common in Norway by the fourteenth century. It is also recorded in the older law of *Gulathing*.[31]

The fifteenth century, and especially the late fifteenth century, seems to have been the period from which most *helmingarfélags* contracts can be found in Iceland. But, even though an equal number of surviving contracts were of *helmingarfélag* as of *máli* from the period of 1401-50, *helmingarfélag* never became the dominant form. Table III indicates that the contract of *máli* was instead the most common type of contract. At the same time, it is important to notice that many of the contracts do not give any indication of what type of contract they were. There are many possible reasons for this. For example, it was possible to make *helmingarfélag* in two ways: at the point at which a marriage was made, or at a later stage, once the couple had children. Some of the contracts which do not indicate their type may thus have been declared as *helmingarfélag* at this later stage. Secondly, it is important to stress that even if *hjónafélag* was not named in the contracts, it is possible that some of the uncertain contracts came to be defined as *hjónafélag* at the point of the division of inheritance. The legal foundation for this could have been the old principle of *félag*, under which a wife owned one-third, and the husband two-thirds of their possessions, since this was (according to *Grágás*) applied when a household was broken up after the death of the couple, if it was not known how much property each partner owned.[32]

a kaupmala." From 1339 DN V, p. 107: "Thorvidar logmadar spurdi thorvald ok Steinbiorn huat felagh edar eighi var millim Leidulfs faudur theira ok Steinnor modor theira".

30 DI III, p. 488.

31 See, generally, for the Norwegian development Græsdal 2000, and Aronsen 2001, compare to 1999. See further: DN from the year of 1335, 1337, 1374, 1386, 1388, 1401, DN V, p. 93, DN III, p. 169, DN I, p. 324, DN IV, p. 398, DN V, p. 290, DN XI, p. 68, as well as DN II, p. 422, DN V, p. 158.

32 To be able to study whether this principle actually was followed in the Late Middle Ages, we would need to study the inheritance practice. It has not been possible within the scope of this study to analyze all the charters concerning inheritance division in the Late Middle Ages. This can provide the subject for another study.

Thirdly, it is also important to remember that contracts concerning property were not standardized. Moreover, because they were in some cases just statements that a contract had been made, there is sometimes no indication of what type of property agreement these statements refer to. Information was not always given about what landed property was involved. This was more of an issue in relation to the *helmingarfélag* than the contracts of *máli*.

Those extended marriage contracts mentioned above are important sources for studies concerning trends in marriage. They will be studied more closely here to discover how the property agreements they describe dealt with the needs of the household of the newly wedded couple and of the extended kin-group. The first issue under consideration concerns what the contracts were about.

9.2.1 From kvennagiptingar *to marital arrangements*

Literally, the word *kaupmáli* means an agreement about the *máli*. The word comes from the *mæla kaup*, discussion of the deal, and often the words *máli í hans garð*, were used to describe what a wife owned in her husband's property. This could be one part of a landed property, or a whole unit of land or even several units that were part of the total possessions of the couple.

The oldest marriage agreements were agreements concerned with the guardianship of the woman, as well as declarations about her share, *máli*, in the couple's property. The woman and the property she brought into a marriage were, according to this scheme, the main objects of the contract. *Kaupmálabréf* was a written testimony concerning this agreement made at marriage. The law code also reflected this interpretation. The word *kvennagiptingar*, the marrying of women, was used in the chapter about marriage regulation in *Jónsbók*.[33]

The contracts were thus to a high degree concerned with the property right of the wife. This can be illustrated by the third oldest Icelandic marriage contract that has survived from the fourteenth century. The

33 *Jónsbók*, p. 70.

contract dates from 1397, and was the marriage contract of Guðríður Ingimundardóttir.[34] The contract states:

> [Witnesses have declared] that they had been nearby and heard the honorable man Vigfús Ívarsson tell that his loving wife, Guðríður Ingimundardóttir, owned 300 hundred in his property in Iceland – or in Norway after the old *markatali*. In addition, she had the gift of one-fourth of all his manorial property, both land and movable property. Then the property owned by Vigfús was 800 hundred. [Her part of the property was then 500 hundred.][35]

Vigfús Ívarsson Hólm was the son of Ívar Hólm and Margrét, and both Vigfús and Ívar held the office of *hirðstjóri* (literally: leader of the king's court), the highest office of the Crown in Iceland.[36] Guðríður was later widowed, and a letter concerning her dealings with the royal administration has survived.[37] This can explain why her marriage contract, as well as the contract of her mother, was kept.[38] These contracts were documentary evidence of what part of the marital property should not be paid to the Crown, because of the outstanding debts of the *hirðstjóri*.

The marriage of Guðríður Ingimundardóttir's parents had also been witnessed in a written document, and this also displays how the marriage agreement was concerned with the woman's position in relation to her future husband. It also dealt with her property rights in relation to her relatives.[39] The division of property between the bride and her brother Gunnar, who was much younger than her, was also covered by the

34 DI III, pp. 616-17. She was daughter of Hólmfríður and Ingimundur, who made a marriage contract in Norway in 1366, compare to DI V, p. 3.

35 "Worum wær j hia ath ærlighr mann wighfus jfuarsson kenndiz firir oss ath gudrid jnnghimundz dotter hans kærligh husfru ææ j hans garde þriu hundroth hundrada a jslande eda j noreghe eftir forngilldu marka tale. þar til fiordunngs giof af öllu sinu godze föstu oc lausu. Reichnadi wighfus bonnde þaa sitt godz viij hunndroth hunndrada."

36 Margrét had become a widow in 1371, and from the document *Máldagi Maríukirkju í Krísuvík* made by the Bishop Oddgeir Þorsteinsson, we know that in her will she had given one-fourth of the landed property at Vatnsleysa and *sæmileg messuklæði* to the church in Krísuvík, see DI III, pp. 290-91. See also Figure 25.

37 DI IV, pp. 284-85. The document states that Guðríður Ingimundardóttir, the wife of Vigfús Hólm, will hand over to the royal authority all the landed property her husband had owned. She also promised to go abroad and meet the king the following summer.

38 The contract of her parents Hólmfríður Ömundardóttir and Ingimundur Uthyrmsson dates from 1366. It is the oldest evidence of a marriage contract published in DI V, p. 3.

39 DI V, p. 3.

contract. The bridegroom gave his bride land, both as a marriage gift[40] and countergift.[41] Some of this property later passed to their daughter Guðríður, as can be seen in the contract from 1397.[42]

Because few contracts have survived from the fourteenth century, it is difficult to say much about trends in these earliest contracts as mentioned before. We can, however, conclude that the oldest marriage contracts provided documentary evidence of the property rights of the wife first and foremost, rather than information about the wider financial arrangements between the couple. Later evidence gives us more information about patterns in contract making. This material indicates that the word *kaupmáli,* which was normally used in the oldest contracts to describe the agreement of a wife's *máli,*[43] gained a wider meaning. Marriage contracts from the early sixteenth century began to be referred to as the *kaupmálabréf* of a couple.[44] This indicates that the contracts began to be more concerned with the entirety of the property of the new household, instead of the emphasis being placed on the property of the future wife. This meant that contracts were no longer only concerned with *kvennagiptingar,* the marriage of women, but also with the union of husbands and wives and the property both partners brought into the marriage.[45] This indicates that the content of the contracts became increasingly concerned with the marital economy.[46]

The lineal principle or the influence of the closest kin in deciding what kind of agreement was made was strong in the earliest contracts. This was related to the fact that the marriage contracts about the financial

40 The marriage gifts were called *bekkjargjöf* and *morghongjöf.* And it was *xx mamata bol* in the land of Horn in Rennisey in Rygjafylki.

41 The countergift *tilgjöf,* was "x marka veð gulls í jörðinni Dal í Rennisey."

42 See DI III, pp. 616-17.

43 As was the case in the contract from 1397. See DI III, pp. 616-17.

44 An example of this is to be found in a contract of 1501. See DI VII, pp. 543-44. On the original document it was written that this was a marriage agreement between Björn Þorleifsson and Ingibjörg Pálsdóttir.

45 Many examples can be cited of this type of contract. Almost all the contracts of *helmingarfélag* were of this type as well as many of the contracts of *máli* from the sixteenth century. See Appendix I.

46 This can also help us to understand the terminological shift in the meaning of the word *kaupmáli,* which was discussed in chapter 6 and 7. In the late fourteenth century the term could be used for both general property contracts, as well as marriage contracts, while at the end of the sixteenth century it was only used in the meaning of marriage. A similar change occurred also for the use of the terms *hjú* and *hjón.* Originally the terms meant a wide group of people who lived in one household. In the sixteenth century the meaning had been more related only to the married couple, and the term *hjón* became used more than *hjú.*

position of the wives were closely related to their role in transferring property from parents to future children. That is why the contract from 1380 of Járngerður Gilsdóttir and Þórður Bessason, witnessed that the fathers of the couple had made this legal marriage agreement.[47] In 1381, Jórunn Brynjólfsdóttir and Ólafur Sigurðsson got married. Björn Brynjólfsson, Jórunn's brother, was her guardian. The contract says that the agreement was made between Jórunn's brother and Björn's father.[48] The closest relatives of the future couple thus made these contracts. It is said in the contract that Ólafur's father provided him with land and movable wealth in order for him to marry Jórunn, and agreed to pay for the wedding from his own resources. The brother of the bride decided the value of the marriage gifts she should receive from her husband. In addition, the brother was to decide whether the agreement should be one for separately-owned property, *tilgjafarkaup*, or shared ownership, *helmingarfélag*.

These oldest contracts show great disparity between law and practice. As mentioned before, according to *Jónsbók* a wife could not deny the husband to make *félag*, which meant that the husband should actually be able to decide what kind of contract the couple made.[49] In the contracts it was, however, not the husband who decided what kind of agreement the couple made, but the brothers or the parents of the bride. Some of the formula used for marriage contracts further illustrate that it was the relatives or parents who decided what kind of contract was made.[50] One example of this parental influence can be taken from a contract made in 1405, which recorded that Guðmundur Þorsteinsson chose that his daughter Sigríður should be *málakona* in her marriage to Arnoddur Brandsson.[51] Because the contracts of *máli* established a wife's separate property within marriage, it is perhaps understandable that some relatives chose this strategy rather than allowing her property to be absorbed into the husband's property in *helmingarfélag*. We can thus

47 DI III, pp. 351-52.
48 DI IV, p. 13.
49 *Jónsbók*, p. 74, compare to NgL II, pp. 76-77.
50 DI V, pp. 505, 582, 611. DI IX, p. 503.
51 DI III, p. 706.

ask whether the principle put forward in *Jónsbók* concerning the role of husbands in determining the type of contract to be used, was greater in the contracts of *helmingarfélag* than *máli.*

Judging on the evidence we have from the surviving contracts this was not in fact the case. The guardians of wives seem also to have played a great role in deciding whether a contract of *helmingarfélag* was made or not. A contract made in 1402 in Reykir in Miðfirði concerned Jón Gunnlaugsson and Þóra Ketilsdóttir. He had three children when this contract was made, and they received the property from his first marriage, before Þóra's father chose that she should be Jón's *helmingarkona.*[52]

Another contract of *helmingarfélag,* concerning the marriage of Brandur Sölvason and Guðlaug Ketilsdóttir, was also made at Reykir in Miðfjörður between the woman's father and a priest, who had a deputy *umboð* from Brandur's father (who was also a priest) to make the deal. It was again the wife's guardian (in this case her father) who decided that she should be *helmingarkona.* The future husband made a *handaband* with her to seal the agreement, while her father gave her property in order to make the agreement with Brandur.[53]

It was thus more common for the guardian of a future wife to decide what kind of agreement was made[54] than it was for the husband to make this decision.[55] According to most of the marriage contracts, it was not the husband but more often the guardian of the bride who decided what form of property ownership the couple should use. As mentioned before, this strong parental control was the reverse of what was dictated by *Jónsbók,* which stressed the importance of the husband's right to rule over his wife. In reality, therefore, while it is possible to identify a shift whereby contracts came to put greater emphasis on marital property rather than simply dealing with *kvennagiptingar,* the strong role of parents

52 Ibid., pp. 678-79. This is the oldest known contract of *helmingarfélag,* even if we have information about marriages made in accordance with that principle before. See also ibid., pp. 488-89 from the year 1393.

53 Ibid., pp. 679-70. In the contract it says: "brandr handlagdi til kaups uid gudlaugu" and "her imot gaf Ketill gudlaugu dottr sinne til kaups uid brand…".

54 Compare to ibid., p. 678. An example can be found in: DI IV, p. 525, of the bride herself deciding the agreement.

55 The only exception to this rule, perhaps, can be found in ibid., p. 358 from 1428. A bridegroom declared that his wife is a *málakona.* Because this is only a declaration about this property agreement of *máli,* it does not give any further information about who had decided she should have separate belongings.

in arranging marriages did not disappear. What is important to underline here is that this parental intervention was not to be concerned with the way the new household was organised. It was rather related to inheritance strategy. Let us study further the inheritance principles behind the different types of contracts.

9.2.2 The different principles of property transfer

In the Old Norwegian legislation the term *málajörð* could mean a landed property which was given away by a family, albeit with the family retaining the right to claim back the same amount of land.[56] The Old Norse meaning of the word *málajörð* was a property that could in part be claimed back from someone else's property.[57] This meaning of the word is not found in the Icelandic documents. There was, however, a possibility for the woman's *máli* to be claimed back by her relatives.

In the contract of Járngerður and Þórður from 1380, it is said that regardless of whether the couple had joint possessions or the wife had separate property, her property would always belong to her, or her heirs, *óbrigðanlega*.[58] This meant that the relatives of the husband could never claim rights over this property. In addition, this land, which was given to her as a dowry, was to be handed over to her on the wedding day. Such contracts clearly aimed at protecting the interests of the wife's family, i.e. the land belonged to the family of the bride, and should not be transferred to those with a consanguineous relationship to the bridegroom.

According to Stig Iuul's study of the Danish *fællig*, the family land, or other land that the couple had inherited, was not part of their joint possessions. The rules concerning Danish *fællig*, along with the English rules concerning joint possession, seem to have been based on excluding inherited land from the contracts. In Denmark inherited land became

56 Arnór Sigurjónsson 1967, p. 25. However, he stressed that in the Icelandic documents from the fifteenth and sixteenth century the word always meant a landed property which was given to a woman.

57 Fritzner II, 1954, p. 627.

58 The meaning of the word *brigð* is 'claim for reversion'. It means that land could be reclaimed by the family from which it had been inherited or bestowed. *Óbrigðanlega* meant that one could not claim the land back. See also discussion here in chapter 3.3, p. 106-107 about the rule of *brigð* in the *réttarbót* of 1294, as well as p. 139-40 about the protest af the clergy against this rule when accepting *Jónsbók*.

a separate property of the woman or man.[59] But in Iceland inherited land as well as the main family manors were more commonly included in the marriage contracts. This was *an important difference.* By including the family land in the joint possessions of the couple, it became difficult to keep the land in the hands of the same family line for generations. Therefore we sometimes find that property was claimed back according to the rules of *brigð.*

One example of this is provided by the marriage of Björn Benediktsson and Elín Pálsdóttir in 1586. The wealth he brought into the marriage amounted to 400 *hundrað* and she brought with her 200 *hundrað.* Included in her wealth was half of the manor at Möðruvellir in Eyjafjörður, as well as the manor at Reykhólar in Reykjanes. He then gave her 60 *hundrað* as a countergift. If the couple did not have any children, the manors involved in the contract could be claimed back by the original families. That is to say that the manors of her family would not be transferred to his family if the couple had no children.[60]

In this way it was possible under a contract of *máli*[61] for the closest kin to make some claim on the property given to a new household. This is also the reason why great variations can be found in contracts of *máli.* These contracts were made according to the needs of the families involved and this is why contracts of *máli,* in contrast to most of the contracts of *helmingarfélag,*[62] were not standardized, but provide detailed information on the terms of the agreements involved.

An example of this is provided by a contract from 1491, which concerned the marriage of Jón Finnbogason and Helga Sæmundsdóttir.[63] His father, Finnbogi Jónsson, was a lawman, and the primary witness to the contract. It was announced that Helga owned a part of her husband's landed property. Moreover, in other forms of wealth she received 80

59 Iuul 1959b, p. 488.

60 NAI, Steinklefi XXXIX, AM Apogr. 1234. No. 60 from 1586. Kaupmálabréf Björns Benediktssonar og Elenar Pálsdóttur. See also the testimony of Jóns Þorlákssonar concerning the same contract number 61. 1586 AM Apogr. 1235.

61 This contract from 1586 was probably a contract of *máli,* because after the husband had given her *tilgjöf,* her possessions amounted to only 260 *hundrað,* while the husband had 340 *hundrað,* which was a common distribution between a couple in a *máli* contract.

62 One exception to this is the contract of Guðmundur Arason and Helga Þorleifsdóttir. See DI IV, p. 312.

63 DI VI, pp. 760-62.

hundrað, and 19 *hundrað* more, as well as the gift he gave to her on their wedding day: this was one-quarter of what he himself had brought to the marriage.[64] The agreement also stated that the husband could decide which possessions – both in land and in movable property – he would transfer to her personal, separate ownership. She consented to this. Then Jón gave her the right to choose the land he would pay her as *máli*, if she became *ein fyrir sér*, which probably means if she became a widow. After that, he gave her the *máli*.[65]

It is not common to find such a full description of the rights granted to a woman. There is also information concerning the woman's property rights during marriage. Jón Finnbogason gave Helga full control during their married life of the landed property of Hafrafellstunga in Öxarfjörður and the land at Gilsbakki, and half the land at Hóll in Skinnastaðaþing. She retained full control of the land she held from his property. The husband claimed all the movable wealth she would own. Following this declaration, she owned no part of his property. This meant that Helga's property had been absorbed into Jón's property, and in return she received certain other lands which she could control during her married life. However, the family land was not to be transferred out of the family line. If she became a widow she would hold the property of Tunga, and one-tenth of the wealth attached to the land. If there was additional wealth it would pass to his heirs. If he became a widower he would retain the following landed properties: Tunga, Gilsbakki and Hóll, and Helga's heirs would retrieve what she had originally contributed to the marriage as dowry. However, Helga's heirs would not get the landed property which her husband had given to her.[66]

This is a very good example showing how the contract of *máli* could be used to bring the possessions of a couple together for the good of their household during their married life. It also illustrates that it remained the right of the bride's family to retrieve their property if she should die without having children.

64 Ibid., pp. 760-61.
65 Ibid., p. 761.
66 Ibid., pp. 761-62.

Thus, even if property was put into the finances of a household, it did not necessarily disappear into the household, and it could be claimed back by the donors. A document from 1574 illustrates the importance of the interests of the closest relatives. It is a property contract concerning land at Víðidalsá, sold by a husband to his wife, if he should live longer than she did, along with a quantity of movable wealth. In return the wife handed over to her husband the land that her father had given her on the day they were married: her dowry. She also gave to her husband what he had given to her. In other words, she exchanged her marriage portion for the land at Víðidalsá. However, if the husband lived longer, then Víðidalsá would be returned to him and his wife's heirs would retrieve her dowry.[67]

This case concerning the preservation of Víðidalsá as a property attached to the husband's family line, also indicates how this couple sought to guarantee the continuation of their marital economy if the wife should be widowed. Víðidalsá would ensure the financial well-being of the widow, but would never become the property of her family. Contracts of *máli* could therefore uphold two important principles: that inherited land should stay in the same family line, and that marital property should be kept together after the death of one of the spouses. This latter principle, to keep the property together, was also one of the main purposes behind *helmingarfélag*.

What then was the difference between the contracts of *máli* and of *helmingarfélag*? The fifteenth century is the period from which most of the *helmingarfélag* contracts emanate. Often these simply stated that a couple had shared goods, but without listing the possessions involved. One example of such a contract was that made between Einar Jónsson and Sigríður Einarsdóttir on their wedding day in 1420. It was a *helmingarfélag*, a very short document, as were many other documents concerned with jointly-owned property.[68] Although some of these docu-

67 AM dipl.isl.fasc. LXV, 27 compare to 25 and 26.
68 DI IV, pp. 277-78.

ments do not give information about the type of contract, it is indirectly possible to see that the couple probably made *helmingarfélag*.[69]

Details given about property in *helmingarfélag* contracts does not seem to have been deemed as important as that contained in a *mála* contract, even if this was not always the case. In 1423 the powerful Guðmundur Arason made an arrangement for jointly-owned property with Helga Þorleifsdóttir. It was the couple, along with the bride's father and mother, that decided that she should be *helmingarkona* with the consent and handshake of Guðmundur and his father's brother, who was Guðmundur's closest relative. This is an example of a marriage settlement agreed between two powerful families.[70] A witness letter from 1453 has also survived in relation to this marriage.[71] In this way an alliance between two of the richest families in the country was made. The marriage contract of Guðmundur and Helga reads as follows:

In dei nomine amen.

On the wedding day [on the farm Vatnsfjörður] this marriage contract was published and confirmed, by Guðmundur Arason and Helga Þorleifsdóttir. … Gudmundur gave 1200 *hundrað*[72] to the settlement with Helga. Her father Þorleifur Árnason gave against this to his daughter the landed property of Bær in Rauðasandur for the settlement with Guðmundur for 100 *hundrað* as well as 100 *hundrað* in other landed property and 100 hundred in movable goods.

Guðmundur gave Helga a gift of one quarter *fjórðungsgjöf*[73] from his 1200 *hundrað* that he had for making this settlement with her. Kristín Björnsdóttir decided that her daughter Helga should be Guðmundur's *helmingarkona* considering their wealth and the wealth they would acquire in the future. Kristín did this with the consent of Guðmundur and Rafn Guðmundsson, his father's brother, who was his closest relative. Helga should also own in addition to this 40 *hundrað* in other useful tools that Guðmundur had given her as *bekkjargjöf*.

69 In 1420 Ari Guðmundsson gave his daughter *til kavps vid* Halldór Jónsson a half part of the landed property of Valþjófsdalur, for making a marriage agreement with her future husband, Halldór. It merely attests that the father gave his daughter half of a farm in order to make an agreement with Halldór, and then sold the other part of this farm to Halldór himself. Probably this agreement was made so that the couple could live at the farm in Valþjófsdalur, and own the possession jointly. See DI IV, pp. 278-79. She probably made another marriage contract with Hákon Jónsson in 1433. See ibid., p. 525.

70 Ibid., p. 312.

71 DI V, pp. 108-109.

72 This was a great amount of wealth. *Höfuðból*, a manor, was 60 *hundrað* or more.

73 A gift that was one-quarter of his property.

The witnesses to this marriage were: Loftur Guttormsson, Rafn Guðmundsson, Auðunn Salamonsson, Árni Einarsson, Gamli Marteinsson, Gunnar Andrésson and Helgi Guttormsson.

And to prove this we those before named men put our seals to this letter, written in the same place, in the same year, two nights after this happened.[74]

According to a copy of this contract, the manor at Bær, also called Saurbær, had been given to Helga by her father, Þorleifur Árnason, for 100 *hundrað*.[75] It is important to notice that no rules excluded the manor from the property, which could be divided amongst the heirs of Helga and Guðmundur. But as the contract illustrates, jointly-owned property could not be established without the consent of the closest relatives of the couple if they had no legitimate children. This could also mean that couples often established their jointly-owned property after they had had children. In order to be certain of the legitimacy of this jointly-owned property witnesses were needed.[76] However, normally there was not the same need to provide details about the property covered by contracts of *helmingarfélag* as was the case for contracts of *máli,* because the couple shared property equally during marriage, and after their death the property should also be divided equally between the heirs.[77] In the case of Guðmundur and Helga, however, property details were indeed necessary with regard to which land Helga brought into the marriage.

The existence of this *helmingarfélag* contract is in part a consequence

74 DI IV, p. 312. "[Í Vatnsfirði]…Jn dei nomine amen. Lýstizt ok stadfestizt suo felldur kaupmale millum gudmundar bonda arasonar ok helgu þorleifsdóttur aa þeirra brudlaupsdege … at nefndur gudmundr hafde tolf hundrud hundrada i sina eigin peninga til kaups med helgu. hier j mot gaf þorleifur arnason helgu dottur sinne til kaups med gudmund jordina j be aa Raudasande firir hundrad hundrada ok þar til hundrad hundrada j audrum jordum. ok hundrad hundrada j lausagoze. gaf optt nefndur gudmundr títt nefndre helgu fiordungs giof af þeim tolf hundrut hundrada sem hann hafde til kaups med hana. kiore Kristínn biornsdotter helgu dottur sina med samþycke ok handabande sialfs guðmundar ok Rafns gudmundzsonar faudurbrodr hans er þar uar þa honum skylldaztur helmingar kono j gard gudmundar allz fiar feingins ok ofeingins. skyllde nefnd helga eiga um framm helming j gard guðmundar fioratige hundrada j semeligum. gripum uoruuirdum. er títt nefndur guðmundur gaf þratt nefndre helgu j sina beckiar giof. Voru þesser brudlaupsuottar … Ok til sanninda hier um settum uer fyr nefnder menn vor jnnciglle firir þetta bref skrifat j sama stad ok are tueim nottum sidar enn fyrr segir." A witness's letter from 1453 concerning this marriage has also survived. See DI V, pp. 108-109.

75 Ibid. This transcription belonged to Guðrún Eggertsdóttir in Bær in 1486.

76 Ibid., pp. 130-31.

77 These agreements usually concerned all of a couple's property, and the property they expected to acquire during their married life. See Hrefna Róbertsdóttir 1986, pp. 33-34.

of a case called *Guðmundarmál*,[78] a long and complicated inheritance dispute about the greatest landholding in Iceland at that time, (see Figure 26). Many of the marriage contracts existed as documents to be used in inheritance disputes, and cannot, thus, be fully understood out of that context. Other documents illustrate the marriage strategy of the involved families. One of these is the contract of Þorvarður Erlendsson and Kristín Gottskálksdóttir, the daughter of the Bishop Gottskálkur of Hólar, which provides detailed information about their *helmingarfélag*.[79] This contract was announced and confirmed and was made between Þorvarður and Kristín themselves in the year of 1508. She received a dowry from her father, Bishop Gottskálkur, and as a countergift from her husband-to-be she was able to choose between two landed properties. Her husband also gave her marriage gifts. Gottskálkur decided that his daughter should be *helmingarkona*. The bishop's intention must have been to ensure that his daughter should get a share in all the future property of the couple. *Helmingarfélag* was a contract intended to expand the household, rather than just preserving the possessions of a wife as under a contract of *máli*.[80]

Gottskálkur made another contract for the second marriage of his daughter, in 1515.[81] At this time she was probably a widow, and after having received half of the possessions from her first marriage, this contract was made to safeguard her personal property. In this situation *máli* was a better strategy for securing the wealth she retained from her first marriage.[82] Her possessions continued to be her personal property, while under her first marriage contract of *helmingarfélag* she and her father probably had the skillfulness to acquire more land than she could otherwise have acquired under a *máli* contract.

A study of joint ownership in other countries also provides further indications as to why people may have preferred to use this type of agreement. According to the English historian Amy Louise Ericksson, a joint tenancy of land by husband and wife in medieval England had

78 DI IV, pp. 264-65.

79 DI VIII, pp. 230-32, compare to *Annálar* 1400-1800, vol. I, p. 78.

80 The wife could not get the profit of her property according to the contract of *máli*.

81 DI VIII, pp. 543-44.

82 Ibid., pp. 725-26. This is a testimony about the conversation of Bishop Gottskálkur and Jón about the marriage agreement.

the advantage that the surviving partner enjoyed the income from land held in this way.[83] This may also explain why *helmingarfélag* became preferred by some families in Iceland; the difference, however, was that the patrimony – or main estate – remained intact for the heir, whilst in England it was not included in this agreement.[84]

Many of the Icelandic *helmingarfélag* contracts concern the wealthiest families.[85] The joint possessions of *helmingafélag* should include all the property of a couple, as well as their future inheritances. This was perhaps the greatest difference between *helmingarfélag* and *máli*. The contract of *helmingarfélag* was thus more suitable for those who were trying to accumulate land, while the contract of *máli* was a better strategy for keeping land inside the family line.

Secondly, not all the property settlements under *helmingarfélag* contracts give clear reasons why it was sometimes preferred to *máli*. It is possible that people who did not own much land got married in accordance with this principle. Not all of these contracts give information about the wealth of the couple. A very short contract from 1562 only informs that the couple made *helmingarfélag*, but it is also stated that no agreements were made about their wealth. The document is preserved in a copy of Árni Magnússon, and he assumed the couple to be very poor.[86] The reason why so little information has been preserved about the contracts of poor people must be related to the fact that extended contracts have survived primarily because of their importance as documentary evidence of property rights. Further contracts of *helmingarfélag* continued to be shorter than contracts of *máli* because in these instances there was not the same need to describe the possessions of each family, since once the jointly-owned property had been established each couple would own half of the property.[87] One example of this kind of contract was made in 1489 and written down in 1503:

83 Erickson 1995, p. 26.

84 Ibid., p. 26. This was also the conclusion of Hrefna Róbertsdóttir about the jointly-owned property of helmingafélag, see Hrefna Róbertsdóttir 1986, pp. 31-40.

85 Ibid., p. 33.

86 DI XIII, p. 687.

87 See for instance from 1489, DI VI, p. 683; from 1491, ibid., p. 738; from 1495, DI VII, pp. 250-51; and from 1498, ibid., p. 406.

[It is announced] that Bjarni Jónsson bonded Guðrún Ólafsdóttir to be his legal wife after the law of God on their wedding day … with the priest Kolbeinn Ingimundarsson and other decent men present. This was done on the condition … [that the couple should] make an agreement for jointly-owned property concerning all the wealth that they had, and that they would get.[88]

A third reason to make a *helmingarfélag* was that the contract of *helmingarfélag* gave the woman and her relatives a stronger position than one of *hjónafélag*. Here we have so far underlined that the wife appeared as an independent actor in the marriage contract as a result of the fact that marriage had become a union between the bride and the bridegroom. This can be interpreted as a result of the fact that the woman's kin became less influential. Previously, the family of a bride had protected her property rights, but from the fourteenth century onwards it was also important according to the law that the bride herself ensured that her husband did not abuse his rights. What matters here is that according to the legal rules of *félag* the husband should decide which parts of their property should be his wife's, and which parts should be his. This limited the power of the wife's relatives in relation to the financial arrangements of her household. Thus, in theory the institution of *félag* clearly strengthened the position of the newly married couple, especially the husband's in relation to the closest heirs of his wife[89] and it was closer to the ideal of the Church model of the sacredness of marriage than to the older rules about making property agreements about separate belongings.[90] At the same time the institution of *félag* was adjusted to accommodate the needs of the closest heirs, so that they would be involved in the making of *helmingarfélag* if no children were born to the marriage.

Both the lack of *hjónafélag* contracts, as well as the trend in contracts of *helmingarfélag* and *máli*, would indicate that property transfers were made while always bearing the interests of parents or the closest kinfolk of the couple in mind.

88 DI VI, p. 683: "ad biarne ionson festi sier gudrvnv olafsdottur til lavgligrar eiginkonu efter guds lavum aa þeirra bryllavfsdegi … ed nærveranda síra kolbeine ingemundarsyne og avdrvm dande monnum med þui skilorde … lavgdv med sier helmingafielag feingens fiar og ofeingens."

89 *Jónsbók*, pp. 73-74.

90 Dübeck 2003, p. 57. See also Brundage 1990, p. 479.

At this point what remains to be considered – against a background of the fact that the interest of the closest relatives of the couple was stronger in *helmingarfélag* than in *hjónafélag* – is the question of what the main differences between contracts of *máli* and contracts of *helmingarfélag* were. The answer is closely related to the matter of inheritance. Firstly, under the contract of *máli*, a wife had no right to what the couple might acquire during her marriage. Any profit would go to her husband or his heirs. Secondly, in contrast to *helmingarfélag* the heirs of a husband and wife would inherit equally. If there were children, the household could remain undivided under the control of the widow or widower until one of the children could take charge. If a contract of *máli* was made, the heirs of the husband would, however, receive what he owned, while the heirs of the wife would get only what she had taken into the marriage if they had no children. If there were children they would inherit from their mother and father separately. This was thus a strategy which was primarily concerned with not transferring inherited property between family lines. If a woman was widowed under this system she had only the right to receive her *máli*.[91] This is one of the reasons why it was important to give detailed information about what possessions belonged to the wife under the contract of *máli*.[92] Thirdly, *máli* did not always necessarily refer to what a woman received as a dowry or as a countergift from her husband. If this property was sold, during the married life of a couple, the value of that *máli* could easily be transferred to another

91 According to the law of *Jónsbók* a wife should retrieve her *máli* if her husband died. If the husband became a widower, the woman's heirs would receive only her dowry and the husband would regain what he had given to her as countergift if they had no legitimate children. See *Jónsbók*, p. 74. This was the case according to the marriage contract of Jón and Helga in 1491. Sometimes there could be problems, however, with declaring whether the gift of the husband was included in the *máli* when division occurred. Compare to *Alþingisbækur Íslands* I, pp. 260-61 from 1574. Many court cases were related to this issue, see for instance DI IX, pp. 268-69. See also *Alþingisbækur Íslands* I, p. 241, and compare to ibid., I, p. 306, which is a judgement concerning the case of Þorbjörg Andrésdóttir.

92 These kinds of documents related to property transfer were of course not only related to marriage. In 1553 a priest declared that Halldór Jónsson, also a priest, had told him that his sister, Ingibjörg Jónsdóttir owned a great deal of wealth in his property, which was her share of the inheritance from her father and mother. See DI XII, p. 628, compare to "ætti under sier stora peninga. sem være fodurarfur hennar og modur." Ownership of a portion within another person's property was a common form by which a woman's belongings could be put at the disposal of her husband or other guardians. See for instance the *máli* of Guðrún Andrésdóttir from 1481 in DI VI, p. 349, and the letter of witness, pp. 417-18 concerning the separate property of a woman. Compare to ibid., pp. 422-23 which is another witness letter concerning Dálkastaðir, and ibid., pp. 423-34 is a witness letter of Hallgeir concerning the same matter.

property. An example of this can be taken from a property contract made in 1377 concerning land at Lýtingsstaðir and Hof.[93] Benedikt Gizurarson sold the land at Lýtingstaðir in Skagafjörður and got instead Hofsjarðir from Sigurður Þorleifsson, with the exception of the land that belonged to the church at Giljar. The children of Benedikt, Böðvar and Solveig, transferred by handshake all their wealth from the land at Lýtingstaðir and Hof. The wife of Sigurður, Guðrún, did the same, transferring her *máli* from Lýtingstaðir to Hof.[94]

What is interesting in this case is that the property of the wife was greater than the land at Lýtingsstaðir. Sigurður made the rest of his wife's possessions part of his best property, and this was sealed by her handshake.[95] Her property could thus be placed with the husband's possessions so that the two were combined. If she wanted to retrieve her property, she could claim the amount of her *máli*, but would not necessarily receive the specific property she had received as dowry.

This same problem could also arise if the couple had *helmingarfélag*. This is why Erlendur Þorvarðsson and Þórunn Sturludóttir made an agreement in 1525 concerning the land she would own if she became a widow.[96] The difference was, however, that under the contract of *helmingarfélag* the widow would always receive half of what belonged to the property of the couple. More importantly, it was a strategy that could leave the property undivided after the death of one of the spouses. The partner who lived longer could decide how to continue managing their land.

In Table III, we can see that by the end of this period it was becoming less common to make a contract of *helmingarfélag*. *Helmingarfélag* was not the preferred marriage strategy of the Icelandic aristocracy in the sixteenth century. Jointly-owned property did not become very common again until after the new legislation of King Christian V in the

93 DI III, pp. 317-19.
94 Ibid., pp. 318-19.
95 Ibid., p. 319.
96 DI IX, pp. 288-89.

late seventeenth century. This can be seen, for instance, in the fact that spouses usually paid taxes separately during the seventeenth century.[97]

One of the reasons why jointly-owned property was not commonly in use could be that inherited property was included in the Icelandic *helmingarfélag*. Couples were to own all their possessions jointly. One of the results of Inger Dübeck's study of the Danish *fællig* is that she actually does not interpret the joint principle as an effort to make the kin-based principle of inheritance transfer weaker. Rather, she assumes that *fællig* actually made it easier to keep landed property inside the family, and as such strengthened the kin in relation to the Church for instance.[98] The situation in Iceland was quite different, because the main manor could be included in the *helmingarfélag*. These agreements did not only concern the wealth that a couple brought into their marriage, but also the wealth they would gain or lose during their married life.[99] As mentioned before, this marriage strategy could thus be used to acquire property, but it was not a useful strategy to keep land within the family from which it came. In times of recession it would probably have been more appropriate to make a contract of *máli*. This pattern of making marriage contracts could thus indicate certain social or economic changes in Icelandic society at the end of the Late Middle Ages.

In the last section of this chapter I shall take a closer look at the strategy behind the different principles of property transfer at the end of the fifteenth and in the sixteenth century in Iceland.

9.3 Property strategies of the aristocracy in the fifteenth and sixteenth centuries

A document has survived from the end of the fifteenth century which includes a statement from Björn Guðnason concerning how his property, as well as that of his wife, Ragnhildur Bjarnadóttir, should be disposed

97 See Jón Pétursson 1863, pp. 235-36, and *Lovsamling for Island* III, p. 3, as well as *Lovsamling for Island* IV, pp. 668-69.

98 Dübeck 2003, p. 87.

99 The contracts referred to all the property which the couple owned or would acquire. It was called *allz fiar feingins og ofeingins* as in DI IX, p. 643 from the year 1532. Or *j feingum peningum ok ofeingnu*m, as in DI V, 1449, p. 30.

of should he die abroad. Björn begged his friends and relatives "father, mother, brother and sister and those in charge of their households, not to ruin his agreement, rather give it strength and support both him and his friends, who are my children and wife."[100] I have previously discussed this person's role in the dispensation case of Þorleifur Björnsson and Ingveldur Helgadóttir.[101] With this dispute in mind, we can better understand how ardent he was about keeping his own property within his closest family. He expresses a husband's earnest concern about the belongings of his family left in Iceland, especially his wife and children. At the same time, however, the document expresses his fear that in his absence, his relatives might lay claim to his property and not respect the property rights of his family. As already discussed in part II, the change in the meaning and making of marriage contracts also affected the social bond that was produced by marriage. It could bring stronger ties between the couple, what we could be termed 'marital solidarity', and this was clearly the case for Björn Guðnason. He was primarily concerned with keeping his family property together, but he was nevertheless perfectly aware of the interests of his relatives. It was for this reason that he decided to make this property agreement on 27 July 1497, before going abroad. His wife had been married with a *máli* contract, which meant that she could only claim her own possessions should anything happen to Björn. It was for this reason also that before he left he gave his wife all those gifts that he was legally allowed to give her. Björn declared that Gunnsteinn Ásgrímsson should be in charge of his wife's property until he returned.[102] If Björn had made a *helmingarfélag* with his wife the situation would have been less critical when he went abroad because this would have given better protection to the interests of his wife and his household against his rivals.[103]

The letter of Björn Guðnason is interesting because it provides information about his strategy for managing his property. He was trying

100 DI VII, pp. 368-70: "födur og modur. brodur og systur. og þeirra husbændur. ad þeir giori i heidur vid mic og fyrir mijna bön og hryggid ekki þennan minn giorning helldur stydied hann og styrked i öllu sem madur vonar uppa alla göda hluti til ydar. bædi til mijn og minna vina. sem er mijn börn og kona."

101 See here discussion in chapter 5.2.3, especially on pp. 185-88.

102 DI VII, pp. 368-70.

103 As mentioned before on pp. 184 ff., Björn Guðnason struggled with many of his relatives to get control of the great wealth of Björn Þorleifsson.

to acquire wealth for himself and his own family. He was not alone in claiming the right to that wealth: his efforts were related to great inheritance disputes between the ruling families at the end of the fifteenth and the start of the sixteenth centuries. Björn Guðnason actually came back to Iceland and made a *helmingarfélag* with his wife at a later stage[104] and also married his children off according to the principle of jointly-owned property: in 1507 he made a marriage contract for his daughter (although this contract was first written down in 1520).[105] His son, Jón Björnsson, made a *helmingarfélag* with Kristín Sumarliðadóttir.[106] A document concerning inheritance divisions after the death of Björn, states that the manor at Ögur should belongs to the widow.[107] This meant that the contract of *helmingarfélag* ensured that the manor did not pass on to any of the rivals among Björn's relatives.

It seems that *helmingarfélag* was often made to further the personal and political aims of powerful men or families. Björn Guðnason's policy of using *helmingarfélag* when marrying his children off reminds us of the policy which had also been employed during the thirteenth century in Iceland by Snorri Sturlason.[108] This illustrates how the use of different principles for making marriage contracts was not necessarily part of a general change in trends in making marriage. Rather, these were possible ways by which inheritance rules could be used to secure the political and financial position of a family. The property could be controlled by the widow, if the husband died, as was also the case when Ólöf ríka was in charge of the manor Skarð in Skarðsströnd after the death of her husband. Moreover, this was the strategy of the ambitious aristocracy of the fifteenth century when, after the plague of 1402-04 it became possible for a great amount of land to become "movable".

Later in the same century great changes occurred in production, which probably also had consequences for economic growth. First the

104 DI VIII, pp. 136-38.

105 Ibid., pp. 165-66. This was the contract of Bjarni Andrésson and Guðrún Björnsdóttir, daugther of Björn Guðnason.

106 Ibid., pp. 217-18. She became a widow in 1508.

107 DI IX, pp. 234-35.

108 See Agnes S. Arnórsdóttir 1995, pp. 161-62.

manors on the coastline started to be more profitable,[109] and many of the rich families of the century such as the Skarðsverjar family used these manors as the foundation for their wealth and power. Another was the before-mentioned Guðmundur Arason, who made a contract with Helga Þorleifsdóttir in 1423.[110] Helga was the daughter of Þorleifur Árnason and Kristín Björnsdóttir of Vatnsfjörður. Guðmundur's family was not well-known until after his father had accumulated his wealth following the Black Death. And because Guðmundur had inherited three manors from his father, and had gained a fourth – Saurbær in Rauðasandur – through marriage, he became a leading figure of his time. He is assumed to have been one of the richest men in Iceland,[111] although he lost his property to the king in 1446,[112] and died four years later. He had been district commissioner, *sýslumaður*, in Húnaþing and was related by marriage to many of the mightiest men in the country. But due to his misdemeanors, which included robbery among other things, in 1457 he was taken to court by his brother-in-law, where half of his property was seized by the Crown as payment for his fine, and the remainder was passed to his heirs. This led to a great inheritance dispute,[113] which – as mentioned before – is probably one of the reasons why we have the marriage contract and many other preserved documents relating to property transfer by Guðmundur ríki, (see Figure 27).

The newcomers of the fifteenth century did not only live at the manors by the coast. They could also combine the old tradition of basing their farming activities at their hinterland manors with the benefits derived from the activities at their coastal manors. An example of this is provided by Jón Finnbogason who married Steinunn Arnfinnsdóttir and

109 See also the discussion on pp. 49-52, and see especially Figure 2. It is not within the scope of this study to examine further the relationship between the change of the fifteenth century manorial culture and the marriage strategy of the aristocracy. That would be a subject for another study. Financial change has been studied partly by Þorkell Jóhannesson, Björn Þorsteinsson Helgi Þorláksson and Árni Daníel Júlíusson.

110 See here the contract in chapter 9.2.2 pp. 316-17.

111 Compare to *Íslenskur söguatlas* I, p. 136. He is assumed to have owned 3217 *hundrað* in landed property, and 788 cow's value.

112 Jón Jóhannesson 1958, pp. 66-67, compare to DI IV, pp. 683-94. Einar Þorleifsson got hold of this property from the king, and later his brother Björn Þorleifsson inherited from him. At that time Björn was the richest man in Iceland, keeping all the wealth of the family of Skarðsverjar, Vatnsfirðingar, as well as the property of Guðmundur.

113 *Íslenskur söguatlas* I, p. 139.

thereby gained land at Ólafsfjörður and in the hinterland of Svarfaðardalur. For most of their married life they lived on the farm at Grund in Svarfaðardalur, which had been the main property of Steinunn's grandfather. Jón benefited further because he was married at the beginning of the fifteenth century, when land in Ólafsfjörður and around Eyjafjörður became more valuable.[114]

Another rich and powerful figure of the fifteenth century who should be mentioned in this context was Björn Þorleifsson, who married Ólöf Loftsdóttir, the daughter of Loftur Guttormsson. Ólöf's family's main manor was Skarð in Skarðströnd in Breiðafjörður.[115] This is one of the few cases in Icelandic history where the same family had been living on the same manor since 1100.[116] The manor in question was among those that gained importance during the fourteenth and fifteenth centuries because of the growing trade in stockfish. However, the wealth of the Skarðverjar family did not only come from their manor. In 1430 Loftur Guttormsson, Ólöf's father, owned seventeen great manors and farms in the north, east and south of Iceland.[117] Loftur Guttormsson was a powerful man and a poet,[118] who was renowned for having many relationships with women.[119] He was born in 1375 or 1376 into a family that was not well known, but came from the district of Eyjafjörður.[120]

The property of two rich families was united in one household by the marriage of Björn Þorleifsson and Ólöf Loftsdóttir. Their marriage contract has not survived, although we do have their probate letter, *skiptabréf*.[121] They owned almost all the land in the district of Vestfirðir, and many farms in the northern and southern parts of Iceland, but little in the eastern region. They had managed to get a portion of the property of Guðmundur Arason, partly by buying it back from the Danish

114 Arnór Sigurjónsson 1967, p. 28.

115 This is the same Ólöf who kept the written confession at her farm; see the discussion here pp. 203-206.

116 Björn Þorsteinsson and Guðrún Ása Grímsdóttir 1990, p. 89, compare to Ólafur Lárusson 1944, pp. 230-43.

117 Compare to DI IV, p. 404, *gjafabréf Lopts Guttormssonar*. He owned: Skarð in Skarðsströnd, Staðarhóll in Saurbæ, Möðruvellir in Eyjafjörður, Sjávarborg in Skagafjörður, Ásgeirsá in Víðidalur, Eiðar in Eiðaþinghá, Ketilsstaðir in Vellir and Dalir under Eyjafjöllum.

118 Jón Þorkelsson 1888, pp. 237-48.

119 See *Annálar 1400-1800*, vol. I, p. 58.

120 Jón Þorkelsson 1888, p. 237. See also pp. 237-38 for information about Loftur Guttormsson.

121 DI XII, pp. 46-53. Their children were Þorleifur, Einar, Solveig and Árni. See *Annálar 1400-1800*, vol. I, p. 51.

Crown, and partly through inheritance from Einar, Björn's brother.[122] Their lifestyle reflected their wealth. According to a later account of their life they were supposed to have always travelled with eighteen mounted men each.[123] Björn Þorleifsson, who was killed by English merchants in 1467, was the son of Þorleifur Árnason and Kristín Björnsdóttir. In 1413 Þorleifur and Kristín lived on the manor at Vatnsfjörður, and they had a *helmingarfélag*.[124]

Björn and Ólöf lived mainly at the manor at Skarð, and after Björn's death in 1467 Ólöf continued to manage the manor until her own death in 1479. After this their son Þorleifur, who was a *sýslumaður* and later also *hirðstjóri* (like his father), received the manors at Skarð and Reykhólar, while Einar and Solveig lived at other manors owned by this family.[125] But, as mentioned in chapter 5, there was a great problem related to the division of the property after the siblings Þorleifur and Solveig had both married within the fourth degree of the line of descent.

The people mentioned here were the "lords and ladies" of the coastal manors during the Late Middle Ages. Their prominence was related to the greater importance of the fishing industry, and the area of Vestfirðir was especially important in this period. The use of *helmingarfélag* as well as marriage dispensations was an important part of their political strategy. This strategy did not, however, secure that the wealth was kept inside the same family for centuries.

Helmingafélag was not a very good strategy for keeping wealth, although it did work as a means by which to acquire it. Several other reasons can also be mentioned why these rich people who made *helmingarfélag* did not manage to keep their wealth inside the family. Guðmundur Arason, for example, did not follow the customary rules of property transfer in that he did not accept his father's widow's right to her belongings. Before Guðmundur himself got married he should have given the

122 Björn Þorsteinsson and Guðrún Ása Grímsdóttir 1990, p. 11.

123 Jón Guðmundson 1902, p. 717.

124 See DI IV, pp. 273-75: in a judgement at Grund in Eyjafjörður from 1420, it is mentioned that Björn Einarsson and Solveig Þorsteinsdóttir had *helmingarfélag*. They were the parents of Kristín. Kristín became a widow, and gained the nickname Vatnsfjarðar-Kristín. *Annálar 1400-1800*, vol. I, p. 51.

125 Björn Þorsteinsson and Guðrún Ása Grímsdóttir 1990, p. 89. The marriage strategy of both Þorleifur and Solveig has been discussed on pp. 182-87 in relation to the forbidden degrees of marriage.

widow Þorgerður her property as it was important to clear all claims to property after an owner's death. So according to an *afhendingarbréf* (a letter), Guðmundur Arason had in 1418 paid to his father's widow her *máli*, separate property. The document was made at the farm of Núpur in Dýrafjörður by Þorgerður and Guðmundur, and Guðmundur is said to have paid her 500 *hundrað*. After this, Guðmundur is supposed – in addition – to have given Þorgerður land at Barðsvík in Strandir, along with other wealth totaling 100 *hundrað*. [126]

This transfer is referred to in another judgement concerning the wealth of Guðmundur Arason which was made on 11 May 1500, called the judgement of *Mýrardómur*.[127] It states that Guðmundur had never paid this sum to Þorgerður, but kept it himself until the end of his life. According to the judgement of *Mýrardómur*, what was at stake was not only Þorgerður's wealth but that of her daughter, Ólöf Aradóttir, which was her inheritance from Ari Guðmundsson and Þorgerður Ólafsdóttir. Her inheritance was about 900 hundred and her brother Guðmundur Arason had no right to it, the document says.[128] Ólöf had forbidden her brother to keep this wealth, which was made up of landed property, movable goods and livestock. She had received four hundred from her father, and five from her mother.[129] Her brother had probably taken this property after their father died. The wealth was judged to belong to Ólöf. Ari Andrésson, who at that time controlled the property of Guðmundur Arason, should have passed this property on to her. However, this affair was complicated by the fact that Ari had received the land from his father, Andrés Guðmundsson, when he made a marriage contract with Þórdís Gísladóttir in 1495.[130] According to the judgement of *Mýrardómur*, Ari was ordered to return the property to Þorgerður's heirs.

126 DI VI, pp. 41-42. This document is also printed in DI IV, pp. 264-65. On the front page of this document it was later written that one "hundrað hundraða" was probably missing from this list, and that was the manor at Reykhólar. The following landed property was given to Þorgerður: Kirkjuból in Romshvalsnesi, Fulavik, Þórirstaðir, Hrafnkelsstaðir for one 100 hundred together, Hrafnseyri in Arnafjörður for one 100 *hundrað*, Horn, Kirkjuból, Skógar, Dynjandi in Mosdal, Half Borg in Mosdal, Skáldfönn in Mosdal, Álfadalur in Ingialdssandur, for one 100 *hundrað* together.

127 DI VII, pp. 479-83.

128 DI VI, pp. 215-17, from 16 July 1479. See also Figure 19.

129 Ibid., pp. 226-27, from 9 October 1479.

130 DI VII, pp. 250-51. See DI VI, pp. 558-59.

Guðmundur Arason is thus a prime example of those newcomers who did not feel themselves bound by the customary inheritance rules of the country. Loftur Guttormsson, the father of Ólöf ríka was a similar figure. He had been a member of the court of King Eric of Pomerania. Loftur was a governor, *hirðstjóri*, over the northern and eastern regions of Iceland between 1427 and 1432, and should have been the royal officer who judged Guðmundur ríki for his plundering in that period. However, Guðmundur was not charged by the royal authority for his illegal activities. It was first in the *Langarréttarbót* of King Christian I from 1450 that laws were introduced to punish that kind of behavior.

The rich men of fifteenth century Iceland could be described as adventurers since they seem to have been able to behave according to their own rules because of their great wealth. For instance, although Loftur was married, he had a relationship with another woman with whom he had many children. He transferred property to them using the institution of legal gifts. Many of these powerful people connected to the royal authority came into conflict with the clerical authorities. For example, Þorvarður Loftsson (d. 1446) drowned Bishop Jón Gerreksson in the river Brúará in 1433. At a later stage Jón Sigmundsson (d. 1520) was in continual dispute with Bishop Gottskálkur of Hólar, which led to Jón being excommunicated several times. Jón Sigmundsson and Björn Guðnason of Ögur had both been fighting the Church authorities, and were among the main protagonists who acted against the Church leaders in 1513 by issuing the document called *Leiðarhólmsskrá*.[131]

The fifteenth century was thus a period of great change and turbulence. It was a time when new families came to power, and because of the high mortality rates after the plague, land was easily concentrated in a few hands. A common problem after the plagues of 1402-04 and of 1494-95, was that the chronological order in which people died was not known. This had great importance for the inheritance strategies of the following generations. An example can be taken from a written testimony of 1567, concerning the death of Solveig Björnsdóttir, the daughter of Björn Þorleifsson and Ólöf Loftsdóttir, and other members of her family. According

131 *Íslenskur söguatlas*, pp. 139, 140-41, Helgi Þorláksson 2003, pp. 45-48.

to the statement, she died in 1495, after her son, Jón Pálsson.[132] Another written statement concerning the same matter says that her son died first, followed by the daughters of Solveig's brother, and then Solveig herself.[133] Because of these different testimonies it was not clear who was the right heir of the great wealth of this family. Other information has survived in relation to another case from the north of Iceland in 1557. It concerned the deaths in the family of Steinn Brandsson, who lived on the manor at Auðbrekka in Hörgárdalur during the Black Death of 1494-95. According to the document Steinn died after his wife, with all Steinn's children dying after him.[134] These cases were both related to the later plague of 1494-95. The situation must have been even worse after the first plague of 1402-04, although there is less written evidence of confusion from this period.

The strategy used to *gain* wealth was not a good strategy for keeping it. This was also related to the situation after the second plague at the end of the fifteenth century. The *Möðruvallaréttarbót* was issued to counteract inheritance disputes of the type that emerged after the Black Death.[135] This new law ruled that when a child inherited from one of his or her parents, with the other parent later inheriting from the child, the surviving parent or their heirs would only receive movable property and not the main manor. The text is as follow:

> If a child inherits from his or her mother and later the father inherits from the child, then the father and his heirs shall not inherit from the child other belongings than property that is movable. The same principle shall also be used if a mother inherits from her child, who had previously inherited from his or her father.[136]

What is at issue here is the transfer of property between two families. It is designed not to let land pass out of the family to which it belonged.

132 DI XIV, pp. 582-84. See also the discussion about her in chapter 5.2.3, pp. 187-89.

133 DI XIV, p. 609.

134 Concerning this case, see Árni Daníel Júlíusson's unpublished thesis 1995, p. 80. See also another case of this type in DI XIII, p. 182. The problem was related to remembering who died first during the Black Death, the parents or the children.

135 DI II, pp. 379-80. See also Figure 28, altar frontal from Möðruvellir.

136 Ibid., p. 382: "Fyrst at upphafe at þar sem barn tok arf eptir moðor sina skilfengna oc faðr eptir sama barn ef þat atte eigi skilgetit barn eptir sik. þa skal faðr heðan af eigi meira erfa eptir barn sitt oc hans. erfingiar en allt lausa goðz æfenliga." See more about this case in ibid., p. 379-80.

The judgement with which the *réttarbót* was connected concerned the heirs of Ingibjörg Þorvarðardóttir, the daughter of Þorvarður Loftsson in Möðruvellir. It was the children of Ingibjörg's sister, Guðríður Þorvarðardóttir, and Guðríður's husband, Erlendur Narfason, who claimed rights to the property on the one side, while on the other side there were heirs of Ingibjörg's husband, Páll Brandsson. This was a complicated case. Ingibjörg and Páll's children had died young, but after their mother, and before their father. When Páll died he had two legitimate grandsons, although they where the sons of Páll's illegitimate son, Grímur. The suit was thus between Páll Brandsson's grandchildren and Erlendur Narfason along with his children Þorvarður, Vigús and Hólmfríður. Erlendur's children's demand was made using the *réttarbót* of King Hákon of 1313, which was originally made only for Norway, but was included in Icelandic manuscripts of the fourteenth century.[137]

When Finnbogi Jónsson judged this case in 1495, he did so using the inheritance law contained in *Jónsbók*, declaring that the Norwegian *réttarbót* had no force in Iceland.[138] This judgement was confirmed at the assembly of *Alþingi* in 1500.[139] However, Erlendur Narfason did not give up the case. It was sent to the royal authority in Denmark, and later King Christian II ruled that the *réttarbót* of 1313 was in fact valid law in Iceland.[140] This demonstrates once again how inheritance regulations were closely related to actual cases. In many instances the legal knowledge of the people involved in these cases may have influenced the outcome more than any fixed rules concerning the division of property.[141] The last judgement in the case of Möðruvellir was not made according to the inheritance rules of *Jónsbók*, but according to the Norwegian *réttarbót*.[142] Changes in the definition of marriage and

137 Björn Þorsteinsson and Guðrún Ása Grímsdóttir 1990, p. 93. DI II, pp. 379-86. See also Figure 10.

138 DI VII, p. 273, compare to p. 264.

139 Ibid., p. 504.

140 DI VIII, pp. 171-75.

141 In this context see also how the "Réttarbót Hákonar konungs háleggs um arftökur ættleiðinga, 28 mars 1318 i Tunsberg," usually called *Herjólfsréttarbót* was also used in Iceland. It was originally made for Norway, but from the mid-fourteenth century it was found in Icelandic copies, and it was used in cases in 1479, 1481, 1512, 1515 and 1554. It is printed in DI II, pp. 411-14.

142 See also how legal knowledge could be shaped by personal involvement in relation to the question of "finding" the right law or "changing" the law, in Bagge 2001, pp. 73-85.

inheritance rules could thus be a consequence of the use of different principles regulating the transfer of goods, and the rules laid down by the authorities could be changed in response to special cases. The judgement on the case of Möðruvellir actually changed the inheritance rules in *Jónsbók*.

Until now we have been discussing how changes in the marriage legislation of the late thirteenth and early fourteenth centuries strengthened the joint principle through the institutions of *félag* and, in Iceland, *helmingarfélag*. In the sixteenth century marriage agreements were, however, generally made in accordance with the principle of *máli* rather than of *helmingarfélag*. An example of this is the contract of Magnús prúði Jónsson and Ragnheiður Eggertsdóttir of 1565.[143] This was a marriage between the richest families in the country and they made a *máli* contract. Many reasons could have prompted this decision. It has already been said that *helmingarfélag* was a better strategy for acquiring property than for preserving it. The extended contracts of *máli* made during the sixteenth century were probably made to stabilize the situation again. The change could even indicate an effort in trying to keep manors within the family.[144] The case of Möðruvellir arose because of the undesirability of transferring property between two family lines. The court material indicates that the Icelandic aristocracy of the sixteenth century tried to transfer property in accordance with this principle, which provided the basis for the contract of *máli*, rather than for the more marriage-orientated contract of *helmingarfélag*.

9.4 Conclusion

In the second part of this book it became clear that marriage contracts and marriage cases from the fourteenth and early fifteenth century that reached the courts, suggest that the custom of the handshake between the bride and bridegroom's guardians or between the prospective husband and his future in-laws was common. This custom was the normal

143 DI XIV, pp. 422-25.

144 Compare to the discussion in Howell 1998 of the strategy in Douai after the economic crisis in the textile industry.

practice. In this chapter we have illustrated how people in the fourteenth century perceived marriage agreements in terms of property transfer, rather than viewing it as a sacrament. There were, however, changes in marriage contracts that emphasized that they should be made between wife and husband, where she put her hand in his and they were joined in holy matrimony. As discussed in chapter 8, witnesses testified that an agreement had been made between the prospective wife and husband. These contracts, which became common in the late fifteenth and the sixteenth century, were thus made both with the consent of the parents and the couple, as they still were very much a property matter.

Two main principles governed the division of marital property in Iceland during the Late Middle Ages. The communal principle, aimed at the maintenance of the marital property after the death of either the husband or the wife, was the basis of the institution of *fēlag*, though modified behind the institution of *helmingarfēlag*. The other principle was more kin-based, because under this system inherited property should be transferred either to the female or male line as soon as one of the spouses died, especially if they did not have children. This was the principle which lay behind the institution of *máli*.

The third type of institution of *fēlag*: *þriðjungsfēlag*, also called *hjónafēlag*, seems not to have been popular in Iceland, which must be a result of the revision of the inheritance and marriage rules of *Jónsbók* in the early fourteenth century. According to the customary law of *Grágás* it was possible to make marriage contracts for both separate ownership and *fēlag*. In these cases, a husband owned double that of his wife, or the spouses each owned as much as they had put into the *fēlag*. The rules of *fēlag* became more defined under the later law of *Jónsbók*, but it was in the *réttarbætur* of the early fourteenth century that the joint ownership of *helmingarfēlag* was first legally defined. The difference between the two types of *fēlag* was that according to the *helmingarfēlag* the spouses should each own a half part, not only of what they put into the marriage, but also of what they acquired later. This made the division of inheritance after the death of a couple more simple, but risked the possibility that the main estate was lost to the original family line if the couple did not have children, instead of only one-third in the contract of *hjónafēlag*.

The joint ownership of *hjónafélag*, with the authority of the husband strengthened in relation to that of his wife's relatives, seems to have existed more in principle than in practice in the Late Middle Ages in Iceland. Its existence in the marriage legislation can be explained because of a strong influence from Norway. The Icelandic property holders reacted by strengthening the principle that secured their ability to control the property of their families. *Helmingarfélag* could not be made without the consent of the closest kin.

According to *helmingarfélag* a couple owned everything jointly, both what they put into the marriage and what they acquired later through inheritance, sale or purchase. According to the principle behind the *hjónafélög* of *Jónsbók*, each partner in a couple should own what they had taken to the marriage, and an agreement for jointly-owned property was made for what they later acquired or lost. If they acquired wealth the husband would own two-thirds of it and the wife one-third. However, their losses would be shared equally. This is why *helmingarfélag* favored the interests of the family of the bride. It automatically gave her family the right to inherit half of the couple's property if they did not have any children.

In the fifteenth century there is evidence of a strengthening of this principle of joint possession when transferring property amongst the richer families, but this does not seem to have been favored as a strategy in the sixteenth century. This can be explained by several factors. First, acceptance of the mutual consent of the couple reinforced the need for paternal consent, and by the Reformation this was strengthened even further. After the influence of aristocratic families in arranging the marriage of their children was weakened, it was necessary to secure the family heritage with new measures. This may explain why *máli* became more common again as a strategy used by the wealthiest families in the sixteenth century.

Secondly, this can be interpreted as a result of the two great plague epidemics of the fifteenth century, in 1402-04, and 1494-95. The rising aristocracy that had acquired land in the wake of these epidemics used the contract of *helmingarfélag* to strengthen their positions. When the new power structure was settled, the ruling elite could go back to use the contract of *máli* to secure their position. However, the sixteenth century contracts of *máli* were not exactly the same type of marriage contracts as those made in the fifteenth century. The reason for this was the new principle of *Möðruvallaréttarbót,* which changed the inheritance rules of *Jónsbók.* After the making of this judgement at the end of the fifteenth century, it was no longer possible for a widow or widower to inherit their spouse's property from their dead children.

It is thus not possible to explain the change in the making of marriage contracts in medieval Iceland as a shift from separate ownership to joint ownership by the couple. *Máli* never disappeared, and was always the most common type of marriage contract. *Máli* could be "moved" from one landed property into another, while the land covered by a contract of *helmingarfélag* was always owned jointly by the couple. However, the surviving contract material from Late Medieval Iceland gives an idea of how the property of the two families involved was kept separate in case the couple did not have children. During married life the finances of husbands and wives tended to be based more on equal sharing, than on the amount of property that each partner had brought into the marriage. The reason for this was that the husband normally gave the wife substantial gifts. Problems arose after the spouse's death. How should their property be divided between their heirs if there were no legitimate children?[145] Could the gifts given by a husband to his wife be inherited by her family? In the next chapter, the principle of reciprocity between the partners in marriage contracts will be further studied.

145 And this was a problem because many marriages were judged not legal, which meant that the relatives of the couple, rather than the children, had the right to inherit.

CHAPTER 10

Exchange of marriage gifts and the problem of inheritance

The Church changed marriage rituals by lending new meaning to old customs. This was also the case in the exchange of marriage gifts. After marriage became a sacred contract, a bride could no longer be bought by the old institution of *mundur*. However, the marriage contract continued to be concerned about financial resources, both land and chattels. As I mentioned in the last chapter, the husband normally contributed two-thirds while the wife provided with one-third.

The marriage contracts surviving from the Icelandic Late Middle Ages demonstrate also that husbands gave their future wives great quantities of land as marriage gifts, especially in the contracts of *helmingarfélag*, and that these were reciprocated with countergifts. One of the preconditions for establishing joint ownership was that there was a high degree of social and financial equality between the couple and their families. This may also be one of the reasons why great gifts were recorded in some contracts of *helmingarfélag*. In some instances men gave their bride large quantities of property in order to be able to establish joint ownership at a later stage. These gifts became especially important if the husband died before the wife. It actually gave the widow the possibility to get hold of more land and thus left the closest heirs with less inheritance.[1] These gifts cannot be seen in isolation from the giver. As a matter of fact, people and their attributes may be seen as "gifts" themselves: A woman may be seen as a gift, as was clearly the case in the old rules of *kvenna-giptingar* in *Jónsbók*. The sacred meaning of the theory of consummation

1 Compare to Dübeck 2003, p. 135.

was, however, based on the fact that both men and women gave part of themselves to the family of their partner through procreation.[2] The exchange of marriage gifts can thus give us an idea about what kinds of obligation the marriage agreement had for the social interaction of the family involved.

This chapter concerns the gift exchange that took place at the conclusion of a marriage, and will in particular consider the effect of the Christianization of marriage practice on the process of gift-giving. It is important to have in mind that marriage continued also to function as a means for making political alliances in medieval Iceland, such as had been the case in earlier times.[3] When marriage contracts were made, personal obligations were bound up with the exchange of land and other forms of wealth.[4] The question here will be what influence the new marriage doctrine had on the making of such alliances, as well as on the reciprocal gifts given at the time of a wedding. Another interesting aspect is to study how Christianization affected the way that the marriage gifts became transferred to the heirs after the death of the couple.[5]

In examining gifts given under the different marriage contracts in use in Iceland during the Late Middle Ages the chapter will treat three main points: The first is concerned with general changes in the institution of the marriage gift during the High and Late Middle Ages, and having established the general background, the reciprocal exchange and the influence of canon law on this process will be examined. The second point concerns the dowry and other marriage gifts given at the start of marriage, while the third will take a look at marital property, also in relation to the exchanges made between spouses through the legal gift.

2 See the discussion on the general meaning of the exchange of marriage gifts in a gender perspective in Melhuus 1992, pp. 40-41. See also Gabriele vom Bruck 1998, pp. 263-98.

3 An example of this is the agreement made between Þorleifur Björnsson and Andrés Guðmundsson in 1483, which was sealed with the marriage of their children. See the discussion about this marriage in Arnór Sigurjónsson 1975, pp. 126-28.

4 This has been confirmed in many studies, also after the Reformation. See for instance in Sabean 1990, p. 416.

5 See Dean and Lowe 1998, pp. 15-19. This discussion in the introduction concerns the different aspects of marriage alliance, especially the reciprocity of the gift in a gender perspective.

10.1 *Historical background*

Several aspects of change in the formation of marriage in the Middle Ages have been discussed so far. As regards property, the change was not a simple shift from one type of contract formation to another. Rather, new principles were introduced to meet the needs of Iceland's landholding aristocracy. Change in marriage legislation aimed at achieving more marriages based on the principle of joint possession through the institution of *félag*. That principle, however, became adapted to accommodate the need for protection of the interests of the family involved through the institution of *helmingarfélag*. The institution of *máli* persisted also during this time as a way of making marriages that allowed for separate ownership of property by the wife. Clearly, property was transmitted through both the male and female lines. The marital gift-giving was closely linked to the type of marriage contracts that were made. In the first section below I shall examine more closely the historical background to this different practice. The focus will be on the influence of canon law as well as on the nature of the gifts that were given according to the older and younger marital rules of *Grágás* and *Jónsbók*.

After that, in the second section I shall proceed to a discussion about the terminology of the exchange of marriage gifts in the Icelandic contracts. The agreement was normally not made according to a fixed formula, so the contracts give information of a non-standardized practice of gift giving. This does not make it easier to use the documents as evidence for changes in the gift-giving system. Because many of the Icelandic contracts use rather old terms for gift giving (such as *mundur*) it is also necessary to give a historical overview over the change in the meaning of those terms.

10.1.1 *Canon law influence on gift-giving in the twelfth and thirteenth century*

Much has been written about the role of marriage gifts in European social history,[6] and very different interpretations of developments within this

6 See the overview in Goody 1988, pp. 240-61.

area have been proposed. Two basic concepts, brideprice and dowry,[7] have been used to describe the two known systems of exchanging gifts at marriage, and especially views on the role of the brideprice in Europe during the Early Medieval Ages differ very much.[8] Jack Goody uses the term "indirect dowry" for brideprice, which refers to the practice of a bridegroom making a payment in return for his bride.[9]

This gift refers to an original system in which a bride actually was bought. The word has its background in the older tradition of Northern Europe, according to which property transfer from the family of the bridegroom to the family of the bride was the usual way of making marriage agreements. Buying here means to make a deal concerning a bride, not to buy in the modern sense of the word. In continental Europe, the assignment of property at marriage had different functions over time. Gifts from the groom to the bride's family may at times have been compensation to her family for the loss of their daughter. However, not even the earliest medieval records give any solid evidence that this was so, on the other hand it is a fact that the gift went directly to the bride. That is why some scholars' doubt whether the brideprice had ever existed in an actual form of marriage, in the way that a husband paid a sum to the father of the bride.[10] In his study of *Marriage in the Western Church* Philip Reynolds gives an overview of the discussion about the different interpretations. It was the German scholars of the so-called *Rechtsschule,* flourishing from the late nineteenth century to the 1940s, who gave an almost universal status to Germanic law. They assumed that marriage everywhere in the Germanic law codes involved the transference of the so-called *mundium* or power in exchange for the brideprice. *Mundium* is the Latin word for what in Icelandic is called *mundur*. Reynolds argues that this school distinguished three modes of marriage: 1) Marriage by purchase or the transference of *mundium*; 2) Marriage by capture; 3) Marriage by mutual consent alone. Although he underlines that these

7 Hughes 1978, p. 262 ff.

8 See for instance Reynolds 1994, p. 72 about the scholar's doubt as to whether a brideprice was ever a fundamental form of dotation in German marriage.

9 Goody 1988, p. 246.

10 Reynolds 1994, p. 72.

suppositions have become deeply entrenched in historiography.[11] Reynolds himself regards such universal norms with deep skepticism.[12] He argues that the law does not always treat the transference of a bride from her kin as the transfer of *mundium*, in the meaning of 'power over her', and generally he underlines that the law is both more heterogeneous and more obscure than this kind of theorizing would suggest.[13]

What is certain is that after the bride had become a more individual partner in the marriage agreement due to the Christian influence, the gift that sometimes is referred to in the literature as the German type of dowry (called *dos* in Latin), was a gift given directly from the husband to the wife. A direct dowry was, on the other hand, a gift that a daughter received from her parents.[14] The technical meaning of the word 'dowry' is a separate property fund given to the bride by her parents and held by herself or them to secure her widowhood, or for her children. The custom of paying dowry in the meaning of giving the daughter the wealth to be married is related to Roman law. According to Roman law, when a woman married she received a dowry (*dos*) which was fixed by a contract. Originally the husband was supposed to have *manus* over the *dos* (dowry), but in more informal marriage arrangements this was the wife's own property.[15]

The Roman *dos* (dowry) had almost disappeared under the customary laws of Early Medieval Europe. Philip Reynolds argues, however, that since the Germans had been used to giving a marriage gift from the husband's side to the wife, the Germanic people, as time passed, easily adopted the Roman laws regarding donations made by the woman's

11 Ibid., p. 71. And he underlines that we still find scholars who accept the theory uncritically, such as Brundage 1990, pp. 128-29, and Gellenik 1967, pp. 557-79, see especially p. 559.

12 Reynolds 1994, p. 71. Note 18 is an overview of the main scholars which discuss this matter. Besnier 1934 has an account on some of the theories and dispute. Köstler 1943 discuss in detail these three kinds of marriage. Wembler 1981 has a brief review of the origins and use of the scheme.

13 Reynolds 1994, pp. 71-72. He cited King 1988, p. 147, about the misleading interpretation of the nature of German law, who wants to see these wrongly interpretations as a part of other relics from the nineteenth century.

14 Goody 1988b, pp. 6-7, 19, 206-207.

15 The Roman historian Tacitus described how the tribes of the north married by giving property to the wife's family. He found this strange because the Romans married their women by giving them dowries. He describes it as something strange "dotem non uxor marito, sed uxori maritus offert." In Tacitus *Germania* 18:1, here after Guðbrandur Vigfússon 1957, p. 438, and Reynolds 1994, p. 81.

fiancé to their own dotal system.[16] So the Roman gift of dowry came back into use during the High Middle Ages, in response to the expectation that both partners should contribute to the household. Clerics in Europe in the Middle Ages encouraged the giving of dowries, which were linked to the condition that marriage should be a public contract. The exchange of gifts also required witnesses, and in this way they served as proof of the marriage. This public approval became a requirement for legitimate matrimony.[17]

In practice, this was also an important step towards securing the economic rights of wives that had been eroded at the beginning of the High Middle Ages. The value of the dowries decreased in the twelfth century, and in many cases the dowry was the only portion a woman received from her family's property. Women could get landed property as dowry although the tendency only to transfer landed property via the male line was strong, especially in France.[18] Previously, women could pass the property of their late husband on to a subsequent spouse, in that they had the inheritance of their children from the first marriage at their disposal. In the eleventh century husbands and their families tried to restrict this practice by obtaining stronger control of the gift which was given by the bridegroom to the bride.[19] At the same time the emphasis had moved away from marriage as a contractual family alliance towards that of providing more financial support to the new conjugal household.[20] A financial agreement was made before marriage between the fathers and the relatives of the bride and the bridegroom. This way of contracting marriage can be compared to the oldest surviving Icelandic contracts which date from the fourteenth century.

The dowry became the central contribution in marital exchanges, particularly in countries that used the revived Roman law. According to Christine Klapisch-Zuber the evolution of the dowry was "complete in the fourteenth and fifteenth centuries when the married woman in

16 Reynolds 1994, p. 76.
17 Brundage 1990, p. 190.
18 Casey 1989, pp. 72-80.
19 Hansen 1996, p. 114.
20 Gies 1989, p. 117.

southern France and in Italy (later in Spain as well) was defined by the dowry her family had provided." However, Klapisch-Zuber also states that in Northern Europe the practice of providing a widow's portion funded by the husband persisted until the early modern era.[21]

In this context it is interesting to compare developments in England to those in Scandinavia. In England marriage agreements were implemented according to two aspects of English inheritance law. The first of these aspects was the principle of primogeniture, which prevailed in most parts of England. The second was the widow's dower, a dower being a life estate to which a wife is entitled on the death of her husband. According to common law a dower should be one-third of the lands and tenements which the husband had acquired. However, a woman could renounce her dower in favor of an agreement for jointly-owned property if this arrangement was completed before marriage. This settlement also stipulated the portion that a bride brought to the marriage, which is the direct dowry.[22] In England, according to the study of Lloyd Bonfield, landed society could therefore choose from a variety of inheritance strategies, and actually adopted several different ways to implement them. These decisions were made on an individual basis since it was the father who could decide the value and timing of transfers to his child.[23]

The Old Icelandic term for payment of a certain price for the bride was called *mundur*. The custom of buying the bride for a certain amount, *mundur*, was recorded in *Grágás*, where *mundur* had the meaning of a payment from the bridegroom to the bride.[24] In Iceland, it was at the betrothal, called *festar*, the agreement was made that the bridegroom had to pay this sum for his bride. The transaction between the bride-to-be's father or guardian and her future husband's party was termed *mundarmál*, the agreement about the payment of this gift. No marriage was lawful without the payment of *mundur*, even if a wedding had been performed in accordance with the law.[25] During the twelfth and thirteenth century

21 Klapisch-Zuber 1990, p. 290.
22 Bonfield 1992, pp. 287-88.
23 Ibid., p. 291.
24 *Grágás* Ib, p. 33; II, p. 159, there it is called *nýmæli*.
25 Guðbrandur Vigfússon 1957, pp. 437-38.

marriage in Iceland was thus an agreement whereby the woman's guardian promised to give her to the prospective husband, and in exchange the future husband had to pay the brideprice. Under Old Norwegian law, the dowry given by the woman's parents to the couple was also included in the marriage agreement. Both gifts, the brideprice and the dowry, remained the separate property of the woman as long as the couple did not make an alternative agreement.[26]

As mentioned before, a dowry according to *Grágás*, was not a legal necessity for a valid marriage. It was the paying of the gift of *mundur* that was one of the conditions for a legal marriage. However, *Grágás* states that if someone had given a woman a dowry, then it should be returned to her family along with the *viðgjöld* if she died without having any children.[27] *Viðgjöld* was a gift given from the bridegroom to the bride, and was considered an augmentation to the woman and her dowry.

Grágás thus describes not only the system of buying the bride through brideprice, but also the system of giving her away by dowry. This would reflect the fact that *Grágás* is a collection of separate laws, whereby the different rules it describes were not necessarily followed at the same time. It is, however, important to underline that from the evidence of our oldest sources there is no indication that marriage took place only through the institution of brideprice. We also know from *Sturlunga saga* that gives information on the late eleventh and twelfth century, that it was a common custom to give a woman a dowry at her marriage.[28]

Research literature in general argues that Germanic marital property law was originally "communal" in structure, meaning that the law did not favor the patrilineal principle of inheritance, but followed the bilateral rules. There is reason to believe, however, that because of the Christian or Roman influence this structure changed. One of the changes was related to the rule that it became more common to marry women with 'direct' dowry, rather than the 'indirect' in Goody's

26 Sandvik 1976, p. 494.

27 *Grágás* Ib, pp. 221-22, II, p. 65.

28 My own studies of twelfth- and thirteenth-century Icelandic marriage practice according to *Sturlunga saga* shows that women got both the brideprice from their husband, as well as the dowry from their parents, see Agnes S. Arnórsdóttir 1995, pp. 147 fff.

terminology. There have been different interpretations of these changes. For instance, Claude Levi-Strauss interpreted the earlier Germanic tradition of brideprice as a transition towards complex structures, inspiring Diana Owen Hughes to argue that the tradition of giving a dowry to a bride indicates change from a tribal, migratory society to a more familial or settled one.[29]

In some societies the two systems coexisted.[30] That this was the case in Iceland during the twelfth and thirteenth century[31] can be related to more general trends in non-centralized societies, where payment of both these gifts seems to have been common.[32] By studying the Icelandic gift-giving system of the twelfth and thirteenth century, it becomes clear that the payment of brideprice and dowry existed without doubt at the same time. It was possible to combine the two systems of brideprice and dowry, or at least elements of both, in arranging the transfer of property and political alliances.[33] This can be explained by the fact that in societies in which marriage exchange had a prominent political purpose, i.e. in societies lacking strong central government, the principle of reciprocity in the exchange of marriage gifts was stronger.[34] This was the case in Iceland during the twelfth and thirteenth centuries,[35] but by the end of the thirteenth century a terminological confusion began to appear about the meaning of the term *mundur*, which originally only meant the brideprice. Even if its legal meaning had disappeared by the introduction of the new marriage law of *Jónsbók* in 1281, the term is used both for the dowry and brideprice in *Njáls saga,* something which probably refers to the author's own confusion about the meaning of these words.[36] As we shall see in the next section this confusion is also to be found in later documents of the Late Middle Ages.

29 Hughes 1978, p. 262.

30 See ibid., pp. 262-91.

31 See Agnes S. Arnórsdóttir 1995, pp. 147-50.

32 On this, see Morris 1986, pp. 105-106.

33 This view is to be found in Hastrup 1985, p. 95, who argues wrongly, however, that the Icelandic way of using both systems was quite exceptional in a comparative context.

34 Morris 1986, pp. 81-138; about this see pp. 105-106, 110.

35 Agnes S. Arnórsdóttir 1995, pp. 147 ff.

36 This usage is to be found in *Njáls saga,* which was written at the end of the thirteenth century. See Einar Ól. Sveinsson ÍF XII, p. lxxvi.

10.1.2 Gift-giving in Iceland during the Late Middle Ages

What constituted a legal marriage was changed by the *New Christian Law* of Bishop Árni from 1275, even if marriage – as mentioned before – continued to be an institution based on the old custom of betrothal. This also means that the older custom of exchanging marriage gifts continued to exist to a certain degree.

In the oldest Norwegian law codes the daughters of a family received no inheritance if there were male siblings. The same rule is found in *Grágás*. According to this custom such daughters would, as mentioned before, receive instead a dowry if they married. Giving a daughter a dowry was, however, not a legal rule according to *Grágás*. In the law code of King Magnús the 'Law-Reformer' from 1274, the inheritance rules were changed. Daughters could now inherit along with their brothers,[37] and the law code not only mentioned dowry for a daughter, but also for a son.[38] According to this new law no more than one-third of the woman's belongings should be in cloth. The rest should be in land or in something that the man could also use.[39]

Jónsbók also granted women more formal rights in the ownership of property compared to the former inheritance law of *Grágás*. They now received the right to inherit half as much as their brothers, as was the rule under Norwegian law, in addition to the right to receive a dowry when they married.

This change in the Norwegian and Icelandic laws indicates that both men and women should bring property into newly-formed households. Firstly, a woman was to receive a dowry from her parents, which her husband could use as the guardian of the household. Secondly, the bridegroom brought property to the marriage sometimes simply called the property he brought to have *kaup við* – to make an agreement – with the woman. This property did not have the same status as it had

37 A son, however, would receive twice as much as a daughter.

38 This rule that a son could also get a *heimanfylgja* should not be understood as being the same gift as a daughter received. A terminological confusion existed in the law when giving the different gifts names. A dowry to a son is the amount he could get to marry, and is probably the gift, which normally was called *tilgjöf* in the Norwegian law.

39 Frimannslund 1966a, pp. 519-20, compare to DN XIII, pp. 71-72, an example from 1427. She states that according to the DN there are many examples of daughters receiving landed property as dowry.

under the old marriage law of *Grágás*. It was not property paid to the woman with the old meaning of *mundur*, brideprice. However, the husband gave a part of this property as his *tilgjöf*, which was a gift given as a countergift for the wife and her property, and had probably the similar meaning as the term dower in England. Sometimes the husband also gave his wife wedding gifts called *morgungjöf*, morning gift, a gift from husband to wife and presented the morning after the wedding; *bekkjargjöf*, a gift given by the bridegroom to the bride on the wedding day; or *línfé*, a gift given by the bridegroom to the bride on the wedding day, often in the form of some cloth.[40] These gifts were given at the wedding feast or the morning after the wedding.[41] Furthermore, the couple could, on marrying or later, give each other *fjórðungsgjöf*, which was a gift of one-fourth of all non-inherited belongings. This gift was a part of what was called legal gift. *Jónsbók* contains a special paragraph outlining what gifts were legal gifts.[42] Legal gifts were of three types: first there were those gifts, which the kings gave to "us and we to them". Secondly there were the gifts of friendship, *vinargjafir* that one could give during one's lifetime. These could be gifts like a horse or a cow, a weapon or other similar things. It was important that these gifts did not belong to one's heirs. Thirdly, there were the gifts called *fjórðungsgjöf* and *tíundarfé*, which were gifts of no more than one-tenth of one's inherited property. The first was a gift that one could present from all of one's non-inherited wealth, and which could either be in land or movable property. This gift could be given to anyone, relative or non-relative. The second gift, called *tíundargjöf*, was a gift that one was allowed to give from inherited property, but could not be more than one-tenth of this property. This could also be a gift of land or movable property, and it was not necessary to obtain the consent of

40 See Appendix 1.

41 If we compare this Icelandic (and partly Norwegian) gift-giving system with what existed in the other Scandinavian countries, we will notice that different rules existed. In Denmark, the law does not mention the *tilgjöf* apparently because widows were provided for through the jointly-owned property of the *fællig*. See Sawyer 1993, p. 207. That the gift of *tilgjöf* is so clearly defined in the Icelandic and Norwegian legislation can only be explained by how common it was, at least in Iceland, that marriage involved a separate portion for the wife.

42 *Jónsbók*, pp. 99-100.

one's heirs before giving it. *Fjórðungsgjöf, vinargjöf* and *tíundargjöf* were all included in the concept of the legal gift, *löggjöf*.[43]

What are the origins of these rules? They are not found in *Grágás* but in the Norwegian laws, both the law of *Frostating* and King Magnús' law code.[44] These rules are related to the principle of making wills and can be traced back to the Roman law of Justinian in the sixth century. According to this law at least a half of one's belongings should go to one's children. Then, in the twelfth century, one of the popes decided that Christ should also have a share of a person's property. These legal principles were brought to Norway in the year 1152 by the papal legate, Nicholas Breakspeare. They became known as the rules stating that one could not give more than-one tenth of inherited wealth away. The rest should form the inheritance of one's legal heirs.[45]

In general it seems that the policy of the Church in Iceland, as elsewhere, "encouraged" a change in the paying of marriage gifts in the direction that the spouses should exchange gifts, which aimed at making them share their property.[46] This was done, amongst other things, by way of an adherence to Roman law and the reason can be explained as a general notion of mutuality that was embedded in the consent theory. There is evidence that this change in Iceland started already during the early thirteenth century or before.[47] Further, at the end of the century, the payment of *mundur* started to lose its formal role and was combined with the other tradition of giving the bride away by dowry.

The evidence for the change in the gift-giving practice in the early thirteenth century is to be found in the legislation. According to *Grágás* the custom of buying a bride with *mundur* was the only legal way to make a marriage as mentioned here before. The concept "added gift",

43 Compare to *Jónsbók*, p. 100: "En þat skal fyrst af lúka tíundargjöf ok fjórðungsgjöf er maðr gefr guði fyrir sál sinni, hverjum manni sem hann gefr löggjöf sína."

44 NgL II, p. 90. These principles were also followed in practice in Norway, see DN II, pp. 181, 323, DN VI, p. 386.

45 Sandvik 1989, pp. 246-47. Nicholas Breakspeare later became Pope Hadrian IV.

46 This is reminiscent of the change that Bonfield identified in England in the Late Middle Ages. Marriage started to be more an issue concerning the household of the future couple than a means of forming a political alliance between families. See Bonfield 1992, pp. 287-308.

47 The existence of the gift of *viðgjöld* and dowry in *Grágás* is an example of that.

viðgjöld, is also mentioned in *Grágás*. Vilhjálmur Finsen believes this term has a similar meaning to *mundur*,[48] because it was a sum paid to the bride, which augmented the dowry.[49] According to Finsen, by making this payment to a woman, one got the right to dispose of her dowry, even if the dowry was the wife's private property in the marriage.[50]

The concepts of *mundur* and *viðgjöld* thus, do not have the same meaning. *Viðgjöld* has the meaning of paying something in addition to the gifts the wife brought with her. By paying the *viðgjöld* to a woman one gained the right to use her dowry.[51] While *viðgjöld* in *Grágás* thus refers to the gift that is added to the gift from the bride's family, *mundur* was the price the husband needed to pay to make the marriage validity. It had the value of one mark, and symbolized the validity of the contract. The main difference here is that the *viðgjöld* was paid against the dowry, and became part of the woman's separate property if the spouses did not make any other type of marriage agreement. This gift was called either *gagngjald* or *viðgjald* in the oldest law code, but in the thirteenth century it was given the new name of *tilgjöf*.[52]

This terminological development cannot be understood without considering the direct and indirect influence of the Church.[53] As mentioned before, the Church encouraged marriage with dowry. Also, as an indirect consequence of the new marriage bond of *hjónaband*, the ideal of a household based on the union of husband and wife came into focus, which influenced the double gift-giving system of marriage.

48 *Grágás* III, p. 653, compare to Ia, pp. 221-22; II, p. 65. See also Vilhjálmur Finsen 1849, p. 251.

49 Dowry was not a formal institution according to *Grágás*, but it did exist as a custom, which could be practised.

50 Vilhjálmur Finsen 1849, pp. 251-52.

51 Ibid., p. 252.

52 Páll Vídalín 1854, pp. 194 ff.

53 This has, however, not always been taken into consideration by scholars who discussed the development of marriage exchange. In Martha Howell's work on marriage exchange in the Low Countries, she discusses the change from customary marriage law, to marriage contracts being made by giving a bride a dowry. She sees this change as a result of financial as well as demographic factors, the Black Death having had a major impact on the organization of property transfers. Her argument focuses on the people of the town Douai and she stresses that they themselves changed the meaning of marriage. See Howell 1998, pp. 197-99, 218.

10.2 Reciprocal exchange of gifts

Details of the double gift-giving system of the High Middle Ages are made clear by *Njáls saga*. There, the gifts are called *mundur allur* or even *heimanmundur*, meaning both the brideprice and the dowry together.[54] These gifts were often combined as one sum that often became the separate belonging of the wife and according to the marriage regulations of *Jónsbók* the woman's guardian, *giftingarmaður*, made the agreement about *heimanfylgja* and *tilgjöf*.[55] These gifts together became the amount of the wife's separate property and could have been altered to this one word, *heimanmundur*. This same word can also be found in the charters, as in a document from 1360,[56] and there is further evidence that in the sixteenth century the word just had the meaning of *heimanfylgja*, dowry. In 1572, it was said that Jón Finnbogason had paid *heimanmundur* to his sisters.[57]

The word *heimanmundur* was used in a contract of 1553,[58] and in a judgement about another contract from 1554.[59] It is also to be found in a contract from 1568,[60] although the word *heimanfylgja* was still used in this instance in relation to the dowry in a contract of 1590.[61] In the marriage contract made between Magnús prúða Jónsson and Ragnheiður Eggertsdóttir of 1565,[62] the words *kaups og kounar mundar* and *heimanmund* were used to describe the marriage gifts. It is apparent that the difference between the words *mundur* and *heimanfylgja*, which had been clear in the earlier text of *Grágás*, had started to lose their distinct meanings.

This raises the question of how this change developed. This process will be studied in three steps. First, I shall analyze the institution of *heimanfylgja*, dowry, and indirect dowry, *kvánarmundur*, gifts given by the husband. Secondly, I shall study the other gifts given by a husband to a

54 See also the discussion on p. 345.

55 *Jónsbók*, pp. 70, 295.

56 DI III, p. 142.

57 AM dipl. isl. fasc. LVII, 8, compare to AM dipl. isl. fasc. LVII, 9 which says that Ragna Finnbogadóttir should get the land at Garður in Ólafsfjörður. See also AM dipl. isl. fasc. LVII, 21, a testimony of selling the land at Garður in Ólafsfjörður, from 1577. See also Appendix III.

58 DI XII, pp. 615-16.

59 Ibid., pp. 734-35.

60 DI XV, pp. 147, 160.

61 Compare to *Alþingisbækur Íslands*, II, p. 202.

62 DI XIV, pp. 422-25.

wife, and thirdly, we shall look at the wider exchange of gifts between wives and husbands according to the rule of legal gifts.

10.2.1 The institution of dowry

The Old Norse name for dowry was the word *heimanfylgja*, or the related words: *heimanferð*, literally meaning leaving the home; *heimanfylgð*, literally meaning to follow one who is moving from her home; or *heimangjöf*, which literally means the gift given to the bride when she leaves her parents home. This was property that a woman received from her closest relatives when she was married. In the Norwegian law codes, this gift was called *heimænfyld*, while the word *heimanfylgja* was frequently used in the saga literature.[63]

By the marriage law of *Jónsbók*, the dowry became a formal part of the drawing up of the marriage contract.[64] In the Late Middle Ages the dowry was the primary payment a woman needed in order to get married. She was given a property so that she could make an agreement with her future husband.[65] Such an agreement needed to be made in front of witnesses.[66] Then the woman's guardian should make the agreement concerning the gifts of both dowry and *tilgjöf* from the husband.[67]

According to *Grágás* a wife could first receive her property after the couple had been in their wedding bed.[68] Some of the marriage contracts inform us, however, that the dowry should be given to the bride on her wedding day.[69] And, even when the dowry was given to the bride, it

63 AM ordbog: with a reference to many sagas as for instance *Harðar saga*, p. 123, *Heiðarvíga saga*, p. 98, see also in *Eyrbyggja saga*, *Kormáks saga* and *Njáls saga* in ÍF IV, p. 45, ÍF VIII, p. 30, ÍF XII, pp. 17, 22.

64 *Jónsbók,* pp. 68, 70.

65 DI VIII, pp. 364-65. Halldór Þorgeirsson gave his daughter Þorgerður land, in order to make a marriage agreement with Jón Bjarnason.

66 DI XIII, p. 491: In 1560 Steinn Jónsson denied having been a witness to an agreement made between the father of the bride and her husband.

67 *Jónsbók,* p. 70.

68 *Grágás* II, p. 199: A woman could receive the gift of *mundur* and all other wealth according to the brideprice contract of *mundarmál.*

69 This becomes clear in a contract from 1381, see DI IV, pp. 13-14. See also about getting the dowry paid on the wedding day DI XII, pp. 74-75.

should be handed over to her husband when he wanted.[70] If, however, the wife died without children, her dowry should return to her family. The role of witnesses could be central in securing those inheritance rights.

In some few instances the word *heimanfylgja* (dowry) was used to indicate what a son received from his parents, and this meaning can also be found in some Norwegian documents. According to an Icelandic charter from 1385, a son received land from his father as a *heimanfylgja*.[71] This confusion was probably related to the double gift-giving system of bilateral inheritance. Because both the husband and the wife brought property into the marriage, it was not always clear what the respective portions should be called.

A dowry could consist of landed property as well as other belongings. The movable parts of the dowry, which could be described as personal effects, were called *þing*. These could be the private belongings of a woman such as clothes and jewelry. These private objects were normally not described in marriage contracts. They could include, for example, things like small shrines, scissors, needles and everyday cloth or fabric. According to law these personal things should never make up more than one-third of a woman's dowry. The other two-thirds should be possessions that her husband could also make use of.[72]

Judged by the existing marriage contracts from Iceland, the word *heimanfylgja* is only mentioned a few times.[73] What is strange is that in all the 193 marriage contracts studied, the term *heimanfylgja* is only mentioned eleven times, the earliest example being in a contract from 1405, and dowry is never mentioned in the *helmingarfélags* contracts. Additionally the word *heimanmundur*, in the same meaning as *heimanfylgja*, is mentioned in six contracts from the period 1525 to 1570. Four of these are *máli* contracts, one is of an unknown type, and one became a *helmingarfélag* after the couple had been married for several years.

70 DI XII, pp. 74-75. This document is a testimony that Þorleifur Grímsson gave to his sister Guðný a gift on her wedding day, when she married Jón Sturlason. The gift was given to the woman, but an agreement was also made that it should be delivered to her husband when he wanted it.

71 DI III, p. 384 compare to IO, p. 76.

72 Páll Vídalín 1854, p. 629: compare to *Jónsbók* the first chapter in *Kvennagiptingar*, pp. 70-71. These private/personal things of the wife could also be given to her as a widow, being as it were the fruits of her dowry.

73 See Table VI, p.367, and Appendix III, 4.

The Icelandic practice of giving a bride a dowry was thus closer related to the custom that a wife should have her own separate property called *máli*. The amount of the dowry and the countergift of the husband was the foundation of this marriage agreement, which allowed the wife to have a separate landholding. Dowries are almost never referred to in the contracts establishing joint ownership of possessions, because of the fact that the couple would each own half of all their property, so it did not matter which belongings initially were given as a dowry from the bride's parents.[74] It was thus difficult to combine the principle of joint ownership of estates with the principle that a woman should own her dowry during marriage.

However, even if the word *heimanfylgja* is not mentioned in the contracts, it does not necessarily mean that the brides were not given a dowry at marriage. The word *heimanfylgja* was simply not used very often in the contracts; instead it was said that a woman was given property by her parents in order to be able to marry.[75] The fact that this property was not always called dowry indicates that this institution maybe did not have legal strength, although there is no doubt that dowry was a common custom in practice.

When a dowry was exchanged for some other property owned by a future husband, the dowry could be lost to the woman's family forever. Sometimes the dowry was not exchanged for other property, but court cases concerning *heimanfylgja* were related to instances in which the heir of the husband did not pay the widow back her dowry. In such cases the written document of *máli* was used as proof of the property rights of the partners involved.[76] In some of the contracts of *máli* it seems that the property usually allotted to the women was the adjacent land, *útjarðir*, i.e. the lands adhering to the estate of the manor, or other less valuable

74 This rule of the Icelandic joint ownership of property was very different from, for instance, the Danish. In the law code from Danish Jutland, the word dowry is termed *hemfærth*. It states that a dowry should be given to a daughter, as the son would obtain property from his parents when he married. If these gifts included landed property, the family property was explicitly excluded from the couple's *fællig*, because this land which belonged to the family estate should never be transferred out of the line. See Iuul 1966, p. 523.

75 This is the common practice in all the extended contracts. Such cases will be discussed further in chapter 11.

76 Compare to DI VII, pp. 270-71, a case from 30 June 1495.

property than the main manor.[77] The sources do not always indicate, however, that this was the case.

It is difficult to find any evidence for the exchange of marriage gifts in Iceland before the Church began to influence marriage practices. However, by comparing the oldest sources from the late twelfth and early thirteenth centuries with the contracts of the Late Middle Ages it becomes apparent that great changes had occurred in the culture of giving and selling property. Thus far the argument in this part of the chapter has been that the existence of the dowry was related to the influence of Roman or canon law. This thesis becomes further strengthened when one is mindful of the fact that the Latin word *dos*, Icelandic *heimanfylgja,* was also used both for endowments to the Church and for the dowry to a woman who was going to get married. This was connected to the fact that the Church was regarded as the bride of Christ.[78]

The word *heimafylgja* had at least two potential meanings.[79] First, it could refer to what a woman received as dowry from her family when she got married. Secondly, it could refer to the property given to a Church as dowry before a place of worship was consecrated. It was first in the thirteenth century that dowry was mentioned in relation to a donation to a church[80] on its foundation in Iceland.[81] The image of the Church as the bride of Christ is also meaningful in relation to the way in which the Church managed the property at its disposal. This also has some similarity to the property-owning relationship between a husband and his wife. The Church was given a dowry, while the person who gave it had it at his disposal and took care of it.[82] The dowry became a distinct portion of property, both when given to the Church and when given to a wife, and it needed to be recorded in a special document called *máldagi*

77 Compare to *vtjarder er þar lau til fyrir hennar malajarder* in DI IX, p. 179 from the year 1523.

78 Guðbrandur Vigfússon 1957, p. 250.

79 This is according to Fritzner I, pp. 766-67.

80 One example can be mentioned: DI VII, pp. 437-38. In 1495 Bishop Stefán declared that there should be a church *hálfkirkja* at Fellisendi in Miðdalur and Þórður Bjarnason should give to the church a certain amount in tithe *tíund* and "ok fim hundrud j þarfligum peningvm j hennar heimanfyllgiu." Many more charters have survived, that give information about the dowry provided to the church.

81 Magnús Stefánsson 1975, p. 74, compare to Magnús Stefánsson 1997, p. 147, and see also *Biskupa sögur* I, p. 287 the B version of *Þorlákssaga* and *New Christian Law* section in NgL V 23, 8. The word *tilgjöf* was also used to describe property donations to the Church, for instance in ibid., p. 23.

82 See Magnús Stefánsson 1997, p. 148.

in the case of the church, or *máli* in the case of woman. By stating in the *máli* that the dowry was the separate property of a woman, it became clear what belonged to her, and in the same way, the property of a church was stated in its *máldagi*. It is in this way that the *kaupmáli* of marriage and the *máldagi* of the church were similar types of document: both were made to prove property rights.

During the period of ecclesiastical reform in the twelfth century, the Church gained jurisdiction over its own property. This occurred in central Europe in the twelfth and thirteenth centuries. Because of this the position of the donor (for instance someone who gave a dowry to the church) and his ability to control this property was altered. The right to control Church property did not follow the secular principle of inheritance. Here I propose to draw similar conclusions in relation to the development of the dowry given to a woman who was going to be married.

The dowry was not the separate property of the wife as it would be understood in the modern meaning of property rights. Instead the dowry consisted of possessions which her husband could absorb into his property and use during their married life with the consent of his wife. In the Icelandic context, giving a woman away with a dowry meant that the bride and her property were given by her family to the newly-established household. Property was thus exchanged for the benefit of the future offspring, who at a later stage would be heirs of the family property of their grandparents. This could happen in two ways: either the inheritance could go first to a woman as a dowry on the understanding that it would later pass to her children as an inheritance or as a legal gift. Alternatively, the woman's parents could give property directly to their grandchildren as legal gifts.[83]

It seems that a similar pattern operated in Iceland to that which Wogan-Brown has identified in Anglo-Norman society. She suggests that women sometimes retained their legal rights over some part of their dowry, at least during married life. However, it was first after she became a widow that a woman could expect to have more control over

83 See further my discussion in chapter 11.

this property. Wogan-Brown describes this as a system in which virginity was exchanged for dower property.[84] The control women could have over their property was closely related to the intention of supporting the offspring of their marriage. A case from 1473 concerning an Icelandic widow who paid back part of her belongings to her parents, who were going to provide for her children, can be cited to illustrate this point that it was first after the death of a husband that his wife could control her own property.[85] The woman who had sacrificed her virginity could, as a widow, use what had originally been paid for her maidenhood. But this property was not always available, and even if the dowry as well as the countergift, *tilgjöf,* was supposed to provide for the household of the widow, it may have lost its value. In such cases the strategy of *helmingarfélag* was a better choice for the wife, as well as in cases in which the relatives of a husband refused to give his widow her *tilgjöf.* In the contracts of *helmingarfélag* the amount of those gifts did not matter, because the wife could always claim half of the couple's belongings.

To sum up: The institution of dowry was formalized by *Jónsbók* in 1281. According to the law a marriage contract was about formalities, which ruled how to give a woman away in marriage. The financial agreement was part of this "gift", and it was very often an agreement concerned with *máli,* the woman's share in the lot. This referred to what a woman received as *heimanfylgja* and the gift from the husband called *tilgjöf.* Let's study further the gifts from the husband to his wife.

10.2.2 The indirect dowry

Jack Goody termed the gifts given by a coming husband to his wife as an "indirect dowry".[86] This was usually paid to her as a dower if she became a widow. The property and gifts brought to the household by a husband according to the Icelandic marriage contracts could be of three types. The first of these was the *kvánarmundur,* which was what a husband brought to the marriage, rather than what he paid for his bride as earlier in the

84 Wogan-Brown 1995, pp. 36-37, 42.
85 DI V, pp. 695-96.
86 Goody 1988b, p. 246.

legislation of *Grágás*. Several new gifts were added to the contracts in the Late Middle Ages. One of these gifts was the before mentioned gift of *tilgjöf*. The bridegroom gave this gift to his bride as a counter gift. Thirdly, certain wedding gifts, as mentioned previously were given during the wedding feast itself or after the marriage had been consummated. These where called morning gift, *morgungjöf*, the gift of bench, *bekkjargjöf*, and *línfé*, which meant wealth in cloth.

All of these were part of a husband's gifts to his wife. *Tilgjöf* was first mentioned in the *Christian law* of King Sverrir Sigurðsson (1184-1202). According to a payment from a husband to his wife in the law of *Gulathing* in Norway, the *tilgjöf* was the same size as the dowry, and here it was called *tilgjöf*, or *gagngjald*. In the law of *Frostathing* and the law of *Borgathing*, these gifts constituted only a half-part of the dowry and were called *þriðjungsauki*.[87] *Þriðjungsauki* did not exist in Icelandic legislation, but the principle that a wife should receive one-third of the property of the couple, or what they earned during their married life, is a principle present in the *félag* of *Grágás*.

The gift of *tilgjöf* is named in *Jónsbók*, but the rule that *tilgjöf* is not allowed to be more than 60 hundrað is first mentioned in the *réttarbót* of King Eiríkur from 1294.[88] This was the same as a minimum size of a manor, *höfuðból*.[89] Other legal documents such as judgements from law courts show that *tilgjöf* became a fixed sum, which could not be higher than 60 *hundrað*,[90] and is mentioned in 44 marriage contracts from 1380 to 1590.[91] Some of these contracts are of unknown type, but most of them were contracts of *máli*, while only five were of *helmingarfélag*.

The legal difference between *mundur* and *tilgjöf* was that the first was a sum of money with which to buy a bride, i.e. an amount which needed to change hands in order to make a contract legal. This meaning

87 Frimannslund 1966a, pp. 519-20.

88 The word *tilgjöf* was first used in Iceland in legislation of the late thirteenth century. It was not initially a fixed gift, but at the end of the thirteenth century it was decided that it could not be more than 60 *hundrað*. See *Jónsbók*, pp. 70, 286.

89 A document from 1524 gives information that the amount a man had for making a marriage agreement was 60 *hundrað*. See DI IX, pp. 249-50.

90 Compare to *Alþingisdómur* 1 July 1480 in DI VI, pp. 275-76. Also here the husband could only give his wife a maximum 60 *hundrað* of his wealth as a *tilgjöf*.

91 See Appendix III. The first contract from 1366 is not from Iceland.

was changed during the High and Late Middle Ages, and it has been stated by the Norwegian legal historian, Ebbe Hertzberg, that the Church wanted the old gift of *mundur* to be renamed and called *gjöf* instead.[92] The new gift of *tilgjöf*, literally meant the gift given as a countergift against the bride's dowry. This gift was commonly used in the contracts of *máli*, and should thus be understood in relation to the rule that the wife had her separate belongings in marriage. Historically it was based on the older form of the less institutionalized gifts of *viðgjöld* or *gagngjöld* named in *Grágás*. The old understanding of property rights as it was formulated in *Grágás* in relation to *viðgjöld* lay behind the payment of *tilgjöf*, in the meaning that it gave the husband a right to control the dowry.[93] *Tilgjöf* was, however, less of an immediate payment than *mundur* had been before, but rather a promise of payment after the husband's death. The woman did not necessarily receive her *tilgjöf* as soon as she was married, as was the case with the old *mundur*. *Tilgjöf* became part of the widow's dower if she became a widow, and the couple did not have joint ownership of this property. The gift of *tilgjöf* was thus only a part of what the husband brought with him into marriage. It could sometimes be part of the gift of one- fourth, *fjórðungsgjöf*, while in other cases it was excluded. The more personal gifts such as the morning gift and the gift of the bench are mentioned in the contracts of *helmingarfélag*. This is a result of the fact that some of these contracts concerned a great amount of wealth and these gifts were used to transfer property from a man to his wife. The payment of *tilgjöf*, which could be a part of the dower if the woman became a widow, could not be retrieved by a woman's relatives if she had no children. In this way it was related to procreation.

When the concept *tilgjöf* was introduced, the word *kvánarmundur* no longer appeared as a legal concept in its former meaning, although the word itself is still present in some of the contracts of the Late Middle Ages. The word *kvánarmundur* is mentioned in fourteen of our 193 mar-

92 Hertzberg 1889, p. 42.
93 Hamre 1960, pp. 653-61.

riage contracts.[94] According to the existing contracts the *kvonarmundur/ kuonarmundur* (also referred to as *quonvmvndar/konumundur*) was all the property a husband took with him into his marriage.[95] *Kvonarmundur* could be given to servants,[96] but it was usually an amount that was given by parents (and especially by fathers) to their sons.[97] The term is used in documents concerning parents who gave land to their sons in *kvánarmundur,* but it is never mentioned that it is a payment or a gift for the bride.[98] There seems to have been more reason to make a special written statement about property given as a *kvonarmundur,* if this gift was made to more distant relatives than to one's own children.[99]

To sum up: There was a clear difference in the meaning of *kvánarmundur* and *tilgjöf* in the contracts. The old brideprice of *mundur* was a payment which made marriage legal. The countergifts in *Grágás, viðgjöf, gagngjald* and according to *Jónsbók tilgjöf,* were not a requirement for a legal marriage, but a gift given towards the dowry in return for gaining the guardianship of a woman. The husband's marriage portion was normally higher than his wife's. Husbands would very often then give *tilgjöf* and *fjórðungsgjöf* from their possessions so that a couple would have the same amount each,[100] as was the case for instance in one wife's *máli,* made in 1537, for 60 *hundrað.* This woman received 40 *hundrað* in her dowry and 20 *hundrað* from her husband as *tilgjöf.* This contract also contained a formula, which determined that the longest living partner

94 See Appendix III, 3. The term *kvánarmundur* had a wide meaning in the Late Middle Ages, and only part of it became the property of the wife. The term disappeared from the law codes in Norway and Iceland during the Late Middle Ages, and it was never mentioned in medieval Danish law. See Frimanslund 1967, pp. 10-11.

95 See for instance DI III, p. 736, IV, p. 536, V, p. 172, VI, p. 207, VII, p. 99, IX, pp. 502, 554, X, p. 69.

96 DI VI, pp. 206-207.

97 DI IX, p. 502.

98 See for instance DI V, pp. 611-12 Parents gave their son Bjarni Ólason land to *kavps og giptingar* with Margrét Ólafsdóttir; DI VI, pp. 509-10. Einar Ólafsson got the land Hvilft in *kuonarmundar* in order to get married to Guðfinna Indriðadóttir. The letter that testifies this is from 21 April 1484. In DI III, p. 736 there is information about a *kvánarmundur* given by an uncle to his nephew in 1410, with the condition that if the nephew did not have any children the amount of the payment should return to the giver.

99 DI XIV, pp. 523-24. See also DI V, pp. 142-43.

100 An example is DI IX, pp. 435-36. In this marriage contract from 1527/1531, the husband brings 20 *hundrað,* the wife 10 *hundrað* and then he gives her the gift of one-fourth of his belongings. It meant that each owned 15 *hundrað.* Her father decided that she should be a *málakona.* See also contracts from 1531 DI IX, pp. 602-603, and from 1531, pp. 603-605, which are made after the same principle.

would receive the gift of *fjórðungsgjöf* from the other.[101] If the husband wanted to give his wife more than the minimum size of a manor, other kinds of marriage gifts, such as the morning gift and the *bekkjargjöf*, were used.[102]

Máli, the separate possessions of a wife,[103] could thus include both the *tilgjöf* from the husband and other marriage gifts he gave her,[104] as was the case in the marriage contract of Járngerður Gilsdóttir and Þórður Bessason which was made in 1380. The witnesses to this contract claimed that the couple's fathers had made a legal marriage agreement, *keyptu löglega hjúskaparkaupi*, between their children. Þórður's father gave him 120 *hundrað*, while Járngerður got 60 *hundrað* from her father.[105] Þórður received land for 90 *hundrað*, the homeland at Eyvindastaðir, with a part of the land at Bollastaðir, the forest in Blöndugil, as well as the common pasture and 20 *kúgildi*, which is equal to the price of 20 cows, and 10 *hundrað* in other movable gods. Járngerður received the landed property at Hamrar in Reykjadalur from her father, to the value of 24 *hundrað*, as well as 20 *kúgildi* and 16 *hundrað* in other movable belongings.[106]

Even if this wife only brought half as much as her husband into their household, it was considered that there was *jafnmæli*, an equal share, between the couple. This was related to a husband's right to control his wife's property and in order to gain this right he needed to bring more property into the new marriage than his wife. According to an agreement

101 DI X, pp. 331-32.

102 See for instance IO, p. 265, a case from the year 1428. Other cases can be mentioned which both stated that the countergift was 60 *hundrað*, and that the 'additional' objects had been transferred as marriage gifts: Se DI IV, p. 562, from the year of 1436; DI V, p. 87, from the year of 1451; and DI VI, p. 93 from the year of 1476.

103 *Máli* could also be used more generally with regard to the property one owned as a portion in another man's wealth. Compare to *Jónsbók*, p. 129, *Um málalands brigð*. There it says: "Ef maðr selr málaland annars manns eða þat er annarr á veð í, þá skal þessi lönd brigða innan næstu.xii. mánaða, nema nauðsyn banni, ella á hann þess máls aldri uppreist." Compare also to p. 127: *Um lögmála á landi*. There it says: "Svá er mælt, þar er maðr selr land sitt öðrum manni ok vill hann leggja á lögmála, þá skulu þeir handsalaz við þann mála sem þeir verða ásáttir. Þat er lögmáli á landi, at hann skal eiga kost fyrsts at kaupa landit með jöfnu verði sem annarr býðr við, þá er landit er falt."

104 Fritzner II, Oslo 1954, p. 630. "*Máli* konu sem lá í bú manns" was "heftelse som paahviler boet for *gagngjald* og *gjöf* som mannen har givet sin hustru."

105 These are typical amounts men and women received for getting married. Very often a husband then gave his wife the gift of one-fourth so they owned the same amount. His gift or *gagngjald* was a payment for receiving the right of having her property at his disposal.

106 DI III, pp. 351-52.

from 1562 between Einar Ásmundsson and Málfríður Bjarnadóttir, she did not bring any riches to the marriage "or contribute to the gifts Einar Ásmundsson gave her."[107] This was not a normal agreement, but shows that a woman could be married even without bringing any wealth into the new household. In this case the gifts referred to did not need to be handed over to Málfríður during her married life, if they only were the gift of *tilgjöf*. This was, however, not the rule applied to certain other gifts given by a husband to his wife as wedding gifts. They will be discussed in the next section.

10.2.3 The morning gift and the bekkjargjöf

The marriage morning gift, called *morgungjöf* and the gift of the bench, called *bekkjargjöf*, are evidenced in the contracts of richer families, and generally this seems to have been the case in other Nordic countries too.[108] This was related to the fact that the amount of the countergift became fixed to be 60 hundrað and if a husband was wealthier he could give more to his wife as a wedding gift.[109]

No rules concerning *morgungjöf* and *bekkjargjöf* were included in the Icelandic law codes. However, all these gifts can be found in both contracts of *helmingarfélag* and of *máli*.[110] Thus, these gifts were never legally defined in Iceland such as was the case for the gift of *heimanfylgja* and the *tilgjöf*.

The name of the morning gift comes from the time at which the gift should be given to a wife: the morning after her wedding. This gift was mentioned in Roman law and in some of the oldest Germanic law codes, but there are different interpretations of its meaning in the Nordic law codes. Especially the Swedish documents concerning morning gifts have been a topic for discussion amongst scholars.[111] It has been suggested that the meaning of the morning gift was related to the loss

107 DI XIII, p. 683 "at hun husfreyan Malfridur lagde eij neina peninga til kaupz nie giafar vid greindan Einar Asmundassin. Og hier epter festi hann hana epter Bokarinnar ordum."

108 Hrefna Róbertsdóttir 1986, p. 39, Magnús Már Lárusson 1966, pp. 699-700, as well as Dübeck 2003, pp. 87-88.

109 Compare to DI VI, pp. 548-49, DI IX, pp. 47-48.

110 Hrefna Róbertsdóttir 1986, pp. 38-39.

111 Carlsson 1966, pp. 695-98.

of a woman's virginity, *pretium virginitatis*, while at the same time it has also been asserted that this was the gift that should support the wife if she became a widow.[112] Thus, the morning gift has been related both to the old idea of marriage as a property agreement and to the new idea of marriage, according to which the morning gift was compensation for the loss of virginity that followed the sacred union of husband and wife.

Under Roman law the morning gift was a gift given by a husband to his wife the morning after their wedding.[113] Surviving Anglo-Saxon documents, suggest that the morning gift differed somewhat from both the joint possessions of the couple conveyed in later marriage settlements, and from the dower. The Anglo-Saxon word *morgen giftu* was the word for the morning gift. While the Anglo-Saxon word *weotuma*, brideprice, was a payment made for the right to guardianship over a woman, the bride received the morning gift, consisting of jewelry or other personal property bestowed upon her by her husband, on the day after their nuptials. The Anglo-Saxons appear to have developed another practice at a later stage, incorporating property arrangements into the betrothal. This alteration is illustrated by the transformation in the nature of the brideprice and the morning gift. The former was no longer paid to the bride's family, but assumed the nature of a gift that the groom bestowed upon his wife The morning gift, on the other hand, came to be an appropriation of estates that were to support the bride if she survived her husband.[114]

It seems that there was confusion among Norwegians in the late twelfth and early thirteenth centuries about the meaning of this gift.

112 See Widén 1983, pp. 71-81. The morning gift was understood by the legal historians of the nineteenth century primarily as a financial support for the widow. Widén names Karl Weinholds's work from 1882 as an example of this, as well as J. Freisen and R. Schröder. In 1926 Ebbe Kock (from Sweden) interpreted the gift as compensation for the loss of the virginity of the maiden, and he was influenced in this by the works of Jan-Erik Almquist. In 1965 Lizzie Carlsson gave her interpretation of the matter, in which she stated that one should understand the use of this gift in the Middle Ages in Sweden as both a property gift for the widow, as well as a gift that was a compensation for the loss of virginity. In Reynolds 1994, p. 351 it is assumed that the morning gift could have been originally associated with the husband's taking of his bride's virginity, but he underlines that it had then lost its significance by the time the law was written. For instance, in the codes of Lombard it was just an additional amount that the man gave to his wife at the time of their marriage.

113 Sandvik 1990, pp. 74, 281-82, compare to NgL II, p. 74.

114 Bonfield 1992, pp. 292-93.

Rigmor Frimannslund has claimed that in the older law code of *Gulathing* the word *mundur* was used as a synonym for the morning gift in the paragraph on marriage.[115] However, if we read this law text more closely, it becomes clear that there was no link between these two gifts. First it says that a man should *kaupa* a woman by *mundur* so that their children would be legally born.[116] The next sentence says that after the couple had spent a night together a morning gift should be given of the same value as the other gifts that had been given at betrothal. After this their children would be legitimate.[117]

The marriage law of *Gulathing* actually contains both the old rules on getting married by the payment of *mundur*, as well as stressing the importance of consummation, i.e. the children born to them as a result of the consummation of their marriage would be legitimate.

In Norway the term morning gift was mainly used in connection with marriage among the aristocracy,[118] probably a result of the fact that the amount of *tilgjöf* became fixed. Richer families transferred more wealth than the gift of *tilgjöf* could contain, in order to get a suitable partner for their children. But there was confusion among contemporaries about what this gift should be called. In 1458 the Norwegian nobleman Henrik Skakt gave his wife Elene Jonsdotter landed property as a betrothal gift or *morgen* gift, or as it says in the document "whatever it was called."[119]

In Iceland the term morning gift did not appear in the law codes, as mentioned earlier. However, it does appear in marriage contracts from 1405-1505.[120] Table IV is a list of these marriage contracts that contained morning gifts and gifts of the bench. Morning gifts were never given alone, but on several occasions gifts of the bench were given alone, as can be seen from Table V.

115 Frimannslund 1966b, p. 699, compare to NgL I, p. 27.

116 Ibid., p. 27: "Þat er nu þvi neft at vér scolom … konor kaupa með mundi. þess at barn se arfgengt. þa skal maðr festa med kono þeirri 12 aura oreigi mund."

117 Ibid., p. 27: "oc geve henne giof of morgon. er þau, hava um nott saman verit. slica sem hann festi við henne., þa er barn þat arfgengt er alet er siðan."

118 Carlsson 1966, pp. 695-98.

119 See DN IX, pp. 297: "j fessnadhæ fæe eller j morghon gaffuo hwadh heller thet heita skal."

120 DI III, pp. 705-706.

Table IV	*Morning gifts and gifts of the bench in marriage contracts 1405-1505*
1405	Arnoddur Brandsson and Sigríður Guðmundsdóttir
1427	Þorsteinn Magnússon and Ólöf Árnadóttir
1434	Ormur Loftsson and Solveig Þorleifsdóttir
1436	Þorvarður Loftsson and Margrét Vigfúsdóttir
1451	Guðmundur Sigurðsson and Guðný Þorsteinsdóttir
1452	Indriði Hákonarsson and Guðrún Gísladóttir
1458	Indriði Jónsson and Ingibjörg Pálsdóttir
1462	Andrés Guðmundsson and Þorbjörg Pálsdóttir
1465	Eyjólfur Böðvarsson and Guðrún Þorkelsdóttir
1467	Hallvarður Ámundarson and Valgerður Kenegsdóttir
1467	Hrafn Brandsson and Margrét Eyjólfsdóttir
1476	Guðni Eyjólfsson and Guðrún Gunnlaugsdóttir
1485	Sveinn Sumarliðason and Guðríður Finnbogadóttir
1489	Sigurður Þorleifsson and Kristín Finnbogadóttir
1505	Þorvarður Erlendsson and Kristín Gottskálksdóttir

Sources: Appendix III, 1 and 2.

Bekkjargjöf[121] was not used in the Icelandic law code, but is found in the marriage contracts of the richest families in Iceland. This was also the case in the other Nordic countries. It was often given together with the morning gift.[122]

The gift of the bench could be part of the legal gift made by a husband and would then be the separate property of his wife.[123] Both these gifts can be found in contracts for joint estates of *helmingarfélag* as well as for separate ownership of *máli.*

Bekkjargjöf was a gift that a bridegroom gave to his bride at their wedding feast. This gift is related to the woman's chastity, as is made clear

121 In England, under manorial law, a widow had the right to claim her husband's copyhold land that was called freebench, widow's bench, or simply bench. See for instance Erickson 1995, p. 25. This should not be confused with the Icelandic meaning of the word *bekkjargjöf.*

122 Hrefna Róbertsdóttir 1986, p. 38, compare to DI III, pp. 705-706. It was first mentioned in Iceland in a document in 1401, where this gift is referred to as a part of the belongings of Þorgerður Ólafsdóttir. See also Magnús Már Lárusson 1966, pp. 699-700, compare to DI III, p. 670.

123 DI V, p. 473.

Table V	*The gifts of the bench in marriage contracts 1402-1505*
1402	Jón Gunnlaugsson and Þóra Ketilsdóttir
1402	Brandur Sölvason and Guðlaug Ketilsdóttir
1423	Guðmundur Arason and Helga Þorleifsdóttir
1427	Þorsteinn Magnússon and Ólöf Árnadóttir
1433	Hákon Jónsson and Oddfríður Aradóttir
1434	Ormur Loftsson and Solveig Þorleifsdóttir
1436	Þorvarður Loftsson and Margrét Vigfúsdóttir
1439	Þórður Sigurðsson and Ingibjörg Halldórsdóttir
1446	Sigríður Þorsteinsdóttir and Ólafur Geirmundsson
1451	Guðmundur Sigurðsson and Guðný Þorsteinsdóttir
1452	Indriði Hákonarsson and Guðrún Gísladóttir
1458	Indriði Jónsson and Ingibjörg Pálsdóttir
1462	Andrés Guðmundsson and Þorbjörg Pálsdóttir
1465	Eyjólfur Böðvarsson and Guðrún Þorkelsdóttir
1467	Finnbogi Jónsson and Málfríður Torfadóttir
1467	Hrafn Brandsson and Margrét Eyjólfsdóttir
1467	Hallvarður Ámundarson and Valgerður Keneksdóttir
1476	Guðni Eyjólfsson and Guðrún Gunnlaugsdóttir
1485	Sveinn Sumarliðason and Guðríður Finnbogadóttir
1489	Sigurður Þorleifsson and Kristín Finnbogadóttir
1505	Þorvarður Erlendsson and Kristín Gottskálksdóttir

Sources: Appendix III, 2.

by the contract of Finnbogi and Málfríður from 1467, which says that he gave her 60 *hundrað* in *bekkjargjöf*, and other gifts which he wanted to give to her chastity.[124]

It seems that these gifts, the morning gift and *bekkjargjöf*, were only given in the fourteenth and fifteenth centuries. No marriage contracts after 1505 mention these gifts.[125] On the other hand the contracts from 1439-1570 do mention that the spouses could give each other a special

124 DI V, pp. 509-510.

125 See Appendix I.

and precious gift called *kjörgripur*, literally meaning a masterpiece,[126] and this was a gift, which was given for the partner who lived longest. One of the reasons why morning gifts and the gift of the bench disappear at the beginning of the sixteenth century, could be that it became less common to make marriage contracts based on the principle of *helmingarfélag*, at that time. In that context it is interesting to compare the Icelandic gift-giving practice with the situation in Denmark.[127] The morning gift was commonly used in the highest rank of society in Denmark during the fifteenth and the sixteenth century, but King Hans (1481-1513) made some law restrictions that limited the amount one could give.[128] There is no indication that this rule became known in Iceland. But as will be discussed in the last section of this chapter, changes did occur in the gift-giving practice of sixteenth century Iceland, compared to the earlier practice. This was related to the more common use of giving the gift of *fjórðungsgjöf*.

10.3 "Legal gifts" and the meaning of the exchange between the spouses

A study of all the gifts given when marriages were concluded according to the written contracts shows that the term *fjórðungsgjöf* was first used in 1423, but soon the gift became most commonly used to transfer property between spouses. It was given with the consent of the parents of the couple, at the point at which a marriage contract was concluded. As a part of this gift the partner who lived longest would receive one-quarter of the other's non-inherited property.

Fjórðungsgjöf was a gift one could make from all the wealth one had, but excluding property one had inherited. Moreover, this could be both land and movable wealth. The gift could be given to anybody, both relatives and non-relatives, but was defined in *Jónsbók* as a part of

126 See Appendix III, 7.

127 There, the *fællig* continued to be a common way of making marriage agreements. And after the Reformation new legislation even strengthened the type of joint agreements that were only between husbands and wives. See Dübeck 2003, p. 84. This was the case in the *Kolding recess* from 13 December 1558.

128 Dübeck 2003, pp. 87-88, 130. In King Hans' *stadsret*, it is stated that the gift is not allowed to be more than 20 mark.

Table VI *Gifts given at marriage 1380-1590*

Type of gifts	total	máli	helmingarfélag	unknown
Kjörgripur 1439-1570	10	5	3	2
Kvánarmundur 1458-1590	14	10	2	2
Heimanfylgja 1405-1590	11	5	0	6
Heimanmundur 1553-70	6	5	1	0
Þing 1458-89	2	1	1	0
Tilgjöf 1380-1590	44	26	5	13
Bekkjargjöf 1402-1505	22	11	9	2
Morgungjöf 1405-1505	15	8	6	1
Löggjöf 1467-1568	20	12	3	5
Fjórðungsgjöf 1423-1570	59	33	11	15

Sources: See Appendix III.

the gifts called legal gifts.[129] They include also the gift called *tíundargjöf*, which was a gift that could be made from inherited property, although limited to be no more than one-tenth of this property. Normally these gifts are mentioned in marriage contracts in relation to cases where the partners promised to give the longest living partner one-quarter of all their possessions, i.e. in *fjórðungsgjöf*.[130] Rules about giving *fjórðungsgjöf* in marriage are found in a *réttarbót* of 1294, in which it was emphasized that the marriage gifts a husband gave to his wife could never be more than one-quarter of his property. Otherwise this would be against the interest of his heirs, who were referred to as *arfasvik* in Icelandic.[131]

The gift of *fjórðungsgjöf* was used more in *helmingarfélags* contracts than in those of *máli* in the fifteenth century.[132] After 1505 husbands did

129 *Jónsbók*, pp. 99-100. It is possible that this gift has its origin in the known principle of gift giving in the Early Middle Ages, for instance according to Langobardian law from 717 the morning gift could not be more than one-quarter of the husband's belongings. Later the morning gift and *mefio* (gift to the bride from the bridegroom) became one gift, called *quarta*. See Dübeck 2003, p. 67, compare to Iuul 1940, pp. 156-57.

130 Hrefna Róbertsdóttir 1986, pp. 37-38, an example of this is a contract of 13 June 1464, see DI V, pp. 415-16.

131 Hrefna Róbertsdóttir 1986, p. 38, compare to *Réttarbót Eiríks konungs* 1294, *Jónsbók*, p. 286.

132 A typical contract of *máli* is printed in: DI IX, pp. 378-80. This is a document made by the husband who was a lawman, and the father of the bride who was a bishop. An interesting document of 1491 gives an idea of how *máli* functioned in its every detail; see DI VI, pp. 760-62. Of those contracts I have registered, only ten of the *máli* contracts mention the word *fjórðungsgjöf*, and bearing in mind that these contracts where more common, it shows that this gift was not automatically used in the contract of *máli*. Those are: DI III,

not give their wives morning gifts or gifts of the bench as mentioned above. It seems that those who continued to transfer property to their wife could do so as *fjórðungsgjöf.* This began to be more common in the sixteenth century. The gift of *fjórðungsgjöf* was thus not only used in the contracts of *helmingarfélag*, but also in the marriage contracts of *máli.* In these instances the gift to the partner who lived longer clearly favored the continuing existence of the household and worked against the possibility that all the wealth would be divided among the heirs.

The intention made by the gifts given by the husband to their wives, or from the wives to the husbands, seems often to have been to keep the household together in the case of the death of one of the spouses. The problem was especially related to the need to protect the widow. On the other hand, the relatives of the wife often tried to protect the belongings of her family. The case of Björn Guðnason has been mentioned already: he had kindly asked his relatives not to do any harm to the interests of his wife and children if he should die abroad.[133] A similar case dates from 1565. This concerned the lawman, Eggert Hannesson, who made a statement concerning his promise to his wife, Steinunn Jónsdóttir, that she would receive 60 *hundrað* from his fortune for her honor *í sæmd sína.* She should get 30 *hundrað* in Túná in Tálknafirði and a sum to the value of 10 cows, and 20 *hundrað* in other movable wealth. He requested his relatives to pay this to his wife if he died before her. In addition, he asked them to be kind to Steinunn, because she had been so faithful to him in spite of the fact that she had encountered many problems because of him and his kin.[134] The gift of the *fjórðungsgjöf* or *tilgjöf* could, however, not be claimed back by the heirs, if the household was in debt.

In 1588 a merchant from Hamburg named Michel Beckin made a claim on the heirs of Eyrek Arnason in Iceland. The claim concerned the *tilgjöf* Eyrek had given to his widow, Anna Korpa Makers. Both husband and wife were dead, but this gift had been given to her on their wedding day in Hamburg. Because the Icelandic heirs of Eyrek could

pp. 616-17, IV, pp. 344-45, 525, 548-49, 602-603, V, pp. 171-72, 506-507, VII, pp. 325-26, VIII, pp. 543-44, *Bréfabók Guðbrands biskups Þorlákssonar*, pp. 463-64.

133 See pp. 323-25.

134 DI XIV, p. 394.

PART 3

Fig. 25. Seal of Vigfús Hólm. *Íslenskur söguatlas.*

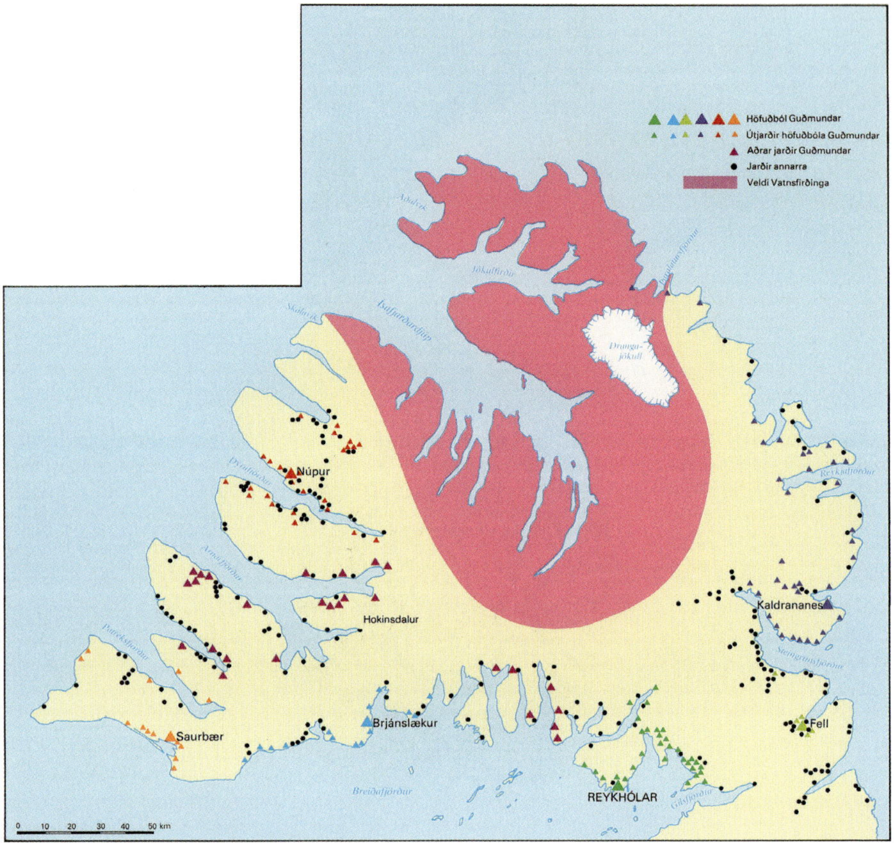

Fig. 26. Map showing the property belonging to Guðmundur ríki. *Íslenskur söguatlas*, p. 136.

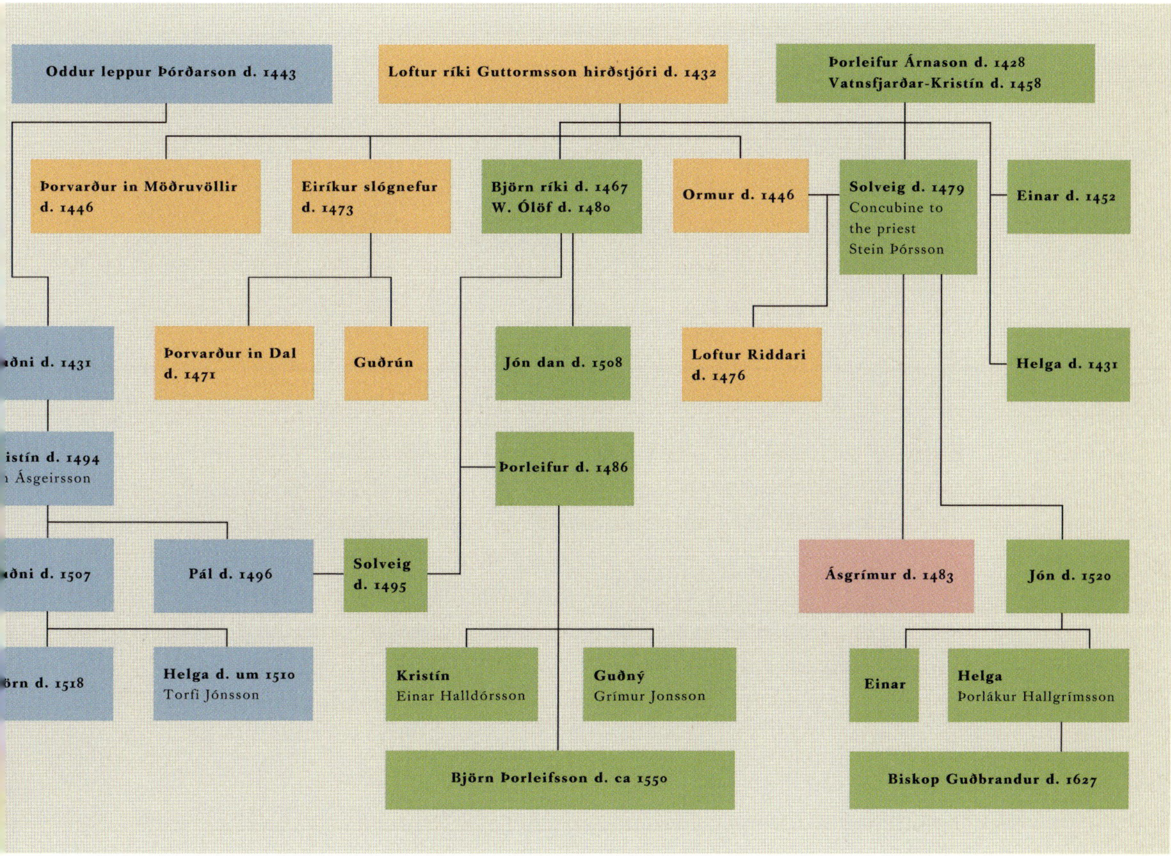

Fig. 27. Family tree, illustrating the most influential persons in Iceland who were fighting for power and wealth from the fourteenth to the sixteenth century. It shows how they were related, both through affinity and kinship. *Íslenskur söguatlas*, p. 139.

Fig. 28. Altar frontal from the fourteenth century, which was made in Norway, and depicts St. Martin of Tours and scenes from his life. It was in the church of Möðruvellir, and is the oldest preserved oil painting in Iceland. *National Museum of Iceland.* Þjms. 6430.

Fig. 29. The bench of the bride from c. 1600 Skarð in Skarðströnd. The couple would sit on the bench during the marriage ceremony. The bench is made from pine and inscribed with: "God have mercy upon me." *National Museum of Iceland.* Þjms. 1916.

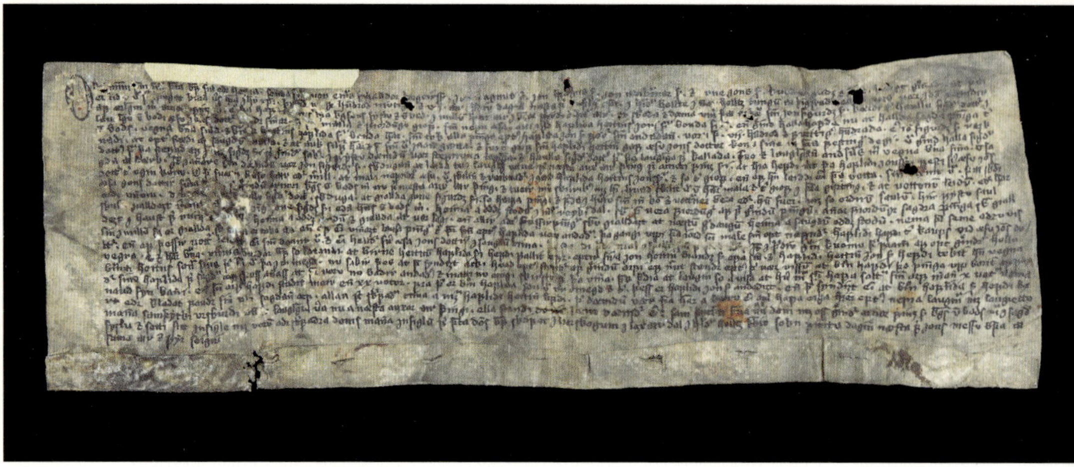

Fig. 30. Judgement about the gift of one-fourth which Æsa Jónsdóttir had given in 1496. *National Archives of Iceland* Bps. A. VIII, fasc. 13

Fig. 31. Seal of Bishop Jón Arason. The bishop's seal depicts a cross and the kneeling bishop in his cope holding his crosier. His mitre lies at his feet together with a shield. *National Museum of Iceland.* Þjms. 768c.

Fig. 32. Ring-shaped buckle from late Medieval Iceland. This buckle has the inscription "Ave Maria, gratia plena". It is possible that the buckle had also included folding hands, as known from other Scandinavian buckles. *National Museum of Iceland.* Þjms. 9047

Fig. 33. A drawing depicting a manor. From a late sixteenth-century manuscript of *Jónsbók. Reykjabók AM 354 folio, Arnamagnæanske Institut*, Reykjavík. *Íslenskur söguatlas*, p. 122.

prove that his household in Iceland was heavily in debt, it was decided that the gift should be paid from Eyrek's property in Hamburg, but if that did not provide enough then part of the amount could be taken from the Icelandic property.[135] Such a declaration was not made without reason. Many court cases reflect the problems that women or their heirs, if the wife was dead, actually had in claiming their property after their husband's death. A judgement from 1558 concerns the efforts of Þórunn Einarsdóttir to claim her property after she became the widow of Bjarni Jónsson. Her claim was about 200 *hundrað*, and 60 *hundrað* more. The result of the case was that she received her property. This judgement was based on the following principles: First, if a man took a wife according to the law of the country, gave her *tilgjöf* and then subsequently died, then she should receive all her things, *þing*, and her dowry from his property as long as he had enough to pay this. Secondly, neither of the spouses should waste the other's wealth. Thirdly, she had a written testimony from her husband that he had lost her fortune. Because the household was in debt, the husband's heirs were obliged to pay this back to his wife and the case ended with her receiving all her property as well as her personal possessions.[136] But the result of some cases was not always in favor of the wife. Another case tells us about a situation in which a lawsuit arose between a widow and the heirs of her husband.

In 1521 a judgment was carried out in *Alþingi* concerning the gifts that Vigfús Erlendsson (who had been *hirðstjóri*) had given to his wife, Salvör Snjólfsdóttir.[137] This case had been prompted by a demand from both Vigfús' widow and his sister, Hólmfríður, that six men should come and judge what gifts Vigfús had given to his wife.[138] The problem was that the wife had no written documents that could prove that her husband had given her 60 *hundrað* in *tilgjöf* and *fjórðungsgjöf*, as well as a silver cross with a golden necklace. That is why the men that came to Vigfús' house wanted the case to be judged at the higher court at Öxará.[139]

135 *Alþingisbækur Íslands* II, pp. 123-24.
136 The whole case DI XIII, pp. 308-10.
137 DI VIII, pp. 816-18.
138 Ibid., pp. 794-811.
139 Ibid., pp. 793-94.

Those who first considered the case had made a list of all the property that Vigfús's children should inherit. This list was made in accordance with Hólmfríður's wishes, and has been preserved in the copybook of herself and her husband, Jón skáld Hallsson.[140] The judgement has also survived in a copy from 1740. The result of the case was that the widow did receive her belongings: everything that Vigfús had given to her in his *tilgjöf*. However, she did not receive her *fjórðungsgjöf*. The reason for this was that his heirs had claimed that the household was in debt, and there was therefore nothing to give as *fjórðungsgjöf*. However, because Vigfús had taken some of Salvör's silver and spent it abroad, this meant that she retrieved the silver cross. The judgement went on to say that if the value of the silver cross was greater than what he had spent, then she should pay back the difference from her *tilgjöf*.[141]

Even though it was not always difficult for a widow to retrieve her portion of the household after her husband's death,[142] there is nevertheless much evidence for cases where the interests of a widow and her husband's heirs did not coincide. Cases like those concerning the widow of Vigfús Erlendsson and the widow of Eyrek Arnason show how the heirs of a husband managed to deny the claims of the widow or her relatives *by declaring the household in debt*. This is related to the fact that in the sixteenth century there was a tendency to protect the belongings of each family better, and to avoid that the inherited property, for example should go to the other line. In 1576 Erlendur Þorgrímsson (a priest) and Ívar Sigurðsson testified that:

> Helga Jónsdóttir gave her daughter a half part of the land at Torfalækur. She gave this land according to the right inheritance division with her brothers, and this should be known if anyone started to claim back this wealth. She also declares that this landed property had not been given as a legal gift or *fjórðungsgjöf*.[143]

140 The inventory is listed in four parts, the first in ibid., pp. 794-802, the second (which is almost the same as the first) in DI VIII, pp. 802-810, the third is a short note in ibid., on p. 811, and the fourth is also a short note in ibid. on p. 811.

141 Ibid., pp. 816-18.

142 In 1548 the brothers of Bishop Gissur paid to his widow, Katrín Hannesdóttir, both the *fjórðungsgjöf* and her *tilgjöf*. See DI XI, p. 650.

143 AM dipl. isl. fasc. LXVIII, 22: "Helga Jónsdóttir gæfi dóttur sinni hálfa jörðina Torfalæk. Jörðina gaf hún til réttra arfaskipta við bræður sína ef að nokkuð yrði aftur klagað þeim peningum sem að hefði fallið henni og bróður. Hún lysir því einnig yfir hún hafi þessa jörð hvorki gefið í löggjöf né fjórðungsgjöf."

The land of Torfalækur was the daughter's inheritance from her mother. That is why it could not be claimed back according to the rules governing legal gifts. It was not a gift, but actually her inherited property.

The gift-giving practice was thus closely related to the different interpretations of belongings given as *gjald*, payment, and *gjöf*, gift.[144] These words are formulated in many documents dealing with property transfer.[145] The common use of the formula[146] is related to the different meaning of the property handed over as marriage payment or inheritance, and that which was given as a legal gift. The main difference was that the first continued to be a requirement for legal marriage, while the other gifts tended to be used more as marriage gifts. *Gjald* is related to the countergift given for the property the woman brought into marriage as an inheritance after her parents, while the gifts were more closely related to the new understanding of marriage as a union. The gift was made for the sake of the marital economy during marriage life, while the payments were made to seal the property elements of the contract and were as such more related to the inheritance pattern.

Thus, in Iceland, just as in England, there was a great difference between the inherited property brought into marriage and the marriage gifts that were not part of the family inheritance. An interesting matter arising from Lloyd Bonfield's study of England in the Late Middle Ages is that there was an important difference in the nature of the gift given by a husband to his wife, and what a woman received from her parents as a dowry. The dowry was seen more as her inherited property. The gift from the husband was more personal, while the inheritance was something that belonged to her family, to be passed on by her to future generations. Both dowry and dower seem to have been regarded as the wife's own property, although administered by her husband. If a couple died without children, the dower should, however, return to the

144 DI VI, p. 296. See for instance the formula of adoption. It reads that one is adopted to *giallds og giafar*.

145 See for instance DI VII, pp. 368-70. In a document of 29 July 1497 Björn Guðnason paid to his wife Ragnhildur Bjarnadóttir some land. He declared: "Lysir eg þennan minn giörning bædi gialld og giof."

146 See also AM ordbog, which gives a reference to *Landsl*, p. 86, *Járnsíða* p. 282, *Byl.* p. 235, *Jónsbók*, p. 89 and the older law of *Gulathing* p. 51.

man's family and the dowry to the woman's.[147] This was also the case in Iceland, but because the main estate of the family could be included in the more personal weddings gifts of the husband to his wife, a great struggle often arose over landed property after the husband's death. The rule of the legal gift should guarantee, however, that only one-tenth of the inherited land could be given to other than legal heirs.[148]

I have indicated that the *fjórðungsgjöf* in the contracts of the sixteenth century merely replaced the morning gift and the gift of the bench from the fifteenth century. The principle behind it was that the partner who lived longest would get one quarter of the non-inherited property. These changes can perhaps be better understood in relation to changes in the social structure between the fifteenth and sixteenth centuries. I have already mentioned that the fifteenth century was a time of great demographic change. More land came into circulation after the plague of 1402-04 and new families gained greater influence. Some of these families used the marriage strategy of *helmingarfélag*. This can explain why the legal gift of *fjórðungsgjöf* became so commonly used. By using it husbands and wives could give each other land or movable wealth, and it was not necessary to get the consent of their heirs. This was especially common in the *helmingarfélag* contracts.

Regardless of whether it was used in the contract of *máli* or *helmingafélag*, this was a strategy that made it possible for the surviving partner to continue to hold a great deal of their property after the death of the other. This strategy was well suited to times of economic growth, especially for the new ruling class. This was the case in the town of Douai in the late

147 Bonfield 1992, pp. 287-308. See also Goody 1988, p. 243. The gift-giving system of paying dowry and dower is often related to "bilateral inheritance."

148 The gift of *löggjöf* made by Elín Jónsdóttir to Magnús Jónsson, her husband, on 13 September 1557, can be used to explain how this could be done. See DI XIII, pp. 236-37. She gave him all her legal gifts, from all her belongings on the condition that: "þo med þui forordi og skildaga at hann lifdi henni leingur. og ætti þau ecki barn sin ä millum þad sem hana lifdi. En ef hün ætti þad sama barn ää lifi epter sig. þa skylldi su giof ecki halldazt". In English translation: "if he lived longer than she, and they did not have any children. If she had children who were alive when she died then this gift should not hold any more." This was a way to transfer property between wife and husband if they did not have any children. Later in another document from 1564 Elín's mother gave her consent to this gift from her daughter to Magnús, and this was sealed by a handshake between Elín's mother and her husband. This concerned land at Þórustaðir in Svalbarðsströnd, which seems to have been the property of Elín's mother's family. This agreement was made on condition that the land should go back to Elín or her heirs, if she had any children. See DI XIV, pp. 229-30.

thirteenth and early fourteenth centuries,[149] and the same tendency was to be found among the new ruling families in Iceland in the fifteenth century. It should, however, be clear that if a man gave something from his best property, *bestu eign*, then his heirs could claim it back and the *fjórðungsjöf* to his wife could be claimed back by declaring the household in debt.[150] This strategy aimed at keeping control of the main property of the family of the bridegroom or the bride, instead of giving it away to the other family. These strategies for maintaining parental influence reflect an ideology which is also found in the rules regarding who should inherit the main manor *höfuðból*, which will be discussed in the last chapter of this book. During the sixteenth century there seems to have been an even greater awareness of not letting the principle of property exchange between the spouses affect the principle of keeping family property inside family.

10.4 Conclusion

How was the reciprocal exchange of gifts at marriage influenced by the Christianisation of marriage in Iceland? One of the clearest effects was that new marriage gifts were introduced, such as the *tilgjöf*. Gifts previously used lost their meaning, such as the payment of the brideprice, *mundur*. This payment did not have any practical legal meaning at the end of the Middle Ages, because by this time it was common to pay gifts as the *tilgjöf* or *fjórðungsgjöf* to the widow. However, the morning gift, which had been used in the fifteenth century, had disappeared in the sixteenth century.

A change occurred from the legally defined system of brideprice to the system of paying both dowry and *tilgjöf* during the thirteenth century in Iceland, and this change was a consequence of the influence of canon law (and the indirect influence of Roman law) on the institution of marriage. In the old marriage law of *Grágás* the institution of brideprice was used as well as dowry, but marriage was based primarily on the first, because

149 Howell 1998, pp. 205-206.

150 *Lovsamling for Island*, I, p. 21: "Eigi skal hér á landi gefa mey eða konu meiri tilgjöf en til Lx hundraða, þo at menn sé ríkir, ok hvergi meiri en sé fjórðungur or fé hans; en ef hann gefr í beztu eign sinni, þá skulu erfingjar hans leysa til sín, ef þeir vilja."

there are no legal demands or definition of paying dowry according to the law of *Grágás*. The gifts of *mundur* and *viðgjöld* were the most important gifts in concluding the contract of marriage. *Jónsbók* formally defined the dowry, and made the indirect dowry (the countergift of the husband, called *tilgjöf*) an important gift. In written marriage contracts from the Late Middle Ages all these gifts were mentioned except the *viðgjöld*. Contracts also mention the morning gift, the gift of the bench, and other legal gifts. The marriage contracts from the fifteenth and sixteenth centuries show that the most common form of contract was *máli*, which very often meant that a wife secured a property of *tilgjöf* in case she became a widow. One of the problems in Iceland was that the dowry could be exchanged for other property owned by the husband.

New types of marriage gifts appear in the marriage contracts of the Late Middle Ages. These are the gifts of the bench and the morning gift. These gifts disappeared again in the sixteenth century, while the legal gift of *fjórðungsgjöf* continued to be the preferred strategy for keeping the household together after the death of one of the spouses.

Two main principles governing transfer of property have been identified. The first aimed to ensure that a woman's dowry, in her *máli*, could not be transferred to her husband's family. The same rules were applied to the countergift, *tilgjöf*, in instances where the couple did not have children. The property of the wife could be used by her husband during their married life, and even exchanged for other property. Added to this were other wedding gifts, of a more personal nature, from a husband to his wife.

The second principle is more concerned with the household, in which joint ownership of the estate was the best way to secure the continuation of the family unit established by marriage and procreation. However, in situations where there were no offspring, the belongings of each family would return to their own line, especially their manors. All possessions were shared under this type of property division, although it was not possible to make this kind of arrangement without the consent of the closest kin until the couple had children of their own.[151] It was in

151 See DI II, pp. 342-45, the *Réttarbót* from 1305.

these types of marriages that couples used the institution of legal gifts to transfer property to each other. However, these legal gifts (and especially the *fjórðungsgjöf*) continued to be used in the contracts of *máli* in the sixteenth century. In this way the household principle continued to operate in the contract of *máli* with regard to non-inherited property.

As mentioned before, the Church changed marriage rituals by lending new meaning to old customs. This was also the case in the exchange of marriage gifts. Old gift-giving institutions gained new meaning. *Heimanfylgja,* which had been an informal custom, became a legally-defined institution. *Kvánarmundur* lost its old legal meaning as a payment for a bride and disappeared from the marriage laws. However, the concept continued to be used in marriage contracts to mean what a husband brought to the new household.

After marriage became a sacred contract, the husband started to give his wife property as a symbolic payment for her virginity. Through consummation they became "one flesh", and having lost her virginity she was repaid as a widow in the form of a dower. The morning gift and the gift of the bench (sometimes called the gift for the woman's chastity) were also related to the reciprocal exchange of virginity and property. When a woman was married, *gift*, the husband gained the right to "use" her and her property. Marriage had come to be primarily an agreement between husbands and wives, and the new marriage gifts symbolised this. The reason why these gifts disappear from marriage contracts in the sixteenth century remains uncertain. This must have been a result of change in the methods for transferring property through marriage. The last chapter of this book will study more closely the principles, which governed the transfer of land, and how the husband's right to use property will also be further discussed.

Different principles governed property transfer in Northern Europe than in the Southern Europe. Seen in a broader European context, patterns in Icelandic marriage generally matched those of the Northern European region more. Throughout the married life of a couple, and during the period after one of the partners had died, it was possible to maintain the household through the use of joint ownership, or through the use of the wife's separate ownership, strengthened by the legal gift.

This structure varied between regions and changed over time, but here the non-inherited wealth or possessions, other than the main manors, were kept within the family through the institution of *fællig* in Denmark and, in Iceland, by claiming that nine-tenths of the inherited property, given as a direct or indirect dowry, should be returned to the heirs of the married couple if they died without leaving legitimate children.

Other rules were applied covering inheritance of the main manors, and these will be studied further in the last chapter of this book.

CHAPTER 11

Transfer of property and property right

Inheritance and marriage practice were closely related issues in sixteenth-century Iceland.[1] A register from around 1541 related to inheritance issues, and other letters that record gifts involving land at Héðinshöfði,[2] provide an insight into the background for preserving so many documents. The documents came to play a major role in the event of disputes over property rights, because even if great change occurred during the Late Middle Ages in the understanding of what constituted a legal marriage, marriage continued to be concerned with political alliance and property transfer. Therefore, the questions which remain to be answered here in this study concern whether the change in marriage legislation influenced the more general understanding of property rights.

As was discussed in the last chapter, property could be transferred through both the female and male lines, although the latter was preferred. This meant that husbands and wives both brought wealth into their marriages, even if the share provided by the husband normally was larger. This was partly a result of the double gift-giving system discussed in the last chapter. This system was also characterized by differences between the inherited property brought into marriage and the marriage gifts. Chapter 9 further demonstrated how the marriage strategy of aristocratic Icelanders changed towards a joint-ownership pattern of sharing property in the fifteenth century. This changed again in the sixteenth century,

1 See *Alþingisbækur Íslands* III, pp. 136-37, about *Reykhólamál* from the year 1598 in which a contract was used, as one among other documents, as proof in an inheritance dispute.

2 See AM dipl. isl. fasc. LXV, 20 only partly published in DI X, pp. 665-66, and in DI IX, pp. 450-51. Without date, place and year according to DI X, p. 666.

when fewer contracts of *helmingafélag* were produced. Marriage during this period was based on making contracts of *máli*, which were primarily designed to secure the interests of the families of the spouses. The use of the principle of joint possession, *helmingarfélag*, can be related to changes in which types of land came to be most valuable. In the fifteenth century the manors of the Vestfirðir districts and other coastal manors like those at Breiðafjörður, Eyjafjörður and around Faxaflói became the centre of political power among the aristocracy. Previously, the manors located in the hinterland centers of agricultural production had been the most important. It was also in the fifteenth century that new families became powerful. These families were mainly based near the coast, behaving as quasi-kings over their territories and owning large quantities of land.[3] The disputing parties in many of the marriage and property cases that have been analyzed here belonged to these families.

In this chapter, aristocratic property strategies will be discussed further, first in relation to the way they affected the property right of the married couple. Secondly, inheritance practices and the different channels through which property could be transferred will be discussed, and in this regard the institutions of adoption and legal gifts are of particular interest. And, finally, the last part of this chapter will discuss how the property strategy of the Icelandic aristocracy of the fifteenth and sixteenth centuries can be understood in the light of the Christian definition of marriage.

We have shown in chapter 3 that the patrilineal principle was stronger under the new marriage and inheritance laws of *Jónsbók* than under those of *Grágás*. A son should take over the main manor while the daughters should receive the *útjarðir*, or more distant lands.[4] Children born legitimately had priority in inheritance matters over those who were illegitimate. According to the law the oldest son should inherit the main manor,[5] and a daughter, who had lived in adultery,[6]

3 Þorkell Jóhannesson 1965, pp. 34-35.

4 Sigurður Líndal 1976b, pp. 591-94, compare to *Jónsbók*, p. 78.

5 Ibid., p. 78.

6 Ibid., p. 79. In the law code it says: *legin í föður garði eða bróður*, which means that someone had intercourse with her in the house of her father or her brother.

should not inherit from her parents unless her father or her brother had mercy on her.[7] In this chapter, we shall study in more detail the meaning of these legal rules, in relation to the patrilineal principle in property transfer that became established as a policy in Iceland by the inheritance and marriage law included in *Jónsbók* in 1281, especially in the section concerning the transfer of the manor. We shall focus especially on the main principle that wealth should not be transmitted between two families in the same generation, and see that the need for this rule became particularly strong in cases where a married couple had no children. It will also be of interest to explore the relation between the fact that this patrilineal principle in manorial transfer and the formal legal definition of dowry became legislation at the same time as the claim for mutual consent to marriage.

11.1 Marital property and the question of inheritance

One result of studies of the patrilineal development in Europe during the High Middle Ages has been to demonstrate that women's power to control property had weakened. This development was reflected in changing practices in the exchange of marriage gifts.[8] These changes can be explained as a result of the stronger influence of Roman law, either directly or indirectly through canon law. Church reformers did not want the old custom of betrothal to be a requirement of a valid marriage. In practice, though, betrothal continued. Clerics accepted this, but tried to influence what gifts were given at the time of wedding. The custom that the husband paid for the bride became less common. Instead, the dowry given to brides became more important. Additionally, it has been documented that in twelfth-century Western Europe women received lower dowries than they had previously done, and seldom in the form of landed property. This was the consequence of increasing patrilineal practices in property distribution.[9] This development does not, however, need to have been a common pattern for

7 Ibid.

8 On patrilineal development see Duby 1985, p. 80 and forward.

9 Casey 1989, p. 74.

the whole European continent. There were indeed great differences between the more Roman law-influenced marriage pattern in the south, and the more mixed system of German and Roman law in the north. However, everywhere the wife's right to use her property was formally limited by her husband's right to dispose of it. In Iceland, even if a wife owned her *máli*, it was her husband's responsibility to maintain it, a responsibility called *varðveiðsla*. The role of the husband in maintaining his wife's property could also include his right to sell it if she gave her consent to the selling.[10]

The gender balance in property transfers clearly favored the husbands. It was never said that a man owned a *máli* in the property of his wife. Moreover, a husband could transfer his own property more freely, without the consent of his wife or children. We have also many examples demonstrating how husbands used their wives' property.[11] This could, however, sometimes work the other way round, with a husband receiving some of his wife's movable goods and giving her land in return.[12]

This part of the chapter will further study the problems concerning how the marital property became disposed of and transferred. Through marriage women had, to a certain degree, the possibility to own and dispose over their own property. But there is no need to discuss all the cases where men could freely dispose over their wives' belongings, as this was the norm. Instead we shall study those cases where the men's rights became limited.

10 In 1390 Álfheiður Flosadóttir made a statement to the monastery of Helgafell that she no longer had any right to claim her *máli* from the land at Miðgarður. Her husband, Eyjólfur Snorrason, had sold the land to the abbot and she had given her consent to this agreement. DI VI, p. 31. This statement by Álfheiður was witnessed by the person who wrote the witness letter, and "vorum vier j hia saum og heyrdum ä handaband." They "were there and both saw and heard the agreement be made" between Þorsteinn *ábóti* in Helgafell and Álfheiður Flosadóttir about this matter.

11 DI V, pp. 466-67. They could sell it in return for other land. Jón Ólason passed land at Ærlækur in Öxarfjörður to his wife, Þorlaug Árnadóttir, in payment for her dowry, which he had sold. Her dowry had been land at Stokkahlaðir in Eyjafjörður. See also DI XI, pp. 512-13 from 1546. Bishop Gissur sold land on behalf of his wife, Katrín Hannesdóttir. See also the discussion in chapter 9.2.

12 Ibid., p. 613.

II.1.1 The limitation of the property rights of the husband

"Judging by how you speak it seems you live under the rule of your wife."[13] These words from the Saga of Njáll are not exceptional in the saga literature. It implies that the man referred to had to act in accordance with the wishes of his wife. The word *kvánríki* was used for that kind of situation, meaning that a wife had authority or power over her husband.[14] The word *kvánríki* had negative connotations and its use in literature probably does not indicate that it had any relation to women's real ability to control their husbands and the couple's property.[15]

This is mentioned here to underline that there is a clear difference between the words meaning to own, *eiga*, and to control, *ráða*. In modern Icelandic the concept of owning, *eiga*, implies full property rights: it means that the person who owns can also use the property. This was not the case in the Middle Ages where rights of property and rights of property use were more complicated.[16] A man owned his wife, as *eiginkona*, but this did not automatically mean that he had unlimited rights to control her and her belongings. The roots of guardianship in Europe, whether the guardian was a husband, a father or another close kin, can be traced back to Roman law. A famous decision, the *Senatus consultum Vellaeanum* from ca. 50 A.D. says that women could by special *exceptio* gain freedom from all obligations. This meant that it could be risky to make a contract with a woman. This is why in practice a woman usually needed to have a man as her guardian. Few people could afford to make themselves exceptions to the rule.[17]

Later Roman law and Germanic law codes both acknowledged that a woman could retain a personal entitlement to property even within marriage. This was true although the woman's degree of freedom to

13 AM ordbog with reference to *kvánríki*, in *Njáls saga*: 321 nr. 5: "Finn ek þat í svörum þínum at þú hefir kvánríki."

14 See AM ordbog with reference to *Finnboga saga ramma*, p. 5: "gestr hafði it mesta kánríki því at hann var mannæli mikit og velingr."

15 The attitude towards women in many of the Icelandic sagas was rather negative. It can be related to the fact that in societies in which women commonly own land, they do not necessarily have the same property rights as men.

16 The king for instance "owned" a quarter share in each boat that travelled between Iceland and Norway, meaning that he had the right to use that space in the ship. See Jón Jóhannesson 1958, p. 155, compare to DI III, pp. 722-25.

17 Sandvik 1990, pp. 282-83.

administer her possessions and the benefit she derived from further family gains differed considerably between the various legal traditions.[18] Earlier Roman law and practice can help us to understand changes in the property arrangements of the spouses, as well as the role of the kin in these affairs during the Middle Ages. It is possible that the right of the husband to control his wife's property became stronger under Roman law influence. However, it seems that the role of women's kin prevented husbands from gaining full power over the property of their wives. The brides' families contributed to the marriage by giving her a dowry, and this is why the influence of her kin continued to be important after their marriage. During the Middle Ages the license to use property was not the same as the *right* to control it.[19] We have seen how a husband had a license to use his wife's property, but this did not mean that he could do whatever he wished with it.

The Church, as the bride of Christ, had an independent *máldagi.* The bride in other marriages also received her own *máli,* which defined her property rights. As has been discussed, the ownership rights of the partners in a marriage were quite separate according to the rule of *máli,* and even when a couple made *helmingarfélag,* their possessions could remain separate after their deaths if they did not have any children. This could happen if the heirs had claimed some of their belongings according to the legal rule of *brigð.*[20] It was only while they were married that the property was joined, but this did not mean that they owned it jointly, but that they owned half of each other's property.

However, a husband's right to dispose of his wife's property was limited by her formal consent. The requirement of women's consent to property transfers was first introduced in a *réttarbætur* of 1280 and again in 1313.[21] The use of this custom in Iceland had its origin in the law

18 Herlihy 1985, p. 91.

19 In this *Opus nonaginta dierum* from 1332 the Franciscan friar William Ockham (1280-1347) argued for this understanding of property right. His discussion of this issue related to the rights of friars, but it may also have been used as a basis for understanding property arrangements between husband and wife. See the discussion in a Scandinavian context in: Mäkinen, 1999, p. 47, concerning William Ockham's interpretation of the 'licentiam utendi' and 'ius utendi'.

20 See the discussion about the legal rule of *brigð* later in this chapter, pp. 395, 413-14, 418, as well as in chapter 9.2.2, p. 312, with a referance to chapter 3.3 and 4.3.2.

21 Sandvik 1994, p. 102.

regulations given by the Norwegian King Eiríkur Magnússon in 1280. These regulations stated that if a couple sold properties then the wife needed to give her consent.[22] The need for consent to property transfer in Iceland, as in other parts of Europe, was related to the Church's influence on marriage.[23] The husband could not dispose of his wife's property, land, chattels or movable goods without her free consent. He could manage the couple's property, but the absence of his wife's consent could limit his right to dispose of the property.

Consent could take different forms. In 1421 Þorleifur sold, with the consent of his wife, land at Hvammur in Hvammsveit to Ásgeir Árnason and his wife Guðfinna Þorgeirsdóttir. In return they received half the land at Auðkúla in Svínadalur and other land in that area. This agreement was confirmed by Guðfinna's handshake. All the aforementioned people shook hands when the agreement was concluded: Þorleifur and Kristín, Ásgeir and Guðfinna.[24] This provides an example of the way in which property that had been transferred by marriage could be sold out of the family. The agreement concerning the sale and purchase of property was made between two couples and illustrates that while the husband ruled over his wife's possessions, the wife was not a passive partner.

Women's consent, and sometimes the consent of relatives, was necessary before landed property was sold. No statistical analysis of all cases concerning the sale of land can be included here. Such an analysis would have to include registers of all transactions of landed property and this is not possible in the context of this study.[25] However, the examples that have been studied show how widespread the custom of the woman's

22 DI II, pp. 196-206, 282-88 compare to NgL III, pp. 3-12: *Réttarbót* from the King Eiríkur Magnússon from the year 1280.

23 Compare to White 1988.

24 DI IV, pp. 292-93.

25 I cannot give a percentage of all the transactions made with the consent of women, because that would imply the use of another kind of documentation than that used here. I have mostly concentrated on registering all marriage cases and contracts, not all transactions of land. But according to analyses of the Norwegian material 25% of all the property transmission in the DN was made with the consent of the woman. See Sandvik, 1994, p. 102 with reference to the study of Per Norseng.

consent was.[26] The cases I have investigated deal with various issues, but one thing they have in common is the consent of the woman to these transactions. There are many examples illustrating how both wives and their sons gave consent to property sales made by their husbands and fathers.[27] Let me mention just few of them: The sale of land by a father to his son was accepted by the mother.[28] Husbands sold property with their wives' consent.[29] A case from 1489 involves a woman consenting to her husband selling her property on the condition that she would receive property of the same value.[30] One case of transfer of property was more complicated because it concerned the rights of daughters. It involved a father giving property to his son. In the document the father makes a distinction between the *máli*, or separate ownership of his wife, and the parts of the property which could be given to the daughters.[31] Another example concerned a woman who consented to her husband giving land, which had belonged to the second husband of her mother.[32] In a document from 1418 concerning the sale of land at Bær in Rauðasandur, a couple sold the land to another man. All those involved took part in the ritual of making the agreement. It is stated "that they all held hands together, on the one side Þorleifur Árnason, but on the other side Þorsteinn Sigurðsson and his wife Helga Þorleifsdóttir."[33] The case illustrates very well that husbands alone did not always make agreements on behalf of the couple.

26 See, for example, DI III, pp. 144-45, 250-51, 291-93, 294-96, 316-17, 322-24, 332-34, 364-65, 624-26, 704-705. DI IV, pp. 262, 273-75, 292-93, 293-94, 361, 369-70, 623-24, 753-56, 756-58. DI V, pp. 288, 231-33, 665-66, 705-707. DI VI, pp. 19-20, 409-10, 451-52, 456-57, 610-11, 612-14, 654-55, 727, 738-39. DI X, p. 620. DI XI, p. 220. DI XIII, pp. 42-43, 561. AM dipl. isl. fasc., LXVIII, 23 for the year 1577. AM dipl. isl.fasc., LXVIII, 26 for the year 1580. AM dipl. isl. fasc., LXIX, 9. *Alþingisbækur Íslands* II, p. 248.

27 See for instance DI III, pp. 291-93.

28 Ibid., pp. 364-65, see also a similar case DI IV, pp. 623-24, and from 1592 *Alþingisbækur Íslands* II, p. 248. Another from 1383 deals with the same issue as the previous case, namely the sale of land by a father to his son, which was accepted by the mother. See DI III, pp. 364-65. The value of the land was 60 *hundrað* and he also got 60 *hundrað* in *kúgildum og vörum*. 120 *hundrað* was often the amount the man brought into a marriage. This case is an example showing that mothers also needed to consent to the marriage of sons and daughters.

29 Many examples of this have survived. See for instance DI III, pp. 144-45, 250-51, 332-34, DI IV, pp. 753-56, 756-58 DI V, pp. 665, 705-707. compare to DI VI, pp. 610-11, 612-14, DI X, p. 620, DI XIII, p. 561

30 DI VI, pp. 654-55.

31 DI XIII, pp. 42-43.

32 DI IV, p. 361 for year 1428.

33 Ibid., p. 262: "at þau helldu haunðum saman þorlæifr arnason af einne alfu enn þorstæin sigurdarson ok helga þordardotter hvstv hans."

There are cases in which women sold property with the consent of their husbands. In 1547 it was witnessed that a husband gave his consent to the agreement that Bishop Jón had concluded with the husband's wife concerning the purchase of some land.[34] In another case a woman transferred a property by handshake to the see of Hólar, in exchange for movable property. This was her inheritance from her uncle and was arranged with the consent of her husband.[35] In another case a woman declared that she had given land to her brother with the consent of her husband.[36] Many other examples could be cited of husbands who consented to their wives' either selling or giving gifts of landed property.[37]

The fact that women became active participants in making property agreements is related to the new Christian understanding of marriage and women's enhanced role in the making of marriage contracts. Previously, according to the legislation of *Grágás*, women had been represented by their guardians. The new role in the Late Middle Ages became even clearer in the records of several court cases concerning women who had not given their consent to the sale of their land by their husbands. One example can be taken from 1431, where Ástríður Jörundardóttir denied that she had given her husband, Sveinn Hallvarðarson permission to sell her landed property, Rípur in Hegranes. Instead, she had made an agreement by handshake with the bishop of Hólar, Jón Vilhjálmsson concerning her part of the land.[38] Many letters are preserved in relation to this case.[39] Because Ástríður had never accepted her husband's right to sell their land, the bishop could take it from the couple. She could thus get protection in Hólar, where the bishop resided, and so could her husband after some negotiation.

34 DI XI, p. 573.

35 DI V, pp. 221-22.

36 DI XIII, p. 563.

37 See for instance DI V, pp. 642-43, DI XIV, p. 250.

38 DI IV, pp. 439-40.

39 Ibid., pp. 440, 440-41, 442-44, 444-45. On the 17 February five men gave their testimony that Ástríður had handed over her property to the bishop *Upp í porcio og annan reikning.* On the same day the bishop forbids Sveinn Hallvarðarson to sell the land *undir banns's pínu.* A letter dated to 24 March indicates that the couple gave the property to the bishop. The day after, the bishop witnessed that he also had taken Sveinn Hallvarðsson under his protection in Hólar.

This case indicates that it was possible to use claims concerning consent (or the lack of it) strategically. It seems that Sveinn had been in debt, and had probably therefore tried to sell the land. Another letter exists which indicates that both of the spouses agreed in the end to give the land to the bishop, in return for Sveinn receiving maintenance – called *próventa* – in old age at Hólar. This was done after his wife had already made the same kind of contract for herself.[40] According to a third letter the bishop agreed to a contract of maintenance for Sveinn, but said there was not enough land left to pay for him, which meant that Sveinn also had to promise to serve ten years as the bishop's servant.

There is evidence concerning other women who refused to agree to the transfer of their property.[41] In a case from 1551, a woman made an oath that she had never given her consent to the sale of a property that she had received from her husband on her wedding day with the acceptance of her father. Another document from 1590 referred to the *réttarbót* of King Eiríkur from the beginning of the fourteenth century, which stated that a husband was not allowed to sell a property without the consent of his wife. According to a witness letter from 17 September 1562 Guðrún Helgadóttir owned the landed property of Gautastaðir.[42] The witness was a man who had been a servant and had heard Guðrún say that the land of Gautastaðir was hers: "because she said that she had never given this land, or sold it, to any soul, and no man had received her permission to sell it."[43] Guðrún knew her rights, and knew that these rights might be challenged later. A number of cases indicate the same awareness among other property-holding women.

Valgerður Gizurardóttir accepted that her husband, Árni Guttormsson, had sold the land of Kvígindisfell in Tálknafjörður to the priest Bjarni Sigurðsson as long as the priest kept his promise to her husband con-

40 DI IV, pp. 440-41.

41 See DI V, p. 425. Margrét Gamladóttir, compare to *Alþingisbækur* II, pp. 4-5 discussion of women who did not consent to their husbands' giving gifts of land.

42 DI XIV, p. 12.

43 Ibid., p. 12. Compare for instance to ibid., pp. 20-21. In 1562 Guðrún Þorleifsdóttir gave Magnús Magnússon *umboð eigna sinna*. Compare to 1565, ibid., pp. 397-98. It was necessary to get the consent of the owner to be *umboðsmaður*.

cerning this deal.[44] She made her acceptance conditional. This case, like many others, clearly indicates that women as well as men were aware of their ability to use different methods to achieve their objectives.

The examples that have been studied here indicate that in a few instances when land was sold without the right consent having been gained, the transfer could be annulled. A case judged by Snorri Þorleifsson, an official in Skálholt, on 1 March 1367 is interesting in this context. The official stated that the deal made between Gyrðir Þorvarðsson and his wife, on one side, and abbot Ásgrímur of Helgafell on the other, had been made freely, *óneydd*. The case concerned land at Vatnsholt and Svarfhóll. The abbot said that he had bought the land at Vatnsholt with the consent of the married couple, but they stated that they had been forced to make the agreement.[45] The witnesses could not prove that the agreement had been forced, and consequently, it was judged legal. The case had begun in 1364 when Gyrðir sold land with the consent of his wife.[46] There must have been some doubts about the legality of this agreement, because another letter from six witnesses has survived from the year after this, stating that: "nobody held their hands together when they joined them together."[47]

This case provides some information about the knowledge of forced agreements, and illustrates how people could be forced to agree by shaking hands or by quickly withdrawing each other's hands. A judgement from 1564 also shows how people sometimes declared that they had been frightened into making an agreement. It concerned a deal made between Bríet Brandsdóttir and Guðmundur Gíslason about a part of the land at Marðargnúpur, for the sum of ten hundrað in 1564.[48] The agreement was judged invalid because Bríet had been intimidated into making the contract.

For the above reasons therefore it can be said that agreements to marry or to sell property, as discussed here in part I, were invalid without

44 DI IV, pp. 609-10. Another example exists of a woman giving her consent on condition that she should receive land in return for that which was sold. See DI VI, pp. 654-55.

45 DI VI, pp. 23-24. See also another testimony in this case, in: Ibid., pp. 18-19.

46 Ibid., pp. 17-18.

47 Ibid., p. 18: "ad sijdustu hiellt og einginn hondum þeirra þa þau logdu hendur sijnar samþyckliga saman."

48 DI XIV, pp. 263-66.

the consent of the people involved. The documents examined indicate that property agreements could be annulled because consent was lacking or had not been freely given.

11.1.2 The property rights of the wife

We have discussed earlier that because a wife's *máli* came to be included in the husband's property (as part of that property),[49] this could sometimes lead to problems in retrieving it after the death of one of the spouses. The separate property of a wife could thus easily be exchanged for some other property belonging to her husband.[50] This gave the husband the ability to use his wife's property, if she gave her consent to it.

In 1390 a wife consented with her handshake to her husband's sale of half of the property of Hvammur. Her *máli* had been part of that land. He transferred her *máli* to the land he had bought at Varðgjá. This agreement was made also with the consent of the sons of the husband.[51] In a letter of 1398 concerning the sale and purchase of land, the wives of the husbands involved gave their consent to the transaction.[52] This was also the case in 1375, when Jón Pétursson sold the landed property, Hólar in Eyjafjörður, in return for the land at Auðbrekka in Hörgárdalur. This agreement was concluded with the consent of the wives.[53]

Women's consent was related to the wife's role in the household, as a partner of her husband. When a woman became a partner in making property agreements during her marriage, it also affected the role of her relatives in taking care of her interests. The need for relatives to represent

49 The situation in Iceland may have been similar to that which developed in England. See Bonfield, 1992, p. 306. There was a great increase in surviving marriage contracts from the English nobility in the fourteenth and fifteenth centuries. These written agreements dealt with more than the widow's maintenance. Surviving contracts note the transfer of property from the bride's family to the groom. In return, a joint life estate was often settled upon the bride and groom in a section of a patrimonial inheritance. The wife could hold these estates for her lifetime if her husband died. Although the frequency of the practice of creating these joint life estates cannot be established quantitatively, the practice was clearly common.

50 An example of this is to be found in DI IV, p. 663.

51 DI III, pp. 449-50.

52 Ibid., pp. 624-26.

53 Ibid., pp. 294-96. The land at Auðbrekka later became the property of Þorleifur Árnason, by inheritance and sale. See Einar Bjarnason 1962, p. 376. The land was valued at 80 *hundrað* according to the property register in 1713, but had a higher value earlier. At the beginning of the fifteenth century it was valued at 100 *hundrað*.

her decreased. This was a result of the fact that the woman herself had become a partner in the contract. However, this new role of the wife did not necessarily mean that she had gained increased property rights. The wife was still under her husband's guardianship and her rights did not extend beyond giving consent to his actions. It can, however, be stressed that the position of the wife was strengthened by the rules of *helmingarfélag*. The most obvious reason for this was because the husband needed his wife's consent to all property transfers under *helmingarfélag*, under which a couple owned all their property jointly. Secondly, if a couple had a *helmingarfélag* agreement there was no doubt that the wife or her heirs could claim the right to half of their possessions, rather than a lesser portion – such as one-third, as would be allowed by *máli* – if she became a widow.[54]

Even if a woman's separate possessions were incorporated into her husband's property it seems that she could sometimes get it "paid back" to her from her husband. In 1482 Benedikt Magnússon gave his wife, Ingibjörg Þorvaldsdóttir, her *mála*, which was the land at Vík and Hóll in Reynistaðarþing.[55] According to the document describing this transfer she should own this land totally, *fullrar eignar*, so that the husband and his heirs would have no claim over it. However, if she died before him then Benedikt would get the land back, whereas Ingibjörg's heirs would receive what was said to be hers in the marriage contract.[56] This division indicates that her heirs could not claim the gifts that her husband had given her after marriage.

Again, this is an example of the way in which efforts were made to ensure that inherited property was not transferred between family lines. This is an example of the strength of the custom of separating the possessions of two family lines.

A woman's legal right to control property was limited according to law. This was made clear in the rules of *Jónsbók*. The wife of a farmer

54 Evidence exists, however, that this claim was not always accepted. According to a judgement from 1586 the agreement for jointly-owned property made between Halla and Þorbjörn was judged illegal because "Halla had declared that she had hardly any wealth when she came to Þorbjörn." See *Alþingisbækur Íslands* II, p. 79 year 1586. The case concerns the inheritance right to the land at Fuglavik.

55 DI VI, pp. 449-50.

56 Ibid., p. 450.

had the right to trade for one *eyrir* each twelve months.[57] The wife of a yeoman was allowed to trade for double this amount, but the wife of a lord could buy for half a pound.[58] If her husband was away from home, a wife could buy everything needed for the household and her husband could also give her full authority to trade. However, the wife was not allowed to sell landed property.[59] But this does not give the full picture of the way in which women could make use of property during their married lives. A comparison of legal regulations with the contents of charters demonstrates that women's freedom to act was greater in practice than in principle. The following examples illustrate the variety of ways in which women seem to have used their property.

Many charters concerning women who sold landed property have survived.[60] In June 1479 in Grund in Grundarfjörður, nine men announced in an open letter that the widow Ólöf Loftsdóttir gave Arnór Finnsson 40 *hundrað* for his service. This included land at Snorrastaðir in Kolbeinstaðarþing, and she also gave him 13 *hundrað* in cow's value, *kúgildi*, and other useful properties. The witnesses were standing by and both heard and saw the words and the handshake between Ólöf and Arnór. She had a written contract for Snorrastaðir that proved that she was the legal owner of this property, and it was made clear that Ólöf gave the land from her and her heirs into the hands of Arnór and his heirs.[61] Ólöf was in a powerful position, being the widow of the *hirðstjóri* Björn Þorleifsson, the ruler of the great manor at Skarð in Skarðströnd. Another widow, Kristín Björnsdóttir, declared that she had given Jón Sigmundsson half the property at Hænuvík in Barðaströnd for his service. The letter was closed with her seal.[62] This is not the only surviving letter marked with a woman's seal. In 1423 Ingibjörg Loftsdóttir took back the authority of *umboð*, which Magnús Jónsson

57 One *eyrir* was an ounce of silver.

58 Sigurður Líndal 1976b, p. 500.

59 *Jónsbók*, pp. 231-32.

60 See, for instance, DI III, pp. 452-53, from 23 August 1390; DI VI, pp. 526-27, from 2 December 1484; ibid., p. 651, from 9 March 1489; and ibid., p. 657, from 8 June 1489.

61 Ibid, pp. 206-207. Another similar case dates from 5 February 1485, according to which Jón Björnsson Dan gave Erlingur Jónsson 20 *hundrað* for his service, and if he needed more to get a good wife, Jón gave a guarantee of the land of Okinsdalur in Arnarfjörður, or in some other land. See ibid., p. 534-35.

62 DI III, p. 698.

had over her wealth, though this agreement did not involve what she owned in the land at Holt in Fljótum. This letter was sealed with her own and another person's seal.[63]

It would be too much to analyze all the surviving transfers of property in which a woman was involved. Many of these transfers were related to the active involvement of widows although it was not only widows that gave, bought or sold landed property.[64] Even if it could be a problem for women to claim their rightful inheritance,[65] they seem to dispose rather freely over their own belongings during their married life. Thus, women whose husbands were guardians of their property could nonetheless make agreements concerning these possessions. One such example dates from 1488, when Margrét Ólafsdóttir gave her relative Ingibjörg Þorvarðardóttir one quarter of the land at Hvassafell in Eyjafjörður as a legal gift. This was achieved by the handshake of these women and with the consent of Margrét's husband. According to the letter recording this arrangement the land was to be handed into the control of Ingibjörg's husband, although it was to be his wife's property of which she could freely dispose.[66]

No general rule can, however, be identified concerning how women under the guardianship of men were to behave. For instance, a husband could make an agreement on behalf of his wife by a handshake, or the wife herself could perform the handshake, as happened in the case of

63 See also DI IV, pp. 309-10, compare to ibid., pp. 259-60, and to Agnes S. Arnórsdóttir 2001b, pp. 38-39.

64 In 1417, Járngerður Ormsdóttir sold land at Torfustaðir and Skálanes in Vopnafjörður to Gunnlaugur Guðmundsson. In return he paid with movable property or wealth. This agreement was confirmed by the two parties with a handshake. See DI IV, pp. 256-57. Another document has survived recording the handshake between a mother and daughter, by which land was transferred as payment for taking care of a grand-daughter. See DI XIII, pp. 393-94.

65 This common practice of women selling land should not be interpreted as women not having problems related to claiming their property right. This was related to the problems that could arise when retrieving a wife's *máli* after her death. Secondly, it is common to find documents concerning this problem of claiming inherited property belonging to women. Some, for instance the case of Sigríður Torfadóttir's from 1369, was that she had not got her inheritance after her mother. See DI III, pp. 254-55, a case from 1369. Another judgement from 1558 is about a similar problem. Einar Oddson claimed on behalf of his wife, Ólöf Pétursdóttir, the right to land at Vallholt, which Ólöf was due to inherit from her mother. See DI XIII, pp. 301-304. Einar claimed her legal right to this property according to the rules of *brigð*. In relation to this case it was stated that Ólöf's parents had been legally married, and a statement of a woman born in the same parish was used to clarify that Ólöf was a legal heir of her parents. According to this statement, this woman had never heard that Ólöf's mother had been anything other than a legal wife to her husband.

66 DI VI, pp. 640-41, from 12 October 1488.

Ingibjörg Þorvarðardóttir.[67] Because of the system of guardianship of women a network of social ties was established.[68] In this way both daughters and widows had responsibility to look after the business of their men. In 1420 the widow of the *hirðstjóri* Vigfús Hólm had in her possession the manors they had controlled. Because of her husband's debt, she promised to go abroad during the following summer in order to put the case to the royal authorities.[69]

More cases can be found in which widows dealt with the representatives of royal power. One of these was Margrét Vigfúsdóttir, the widow of Þorvarður Loftsson.[70] Danish King Christopher of Bavaria (1439-48) claimed that he had problems in getting hold of certain lands which belonged to the Crown in the north of Iceland. The reason for this was that the widow Margrét was holding these lands.[71] The freedom of the widows both according to law and in more everyday practice of selling property was clearly stronger than was the case with wives or unmarried women. It was, however, not only widows who were actively involved in disposing over property. The problem which could be related to getting their rightful share of inheritance as well as the rules of women getting less inheritance than men was thus not a hindrance for married women to act independently in property matters.

This chapter has brought into focus that writing a contract to confirm a marriage agreement constituted a statement of the property rights of the partners involved. These contracts were designed to ensure that inherited property would not be transferred between family lines without

67 DI IV, pp. 351-52. An agreement made in 1428 between Kristín Björnsdóttir and the heirs of Þorleifur Marteinsson gives an idea of how women's role in making agreements was not fixed. In January 1428 Kristín arranged for the church in Víðidalstunga to be rebuilt, while the heirs of Þorleifur were to give her landed property to cover the expenses of this project. This agreement was first confirmed with a handshake between Kristín and Sveinn Björnsson, who was the guardian of Þuríður Ólafsdóttir (his wife), who was one of these heirs. A second handshake took place between Kristín and Guðmundur Þorláksson, who was the guardian of Solveig Ólafsdóttir. In return for the land paid to Kristín, she would rebuild the church.

68 Loftur Guttormsson made an agreement concerning the property of his wife Ingibjörg Pálsdóttir with her ex-guardian and the bishop. It concerned an amount she had inherited. The bishop paid part of this wealth to Loftur in landed property, and another part was absorbed by his wife's debt, which she had got because of the *hirstjórnarumboð* of her father Páll Þórðarson. See DI IV, pp. 251-52.

69 DI IV, pp. 284-85.

70 *Annálar 1400-1600,* I, p. 60, from the year 1447. See also DI IV, pp. 705-706.

71 This case was probably related to the testament of Þorvarður Loftsson, see DI IV, pp. 674-77, and the gift of one fourth, which Margrét Vigfúsdóttir got.

the consent of the heirs. Secondly, these contracts concerned the property that the couple brought into their marriage and the agreement they made about it, which was normally either one establishing joint possession or establishing the separate property of the wife. It can be concluded that even if a husband had disposed of his wife's wealth, in which case it could be difficult for the widow to retrieve this wealth after his death, she had a legal right to claim it back.[72] This underlines the potential for a woman's relatives to retrieve her dowry in the event of the woman dying before her husband, without having had children with him.

11.1.3 The rights of the relatives of the wife

Documents concerning property transfer seem in some instances to have had greater meaning after the death of the spouses than during their marriage. The documents that deal with property transfer through marriage are therefore very much related to the question of inheritance.[73] A document from 1576 concerning the division of the wealth left after the death of Magnús Magnússon and Guðrún Þorleifsdóttir illustrate this point.[74] They had received a dispensation to marry from the king in 1565. This was needed because a relative of Magnús was said to have had a sexual relationship with Guðrún before she became Magnús's wife.[75] According to the document concerning the inheritance division, Guðrún had also had children with Egill Jónsson before her marriage to Magnús. She was probably Egill's widow. This double problem (Guðrún's children from her first marriage and the possibility that Guðrún and Magnús's marriage could be declared to be within the forbidden degrees) prompted the production of the document concerning the inheritance division. Magnús

72 More information has survived about this practice. For example, a case from 1527 shows how it was necessary for a husband to give his wife land, other than that she originally owned when they made their contract. See DI IX, pp. 403-404.

73 It is clear that one of the preconditions for marriage was to acquire land on which to live. In 1387 the owner of half the manor at Vatnsfjörður planned to go abroad. He handed the property to another person, according to a written document concerning an agreement. In the agreement it also said that if the son of the new owner got married, then he should have this part of Vatnsfjörður. DI III, pp. 399-400.

74 AM dipl. isl. fasc. LXVIII, 21.

75 DI XIV, pp. 363-64.

and Guðrún called witnesses to the farm at Höskuldsstaðir in Skagaströnd to testify to the property transfer made by Guðrún to her children. This concerned the inheritance she left to the children of her first marriage. These children inherited the land from their father.[76] All the children gave their consent to this division and they accepted all the arrangements their mother had made previously. Among other such arrangements, Guðrún had given her husband Magnús land at Fremri Núpur.

This document shows that marrying a widow gave a man a chance to enjoy the use of some of her possessions during their married life. However, this property was "transferred" back to the woman's rightful heirs after her death. This emphasizes the importance of the role women had in transferring property between generations. The property of Guðrún Þorleifsdóttir, who was either a widow, or had had illegitimate children before her marriage, was inherited by her children rather than her second husband. Women did not only transfer wealth within their family lines, but also had a duty to act as guardians of their family property during their married life.

It was after the owner of a property had died that marriage contracts might be used as evidence for inheritance rights. This is why a lawman like Jón Finnbogason knew it was important to have written documents concerning the property division in his family. In 1555 he gave his son Finnbogi land with the consent of his wife, Sigríður Einarsdóttir, and his three daughters. At the same time Jón made a statement concerning his wife's *máli*.[77] This kind of document could have great value at a later stage when the property of the couple came to be divided between their heirs.

Another example can be taken from a letter concerning inheritance division, *skiptabréf*, of Þórður Helgason in Staðarfell from May 1493. The wife claimed the amount of her *máli*, and two legal witnesses stated that Þórður had declared in his will what his wife's possessions were.[78] If they had made a marriage contract, it would have been easier to prove what her property consisted of. In this case no contract existed, only the witnesses to their arrangements. The old tradition of oral evidence

76 Appendix II indicate this.

77 DI XIII, pp. 42-43.

78 DI VII, pp. 183-84.

was still alive, and was useful in cases for which no written documents existed. It was in this way that witnesses, oral or written, could fulfill the same function as written contracts.

When discussing the role of women as guardians over their family property during their married life, it is worth remembering that even if their relatives did have fewer possibilities to control the properties of the married women, according to the law of *Jónsbók* rather than *Grágás*, there was still a possibility to interfere. The rules of *brigð*[79] indicate that inherited land could not be sold or exchanged for another property without the consent of the closest heirs. In some instances the relatives of a wife gave their consent to her husband's sales. Páll Grímsson handed over to his wife, Margrét Erlendsdóttir, three *útjarðir*, called Brekkur and Hraun in Höfðaströnd, in return for her *máli* at Austfirðir.[80] This happened in 1556, one year after they were married. It seems that this agreement could not have been made without the knowledge of her relatives. The householder Þorsteinn Finnbogason and Bjarni Ellendsson, Margrét's brother, were witnesses to this agreement between Páll and Margrét.[81] This indicates that if the couple changed their agreement concerning *máli* this should be done with the acceptance of her family. This meant that it was possible for a wife's relatives to play a part in the property settlement after her marriage. There is, however, limited evidence that this happened in practice, something that highlights the fact that the new role of the wife, as a partner of her husband, was widely accepted, even if it did not mean that a wife would no longer need the help of her relatives.

Even if a wife could receive payment for her property from her husband, many problems arose when a wife tried to retrieve her possessions, as discussed previously. The rules concerning *brigð* did not ensure that a wife's land was not lost. People therefore used the courts to claim the right to *máli*. In 1496 Jón Sigurðsson on behalf of his mother Æsa Jónsdóttir claimed her *mála* and her gift, *fjórðungsgjöf*, which was included in the property of her dead husband, Hafliði Jónsson, (See Figure 30).

79 As mentioned earlier the term *brigð* refers to the right of the relatives to claim back or buy inherited land.

80 DI XIII, pp. 121-22.

81 Ibid., p. 122.

Bjarni Hafliðason was Hafliði's son and heir, but Bjarni was also dead and it was Bjarni's wife, Halla Sigurðardóttir, who had retained all this wealth as a guardian for their children.[82]

Further information has survived from other cases concerning the problem of retrieving a wife's *máli* from the heirs of her dead husband. A case concerning Arnór Finnson and Bjarni Halldórsson should be cited.[83] Arnór accused Bjarni of retaining the *mála* of Ingigerður Þorsteinsdóttir after the death of her husband, Sigmundur Halldórsson. Arnór was Ingigerður's guardian. Bjarni claimed that the land was his because he was Sigmundur's brother and his legal heir, and said that the land had been given by Ingigerður to her husband as a gift before his death. Bjarni Halldórsson did not win the case, but was ordered to pay all the *máli* that Ingigerður had in Sigmundur's property. This was in accordance with the law that stated that if a man made a legal marriage and gave his wife a marriage gift, and then later died, she would receive the value of her own possessions and her dowry from his wealth. If he did not have this wealth his heirs were to pay the amount to his widow from their own possessions.[84]

Problems in retrieving a wife's *máli* could be related to what her husband did with her land. In 1555 Þorsteinn Torfason declared the extent of the possessions of his wife, Þorgerður Sturludóttir, saying that the land of Hjörsey at Mýrar was hers. The reason for this statement was that earlier she had asked him to reveal which of their belongings were hers, but he had not been willing to tell her. In the end he was forced to tell the truth: he had disposed of all her wealth so he needed to give her another property. This was the land at Hjörsey.[85] Another case from 1558 exemplifies this problem. Bjarni Jónsson had used all his wife's wealth, and because she was able to claim this back after his death,

82 See a judgement about the *máli* of Æsa Jónsdóttir and her *fjórðungsgjöf.* DI VII, pp. 300-302, 354-55. This was about: "alla jörðina Oddstaði í Lundarreykjadal með tilskildum torfskurði í Brautártungu jörð, ásamt kúgildum og fríðum peningum." The value of Æsa's belongings was 6 *hundrað* and 40 *hundrað*, as well as some silver and the contents of the house and the countergift which the husband had given her on the day of their betrothal.

83 DI VIII, pp. 103-106.

84 Ibid., pp. 103-104.

85 DI XIII, pp. 44-45.

his heirs were ordered to repay her in accordance with the agreement that had been made when they were married.[86]

It is thus possible to sum up by saying that even though the role of a woman – actively participating in making property agreements on behalf of herself and her husband – became stronger, the right of her kin to interfere on her behalf had not diminished. This meant also that a husband's right to rule over the marital property during his married life could also be limited by the interference of the closest kin.

11.2 The consequences of the new marriage practice for property transfer

As has already been discussed, during the twelfth and thirteenth centuries the principle requiring the mutual consent of a couple became one of the main criteria for a legal marriage. The need for the consent of the parents was asserted in reaction to these new criteria. The consent of the closest relatives represents the parents' need to control the marriage of their offspring, and was not in opposition to the ecclesiastical authority. The bilateral inheritance structure of Icelandic society was influenced by the new marriage doctrine. The position of the couple came to be ideologically strengthened, but at the same time the parental consent also was strengthened. The question here will be how this affected the more general pattern of property transfer. The first section concerns the consent of heirs to property transfer, while the second section deals with how property was transferred to people of illegitimate status.

11.2.1 The consent of heirs to property transfer

In 1592 a property was judged to belong to a man and his heirs.[87] This expression clearly indicates that property rights were not just personal, but also related to the inheritance rights of an individual's closest heirs. This can be called a shared ownership right. An expression that means

86 Ibid., pp. 308-10. This is a judgement from 1558: "Um málakröfu Þórunnar Einarsdóttir í garð bónda síns Bjarna heitins Jónssonar."

87 *Alþingisbækur Íslands* II, p. 248.

to get property in perpetuity, to *æfinlegrar eignar*, is also included in some marriage contracts. In a contract from 1505, a man took a woman as his legal wife, and received property from his father to *æfinlegrar eignar*.[88] This expression is concerned with describing the full ownership of the members of the new household. However, when property was given away like this, it did not mean that the land became the private property of the couple, at least not if it was one of the family's main manors. According to the general phrase of sales agreement, *kaupbréf*,[89] property was something which belonged to the person or persons who would inherit from the owner as well. This explains why it was so important for the owner to get wide acceptance for sales of property. In 1479 Halldór Brandsson gave his son the land at Barð in Fljótum with the consent of his wife and his brother.[90] This is an example of the inclusion of the institution of *laudatio parentum* in a late fifteenth-century Icelandic document. It was an institution based on the consent of the lineal relatives to the transfer of part of the ancestral inheritance, which meant that one needed to get consent of the close relatives for selling property.[91]

It was never necessary for large numbers of relatives to participate in the formal ritual of making a property contract.[92] What was usually important was the consent of the closest kin to property transfer. This also included the consent of both wife and husband to different kinds of property transfer, as discussed in section 11.1.

Consent of the closest relatives is found in almost all documents that refer to the sale of land.[93] A father sold land to one of his sons with the

88 DI VII, pp. 747-48.

89 See, for instance, DI VI, pp. 51-52 from the year c.1450 or later: "til æfinligrar eignar vndan mier og mijnvm erfingium enn vnder hann og hanz erfingia."

90 DI VI, p. 208.

91 White 1988, pp. 180-81.

92 DI III, pp. 704-705. The most usual form for collective handling was when a couple sold land together as the following case illustrates: See ibid., p. 705: "woro þau þa oll j æinu handabande benedik[t]. biorn. þorgýls ok ingunn sæm samþycktu þetta þeirra kaup." Compare to ibid., pp. 635-36 from 1398, which is an example of a couple and their son selling land together. See also DI VI, pp. 120-21.

93 See for instance DI III, pp. 372-73, 449-50. DI IV, pp. 278-79, 303, 531, 583. DI V, pp. 205-206, 221-22, 451. DI VI, pp. 32-33, 33-34, 43-44, 45-46, 51-52, 108-10, 119, 120-21, 147-48, 161-62, 202-203, 217, 342-43, 369-70, 409-10, 411-12, 451-52, 456-57, 475-76, 479, 567-68, 610-11, 612-14, 694-95, 727-28, 738-39. DI IX, pp. 450-51. DI XIII, pp. 517-19.

consent of another son.[94] Sons consented when their fathers sold land.[95] A daughter consented when her mother gave a legal gift,[96] *löggjöf*, from her property.[97] One case survives that testifies to the consent of a son when his mother gave land to a monastery for the good of her husband's soul.[98] Another case involves a woman who sold land with the consent of her son.[99] The documents widely show us how women sold land with the consent of their sons,[100] or daughters,[101] just as they gave land to their sons with the consent of their husbands and their other sons, or with the consent of their husbands alone.[102]

To sum up, the law court material gives no indication that transfers of property were annulled because the consent of relatives was lacking, but many court cases stated that land was transferred with the consent of the closest heirs. This is remarkable in a comparative respect. The institution of *laudatio parentum*, implying the consent of relatives from either the male or female line, grew in importance in France during the twelfth century, but lost ground during the following century, disappearing totally before 1300.[103] In Iceland, this institution seems to have survived at least until the end of the sixteenth century.

It has been assumed that the increasing influence of the Church and the consolidation of the state may have meant that the institution disappeared in France. Similar transformations are assumed to have taken place in many other Western European societies from the end of the eleventh century to the beginning of the twelfth century.[104] However, it seems that no such transformation took place in Iceland during the

94 DI III, pp. 372-73.
95 DI IV, p. 303.
96 This was a gift that could not be greater than one-tenth of one's wealth. See discussion above in section 10.3.
97 DI VI, p. 479.
98 DI IV, p. 531.
99 DI VI, p. 217. Compare also that Jón Sæmundsson accepted that his mother Sigríður Árnadóttir bought Stokkseyri in Eyrarbakki in the year 1465, from Jón Ólafsson. See DI V, p. 451.
100 DI VI, p. 217, DI IV, pp. 516-17.
101 DI VI, p. 479.
102 DI V, pp. 221-22, VI, pp. 765-67.
103 White 1988, pp. 180-81. White has showed that the institution varied with regard to which relatives could belong to it. For instance it did not only concern the agnate group.
104 Hansen 1996, pp. 150-52. He mentions that David Herlihy, George Duby, Guy Bois and Stephen White have done research on this question.

Middle Ages. This does not indicate that the state and the Church were not important in Iceland in the Middle Ages, but rather that there was a different type of state control and Church influence. Not surprisingly, the transformation of medieval Icelandic society into a state seems to have occurred later than in France. Another way in which Iceland seems to have been special was that property could often be transferred to illegitimate children.

11.2.2 Adoption and legal gifts as means by which to transfer property

Illegitimate children could be made legitimate through the institution of *ættleiðing*, which literally means to take a child into one's kin. The word adoption will be used for this practice.[105] Children were adopted with the consent of the relatives of the adopter.[106] This was a common practice among clerics in particular.[107] Adoption could be used to ensure that children born out of wedlock received their share of property. This was first mentioned in the law code of *Jónsbók*. The ceremony of adoption should take place in front of the church door.[108] These rules were reinforced by a *réttarbót* of 1314.[109] Children born in adultery or the children of concubines were not accepted as equal heirs as the legitimately born children, until they had been adopted into the family with the consent of relatives.

The fathers of children not born in marriage also needed to be identified. Women had to make oaths stating who the father of their children was.[110] An example of such an oath has survived from 1561 when a woman swore that a priest was the father of her illegitimate children.[111] The formula was as follows:

105 On this institution see Agnes S. Arnórsdóttir 2005, pp. 211-12.

106 DI XIII, pp. 517-19, from the year 1560.

107 Several cases demonstrate this practice: in 1439 a priest adopted his son with the consent of the son's grandfather, see DI IV, p. 583. And in 1528 a priest gave landed property to his daughter with the consent of his brother, and gave other children wealth; see DI IX, pp. 450-52.

108 *Jónsbók*, p. 87: "Nú má maðr bæta ráð sonar síns ok leiða hann í ætt."

109 Ibid., p. 296.

110 See for instance DI XIII, pp. 599-600, a judgement about *ósvarin frillubörn* from 1561, with reference to the Christian law and *Jónsbók* about the rules for this kind of ceremony.

111 Ibid., pp. 598-99.

I put my hand on the Holy Book and put my case to the judgement of God, and declare that the priest Þorleifur Björnsson is as true the father of my children as I am the mother.[112]

This kind of evidence became important when, for instance, those who were born outside marriage claimed to be the heirs of their parents.[113] Many of the surviving documents of adoption concern the adoption of the children of priests.[114] A letter of adoption from 1401 shows how the rules from *Jónsbók* were followed. As regard the adoption, the ceremony was performed in front of the church door with the consent of the closest kin of the adopter.[115] The consent of the closest kin was very important in guaranteeing that they would not sue the children in court at a later stage. Some statements of adoption were also made with special reference to certain legal regulations.[116]

It was not only the clerics of lower rank who adopted their children. Bishop Jón Arason adopted his four children. By doing this he gave them all share in his property. This was done with the consent of his mother's sister, who was his closest legal heir. At the same time the bishop gave each of his three sons a book, and his daughter a silver buckle.[117] In the same year, 1522, the mother of these children, Helga Sigurðardóttir,

112 Ibid., p. 598: "Til þess [legg] ec hond a helga bock og so skyt ec minu male til gudz at sira Þorleifur Biornsson er so sannur holldligur fader sem ec holldlig moder at þessum minum bornum."

113 A testimony given by a priest in 1479, which stated that a woman had declared who the father of her son was, was used by the son to take his claim to inherit from this man. See DI VI, pp. 189-90. It was important to find the right paternity to children, not only because of the child inheritance right, but also to know who had the obligation to care for the child. Children born outside marriage were not totally without maintenance as the example of the poor woman, Guðlaug Sveinsdóttir, in ibid., pp. 532-34 illustrates. She could not take care of her newborn baby but claimed that the father was Runólfur Höskuldsson. They were not married, but according to this document he was obliged to take care of both the woman and the child.

114 See, for instance, DI III, pp. 666-67, 2 June 1401, compare to ibid., pp. 668-69. See also DI IV, pp. 357-58, 27 April 1428; DI IX, pp. 609-10, 18 February 1532; and DI X, pp. 330-31, 23 October 1537. During the Reformation, it was common for a priest to make a marriage contract with his concubine and after doing this, to make other documents declaring that their children were adopted. Ibid., pp. 666-67, 21 September 1541, but testified in the year of 1587. See also DI XI, pp. 252-53, 31 August 1543, and pp. 658-59, 25 July 1548.

115 DI III, pp. 666-67.

116 DI VI, pp. 351-52, from 30 April 1481: The lawman Hrafn Brandsson declared that the adoption of Stefán Loftsson was legal according to the law of *Herjólfsréttarbót*.

117 DI IX, pp. 94-95, from 29 May 1522, testified 21 April 1541. Figure 32 shows a ring-shaped buckle. See also Figure 31, his seal.

adopted two of the sons, with the consent of her brother.[118] Through this double ceremony the children got the full right to claim inheritance from both their father and mother. This case is just one of many described in surviving letters of adoption.[119]

The clerics could also marry their children to other high ranking persons in society. Several existing marriage contracts from the fifteenth and sixteenth century concern the children of lawmen and bishops. Þórunn Jónsdóttir, the daughter of Bishop Jón Arason, was for instance given in marriage to the lawman Rafn Brandsson.[120] Bishop Jón Arason used the form of an old-style property contract when marrying his children off.[121] This was related to the importance of the financial elements of marriage contracts to clerics. It was essential for clerics to make good contracts for their children, in order to give their illegitimate children a legal status.[122] These contracts were thus important in order to establish the status of the children.

Secondly, people who had children outside marriage could make wills and in that way give part of their property to children who were not legally born. Wills, along with letters of adoption, could be used to transfer property if the existing inheritance rules did not suit the purpose of the property owner. But, as mentioned before, only one-tenth of one's inherited property could be given away – to the disadvantage of the legal heirs – and one-quarter of property that had been acquired by other means.[123]

Testamentary dispositions had been common, at least among the rich, in late Roman antiquity. Although it never quite disappeared, this

118 Ibid., pp. 74-75, from 25 April 1522, testified 8 November 1523.

119 See, for instance, DI VI, p. 693; DI IX, pp. 219-21, 490-91; and DI XII, pp. 553-54.

120 DI IX, pp. 378-80.

121 It is interesting to look at these contracts as evidence of the high levels of marriage between the secular and ecclesiastical groups. In this case the *handaband* was performed by the bishop and the lawman, and the bishop gave away his daughter with her consent. It was actually the older forms of marriage-making that predominated in this instance, with the principle of the woman's consent appearing as an element added to the handshake between the men. Other contracts from this period placed greater emphasis on the central place of the couples themselves, in the sense that the documents were more a statement of the financial relationship between the spouses than a financial contract between their families; see, for instance, 1531 Ibid., pp. 602-603, 604-605.

122 Ibid., pp. 498-99.

123 *Jónsbók*, pp. 99-100.

practice certainly diminished markedly in importance during the Early Middle Ages. The Germanic peoples who settled in Western Europe preferred to transmit property by intestate succession rather than by testamentary dispositions. Roman observers in antiquity, notably Tacitus (c.56-c.115), had found it remarkable that the will had no place in the Germanic legal systems and that property usually passed from one generation to the next according to fixed rules. This presumably reflected the intimate relationship that Germanic society saw between the possession of family property and personal identity. Thus custom dictated that property holders in any given generation must allow their survivors to share their family goods according to community norms, rather than expressing a personal preference about the matter through a will. These Germanic inheritance practices persisted through the Early Middle Ages, but both canon law and new social structures changed practice to introduce more flexibility.[124] This canon law influence can clearly be found in the Icelandic legislation of the High Middle Ages.

According to Icelandic law it was possible to give one's illegitimate children a part of one's property as a legal gift. Steinunn Jónsdóttir did so in November 1567, to the benefit of four of her children.[125] She had previously given her other children a share in their inheritance. It seems that her intention was to make clear that her illegitimate children had not been given more than these legal gifts,[126] and that the legitimate children should not start to claim rights to the belongings she had thus given.[127] Such legal gifts were given by both women[128] and men[129] and

124 Brundage 1995a, pp. 87-88.

125 DI XV, p. 37.

126 Compare to DI XV, pp. 37-38.

127 Compare to ibid., p. 38.

128 One example of *fjórðungsgjöf* was that which Guðrún Þorsteinsdóttir gave to her son Þorsteinn Þórarinsson in 1464. See DI VI, pp. 54-55. Þorsteinn got part of the property Arnastapi *undir Jökli*, but paid some chattles to his mother for this. A part of the property transfer was his legal inheritance, of which he got the same amount as his brothers, but then he also got the *fjórðungsgjöf* of her property. See also ibid., pp. 55-56 when he *handleggur* (relinquishes) all his claim in this land to his brother; and further ibid., pp. 56-57 about the same landed property.

129 One example can be taken from DI VII, pp. 591-92. In 1502 Guðni Jónsson gave his daughter Helga,"full property right", to the land at Bræðratunga in Biskupstungur, as his legal gift, both *fjóðrungsgjöf* as well as *tíundargjöf*. He had gotten this land from his brother Páll Jónsson, who had received it as an inheritance from his dead son Jón Pálsson, who had received it as a gift from his mother in her testament. This was the testament of Solveig Björnsdóttir.

give the impression that there was greater individual freedom of action in property transfer than the general inheritance rules would suggest.[130]

Legal gifts are frequently mentioned in the documents concerning property transfer.[131] *Fjórðungsgjöf* could be used in order to transfer land between persons more widely than the gift of *tíundargjöf*, as it was mentioned above in relation to the exchange of marriage gifts.[132] Sometimes such property transfers were recorded in special letters describing the legal gifts.[133] The legal gifts could be used for different types of property transfer. They could be given as a payment to servants,[134] but it is striking to see how often they were used to transfer property from parents to children.[135] The way in which such legal gifts were given demonstrates the inheritance strategy of the people involved.[136] Priests also commonly used legal gifts to transfer property to their concubines.[137] Thus these gifts, along with the adoption of children, were used to transfer property to people other than the legal heirs.[138]

To sum up: Many documents concerning adoption and wills have survived as a consequence of these institutions being the available method

130 Examples of legal gifts between spouses are many. See for example DI XIII, pp. 236-37, *löggjafarbréf* of Elín Jónsdóttir to her husband Magnús Jónsson, from 1557. See also the example of *fjórðungsgjöf* in DI VIII, pp. 154-55, a *fjórðungsgjöf* which Þorbjörg Brandsdóttir gave to her husband Ásgrímur.

131 These gifts were for instance still given in 1573, compare to *Alþingisbækur Íslands* I, p. 157. See also Agnes S. Arnórsdóttir 2005.

132 Compare to *Jónsbók*, p. 100.

133 AM dipl. isl. fasc. LIX, 10. This letter about the *löggjafir* of Eiríkur Stefánsson survive from 1593. This kind of gift is often mentioned in other types of Icelandic charters related to the question of ownership of property. See for instance from the years 1434-46: DI IV, pp. 656, 663, 677.

134 DI VI, p. 415.

135 One such example is that a priest gave a legal gift to his son in 1391, see DI III, pp. 454-55. We can find a document about a gift from a father to his daughter in 1531, see DI IX, pp. 605, from a father to his son in 1565 see DI XIV, p. 400, and a mother to her son in 1464, see DI VI, pp. 54-55.

136 Those difference inheritance strategies where the changing factor of the social structure. A definition of the word social structure is here borrowed from Burke 1980, p. 42, "To speak of the "social structure" … is to suggest that the major institutions … and the major groups in society … depended on one another, in the sense that a change in one group or institution would be followed by change in the other."

137 Magnús Jónsson was one such priest. In 1533 he gave Kristín Vigfúsdóttir *fjórðungsgjöf* of all his belongings. The letter says that if they had children this wealth should go to them; otherwise the property should be transmitted in accordance with the inheritance rules. See DI IX, p. 684.

138 Either adoption or a legal gift could be arranged for children born out of wedlock. See for instance ibid., p. 490: In 1529 Bishop Jón Arason of Hólar gave his son Ari the land at Holtastaðir in Laugardalur, as well as the land at Vatnahverfi, Lækjardalur, Sæunnarstaðir, Gautsdalur, Strútur and Refstaðir. The same bishop had three years earlier given wealth to Helga Sigurðardóttir, who was his "wife", but she had immediately given that amount to the church at Hólar, in return for her maintenance, called *próventa*, in her old age. See ibid., pp. 351-52.

through which children born outside of marriage could gain some of the rights as the legitimately born children. This demonstrates how society adjusted to the new marriage rules. This is compatible with Thyra Nors' conclusion that there were two, irreconcilable perceptions of legitimacy in the High Middle Ages. First there was the international Church's new legal view of marriage. The other perception of legitimacy was a product of a more traditional culture.[139]

Auður Magnúsdóttir's study of concubines, companions and consorts in Iceland between 1120 and 1400 further emphasizes this. She states that during that period several other forms of cohabitation were to some degree accepted by the laity, and more or less tolerated by the Church.[140] In the context of the study here, the main point to bear in mind is that the boundaries between what was legitimate and illegitimate were moved and redefined during the Middle Ages.[141] Secondly this does not mean that those who were born out of wedlock could not claim the right of being a legal heir after one's parents. Alternative channels of legitimizing their status were taken in use. This was possible through the oral ritual of adoption as well as by making a written will. This clearly underlines that there where different channels of property transfer available. Property came to be transferred through legally born heirs, or through children who had been adopted. Thirdly, one-fourth of one's non-inherited wealth, and one-tenth of inherited wealth, could be given to children born from other cohabitation relationships. This was done by making a will. It is important to remember that these alternative institutions were not acting in opposition to the practices of the Church, because they were closely related to religious rituals. Wills were often drawn up on a deathbed by a priest, and a person could only be adopted through the Christian rite of adoption.[142]

139 Nors 1996, p. 20.
140 Auður Magnúsdóttir 2001, p. 220.
141 Nors 1996, p. 17.
142 Agnes S. Arnórsdóttir 2005, pp. 205-19.

11.2.3 Preliminary conclusion

The legal culture of Iceland in the twelfth and thirteenth centuries has been described as a *ius particulare*, a special compromise between canon law and customary law in a specific region – as opposed to a common European *ius commune*.[143] This legal culture continued into the Late Middle Ages. Priests had their companions, as in many other regions of Europe, but what seems to have been different in Iceland was that it was not assumed to be immoral even for bishops to live in this kind of relationship. Moreover the children born of these relationships were adopted after the parents had paid fines to the Church. Bishop Jón Arason not only lived with a female companion, but also had children. One of his sons, Magnús Jónsson, later became a priest himself and made a contract with Kristín Vigfúsdóttir in 1553 concerning the financial arrangements of their marriage.[144]

Clearly, the ecclesiastical definition of what constituted a legal marriage also had great influence on the way in which property was transferred. However, it cannot be said that this influence had the same results everywhere in Europe. The institution of *laudatio parentum*, as well as the alternative channels for making children legitimate heirs, survived longer in Iceland than in the more centralized societies of Western Europe.

11.3 Patrilineal strategy

According to Georges Duby a fundamental change occurred in the organization of aristocratic families during the eleventh and twelfth centuries in France. This change was towards primogeniture, which placed a strong emphasis on transmission of the family estate through the male line.[145] This change took place most noticeably in the central agricultural area in Western Europe, while the traditional, more bilateral system prevailed in both Northern and Southern Europe.[146] The system in the north was

143 Einar Arnórsson 1953-54, p. 5. He translates *jus particulare* as *staðbundinn kirkjuréttur*.

144 See DI IX, pp. 682-84. She got 100 *hundrað* for being his concubine. See also DI VIII, pp. 685-86, 4 May 1519, where Jón Arason and Helga Sigurðardóttir received absolution for having nine illegitimate children.

145 Duby 1985, pp. 80-82.

146 See also Winberg 1985, pp. 27-29, Casey 1989, pp. 30-31, 74, Bagge 1992, pp. 343-50.

based on the principle that property could be transferred through both the female and the male lines, such as was the case in Iceland.

In earlier times aristocrats in Central and Western Europe had regarded their families as a horizontally-organized group, formed from relatives through marriage as well as blood relatives. Men and women were linked as much by marriage as by blood. At this time the relation of men to their king was more important than the bonds formed by ancestry.[147] Kings and dukes were the sources of offices, gifts and honors. However, the bilateral system was socially unstable. Abrupt change could take place in every generation, where property could be dispersed via both the male and the female lines. These were some of the problems related to bilateral inheritance practice.

Bilateral land transactions between families in Iceland could lead to the erosion of the family estate. The instances of consent of the closest relatives that can be found in Icelandic documents can be seen as an attempt to solve this problem by establishing greater lineal control.[148] This policy occurred at the same time as the rules about legal marriage were formally accepted, as has been discussed. We can thus ask whether there is any reason to believe that regulation of property transfer came to be influence by the redefinition of what constituted legal marriage. Did canon law directly influence property strategy towards stronger patrilineal transmission of land? The remaining question is whether the patrilineal emphasis in *Jónsbók* was more the product of an "importation" of Norwegian legal thinking than a result of Icelandic policy?

11.3.1 Patrilineal ideology and bilateral inheritance practice

The introduction of a stronger lineal principle of inheritance in Iceland was a consequence of the new legislation of *Jónsbók* and the *réttarbætur*.[149] An example of patrilineal ideology can also be found in the

147 This view of Duby has been criticized by Van Houts 1999, pp. 146-47.

148 Agnes S. Arnórsdóttir 1995, p. 199.

149 The inheritance law of *Jónbók* was more closely related to the Norwegian inheritance rules, than to the inheritance law in *Grágás*. Recently Michael Gelting has stated that the principle of pre-emption by members of the kin to heritable land which had been sold to non-kin is related to the codification of the kin's right that was introduced through royal legislation during the twelfth and thirteenth centuries. This was

inheritance law of the oldest Icelandic law code *Grágás*, which limited women's ability to inherit and dispose of landed property. The ideology present in *Grágás* was, however, not as strong as that in the later law code of *Jónsbók,* from 1281, in which the role of the male rather than the female line in inheriting the main manor, *höfuðból,* was strengthened. According to the rules about the manor in *Jónsbók*, a woman's dowry could only consist of land from outlying areas rather than manors.[150] One such example can be taken from the beginning of the sixteenth century. In 1501 Björn Þorleifsson, the son of Þorleifur Björnsson, made a marriage contract with Ingibjörg Pálsdóttir, including amongst other things the land at Flatey in Breiðafjörður. If they died without children this land should go back to his relatives. This was done with the consent of Ingveldur Helgadóttir, Björn's mother.[151] The question here is why this claim of the right to keep family land inside the family line of Björn was made. Was it a defensive tactic, aimed at securing the rights of the husband's heirs against the possibility that the land could be lost to the heirs of his wife?

It had been very difficult to gain acceptance of the legality of the marriage of Björn's mother and father, Ingveldur and Þorleifur, and the strategy they used in making their son's marriage contract must be understood in the same way as their efforts to gain dispensation for their marriage. Both of these choices were strategies for legitimating relationships, so that their children could become the owners of their property.

The same principle was applied to the manor at Grund in Eyjafjörður in a contract of 1533. It says that this land belonged to a woman, Þórunn Jónsdóttir, and if her husband, Ísleifur Sigurðsson, died before she did, and they had no children, she would retain the manor and, from their

the so-called *odelsret* in the Norwegian law, *lovbydelse* in the Danish law, or *bördsrett* in the Swedish law, named *retrait lignager* in French. This right to claim back heritable land has traditionally been interpreted either as an old institution of supposedly kin-based society in prehistoric times, or as a defensive reaction on the part of the traditional society against the increasing influence of the royal and ecclesiastical power. See Gelting 2000.

150 Generally women did, however, get more right to inheritance according to *Jónsbók*, than was the case in *Grágás*. See the inheritance law in *Jónsbók*, pp. 78 ff.

151 DI VII, pp. 543-44.

other land, be able to settle her husband's share of their property with his heirs.[152]

In this way, if the principal manors of a family were part of the land transferred through marriage, the rule that this land should not be alienated from the family line, should the spouses not have children, was often stated. However, these rules were not institutionalized, but used on an *ad hoc* basis. Marriage regulation in the early fourteenth century reinforced the need for the consent of relatives. The approval of the kin for the transfer of property ensured that parents could control the marriages of their children. But was parental control related to the idea of keeping the main family land within the family for generations?

The strengthening of agnate kinship relationships and the general tightening of control over patrimony during the European High Middle Ages, are normally viewed in contrast to the liberal inheritance practices of the Early Middle Ages.[153] Georges Duby[154] described how the change in the strategy of the French aristocracy as a change from a bilaterally defined (cognate) kinship system to one where patrilineal (agnate) relationships were given priority.[155] It has therefore been assumed that the institution of *laudatio parentum* was strengthened as a reaction against the Church's influence on marriage. Georges Duby says that in France *laudatio parentum* became a necessity from the middle of the eleventh century onwards. There was a general tendency to exclude women who no longer received anything but the dowry from the paternal home, so that they often only received negligible amounts for their funeral costs, generally drawn from their mother's dowry. Through the practice of joint ownership between brothers, and especially through the policy of limiting the number of marriages, knightly lineages were instrumental in averting the division of inheritances. Families united to defend their

152 DI IX, pp. 655-57.

153 Hansen 1996, p. 152.

154 See, for instance, Duby 1968, 1984, 1990, 1991a (first published 1978), 1991b, 1991-92. Duby's work has been criticized in *Aristocratic Women in Medieval France*, 1999, for drawing too many conclusions about practice from the normative documents, like the law codes and the writings of the clerics or the aristocrats. Even when he looks behind the formal political institutions, his interpretations are colored by his male point of view. See also a similar criticism in Jacqueline Murray in 1995, p. 8.

155 See the definition and discussion of this principle, pp. 398-99.

economic position. Because of this the seigniorial society remained stable for two centuries, according to Duby.[156]

Stephen White has shown that the scope of the group of relatives who used the institution of *laudatio parentum*, varied. For instance, it was not only an issue for the agnate kin-group.[157] An aristocrat felt like a member of a lineage, of a stock. The inheritance was handed down from a father to his oldest son.[158] This development changed the understanding of property rights and power relationships.[159] "The house was willing to give up the blood of its women, but restricted their claims to the ancestral inheritance."[160]

This change emphasized the need to keep property together by strengthening the solidarity of blood relationships in inheritance matters. Agnate descent (descent through the male line from the same male ancestor) with a vertical structure should ensure that property could be kept inside the same family for many generations.

This in turn influenced marriage strategies. The eldest son would now inherit the house of the family and he alone should be allowed to marry. Other male siblings would have to find other ways of supporting themselves. Some of the daughters were married off, but they received smaller dowries than before. Change in the political structure ensued. The authority of the state fragmented, while aristocratic families strengthened their position through the strategy of primogeniture. In addition, personal bonds became stronger within families. This meant that around 1300 we find estates in many areas of Europe bearing a family name. The estate was transmitted through the male line by primogeniture.

This principle has the name *retrait lignager* in French. Younger sons, wives and daughters were left out of this arrangement altogether. The rules governing Icelandic manors, *höfuból*, are related to this principle. A manor should revert to the male line rather than be passed to the female

156 Duby 1994, pp. 108-109.
157 Hansen 1996, pp. 114-15, compare to White 1988, pp. 180-81.
158 Duby 1994, pp. 117-18.
159 Ibid., pp. 105, 107.
160 Duby, 1991a, p. 11.

line, and if a manor was transferred out of the male line it was possible to claim it back.[161] However, in other respects the situation in Iceland during the twelfth and thirteenth centuries seems to have been very different from that in France. In reality primogeniture was not practiced very much.[162]

How should the patrilineal tendency found in the Icelandic law codes then be interpreted? Was it just an ideology enforced from abroad, transferred mainly from the Norwegian legal context? Or did it have practical significance in Iceland too?

The patrilineal ideology is stronger in the inheritance rules of *Jónsbók* than in *Grágás*,[163] and is the primary basis for the inheritance rules of *höfuðból* in *Jónsbók*. The male line was strengthened, especially in property matters. Was this a reaction against the stronger marriage ideology of the *New Christian Law*? In Norway the principle of *óðalsréttur* ensured that family land was not transferred out of the family by marriage, just like in Denmark the family manor was not included in the *fællig*.[164] Maybe the rules of *höfuðból* were intended to have the same effect in Iceland. It seems, however, that the principle of *höfuðból* did not prevent the division of familial landed property in Iceland. Property was widely transferred according to a bilateral pattern. Consent to property transfers was thus commonly sought in order to gain acceptance from a group of close heirs to the use of property.

11.3.2 The influence of the óðalsréttur *in Icelandic legal thinking*

Even if the law code of King Magnús the "Law-Reformer" in the Norwegian *Landslov* and the Icelandic *Jónsbók* were products of the same legal thinking, there was a difference between the two regions.[165] *Óðal* means

161 See documents about transfer of manors, DI VII, p. 317, DI IX, pp. 54 ff, 484. About the right to claim back manors DI VI, p. 201. Open letters from the king about manors see: Ibid., pp. 361-62, and compare to p. 358.

162 See Jochens 1985, who assumed that primogeniture was developed in Iceland in the thirteenth century. This interpretation is modified in Agnes S. Arnórsdóttir 1995, pp. 79-85.

163 Ibid., pp. 85-90.

164 Iuul 1959b, pp. 487-88.

165 See Sveinbjörn Rafnsson 1974, p. 139: "Likheterna mellom Grágásen och Jónsbók ar stora. Jónsbokens legale förutsattninga var … receptio av norska konstitionella lagar och continuatio av fristatens rätt."

patrimony, and is related to the German word *edel, adel,* which means noble or nobility and was applied to the nobility of the earlier Teutonic communities that consisted of landowners. The conditions which in the Norse law constituted an *odal,* were either an unbroken succession from father to son through three or more generations,[166] or unbroken possession for thirty or more years,[167] or sixty years.[168] The *odal* in Norway should be passed to sons, while the *útjarðir* (outlying lands) and *lausafé* (movable property) were passed to daughters. The *óðal* was in a certain sense inalienable within a family, so that even when separated from the owner it still retained a title. Examples of this are the words *land-brigð* and *máldagi á landi.*[169]

In the prologue to the law code of *Jónsbók,* King Magnús introduced the idea of *óðal* to the Icelanders.[170] The principle of *óðalsréttur* had clearly not been very important during the early years of settlement in Iceland. As early as 1849 Vilhjálmur Finsen stated that movable properties were seen as being just as important as landed property.[171]

Finsen was examining Icelandic society as he knew it from the period of *Grágás.* But as Sveinbjörn Rafnsson has underlined, this does not mean that the Icelanders were not aware of these patrilineal inheritance rules. In his study of the book of settlement, *Landnámabók,* he argued that the text contains a register of the families that owned land in Iceland around 1300, and that this register reflects patrilineal interests.[172] However, the word *óðal* was only used once in this text, although it can also be found in the *Íslendinga saga* of Sturla Þórðarsson. The word was more common in translated literature in Iceland, where it was used as a translation for the word *patria.* Sveinbjörn Rafnsson assumes that patrimonial inherit-

166 Guðbrandur Vigfússon 1957, p. 470, compare to NgL I, pp. 91, 277, 284. The word *feudal* is a composed word, *fee-odal* or *anodal* meaning fiefs held from the king.

167 NgL I, p. 249.

168 Ibid., p. 284.

169 Guðbrandur Vigfússon 1957, p. 470.

170 *Jónsbók,* p. 3: "Eptir erfðatal hefr landabrigði, því at þann tíma sem maðr erfir nokkurar jarðir, þá hæfir honum at skoða um sín óðul ok annarra manna, at hann haldi engra manna óðulum með lögum sóttum, ok kunni sjálfs síns óðulum með lögum at brigða."

171 He explains this by saying that the population was never large in Iceland compared to the space available. That is why there was no reason to organise *óðalsréttur.* See Vilhjálmur Finsen 1849, p. 155.

172 Sveinbjörn Rafnsson 1974, pp. 141-42.

ance rights were known in Iceland even before the country came under the rule of the Norwegian king in 1262/64.[173]

After *Jónsbók*, the *réttarbót* of King Eiríkur (written in 1291) contains further rules relating to patrimonial rights. It says that if one wants to claim back a patrimony one should find six men (to whom one is not related) to judge the case.[174] According to Vilhjálmur Finsen[175] this text may have had its origin in *Staðarholtsbók* of *Grágás* or it may have been taken from the law of King Magnús.[176] This raises the question of whether it is possible to trace any further evidence in *Grágás* concerning patrimonial rights.

The rules about a claim for reversion, called *brigð* in *Grágás*, gave the relatives some power to a claim back family land that had been sold.[177] There is reason to relate this to the early influence of canon law on Icelandic property law. Patrimonial inheritance rights were a novel phenomenon in twelfth century France, and were the result of the influence of Roman law. If family property was transferred outside the line, the legal heirs could claim it back. The institution *retrait lignager* came to be strong in France in the thirteenth and fourteenth centuries. The oldest legal rules from Iceland, concerning the rights of heirs to claim back their inheritance thus dates from a similar time as those in France.

This principle of *brigð* was more fully developed in *Jónsbók* than in *Grágás*. The sixth chapter of *Jónsbók* is called the chapter of claim for reversion of landed property, *landsbrigðabálkr*, with the word *brigð* meaning that one could reclaim the land. For instance a young man could claim *brigð* of the land his guardian had kept, and he was able to claim it back ten years after he reached maturity.[178] This principle guaranteed that kinsfolk could retrieve family property that had been alienated by

173 Ibid., p. 112, compare to Sts. I, 1946, p. 260.

174 DI II, p. 291: "Hverr óðal sitt vill brigða nefni.vj. menn hvor þeirra til dóms; í þeim skulu hvárki vera frændr né mágar; eigi fjórmenningar at frændsemi ok ei[gi] vitni beri fjandmenn eðr öfundarmenn. Enn ef einhverr setr þann í dóm, þá skal nefna hann úr með tveggja manna vitni ok setja skilvísan mann í staðinn."

175 Ibid., pp. 290-91.

176 Ibid., p. 291. Compare to chapter 8 in *Óðalsbálkur*, NgL, II, pp. 97-98.

177 This was thus a rather weak principle compared to the *odelsréttr* in Norway or what has been called *retrait lignage* in France.

178 *Jónsbók*, p. 117.

way of sale or gift.[179] Cases concerning claims to rights to land through the institution of *brigð* can be found in the Icelandic court records. For instance, one example from 1587 concerned the land at Skarfanes.[180] However, these rules did not apply to those who had wanted to give property to a monastery or bishopric before the Reformation.

Another property strategy related to shared-property rights arose from the rules governing those situations in which the separate part of property called *máli*, was part of another person's holdings and to have a *lögmáli* in land was a legal expression for describing the right to claim back this share in a property.[181] The concept seems to have been very common from the late sixteenth century onwards,[182] and it was a safeguard against that land could be freely given away or sold.

In the sixteenth century this principle of *lögmáli* was used frequently. For instance, in 1562 it was testified that Páll Jónsson had declared a right of *lögmáli* in land at Reykhólar.[183] One year later further documents were produced which stated that Páll Jónsson legally bound his share (called *lögfestir landsmála*) in the manor. According to this declaration the following words were written: "I forbid anyone to receive this land at Reykhólar as a gift, or payment, without my permission."[184] This resistance to selling land was related to the fact that land could not be sold without the owner's consent, and as these cases concerning *lögmála* indicate many people could share the ownership rights to one property. Did the common use of *lögmáli*, along with the wife's *máli*, have anything to do with changes in the patrilineal transfer of property?

179 Ibid., p. 109: "skal fyrst bjóða frændum sínum nánustum með vitnum við honum at taka."

180 A son claimed from a priest the right to the land, because he claimed the land had been given by his mother in a testament, but the father had later given the land to the priest. See *Alþingisbækur Íslands* II, p. 95.

181 Compare to Fritzner II, Oslo 1954, p. 605. Compare to *málajörð* in *Jónsbók*. p. 286. See also DI XV, pp. 105-106. from 28 May 1568: "Lýsing á lögmála í Laugaból og Laugaland."

182 See, for instance, AM dipl.isl.fasc. LXII, 5, from 1633, *Lýst afhendingu lögmála á hálfri jörðinni Hóli í Svarrárdal.* AM dipl.isl.fasc.LXVIII, 15, from 1569, *Vitnisburður um afhendingu lögmála í Látrum.* Also in Apogr 818, and printed in DI XV, p. 158; compare to AM dipl.isl.fasc.LXIX, 16, from 1595 *Lýsing á lögmála lögðum á Látra á Ströndum*; AM dipl.isl.fasc.LXIX, 21, from 1597, *Vitnisburður um loforð fyrir lögmála í jörðunni Refseyri í Sauðlauksdal.* See also the use of this word in DI XV, p. 13 and in DI XVI, p. 210, as well as in *Alþingisbækur Íslands,* I, p. 153, from the year of 1573; compare to *Alþingisbækur Íslands* I, p. 239, the year of 1574, a declaration about *lögmáli* in two landed properties. See also ibid., p. 353, Anno 1578, several letters of *lögmáli* in landed property; compare to *Alþingisbækur Íslands* II, p. 97.

183 DI XIV, p. 13.

184 Ibid., p. 87.

This question is interesting in relation to the question of how widely the custom of getting the consent of close relatives to transfer of property was followed. My study of the *laudatio parentum* shows that the principle requiring the consent of the kin never disappeared in Iceland.[185] This was a lineal inheritance strategy, but not patrilineal. The institution of *retrait lignage* was, however, patrilineal.

The Icelandic sources from the Late Middle Ages thus give us a picture of a society in which both the institutions of consent of the closest relatives (*laudatio parentum*) and the ability to claim patrimonial rights (*retrait lignage*) were known and used to some degree.

The patrilineal ideology found in *Jónsbók* can easily be explained by the influence from Norway. *Jónsbók* was a result of a stronger royal influence in Iceland, and this influence seems to be evident in relation to the inheritance rules concerning manors. However, as discussed in chapter 4, the royal authority was not as strong in fourteenth- and fifteenth-century Iceland as the law codes of the thirteenth century suggest. During the period 1350 to 1450 royal authority in Iceland was actually very weak. It was first under King Christian I, in the fifteenth century that this situation changed.[186]

The patrimonial interest expressed in the law of *Jónsbók* seems to have had relevance. All the copies and transcriptions of the Norwegian law codes concerning these matters in Icelandic manuscripts are evidence of an interest in these issues. These laws have been preserved in Icelandic law collections owned by legal experts,[187] just like many other rules concerning inheritance.[188] This reflects an interest for a patrilineal inheritance policy. This interest can be understood as one way of trying to deal with the special Icelandic situation of a rather weak central government, in that the foundation of the Icelandic elite's power lay in trying to keep their principal manors within their families, rather than

185 See the discussion earlier in this chapter.

186 Compare to the discussion above in chapter 4, p. 134. This change is related to the *Lönguréttarbót* of 1450.

187 See, for instance, AM 59a, 4to, from the late seventeenth century, *Óðalsbálkr* (Chapters 1-17), from the King Magnús law code. This copy was owned by the lawman Magnús Jónsson, but Árni Magnússon got it later from Guðrún Þorsteinsdóttir.

188 Compare to AM 211d, 4to pap, *Seks isl. skiftebrev efterfulgt af en kort definition af óðalsjörð.* Compare to AM 214b, 4to, partly about inheritance and *óðalssölu,* and another chapter in the same document: *Ágrip um kvenlegg og föðurætt, kvenlegg og móðurætt um erfðir og óðalsbálk.* See also: AM 224a, 4to, *Óðalsrétt.*

under the royal government. This background, also discussed in chapter 9.1 here about the historical background of the practice of making marriage contract, is important to have in mind when analyzing the property strategy. The patrilinial ideology could never be put into real practice as in the neighboring Nordic countries or elsewhere on the Continent, because of the lack of privileged position.[189]

The interest in patrilineal inheritance rights was thus related both to the lack of strong central authority, and the problem of the bilateral inheritance structure. It would be reasonable to talk of a patrilineal stratification of the Icelandic aristocracy in the Late Middle Ages, although this was also based on gaining royal offices.

The bilateral principle of transmitting property is widely evidenced in the documents. It can be seen, for instance, in a case in which sons were free to do what they wanted with their property after their father had died, but as long as the father lived, the land was to stay under the control of the family. Because it was difficult to keep property within the same family, other strategies were used as *ad hoc* solutions. One of these strategies was to transfer property to children in the family who had the same name as the donor.[190] This strategy is reminiscent of the development of entail in England. An entail was an interest in land, with the limitation that the estate could only pass to a particular category of heir. As Larry Poos and Lloyd Bonfield have stated the "employment of entails was one method of fashioning flexible transmission strategies, which we believe was the thrust behind many land transfers."[191] They stress that preferences in inheritance strategies were as likely to have

189 See also the discussion her in chapter 1, pp. 32-33.

190 See the witnesses' letter from 1482 in DI VI, p. 443. It states that Björn Þorleifsson had given his daughter Solveig the manor at Vatnsfjörður, so that the land should be transferred to heirs who had that name. See also *Alþingisbækur Íslands* I, pp. 25-26. According to this will the daughter of her brother, Ragnheiður Eggertsdóttir, should have the land at Breiðdalur, and if she had a daughter and named her Katrín, the land should follow that name. See also DI XIII, pp. 640-41. In 1561 Jón Magnússon declared that his mother had given the landed property at Hvammur in Höfðahverfi to the son who was to be named Magnús. See also AM. dipl.isl. fasc. LXIX, 22, from 1598 "Vitnisburðarbréf um lesinn vitnisburð þess að Elen Magnúsdóttir hefði gefi Þórustaði gegn því skilyrði að stúlkubarn yrði skírt Elen og að skyldi jörðin fylgja nafni." Compare to AM dipl. isl. fasc. LXXIII, 20 from 1595 "Vitnisburður um að Magnús Jónsson hefði lyst því yfir að hann hefði gefið dóttur sinni Elenu jörðina Þórustaði."

191 Bonfield and Poos 1988, p. 299.

been governed by self-generated normative rules as to have been directed from above by positive law.[192]

Another way of solving inheritance problems was to change the inheritance laws. The case of Möðruvellir from 1499 can be mentioned here again in order to illustrate more fully the problems that arose. This judgement was made with reference to a Norwegian *réttarbót* from the early fourteenth century. It stated that if a child was the heir of his mother or father, and the child subsequently died, the father and mother could not inherit more than just the movable portion of this wealth.[193] Thus, it was a rule, which forbade reverse inheritance.[194] The family at Kolbeinsstaðir called Erlendungar was involved in this case. Erlendur Erlendsson and his children, Þorvarður, Vigfús and Hólmfríður, claimed to be heirs to the manor at Möðruvellir after Páll Brandsson. The lawman Finnbogi Jónsson protested both in a judgement issued in Spjaldhagi in 1495, and again in a judgement from 1499 which was made at the Alþingi. This judgement concerned the transfer of property between the two families involved. If a child inherited from his or her mother, and the father later inherited from the child, then the father and his heirs should not inherit from the child anything other than movable goods. The same principle was used if a mother inherited from her child, who had previously inherited from his or her father.[195]

At the same time as the case concerning Möðruvellir was under consideration, the priest Eiríkur Sumarliðason claimed the right to the manor at Grund in Eyjafjörður as an inheritance from his brother Sveinn, under the same law of *Möðruvallaréttarbót*. This claim was contested by the lawman Finnbogi Jónsson, who asserted a right to the land on behalf of his daughter. In the end Eiríkur received the land on 22 November 1507 when the king confirmed all the *réttarbætur* from King Hákon, including this one. This became a problem in many cases over the following

192 Ibid., pp. 300-301.

193 DI II, pp. 379-80; see also the discussion of this case in chapter 3, above.

194 On the concept of "reverse inheritance" in a Scandinavian context, see Sawyer and Sawyer 1993, pp. 180-85.

195 Compare for instance to: DI II, pp. 379-80.

century, but the principle established by *Möðruvallaréttarbót* remained in place until the law was changed in 1711 by King Frederik IV.[196]

Both the cases of Möðruvellir and Grund show how the principle of not transferring property between the family lines was strengthened in the sixteenth century. This contrasts with the fifteenth century, during which it had been more common to transfer property between families by marriage, as was discussed above in chapter 9. This different property strategy can best be seen by studying closer the principle behind the transfer of the manors.

11.3.3 Höfuðból

Höfuðból was a landed property, a manor usually assessed at 60 *hundrað* or more, and such manors became the new centers of power in Iceland after the fall of the Commonwealth in 1262-64. So far it has been argued that the patrimonial principle was "imported" to Iceland from Norwegian legal thinking. However, while the concept *höfuðból* was first legally introduced in *Jónsbók*, the word *aðalból* used in *Grágás* had a similar meaning before this time, although the inheritance rules of *aðalból* were not the same.[197] During the late thirteenth century, the manor thus became a special legal concept. According to the law a manor was to be transferred via the male line, rather than the female, although in some special cases a woman could inherit such a property. Magnús Már Lárusson has studied inheritance practice concerning manors in the Late Middle Ages. He identified approximately thirty manors in the Icelandic sources.[198]

Sometimes manors were transferred via the female line through marriage. This study has demonstrated situations in which the manors could be claimed back under the rules of *brigð*. It means that if a husband gave

196 This *réttarbót* is printed in NgL III, pp. 98-102.

197 Björn Þorsteinsson and Guðrún Ása Grímsdóttir 1989, p. 90 compare to Magnús Már Lárusson 1971, pp. 41-42.

198 Ibid., pp. 40-90, compare to Magnús Már Lárusson 1961, pp. 707-10. Charters that show practice relating to manors are: DI IV, p. 404-406; the letter of gift of Loftur ríki Guttormsson; the description of the property of Guðmundur ríki Arason from the fifteenth century provides a good example of what kind of property the richest aristocrats had, see DI IV, pp. 683-94.

his wife something from his best property, *beztu eign,* then his heirs could claim it back if they wanted.[199]

A judgement from 1420 concerning the land at Grund in Eyjafjörður is helpful in understanding this problem.[200] In 1420 Þorleifur Árnason, the husband of Kristín Björnsdóttir, claimed on her behalf a half part of the land at Grund as her heritage, although it was in the possession of her mother, Solveig Þorsteinsdóttir. He used the marriage contract made between Solveig and Björn Einarsson as proof that they had *helmingarfélag* on their wedding day, so Kristín the daughter could claim inheritance right to the manor.

Another document shows that Björn had sold the half part of the land to the priest Halldór Loftsson, but that another man Magnús Jónsson holds it.[201] This transfer was judged illegal as it was not allowed to sell the property of one's wife without her consent. Magnús therefore had to prove that Solveig had approved of the sale. This case illustrates the importance of the consent of the wife and the documents from 1421 indicate that Þorleifur and Krístin were fully aware of this and acted accordingly.[202]

Because of the bilateral principle manors sometimes passed through the female line, but then usually from a woman to her grandson. In 1433 Solveig Þorsteinsdóttir gave her daughter's son, Björn Þorleifsson, a half part of the manor at Vatnsfjörður.[203] This was done with the consent of his mother, Kristín Björnsdóttir, and it was stated that Björn was not allowed to give the property away. He should not "sell the manor or give it away, or put a *máli* into this land even if he got married." He could only give the land to Saint Olav, or to God. Solveig declared that this

199 This practice is found in some of the marriage contracts: see for instance the rules concerning Flatey in Breiðarfjörður in the contract of Björn Þorleifsson, discussed before.

200 DI IV, pp. 273-75. Judgement about who had property right to the landed property at Grund in Eyjafjörður. About Kristín Björnsdóttir (Vatnsfjarðar-Kristín 1420-1448) see ibid.; pp. 274, 275, 290-93, 312, 351-53, 529-30, 549, 598, 714. She was the wife of Þorleifur Árnason, but Solveig Þorsteinsdóttir was her mother. Solveig was the wife of Björn Einarsson, see ibid., pp. 274, 529-30. They had *helmingarfélag*. Þorleifur Árnason lived in Vatnsfjörður and Víðidalstunga (d. 1433), see ibid., pp. 245-47, 262, 273-75, 282, 290-93, 294-96, 312, 325, 335-36, 352, 601. See also family tree in Figure 14.

201 Ibid., pp. 259-60. In 1417 Ingibjörg Loftsdóttir had handed half of the land at Grund over to Magnús Jónsson and his wife Ingunn, compare to ibid, pp. 309-10.

202 Ibid., pp. 292-93. See also family tree in Figure 14.

203 Ibid., pp. 529-30. The other part of Vatnsfjörður belonged to the local church.

was a legal gift, *löggjöf,* in case anyone questioned this property transfer.[204] The family land was to stay inside the family, and even if it was given to God it would probably have remained the right of Björn Þorleifsson's family to dispose over the land. In case there were any disputes about this matter it was made clear that this gift was the *löggjöf,* legal gift, of his grandmother to Björn Þorleifsson.[205]

In the district of Vestfirðir more land was controlled by members of the richest families than by the Church.[206] The properties of the wealthy families of Vatnsfirðingar and Seldælir were successfully kept within the families during at least some periods, as for instance when Kristín Björnsdóttir was head of her family. Her will from 1458 gives an idea of how she managed to keep the property within the family. However, in the late fifteenth and early sixteenth centuries the property came to be divided because of disputes between the different members of the family. The efforts to keep wealth inside the same family thus seem to have only been partly successful. As the historian Arnór Sigurjónsson has emphasized, the main landholders named in the register of landed property from 1710 were not related to the landholding families of the fifteenth century.[207] Finally let's take a look at the reason for this development.

Even if *Jónsbók* represented a stronger patrilineal ideology than *Grágás,* the kinship structure continued to be bilateral in *Jónsbók*. For instance, a manor should go to a daughter rather than to a more distant relative from the male line. This same kinship pattern is also found in the King Magnús "Law-Reformer's" Norwegian law codes from 1274.

According to the King Magnús' law codes the kinship system was bilateral with a slight tendency towards a patrilineal organization. Lars Ivar Hansen has formulated a theory about this development. His observations are based on Torben Vestergaard's study of the three-generation

204 Ibid., p. 530.

205 As mentioned before, this was a gift that could not be more than one-tenth of the wealth one had got in inheritance. See *Jónsbók,* p. 100.

206 Arnór Sigurjónsson 1973, pp. 74-115, see especially pp. 98-100.

207 Ibid., pp. 74-115, see especially pp. 105-106, 111. See also Jakob Benediktsson 1939, pp. 57-65, referring to an article by Vísi-Gísli, about kinship. There he mentioned that only three of the ruling families inherited their manors according to the patrimonial inheritance rules.

patrilineal system found in the oldest Norwegian provincial law.[208] Hansen suggests

> that the strong patrilineal bias observed in the oldest Norwegian provincial laws, with the clearly defined three-generation patrilineage, should be regarded as evidence of a reaction on the part of the traditional aristocracy. Feeling the pressure from the new, expanding social authorities of the monarchy and of the church, which wanted to establish new premises for the institution of marriage and new conditions for making property transfer, the aristocracy may have sought to strengthen those aspects of the inheritance law that would serve to keep the patrimony together.

This meant that the oldest Norwegian law thus represents not an old patrilineal structure, but rather a new one, and the writing of the code is perhaps a result of that process.[209] Hansen states further:

> However, in the end these initiatives were undermined and curtailed by the victorious influence of Canon Law in the national law codes. The relevant context is here seen as the fundamental transition process that Norwegian society underwent during the eleventh and twelfth centuries, involving the establishment of a hierarchically structured state power on the basis of pre-state structure.[210]

In the Norwegian context the patrilineal tendency was thus weakened by the legislation of King Magnús. But the Icelandic kinship structure of *Grágás* did not reflect the same pattern as that contained in the oldest Norwegian law codes.[211] This was a result of the differences between the political structures of these two societies, Icelandic society being much more decentralized than the Norwegian. It is thus important to emphasize that even if there was a stronger lineal tendency in *Jónsbók* than in *Grágás*, the bilateral structure was very strong in relation to inheritance practice in the Late Middle Ages. There was thus not an evolutionary change, from a bilateral to a lineal inheritance structure.

The study by Lloyd Bonfield of kinship organization in England is

208 Hansen 1996, p. 153; compare to Vestergaard 1988, pp. 160-93.

209 See also Iversen 2001, on the influence of Roman law on Norwegian law.

210 Hansen 1996, p. 153. See also the discussion in Hansen 2005.

211 See discussion in the introduction above concerning kinship structure. For more on the differences, see Vestergaard 1988 and Agnes S. Arnórsdóttir 1995, pp. 33-38.

useful in enabling us to understand how change in kinship structure did not have to be evolutionary. In an interesting paper on property settlements on marriage from the Anglo-Saxon period to the mid-eighteenth century, he provides empirical evidence for the theory of cyclical change in the social structure. He assumes that the marriage pattern of the Late Middle Ages in many respects was similar to that which had existed before the Norman Conquest:

> The English landed society had by the beginning to the early modern period returned to the flexible arrangements of the later Anglo-Saxons ... the widow had recouped her losses brought about by the introduction of feudalism.[212]

When trying to explain the changes in property transfer via marriage during the Middle Ages, it is important not only to focus on explanations of an evolutionary character. Change does not necessarily imply the substitution of one system for another, but may be perceived as waves of change provoked by internal as well as external factors.[213] What was at work in the Late Middle Ages was not a change from one system of transferring property to another, but rather waves of change from internal sources (social organization of the family) and from external sources (demographic change, state formation, the Church and so on).

Those who have been studying change in property transfer via marriage during the Middle Ages have emphasized change from one form of marital property law to another, from what legal historians have characterized as an aggressively "conjugal" system to a more "lineal" or even "patrilineal" system. This change is supposed to have taken place over 300 years, beginning in the thirteenth century and not ending until the late sixteenth or early seventeenth century.[214] In her study of marriage exchange in the cities of the Low Countries, Martha C. Howell indicates that this did not mean that social structures were moving towards a clan organization. There was in fact a double process at work. One was a

212 Bonfield 1992, p. 308.

213 Hansen 1996, p. 116. Compare to Burke 1980, p. 103: "Indeed it is likely that in pre-industrial societies, social change is cyclical."

214 Howell 1998, p. 9.

lineal principle, called "lineal regrouping" by some historians, and the other the principle of "liberation" of the individual rights of households on another level. Howell refers to Henri Bresc's paper of 1996, which considers whether the family progressed steadily from the extended model of the Early Middle Ages to the nuclear family of modern Europe. He states that family relationships were consolidated among the lower orders of society as a result of the demographic crisis following the Black Death. This is what historians have called "linear regrouping":

> We are thus faced with two competing explanations: a gradual legal liberation of the individual as he became progressively more aware of his rights and master of his fate: or a malleable set of relationships manipulated by an extended family which used them to occupy new territory, gather capital and useful connections, and build up a power base.[215]

Here in the third part of this book we have studied what Martha Howell calls the double process of "lineal regrouping" and the "liberation" of individual rights as illustrated in the Icelandic sources concerned with the transfer of property through marriage. This double process is evident in the institutions studied. The institutions produced by the lineal principle were the institutions of *máli*, and the right of the relatives to give consent to property transfers (*laudatio parentum*) as well as the right of relatives to retrieve family property by claiming a *brigð* on the property. The principle concerned with the "liberation" of individual rights favoured the making of marriage through the institution of *félag*, modified as the institution of *helmingarfélag*, as well as the legislation of the legal gifts of *fjórðungsgjöf*. The rules of the legal gifts in *Jónsbók* were used effectlivly in fifteenth and sixteenth century Iceland. These rules had their origins in canon law, and strengthened, in Iceland as in England for instance, the testamental freedom.[216] This principle also lay behind some of the inheritance cases which aimed at preserving property within the houshold as long as the owner lived. It makes sense to explain this change partly as a consequence of the influence of canon law on marriage. It strengthened the individual rights

215 Howell 1998, p. 13, with reference to Bresc 1996, see especially p. 432.
216 On making testaments in England see Sheehan 1996, pp. 24-25.

of spouses against the kin-group. The introduction of the consent theory is an example of this, and in the first part of this study we have considered this topic in detail. This change in the definition of marriage also affected property transfer through marriage and inheritance principles, as discussed in chapters 9 and 10. When the mutual consent of spouses became a legal requirement the need to reinforce parental consent arose. This resulted in a stronger legal basis for parental or kin-based control of marriage and inheritance, such as the laws that appeared in Iceland and found in the *réttarbœtur* of the early fourteenth century.

11.4 Conclusion

Gender relations had been changed by the Christian doctrine of marriage. Under the new meaning of marriage a husband gained an increased right to control his wife's property, after this had previously been her relatives' role. At the same time a wife's right to consent the property transfers of her husband was enshrined in law. The wife's property, or that of the couple if they had joint ownership, could not be validly transferred without the consent of the woman. This meant that the husband's right was not an absolute right to the *dominus*. Because of the medieval understanding of property rights as *actio-utilis*, the right of a husband to use this property was limited by his wife's consent. Also, because of the right to claim back property *actio rei vindicationis*, absolute property rights in the modern sense did not exist. Because of this, many people had different claims to the same property, linking them together in a complex social structure. Parental control had been a central part of all property transfers in the Middle Ages. The need for this control lay behind the institution of *laudatio parentum*, the consent given by relatives to a property transfer. From the early fourteenth century the consent of one's wife or husband also became necessary to sales of property. Property could not be transferred through marriage, wills, gifts, sale or purchase without the consent of the people involved. This change not only affected the distribution of property but social relations too.

In the same way that change in the English social structure was influenced by the Norman Conquest, Icelandic social structure came under the influence of Norwegian legislation. Cyclical change in Icelandic social structure should, thus, be understood as closely related to the influence of the Norwegian system in the twelfth and thirteenth centuries.

The influence of the Church on the property concerns of couples meant that both wives and husbands should bring property into marriage. According to the old law of *Grágás* a husband should pay *mundur* for his bride, while the later law code of *Jónsbók* demanded that the parents also should give their daughter away with a dowry. Instead of paying for his bride, a man gained a wife and her dowry. This influenced inheritance practice. The strengthening of the patrilineal organization of marriage in *Jónsbók*, as well as the rules concerning parental consent, were among the results of this process. Legitimate children, born to parents in a legally contracted marriage, and made according to the law of God, gained better inheritance rights than illegitimate children. In addition, the new rules stating what property a couple should bring into a new marriage, along with the rules governing how a couple should divide their property, also influenced the inheritance disputes brought to court.

As a reaction to change in the inheritance and marriage regulation of the late thirteenth and early fourteenth centuries, change occurred in the way the aristocracy transferred property. When the definition of what was a legal or illegal marriage changed, the channels of property transfer through marriage and inheritance changed too. It was accepted that property could also be transferred to those born out of wedlock. The institutions of adoption and legal gifts were used to transfer property to illegitimately born children. The adoption of illegitimate children became common because the need for legal property transfer had become a subject for the courts. Another possible way to give property to illegitimate children was to use the institutions of legal gifts, the *tíundargjöf* and *fjórðungsgjöf*, for the transfer of wealth to them.

The principle in favor of transferring property through marriage between the generations was safeguarded by making a marriage contract for separate ownership. At the same time the new ideal of marriage gained greater importance: couples should love one another. The idea of the *hjónaband* was, however, never fully realized in the property relations between couples. The communal-based strategy of *félag* was not suitable for the Icelandic elite. This was a result of the fact that Iceland remained a thoroughly decentralized society until the late eighteenth century and the main power base for the Icelandic elite was landed property. This is probably the main reason why the illegitimate children of Icelandic priests were adopted, so that they could inherit property. In other parts of Europe priests also had children, but these children were able to earn a living within the growing administration of the Church or state. However, as long as landed property was transmitted in accordance with bilateral inheritance rules the ability of aristocratic families to retain their property over generations was never more than a dream. Because of the weak patrimonial inheritance practice the institution of *máli* was preferred since it provided better security against land being transferred between families, something that could easily happen under contracts of *helmingarfélag*. In this respect it is interesting to compare the situation in Iceland with other regions. In both France and Denmark, for instance, family land was excluded from marriage contracts, while in Norway women did not get the main family land as a dowry but only outlying land.

There was no institution stable enough to ensure that the main land or manor came under family control. In this case the rules about *höfuðból*, and the *heimaland* more generally, favored the continuation of the family line. All this was important in a bilaterally organized society. However, it was difficult to keep land within the same family over many generations because of the bilateral inheritance practice, and that is why the institution of *brigð* was sometimes used to claim back family property.

The development in Iceland was as much a result of self-generated normative rules as of rules imposed by a strong royal authority. The same legal culture lay behind the practice of adopting illegitimate children so they could gain the right to inherit. The question of when this practice changed would need to be studied in another project, but the *Judgement of Stóridómur* from 1564-65 was probably the turning point in the history of Iceland. This was made in accordance with the wishes of the Icelandic bishops, and was reinforced by a powerful royal authority that was now more successful than ever at imposing its will. Thus Iceland, like other regions of Christian Europe, also started to undergo a transition towards a more modern society.

CHAPTER 12

Conclusion and discussion

This study of the Christianization of marriage in Iceland c. 1200-1600 has examined how the definition of what constituted a legal marriage changed, and how the secular and ecclesiastical models of marriage co-existed. The two concepts of property and virginity have been used as symbols of the two types of marriage contract, the secular and the ecclesiastical. Property symbolized the secular contract, while virginity had become a key symbol in the sacred contract, something that could be clearly seen by the end of the sixteenth century, a long time after marriage was supposed to have lost its sacramental status in the Protestant Church. This last chapter of the book provides an overview of the main conclusions of the study, and then discusses which significance the process of Christianization had on the understanding of property rights and gender relations.

Partly, my study of Icelandic marriage contracts and related material has been a study that aims at explaining the existence of the source material. I soon realized that evidence for a large number of marriage cases survived, and that contracts were only one part of this body of material. The study of the legal regulation of marriage over an extended period enables us to understand how the fundamental change in the law that came at the end of the thirteenth century slowly gained practical meaning over the period that followed. Documents related to court proceedings and marriage contracts are the products of this change. The survival of these sources is closely related to the marriage and inheritance strategies of the most powerful Icelandic families. The re-definition of what constituted a legal marriage meant that documents concerning marriage were preserved because they were invaluable should property disputes arise.

12.1 *Conclusion*

During the twelfth century, the mutual consent of the couple became one of the main criteria for a valid marriage. The absence of a woman's consent meant that marriage had not been legitimately performed. At the same time the ecclesiastical authorities stressed that the consent of the parents was also important. The ecclesiastical model was introduced in Iceland during the late twelfth and early thirteenth centuries, by way of letters from the pope in Rome and the Norwegian archbishops in Niðarós. This resulted in a new marriage legislation strongly influenced by canon law. The influence can be found in the oldest Icelandic law of *Grágás*, which provides the foundation for the rules concerning divorce, in addition to the changes made by the Lateran Council of 1215 concerning the forbidden degrees of marriage. The new law in *Grágás*, called *nýmæli*, reflected the influence of canon law on marriage regulation. This Christian influence was more widely developed in the *New Christian Law* of Bishop Árni Þorláksson of 1275, as well as in the later secular law of *Jónsbók* from 1281. It is nonetheless important to emphasize that the *New Christian Law* was not only canon law received from abroad, but also a text "translated" into the Icelandic context. The marriage regulations in *Grágás* and *Jónsbók* were not only influenced by canon law, but also by the customary law of the Icelanders. I have even argued that because of the influence of the Church, the need to redefine the secular contract increased. Thus, new regulations were shaped by a compromise between old and new rules.

In my overview of marriage regulations from 1280 to 1600, I showed that new regulations were aimed at defining what constituted a legal marriage. Judgements made in local courts sometimes also gained the status of law, so it was not only the legislation of the authorities that mattered. It is important to consider how people used the law and how the courts were used to ensure that people were legally married. The *réttarbætur*, that is the supplementary laws of the Norwegian and

Danish kings from the fourteenth and fifteenth century, were intended to define what constituted a legal marriage. They aimed at dealing with the problem of clandestine marriage, while making the rules concerning inheritance and property division clearer, while church statutes were more concerned with the marriage ritual. Because marriage was under ecclesiastical jurisdiction, but was also a matter involving inheritance, both secular and ecclesiastical authorities were concerned with defining the institution of marriage.

It makes sense to describe the change in medieval marriage in Iceland, as elsewhere in Western Europe, as a slow progression towards the Christian model, which at the same time retained many aspects of the secular model. I propose that the changes in the models of marriage should be viewed in terms of two factors: the acceptance of new marriage rituals and legislation, and the internalization of new Christian norms.

With regard to the former issue, it is clear that the acceptance of the Christian marriage doctrine did not simply replace the older custom of the kin-based marriage contracts. Too much emphasis has been placed on a possible conflict between the bride's consent and parental consent as an explanation for the developments in marital custom and marriage law in the Middle Ages. The family of the bride did not lose its influence because of the introduction of bridal consent. Parental consent continued to be important to the position of every potential spouse and this importance actually increased, especially after the Reformation. There would not be any sound basis for a marriage, at least not among the aristocracy, unless families provided the land and the income necessary to sustain the couple and their children.

The Church became stronger as an institution during the fourteenth and fifteenth centuries. There is evidence that during the same period Christian norms and values were increasingly internalized, not only by individuals, but also by institutions. It became possible to impose fines for incorrect behavior because a new way of living had been accepted, as covered in my discussion of the control of sexuality inside and outside marriage. Changes in marriage practices were closely related to general changes in moral codes and sexual behaviour. The different interpretations of what constituted legal marriage are signs of the efforts to control sexuality. This control was not only related to the making of marriage contracts, but also to governing sexual behavior before and during marriage. The Church defined legal marriage and made rules about correct Christian behavior. This made it possible both to impose penances and to allow those people who had sinned to re-make their marriage agreements. At the same time, it also became simpler to question the legality of marriage contracts. This explains the large quantity of court material produced in relation to marriage. In order to ensure inheritance, marriage needed to follow specific protocols.

It remained the case that the common people provided the most important testimonies of behavior. This was related to the development of the judicial system. The local court material indicates that regional differences existed when it came to dealing with problems associated with legal marriage. It was not just a question of how the royal and Church authorities abroad had defined a valid marriage. This authority was also closely related to personal rather than institutional strength.

Thus, it was first in the sixteenth century, by the judgement of *Stóridómur* and by the marital ordinance of King Frederik II of 1587, that stronger control over sexual behavior was exercised by the central authority in Denmark. Of course, previous cases had been judged according to canon law in Iceland, although it had been primarily for the local bishops to judge and impose penalties in such matters. With the judgement of *Stóridómur* in 1564-65 and the marriage ordinance of 1587, the death penalty was first introduced in cases concerning sexual behavior. What earlier had been considered unacceptable sexual behavior was now considered a sexual crime. Another novelty of the legislation of 1587 was the actor behind it: the king had replaced the pope as the instigator of such regulations.

When it became mandatory to make a written contract concerning financial matters associated with marriage, changes occurred as to who should be involved in making the agreement. Both women and priests became involved in the formal making of contracts, but little was removed from the previous formula of marriage, although new elements were added. There continued to be an oral aspect to contracting marriage, and the spoken word continued to have legal importance.

The sacred meaning of marriage was "translated" to people through rituals.

The evidence of marriage contracts from the fourteenth century indicates that the agreement was made by parents rather than the couple themselves. All the contracts from the fourteenth century concern property arrangements. Surviving contracts represent the former understanding of marriage as a property agreement between two families. The contracts of the fifteenth century suggest something else. In these cases the couple was central to the agreement, although while the mutual consent of marriage had become an accepted norm, parental control seems also to have been strengthened. The contracts of the late fifteenth and sixteenth centuries show that the old financial aspects and the new Christian values existed side by side. All such contracts are concerned with financial commitments. In some cases the religious significance of the arrangement was mentioned, but more often it was merely added that the contract was made according to the law of God. However, the greatest change evident in these contracts was that they concerned the union of individuals, and not only the union of the fathers of brides and their future husbands. This constituted a new construct in gender identity.

The couple, who had become the main subject of marriage, should love each other as well as their God. The meaning of marriage thus became a personal matter, not only a contract involving wealth and social alliances. This affected both the relationships between the sexes and the understanding of gender roles. Chastity became a highly regarded virtue for both men and women, and adultery was not only a sin but also a crime.

Seen thus, the end of the sixteenth century marks the final change in a process that had been under way since the thirteenth century. The marriage ordinance of 1587 clearly stresses the importance of the virginity of the bride. If a woman was not a virgin, her husband could divorce her. Only through full parental control could the beauty and the pureness of the virginity be guaranteed. This was the result of the understanding of sacred marriage. However, the importance of virginity emerged much later in the legislation than that of consent. Through the emphasis on virginity brides came to be idealized as innocent and clean, which was in turn related to the new social bonds made through the marriage contract.

Before the Reformation the Church authorities had full jurisdiction over marriage cases. Even if their authority was personal rather than autonomous in character, this power developed gradually during the fourteenth and fifteenth centuries. Change in marriage practice was also related to a more general change in moral codes and sexual behavior. This was related to the fact that it was possible to declare a marriage illegal by claiming that the couple had been having an incorrect relationship before their contract was made. Such a process would frequently start with rumors.

At the same time the Church gradually succeeded in giving the secular marriage ceremony a religious character. The oldest rituals are described in *Grágás*, according to which men shook hands and announced the financial contract before witnesses. In the late thirteenth century, women entered into the ritual and their consent in front of witnesses became a sign of sacred marriage. After the marriage contract had gained this new element the consent of the parents became even more important than before. This was related to the transfer of property and property rights. On the other hand, marriage became a more personal matter since it was understood that the couple should love each other as well as their God.

My study has shown that the question of what constituted a legal marriage was not resolved by the marriage legislation from the end of the thirteenth century. Both the *réttarbætur* and the Church statutes demonstrate that this was an ongoing process which was concerned with, among other things, securing the place of elements of the former secular marriage contract. That is made clear by examining what types of property agreements were made at marriage. Marriage contracts dealt with the property agreement made by the couple, and the way in which they shared property was important to the inheritance rights of their heirs. Thus the principle was established that couples should not combine the property of their families if no children were born to them.

The two main principles governing marital property division – the first a communal one, aimed at maintaining the household after the death of either of the spouses, and the second a more kin-based principle, aimed at keeping family land within the family – provided the bases for the two different types of contracts, on the one hand *helmingarfélag*, on the other *máli*. These different ways of organizing marriage through property transfer were symbolized differently. The wedding ring symbolized the sacred marriage. The ring was a symbol of the union of the couple, which could not be broken. On the other hand the coat of arms symbolized the kin-based structure, which was behind the principles of organizing property transfer according to the contract of *máli*. It was a symbol, which followed the members of the same family line over many generations. These two forms of making marriage could easily exist in the same society at the same time during the medieval period, but they represent different ways of organizing social bonds. The change in the making of marriage contracts should, thus, not be seen as a shift from separate property ownership to joint possession by the couple, even if the fifteenth century saw a strengthening of the communal principle that provided for joint possession. Also the contracts of *máli* became more influenced by this communal principle, since it became more common during the sixteenth century to give the husband or the wife – whoever lived longest – one-fourth of each other's belongings. The *máli* contracts, however, could also generally secure the inheritance interests of the families of the spouses better than the contracts of *helmingarfélag*, because the main manor could be hold out of the separate property, while it was always included in jointly-owned property. That is probably the reason why the contracts of *helmingarfélag* never became as popular a strategy as having the separate property of the wife recorded in an agreement of *máli*.

Changes in marriage regulation were also related to the exchange of marriage gifts. Both partners brought property into their new household. The institution of brideprice (*mundur*) lost its old value as the symbol of legal marriage, and new marriage gifts such as the gift of the bench (*bekkjargjöf*) and the morning gift became common. During the fifteenth century, when agreements for jointly-owned property were frequently made, these gifts were common. They disappeared, however, in the sixteenth century, when legal gifts came to be used for transferring property within marriage. This meant that a couple could give each other one quarter of their non-inherited property. The communal-oriented gift of the morning gift was never legally defined in Iceland.

The institution of legal gifts meant that only one-tenth of the family land could be given away to people other than those who would otherwise inherit the land. Consent given by relatives to property transfers was widely sought and recorded in the sixteenth century. However, the morning gift had been used for transferring wealth to a future wife so that the couple could make an agreement for joint ownership. This strategy came to be unsuitable for Icelandic property transfers because the family land or the main manor could be included in the jointly-owned property. One can thus say that the idea of *hjónaband* was never fully realised in terms of the property agreements made between spouses. We can thus sum up by saying that a husband's right to control the property within his marriage was reinforced by the law of *Jónsbók*, but his license to use the property was limited by the requirement for his wife's consent in affairs concerning her land, and the right of her relatives to claim back inherited property, as both the *réttarbœtur* and the court cases illustrate.

The property contract of *máli* did not, however, remain totally unaffected by this development. The new emphasis on the sacred contract made by a couple meant that there was a different type of commitment between spouses, which included a new gender identity. This new union was built into the property contract; the ties between spouses were sealed with financial commitments even if contracts continued to have great value in the making of political alliances. In this way the sacred meaning of marriage was incorporated within the old property contract. Among other things, this meant that a husband's right to control his wife's *máli* was stronger than had previously been the case. For instance, a wife could not divorce her husband and return with her property to her parents. This is how changes in social relations (through property relations) were closely connected to the introduction and use of canon law in the thirteenth and fourteenth centuries. This development continued in the fifteenth and sixteenth centuries, when the gift called *fjórðungsgjöf*, which aimed at transferring non-inherited property between the couple, became commonly used.

Even if there were some restrictions on transferring family land or inherited property between families, this tradition was not strong enough to ensure that manors would stay in the same families for centuries.

Primogeniture was unknown, and bilateral inheritance practice (which allowed land to be transferred by marriage) made it impossible to keep property in the hands of the same families for many generations. It made it easier for a new group of landowners to acquire wealth during the fifteenth century. The families that married according to the principle of joint possession of the spouses were newcomers to the elite. They were the lords and ladies of the coastal manors, which had gained new importance as a result of the stockfish trade in the fifteenth century. However, this did not mean that the aristocracy did not try to keep their manors within their families. The desire to keep property inside the same family was strongly expressed, as the interest in the Norwegian *óðalsrétt* among Icelandic property holders of the sixteenth and seventeenth centuries demonstrates.

12.2 Discussion: Christian influence on property rights and gender relations

The Christianization of marriage in Iceland during the Middle Ages was not only a change that had great meaning for the institution as such, it also had a great effect on the social and political structure. Here this influence will be discussed in relation to changes in the understanding of property rights as well as changes in gender relations. I have discussed in detail how the terminological change in the Icelandic marriage contracts from the fourteenth to the sixteenth century reflects the growing influence of the Church. Because of the influence of canon law, the old ritual of betrothal changed into the "sacred" marriage. At the same time, marriage in the Late Middle Ages included many elements of the older understanding of marriage as a contract concerning property transfer between families. In this way marriage contracts of the fourteenth to sixteenth centuries were at the same time religious contracts and property contracts. The content of the written contracts was concerned mostly with the property transfer, whilst the Christian formula for marriage was spoken out loud. Nonetheless, many property contracts also state that the marriages they describe were made according to the law of God as well as the country. This can help us to understand how the former understanding of the property agreement could continue to be the basic element of these written Icelandic contracts. What I have not discussed so much, however, is how these bonds that were made through exchanging property by marriage, also became Christianized.

I have argued that Christian marriage doctrine changed the definition of what constituted a legal marriage, and it changed the form as well as the content of the property contract too. A legal marriage was not made by buying the bride through *mundur*, but with the consent of the couple. A new understanding of gender relations arose. Women became partners in the contract-making; the handshake was between the husband and wife, instead of between the father of the bride and her future husband. The rituals connected to these different kinds of bonds thus gained new meaning. Marriage was no longer a financial matter alone, but also involved religious beliefs and a closer union of the spouses.

At the same time marriages within the Icelandic aristocracy in the Late Middle Ages continued to be very much concerned with landed property. Property was the main basis for political power. It is useful to have in mind Foucault's definition of power in this context. According to him, power is not: "an institution, and not a structure; neither is it a certain strength we are endowed with; it is the name that one attributes to a complex strategical situation in a particular society."[1]

Behind the number of documents concerning property transfer, which survive from the Late Middle Ages, lies a "complex strategical situation" in Icelandic society. There was no institution that could guarantee that family land would stay within the line for generations. In addition, because of the weak central power there was an inability to enforce the law. The courts of late medieval Iceland were centers for dispute resolution, used by the most powerful members of society. Autonomous structures of law enforcement were often absent. Of course, there were limits as to what kind of strategies different persons or groups could use in resolving their disputes. For instance, there was a limit as to how much landed property one could transfer through a marriage settlement. Correspondingly, there was a limit as to how much one could receive. However, the

1 Foucault 1984, p. 93.

main point of this study has been to underline that these strategies were affected by the Church's influence on marriage and inheritance laws. The complexity of this process was a result of the fact that this influence did not only have consequences for the Church as an institution. The Icelandic elite used the new rules for their own purposes. In this way the management of property in the Middle Ages was not only governed by rules imposed from above (by the state or the Church), but were also shaped by the actions and ideas of men and women of the aristocracy.[2]

The legislation of the late sixteenth century shows how virginity became one of the preconditions for marriage. The earlier development of the need for the consent of the woman in matrimonial cases seems to have changed attitudes towards women. A cruel treatment of women had never been accepted in Iceland in the Commonwealth period,[3] but by the end of the sixteenth century these principles had a firm legal grounding. The rules of courtship were related to issues of marriage regulation and property. Control of marriage meant control of both sexuality and property. This was reflected in legal regulations as well as in much of the court material, although literature and the poems reflect a more emotional view of this change.

Secondly, when considering change in marriage regulation and views on the functionality of marriage, one can see a change in interpretations from the 1970s to the present. The traditional view, that marriages were made only by men in the interests of family strategy, and not in the interests of individuals, whether male or female, has been cast into doubt. This traditional view, that strategy was placed before individual behavior, can be traced back to Lawrence Stone's studies made in the 1970s. He had stated that the origins of the modern family were to be found in the eighteenth century, based on the personal choice of partner and strong emotional ties within the nuclear family. An interesting momentum in this discussion is the change from looking at women as objects to looking at women as subjects.[4] One can easily see how the study of women has changed from this object-oriented perspective towards

2 Compare to Hansen 1996, p. 136. See also Hansen 2000, introduction.
3 Agnes S. Arnórsdóttir 1990, pp. 62-76.
4 Dean and Lowe 1998, pp. 10-11.

a greater awareness of the importance of their subjective existence, in which women are seen as actors with their own wishes and abilities to achieve their goals. These aspects have been emphasised in this study of Icelandic marriage practice and theory in the Middle Ages.

The question that remains to be answered is whether there is any information available as to how changes in marriage affected women's own identity and self-image. As mentioned earlier, there is evidence that women could claim their rights in court. They were also members of that group of people who used the court system for dispute resolution. The historian Arnór Sigurjónsson in *Vestfirðingarsaga* assumed that because of this women had a strong position in marriage, and could often control their children's inheritance from their father after being widowed.[5] Women's role in keeping information about ownership rights has not been fully explored.[6] It is clear that their role in remembering and transmitting genealogical information was great, and judging by the catalogue of documents in the Arnamagnean collection it seems that many of the manuscripts Árni Magnússon collected had been in the hands of women.[7] One of the reasons for this seems to be that women often lived longer than their husbands.[8] Another possible explanation arises from the bilateral kinship structure. The matrimonial system of property transfer, which meant that property was transferred through both the female and male lines, resulted in a situation where women as well as men were actively aware of the importance of keeping documents which could prove either their, or their families', property right to land.

Different kinship systems and different family structures can be expected to produce different types of space for men and women, young and old.[9] In this way kinship is something more than the "transmission of patrimony". It is also related to the transmission of memory and the construction of identity.[10] Studies of both "gender" and "kinship" have

5 Arnór Sigurjónsson 1975, pp. 9-10.

6 On this, see van Houts 1992, pp. 53-68, and compare to van Houts 2001, pp. 1-2.

7 Compare to AM dipl.isl.fasc. LX VIII, 8, from 1542. *Transkriftarbréf* kept with Ragnheiður Jónsdóttir, about Gröf in Höfðaströnd. She was the widow of Bishop Einar Þorsteinsson.

8 This is obvious because it is stated that they are widows.

9 Goddard 1996, p. 82.

10 Ibid., p. 70.

been concerned with understanding the rights and duties that regulate relations between people defined by their *difference*. This construction can be used to examine groups, even whole societies, as well as different identities among the members of these groups. Bourdieu has, for instance, suggested that men and woman use and interpret the same field of genealogical relationships in different ways.[11] This change from object-orientation of women's property rights towards subject-orientation is visible in the Icelandic source material from the earliest time till the end of the sixteenth century. In the context of this study it should be stressed that the change which our documents describe was related to a new understanding of gender relations: The new understanding of the relationship between a woman and a man within marriage also affected the way relationships between men and women were understood within wider society. This was partly a result of the Church's influence on married life during the Middle Ages, which changed the view of women's role in marriage. A woman came to be seen not as a member of her own family, but as the wife of her husband. Women acted in accordance with this new role. Women's, especially widow's, relatively strong position in the society of the Late Middle Ages is evidenced by those documents on which they used their own seals.[12] In addition, women's role in bringing about the internalization of Christian norms can be cited as proof of their strong position. A good example of this is that Ólöf Loftsdóttir gave her permission for the marriage of her daughter, Solveig Björnsdóttir, to Páll Jónsson in 1479.[13] Women became actors in such matters, instead of only being members of their kin-group, represented by their relatives in the courts.

It has been important to distinguish between ideology and everyday social life while focusing on the interaction between these two levels. At the end of the seventeenth century references to the *New Christian Law* of Bishop Árni of 1274 were still being made. This demonstrates that canon law shaped Icelandic legal culture for many centuries. This was the result of the fact that the use of different law codes and principles

11 See the overview in ibid., pp. 71-72, 82, 86.

12 Agnes S. Arnórsdóttir 2000b, pp. 38-39.

13 DI VI, p. 182.

was a weapon in the armoury of participants in the political battles of the Late Middle Ages and the Early Modern period. When discussing change in marriage making during the Middle Ages, it is obvious in the Icelandic context that change was often based not only on merely adding new rules to older ones, but also on making some compromises. One of the compromises was related to the question of how a legal marriage was related to the issue of inheritance. Here in the end we shall discuss how these changes and compromises in the definition of marriage interacted with people's understanding of what made a marriage legal. The first phase of the legal regulation of marriage can be described as a period during which ideas concerning marriage, in both its secular and ecclesiastical models, were put into practice and explained. This was not only a question of explaining the law codes of *Jónsbók* and the *New Christian Law*, but also of correcting and changing these law codes to meet the needs of the Icelanders. The new rules about joint possession illustrate this point. Motivating these new rules was the wish to secure the rights of the family group against a loss of control in marriage transactions. In short, these changes were first made in marriage legislation and Church statutes. The next step was an expectation that both women and men should behave differently during the period of their engagement, at the time of their wedding and also later in their married life. Change in social structure can also be identified as a long-term result of change in the institution of marriage. What took place was change in the legal culture, change in ritual behavior and change in the socio-economic structure.

Change in the family structure in the Late Middle Ages was closely connected to change in the making of marriage contracts, as previously described. The contract became a sign of the agreement between families, with the couple at its centre. Memories concerning ancestry, which were frequently recorded in genealogical lists, had previously performed a similar function. It is important to emphasize that this is not a revolutionary shift from one form of contract to another, because making a formal marriage agreement had a long history. The making of marriage contracts had merely been transferred "from memory to written record",[14]

14 Thanks to Clanchy 1979.

but in its written form it included both old and new rituals. The new element in the Christian marriage contract came to affect the transfer of property between families. Many lawsuits concerning inheritance were related to the fact that the closest relatives of the parents of "illegitimate" children could claim the inheritance.

One element in this struggle was the strengthening of parental consent to marriage, partly in reaction to the influence of canon law in defining marriage as a sacrament. This reaction could also be seen as a compromise, or even as a desire to conserve elements of the old property contract. However, my point is that parental consent gained new meaning in the Late Middle Ages. It was not only concerned with deciding what property should be given upon the marriage of their child, or with who their daughter's husband should be. By the end of the sixteenth century court cases began to reflect a parental interest in chastity, and the woman's virginity became a virtue. The couple to be married should be free of the stain of any sexual relationship before marriage. Thus, at this time a new gender identity had been established. The love of God came to be symbolized by the loving earthly relationship between a husband and a wife.

Bibliography

Unprinted sources

1. Arnamagnæanske Institut, Copenhagen/Reykjavík

AM: Den Arnamagnæanske Håndskriftsamling. Det Arnamagnæanske Institut, Copenhagen. Stofnun Árna Magnússonar á Íslandi, Reykjavík.

AM dipl. isl. fasc. LXV, 2 – LXX, 31.

AM 59a, 4to, *Ódalsbálkr.*

AM 186, 4to, 1-4v, *Om skriftemål og anger.*

AM 211d, 4to, *Seks isl. skiftebrev efterfulgt af en kort definition af óðalsjörð.*

AM 214a, 4to, pp. 42-43, *Félag.*

AM 214b, 4to, *Ágrip um kvenlegg og föðurætt, kvenlegg og móðurætt um erfðir og óðalsbálk.*

AM 215, fol, pap, bl. 21v, *Skiptabref barna Lopts ryka.*

AM 224a, 4to, *Óðalsrétt.*

AM 229, 4to. Number 6, *Kommentarer til Ægteskabskontrakt.* Number 9, *Om straf for hævet trolovelse fra 1642 med efterskrift fra 1646.* Number 10, *Om odels-salg.*

AM 241b, fol, vii, *Brudstykker af formularer til brug ved brudevielser.*

AM 267, 4to, *Optegnelser om jordegods.*

AM 382, fol, 2, *Islandske dokumenter de fleste i afskrift.*

AM 391, fol, pap. 36, pp. 7-12, *Dialog mellem tvende Elskende.*

AM ordbog: *A Dictionary of Old Norse Prose.*

Rask Samling: Rask. 52. Pap. 15, pp. 397-99, *Um Grundar-Helgu.*

2. Archivio Segreto Vaticano, Rome

Penitenzienia Ap., Registri delle Suppliche
Vol. 25, fol. 13v.
Vol. 42, fol. 47v., 48r.

3. Bryggens Museum, Bergen

BRM 0/95078 Ring brooch.

4. British Library, London

Collectio Cottoniana. MS, Cott. Vitellius E 13.

5. Danmarks Nationalmuseum, Copenhagen

D423/1994 Ring-shaped buckle. "Trolovelsesring med hænder foldet omkring et hjerte". From the sixteenth century, found in 1894 in Aalborg, Denmark.

6. National and University Library of Iceland, Reykjavík

Marriage contract from 1591. Dip. Isl. nr. 25.

7. National Archives of Iceland, Reykjavík

Ministerialbók fyrir Reykjavíkurdómkirkju (Prestþjónustubók), 1816-1838.
Prestþjónustubækur. Prestþjónustubók Reykholts, Borg, 1664-1788.
Steinklefi XXXIX. AM Apogr. 1234. "Handrit dr. Jóns Þorkelssonar". Nr. 60. 1586."
Steinklefi XXXIX. AM Apogr. 1235. "Vitnisburður Jóns Þorkelssonar". Nr. 61. 1586."
Steinklefi XXXIX. MS STEPH. 216, 274 to, pp. 244-46. "Handrit dr. Jóns Þorkelssonar."
Steinklefi XXXIX. MS STEPH. 217, 274 to, pp. 244-46. "Handrit dr. Jóns Þorkelssonar."

8. Peterhouse College, Cambridge

Collectio Petrihugensis. cod. 114, 180, 193, 203.

Printed primary sources

Alþingisbækur Íslands, I (1570-1581), Reykjavík 1912-1914.

Alþingisbækur Íslands, II (1582-1594), Reykjavík 1915-1916.

Alþingisbækur Íslands, III (1595-1605), Reykjavík 1917-1918.

Annálar 1400-1800, eds. Hannes Þorsteinsson, Jón Jóhannesson, Þórhallur Vilmundarson and Guðrún Ása Grímsdóttir, vol. I-VI, Reykjavík 1922-88.

Árna saga biskups, ed. Þorleifur Hauksson, Reykjavík 1972.

Bréfabók Guðbrands byskups Þorlákssonar, eds. Jón Þorkelsson and Páll Eggert Ólason, Reykjavík 1919-1942.

Bsk. Bmf: *Biskupa sögur,* eds. Guðbrandur Vigfússon et al, vol. I-II, Copenhagen 1858-1878.

Corpus Iuris Canonici, ed. Emil Friedberg, vol. I-II, Leipzig 1879-1881, reprinted Graz 1959.

Decretales ineditae saeculi, eds. S. Chodorow and Ch. Duggan, vol. XII, Città del Vaticano 1982.

DI: *Diplomatarium Islandicum, Íslenzkt fornbréfasafn, sem hefir inni að halda bréf og gjörninga, dóma og máldaga, og aðrar skrár, er snerta Ísland eða íslenzka menn,* eds. Jón Sigurðsson, Jón Þorkelsson, Páll Eggert Ólason and Björn Þorsteinsson, vol. I-XVI, Copenhagen and Reykjavík 1857-1972.

Diplomatarium Poenitentiariae Norvegicum. Synder og pavemagt: Botsbrev fra Den Norske Kirkeprovins og Suderøyene til Pavestolen 1438-1531, eds. Thorstein Jørgensen and Gastone Saletnich, Stavanger 2004.

DN: *Diplomatarium Norvegicum,* eds. Chr. C. A. Lange, Carl R. Unger, H. J. Huitfeldt-Kaas, Alexander Bugge and Hallvard Magerøy, vol. I-XXI, Christiania/Oslo 1847-1976.

Drei lygisögur: Egils saga einhenta ok Ásmundar bersekjabana/ Álaflekks saga/Flóres saga konungs ok sona hans, ed. Åke Lagerholm, Halle 1927.

Finnboga saga hins ramma, ed. Hugo Gering, Halle 1879.

Flateyjarbók. En Samling af norske Konge-Sagaer med indskudte mindre Fortællinger om Begivenheder i og udenfor Norge, samt Annaler, eds. Guðbrandur Vigfússon and Unger, Christiania 1860.

Grágás (Ia, Ib, Ic and Id): *Grágás, Islændernes lovbog i fristatens tid, udgivet efter det kongelige Biblioteks Haandskrift,* ed. and translated by Vilhjálmur Finsen, Ia, First vol., Copenhagen 1852. Ib, Second vol., Copenhagen 1852. Ic and Id, Third vol., Oversættelse, Copenhagen 1870.

Grágás (II): *Grágás efter det Arnamagnæanske Haandskrift Nr. 334 fol., Staðarhólsbók,* Copenhagen 1879.

Grágás (III): *Grágás Stykker, som findes i det Arnamagnæanske Haandskrift. Nr. 351 fol., Skálholtsbók og en Række andre Haandskrifter,* Copenhagen 1883.

Grágás. Lagasafn íslenska þjóðveldisins, eds. Gunnar Karlsson, Kristján Sveinsson and Mörður Árnason, Reykjavík 1992.

Harðar saga, ed. Sture Hast, Copenhagen 1960.

Heiðarvíga saga, ed. Kr. Kålund, Copenhagen 1904.

ÍF: *Íslenzk fornrit,* vol. I-XXXV, Reykjavík 1968-2003.

IO: *Islandske Originaldiplomer indtil 1450,* ed. Stefán Karlsson, Copenhagen 1963.

Islandske Annaler indtil 1578, ed. Gustav Storm, Christiana 1888.

Íslandslýsing. Qualiscungue descriptio Islandiae. Translated by Sveinn Pálsson, Reykjavík 1971.

Járnsíða eður Hákonarbók, Copenhagen 1847.

Járnsíða og Kristinréttur Árna Þorlákssonar, eds. Haraldur Bernharðsson, Magnús Líndal Magnússon and Már Jónsson, Reykjavík 2005.

Jón Helgason, "Islandske bryllupstaler fra senmiddelalderen", *Bibliotheca Arnamagnana,* vol. XX, Copenhagen 1960, pp. 151-74.

Jón Þorkelsson, *Digtningen på Island i det 15. og 16. århundrede,* Copenhagen 1888.

Jónsbók. Kong Magnus Hakonssons lovbog for Island vedtaget paa Altinget 1281 og réttarbætur, de for Island givne retterbøder af 1294, 1305 og 1314, ed. Ólafur Halldórsson, Copenhagen 1904.

Ketils saga høings. Fornaldarsögur Norðrlanda, ed. C.C. Rafn, vol. 2, Copenhagen 1829.

Kirkeordinansen 1537/39. Det danske Udkast til Kirkeordinansen (1537). Ordinatio Ecclesiastica Regnorum Daniæ et Norwgiæ et Ducatuum Sleswicensis Holtsatice etc. (1537). Den danske Kirkeordinans (1539), ed. Martin Schwarz Lausten, Copenhagen 1989.

Laurentius saga biskups. Rit Handritastofnunar Íslands III, ed. Árni Björnsson, Reykjavík 1969.

Lovsamling for Island, vol. I, (1096-1720), Copenhagen 1853.

Medieval Handbooks of Penance: a Translation of the Principal Libri Poenitentiales and Selections from related documents, eds. John T. McNeill and Helena M. Gamer, New York 1990.

Middelalderens danske bønnebøger, ed. Karl Martin Nielsen, vol. II, Copenhagen 1949.

NgL: *Norges gamle love indtil 1387,* eds. R. Keyser, P.A. Munch, Gustav Storm and Edde Hertzberg, vol. 1-5, Christiania 1846-1895. *Norges gamle love. Anden række. 1388-1604,* eds. Absalon Taranger, Oscar Albert Johnsen, Oluf Kolsrud, Grethe Authén

Blom, Halvor Kjellberg, Ferdinand Linthoe Næshagen and Gösta Åqvist, vol. 1-3, Christiania/Oslo 1912-81.

Olaus Magnus, *Historia de gentibus Septentrionalibus*, Rome 1555.

Ordinatio Ecclesiastica Regnorum Daniæ et Norwegiæ et Ducatuum/Sleswicensis/Holtsatiæ etc., Copenhagen 1537.

Regesta Norvegica 1264-1300, eds. Narve Bjørgo and Sverre Bagge, vol. II, Oslo 1978.

Regesta Norvegica, ed. Erik Gunnes, vol. V, 1337-1350, Oslo 1979.

Strengleikar. An Old Norse Translation of Twenty-one Old French Lais, eds. R. Cook and M. Tveitane, vol. 3, Oslo 1979.

Sts: *Sturlunga saga*, eds. Jón Jóhannesson, Magnús Finnbogason and Kristján Eldjárn, vol. I –II, Reykjavík 1946.

Trístrams saga ok Ísöndar, ed. Gísli Brynjólfsson, Copenhagen 1878.

Women's Lives in Medieval Europe. A Sourcebook, ed. Emilie Amt, London 1993.

Zwei fornaldarsögur, Hrólfssaga Gautrekssonar und Ásmundarsaga kappabana nach Cod. Holm. 7; 4to, ed. Ferdinand Detter, Halle 1891.

Þorsteins saga Víkingassonar, Fornaldarsögur Norðrlanda, ed. C.C. Rafn, vol. 2, Copenhagen 1829.

Unpublished theses and papers

Agnes S. Arnórsdóttir, *Kvinner og "krigsmenn". Kjønnenes stilling i det islandske samfunnet på 1100- og 1200-tallet*, Master thesis in history, University of Bergen 1990.

Árni Daníel Júlíusson, *Bønder i pestens tid. Landbrug, godsdrift og social konflikter i senmiddelalderens islandske bondesamfund*, PhD thesis in history, University of Copenhagen 1995.

Aronsen, Elisabeth, *Skrift og rett. Utviklingen av en skriftkultur i Telemarks rettssystem i perioden 1300-1450*, Master thesis in history, University of Oslo 1999.

Bandlien, Björn, *takask með þeim góðar ástir. Kjærlighet og ekteskap i norrøn høymiddelalder*, Master thesis in history, University of Oslo 1998.

Magnús Lyngdal Magnússon, *Kristniréttur Árna frá 1275. Athugun á efni og varðveislu í miðaldahandritum*, Master thesis in history, University of Iceland 2002.

Napran, Laura Marie, *Marriage contracts in the southern Low countries and the north of France in the twelfth century*, PhD thesis in history, University of Cambridge 2001.

Orri Vésteinsson, *The Christianization of Iceland. Priests, Power and Social Change 1000-1300*, PhD thesis in history, University of London 1996.

Ragnheiður Kristjánsdóttir, *Makaval Íslendinga 1750-1900,* Master thesis in history, University of Iceland 1994.

Riisø, Anne Irene, *Stat og kirke: Rettsutøvelsen i kristenrettsaker mellom Sættargjerden og reformasjonen,* Master thesis in history, University of Oslo 2000.

Sørensen, Helle, *Det kanoniske slægtskab. En undersøgelse af kirkerettens betydning for den nordiske landskabslovgivning i det tolvte og trettende århundrede,* Master thesis in history, University of Copenhagen 2000.

Secondary sources

Agnes S. Arnórsdóttir, "Viðhorf til kvenna í Grágás", *Sagnir,* 1986, pp. 23-30.

Agnes S. Arnórsdóttir, *Konur og vígamenn. Staða kynjanna á Íslandi á 12. og 13. öld.* Sagnfræðirannsóknir, Studia Historica 12, Reykjavík 1995.

Agnes S. Arnórsdóttir, "Um brúðarkaup, kvennagiftingar og kanóniskan rétt", *Þættir úr kristnisögu Íslands. Konur og kristsmenn,* Reykjavík 1996, pp. 65-89.

Agnes S. Arnórsdóttir, "Review of Inger Holtan: Ekteskap, frillelevnad og hor i norsk høgmellomalder", *Hifo-nytt,* number 5, 1997, pp. 15-18.

Agnes S. Arnórsdóttir, "Review of Trevor Dean & Kate Lowe", *Marriage in Italy 1300-1650*", *Nyt fra historien,* XLVII, 2, 1998, pp. 97-98.

Agnes S. Arnórsdóttir, "Two models of Marriage? Canon Law and Icelandic Marriage Practice in late Middle Ages", *Nordic Perspectives on Medieval Canon Law,* ed. Mia Korpiola, Helsinki 1999, pp. 79-92.

Agnes S. Arnórsdóttir and Thyra Nors, "Ægteskabet i Norden og det europæiske perspektiv – overvejelser om især danske og islandske normer for ægteskab i 12.–14. århundrede", *Ægteskab i Norden fra Saxo til i dag:* eds. Kari Melby, Anu Pylkkänen and Bente Rosenbeck, (*Nord* 1999:14), Copenhagen 1999, pp. 27-51.

Agnes S. Arnórsdóttir, "Marriage in the Middle Ages. Canon Law and Nordic Family Relations", *Rapporter til Det 24. Nordiske Historikermøde 1, Norden og Europa i middelalderen,* eds. Per Ingesman and Thomas Lindkvist, Aarhus 2001a, pp. 174-202.

Agnes S. Arnórsdóttir, "Hlaupin í fjarlæga fjórðunga. Nokkur orð um réttarstöðu íslenska kvenna á 15. og 16. öld", *Kvennaslóðir. Rit til heiðurs Sigríði Th. Erlendsdóttur sagnfræðingi,* Reykjavík 2001b, pp. 33-45.

Agnes S. Arnórsdóttir, "Icelandic Marriage Dispensations in the Late Middle Ages", *The Roman Curia, the Apostolic Penitentiary and the Parties in the Later Middle Ages,* eds.

Kirsi Salonen and Christian Krötzl, *Acta Instituti Romani Finlandiae,* vol. 28, Rome 2003, pp. 159-169.
Agnes S. Arnórsdóttir, "Death and donation: different channels of property transfer in late medieval Iceland", *The Marital Economy in Scandinavia and Britain 1400-1900*, eds. Maria Ågren and Amy Louyde Erickson, Aldershot 2005, pp. 205-19.
Agnes S. Arnórsdóttir, "Icelandic Marriage contracts", *To have and to hold. Marrying and Its Documentation in Western Christendom, 400-1600,* eds. Philip Reynolds, and John Witte, Jr., Cambridge 2007, pp. 360-89.
Agnes S. Arnórsdóttir, "Sjælegaver i islandsk senmiddelalder – religiøs formidling og familiestruktur", *Konge, kirke og samfund. De to øvrighedsmagter I dansk senmiddelalder,* eds. Agnes S. Arnórsdóttir, Per Ingesman and Bjørn Poulsen, Aarhus 2007, pp. 415-42.
Agnes S. Arnórsdóttir, "Eigi skal gráta Björn bónda heldur safna liði." Ólöf ríka, göðsögn og saga", *Heimtur. Ritgerðir til heiðurs Gunnari Karlssyni sjötugum,* eds. Guðmundur Jónsson, Helgi Skúli Kjartansson and Vésteinn Ólason, Reykjavík 2009, p. 19-34.
Andersen, Randi, "Kvinnas økonomiske rettsstode i norsk mellomalder", *Kvinnans ekonomiska ställing under nordisk medeltid. Uppsatser framlagda vid ett kvinnohistoriskt symposium i Kungälv 8.-12. oktober 1979,* eds. Hedda Gunneng and Birgit Strand, Lindome 1981, pp. 81-88.
Anderson, Gudrun, "Kvinnans underordning axiom eller öppen fråga?", *Historisk Tidskrift* 3, 1997, pp. 452-58.
Anderson, Gudrun and Maria Ågren, "Kvinnor och egendom under tidigmodern tid – forskningsläge och forskningsstrategier", *Scandia,* 62:1, 1996, pp. 25-53.
Ariès, Philippe and Georges Duby, eds. *A History of Private Life. Relations of the Medieval World,* vol. II, Cambridge 1988.
Árni Daníel Júlíusson, "Áhrif fólksfjöldaþróunar á atvinnuhætti gamla samfélagsins", *Saga* XXVIII, 1990, pp. 149-156.
Árni Daníel Júlíusson, *Bønder i pestens tid: landbrug, godsdrift og social konflikt i senmiddelalderens islandske bondesamfund,* Copenhagen 1996.
Árni Daníel Júlíusson, "Þurrabúðir, býli og höfuðból", *Íslenska söguþingið 28.–31. Maí 1997. Ráðstefnurit,* eds. Guðmundur J. Guðmundsson and Eiríkur K. Björnsson, Reykjavík 1998a, vol. II, pp. 57-69.
Árni Daníel Júlíusson, "Valkostir sögunnar. Um landbúnað fyrir 1700 og þjóðfélagsþróun á 14. – 16. öld", *Saga* XXXVI, 1998b, pp. 77-111.
Arnór Sigurjónsson, *Ásbirningasaga,* Reykjavík 1967.

Arnór Sigurjónsson, "Jarðamat og jarðeignir á Vestfjörðum 1446, 1710 og 1842", *Saga* X, 1973, pp. 74-115.

Arnór Sigurjónsson, *Vestfirðingasaga 1390-1540*, Reykjavík 1975.

Aronsen, Elisabeth, "Innføringen av praktisk skriftkultur i norsk senmiddelalder – et ledd i sentraliseringsprosessen", *Historisk Tidsskrift* 80:4, 2001, pp. 419-43.

Auður Magnúsdóttir, "Ástir og völd. Frillulíf á Íslandi á þjóðveldisöld", *Ný Saga*, 1988, pp. 4-12.

Auður Magnúsdóttir, "Hövdingar, hustrur och frillor: Frilloväsendet på Island under fristatstiden", *Kirkehistorier. Rapport fra et middelaldersymposium*, Copenhagen 1996, pp. 93-113.

Auður Magnúsdóttir, *Frillor och fruar. Politik och samlevnad på Island 1120-1400*, Göteborg 2001.

Axel Kristinsson, "Íslenskar ríkisættir á 12. og 13. öld", *Íslenska söguþingið 28.-31. Maí 1997. Ráðstefnurit*, eds. Guðmundur J. Guðmundsson and Eiríkur K. Björnsson, vol. II, Reykjavík 1998a, pp. 70-82.

Axel Kristinsson, "Embættismenn konungs fyrir 1400", *Saga* XXXVI, 1998b, pp. 113-52.

Axel Kristinsson, "Lords and Literature: The Icelandic Sagas as Political and Social Instruments", *Scandinavian Journal of History*, 28, 1, 2003, pp. 1-17.

Bagge, Sverre, "Europa 300-120", *Cappelens Kvinnehistorie I, Urtid, oldtid, middelalderen til ca. 1500*, Oslo 1992, pp. 315-77.

Bagge, Sverre, "Law and Justice in Norway in the Middle Ages: A case study", *Medieval Spirituality in Scandinavia and Europe. A Collection of Essays in Honour of Tore Nyberg*, eds. Lars Bisgaard, Carsten Selch Jensen, Kurt Villads Jensen and John Lind, Odense 2001, pp. 73-85.

Bandlien, Bjørn, "Kvinnens vilje og mannens ære. Om ekteskapsinngåelse på Island i middelalderen", *Historie*, 4, 1997, pp. 46-56.

Bandlien, Bjørn, "The Church's teaching on women's consent: a threat to parents and society in Medieval Norway and Iceland?", *Family, Marriage and Property Devolution in the Middle Ages*, ed. Lars Ivar Hansen, Tromsø 2000, pp. 55-79.

Bandlien, Bjørn, *Å finne den rette. Kjærlighet, individ og samfunn i norrøn middelalder*, Oslo 2001.

Bandlien, Bjørn, "Strategies of passion. Love and Marriage in Medieval Iceland and Norway". *Medieval Texts and Cultures of Northern Europe*, 6, Turnhout 2005.

Barnard, Alan, *History and Theory in Anthropology*, Cambridge 2000.

Barth, Fredrik, *Balinese Worlds*, Chicago 1993.

Bartlett, Robert, *The Making of Europe. Conquest, Colonization and Cultural Change 950-1350*, London 1994.

Benadusi, Giovanna, "Rethinking the state: family strategies in early modern Tuscany", *Social History,* vol. 20, 2, 1995, pp. 157-78.

Berulfsen, Bjarne "Formularbok", *KLNM* IV, Copenhagen 1959, pp. 491-92.

Besnier, Robert, "Le mariage en Normandie des origines au XIIIe siècle", *Normannia,* 7 1934, pp. 69-110.

Bitel, Lisa M., *Land of Women. Tales of Sex and Gender from Early Ireland,* London 1996.

Bjarni Einarsson, "Málvöndun og fyrnska", *Skírnir. Tímarit hins íslenska bókmenntafélags,* 148, 1974, pp. 41-59.

Björn Björnsson, "Um hjúskaparmál í lútherskum sið", *Lúther og íslenskt þjóðlíf. Erindi flutt á ráðstefnu 4. Nóvember 1983,* Reykjavík 1989, pp. 141-52.

Björn Lárusson, "Valuation and distribution of landed property in Iceland", *Economy and History,* 4, 1961, pp. 34-64.

Björn Lárusson, *The Old Icelandic land registers,* Lund 1967.

Björn Þorsteinsson, "Fall Björns Þorleifssonar á Rifi og afleiðingar þess", *Safn til sögu Íslands og íslenskra bókmennta,* I:4, Reykjavík 1956, pp. 3-22.

Björn Þorsteinsson, *Enska öldin í sögu Íslendinga,* Reykjavík 1970.

Björn Þorsteinsson and Bersteinn Jónsson, *Íslandssaga til okkar daga,* Reykjavík 1991.

Björn Þorsteinsson and Sigurður Líndal, "Lögfesting konungsvaldsins", *Saga Íslands,* vol. III, Reykjavík 1978, pp. 19-108.

Björn Þorsteinsson and Guðrún Ása Grímsdóttir, "Norska öldin, með viðaukum eftir Sigurð Líndal", *Saga Íslands,* vol. IV, Reykjavík 1989, p. 61-260.

Björn Þorsteinsson and Guðrún Ása Grímsdóttir, "Enska öldin, með viðaukum eftir Sigurð Líndal", *Saga Íslands,* vol. V, Reykjavík 1990, pp. 3-216.

Bloch, Maurice, "Ritual, History and Power. Selected Papers in Anthropology". *Monographs on Social Anthropology,* 58, London 1989.

Blom, Ida, "En annen historie? Kvinnehistorie i et internasjonalt perspektiv", *Historiskt Tidskrift* 69:4, 1990, pp. 416-34.

Bonfield, L., "Property Settlements on Marriage in England from the Anglo-Saxons to Mid-Eighteenth Century", *Marriage, Property, and Succession.* ed. Lloyd Bonfield, Berlin 1992, pp. 287-308.

Bonfield, L., and Larry R. Poos, "Law and individualism in Medieval England", *Social History,* vol. II: 3, 1986, pp. 287-301.

Bonfield, L., and Larry R. Poos, "The Development of the deathbed transfer in Medieval English manor courts", *Cambridge Law Journal,* 47:3, 1988, pp. 403-27.

Bourdieu, Pierre, *Outline of a theory of practice,* Cambridge 1995.

Boyle, Leonard E., "Diplomatics", *Medieval Studies. An Introduction,* ed. James M. Powell Syracuse 1976, pp. 69-101.

Bresc, Henri, "Europe: Town and Country (Thirteenth-Fifteenth century), *A History of the Family,* vol. 1, Cambridge 1996, pp. 430-66.

Brooke, Christopher, *The Medieval Idea of Marriage,* Oxford 1991.

Bruck, Gabriele, "Kinship and Embodiment of History", *History and Anthropology,* 10:4, 1998, pp. 263-98.

Brundage, James A., "Concubinage and Marriage in Medieval Canon Law", *Journal of Medieval History,* 1975, pp. 1-17.

Brundage, James A., *Law, Sex and Christian Society in Medieval Europe,* Chicago 1990.

Brundage, James A., "Implied Consent to Intercourse", *Consent and Coercion to Sex and Marriage in Ancient and Medieval Societies,* ed. Angeliki A., Laiou, Washington D.C. 1993, pp. 245-56.

Brundage, James A., *Medieval Canon Law,* New York 1995a.

Brundage, James A., "The Merry Widow's Serious Sister: Remarriage in Classical Canon Law", *Matrons and Marginal Women,* eds. Robert R. Edwards and Vickie Ziegler, Woodbridge 1995b, pp. 33-48.

Burguière, André, Christiane Klapisch-Zuber, Martine Segalen and Francoise Zonabend, eds. *Histoire de la famillie,* vol. 1-2, Paris 1986.

Burke, Peter, *Sociology and History. Controversies in Sociology,* London 1980.

Butler, Judith, *Gender Trouble: Feminism and the Subversion of Identity,* London 1999.

Byock, Jesse, *Viking Age Iceland,* London 2001.

Bøe, Arne, "Lysing", *KLNM* XI, Copenhagen 1966, p. 26.

Børresen, Kari E., Sara Cabibbo and Edith Specht, eds. *Gender and Religion, Genre et Religion.* European Studies/Etudes européennes, Rome 2001.

Calvi, Giulia, "Reconstructing the family: widowhood and remarriage in Tuscany in the early modern period", *Marriage in Italy 1300-1650,* eds. Trevor Dean and K. J. P. Lowe, Cambridge 1998, pp. 275-96.

Carlsson, Lizzie, *Jag giver dig min dotter. Troloving och äktenskap i den svenska kvinnans äldre historia, vol. 1-2,* Skrifter utg. av Inst. för Rättshistorisk forskning, Lund 1965.

Carlsson, Lizzie, "Morgongåva", KLNM XI, Copenhagen 1966, pp. 695-98.

Carlsson, Lizzie, "Skyldskap", KLNM XVI, Copenhagen 1971, pp. 42-43.

Casey, James, *The History of the Family*, Oxford 1989.

Clanchy, M. T., *From Memory to Written Record: England 1066-1307*, London 1979.

Crouzel, Henri, *Virginité et mariage selon Origène*, Paris 1963.

Damsholt, Nanna, "Ægteskab i dansk middelalder", *Ægteskab i Norden fra Saxo til i dag*, eds. Kari Melby, Anu Pylkkänen and Bente Rosenbeck, (Nord 1999:14), Copenhagen 1999, pp. 55-70.

Dauphin et al., "Culture et Pouvoir des Femmes. Essai d'Historigraphie", *Annales ESC*, 1986:2, pp. 271-93. English translation in *Journal of Womens History*, 1989, I, pp. 63-88.

D'Avray, David, ed. *Medieval Marriage Sermons: mass communication in a culture without print*, Oxford 2001.

Dean, Trevor, "Fathers and daughters: marriage laws and marriage disputes in Bologna and Italy, 1200-1500", *Marriage in Italy 1300-1650*, eds. Trevor Dean and Kate Lowe, Cambridge 1998, pp. 85-106.

Dean, Trevor and Kate Lowe, eds. *Marriage in Italy 1300-1650*, Cambridge 1998.

Donahue, Charles, Jr., "The Policy of Alexander the Third's Consent Theory of Marriage", *Fourth International Congress of medieval Canon Law*, ed. Stephan Kuttner, Città del Vaticano 1976, pp. 251-81.

Donahue, Charles, Jr., "English and French Marriage Cases in the Later Middle Ages: Might the Differences be Explained by Differences in the Property Systems?", *Marriage, Property, and Succession*, ed. Lloyd Bonfield, Berlin 1992, pp. 339-66.

Duby, Georges, *Rural Economy and Country Life in the Medieval West*, London 1968.

Duby, Georges, *The Knight, the Lady and the Priest*, London 1984.

Duby, Georges, *Makten och Kärleken. Om äktenskapet i feodaltidens Frankrige*, Stockholm 1985.

Duby, Georges, *Mâle moyen âge. De l'Amour et autres essais* Champs, Flammarion 1990.

Duby, Georges, *Medieval Marriage. Two Models from Twelfth-Century France*, London 1991a (first published 1978).

Duby, Georges, *L'Histoire Continue,* Paris 1991b.

Duby, Georges, *Love and Marriage in the Middle Ages*, Chicago 1994.

Duby, Georges, and Michelle Perrot, *Histoire des Femmes en occident. Le Moyen Age 2,* eds. Christiane Klapisch-Zuber, Paris 1991-1992.

Duggan, Ch., *Twelfth century Decretal Collections and their Importance in English History*, London 1963.

Dumont, Louise, *Essays on Individualism. Modern Ideology in Anthropological Perspective*, London 1992.

Durrenberger, E., Paul, *The Dynamics of Medieval Iceland. Political Economy and Literature,* Iowa City 1992.

Dübeck, Inger, *Kvinder, familie og formue,* Copenhagen 2003.

Dübeck, Inger, "Property and authority in Danish marital law." *The Marital Economy in Scandinavia and Britain 1400-1900,* eds. Amy Louise Erickson and Maria Ågren, Aldershot 2005, pp. 127-39.

Einar Arnórsson, *Íslenzkur kirkjuréttur,* Reykjavík 1912.

Einar Arnórsson, "Þáttur Bjarna Ólasonar í Hvassafelli", *Blanda,* 5, 1932-1935, pp. 343-87.

Einar Arnórsson, "Athugasemdir og viðaukar við þátt Bjarna Ólason í Hvassafelli", *Blanda,* 6, 1936-1939, pp. 37-49.

Einar Arnórsson, "Víg Páls á Skarði", *Saga* IX, 1949-53, pp. 127-76.

Einar Arnórsson, "Gottskálk biskup Nikulásson og Jón lögmaður Sigmundsson", *Safn til sögu Íslands og íslenzkra bókmennta,* Reykjavík 1953-1954, pp. 5-69.

Einar Arnórsson, "Lög rómversk katólsku kirkjunnar um hjónaskilnaði", *Afmælisrit helgað Ólafi Lárussyni,* Reykjavík 1955, pp. 55-62.

Einar Bjarnason, "Skilgreining á Jónunum tveimur sonum Finnboga gamla í Ási í Kelduhverfi", *Afmælisrit helgað Ólafi Lárussyni,* Reykjavík 1955, pp. 63-88.

Einar Bjarnason, "Auðbrekkubréf og Vatnsfjarðarerfðir", *Saga* III, 1960-63, pp. 371-411.

Einar Bjarnason, "Undanþágur frá banni við hjónabandi fjórmenninga að frændsemi eða mægðum í kaþólskum sið á Íslandi", *Saga* VII, Reykjavík 1969, pp. 140-59.

Einar Bjarnason, *Íslenzkir ættstuðlar,* vol. I-III, 1969-1972.

Einar Bjarnason, "Erfðamál frá 15. öld", *Úlfljótur* 24, 1971, pp. 286-92.

Einar Gunnar Pétursson, "Skarð á Skarðsströnd og kirkjan þar", *Lesbók Morgunblaðsins,* 43, Reykjavík 1983.

Einar Gunnar Pétursson, "Hugvekja við afhendingu fornbréfa", *Bókahnútur brugðinn Ólöfu Benediktsdóttur fimmtugri 4. febrúar 1997,* Reykjavík 1997, pp. 26-29.

Einar Laxness, *Íslandssaga,* vol. I-III, 1995.

Einar Ólafur Sveinsson "Formáli", *Íslenzk fornrit,* XII, Brennu – Njálssaga, Reykjavík 1954, pp. v-clxiii.

Einar Sigmarson, "Rýnt í gamla gátu? Hver er höfundur Qualiscunque descriptio Islandiae?", *Saga* XLI:2, 2003, pp. 97-133.

Eiríkur Tómasson, "Var réttarfar á þjóðveldisöld nútímalegt", *Líndæla. Sigurður Líndal sjötugur, 2. júlí 2001,* Reykjavík 2001, pp. 95-111.

Elliott, Dyan, *Spiritual Marriage: Sexual Abstinence in Medieval Wedlock,* Princeton 1993.

Ennen, Edith, *The Medieval Women,* Oxford 1989.

Erickson, Amy Louise, *Women and Property in Early Modern England,* London 1995.

Erickson, Amy Louise, "The marital economy in comparative perspective", *The Marital Economy in Scandinavia and Britain 1400-1900,* eds. Amy Louise Erickson and Maria Ågren, Aldershot 2005, pp. 3-20.

Erickson, Amy Louise and Maria Ågren, eds. "Women and Gender in the early Modern world", *The Marital Economy in Scandinavia and Britain 1400-1900,* Aldershot 2005.

Esmein, Adhémar, *Le mariage en droit canonique,* eds. Robert Génestal and Jean Dauvillier, vol. I-II, Paris 1929-1935.

Evergates Theodore, ed. *Aristocratic Women in medieval France,* Philadelphia 1999.

Fenger, Ole, *Gammeldansk ret. Dansk rets historie i oldtid og middelalder,* Viborg 1983.

Foucault, Michel, *The History of Sexuality. An introduction,* London 1984.

Frank, Roberta, "Marriage in the Middle Ages: Marriage in Twelfth – and Thirteenth Century Iceland", *Viator,* 4, 1973, pp. 473-84.

Fransen, Gérard, *Les décretales et les collections des décrétales,* Typologie des sources du moyen âge occidental, vol.A-III*, fasc.2, Turnhout 1972.

Frimannslund, Rigmor, "Medgift", KLNM XI, Copenhagen 1966a, pp. 519-20,

Frimannslund, Rigmor, "Morgongåva", KLNM XI, Copenhagen 1966b, pp. 699.

Frimannslund, Rigmor, "Mundr", KLNM XII, Copenhagen 1967, pp. 10-11.

Fritzner, Johan, *Ordbog over det gamle norske Sprog,* vol. I-IV, Oslo 1954-72.

Gaunt, David, *Familjeliv i Norden,* Malmö 1983.

Geertz, Clifford, *The interpretation of Cultures. Selected Essays,* London 1993.

Gellenik, Christian, "Marriage by Consent in Literary Sources of Medieval Germany." *Studia. Gratiana,* 12, 1967, pp. 557-79.

Gelting, Michael H., "Det komparativ perspektive i dansk højmiddelalderforskning. Om Familia og familie, Lið, Leding og Landeværn", *Historisk tidsskrift,* vol. 99, 1999a, pp. 145-88.

Gelting, Michael H., "Marriage, Peace and the Canonical Incest Prohibitons: Making Sense of an Absurdity?", *Nordic Perspectives on Medieval Canon Law,* ed. Mia Kopiola, Helsinki 1999b, pp. 93-124.

Gelting, Michael H., "Odelsrett – lovbydelse – bördarätt – retrait lignager. Kindred and Land in the Nordic Countries in the Twelfth and Thirteenth Centuries", *Family, Marriage and Property Devolution in the Middle Ages,* ed. Lars Ivar Hansen, Tromsø 2000, pp. 133-65.

Gelting, Michael H., "Kanonisk ret og de nordiske slægtssamfund", *Historie,* 2003, pp. 410-30.

Giddens, Anthony, *Sociology,* Oxford 1993.

Gies, Joseph and Frances Gies, *Marriage and the Family in the Middle Ages,* New York 1989.

Gísli Ágúst Gunnlaugsson, "Ást og hjónaband á fyrri öldum. Um ástina og hjónabandið í erlendum sagnfræðirannsóknum og íslensku samfélagi 1780-1900", *Ný Saga,* 1988, pp. 76-87.

Gísli Ágúst Gunnlaugsson, "Siðferðisbrot á Norðurlöndum 1550-1850", *Saga og samfélag. Þættir úr félagssögu 19. og 20. aldar,* Reykjavík 1997, pp. 62-82.

Gjerløw, Lilli, *Liturgica Islandica I. Text.* Bibliotheca Arnamagnæana, Vol. XXXV, Copenhagen 1980.

Goddard, Victoria, A., "From the Mediterranean to Europe: Honour, Kinship and Gender", *The Anthropology of Europe. Identity and Boundaries in Conflict,* eds. Victoria A. Goddard, Josep R. Llobera and Cris Shore, Oxford 1996, pp. 57-92.

Goody, Jack, *Production and Reproduction. A Comparative Study of the Domestic Domain,* Cambridge 1988a, (org. 1976).

Goody, Jack, *The Development of the Family and Marriage in Europe,* Cambridge 1988b.

Goody, Jack, *The Logic of Writing and the Organization of Society,* Cambridge 1992.

Goody, Jack, *The East in the West,* Cambridge 1996.

Granquist, Karin, "Til hvem gir du din sjel?", *Hekseprosesser og trolldom, Ottar,* No. 234, 1, 2001, pp. 36-40.

Granqvist, Karin, *Samerna, staten och rätten i Torne lappmark under 1600-talet. Makt, diskurs och representation.* Skrifter från Institutionen för historiska studier 8, Umeå 2004.

Gravdal, Kathryn, *Ravishing maidens. Writing rape in Medieval French Literature and Law,* Philadelphia 1991.

Græsdal, Kathrine, "Joint Ownership in Medieval Norway", *Family, Marriage and Property Devolution in the Middle Ages,* ed. Lars Ivar Hansen, Tromsø 2000, pp. 81-97.

Guðbrandur Vigfússon and Richard Cleasby (eds.), *An Icelandic-English Dictionary,* Oxford 1957.

Guðmundur Hálfdánarson, *Historical Dictionary of Iceland,* European Historical Dictionaries, London 1997.

Guðni Jónsson, ed. "Formáli", *Byskupasögur III,* Reykjavík 1962, pp. vii-x.

Guðrún Ása Grímsdóttir, "Um afskipti erkibiskupa af íslenzkum málefnum á 12. og 13. öld", *Saga* XX, 1982, pp. 28-62.

Guðrún Ása Grímsdóttir, "Um íslensku prestkonuna á fyrri öldum", *Þættir úr kristnisögu Íslands", Konur og kristmenn,* ed. Inga Huld Hákonardóttir, Reykjavík 1996, pp. 215-48.

Guðrún Nordal, Sverrir Tómasson and Vésteinn Ólason, *Íslensk bókmenntasaga I,* Reykjavík 1992.

Gunnar F. Guðmundsson, *Kristni á Íslandi, Íslenskt samfélag og Rómarkirkja,* ed. Hjalti Hugason, vol. II, Reykjavík 2000.

Gunnar F. Guðmundsson, "Iðrun og yfirbót. Nokkur orð um skriftarmál á miðöldum", *Líndæla. Sigurður Líndal sjötugur, 2. júlí 2001,* Reykjavík 2001, pp. 213-77.

Gunnar Karlsson, "Kenningin um fornt kvenfrelsi á Íslandi", *Saga* XXIV, 1986, pp. 45-77.

Gunnar Karlsson, "Nafngreindar höfðingjaættir í Sturlungu", *Sagnaþing helgað Jónasi Kristjánssyni sjötugum. 10. apríl, 1994,* Reykjavík 1994a, pp. 307-15.

Gunnar Karlsson and Skúli Kjartansson, "Plágurnar miklu á Íslandi", *Saga* XXXII, 1994b, pp. 11-74.

Gunnar Karlsson, "Plague without rats: the case of fifteenth-century Iceland", *Journal of Medieval History,* Vol. 22, 3, 1996, pp. 263-84.

Gunnar Karlsson, "Um fræðilegan hernað og plágurnar miklu", *Saga* XXXV, 1997, pp. 223-39.

Gunnar Karlsson, "Íslensk þjóðernisvitund á óþjóðlegum öldum", *Skírnir,* 173, 1999, pp. 141-78.

Gunnar Karlsson, *A Brief History of Iceland,* Reykjavík 2000a.

Gunnar Karlsson, *Iceland's 1100 Years. The History of a Marginal Society,* Reykjavík 2000b.

Gunnar Karlsson, *Goðamenning. Staða og áhrif goðorðsmanna í þjóðveldi Íslendinga,* Reykjavík 2004.

Gunnar Karlsson, "Kristnitaka Íslendinga og menningaráhrif hennar", *Andvari,* 125, 2005, pp. 107-27.

Gunneng, Hedda, "Kvinnlig arvsrätt under svensk medeltid. En forskningsrapport", *Manliga strukturer och kvinnliga strategier. En bok til Gunhild Kyle,* eds. Birgit Sawyer and Anita Göransson, Göteborg 1987, pp. 79-90.

Gunneng, Hedda and Birgit Strand, eds. *Kvinnans ekonomiska ställning under nordisk medeltid. Uppsatser framlagda vid ett kvinnohistoriskt symposium i Kungälv 8-12. oktober 1979,* Stockholm 1981.

Gunneng, Hedda et al., *Kvinnors rosengård: medelstidskvinnors liv och hälsa, lust och barnefödende,* Stockholm 1989.

Gunnes, Erik, "Erkibiskop Øystein som lovgiver", *Nye middelalderstudier: Kongedømme, kirke, stat,* eds. Claus Krag and Jørn Sandnes, Norske historikere i utvalg, vol. VI, Oslo 1983, pp. 94-109.

Gunnes, E. and Kari Vogt, "Kvinnekår og kvinnesyn", *Norges kulturhistorie* II, Oslo 1979, pp. 181-210.

Hajnal, John, "Two Kinds of Pre-industrial Household formation systems", *Population and Development Review,* 8:3, 1982, pp. 449-94.

Hamre, Lars, "Gåve", KLNM V, Copenhagen 1960, pp. 653-61.

Hamre, Lars, " Skrift og Samfunn. Eit møte mellom nytt og gammalt. Små refleksjonar om eit stort emne", *Rett og historie. Festskrift til Gudmund Sandvik,* eds. Dag Michalsen and Knut Sprauten, Oslo 1997, pp. 126-37.

Hansen, Lars Ivar, "Slektskap, eiendom og sosiale strategier i nordisk middelalder", *Collegium Medievale,* vol. 7, 2,1996, pp. 103-154.

Hansen, Lars Ivar, "The Consept of Kinship According to the West Nordic Medieval Law" *How Nordic are the Nordic Medieval Laws?* eds. Ditlev Tamm and Helle Vogt, Medieval Legal History I, Copenhagen 2005, pp. 170-201.

Hansen, Lars Ivar, ed., *Family, Marriage and Property Devolution in the Middle Ages,* Tromsø 2000.

Hareven, Tamara K., "The History of the Family and the Complexity of Social Change", *The American Historical Review,* 96:1, 1991, pp. 95-124.

Harrington, Joel F., *Reordering Marriage and Society in Reformation Germany,* Cambridge 1995.

Hastrup, Kirsten, *Culture and History in Medieval Iceland. An anthropological analysis of Structure and Change,* Oxford 1985.

Haug, Eldbjørg, *Provincia Nidrosiensis i dronning Margretes unions- og maktpolitikk,* Skriftserie fra Historisk Institutt, no.13, Trondheim 1996.

Helander, Sven, "Sakrament", KLNM XIV, Copenhagen 1969, pp. 665-68.

Helgi Þorláksson, *Vaðmál og verðlag. Vaðmál í utanlandsviðskiptum og búskap Íslendinga á 13. og 14. öld,* Reykjavík 1991.

Helgi Þorláksson, *Saga Íslands* VI, Reykjavík 2003.

Helle, Knut, *Norge bliver en stat 1130-1319,* Oslo 1993.

Helmholz, Richard H., *Marriage Litigation in Medieval England,* Cambridge 1974.

Helmholz, Richard H., *The Canon Law and Ecclesiastical Jurisdiction from 597 to the 1640s.* The Oxford History of the Laws of England, vol. I, Oxford 2004.

Herlihy, David, "Family Solidarity in Medieval Italian History", *The Social History of Italy and Western Europe, 700-1500. Collected Studies,* London 1978, pp. 173-84.

Herlihy, David, *Medieval Households,* Cambridge 1985.

Herlihy, David, "The Family and Religious Ideologies in Medieval Europe", *Family History at the Crossroads*, eds. Tamara Hareven and Andrejs Plakans, Princeton 1987.

Herlihy, David, *Women, Family and Society in Medieval Europe. Historical Essays, 1978-1991*, Oxford 1995.

Hertzberg, Ebbe, "De gamle loves mynding", *Christiania videnskabs – selskabs forhandlinger*,1889, pp. 1-51.

Hirdman, Yvonne, "Genussystemet", *Kvinnovetenskaplig Tidskrift*, 3, 1988, pp. 49-63.

Hirdman, Yvonne, "Skevläsning – till debatten om genussystem", *Kvinnovetenskaplig tidskrift* 2, 1993, pp. 57-61.

Hjalti Hugason, "Gísli Ágúst Gunnlaugsson, Saga og samfélag. Þættir úr félagssögu 19. og 20. aldar", *Saga*, XXXVI, 1998, pp. 265-70.

Hjalti Hugason, ed., *Kristnisaga Íslands* vol. I-IV, Reykjavík 2000.

Holtan, Inger, *Ekteskap, frillelevnad og hor i norsk høgmellomalder*, Oslo 1996.

Holtzmann, W., "Krone und Kirche in Norwegen im 12. Jahrundert", *Deutsches Archiv für Erforschung des Mittelalters*, 2, 1938, pp. 341-400.

Howell, Martha C., *The Marriage Exchange. Property, Social Place, and Gender in Cities of the Low Countries, 1300-1550*, Chicago 1998.

Hrefna Róbertsdóttir, "Helmingarfélag hjóna á miðöldum", *Sagnir*, 1986, pp. 31-40.

Hughes, Diana Owen, "From Brideprice to Dowry in Mediterranean Europe", *Journal of Family History*, 1978, pp. 262-91.

Icelandic-English Dictionary, eds. Richard Cleasby and Guðbrandur Vigfússon, Oxford 1957.

Inga Huld Hákonardóttir, *Fjarri hlýju hjónasængur. Öðruvísi Íslandssaga*, Reykjavík 1992.

Ingesman, Per, "Kirkeordinansen i ny udgave", *Historie* 19: 1, 1991, pp. 163-73.

Ingesman, Per, "Fra Pønitentiariatets supplikregistre", *Nyt fra historien* XLVI, 2, 1997, pp. 193-99.

Ingesman, Per, "De ukendte pavebreve", *Humaniora*, vol. 12, 1998, pp. 3-6.

Ingesman, Per, "Nådens og retfærdighedens kilde. Brugen af pavemagten i nordisk senmiddelalder", *Rapporter til Det 24. Nordiske Historikermøde 1, Norden og Europa i middelalderen*, eds. Per Ingesman and Thomas Lindkvist, Århus 2001, pp. 130-73.

Iuul, Stig, *Fællig og Hovedlod. Studier over Formueforholdet mellem Ægtefæller i Tiden før Christian V's Danske Lov*, Copenhagen 1940.

Iuul, Stig, "Formkrav", KLNM IV, Copenhagen 1959a, pp. 486-87.

Iuul, Stig, "Formuefællesskab", KLNM IV, Copenhagen 1959b, pp. 487-91.

Iuul, Stig, "Medgift. Danmark", KLNM XI, Copenhagen 1966, p. 523.

Ivarsen, Tore, "Landskapslovene og kanonisk ret", *Nordiske middelalderlover. Tekst og kontekst,* eds. A. Dybdahl and J. Sandnes, Trondheim 1997, pp. 69-87.

Ivarsen, Tore, "Jordeie og jodleie. Eiendomsbegrepet i norske middelalderlover", *Collegium Medievale,* vol. 14, 2001, pp. 79-114.

Ivarsen, Tore, "Den kanoniske retten som bindeledd mellom Romakirken og Bygdenorge", *Den kirkehistoriske udfordring,* ed. Steinar Imsen, Trondheim 2005, pp. 75-90.

Íslenskur söguatlas. Frá öndverðu til 18. aldar, vol. I, ed. Árni Daníel Júlíusson, Jón Ólafur Ísberg and Helgi Skúli Kjartansson, Reykjavík 1991.

Jacobsen, Grethe, *Kvinder, køn og købstadslovgivning 1400-1600. Lovfaste mænd og ærlige kvinder,* Copenhagen 1995.

Jakob Benediktsson, *Gísli Magnússon (Vísi-Gísli) Ævisaga, ritgerðir, bréf,* Safn fræðafélagsins, vol. XI, Reykjavík 1939.

Jexlev, Thelma, "Anna Brades bønnebog – et Birgittinsk håndskrift fra Maribo", *Birgitta, hendes værk og hendes klostre i Norden,* ed. Tore Nyberg, Odense 1991, pp. 323-29.

Jochens, Jenny, "The Church and sexuality in medieval Iceland", *Journal of Medieval History,* 6, 1980, pp. 377-92.

Jochens, Jenny, "En Islande Mèdièvale: à la recherche de la famille nucléaire", *Annales ESC,* 1985, pp. 95-112.

Jochens, Jenny, "The Medieval Icelandic Heroine: Fact or Fiction?", *Viator* 17, 1986a, pp. 35-50.

Jochens, Jenny, "Consent in Marriage: Old Norse Law, Life, and Literature", *Scandinavian Studies,* 58: 1986b, pp. 142-76.

Jochens, Jenny, ""Með jákvæði hennar sjálfrar". Consent as Signifier in the Old Norse World", *Consent and Coercion to Sex and Marriage in Ancient and Medieval Societies,* ed. Angeliki A. Laiou, Washington D. C. 1993, pp. 271-89.

Jochens, Jenny, *Women in Old Norse Society,* London 1995.

Johnsen, Arne Odd, *Fra ættesamfunn til statssamfunn,* Oslo 1948.

Joyce, G. H., *Christian Marriage: An Historical and Doctrinal Study,* London 1933.

Jón Guðmundsson, "Um ættir og slekti.", *Safn til sögu Íslands og íslenzkra bókmennta að fornu og nýju,* 3, Copenhagen 1902, pp. 701-28.

Jón Helgason, "Islandske Bryllupstaler fra senmiddelalderen", *Bibliotheca Arnamagnana,* Vol. XX, Copenhagen 1960.

Jón Jóhannesson, *Íslendinga saga,* vol. I, Reykjavík 1956.

Jón Jóhannesson, *Íslendinga saga,* vol. II, Fyrirlestrar og ritgerðir um tímabilið 1262-1550, Reykjavík 1958.

Jón Ólafur Ísberg, "Sóttir og samfélag", *Saga* XXXIV, 1996, pp. 177-218.

Jón Ólafur Ísberg, "Plága", *Saga* XXXVI, 1998, pp. 238-43.

Jón Pétursson, *Íslenzkur kirkjurjettur*, Reykjavík 1863.

Jón Viðar Sigurðsson, *Frá goðorðum til ríkja. Þróun goðaveldis á 12. og 13. öld*, Sagnfræðirannsóknir. *Studia Historica*, vol. 10, Reykjavík 1989.

Jón Viðar Sigurðsson, "The Icelandic Aristocracy after the Fall of the Free State". *Scandinavian Journal of History*, 20, 1995a, pp. 153-66.

Jón Viðar Sigurðsson, "Forholdet mellom frender, hushold og venner på Island i fristatstiden", *Historisk Tidskrift*, 3, 1995b, pp. 311-30.

Jón Viðar Sigurðsson, "Heimili þingmennska, frændur og vernd á þjóðveldisöld", *Íslenska söguþingið 28. - 31. Maí 1997, Ráðstefnurit*, vol. I, eds. Guðmundur J. Guðmundsson, and Eiríkur K. Björnsson, Reykjavík 1998, pp. 107-16.

Jón Þorkelsson, *Om digtningen på Island i det 15. og 16. århundrede*, Copenhagen 1888.

Jón Þorkelsson, "Islandske haandskrifter i England og Skotland", *Arkiv for nordisk filologi*, 8, 1892, pp. 217-35.

Jørgensen, Jens Ulf, "Ægteskab. Alment og Danmark", KLNM XX, Copenhagen 1976, pp. 481-86.

Den Jyske Historiker, "Kønnet i historien", vol. 58-59, 1992.

Katalog over den Arnamagnæanske håndskriftsamling, vol. 1-2, Copenhagen 1889.

Keesing, Roger M., *Cultural Anthropology. A Contemporary Perspective*, London 1981.

Kelly, Kathleen Coyne, *Performing Virginity and Testing Chastity in the Middle Ages*, London 2000.

King, P. D., "The Barbarian Kingdoms", *The Cambridge History of Medieval Political Thought*, Cambridge 1988, pp. 123-53.

Klapisch-Zuber, Christine, "Women and the Family", *The Medieval World*, ed. Jacques Le Goff, London 1990, pp. 285-311.

Kleven, Hans I., *Norrøn arverett og samfunnsstruktur*, Larvik 2001.

KLNM: *Kulturhistorisk leksikon for nordisk middelalder fra vikingetid til reformationtid*, I-XXII, Copenhagen 1956-1978.

Korpiola, Mia, "An Uneasy Harmony: Consumation and Parental Consent in Secular and Canon Law in Medieval Scandinavia", *Nordic Perspectives on Medieval Canon Law*, ed. Mia Korpiola, Helsinki 1999a, pp. 125-50.

Korpiola, Mia, "Controlling Their Children's Choice: Strategies of Parental Control of Marriage in Medieval Europe and Scandinavia", *Ægteskab i Norden fra Saxo til i dag*, eds. Kari Melby, Anu Pylkkänen and Benthe Rosenbeck, *Nord* 1999:14, Copenhagen 1999b, pp. 71-106.

Korpiola, Mia, ed., *Nordic Perspectives on Medieval Canon Law,* Helsinki 1999.

Korpiola, Mia, *Between Betrothal and Bedding: The Making of Marriage in Sweden, ca. 1200-1600,* Helsinki 2004.

Kuber, Adam, *Wives for cattle. Bridewealth and Marriage in Southern Africa,* London 1982.

Kvinnearbeid i Norden fra vikingtiden til reformasjonen. Foredrag fra et nordisk kvinnehistorisk seminar i Bergen 2-7 august 1983, Bergen 1985.

Köstler, Rudolf, "Raub-, Kauf- und Friedelehe bei den Germanen", *Zeitschrift der Savigny-Stiftung für Rechtsgeschichte,* Germanistische Abteilung 63, 1943, pp. 92-136.

Lahtinen, Anu, "So the respectable widow sold her land to him", *Family, Marriage and Property Devolution in the Middle Ages,* ed. Lars Ivar Hansen, Tromsø 2000, pp. 107-116.

Laiou, Angeliki E. ed. *Consent and Coercion to Sex and Marriage in Ancient and Medieval Societies,* Washington D.C. 1993.

Landau, Peter, "The importance of Classical Canon Law in Scandinavia in the 12th and 13th centuries", *How Nordic are the Nordic Medieval Laws?* eds. Ditlev Tamm and Helle Vogt, *Medieval Legal History* I, Copenhagen 2005, pp. 24-39.

Lára Magnúsardóttir, "Agameðöl kirkjunnar fyrir siðaskipti: Bannfæringar", *Íslenska söguþingið 28.–31. Maí 1997. Ráðstefnurit,* vol. II, eds. Guðmundur J. Guðmundsson and Eiríkur K. Björnsson, Reykjavík 1998, pp. 210-20.

Lára Magnúsardóttir, *Bannfæring og kirkjuhald á Íslandi 1275-1550. Lög og rannsóknarforsendur,* Reykjavík 2007.

Le Play, F., *L'Organistation de la famille suvivant le vrai modèle signalé par l'histoire de toutes les races et tous les temps,* Tours 1871.

Lehman, K., *Verlobung und Hochzeit nach den nordgermanischen Rechten des früheren Mittelalters,* München 1882.

L'Hermite-Leclercq, "L'Ordre Féodal (XIe – XIIe Siécles)", *Histoire des femmes en occident,* eds. Georges Duby and Michelle Perriot, vol. II, Paris 1991.

Ljungfors, Åke, "Formelbyggnad", KLNM IV, Copenhagen 1959, pp. 484-86.

Loftur Guttormsson, "Hjúskapur og hugarfar. Árstíðasveiflur hjónavígslna 1660-1860. Samanburðarathugun", *Saga* XXX,1992, pp. 157-96.

Loftur Guttormsson, *Kristni á Íslandi. Frá siðaskiptum til upplýsingar,* ed. Hjalti Hugason, vol. III, Reykjavík 2000.

Lowe, Kate, "Secular Brides and Convent Brides: Wedding ceremonies in Italy during the Renaissance and Counter-Reformation", Trevor Dean and Kate Lowe (eds.), *Marriage in Italy 1300-1650*, Cambridge 1998, pp. 41-65.

McCarthy, Conor, *Marriage in Medieval England: Law, Literature and Practice,* New York 2004.

Magnús Már Lárusson, "Festermål", KLNM IV, Copenhagen1959a, pp. 236-40.

Magnús Már Lárusson, "Formulabok", KLNM IV, Copenhagen 1959b, p. 492.

Magnús Már Lárusson, "Félag", KLNM IV, Copenhagen 1959c, pp. 212-13.

Magnús Már Lárusson, "Hovedgård", KLNM VI, Copenhagen 1961, pp. 707-10.

Magnús Már Lárusson, "Incest", KLNM VII, Copenhagen 1962a, pp. 374-75.

Magnús Már Lárusson, "Jónsbók", KLNM VII, Copenhagen 1962b, pp. 612-18.

Magnús Már Lárusson, "Jordejendom", KLNM VII, Copenhagen 1962c, pp. 671-77.

Magnús Már Lárusson, "Morgongave", KLNM XI, Copenhagen 1966, pp. 699-700.

Magnús Már Lárusson, "Odelsrett", KLNM XII, Copenhagen 1967, pp. 499-502.

Magnús Már Lárusson, "Á höfuðbólum landsins", *Saga,* IX, 1971, pp. 40-90.

Magnús Stefánsson, "Kirkjuvald eflist", *Saga Íslands,* II, Reykjavík 1975, pp. 57-144.

Magnús Stefánsson, "Frá goðakirkju til biskupakirkju", *Saga Íslands* III, Reykjavík 1978, pp. 111-260.

Magnús Stefánsson, "Seksualitet og synd i middelalderen", *Liv og helse i middelalderen,* vol. VI, ed. Ingvild Öye, Onsdagskveld i Bryggen Museeum Bergen 1991, pp. 49-60.

Magnús Stefánsson, "Islandsk egenkirkevesen", *Rett og Historie. Festskrift til Gudmund Sandvik,* eds. Dag Michalsen and Knut Sprauten, Oslo 1997, pp. 138-62.

Magnús Stefánsson, *Staðir og staðamál. Studier islandske egenkirkelige og beneficialrettslige forhold i middelalderen,* vol. I, Historisk Institutt, Universitetet i Bergen skrifter, Bergen 2000.

Makowski, Elizabeth, "The Conjugal Debt and Medieval Canon Law", *Journal for Medieval History,* 3, 1977, pp. 99-114.

Margrete I. Regent of the North. The Kalmar Union 600 Years, Essays and Catalogue, Danish National Museum, Copenhagen 1997.

Maurer, Konrad, *Die Bekehrung des norwegischen Stammes zum Christenthume in ihrem geschichtlichen Verlaufe quellenmässig geschildert,* vol. 1-2, Osnabrück 1855-1856.

Maurer, Konrad, *Udsigt over de nordgermaniske retskilders historie,* Christiania 1878.

Mauss, Marcel, *The Gift. The form and reason for exchange in archaic societies,* London 1990.

Már Jónsson, *Blóðskömm á Íslandi 1270-1870,* Reykjavík 1993.

Már Jónsson, "Textatengsl nokkurra elstu handrita Jónsbókar", *Líndæla. Sigurður Líndal sjötugur 2. júlí 2001,* Reykjavík 2001, pp. 373-87.

Melhuus, Mari, Ingrid Rudie and Jorun Solheim, "Antropologien og kjønnet", *Forståelser av kjønn*, eds. Arnhild Taksdal and Karin Widerberg, Oslo 1992.

Miller, William Ian, *Bloodtaking and Peacemaking, Feud, Law and Society in Saga Iceland,* Chicago 1990.

Molho, Anthony, *Marriage alliance in late medieval Florence,* Cambridge 1994.

Morris, Ian, "The Use and Abuse of Homer", *Classical Antiquity*, 1986, pp. 81-138.

Murray, Jacqueline, "Thinking about gender: The Diversity of Medieval Perspectives", *Power of the weak*, Chicago 1985, pp. 1-26.

Murray, Jacqueline, "Historicizing sex, sexualizing history", *Writing Medieval History*, ed. Nancy Partner, London 2005, pp. 133-52.

Mäkinen, Virpi, "The Rights of the Poor: An Argument against Franciscans", *Nordic Perspectives on Medieval Canon Law*, ed. Mia Korpiola, Helsinki 1999, pp. 41-49.

Napran, Laura, "Marriage Contracts in the Twelfth Century: the Case of Renaud of Saint-Valéry and Edela of Ponthieu", *Family, Marriage and Property Devolution in the Middle Ages*, ed. Lars Ivar Hansen, Tromsø 2000, pp. 117-32.

Natvig Aas, Kristin, "Patriarkatsteoriernas maktförståelse bör nyangeras", *Kvinnoveten-skaplig tidskrift*, 2, 1993, pp. 27-44.

Nielsen, Hanne R., "Køn, kultur, repræsentation. Nyere tendenser i international kvinde-historisk forskning", *Kønnet i historien, Den Jyske Historiker,* 58-59, 1992, pp. 7-51.

Nors, Thyra, "Kampen om ægteskabet. En konfliktfyldt historie om kirkens forsøg på at genne lægfolk ind i den hellige ægtestand", *Den jyske Historiker*, 42, 1987, pp. 28-46.

Nors, Thyra, "Illegitimate Children and Their High-Born Mothers. Change in the Perception of Legitimacy in Mediaeval Danmark", *Scandinavian Journal of History*, 21, 1996, pp. 17-37.

Nors, Thyra, "Anders Sunesen, det internationale ægteskab og dansk politik", *Anders Sunesen – Danmark og verden i 1200-tallet,* ed. Kurt Villad Jensen, Odense 1998a, pp. 37-52.

Nors, Thyra, "Ægteskab og politik i Saxos Gesta Danorum", *Historisk Tidskrift*, 98:1, 1998b, pp. 1-33.

Nors, Thyra, "Slægtstrategier hos den danske kongeslægt i det 12. århundrede: svar til Helge Paludan", *Historie* 1, 2000, pp. 55-68.

Norseng, Per, "Lovmaterialet som kilde til tidlig nordisk middelalder", *Kilderne til den tidlige middelalders historie. Rapporter til den XX nordiske historikerkongres,* vol. I, ed. Gunnar Karlsson, Reykjavík 1987, pp. 48-77.

Nylander, Ivar, "Kanonisk rätt", KLNM VIII, Copenhagen 1963, pp. 222-24.

Olivecrona, S. R. D. K., *Om makars giftorätt i bo,* Uppsala 1882.

Ordbog over det norrøne prosasprog, Registre, Copenhagen 1989.

Ordbog til det ældre danske sprog (1300-1700), vol. I-V, Copenhagen 1881-1918.

Ormøy, Ragnhild, "Inheritance and Division of Wealth on the Death of a Husband", *Family, Marriage and Property Devolution in the Middle Ages,* ed. Lars Ivar Hansen, Tromsø 2000 pp. 99-106.

Orri Vésteinsson, "Skjalagerð og sagnaritun", *Samtíðarsögur,* vol. II, Akureyri 1994, pp. 625-37.

Orri Vésteinsson, *The Christianization of Iceland. Priests, Power, and Social Change 1000-1300,* Oxford 2000.

Ólafur Lárusson, "Lögbók Íslendinga (Jónsbók)", *Monumenta typographica Islandica 3,* Copenhagen 1934, pp. 49-88.

Ólafur Lárusson, "Elzta óðal á Íslandi", *Byggð og saga,* 1944, pp. 230-43.

Partsch, Gottfried, *Das Witwirkungsrecht der Familiengemeinschaft im alteren walliser Recht,* Genève 1951.

Patersson, Hans, *Morgongåvoinstitutet i Sverige under tiden fram till omkring 1734 års lag,* Lund 1973.

Payer, Pierre, J., *Sex and the Penitentials: The Development of a Sexual Code 550-1150,* London 1983.

Páll Eggert Ólason, *Íslenzkar æviskrár. Frá landnámstímum til ársloka 1965,* vol. I-VI, Reykjavík 1948-1976.

Páll Vídalín, *Skýríngar yfir Fornyrði lögbókar þeirrar, er Jónsbók kallast,* Reykjavík 1854.

Pedersen, Frederik, "The *fællig* and the family: the understanding of the family in Danish medieval law", *Continuity and Change,* 7 (1), 1992, pp. 1-12.

Pedersen, Frederik, "Romeo and Juliet of Stonegate. A Medieval Marriage in Crisis", *Bortwick Paper,* No 87, 1995, pp. 1-31.

Pedersen, Frederik, "Maritalis Affectio": Marital Affection and Property in Fourteenth-Century York Cause Papers", *Women, Marriage and Family in Medieval Christendom: Essays in Memory of Michael M. Sheehan,* eds. C. M. Rousseau and J. Rosenthal, Kalamazoo 1998, pp. 175-209.

Pedersen, Frederik, *Marriage Disputes in Medieval England,* London 2000.

Peters, Christine, "Gender, Sacrament, and Ritual. The making and meaning of Marriage in late Medieval and early Modern England", *Past and Present,* vol. 169, 2000, pp. 63-96.

Phillpotts, Bertha S., *Kindred and Clan in the Middle Ages and after. A Study in the Sociology of the Teutonic Races*, New York 1913.

Poos, Larry R., "Ecclesiastical Courts, Marriage, and Sexuality in Late Medieval Europe", *New Approaches to the History of Late Medieval and Early Modern Europe.* Selected Proceedings of Two International Conferences at The Royal Danish Academy of Sciences and Letters in Copenhagen in 1997 and 1999, eds. Troels Dahlerup and Per Ingesman, The Royal Danish Academy of Sciences and Letters, Copenhagen 2009.

Reynolds, Philip L., *Marriage in the Western Church. The Christianization of Marriage during the Patristic and Early Medieval Periods*, New York 1994.

Reynolds, Philip L., and John Witte, Jr., eds. *To have and to hold. Marrying and Its Documentation in Western Christendom, 400-1600*, Cambridge 2007.

Rian, Østein, "Giftermål og familie som elitedannende faktorer i 1600-tallets Bratsberg", *Historisk Tidskrift*, 4, 1990, pp. 471-83.

Michael Rouche, ed., *Mariage et sexualité au Moyen Age. Accord ou crise?*, Paris 2000.

Rowlands, Alison, "Book Review on Reordering Marriage and Society in Reformation Germany, by Joel F. Harrington", *Social History*, vol. 23, I, 1998, pp. 103-104.

Sabean, David Warren, *Property, production, and family in Neckarhausen, 1700-1870*, Cambridge 1990.

Sabean, David Warren, *Kinship in Neckarhausen 1700-1870*, Cambridge 1998.

Safley, Thomas Max, *Let no Man put asunder. The control of Marriage in the German Southwest: a Comparative Study, 1550-1600*, Missouri 1984.

Salisbury, J. E., "Bestiality in the Middle Ages", *Sex in the Middle Ages. A Book of Essays*, ed. J. E. Salisbury, New York, 1991, pp. 173-86.

Salonen, Kirsi, *The Penitentiary as a Well of Grace in the Late Middle Ages. The example of the Province of Uppsala 1448-1527*, Helsinki 2001.

Sandvik, Gudmund, "Ægteskab. Norge", KLNM XX, Copenhagen 1976, p. 494.

Sandvik, Gudmund, "Rettshistorie. Europeisk rettshistorie i mellomalderen. Førelesninger", *Jussens venner* 5, Oslo 1989.

Sandvik, Gudmund, "Rettshistorie", *Jussens venner* 6/7, Oslo 1990.

Sandvik, Hilde, '*Umyndige*' *kvinner i handel og håndverk. Kvinner i bynæringer i Christiania i siste halvdel av 1700-tallet*, Oslo 1992.

Sandvik, Hilde, "Kjønnsperspektiv på tidlig moderne tids økonomi – med vekt på arbeid og økonomisk rådighet i familieøkonomien", *Rapport III, Fra kvinnehistorie til kjønnshistorie? Det 22. nordiske historikermøte Oslo 13.-18. august 1994*, Oslo 1994, pp. 93-106.

Sandvik, Hilde, "Decision-making on marital property in Norway, 1500-1800", *The Marital*

Economy in Scandinavia and Britain 1400-1900, eds. Amy Louise Erickson and Maria Ågren, Women and Gender in the early Modern world, Aldershot 2005, pp. 111-26.

Sawyer, Birgit, *Kvinnor och familj i det forn- och medeltidiga Skandinavien*, Skriftserie fra Historisk Institutt, no. 34, Trondheim 1998.

Sawyer, Birgit, *The Viking-Age Rune Stones. Custom and commemoration in Early Medieval* Scandinavia, Cambridge 2000.

Sawyer, Birgit and Peter Sawyer, *Medieval Scandinavia. From Conversion to Reformation circa 800-1500*. The Nordic series, vol. 17, London 1993.

Schneider David M., *A Critique of the Study of Kinship*, Michigan 1992.

Scott, Joan Wallach, *Gender and the Politics of History*, New York 1988 (revised second edition 1999).

Scott, Joan Wallach, "Gender. A Useful Category of Historical Analyses", *Feminism and History*, 1996, pp. 152-80.

Scott, Joan and Linda Gordon, "Review and Reply", *Signs*, vol. 15, no. 4, 1990, pp. 848-60.

Segalen, Martine, *Historical Anthropology of the Family*, Cambridge 1996.

Sheehan, Michael M., *Marriage, Family and Law in Medieval Europe: Collected Studies*. ed. James K. Farge, Cardiff 1996.

Sheehan, Michael M. and Jacqueline Murray, *Domestic Society in Medieval Europe. A select Bibliography*, Toronto 1990.

Sigurður Líndal, "Upphaf kristni og kirkju", *Saga Íslands I*, Reykjavík 1974, pp. 227-88.

Sigurður Líndal, "Ægteskab", KLNM XX, Copenhagen 1976a, pp. 495-501.

Sigurður Líndal, "Ætt", KLNM XX, Copenhagen 1976b, 591-94.

Sigurður Líndal, "Lögfesting Jónsbókar 1281", *Tímarit lögfræðinga*, 32, 1982, pp. 182-95.

Sigurður Líndal, "Um þekkingu Íslendinga á rómverskum og kanónískum rétti frá 12. öld til miðrar 16. aldar", *Úlfljótur. Afmælisrit*, vol. 50. no. 1, 1997, pp. 241-73.

Silja Aðalsteinsdóttir and Helgi Þorláksson, eds., *Förändringar i kvinnors villkor under medeltiden. Uppsatser framlagda vid ett kvinnohistoriskt symposium i Skálholt, Island, 22.-25. juni 1981*. Ritsafn Sagnfræðistofnunar 9, Reykjavík 1983.

Sjöberg, Maria, "Kvinnans underordning en undtagshistorie?", *Historisk Tidskrift*, 3. 1997, pp. 459-62.

Smith, Richard, "Kin and Neighbors in a Thirteenth-Century Suffolk Community", *Journal of Family History*, 4, 1979, pp. 219-56.

Sommerstadt, Lena, "Mejerskor, industrialisering och välfärds-politik. Argument för en komparativ genusforskning", *Rapport III, Fra kvinnehistorie til kjønnshistorie?* Det *22. nordiske historikermøte Oslo 13.-18. august 1994*, Oslo 1994, pp. 107-20.

Stefán Karlsson, "Ég aum, sek og syndug. Skriftarmál Ólafar Loptsdóttur", *Morgunblaðið* 22/5,1988.

Sveinbjörn Rafnsson, *Studier i Landnámabók. Kritiska bidrag till den isländska fristatstidens historia,* Bibliotheca Historica Lundensis 31, Lund 1974.

Sveinbjörn Rafnsson, "Skjalabók Helgafellsklausturs. Registrum Helgafellense", *Saga,* XVII, 1979, pp. 165-186.

Sveinbjörn Rafnsson, "Þorláksskriftir og hjúskapur á 12. og 13. öld", *Saga,* XX, 1982, pp. 114-29.

Sveinbjörn Rafnsson, "Forn hrossreiðalög og heimildir þeirra. Drög til greiningar réttarheimildar Grágásar", *Saga,* XXVIII, 1990, pp. 131-48.

Sveinbjörn Rafnsson, *Sögugerð Landnámabókar. Um íslenska sagnaritun á 12. og 13. öld.* Ritsafn sagnfræðistofnunar 35, Reykjavík 2001.

Sverrir Jakopsson, "Friðarviðleitni kirkjunnar á 13. öld", *Saga,* XXXVI, 1998a, pp. 7-46.

Sverrir Jakopsson, "Griðarmál á ófriðaröld", *Íslenska söguþingið 28. –31. Maí 1997. Ráðstefnurit,* vol. I, eds. Guðmundur J. Guðmundsson and Eiríkur K. Björnsson, Reykjavík 1998b, pp. 117-134.

Sýslumannaævir, vol. II. Með skýringum og viðaukum eftir Jón Pétursson og Hannes Þorsteinsson, Reykjavík 1889-1904.

Tentler, Thomas N., *Sin and Confession on the Eve of the Reformation,* Princeton 1977.

Torfi Tulinius, "Guðs lög í ævi og verkum Snorra Sturlusonar", *Ný Saga,* 1996, pp. 31-40.

van Houts, Elisabeth, "Women and writing of history in the early Middle Ages: the case of Abbess Mathilda of Essen and Aethelweard", *Early Medieval Europe,* vol. 1, 1992, pp. 53-68.

van Houts, Elisabeth, *Memory and Gender in Medieval Europe 900-1200,* London 1999.

van Houts, Elisabeth, ed., *Medieval Memories. Men, Women and the Past, 700-1300,* Essex 2001.

Vauchez, André, "La question du célibat ecclésiastique dans l'Occident médiéval: un état de la recherche", *Medieval Spirituality in Scandinavia and Europe. A Collection of Essays in Honour of Tore Nyberg,* eds. Lars Bisgaard, Carsten Selch Jensen, Kurt Villads Jensen and John Lind, Odense 2001, pp. 21-32.

Vestergaard, Torben Anders, "The system of kinship in early Norwegian law", *Mediaeval Scandinavia,* 1988, pp. 160-93.

Vésteinn Ólason, *Íslensk bókmenntasaga,* vol. II, Reykjavík 1993.

Vilhjálmur Finsen, "Fremstilling af den islandske familieret efter Grágás", *Annaler for Nordisk oldkyndighed og historie,* København 1849, pp. 150-331.

Vogt, Helle, *Slægtens funktion i Nordisk højmiddelalderret – kanonisk retsideologi og fredsskabende lovgivning,* København 2005.

Wemble, Suzanne F., *Women in Frankish Society: Marriage and the Cloister 500-900,* Philadelphia 1981.

Wetterberg, Christina Carlsson., "Från patriarkat till genussystem – och vad kommer seden?", *Kvinnovetenskaplig tidskrift,* 3, 1992, pp. 34-48.

White, Stephan D., *Custom, Kinship and Gifts to Saints: The Laudadio Parentum in Western France 1050-1150,* Chapel Hill 1988.

Widén Solveig, "Morgongavan som grund for ankeförsörjning", *Förandringar i kvinnors villkor under medeltiden. Uppsatser framlagda vid ett kvinnohistoriskt symposium i Skálholt, Island, 22.-25. juni 1981,* eds. Silja Aðalsteinsdóttir and Helgi Þorláksson, Ritsafn Sagnfræðistofnunar 9, Reykjavík 1983, pp. 71- 81.

Wiesner-Hanks, Merry E., *Gender in History,* Oxford 2001.

Winberg, Christer, *Grenverket. Studier rörende jord, släktskapssystem och ståndaprivilegier.* Skrifter utgivna av institutet för rättshistorisk forskning. Serien I. Rättshistoriskt bibliotek, vol. 38, Stockholm 1985.

Witte, John, Jr., *From Sacrament to Contract. Marriage, Religion and Law in Western Tradition,* Louisville 1997.

Wogan-Browne, Jocelyn, "Rerouting the Dower, The Anglo – Norman Life of St. Audrey by Marie (of Chatteris?)", *Power of the Weak,* eds. Jennifer Carpenter and Sally-Beth Maclean, Chicago 1995, pp. 27-55.

Þorkell Jóhannesson, *Lýðir og landshagir,* vol. I, Reykjavík 1965.

Þorkell Jóhannesson, *Saga Íslendinga,* vol. VII, Tímabilið 1770-1830, Reykjavík 1950.

Øye, Ingvild, "Middelalderkvinner i tverrfaglig belysning", *Historisk tidskrift,* 4, 1990, pp. 435-54.

Appendices

Appendix I. Marriage contracts 1351 to 1600

Abbreviations used:
A: delivering letter = *afhendingarbréf*
B: gift of the bench = *bekkjargjöf*
C: contract of marriage = *kaupmáli*
D: declaration = *lýsing*
Dis: dispensation = *leyfisbréf*
F: the gift of one fourth = *fjórðungsgjöf*
G: letters of gift = *gjafabréf*
H: joint possession = *helmingarfélag*
Hm: dowry = *heimanmundur/heimanfylgja*
Kjörgripur: masterpiece
K: brideprice = *mundur*
L: legal gift = *löggjöf*
M: separate property = *máli*
Morn: morning gift = *morgungjöf*
R: report concerning contract = *skýrsla um kaupmála*
S: agreement = *samþykktarbréf*
T: countergift = *tilgjöf*
Túndarg: the gift of one tenth, compare to legal gift
ú: summary of a contract = *útdráttur*
U: type of contract uncertain
W: letter of witnesses = *vitnisburðarbréf*
Þ: personal things = *þing*

The year is the year of the entry into marriage. Where this date is not known the date of the relevant document is given. Types of document are related to the kind of documents in which the information about the contract is to be found. Types of agreements are either uncertain, joint possessions or separate belongings of the wife. Types of gifts covers those types mentioned in the contracts.

1. The period 1351 to 1400

Year and source	**names of the couple**	**types of document**	**types of agreement**	**types of gifts**
1366: DI V, p. 3.	Ingimundur Uthyrmisson Hólmfríður Ögmundsdóttir	Ú	U	B, M, T
1380: DI III, pp. 351-52.	Þórður Bessason[1] Járngerður Gilsdóttir	C	U	B, Morn, T
1381: DI IV, pp. 13-14.	Ólafur Sigurðsson Jórunn Brynjólfsdóttir	C	U	
1383: DI IX, pp. 19-20	Gudbjartur Ásgrímsson[2] Þorbjörg Þorsteinsdóttir	R	U	
1397: DI III, pp. 616-17.	Vigfús Hólm Guðríður Ingimundardóttir	C	M	

2. The period 1401 to 1450

Year and source	**names of the couple**	**types of document**	**types of agreement**	**types of gifts**
1402: DI III, pp. 678-79.	Jón Gunnlaugsson Þóra Ketilsdóttir	C	H	B
1402: DI III, pp. 679-70.	Brandur Sölvason Guðlaug Ketilsdóttir	C	H	B
1405: DI III, pp. 705-706.	Arnoddur Brandsson Sigríður Guðmundsdóttir	C	M	Heim, T, Morg, B
1408: DI III, p. 756, see also III, pp. 720-21, IV, pp. 316-17.	Þorsteinn Ólafsson Sigríður Björnsdóttir	W	U	
1418: DI IV, pp. 264-65.	Ari Guðmundsson Þorgerður Ólafsdóttir	A	M	
1420: DI IV, pp. 277-78.	Einar Jónsson Sigríður Einarsdóttir	C	H	

Continued →

1 He received "heimanjörð", the main land of the family.

2 DI IX, p. 19. It is said that when he was young he studied in "Paris in Germany".

Year and source	names of the couple	types of document	types of agreement	types of gifts
1420: DI IV, pp. 278-79.	Halldór Jónsson Oddfríður Aradóttir	G	U[3]	
1423: DI IV, p. 312.[4]	Guðmundur Arason Helga Þorleifsdóttir	C	H	F, B
1427: DI VIII, pp. 344-45.	Þorsteinn Magnússon Ólöf Arnadóttir	C	U	T, B, Morg, F
1428: DI IV, p. 358.	Þorleifur Egilsson Sigríður Þórarinsdóttir	C	M	
1429: DI IV, pp. 391-92.	Sigmundur Oblandsson Ingveldur Erlendsdóttir	W	U	
1433: DI IV, p. 525.	Hákon Jónsson Oddfríður Aradóttir	C	M	F, B
1434: DI IV, pp. 548-49.	Ormur Loftsson Solveig Þorleifsdóttir	C	M	F, T, B, Morg
1436: DI IV, pp. 562-63 for *máli*, DI IV, pp. 588-89 for *helmingarfélag*	Þorvarður Loftsson[5] and Margrét Vigfúsdóttir	C	M OG H[6]	T, B, Morg, F[7]
1439: DI IV, pp. 602-603.	Þórður Sigurðsson[8] Ingibjörg Halldórsdóttir	C	M	B, F, K
1445: DI IV, pp. 667-78.[9]	Steindór Jónsson Ingunn Ólafsdóttir	W	H	
1446: DI IV, pp. 673-74.	Ólafur Geirmundsson Sigríður Þorsteinsdóttir	C	M	T, B
1449: DI V, p. 30.	Þorkell Einarsson Ólöf Narfadóttir	C	H	F, K

3 This is probably a *helmingarfélag*, because the father of the bride gave her a half part of a property and her coming husband the other half.

4 See also DI V, pp. 108-109, witnesses' letter concerning the same contract.

5 He had the landed property at Eiðar, but she had Hlíðarenda in Fljótshlíð. The description of the marriage of Margrét and Vigfús appears in *Annálar* I, p. 57 for the year 1436.

6 Made in 1439, see DI IV, pp. 588-89, 589-90.

7 *Fjórðungsgjöf*, it was given when they made a *helmingarfélag* in 1439. In DI IV, p. 589 it is stated that according to the *Réttarbót* of King Hákon from 1306 a wife could not deny her husband to make a *félag*, but could do so when they had children.

8 He had the landed property at Hagi in Barðaströnd *til kaups* with her, and the land was 60 *hundrað*. Her *máli* was put into the land, but she had brought the landed property at Þorfinnstaðir in Valþjófsstaður into the marriage. The heirs of the husband could claim back the land at Hagi.

9 This document was made many years after their marriage.

3. The period 1451 to 1500

Year and source	names of the couple	types of document	types of agreement	types of gifts
1451: DI V, pp. 87-88.	Guðmundur Sigurðsson Guðný Þorsteinsdóttir	C	M	T,B, Morg
1452: DI V, pp. 98-99.	Indriði Hákonarson Guðrún Gísladóttir	C	M	T, B, Morg
1455: DI V, pp. 130-31.	Jón Alexisson Bergljót Jónsdóttir	C	H	F
1458: DI V, pp. 171-72.	Indriði Jónsson Ingibjörg Pálsdóttir	C	M	F, K, Þ, B, Morg
1460: DI V, pp. 205-206.	Gísli Filuppusson[10] Ingibjörg Eyjólfsdóttir	C	H	K
1461: DI V, pp. 610-11.	Bjarni Ólason, Margrét Ólafsdóttir	C	M	
1462: DI V, pp. 372-73.	Andrés Guðmundsson Þorbjörg Ólafsdóttir	C	H[11]	F, B, Morg, Tíundarg.
1463: DI VI, pp. 396.	Hallur Jónsson Guðný Jónsdóttir	G	U	
1464: DI V, pp. 415-16.	Björn Sæmundsson Snjófríður Björnsdóttir	C	M	
1465: DI V, pp. 454-55.[12]	Eyjólfur Böðvarson Guðrún Þorkelsdóttir	C	M	Hm, Morg, B, T
1466: DI V, pp. 466-67.	Jón Ólason Þorlaug Árnadóttir	W	U	
1467: DI V, pp. 504-506.[13]	Hrafn Brandsson Margrét Eyjólfsdóttir	C	M	B, Morg, T

Continued →

10 Filippus and Gróa gave their son Gísli the landed property at Hagi in Barðaströnd, for 100 *hundrað.*

11 In 1471 they made a *helmingarfélags* see DI V, pp. 646-47. In 1473 he sold land with the consent of his wife; see DI, V, pp. 705-706. This Andrés was an illegitimate son of Guðmundur Arason.

12 At the end of this document it states that after this written agreement concerning property transfer had been made, the husband *festa* the wife to be a legal wife according to the law of God with the right words being said.

13 At the end of this contract concerning the property agreement it is mentioned that the contract had been made according to the law of God.

Year and source	**names of the couple**	**types of document**	**types of agreement**	**types of gifts**
1467: DI V, pp. 506-507.	Magnús Magnússon Sigríður Jónsdóttir	C	M	F
1467: DI V, pp. 508-509.	Finnbogi Jónsson Málfríður Torfadóttir	C	U	T, B[14]
1467: DI V, p. 473.	HallvarðurÁmundarson [15] Valgerður Kenegsdóttir	C	M	B, Morg, L
1468: DI V, pp. 532-33.	Sumarliði Eiríksson Guðrún Árnadóttir	C[16]	U	
1469: DI V, pp. 554-55.	Páll Jónsson Margrét Eyjólfsdóttir	C	U	
1470: DI V, pp. 580-81.	Bárður Jónsson Guðrún Halldórsdóttir	C	M	T
1470: DI V, pp. 560-61, compare to DI VI, pp. 275-76, DI VI, pp. 276-78, DI VI, pp. 347-48, 350-51.	Loftur Ormsson Gunnhildur Pétursdóttir	C	H	T
1476: DI VI, pp. 92-93.	Guðni Eyjólfsson Guðrún Þorkelsdóttir	C	H	B, Morg
1477: DI VI, pp. 118-19.	Magnús Þorkelsson Kristín Eyjólfsdóttir	C	H	F
1479: DI VI, pp. 226-29.	Ásgrímur Sigmundsson Steinunn Þórarinsdóttir	C	M	L
1480: DI VI, pp. 295-96.[17]	Einar Oddson Ása Egilsdóttir	C	U	T
1481: DI VI, p. 392.	Jón dan Björnsson Kristín Sumarliðadóttir[18]	C	H	F

Continued →

14 And other gifts he wanted to give to her honor.

15 After they had made a contract, he *festa* the woman according to the law of God, using the words that should be spoken. He had 300 *gyllini* and 100 of these became her *bekkjargjafa*, morning gift and legal gift.

16 See also *Tylftardómur* from 1 July 1504: "um úrskurð Finnboga Jónssonar lögmanns um peninga eptir Sumarliða Eiríksson og Guðrúnu konu hans Arnadóttir". DI IX, pp. 46-48.

17 "För þesse giorningur fram … med laugligri festingu."

18 See also DI, VIII, pp. 217-18, "transkriftarbréf eftir Jón dan Björnsson og Björn Guðnason", and VIII, p. 262-63. There was a problem as to what land the couple should receive. Kristín got Hrafnseyri in Arnarfjörður, but Björn got Sæból in Ingjaldssandi. Then it all came to be shared in two equal portions, and it was specifically mentioned that she accepted this division.

Year and source	names of the couple	types of document	types of agreement	types of gifts
1483: DI VI, pp. 501-502.	Jón Jónsson Dýrfinna Gísladóttir	G	U	Hm
1485: DI VI, pp. 547-49, see also DI VII, pp. 317-18.	Sveinn Sumarliðason Guðríður Finnbogadóttir	C[19]	H	T, B, Morg[20]
1489: DI VI, pp. 675-76.	Magnús Áskelsson Guðríður Jónsdóttir	C	U	
1489: DI VI, pp. 648-49.	Þorvarður Bjarnason Ingibjörg Ormsdóttir[21]	W	U	
1489: DI VI, pp. 660-61.	Sigurður Þorleifsson Kristín Finnbogadóttir	C	H,	T, B, Morg,[22] Þing
1489: DI VI, p. 683.	Bjarni Jónsson Guðrún Ólafsdóttir	W	H	
1491: DI VI, p. 738.	Þorgils Þorsteinsson Guðrún Jónsdóttir	C	H	F, L
1491: DI VI, pp. 760-62.[23]	Jón Finnbogason Helga Sæmundsdóttir	C	M	T, L
1491: DI VI, p. 746.	Vigfús Bjarnason[24] Steinunn Gunnarsdóttir	W	U	
1492: DI VII, pp. 138-39 (see also DI VII, pp. 136-37).	Ólafur Filippusson Vigdís Jónsdóttir	C	U	F, T

Continued →

19 See also "Tylftardóm frá 1. júli 1504 um úrskurð Finnboga Jónssonar lögmanns um peninga eptir Sumarliða Eiríksson og Guðrúnu konu hans Arnadóttir." DI IX, pp. 46-48. See also DI VIII, pp. 169-70 the judgement made according to the *réttarbót* from 1313.

20 "Gagngjald og gjöf sem kallast morgungjöf og bekkjargjöf".

21 She was legally betrothed according to the law of God, and then her property agreement was mentioned.

22 *Tilgjöf* and *bekkjargjöf* are called *gagngjald og gjöf.*

23 This contract is very detailed, and gives also information about movable wealth.

24 He had been married first to Kristrún Ormsdóttir, but she had died. This information is given in a witness's letter recording Vigfús' declaration that he did not own more than the land at Meðaldal in Dýrafjörður and four *kúgildi.* Everything else from his earlier marriage was the property of his children from his first marriage.

Year and source	names of the couple	types of document	types of agreement	types of gifts
1494: DI VII, pp. 223-34.	Finnbogi Jónsson Málfríður Torfadóttir	C	U	
1495: DI VII, pp. 250-51.	Ari Andrésson[25] Þórdís Gísladóttir	C	H	
1497: DI VII, pp. 325-26.	Jón Sigmundsson Björg Þorvaldsdóttir	C	U	F, L, T
1498: DI VII, p. 406.	Hallvarður Eiríksson Þorgerður Jónsdóttir	C	H	F
1499: DI VII, p. 424.	Bárður Jónsson Sigríður Jónsdóttir	W	U	

4. The period 1501 to 1550

Year and source	names of the couple	types of document	types of agreement	types of gifts
1501: DI VII, pp. 543-44.	Björn Þorleifsson Ingibjörg Pálsdóttir[26]	C	U	Hm
1505: DI VII, pp. 747-48.	Sumarliði Bjarnason Agnes Hallbjarnardóttir	C	M	
1505: DI VIII, pp. 230-31.[27]	Þorvarður Erlendsson Kristín Gottskálksdóttir	C	H	T, B, Morg
1505: DI VII, p. 755.	Þorsteinn Finnbogason Cecilia Torfadóttir	C	U	Hm, L
1506: DI VIII, pp. 103-107.	Sigmundur Halldórsson Ingigerður Þorsteinsdóttir	J	M	
1507: DI VIII, pp. 136-38.	Bjarni Guðnason Ragnhildur Bjarnadóttir	C	H[28]	

Continued →

25 Andrés Guðmundsson had given the land at Saurbæ in Rauðasandur "með Ara" in accordance with the rules concerning *langfeðgaeign*.

26 The landed property, at Flatey in Breiðafjörður should revert to her parents if she did not have any children.

27 *Skarðsannáll* for 1510. See also DI VIII, pp. 281-82, *gjafabréf* from 1509.

28 She could choose which *höfuðból* she should have, if they had legitimate children.

Year and source	names of the couple	types of document	types of agreement	types of gifts
1507: DI VIII, pp. 165-66.	Björn Andrésson Guðrún Björnsdóttir[29]	C	H	K, F, Kjörgripur
1510: DI VIII, p. 331.	Ólafur Guðmundsson Þorbjörg Guðmundsdóttir	W[30]	U	
1512: DI VIII, pp. 364-65.	Jón Bjarnason Þorgerður Halldórsdóttir	C	U	
1515: DI VIII, pp. 543-44.	Jón Einarsson Kristín Gottskálksdóttir	C	M	F
1517: DI XII, pp. 74-75.	Jón Sturlason Guðný Grímsdóttir	W	U	
1521: DI VIII, pp. 812-13.	Jón Hallgrímsson Helen Þórarinsdóttir	J	U	
1523: DI IX, pp. 178-80.	Páll Grímsson Margrét Erlendsdóttir	C	M	F, T
1524: DI XI, p. 89.	Jón Þórðarson Sigríður Halldórsdóttir	C	U	K
1524: DI IX, pp. 249-50.	Jón Hallson Guðrún Finnbogadóttir	W	U	
1525: DI IX, pp. 286-87.	Jón Torfason Þórunn Einarsdóttir	C	M	F
1525: DI IX, pp. 288-89, compare to a judgement from 1554, see DI XII, pp. 734-35.	Erlendur Þorvarðsson Þórunn Sturludóttir	C	H	K, Hm, F
1526: DI IX, pp. 378-80.	Rafn Brandsson Þórunn Jónsdóttir	C	M	T
1527: DI IX, pp. 435-36.	Sveinn Jónsson Halldóra Einarsdóttir	C	M	F
1527: DI IX, pp. 473-74.	Þórarinn Steindórsson Oddný Jónsdóttir	C	M	F, Kjörgripur
1528: DI IX, pp. 476-77.	Lazarus Mattheusson Guðrún Ólafsdóttir	C	H	F

Continued →

29 She was 18 years old when they got married.

30 This is a testimony about publications of banns from a priest.

Year and source	names of the couple	types of document	types of agreement	types of gifts
1528: DI IX, pp. 466-67.	Koðran Ólafsson Guðný Brandsdóttir	C	M	F
1529: DI IX, pp. 498-99.	Þorsteinn Einarsson Guðrún Bessadóttir	C	M	
1529: DI IX, pp. 502-504.	Jón Einarsson Margrét Björnsdóttir	C	M	K, F
1530: Letter of *fjórðungsgjöf.* DI IX, pp. 553-54, and the contract DI IX, pp. 554-55.	Ari Jónsson Halldóra Þorleifsdóttir[31]	C	U	F
1531: DI IX, pp. 602-603.	Oddur Tumason Cecilia Ormsdóttir	C	M	F
1531: DI IX, pp. 603-605.	Eyjólfur Einarsson Helga Jónsdóttir	C	U	F, T
1532: DI IX, p. 643.	Ari Andrésson Þórdís Gísladóttir	C	H	
1533: DI XI, p. 113.	Jón Ólafsson Þóra Björnsdóttir	C	U	
1533: DI IX, pp. 655-57, compare to *löggjafar-bréf* from 1541, DI X, pp. 673-74.	Ísleifur Sigurðsson Þórunn Jónsdóttir[32]	C	U	T, L
1533: DI IX, pp. 658-59.	Björn Jónsson Steinunn Jónsdóttir	C[33]	U	
1534: DI IX, pp. 713-14.	Páll Vítusson Helga Jónsdóttir	C	U	
1534: DI IX, pp. 711-12.	Björn Þorvaldsson Herdís Gísladóttir	C	M	T
1535: DI IX, pp. 748-49.	Guðmundur Ólafsson Bergljót Sigmundsdóttir	W[34]	M	

Continued →

31 In this case she received all the land at the manor at Möðruvellir, although her father should hold it as long as he lived.

32 The land at Grund in Eyjafjörður should be held by her family.

33 He was a priest.

34 Witnesses' letter concerning legal marriage.

Year and source	names of the couple	types of document	types of agreement	types of gifts
1535: DI IX, pp. 739-40.	Ormur Sturluson Þorbjörg Þorleifsdóttir	C	M	T
1537: DI X, p. 116.	Jón Narfason Sesselía Bassadóttir	W	U	
1537: DI X, pp. 331-32.	Andrés Björnsson Guðlaug Jónsdóttir	C	M	K, F
1538: DI XII, p. 89.	Hallur Ólafsson Cecilia Guðmundsdóttir	C	H	
1539: DI X, pp. 421-22.	Grímur Jónsson Geirlaug Jónsdóttir	C	M	F, K
1539: DI X, p. 497.	Þórólfur Eyjólfsson Margrét Erlendsdóttir	G	U	
1540: DI X, pp. 546-47.	Þorvarður Helgason Guðrún Höskuldsdóttir	C[35]	U	
1541: DI X, pp. 652-54.	Einar Árnason Arndís Snorradóttir	Dis[36]	U	
1541: DI X, pp. 667-68, compare to DI XI, pp. 146-47.	Erlendur Þorvarðsson Guðrún Jónsdóttir	C	M	Hm, L, F
1542: DI X, p. 703.	Jón Grímsson Þórunn Helgadóttir	D[37]	U	
1542: DI X, pp. 716-17.	Jón Skúlason Ingibjörg Sigurðardóttir	C	M	T
1542: DI XI, pp. 162-63.	Guðmundur Skúlason Guðný Brandsóttir	C	M	F
1542: DI XI, pp. 165-66.	Árni Pétursson Þuríður Þorleifsdóttir	C	M	T
1543: DI XI, pp. 193-94.	Þorleifur Björnsson Ragnhildur Jónsdóttir	C[38]	U	

Continued →

35 Contract concerning landed property as well as declaration of legal marriage.

36 Dispensation from Bishop Gissur Einarsson, with reference to the Church Ordinance stating that couples related within four degrees were allowed to marry. This contract is in Latin.

37 Dispensation from Bishop Gissur Einarsson.

38 He was a priest. It says in the contract that if they were not allowed to marry their children should be adopted, and given the gift of *fjórðungsgjöf.*

Year and source	names of the couple	types of document	types of agreement	types of gifts
1543: DI XI, p. 257 the contract, DI XI, pp. 259-60 *festingarbréf.*	Gissur Einarsson Katrín Hannesdóttir	C	U	T, F
1543: DI XI, pp. 260-61.	Hallgrímur Pétursson Sigríður Einarsdóttir	C	M	T
1544: DI XI, p. 305.	Þorlákur Einarsson Guðrún Hannesdóttir	C[39]	U	F
1544: DI XI, pp. 414-15.	Ólafur Árnason Ragnhildur Þorsteinsdóttir	C	H	Kjörgripur
1544: DI XII, pp. 93-94.	Jón Þórarinsson Guðný Einarsdóttir	C	M	T
1545: DI XI, p. 435.	Bessi Þorsteinsson Guðrún Tumadóttir	C[40]	U	F
1546: DI XI, pp. 526-27.	Björn Hannesson Þórunn Daðadóttir	C	M	F
1547: DI XI, pp. 606-607.	Jón Arngrímsson Sigríður Narfadóttir	C[41]	M	
1547: DI XII, pp. 103, 104, 104-105.[42]	Jón Pálsson Ásdís Fúsadóttur	S	M	
1548: DI XI, pp. 667-68.	Nikulás Þorsteinsson Sigríður Einarsdóttir	C	U	K, F, T
1548: DI XII, pp. 119-20.	Pétur Vigfússon Þóra Jónsdóttir	C	H	
1549: DI XI, pp. 734-35.	Eiríkur Böðvarsson Guðrún Þorvarðardóttir	C	M[43]	
1549: DI XI, p. 739.	Örnólfur Jónsson Steinunn Ólafsdóttir	C	M	K, F

Continued →

39 Compare a personal letter of Bishop Gissur Einarsson about this marriage to the mother of the bride in DI XI, pp. 364-65.

40 This is a copy of a contract, and something is missing at the end of the document, but two women testify this contract.

41 "Minnisgreinar Gissurar biskups um kaupmálann."

42 There exist three testimonies of this contract.

43 This contract has the following statement: "og giördu þad fielag med sier. ad hennar mäle skylldi vera og standa oskert". It means that they had made that agreement (*fielag*) that her separate property (*mäle*) should continue to hold.

Year and source	names of the couple	types of document	types of agreement	types of gifts
1549: DI XI, pp. 719-20.	Jón Sigurðsson Margrét Eiríksdóttir	W	M	K
1549: DI XI, pp. 688-89.	Jón Þorsteinsson Halldóra Jónsdóttir	C, W	M	Hm, F
1550: DI XI, pp. 796-97.	Bjarni Marteinsson Guðríður Þorsteinsdóttir	C	M	
1550: DI XI, pp. 824-25.	Tumi Þorgrímsson Sigríður Magnúsdóttir	C	M	
1550: DI XI, pp. 822-23, *Alþingisbækur Íslands* I, pp. 172-73. [44]	Magnús Jónsson Elen Jónsdóttir	C	M	T, Þriðjun-gagóss

5. *The period 1551 to 1600*

Year and source	names of the couple	types of document	types of agreement	types of gifts
1551: DI XII, pp. 302-303.	Jón Einarsson Málmfríður Bjarnadóttir	C	M, L, T	L, T
1551: DI XII, p. 313.	Eggert Hannesson Sigríður Þorleifsdóttir	C	U	Hm
1552: DI XII, pp. 467-68.	Þorvarður Björnsson Guðrún Halldórsdóttir	C	M[45]	
1552: DI XII, p. 481.	Árni Guðmundsson Halldóra Loftsdóttir	W	H	
1553: DI XII, pp. 501-502.	Þorleifur Grímsson Solveig Halldórsdóttir	C	M	

Continued →

44 "Eftir kaupmála lögleg festing með þeim orðum sem tilheyra." In this contract the word *þriðjungagóss* is mentioned, but it is said to be in movable wealth.

45 In this contract the word *samvíxludagur* is mentioned.

Year and source	names of the couple	types of document	types of agreement	types of gifts
1553: DI XII, pp. 502-503.	Þorsteinn Guðmundsson Þórunn Jónsdóttir	C[46]	U	T, F, L
1553: AM dipl.isl.fasc. LXIX, 4.[47]	Jón Oddsson Hallotta Magnúsdóttir	W	U	
1553: DI XII, pp. 559-60.	Jón Magnússon Ragnheiður Pétursdóttir	W	U	Hm
1553: DI XII, pp. 627-28.	Torfi Þorsteinsson Guðný Magnúsdóttir	C[48]	U	T
1553: DI XII, pp. 619-21.	Steinn Ólafsson Arnbjörg Brandsdóttir	C	M	
1553: DI XII, pp. 615-16.	Jón Sigurðsson Þórunn Árnadóttir	C	M	T, F, Hm
1553: DI XII, pp. 502-503.	Þorsteinn Guðmundsson Þórunn Jónsdóttir	C	U	
1553: DI XII, pp. 628-69.	Ólafur Jónsson Steinunn Jónsdóttir	C	U	T
1554: DI XII, pp. 745-46, compare to 775.	Egill Jónsson Guðný Þorleifsdóttir	C	M	F, Kjörgipur
1554: DI XII, pp. 711-12.	Árni Einarsson Vilborg Eiríksdóttir	W	U	
1554: DI XII, p. 699.	Gísli Jónsson Kristín Eyjólfsdóttir	W	M	L
1555: DI XIII, pp. 89-90.	Finnbogi Tumason Þórunn Þórðardóttir	C	U	
1555: DI XIII, pp. 72-73.	Séra Bjarni Gíslason Málfríður Torfadóttir	C	M	T
1555: DI XIII, pp. 96-97.	Hrólfur Bjarnason Ingibjörg Bjarnadóttir	C	U	F, L

Continued →

46 Compare to DI XII, pp. 534-35, *samþykktarbréf* and witnesses letter of ibid., p. 504, and of ibid., pp. 507-509.

47 Compare to *Bréfabók Guðbrands biskups* for the year 1588, p. 436. This is a testimony about this marriage of 1553.

48 The word *hjonavixla* is mentioned in this contract.

Year and source	names of the couple	types of document	types of agreement	types of gifts
1555: DI XIII, p. 81.	Séra Þorlákur Hallgrímsson Helga Jónsdóttir	C	U	
1555: DI XIII, p. 80.	Eiríkur Snjólfsson Þuríður Þorleifsdóttir	C	M	L
1555: DI XIII, pp. 100-101.	Séra Jón Halldórsson Helga Þórðardóttir	G	M	
1555: DI, pp. 44-45.	Þorsteinn Torfason Þorgerður Sturludóttir	U	U	
1556: DI XIII, pp. 131-33.	Þórður Þorleifsson Steinunn Ólafsdóttir	C	M	K, F
1556: DI XIII, pp. 127-28, 270-73, 278-81.	Páll Jónsson Helga Aradóttir	J	U	L, F
1557: DI XIII, pp. 240-41.	Benedikt Halldórsson Valgerður Björnsdóttir	C	M	T
1558: DI XIII, pp. 342-43.	Jón Ormsson Þórunn Gísladóttir	C	M	F, Kjörgripur
1558: DI XIII, pp. 343-44.	Sigurður Bjarnason Ragnheiður Björnsdóttir	C[49]	M	F
1559: DI XIII, p. 394.	Ólafur Ormsson Margrét Jónsdóttir	C	U	
1559: DI XIII, pp. 439-40.	Jón Ólafsson Guðrún Árnadóttir	C	U	
1559: DI XIII, pp. 440-44.	Eggert Hannesson Sessilía[50] Jónsdóttir	C	U	
1559: DI XIII, p. 394.	Jón Sigurðsson Halldóra Þorbergsdóttir	C	M	L
1560: DI XIII, pp. 463-64.	Ólafur Ólafsson Sigríður Þorsteinsdóttir	W	U	F
1560: DI XIII, pp. 506-507.	Magnús Þorleifsson Agnes Magnúsdóttir	C	M	K, F

Continued →

49 "Lögleg samvíxla í kirkju eftir ordinansen."

50 Her name may have been Steinunn, compare to *leyfisbréf konungs* from 1563, in DI XIV, p. 76.

Year and source	names of the couple	types of document		types of agreement	types of gifts
1560: DI XIII, pp. 530-31.	Jörundur Steinmóðsson Andrésa Einarsdóttir	C		M	
1560: DI XIII, pp. 543-44.	Ólafur Guðmundsson Margrét Halldórsdóttir	C		H	
1561: DI XIII, pp. 628-29.	Halldór Ormsson Þórdís Eyjólfsdóttir[51]	C		M	
1561: DI XIII, pp. 660-61.	Jón Björnsson Guðlaug Þorgilsdóttir	C		M	K, F, L
1562: DI XIII, p. 687.[52]	Jón Magnússon Guðlaug Björnsdóttir	C		H	
1562: DI XIV, pp. 18-19.	Jón Þórðarson Guðrún Jónsdóttir	C		U	
1562: DI XIII, pp. 683-86.	Einar Ásmundsson Málfríður Bjarnadóttir	C		U[53]	
1562: DI XIV, pp. 18-19.	Jón Þórðarson Ingveldur Jónsdóttir	C		H	
1562: DI XIII, pp. 758-59.	Einar Eyjólfsson Vilborg Bjarnadóttir	C		M	F, T
1563: DI XIV, pp. 170-71.	Sigurður Jónsson Guðný Jónsdóttir	C		M	F
1564: DI XIV, pp. 256-57	Séra Sveinn Bárðarson Ingunn Guðmundsdóttir	C		M	
1564: DI XIV, pp. 323-24.[54]	Þorleifur Björnsson Ragnhildur Jónsdóttir	C[55]		U	
1565: DI XIV, pp. 422-25.	Magnús Jónsson prúði Ragnheiður Eggertsdóttir	C		M	K, F, Hm
1565: DI XIV, pp. 413-15.	Gottskálkur Magnússon Guðrún Gottskálksdóttir	C	M	M	L, T

Continued →

51 Þórdís was not allowed to give the land which he had given to her, to any other persons than Halldór or his heirs.

52 Árni Magnússon, the editor of the document mentions that this couple was very poor.

53 She did not give any wealth to *kaups né gjafar*.

54 Compare to the *hjúskaparleyfi*, marriage dispensation: DI XIV, pp. 277-80.

55 *Festi hana fyrir kirkjudyrum.* (Betrothed her in front of the church door).

Year and source	names of the couple	types of document	types of agreement	types of gifts
1565: DI XIV, pp. 365-68.	Séra Halldór Benediktsson Helga Illugadóttir	J[56]	U	
1563: DI XIV, pp. 170-71.	Sigurður Jónsson Guðný Jónsdóttir	C	M	F
1565: DI XIV, pp. 363-64.	Magnús Magnússon Guðrún Þorleifsdóttir	Dis	U	
1567: DI XV, pp. 46-47.	Eiríkur Böðvarsson Guðrún Þórðardóttir	W	H	
1567: DI XIV, p. 575.	Sveinn Bjarnason Halldóra Loftsdóttir	C	M	
1568: DI XV, pp. 159-60.	Bjarni Sturluson Ingibjörg Pálsdóttir	C	M	Hm, T, L
1568: DI XV, pp. 147-48.	Jón Grímsson Hildur Magnúsdóttir	C	M	Hm, T, F
1569: DI XV, pp. 190-92.	Jón Einarson Helga Guðmundsdóttir	C	M	
1570: DI XV, pp. 422-23.	Þorvarður Þorólfsson Vilborg Gísladóttir	C	M	Hm F,
1570: DI XV, pp. 411-12.	Finnbogi Einarsson Þuríður Þorgrímssdóttir	C	U	Kjörgripur
1573: AM dipl. isl. fasc. LVII, p. 14.	Ólafur Örnólfsson Sigríður Jónsdóttir	C	U	
1574: AM dipl.isl.fasc. LXV, p. 27.	Erlendur Þórðarson Guðfinna Arnfinnsdóttir	C	U	
1586:[57]	Björn Benediktsson Elen Pálsdóttir	C	U	
1588: AM dipl. isl. fasc. LXIX, 8.[58]	Sæmundur Árnarson Elen Magnúsdóttir	W	U	

Continued →

56 Judgement concerning divorce.
57 NAI, Steinklefi XXXIX, 60, AM Apogr. 1234, compare also to 61, AM Apogr. 1235.
58 See also NAI, Steinklefi XXXIX, 216, pp. 244-46.

Year and source	**names of the couple**	**types of document**	**types of agreement**	**types of gifts**
1588: No. 217 in MSTeph. 27 4to pp. 244-46[59]	Daði Bjarnason Solveig Gunnarsdóttir	T	U	
1590: *Alþingisbækur Íslands* II, p. 202.	Jón Guðmundsson Kristín Einarsdóttir	C	M	K, Heiman, T
1591: Dip. Isl. nr. 25.[60]	Daði Bjarnason Arnfríður Benediktsdóttir	C	U	
1598: *Alþingisbækur Íslands* III, pp. 136-37.	Björn Benediktsson Elín Pálsdóttir	D	U	

59 NAI, Steinklefi XXXIX "Handrit dr. Jóns Þorkelssonar".

60 In the National and University Library of Iceland.

Appendix II. Contract of helmingarfélög *1402-1567*

Year	source	couple
1402	DI III, pp. 678-79.	Jón Gunnlaugsson and Þóra Ketilsdóttir
1402	DI III, pp. 679-80.	Brandur Sölvason and Guðlaug Ketilsdóttir
1420	DI IV, pp. 277-78.	Einar Jónsson and Sigríður Einarsdóttir
1423	DI IV, p. 312.	Guðmundur ríki Arason and Helga Þorleifsdóttir
1436	DI IV, pp. 562-63, for *máli*, DI IV, pp. 588-89 for *helmingarfélag*, made 1439.	Þorvarður Loftsson and Margrét Vigfúsdóttir
1445	DI IV, pp. 667-78.	Steindór Jónsson and Ingunn Ólafsdóttir
1449	DI V, p. 30.	Þorkell Einarsson and Ólöf Narfadóttir
1455	DI V, pp. 130-31.	Jón Alexisson and Bergljót Jónsdóttir
1460	DI V, pp. 205-206.	Gísli Filuppusson and Ingibjörg Eyjólfsdóttir
1462	DI V, pp. 372-73.	Andrés Guðmundsson and Þorbjörg Ólafsdóttir[61]
1470	DI V, pp. 560-61.	Loftur Ormsson and Gunnhildur Pétursdóttir
1476	DI VI, pp. 92-93.	Guðni Eyjólfsson and Guðrún Þorkelsdóttir
1477	DI VI, pp. 118-19.	Magnús Þorkelsson and Kristín Eyjólfsdóttir
1481	DI VI, p. 392.	Jón dan Björnsson and Kristín Sumarliðadóttir[62]
1485	DI VII, pp. 317-18.	Sveinn Sumarliðason and Guðríður Finnbogadóttir[63]
1489	DI VI, pp. 660-61.	Sigurður Þorleifsson and Kristín Finnbogadóttir
1489	DI VI, p. 683.	Bjarni Jónsson and Guðrún Ólafsdóttir
1491	DI VI, p. 738.	Þorgils Þorsteinsson and Guðrún Jónsdóttir
1495	DI VII, pp. 250-51.	Ari Andrésson and Þórdís Gísladóttir
1498	DI VII, p. 406.	Hallvarður Eiríksson and Þorgerður Jónsdóttir

Continued →

61 In 1471 they made a *helmingarfélagskontrakt*, see DI V, pp. 646-47.

62 See also DI VIII, pp. 217-18, 262-63.

63 See also: "Tylftardóm frá 1. júli 1504 um úrskurð Finnboga Jónssonar lögmanns um peninga eptir Sumarliða Eiríksson og Guðrúnu konu hans Arnadóttir;" DI IX, pp. 46-48.

Year	source	couple
1505	DI VIII, pp. 230-31, *Skarðsannáll* anno 1510. See also DI VIII, pp. 281-82, *gjafabréf* from 1509.	Þorvarður Erlendsson and Kristín Gottskálksdóttir
1507	DI VIII, pp. 136-38.	Bjarni Guðnason and Ragnhildur Bjarnadóttir
1507	DI VIII, pp. 165-66.	Björn Andrésson and Guðrún Björnsdóttir
1525	DI IX, pp. 288-89.	Erlendur Þorvarðsson and Þórunn Sturladóttir
1528	DI IX, pp. 476-77.	Lazarus Mattheusson and Guðrún Jónsdóttir
1532	DI IX, p. 643, see also DI VII, pp. 250-51.	Ari Andrésson and Þórdís Gísladóttir
1538	DI XII, p. 89.	Hallur Ólafsson and Cecilia Guðmundsdóttir
1544	DI XI, pp. 414-15.	Ólafur Árnason and Ragnhildur Þorsteinsdóttir
1548	DI XII, pp. 119-20.	Pétur Vigfússon and Þóra Jónsdóttir
1552	DI XII, p. 481.	Árni Guðmundsson and Halldóra Loftsdóttir
1560	DI XIII, pp. 543-44.	Ólafur Guðmundsson and Margrét Halldórsdóttir
1562	DI III, p. 687.	Jón Magnússon and Guðlaug Björnsdóttir
1562	DI XIV, pp. 14-15.	Jón Þórðarson and Ingveldur Jónsdóttir
1567	DI XV, pp. 46-47.	Eiríkur Böðvarsson and Guðrún Þórðardóttir

Appendix III. Marriage gifts

All references to the sources can be found in Appendix I: Marriage contracts.

1. Bekkjargjöf: *the gift of the bench 1402-1505*

Year	couple	type of contract
1402	Brandur and Guðlaug	Helmingarfélag
1402	Jón and Þóra	Helmingarfélag
1405	Arnoddur and Sigríður	Máli
1423	Guðmundur and Helga	Helmingarfélag
1427	Þorsteinn and Ólöf	Unknown
1433	Hákon and Oddfríður	Máli
1434	Ormur and Solveig	Máli
1436	Þorvarður and Margrét	Máli and helmingarfélag
1439	Þórður and Ingibjörg	Máli
1446	Ólafur and Sigríður	Máli
1451	Guðmundur and Guðný	Máli
1452	Indriði and Guðrún	Máli
1458	Indriði and Ingibjörg	Máli
1462	Andrés and Þorbjörg	Helmingarfélag
1465	Eyjólfur and Guðrún	Máli
1467	Hrafn and Margrét	Máli
1467	Finnbogi and Málfríður	Unknown
1467	Hallvarður and Valgerður	Máli
1476	Guðni and Guðrún	Helmingarfélag
1485	Sveinn and Guðríður	Helmingarfélag
1489	Sigurður and Kristín	Helmingarfélag
1505	Þorvarður and Kristin	Helmingarfélag

Sources: See Appendix I

2. Morgungjöf: *the morning gift 1405 to 1505*

Year	**couple**	**type of contract**
1405	Arnoddur and Sigríður	Máli
1427	Þorsteinn and Ólöf	Unknown
1434	Solveig and Ormur	Máli
1436	Þorvarður and Margrét	Máli and helmingarfélag
1451	Guðmundur and Guðný	Máli
1452	Indriði and Guðrún	Máli
1458	Indriði and Ingibjörg	Máli
1462	Andrés and Þorbjörg	Helmingarfélag
1465	Eyjólfur and Guðrún	Máli
1467	Hrafn and Margrét	Máli
1467	Hallvarður and Valgerður	Máli
1476	Guðni and Guðrún	Helmingarfélag
1485	Sveinn and Guðríður	Helmingarfélag
1489	Sigurður and Kristín	Helmingarfélag
1505	Þorvarður and Kristín	Helmingarfélag

Sources: See Appendix I

3. Kvánarmundur *1458 to 1590*

Year	couple	type of contract
1458	Indriði and Ingibjörg	Máli
1460	Gísli and Ingibjörg	Helmingarfélag
1507	Björn and Guðrún	Helmingarfélag
1524	Jón and Sigríður	Unknown
1525	Erlendur and Þórunn	Helmingarfélag
1529	Jón and Margét	Máli
1537	Andrés and Guðlaug	Máli
1548	Nikulás and Sigríður	Unknown
1549	Örnólfur and Steinunn	Máli
1549	Jón and Margrét	Máli
1556	Þórður and Steinunn	Máli
1560	Magnús and Agnes	Máli
1561	Jón and Guðlaug	Máli
1565	Magnús and Ragnheiður	Máli
1590	Jón and Kristín	Máli

Sources: See Appendix I

4. Heimanfylgja: *dowry 1405 to 1590*

Year	couple	type of contract
1405	Arnoddur and Sigríður	Máli
1465	Eyjólfur and Guðrún	Máli
1483	Dýrfinna and Jón	Unknown
1501	Björn and Ingibjörg	Unknown
1505	Þorsteinn and Cecilia	Unknown
1541	Erlendur and Guðrún	Máli
1543	Gissur and Katrín	Unknown
1549	Jón and Halldóra	Máli
1551	Eggert and Sigríður	Unknown
1553	Ragnheiður and Jón	Unknown
1590	Jón and Kristín	Máli

Sources: See Appendix I

5. Heimanmundur: *dowry 1525 to 1570*

Year	couple	type of contract
1525	Erlendur and Þórunn	Unknown
1553	Jón and Þórunn	Máli
1565	Magnús and Ragnheiður	Máli
1568	Bjarni and Ingibjörg	Máli
1568	Jón and Hildur	Máli
1570	Þorvarður and Vilborg	Unknown

Sources: See Appendix I

6. Þing: *personal thing 1458 and 1489*

Year	**couple**	**type of contract**
1458	Indriði and Ingibjörg	Máli
1489	Sigurður and Kristín	Helmingarfélag

Sources: See Appendix I

7. Kjörgripur *1439 to 1570*

Year	**couple**	**type of contract**
1439	Þórður and Ingibjörg	Máli
1449	Þorkell and Ólöf	Helmingarfélag
1507	Bjarni and Ragnhildur	Helmingarfélag
1527	Þórarinn and Ragnhildur	Máli
1539	Grímur and Geirlaug	Máli
1544	Ólafur and Ragnhildur	Helmingarfélag
1546	Björn and Þórunn	Máli
1554	Árni and Vilborg	Unknown
1558	Jón and Þórunn	Máli
1570	Finnbogi and Þuríður	Unknown

Sources: See Appendix I

8. Tilgjöf: *countergift 1366 to 1590*

Year	**couple**	**type of contract**
1366	Ingimundur and Hólmfríður	Unknown
1380	Þórður and Járngerður	Unknown
1404	Arnoddur and Sigríður	Máli
1427	Þorsteinn and Ólöf	Unknown
1434	Ormur and Solveig	Máli
1436	Þorvarður and Margrét	Máli and helmingarfélag
1446	Ólafur and Sigríður	Máli
1451	Guðmundur and Guðný	Máli
1452	Indriði and Guðrún	Máli
1465	Eyjólfur and Guðrún	Máli
1467	Hrafn and Margrét	Máli
1467	Finnbogi and Málfríður	Unknown
1470	Bárður and Guðrún	Máli
1476	Guðni and Guðrún	Helmingarfélag
1480	Einar and Ása	Unknown
1485	Sveinn and Guðríður	Helmingarfélag
1489	Sigurður and Kristín	Helmingarfélag
1491	Jón and Helga	Máli
1492	Ólafur and Vigdís	Unknown
1497	Jón and Björg	Unknown
1505	Þorvarður and Kristín	Helmingarfélag
1523	Páll and Margrét	Máli
1526	Rafn and Þórunn	Máli
1531	Eyjólfur and Helga	Unknown
1533	Ísleifur and Þórunn	Unknown

Continued →

Year	couple	type of contract
1535	Ormur and Þorbjörg	Máli
1542	Jón and Ingibjörg	Máli
1542	Árni and Þuríður	Máli
1543	Gissur and Katrín	Unknown
1543	Hallgrímur and Sigríður	Máli
1544	Jón and Guðný	Máli
1548	Nikulás and Sigríður	Unknown
1550	Magnús and Elen	Máli
1551	Jón and Málmfríður	Máli
1553	Þorsteinn and Þórunn	Unknown
1553	Torfi and Guðný	Unknown
1553	Jón and Þórunn	Máli
1553	Ólafur and Steinunn	Unknown
1555	Bjarni and Málfríður	Máli
1557	Benedikt and Valgerður	Máli
1562	Einar and Vilborg	Máli
1565	Gottskálk and Guðrún	Máli
1568	Bjarni and Ingibjörg	Máli
1568	Jón and Hildur	Máli
1590	Jón and Kristín	Máli

Sources: See Appendix I

9. Löggjöf: *legal gift 1467 to 1568*

Year	**couple**	**type of contract**
1467	Hallvarður and Valgerður	Máli
1479	Ásgrímur and Steinunn	Máli
1491	Þorgils and Guðrún	Helmingarfélag
1491	Jón and Helga	Máli
1497	Jón and Björg	Unknown
1505	Þorsteinn and Cecilia	Unknown
1533	Ísleifur and Þórunn	Unknown
1541	Erlendur and Guðrún	Máli
1551	Jón and Málmfríður	Máli
1553	Þorsteinn and Þórunn	Unknown
1554	Gísli and Kristín	Máli
1555	Hrólfur and Ingibjörg	Unknown
1555	Eiríkur and Þuríður	Máli
1556	Páll and Helga	Helmingarfélag
1559	Jón and Halldóra	Máli
1561	Jón and Guðlaug	Máli
1562	Einar and Vilborg	Máli
1565	Gottskálkur and Guðrún	Máli
1568	Bjarni and Ingibjörg	Máli

Sources: See Appendix I

10. Fjórðungsgjöf *1423 to 1570*

Year	couple	type of contract
1423	Guðmundur and Helga	Helmingarfélag
1427	Þorsteinn and Ólöf	Unknown
1433	Hákon and Oddfríður	Máli
1434	Ormur and Solveig	Máli
1436	Þorvarður and Margrét	Máli and helmingarfélag
1439	Þórður and Ingibjörg	Máli
1449	Þorkell and Ólöf	Helmingarfélag
1455	Jón and Bergljót	Helmingarfélag
1458	Indriði and Ingibjörg	Máli
1462	Andrés and Þorbjörg	Helmingarfélag
1467	Magnús and Sigríður	Máli
1470	Bárður and Guðrún	Máli
1477	Magnús and Kristin	Helmingarfélag
1481	Jón and Kristín	Helmingarfélag
1491	Þorgils and Guðrún	Unknown
1492	Ólafur and Vigdís	Unknown
1497	Jón and Björg	Unknown
1498	Hallvarður and Þorgerður	Helmingarfélag
1507	Björn and Guðrún	Helmingarfélag
1515	Jón and Kristín	Máli
1523	Páll and Margrét	Máli
1525	Jón and Þórunn	Máli
1525	Erlendur and Þórunn	Helmingarfélag
1527	Sveinn and Halldóra	Máli
1527	Þórarinn and Oddný	Máli
1528	Lazarus and Guðrún	Helmingarfélag

Continued →

Year	couple	type of contract
1528	Koðran and Guðný	Máli
1529	Jón and Margrét	Máli
1530	Ari and Halldóra	Máli
1531	Oddur and Cecilia	Máli
1531	Eyjólfur and Helga	Unknown
1537	Andrés and Guðlaug	Máli
1539	Grímur and Geirlaug	Máli
1541	Erlendur and Guðrún	Máli
1542	Guðmundur and Guðný	Máli
1543	Þorleifur and Ragnhildur	Máli
1543	Gissur and Katrín	Unknown
1544	Þorlákur and Guðrún	Unknown
1545	Bessi and Guðrún	Unknown
1546	Björn and Þórunn	Máli
1548	Nikulás and Sigríður	Unknown
1549	Örnólfur and Sigríður	Unknown
1549	Jón and Halldóra	Máli
1553	Þorsteinn and Þórunn	Unknown
1553	Jón and Þórunn	Máli
1554	Árni and Vilborg	Unknown
1555	Hrólfur and Ingibjörg	Unknown
1556	Þórður and Steinunn	Máli
1556	Helga and Páll	Unknown
1558	Jón and Þórunn	Máli
1558	Sigurður and Ragnheiður	Máli
1560	Ólafur and Sigríður	Unknown
1560	Magnús and Agnes	Máli
1561	Jón and Guðlaug	Máli

Continued →

Year	couple	type of contract
1562	Einar and Vilborg	Máli
1563	Sigurður and Guðný	Máli
1568	Jón and Hildur	Máli
1568	Bjarni and Ingibjörg	Máli
1570	Þorvarður and Vilborg	Máli

Sources: See Appendix I

Appendix IV. List of Icelandic bishops appointed directly by the Papacy

In the see of Skálholt	In the see of Hólar
Michael 1382/83-92, Denmark	Jón Skalli Eiríksson 1357-90, Norway
Vilchin Henriksson 1394-1405, Denmark	Pétur Nikulásson 1391-1411, Denmark
Jón 1406-13, Denmark	Jón Tófason (Henriksson) 1411-23, Denmark
Árni Ólafsson 1413-20/26, Iceland	Jón Vilhjálmsson Craxton 1426-35, England
Jón Gerreksson 1426-33, Denmark	Jón Bloxwich 1435-41, England
Jón Vilhjálmsson Craxton 1435-38, England	Robert Wodborn 1441, England
*Godsvin Comhaer 1437-47, Holland	
Marcellus de Nieveriis 1448-62, Germany	
*Jón Stefánsson Krabbe 1436-64, Denmark	

** Uncertain if appointed directly by the Papacy.*

Source: Björn Þorsteinsson and Guðrún Ása Grímsdóttir, "Enska öldin, með viðaukum eftir Sigurð Líndal", Saga Íslands, *V, Reykjavík 1990, p. 41.*

List of abbreviations

AM: Arnamagnean collection of manuscripts in the Arnamagnean Institute.

AM dipl. isl. fasc.: Diplomatarium Islandicum, unpublished charters in the National Archives of Iceland.

AM ordbogen: A Dictionary of Old Norse Prose in the Arnamagnean Institute. The Dictionary is to be published.

Bsk. Bmf: *Biskupa sögur*. The Sagas of the Icelandic bishops.

DI: *Diplomatarium Islandicum, Íslenzkt fornbréfasafn* (published Icelandic charters from the Medieval Ages), Copenhagen and Reykjavík 1857-1972.

DN: *Diplomatarium Norvegicum* (published Norwegian charters from the Medieval Ages), Christiania/Oslo 1847-1976.

ÍF: *Íslenzk fornrit* (the Sagas of the Icelanders), Reykjavík 1968-2003.

IO: *Islandske Orginaldiplomer indtil 1450* (Icelandic original charters), Christiania 1888.

KLNM: *Kulturhistorisk leksikon for nordisk middelalder fra vikingetid til reformationtid*, Copenhagen 1956-1976, 2. publication 1980.

NAI: National Archives of Iceland, Þjóðskjalasafn Íslands.

NgL: *Norges gamle love* indtil 1387 (the old Norvegian law codes), Christiania 1846-1895.

Sts: *Sturlunga saga* (the Saga of the Sturlunga family), Reykjavík 1946.

Þjsks: Þjóðskjalasafn Íslands, the National Archives of Iceland.

Glossary and explanation

Aðalból: Main estate.

Affinity: Relationship created through marriage.

Agnate: Related through the paternal line or by patrilinear descent.

Alin, pl. álnir: Ell. A measure, 47.7 cm or 55.6 cm. As a length of homespun, the basic medium of exchange, the *alin* was a currency unit; one *hundrað* equalled 120 *álnir*.

Alþingi: The general assembly which was convened at Þingvellir at the end of June every year and lasted for two weeks.

Alþingisdómur: General assembly court.

Arfskot: Dispossession of heirs.

Bekkjargjöf: "Gift of the bench", gift given by the bridegroom to the bride on the wedding day.

Betrothal: *Festar.* A property agreement which took place at marriage according to a set of formalities and according to the oldest marriage legislation in *Grágás*, a minimum property qualification was prescribed as a condition for entering marriage.

Bilateral kinship: Kinship transmitted separately by the mother and by the father, with each filiation serving different ends.

Biskupasögur: The Sagas of the Icelandic bishops.

Bóndi, pl. bændur: It is difficult to translate the Icelandic word *bóndi* (pl. *bændur*) into English, both because the meaning of the word in the Icelandic language has changed through time, and because it has very different connotations from similar words in English. In medieval texts, the word *bóndi* could best be translated as yeoman or franklin, that is, a freeholder. Thus, the term first involved some form of landownership, although etymologically it means simply a tiller of the earth. In the late Middle Ages *bóndi* was either one who lived on his own land or those who had leasehold. The term head of household can also be used.

Brigð: (Claim for) reversion.

Brideprice: The goods and/or service is assumed to have originally been paid by the parents of the future husband to the parents of the future wife. In Icelandic documents there is no evidence that this amount was given to the parents of the bride. It is instead an amount paid directly from the bridegroom or his parents to the bride. See also *Kvánarmundur, mundur.*

Brúðkaup/hlaup: Wedding.

Bú: Houshold, stock.

Cognatic kinship. See bilateral kinship.

Commonwealth: Period of ca. 930-1262/64 in Icelandic history. It was a period in which the inhabitants were not under any kingship, but when the general assembly, *Alþingi*, convened at Þingvellir, the Icelanders developed both a legislative and a judiciary system. They did not, however, create any centralised mechanism for enforcing the law. See *þjóðveldi.*

Consanguinity: Kinship between individuals claiming descent from a common ancestor.

Dower: A life estate to which a wife is entitled on the death of her husband.

Dowry: The goods and/or sevices offered by the family of the bride to her future husband. By extension, the term dowry has come to denote all matrimonial presents, whether from the husband's or the wife's family.

Eyrir, pl. aurar: An ounce of silver.

Festar: Betrothal. Binding a woman by contract before entering into marriage. Compare to making the agreement of *festarmál.*

Festarmál: See *festa.*

Fékaup: Agreement about financial affairs.

Félag: See *hjónafélag.*

Fjórðungsgjöf: A gift of one-fourth. One was allowed to give a quarter of one's non-inherited belongings to someone other than an heir, according to the law of *Jónsbók* from 1281. See also legal gift and *löggjöf.*

Forsagnarvottur: Primary witnesses.

Fylgikonur: Female followers. Often used about the concubines of the priests.

Gagngjald: A gift given against the dowry, *heimanfylgja*, called countergift. Used in *Grágás*, but later in *Jónsbók* it became designated *tilgjöf.*

Gamli Sáttmáli: "Old Covenant" from 1262-64 when Iceland became a tributary province in the Norwegian monarchy.

Gifta: To give a woman away in marriage.

Giftingamaður: Guardian of the bride.

Gratian's Decretum: Compilation of canon law made by Gratian around 1140, including extracts from Christian writers and Church council decisions.

Grágás: "Gray goose", the law of the Icelandic Commonwealth preserved in two manuscripts dated from around the mid-thirteenth century. The name is a fairly late creation, from the sixteenth century, and its origins are unclear.

Handaband: Handshake between members of two or more families, when agreeing on a deal, for instance concerning marriage.

Handsöl: Making an agreement by handshake.

Heimanfylgja: Dowry. A gift given by the parents to the bride to be married.

Heimanmundur: See *mundur* or *heimanfylgja.*

Helmingarfélag: A jointly owned property in marriage, where each part owned half of every property.

Hirðstjóri: The highest royal office in Iceland. The literal meaning of the term *hirðstjóri* is courtier, or a man of the court, and at first the function of the office was to lead the king's men in Iceland. The name *hirðstjóri* was used from 1271 until the mid-sixteenth century, when the title changed to *höfuðsmaður.*

Hjón: A married cople.

Hjónaband: Marriage. Literally meaning personal union between husband and wife.

Hjónafélag: Marriage agreement between a husband and a wife. Jointly-owned property in marriage where the woman owned one-third and the husband owned two-thirds, sometimes named *þriðjungsfélag.*

Hjónavígsla: The blessing of the spouses by a priest. Nuptial ceremony, wedding ceremony.

Hjúskapur: Agreement of the *hjú*, that is marriage made according to the rules of *festar.* An older term for marriage than *hjónaband.*

Hólar: One of the two bishop sees in Iceland, placed in the district of Eyjafjörður in the North of Iceland.

Höfuðból: Manor. Landed property, 60 hundred or more.

Höfuðsmaður: See *hirðstjóri.*

Hundrað: Measurement. One hundred = 120 alen *vaðmál* (cloth) or the same value as six cows. Thus "tólf, tuttugu, sextíu ... hundraða jörð" means land of twelve, sixty ... hundreds value. See also *jörð.*

Íslendinga sögur: The Sagas of the Icelanders written mainly in the thirteenth and fourteenth century about the period of the Icelandic settlement and life in Iceland in the decades afterwards.

Jarðarbrigð: Reclamation of land.

Jarðareigandi: Landowner.

Jarðareign: Possessions of land.

Jarðarhundrað: A hundred in an estate.

Jarðarkaup: The purchase of land.

Járnsíða: "Ironside", name of a law book which in 1271-73, after Iceland entered into union with Norway, superseded *Grágás.*

Jomfrukrenkere: "Those who had a sexual contact with maidens." Word used in Danish legal documents from the end of the sixteenth century about men who had a sexual relationship with maidens, with the result that they lost their maidenhood.

Jónsbók: *Jónsbók* is a written law code, called "Jón's book" after the law speaker Jón Einarsson, one of its authors. The code was first accepted in *Alþingi* in 1281, superseding the existing law book called *Járnsíða,* and it was to serve as the basis for the Icelandic legal system for centuries. After certain amendments and revisions had been made to the original version of *Jónsbók,* at the request of Icelanders, it took its final form in the early fourteenth century. In this form, it remained valid for around 400 years until absolutism was introduced in Iceland (1662). *Jónsbók* is not preserved in an original redaction, but the code exists in numerous medieval and later manuscripts.

Jörð: Land, an estate: in Icelandic very frequently equivalent to the Norse word "ból", or the Danish word "gaard". Thus "tólf, tuttugu, sextíu ... hundraða jörð" means land of twelve, twenty, sixty ... hundreds value.

Kaupbréf: A letter about a general agreement about transfer of landed property.

Kaupmáli: Contract, or an agreement usually about some financial affair and, in its most common use, about the marriage agreement.

Kaupmálabréf: A letter of marriage contract, referring to the financial agreement and sometimes also to some Christian elements of making marriage according to canon law.

Kjörgripur: A masterpiece, things or other valuable belongings which the spouses could give each other in marriage.

Konungasögur: The Sagas written by the Icelanders about the Norwegian and Danish kings.

Kúgildi: The price of a cow.

Kristniréttur hinn eldri: The old Christian law of *Grágás.*

Kristniréttur hinn nýi: New Christian law of Bishop Árni Þorláksson 1274.

Kvánarmundur: The wealth the husband brought into marriage. In the contract of the Late Middle Ages this term was used about all the material wealth the husband brougt in to marriage. The older meaning of the word was brideprice. See *Mundur.*

Kvánga: To marry a woman.

Kvennagiptingar: "Marriage of women", is a special chapter on women and marriage, in *Jónsbók.*

Landnámabók: Book of Settlement. An Icelandic telling about the persons who settled down in Iceland during the period 870-930.

Langaréttarbót: A law amendment issued to the Icelanders by the Danish king, Christian I in 1450, see *réttarbót.*

Laudatio Parentum: An institution based on the consent of the lineal relatives to transfer a part of the ancestral inheritance.

Lausafé: Movable goods.

Lawman: Presiding judge. See *lögmaður.*

Legal gift: See *löggjöf.*

Liber Extra: Papal lawbook from 1234, also called Gregory IX's decretals.

Lineage: A kinship-group descended from the same ancestor within the space of a few generations.

Línfé: Gift given by the bridegroom to the bride on the wedding day, often in the form of cloth.

Lýrit: (Power of) veto.

Lýsing: Publication of marriage banns.

Löggjöf: "Legal gift" introduced to the Icelanders in the law book of *Jónsbók.* Three types of legal gifts existed: a *vinargjöf,* literally meaning a gift to a friend, normally some personal thing; *fjórðungsgjöf,* a gift containing one-fourth of one's non-inherited belongings; and finally *tíundargjöf,* a gift which could not include more than one-tenth of one's inherited property.

Lögmaður: Lawman. Presiding judge, an office established in 1271 shortly after Iceland entered into a union with Norway. The lawman presided over the *Alþingi,* and its proceedings were illegal without his presence. The lawmen also served as presidents of the courts in *Alþingi,* selected judges, and directed the different functions of the assembly. There was initially only one lawman in Iceland, but from 1277 until the *Alþingi* was abolished in 1800, there were two at a time, one for the northwestern part of the country, another for the southeastern part.

Lögmáli: Lawful pre-emption right. First right to buy a share in a property.

Lögrétta: Law Council.

Lögsögumaður: The lawspeaker at the *Alþingi.*

Málakona: Wife married according to a contract of separate ownership.

Máldagi, pl. máldagar: A term for an agreement about property: an endowment agreement. A particular type of document recording the property belonging to a church and the condition of the endowment. The word could also be used about the endowment agreement in a marriage, compare to *máli.*

Máli: (Exercise of) pre-emption right, pre-emption agreement. Here normally used over the special type of marriage agreement, which allowed the wife to have a separate landholdning.

Málaland: Land subjected to pre-emption right.

Morgungjöf: "Gift of giving in the morning", a gift from husband to wife paid the morning after the wedding. Called "morning gift" in English.

Mundur: A sum, of at least one *mark,* which according to *Grágás* was promised by the prospective husband at the betrothal but usually paid later. Without the payment of *mundur* the marriage was invalid.

Mutual consent: Also named principal consent. According to canon law both the husband- and wife-to-be should give their consent to marriage.

New Christian law: See *Kristniréttur hinn nýi.*

Nýmæli: New law in *Grágás.*

Old Christian Law: See *Kristniréttur hinn eldri.*

Óðal: Patrimony.

Parental consent: Parental consent to marriage of their children.

Patrilineal system: A kinship system which counts only links through males.

Penitential: A handbook, containing a compilation of sins (the majority relating to sexuality) and the penalties they incur, drawn up for the use of clerics in the Middle Ages.

Primogeniture: Principle of inheritance, systematically favouring the oldest child, usually the oldest son, to the disadvantage of his younger siblings.

Próventa: Maintenance in old age.

Púsa: See *púsunarmessa.*

Púsunarmessa: Nuptial mass.

Retrait lignager: The "lineal re-purchase right" of the kin.

Réttarbót, pl. réttarbætur: Law amendments or corrections to the law. Most of those amendments were made at the end of the thirteenth and the beginning of the fourteenth century.

Skálholt: One of the two bishop sees in Iceland, placed in the south district of *Árnessýsla.*

Stóridómur: The "Large" or "Long Judgement" in literal translation, a statute passed in *Alþingi* on 30 June 1564, and ratified by the king the following year. *Stóridómur* redefined the penal code for moral offences, especially in cases connected with adultery and sexual intercourse between persons related either through affinity or consanguinity.

Sturlunga saga: A compilation of sagas from around 1300, containing several accounts of which the *Íslendinga saga* of Sturla Þórðarson is the greatest. Some of the Sagas in the collection were almost contemporary accounts about the political situation in Iceland in the thirteenth century.

Sýsla: County, the traditional administrative and juridical district in Iceland in the Middle Ages. The term itself was first used in *Jónsbók,* the code of law enacted in 1281, but it was only at the close of the Middle Ages that the geographical division of the country into counties was finished. In each county there was a bailiff (*sýslumaður*) who served as district judge, sheriff, and representative of the state in the county.

Sýslumaður: Baliff or sheriff, a district judge or commissioner. See *sýsla.*

Tilgjöf: Countergift. A gift given by the husband to the wife as a countergift for the dowry she brought with her.

Tíundargjöf: A gift of one-tenth. One could only give one-tenth of one's inherited property out of the family. See *legal gifts.*

Trolovelse: Engagement, Danish word for a promise of marriage.

Útjarðir: Outlying lands. Land attached to the manor or other less important landed property.

Viðgjald: "Payment added to other wealth", a term meaning the same as *gagngjald, tilgjöf, countergift*. It was a gift from the husband to augment the dowry of the bride. This term *viðgjald* was only known in *Grágás*, but not in later law regulations.

Þing: A personal thing which a woman brought with her into marriage, or received in a marriage contract. *Þing* was also used in the meaning assembly, see *Alþing*.

Þjóðveldi: Commonwealth. The Icelandic "republic" in the period from the establishment of the general assembly the *Alþingi* in 930, until Iceland became part of the Norwegian kingdom in 1262/64.

Þriðjungsfélag: See *hjónafélag*.

Ættleiðing: Adoption, literally in the meaning of taking a child into one's kin.

Danish summary

Ejendom og jomfrudom

Kristningen af ægteskabet på Island i middelalderen 1200-1600

På en vis måde drejer afhandlingen "Ejendom og jomfrudom. Kristningen af ægteskabet på Island i middelalderen 1200-1600" sig om at give en forklaring på selve eksistensen af det bevarede kildemateriale vedrørende ægteskab og ægteskabsindgåelse på Island i senmiddelalderen. Det gælder først og fremmest de knap 200 skriftligt opsatte ægteskabskontrakter, der er bevaret fra perioden mellem 1380 og 1600. Dette materiale er bevaret på grund af den politiske kamp om retten til ejendom og ressourcer, i hvilken ægteskabsindgåelser og familiealliancer spillede en central rolle. Alligevel handler afhandlingen ikke bare om kampen om jord, men snarere om kirkens indflydelse på ægteskabet på Island i middelalderen. Målet har været at analysere, hvordan kirken ændrede forståelsen af, hvad et gyldigt ægteskab var. En vigtig del af denne forandring bestod i, at der dannedes en ny forståelse af forholdet mellem kønnene i ægteskabet. Det er disse forandringers samfundsmæssige betydning, afhandlingen sætter sig for at afdække.

Undersøgelsen bygger i vid udstrækning på teoretiske overvejelser fra historisk antropologi og på anlæggelsen af et kønsperspektiv, noget der gøres nærmere rede for i *kapitel 1*. Det antropologiske perspektiv bruges til at analysere forandringer i den slægtsmæssige organisering i et førindustrielt og delvis førstatsligt samfund som det islandske og til at belyse sammenhængen mellem social organisering og kønsmæssig identitetsdannelse. Kønsperspektivet er særlig vigtigt for at analysere forskellen mellem konstruktionen af det kvindelige og det mandlige, både ifølge kanonisk ret og i den konkrete sociale praksis. Forandringer i ægteskabsritualer undersøges specielt som udtryk for en forandring i ægteskabets symbolske betydning. Ved siden af det historisk-antropologiske perspektiv og kønsperspektivet er det tredje perspektiv, afhandlingen anlægger, et strategiperspektiv. Aristokratiets magtgrundlag var jordejendom og andre naturgivne ressourcer, som var genstand for en stadig kamp mellem de forskellige slægter, og ved kirkens omdefinering af, hvad et gyldigt ægteskab var, forandredes betingelserne for denne kamp og dermed også hele det politiske landskab.

Kapitel 2 handler om undersøgelsens historiografiske baggrund, samtidig med at det redegør for kildematerialet og problemer relateret til studier af det. *Kapitel 3* er om det retslige grundlag for ægteskabet og den ændring heri, som tilvejebragtes ved kirkens introduktion af samtykkelæren, hvorefter et ægteskab etableredes ved parternes frie samtykke. Introduktionen af den nye lære, som var den internationale pavekirkes officielle politik fra anden halvdel af 1100-tallet, følges igennem undersøgelser af kanonisk ret, islandske kirkelige statutter, islandsk verdslig lovgivning og, i nogen grad, retspraksis. Det vises, hvorledes det nye syn på ægteskabet og den traditionelle islandske opfattelse heraf efterhånden kom til at samvirke. Kirken fik kontrol med det, som var det vigtige for den, især indgåelsen og opløsningen af ægteskabet, mens verdslig lovgivning regulerede den økonomiske side af ægteskabet. I kapitlet drøftes den islandske udvikling i et bredere europæisk perspektiv. Konklusionen er, at ægteskabet på Island forandredes på samme måde som i andre dele af den vestlige kristenhed, det vil sige ved indgåelse af et kompromis mellem nye og gamle traditioner. Hver region havde sit særpræg i denne proces, og det, som var særligt karakteristisk for Island, var fraværet af en central fyrstemyndighed med en udøvende magt i forhold til samfundet. Det var i vid udstrækning også situationen, efter at Island var blevet en del af det norske kongedømme i 1262-64. Det betød, at ægteskabet fortsat havde stor betydning som politisk alliancemiddel inden for de ledende slægter, således som det havde været i 1100- og 1200-tallet. Et andet forhold, som gav det islandske samfund et særpræg, var en meget stærk bilateral slægtskabsstruktur, som betød, at der ved et ægteskab blev overført ejendom til den nyetablerede husstand fra begge de involverede familier. Både fra et aristokratisk og et kirkeligt synspunkt førte det til et behov for stærkere kontrol med ejendomsoverføringerne. Det kan forklare, hvorfor den såkaldte "nye kristenret", med dens af kirken formulerede regler om ægteskab og arv, blev godkendt på Altinget i 1275 og siden blev yderligere cementeret med den nye civile ret i lovbogen *Jónsbók* fra 1281.

Kapitel 4 handler om, hvad der var et lovligt ægteskab. Trods den ny ægteskabsordning, der var etableret på Island ved slutningen af 1200-tallet, fandtes der i senmiddelalderen ikke nogen entydig definition af, hvad der var et "ægte" ægteskab. Dette skyldtes ikke mindst, at et lovligt ægteskab skulle opfylde flere kriterier. Det skulle være indgået med begge parters frivillige samtykke, efter at der havde været lyst for ægteparret tre søndage i træk. Således skulle ægteskabet være indgået ifølge "Guds lov", det vil sige den kanoniske ret, men ægteskabsindgåelsen skulle helst være sket med samtykke af de nærmeste slægtninge til parret, først og fremmest forældre eller værger. Alligevel var forældrenes samtykke ikke nødvendigt for, at ægteskabsindgåelsen var gyldig. Af afgørende betydning, blandt andet i de retslige kampe om ejendom, var, at forskellige kirkeretslige regler kunne gøre et ægteskab ugyldigt.

Den kongelige lovgivning, således som den findes først og fremmest i de såkaldte *retterbøter* (det vil sige kongelige enkeltbestemmelser af forordningskarakter, der kom til at fungere som tillægsbestemmelser til eller modifikationer af de gamle lovbøger), beskæftiger sig primært med ægteskabet som en økonomisk kontrakt. Samtidig tilsigter den dog også at definere grænsen mellem den ulovlige og lovlige ægteskabsaftale. Heroverfor handler de kirkelige statutter, udstedt dels af ærkebisperne i Trondheim, dels af de islandske biskopper selv, i højere grad om de kirkelige ceremonier end om ejendomskontrakten. Derfor var der egentlig ingen modsigelse mellem de kongelige retterbøter og de kirkelige statutter; de supplerede snarere hinanden.

Ved reformationen kom en lovgivning, ifølge hvilken staten skulle overtage jurisdiktionen over ægteskabet, samtidig med at det blev påbudt, at præsten skulle vie ægteparret i kirken. I kølvandet på reformationen fulgte flere love og domme, som tilsigtede at etablere en strengere kontrol med seksualiteten såvel inden for som uden for ægteskabet.

Afhandlingen påviser klart, at de islandske domstole blev en arena, hvor de mægtige slægter brugte de forskellige opfattelser af et lovligt ægteskab i deres kamp om politisk magt over jord og ressourcer, samtidig med at både kirken og staten brugte domstolene til at kontrollere befolkningens seksualitet. Før reformationen kunne lægfolket i højere grad spille bispemagt, pavemagt og kongemagt ud mod hinanden, hvad der gav en betydelig mulighed for at handle strategisk. Det blev vanskeligere ved slutningen af 1500-tallet, fordi kontrollen med ægteskabet mere og mere samledes på én hånd, kongemagtens. Det var således først og fremmest i perioden mellem slutningen af 1200-tallet og slutningen af 1500-tallet, at den retslige scene var velegnet for strategiske manipulationer, fordi der eksisterede så komplekse kriterier for, hvad der var et lovligt ægteskab, og fordi så mange instanser kunne godkende det og give dispensationer. Situationen var et resultat af det kompromis mellem gamle og nye traditioner, der var etableret i 1200-tallet: Den nye forståelse af, hvad der konstituerede et gyldigt ægteskab, var trængt ind, men gamle opfattelser stod fremdeles stærkt.

Ægteskabslovgivningen var i udvikling igennem hele perioden fra 1200 til 1600, og det indebar en forandring af ægteskabet, således at det i tillæg til at være en ejendomskontrakt også fik en religiøs betydning. Denne udvikling førte også til et nyt syn på kønsmoralen. Både mænd, men især kvinder skulle ved slutningen af 1500-tallet være jomfruer ved ægteskabsindgåelsen.

Kapitel 5 handler om lovgivningens regulering af seksualiteten, både inden for og uden for ægteskabet. Der måtte ikke indgås ægteskab mellem for nært beslægtede personer. Ifølge en vedtagelse af Det fjerde Laterankoncil i 1215 skulle der en dispensation til, for at personer nærmere beslægtet end fjerde led kunne indgå ægteskab, og det gjaldt også for dem, som var beslægtede igennem svogerskab eller fadderskab. Ægteskabet skulle også fuldbyrdes, og impotens kunne være en gyldig grund til at annullere et ægteskab. Det samme var tilfældet, hvis det kunne bevises, at den ene af parterne levede i hor. Hvis det blev påvist, at en mand før sin ægteskabsindgåelse havde haft samleje med en kvinde, der var beslægtet med hans hustru i fjerde led eller nærmere, kunne det også føre til, at hans ægteskab betragtedes som incestuøst og derfor kunne opløses.

Problemer kunne opstå, hvis bare nogle af de forskellige kriterier for et gyldigt ægteskab ikke var opfyldt. I tillæg var der åbenbart heller ikke altid enighed om, hvilke kriterier der var de vigtigste. Det var muligt at få dispensation for at have indgået ægteskab i forbudne led, men der var stor uenighed om, hvem der kunne give sådanne dispensationer. I udgangspunktet var det biskopperne, som sad inde med denne myndighed, men det var muligt at henvende sig direkte til pavestolen og søge om dispensation, ligesom også verdslige myndigheder gav ægteskabsdispensationer. Her skiftes fokus fra udviklingen af retten til, hvordan den blev brugt og af hvem. Det femte kapitel behandler, hvordan netop de forskellige definitioner af, hvad der var et lovligt ægteskab, blev anvendt i retssager, og hvordan retsdokumenterne ofte afspejler en usikkerhed eller uklarhed blandt folk om, hvem der var lovformeligt gift og hvem ikke. Magteliten brugte denne usikkerhed i kampen om jordejendom. F.eks. viser arvetvister, at personer beslægtede i fjerde led fik dispensationer til at blive ægtefolk, men at deres fjernere slægtninge ofte nægtede at godkende sådanne dispensationer for at sikre egen ret til en omtvistet ejendom. Man kan således nemt dokumentere en politisk kamp om ejendom og ressourcer. Denne kamp fandtes imidlertid ved siden af en ideologisk kamp for at højne moralen på Island. Kapitlet omhandler også, hvordan kirken krævede bøder i samlivssager. På den måde styrkede den doktrinen om, hvad der var rigtigt, og hvad der var forkert samliv. På langt sigt førte dette til en internalisering af kristne normer og værdier. I bevarede kvindelige skriftemål fra 1400-tallet finder man udtryk for dette møde mellem den kirkelige diskurs og det praktiske liv.

Afhandlingen behandler ikke forståelsen af seksualiteten før og uafhængigt af den kanonisk retslige indflydelse, især på grund af vanskeligheder ved at anvende kildematerialet retrospektivt. Derimod konstateres det, at når spørgsmålet om seksualmoralen dukker op som et retsligt fænomen i den tidligste periode, som er behandlet i afhandlingen, så er det i høj grad i tilknytning til arvetvister. Det kunne tyde på, at lægfolks interesse for seksualmoralen var knyttet mere til arvespørgsmål end til religion. Dette ændrer sig imidlertid, og retssager fra det sene 1400-tal og fra 1500-tallet viser tydeligt, at man begynder at håndhæve seksualmoralen uafhængigt af arvespørgsmål. Kirken kunne placere sit krav om at kontrollere befolkningens seksuelle adfærd inden for den kontrol, som lægfolk allerede havde etableret over arveretten. Kirken introducerede sin seksualmoral med både lovgivning, skriftemål, prædikener og helgenfortællinger. I afhandlingen er undersøgelsen i hovedsagen begrænset til den kontrol, som var knyttet til lovgivningen, og til håndhævelsen af seksualmoralen inden for retssystemet. De, som bragte sagerne for domstolene, og som dømte i dem, var til dels præsterne, men også verserende rygter i bygderne førte til rejsning af sager ved domstolene. En del af kontrollen med seksualmoralen foregik før reformationen bag lukkede døre, så at sige når lægfolk bekendte deres synder i skriftemål.

I *kapitel 6* diskuteres de forandringer, som ægteskabsritualerne afspejler. Ritualerne blev mere religiøse, mere individuelt orienterede og mere kontrolleret af embedsmænd i den behandlede periode. Denne udvikling viser sig på det sproglige plan, hvor der sker en ændring fra en mundtlig til en skriftlig tradition, idet vidnerne i den mundtlige tradition var lægfolk, mens vidnerne i både vidnesbyrd og ægteskabskontrakter i den skriftlige tradition også var præster. Ægteskabet blev forandret fra at være en kontrakt om ejendom til også at blive en kontrakt om helligdom. *Kapitel 7* diskuterer mere konkret, hvordan de skriftlige ægteskabskontrakter over tid blev mere påvirket af den kristne ægteskabsideologi. Således kan det konstateres, at samtidig med at præsternes rolle gradvis bliver vigtigere, blandt andet som vidner til selve kontrakten mellem ægtefællerne, så blev forældrenes samtykke ikke mindre vigtigt. *Kapitel 8* handler om, hvordan det hellige ægteskab påvirkede også de sociale bånd, som blev skabt ved ægteskabsindgåelsen, særlig i forhold til det nye syn på kønskontrakten. En del af kapitlet giver nærmest en billedlig fremstilling af forandringer i, hvordan ægteskabsaftalen blev indgået. Ægteskabet forandredes fra at være et *handaband* (et ved håndslag bekræftet bånd) mellem to familier til at blive også et *hjónaband* (et ægteskabsbånd) mellem en mand og en kvinde, givet til dem af Guds nåde. Forandringer som følge heraf fandt sted både i den økonomiske del af ægteskabsaftalen og i selve fejringen af brylluppet.

Der tages også udgangspunkt i et konkret empirisk materiale, nemlig en række bevarede bryllupstaler fra 1400-tallet, i hvilke især brudgommens tale til bruden fremhæves som illustrativ for forandringerne i ægteskabsritualerne. Forandringerne skyldtes ikke bare kristen påvirkning, men var også knyttet til ændringer i den sociale organisering af familieforbindelser. I den forbindelse berøres, hvorledes kirkens syn på seksualiteten forandrede brudens rolle ved den gaveudveksling, som i øvrigt diskuteres nærmere i kapitel 10. Disse forandringer i ritualerne, kontrakterne og ceremonierne afspejler en ny forståelse af ægteskabet. Det bliver i stigende grad opfattet religiøst og individuelt. Men forandringerne afspejler også en anden udvikling. Ægteskabet bliver mere kontrolleret af offentligheden. I praksis først og fremmet af præsten, som i første del af den behandlede periode er kirkens repræsentant, men efter reformationen går over til at være statens. Ægteskabsritualerne gik fra at være "offentlige" i betydningen kendt af alle til også at blive offentlige i betydningen kontrolleret af staten. Denne forandring var udtryk for dybtgående ændringer i ægteskabets samfundsmæssige betydning.

Kapitel 9 omhandler, hvordan aftaler om ejendom i ægteskabet fungerede på Island i middelalderen. Lovgivning, ægteskabskontrakter og retssager analyseres for at kunne forklare forskellen på særeje og fælleseje. Hensigten er at vise, hvordan to forskellige hensyn, til henholdsvis hushold og slægt, virkede sammen om at bestemme, hvordan der blev disponeret over ejendom. Der var to hensyn at tage, når et ægtepars ejendomsbesiddelse skulle organiseres juridisk. Det ene var hensynet til husholdet og specielt til den ægtefælle, der levede længst. Det andet var hensynet til slægtningene til de to ægtefæller. Kapitlet handler om, hvordan disse hensyn manifesterede sig i ægteskabskontrakterne. Det drøftes for det første, hvilke rammer lovgivningen satte for ægteskabskontrakterne. Derefter ses for det andet på, hvilke typer af aftaler der blev gjort ved ægteskabsindgåelsen. Og endelig undersøges for det tredje, hvordan praksis var i administreringen af ejendommen. Det påvises, at der var to principielt forskellige valgmuligheder, når man ønskede at lægge vægt på henholdsvis slægten og husholdet, nemlig *máli* (særeje) og *helmingarfélag* (fælleseje). En undersøgelse af forandringer i kontraktindgåelsen over tid viser, at der hele tiden blev indgået ægteskabskontrakter efter *máli*-princippet. 1400-tallet var imidlertid den periode, hvor den største del af de rigeste familier indgik kontrakter efter fællesejeprincippet, noget som var særlig karakteristisk for det nye aristokrati, som kom til magten i denne periode. Fælleseje var derimod dårligt egnet til at bevare ejendom inden for disse familier. Dette samt problemer i kølvandet på en stor pestepidemi i 1495 kan sandsynligvis forklare, hvorfor magteliten i 1500-tallet ser ud til generelt at have foretrukket særejekontrakter. På Island fandtes der ingen tradition, som kunne sikre, at ejendom blev bevaret inden for den samme familie igennem flere generationer. Sammen med det forhold, at kvinder kunne få jord i medgift, ja endda kunne få en slægts hovedgård, førte dette til, at ejendom havde nemt ved at blive overført mellem familier ved giftermål. Og hovedgårdene kunne også blive en del af et fælleseje, således at en hovedgård kunne gå ud af en slægts eje, hvis der ikke var noget ægtefødt barn til at arve den. Derfor blev særejekontrakter foretrukket frem for fælleseje af aristokratiet i 1500-tallet.

Kapitel 10 handler om gaveudveksling ved ægteskabsindgåelsen, især spørgsmålet, om gaver blev givet på en måde, som favoriserede ægtefællerne og deres fælles hushold, eller på en måde, så hensynet til ægtefællernes respektive slægtninge var størst. På baggrund af en almen redegørelse for forholdet mellem brudekøb og medgift, dels generelt i Vesteuropa, dels specielt i Norden, behandles de islandske forhold. Det vises, at den nye forståelse af ægteskabet, der slog igennem fra 1200-tallet og frem, også havde konsekvenser for gaveudvekslingen i forbindelse med ægteskaber. Den medførte, at der ved en ægteskabsindgåelse overførtes store ejendomme fra ægteparrets forældre på begge sider til det nye ægtepar. Ligeledes blev der skabt nye arveregler, som skulle udelukke uægte børn fra arv. Husholdet blev således afgørende styrket i økonomisk henseende.

Kapitel 11 handler om forskellen mellem overførsler af ejendom igennem forskellige kanaler. Islændingene tilpassede lovgivning og praksis på en måde, så der skabtes et kompromis mellem den nye kirkelige forståelse af ægteskabet og det islandske samfunds gamle traditioner. For det første drøftes de to køns forskellige ejendomsret særlig med hensyn til, hvordan den kristne lære påvirkede ejendomsretten. Den nye situation skabte interessekonflikter mellem et ægtepars hushold på den ene side og parrets slægtninge uden for husholdet på den anden side. Den nye forståelse af ægteskabet styrkede ægteparret både juridisk og økonomisk i forhold til parrets slægtninge. Dette skabte en "patrilineær reaktion", som førte til, at visse bestemmelser blev modificeret og nye praksisformer udviklet på en måde, som også tog hensyn til slægtens interesser. Den bilaterale slægtskabsstruktur førte til et behov for en patrilineær organisering, hvor de nærmeste slægtninge blev givet en vis kontrol over ejendomsoverførslerne og fik sikret deres ret gennem den institution, der kaldtes *brigð*, den islandske form for det, som i dansk middelalder kaldes lovbydelsesret.

I den behandlede periode blev ægteskabet en mere personlig kontrakt mellem en mand og en kvinde, samtidig med at det fortsat havde en politisk alliancefunktion for magteliten. Dette er udgangspunktet for den konklusion på afhandlingen, der gives i *kapitel 12*. Her drøftes undersøgelsens empiriske konklusioner set i relation til den teoretiske diskussion, der er præsenteret i indledningskapitlet. Målet med denne drøftelse er at vise, hvordan de af kirken hidførte forandringer i opfattelsen af ægteskabet også afspejlede sig i nye opfattelser af ejendomsforhold. De havde en stærk forankring i en kønsbestemt ideologi, som var drivkraften bag den strategi, både gejstlige og verdslige brugte i "kampen" om at definere det gyldige og lovlige ægteskab. På den måde kan forandringer i den islandske samfundsstruktur belyses igennem de forandringer, som foregik af ægteskabet som institution. Forandringer i definitionen af, hvad der var et lovligt ægteskab, gav mulighed for vidt forskellige slægtsstrategier, og netop de var drivkraften bag udviklingen af samfundet i sin helhed.

Index of Persons

A

Agnes, Abbess 192
Alexander III, Pope, (1159-81) 68, 70-71
Álfheiður Arnardóttir 159
Álfheiður Flosadóttir 380
Ambrose of Milan 281
Andersen, Randi 99
Andrés Guðmundsson 240, 329, 338, 364-65, 474, 477, 488
Anna Korpa Maker 368
Ari Andrésson 329, 479, 488-89
Ari Guðmundsson 316, 329, 472
Ari Jónsson 290, 479
Arnbjörg Brandsdóttir 261, 483
Arndís Snorradóttir 260, 480
Arngrímur Björnsson 265
Árni Daníel Júlíusson 8
Árni Einarsson 228, 317, 483
Árni Einarsson, Archbishop, (1346-49) 93, 107, 120-21, 226
Árni Guttormsson 386
Árni Magnússon 319, 438
Árni Steingrímsson 170, 234
Árni Steinólfsson 265
Árni Þorláksson, Bishop, (1269-98) 53, 87-88, 90-93, 96, 106, 111, 120, 132, 143, 166, 186, 202, 209, 213, 271, 346, 428, 439
Arnoddur Brandsson 310, 364, 472
Arnór Finnson 396
Arnór Sigurjónsson 420, 438
Ásbjörn Guðmundsson 58
Ásdís Fúsadóttir 163
Ásgeir Árnason 383
Ásgeir Bjarnason 204
Ásgrímur of Helgafell 387
Ástríður Jörundardóttir 385
Auðunn Salamonsson 317
Auður Magnúsdóttir 8, 22, 79, 405

B

Bandlien, Bjørn 86
Bárður Jónsson 242, 475, 477
Bartlett, Robert 28
Beckin, Michel 368
Benedikt Gizurarson 322
Benedikt Halldórsson 484, 496
Benedikt Magnússon 389
Benedikt Pétursson 159
Bergur Ingimundarson 143
Bergur Jónsson 171
Bernard of Clairvaux 81
Bessi Þorsteinsson 236, 481
Birgit Gísladóttir 159
Bitel, Lisa M. 274
Bjarni Andrésson 325
Bjarni Ellendsson 395
Bjarni Hafliðason 396
Bjarni Jónsson 320, 369, 396, 476, 488
Bjarni Narfason 193
Bjarni Ólason 211, 240, 474
Bjarni Sigurðsson 386
Bjarni Skeggjason 198
Bjarni Snorrason 58
Björg Þorvaldsdóttir 189-91, 477

Björn Benediktsson 313, 486-87
Björn Brynjólfsson 249, 310
Björn Guðnason 186, 189, 193-94, 323-25, 330, 368
Björn Halldórsson 204
Björn Jónsson 479
Björn Jórsalafari 184
Björn Magnússon 175
Björn Þorleifsson 182, 185-86, 189, 327-28, 330, 390, 408, 419-20, 477
Björn Þorsteinsson 501
Böðvar Arason 168
Böðvar Benediktsson 322
Böðvar Jónsson 255
Bois, Guy 399
Bonfield, Lloyd 343, 371, 416, 421
Bourdieu, Pierre 35, 439
Brahe, Anna 282
Brandur Sæmundsson 82
Brandur Sölvason 311, 365, 472, 488
Bresc, Henri 423
Bríet Brandsdóttir 387
Brooke, Christopher 25
Brother Robert 224
Brundage, James 25, 71, 73-74, 297

C

Carlsson, Lizzie 362
Casey, James 25
Cecile Þorsteinsdóttir 183
Cecilia Loftsdóttir 198
Christian I, King 330
Christian II, King 332
Christian III, King 115, 122, 238
Christian V, King 322
Christopher of Bavaria, King, (1439-48) 392

D

Daði Arason 182
D'Avray, David 277
Dean, Trevor 25, 109
Donahue, Charles 300-301
Dübeck, Inger 323
Duby, Georges 21, 25, 31, 75, 219, 239, 406, 409
Dumont, Louise 293-94

E

Eggert Hannesson 182, 264, 368, 482, 484
Egill Eyjólfsson, Bishop, (1331-41) 196
Egill Grímsson 198
Egill Jónsson 393, 483
Einar Arnórsson 78
Einar Bjarnason 187-88
Einar Eiríksson 184
Einar Eyjólfsson 182, 485
Einar Hafliðason 60
Einar Jónsson 315, 472, 488
Einar Oddson 475
Einar Ólafsson 359
Einar Ormsson 183, 187
Einar Salomonson 170
Eiríkur, Archbishop, (1188-1213) 82-83, 87
Eiríkur Böðvarsson 259, 481, 486, 489
Eiríkur Magnússon, King, (1268-99) 113, 116, 140, 357, 383, 386, 413
Eiríkur Stefánsson 404
Eiríkur Sumarliðason 417
Elen Magnúsdóttir 486
Elín Pálsdóttir 313, 487
Erickson, Amy Louise 38, 40
Erlendur Erlendsson 417
Erlendur Narfason 332
Erlendur Þorgrímsson 370
Erlendur Þorvarðsson 257, 322, 478, 480, 486, 489, 492-93, 497-99
Erlendur Þórisson 169
Erlendur Þórðarsson 486
Erlingur Jónsson 390
Eyjólfur Böðvarsson 240, 364-65
Eyjólfur Snorrason 380
Eysteinn, Archbishop, (1120-88) 80-82

F

Finnbogi Einarsson 182, 486, 494
Finnbogi Jónsson 178, 193, 256, 313,

332, 365, 394, 417, 475, 477, 490, 495
Finnbogi Tumason 261, 483
Frank, Roberta 77
Frederik II, King, (1559-88) 58, 114-15, 128-29, 146, 171, 173, 209, 225, 237, 430
Frederik IV, King, (1699-1730) 418
Frimannslund, Rigmor 363

G

Gamli Marteinsson 317
Gauti, Archbishop, (1475-1510) 186
Geertz, Clifford 244
Gelting, Michael 36, 407
Gies, Joseph 50
Gilsson, Gils 144
Gísli Jónsson 144, 483
Gísli Jónsson, Bishop, (1556-87) 144
Gísli Magnússon 58
Gissur, Bishop, (1082-1118) 122, 141-44, 150, 170, 208, 238, 260, 268
Goody, Jack 25, 27, 33-34, 36, 72, 158, 340, 345, 356
Gordon, Linda 38
Gottskálkur Nikulásson, Bishop, (1498-1520) 191-92, 318, 330
Gottskálkur Jónsson 235
Grafar-Gunna 172-74, 209, 285
Gratian 68, 70, 81, 284
Gregory IX, Pope, (1227-41) 68
Grímur Pálsson 332
Grímur Jónsson 480, 494, 499
Grundar-Helga 184
Guðbjartur flóki 124
Guðbrandur Þorláksson, Bishop, (1542-1627) 148, 163
Guðfinna Arnfinnsbóttir 486
Guðfinna Indriðadóttir 359
Guðfinna Jónsdóttir 198
Guðfinna Þorgeirsdóttir 383
Guðlaug Ketilsdóttir 311, 365, 472, 488
Guðlaug Sveinsdóttir 401
Guðmundur Arason 316, 326-30, 365, 473, 488
Guðmundur Gíslason 387
Guðmundur Ingimundarson 165
Guðmundur Sigurðsson 364-65, 474
Guðmundur Þorláksson 392
Guðmundur Þorleifsson 58
Guðmundur Þorsteinsson 164, 310
Guðni Einarsdóttir 481, 496
Guðni Eyjólfsson 177, 364-65, 475, 488, 490-91, 495
Guðni Jónsson 60, 403
Guðni Jónsdóttir 485-86, 500
Guðni Þormóðsson 264
Guðný Brandadóttir 479-80, 499-500
Guðný Grímsdóttir 478
Guðný Magnúsdóttir 259, 483
Guðný Þorleifsdóttir 483
Guðný Þorsteinsdóttir 364-65, 474, 490-91, 495
Guðríður Finnbogadóttir 364-65, 476
Guðríður Ingimundardóttir 250, 289, 308, 472
Guðrún Árnadóttir 241, 475, 484
Guðrún Bessadóttir 479, 498
Guðrún Björnsdóttir 268, 489, 492
Guðrún Eggertsdóttir 317
Guðrún Eiríksdóttir 169
Guðrún Finnbogadóttir 177, 478
Guðrún Gísladóttir 364-65, 474, 490-91, 495
Guðrún Gottskálksdóttir 496-97
Guðrún Guðmundsdóttir 178
Guðrún Gunnlaugsdóttir 177, 364-65
Guðrún Halldórsdóttir 259, 475, 482, 495, 498
Guðrún Hannesdóttir 481, 499
Guðrún Helgadóttir 386
Guðrún Jónsdóttir 170-71, 257, 476, 480, 485, 488-89, 493, 497-99
Guðrún Magnúsdóttir 165
Guðrún Ólafsdóttir 320, 476, 478, 488
Guðrún Ormsdóttir 58
Guðrún Sigmundsdóttir 148
Guðrún Tumadóttir 236, 481, 499
Guðrún Þórðardóttir 259, 486, 489
Guðrún Þorkelsdóttir 240-41, 36-65, 474-75, 488, 495
Guðrún Þorleifsdóttir 82, 393-94, 486

Guðrún Þorsteinsdóttir 403, 415
Gunnar Andrésson 156, 317
Gunnar Jónsson 134
Gunnhildur Pétursdóttir 275, 475, 488
Gunnlaugur Ormstunga 226
Gunnsteinn Ásgrímsson 257-58, 324
Gyrðir Ívarsson, Bishop, (1350-60) 121

H

Hadrian IV, Pope, (1154-59) 348
Hafliði Jónsson 395
Hákon Hákonarson, King, (1217-63) 224, 287
Hákon Jónsson 365, 473
Hákon Magnússon, King, (1270-1319) 49, 102-03, 113, 161
Hákon V, King, (1299-1319) 49
Halla Sigurðardóttir 396
Halla Vilhjálmsdóttir 162
Halldóra Guðbrandsdóttir, Abbess 143, 290
Halldór Benediktsson 285, 290, 486
Halldór Brandsson 398
Halldór Þorgeirsson 351
Hallgerður Höskuldsdóttir 287
Hallvarður Ámundarson 364-65
Hansen, Lars Ivar 8, 34, 420
Hans, King, (1481-1513) 366
Hareven, Tamara K. 32
Harrington, Joel F. 23
Helena Þórarinsdóttir 231
Helga Aradóttir 266, 289, 484
Helga Einarsdóttir 156, 162
Helga Fúsadóttir 164
Helga Guðmundsdóttir 486
Helga Illugadóttir 285, 290, 486
Helga Jónsdóttir 262, 370, 479, 484
Helga Sæmundsdóttir 313, 476
Helga Sigurðardóttir 266, 401
Helga Snorradóttir 170
Helga Þorleifsdóttir 316, 326, 365, 384, 473, 488
Helga Þorsteinsdóttir 226
Helga Þorvarðardóttir 161
Helgi Guttormsson 317
Helgi Þorláksson 8
Helgi Þórólfsson 210
Helmholz, Richard 25, 56, 172, 286
Herlihy, David 399
Hertzberg, Ebbe 358
Hólmfríður Erlendsdóttir 182, 332, 369-70, 417
Hólmfríður Ögmundsdóttir 250, 472, 495
Hrafn Brandsson 187, 212, 364-65, 474
Hrefna Róbertsdóttir 9, 28, 51
Hrútur Herjólfsson 227

I

Indriði Hákonarsson 364, 365
Indriði Jónsson 364, 365, 474
Inga Huld Hákonardóttir 302
Ingibjörg Eiríksdóttir 181-82, 480, 483
Ingibjörg Halldórsdóttir 365, 473
Ingibjörg Loftsdóttir 390
Ingibjörg Ormsdóttir 476
Ingibjörg Ólafsdóttir 171
Ingibjörg Pálsdóttir 193, 364-65, 408, 474, 477, 486
Ingibjörg Sturludóttir 138, 206
Ingibjörg Þorvaldsdóttir 389
Ingibjörg Þorvarðardóttir 332, 391-92
Ingigerður Þorsteinsdóttir 396, 477
Ingilbrikt Jónsson 162
Ingimundur 250, 472, 495
Ingimundur Uthyrmsson 308
Ingiríður Þórisdóttir 157
Ingunn Ólafsdóttir 473, 488
Ingveldur Erlendsdóttir 161
Ingveldur Helgadóttir 184, 324, 408
Innocent III, Pope, (1198-1216) 68
Ísleifur Sigurðsson 408, 479
Iuul, Stig 312
Ívar Hólm 308
Ívar Sigurðsson 370

J

Járngerður Gilsdóttir 249, 310, 312, 360, 472, 495
Jochens, Jenny 104, 286
Jón Arason, Bishop, (1522-50) 47, 125, 161, 385, 401-02, 406

Jón Jóhannesson 135, 136
Jón at Móberg 192
Jón Bjarnason 478
Jón Björnsson 325, 485
Jón Egilsson 46
Jón Finnbogason 313-14, 326, 350, 394, 476
Jón Gerreksson, Bishop, (1426-33) 330
Jón Grímsson 257, 480, 486
Jón Guðmundsson 146, 487
Jón Gunnlaugsson 311, 365, 472, 488
Jón Halldórsson, Bishop, (1322-39) 114, 119, 197-98, 203, 484
Jón Hallgrímsson 231, 478
Jón Helgason 279
Jón Jónsson 172-74, 192, 476
Jón Loftsson 148-49
Jón Magnússon 483, 485, 489
Jón Narfason 182, 480
Jón Ólafsson 479, 484
Jón Pálsson 331, 481
Jón Pétursson 162, 388
Jón rauði, Archbishop, (1268-82) 87, 89-90
Jón Sæmundsson 399
Jón Sigmundsson 139, 182, 189, 191-92, 330, 390, 477
Jón Sigurðsson 258
Jón Sigurðsson, Bishop, (1343-48) 118-19
Jón Sturlason 478
Jón Vilhjálmsson, Bishop, (1426-35) 134, 136, 206, 385, 501
Jón Þorláksson 188
Jón Þorvaldsson 182, 190
Jörundur, Archbishop, (1287-1309) 120
Jörundur Þorsteinsson, Bishop, (1267-1313) 196
Jórunn Brynjólfsdóttir 249, 310, 472
Justinian 288, 348

K

Katla Þorláksdóttir 210
Katrín Hannesdóttir 481, 493, 496, 499
Klapisch-Zuber, Christine 26, 342-43
Knútur Einarsson 157
Kolbeinn Böðvarsson 169
Kolbeinn Ingimundarsson 320
Kolbeinn Ólafsson 141
Kristín 326
Kristín Björnsdóttir 183, 253, 316, 326, 328, 390, 419-20
Kristín Eyjólfsdóttir 475, 483, 488
Kristín Einasdóttir 487
Kristín Finnbogadóttir 364-65, 476, 488
Kristín Gottskálksdóttir 477-78
Kristín Jónsdóttir 169
Kristín Sumarliðadóttir 325
Kristín Vigfúsdóttir 406

L

Landau, Peter 77, 82
Lárentíus Kálfsson, Bishop, (1323-31) 196
Loftur Guttormsson, Icelandic historian 24, 330
Loftur Guttormsson (d. 1432) 137, 183, 317, 327
Loftur Ormsson 183, 275, 475, 488
Lombard, Peter (1095-1160) 69-70, 91
Lowe, Kate 25, 281

M

Magnús Eyjólfsson, Bishop, (1479-90) 185, 187, 188, 194, 225
Magnús Gissurarson 264
Magnús Gizurarson, Bishop, (1216-37) 203
Magnús Jónsson 390, 406, 419, 482, 485
Magnús lagabætir ('Law-Reformer'), King, (1263-80) 54, 90, 95, 140, 157, 287, 346, 348, 411-13, 420-21
Magnús Lyngdal Magnússon 88-89
Magnús Magnússon 182, 241, 393, 475, 486
Magnús Már Lárusson 28, 233, 418
Magnús prúði Jónsson 333
Magnús Stefánsson 9, 203, 206
Málfríður Bjarnadóttir 361, 485
Málfríður Torfadóttir 365, 475, 477, 483
Margrét Eiríksdóttir 258, 482
Margrét Erlendsdóttir 395, 478, 480

Margrét Eyjólfsdóttir 242, 364-65, 474-75
Margrét Gamladóttir 386
Margrethe I, Queen, (1375-1412) 135
Margrét Ólafsdóttir 240, 391, 474
Margrét Vigfúsdóttir 253, 364-65, 392, 473, 488
Michael, Bishop, (1382/83-92) 135
Miller, William Ian 31
Mörður Valgarðsson 227
Murry, Jacqueline 81

N

Nicholas I, Pope, (858-67) 274
Nors, Thyra 35, 405

O

Oddfríður Aradóttir 253, 365, 473
Oddný Jónsdóttir 175, 478
Oddur Einarsson, Bishop, (1589-1630) 61, 146-47, 149-50, 172
Oddur Þorleifsson 250
Ögmundur Pálsson, Bishop, (1520-40) 139
Ólafur, Archbishop, (1350-70) 119
Ólafur Geirmundsson 365, 473
Ólafur Hjaltason, Bishop, (1552-69) 261-62
Ólafur Marteinsson 158
Ólafur Rögnvaldsson, Bishop, (1460-95) 139, 180,187
Ólafur Sigurðsson 249, 310, 472
Ólafur Tryggvason, King, (968-1000) 275
Olav, Saint 419
Ólöf Aradóttir 329
Ólöf Árnadóttir 364-65
Ólöf Arnardóttir 236
Ólöf Guðmundsdóttir 58
Ólöf Loftsdóttir 185, 188-89, 203, 325, 327, 390, 439
Ólöf Pétursdóttir 391
Ormur Jónsson 181-82
Ormur Loftsson 183-84 252, 364-65, 473
Ormur Sturluson 107, 264, 480
Orri Vésteinsson 9, 47

P

Páll Brandsson 332, 417
Páll Grímsson 395, 478
Páll Jónsson 181-82, 185, 188, 266, 289-90, 414, 439, 475, 484
Páll Stígsson 129, 263
Páll Þorsteinsson 200
Pétur Hálfdánarson 156
Pétur Vigfússon 259, 481, 489
Philpot, Bertha 100

R

Rafn Brandsson 242, 402, 478
Rafn Guðmundsson 316-17
Ragnheiður Eggertsdóttir 333, 350, 485
Ragnhildur Jónsdóttir 263, 480, 485
Randíður Bjarnadóttir 211-12
Runólfur Höskuldsson 401

S

Sabean, David Warren 36
Sæmundur Oddson 251
Safley, Thomas Max 126
Salvör Nikulásdóttir 171
Salvör Snjólfsdóttir 369
Saxo 35
Schneider, David M. 30
Scott, Joan 38-39
Sesselía Bassadóttir 480
Sesselía Jónsdóttir 264-65
Sigmundur Halldórsson 396, 477
Sigríður 499
Sigríður Árnadóttir 399
Sigríður Björnsdóttir 251, 472
Sigríður Einarsdóttir 141-42, 315, 394, 472, 481, 488
Sigríður Guðmundsdóttir 310, 364, 472
Sigríður Jónsdóttir 182, 241-42, 475, 477, 486
Sigríður Torfadóttir 391
Sigríður Þorsteinsdóttir 365, 473, 484
Sigurður Jónsson 266, 485-86

Sigurður Líndal 78, 88
Sigurður Nordal 227
Sigurður Oblandsson 161
Sigurður Stefánsson (1570-95) 61
Sigurður Þorleifsson 322, 364-65, 476, 488
Skeggi Allason 168-69
Snorri Hákonarson 58
Snorri Sturluson 78
Snorri Þorleifsson 387
Solveig Björnsdóttir 181-82, 184-85, 187-89, 192, 194, 203, 206, 328, 330-31, 439
Solveig Ólafsdóttir 392
Solveig Þorleifsdóttir 183, 252, 364-65, 473
Solveig Þorsteinsdóttir 419
Stefán Jonsson, Bishop, (1491-1518) 139, 177-78, 186, 192, 238, 258
Stefán Karlsson 203
Steingrímur Böðvarsson 198
Steinn Brandsson 331
Steinn Jónsson 351
Steinn Ólafsson 261, 483
Steinunn Arnfinnsdóttir 326-27
Steinunn Bjarnadóttir 177
Steinunn Gunnarsdóttir 158
Steinunn Jónsdóttir 182, 368, 403, 479, 483
Steinunn Ólafsdóttir 266, 481, 484
Stigsen, Otte 124
Stone, Lawrence 437
Sturla Þórðarson 177-78, 182, 412
Sumarliði Eiríksson 241, 475
Sveinbjörn Rafnsson 9, 78-79, 286, 412
Sveinn Björnsson 392
Sveinn Hallvarðarson 385-86
Sveinn Pétursson 187
Sveinn Símonarson 264
Sveinn Sumarliðason 364-65, 417, 476, 488
Sverrir Jakobsson 79
Sverrir Sigurðsson, King, (1177-1202) 357

T

Tacitus 403
Tertullian 281
Thomas Jónsson 202
Tómas Arnarson 171
Tómas Hjálmarsson 162
Torfi Tulinius 78

U

Unnur Marðardóttir 287

V

Valdís Helgadóttir 124
Valgerður Gizurardóttir 386
Valgerður Keneksdóttir 364-65, 475
Vatnsfjarðar-Kristín 18, 328, 419
Vestergaard, Torben 420
Viðnæmur Jónsson 156, 162
Vigdís 257-58, 476, 495, 498
Vigfús Erlendsson 182, 369, 370
Vigfús Ívarsson Hólm 281, 289, 308, 392, 472
Vigfús Þorsteinsson 182
Vilborg Eiríksdóttir 228, 483
Vilchin Henriksson, Bishop, (1394-1405) 136
Vilhjálmur Finsen 349, 412-13
Vísi-Gísli 420

W

White, Stephen 410
Wogan-Brown, Jocelyn 356

Þ

Þóra Bjarnadóttir 264
Þóra Jónsdóttir 259, 481, 489
Þóra Ketilsdóttir 311, 365, 472, 488
Þorbjörg Brandsdóttir 163, 404
Þorbjörg Ólafsdóttir 240, 474
Þorbjörg Pálsdóttir 364-65
Þorbjörg Þorsteinsdóttir 124, 472
Þórdís Magnúsdóttir 168-69
Þórður Bessason 249, 310, 312, 360, 472
Þórður Bjarnason 354

Þórður Helgason 394
Þórður Ketilsson 182
Þórður Sigurðsson 365, 473
Þorgerður Böðvarsdóttir 138, 167
Þorgerður Halldórsdóttir 478
Þorgerður Ólafsdóttir 329, 472
Þorgerður Sturludóttir 396, 484
Þórkatla Bjarnadóttir 58, 264
Þorkell Einarsson 473, 488
Þorkell Guðbjartsson 240
Þorlákur Einarsson 268, 481
Þorlákur Eyjólfsson 236
Þorlákur Hallgrímsson 262, 484
Þorlákur Þórhallson, Bishop, (1178-93) 22, 80, 81, 84, 196, 197
Þorlaug Árnadóttir 474
Þorleifur Björnsson 181-82, 184-87, 189, 192-94, 263, 324, 401, 408, 480, 485
Þorleifur Grímsson 182, 266, 482
Þorleifur Marteinsson 392
Þorleifur Þórðarson 138, 167-68, 316-317, 326, 328, 383-84, 419
Þorleifur Þóroddson 142
Þorsteinn Arviðsson 182
Þorsteinn Finnbogason 395, 477
Þorsteinn Guðleiksson 198
Þorsteinn Guðmundsson 107, 483
Þorsteinn Magnússon 364-65, 473
Þorsteinn Ólafsson 251, 472
Þorsteinn Sigurðsson 384
Þorsteinn Torfason 396, 484
Þorsteinn Þórarinsson 403
Þórunn Jónsdóttir 107, 266, 402, 408, 478, 483
Þórunn Sturludóttir 322, 478
Þórunn Þórðardóttir 261, 483
Þorvarður Björnsson 259, 482
Þorvarður Erlendsson 318, 364-65, 417, 477, 489
Þorvarður Loftsson 253, 330, 332, 364-65, 392, 473, 488
Þuríður Arnardóttir 201
Þuríður Ólafsdóttir 392
Þuríður Þorleifsdóttir 480, 484

Æ

Æsa Jónsdóttir 395

Ö

Örnólfur Jónsson 266, 481

Geographical Index[1]

A

Aalborg 274
Ásgeirsá in Víðidalur 327
Auðbrekka in Hörgárdalur 331, 388
Austfirðir 395

B

Bær in Rauðasandur 316-17, 384
Barð in Fljótum 398
Barðsvík in Strandir 329
Bergen 7, 113, 187, 274-75, 278, 287
Bessastaðir 129
Bjarnanes in Hornafjörður 52
Blöndugil 360
Bollastaðir 360
Borg 58, 230, 250
Borg in Mosdal 329
Breiðafjörður 57, 327, 378, 408, 477
Brekkur 395

C

Copenhagen 7, 47, 55, 60, 123-24, 128, 141, 174, 274, 287, 446

D

Denmark 26, 35, 46, 60, 80, 99, 122-23, 126, 129, 170, 187, 238, 274, 282, 289, 301-02, 312, 332, 347, 366, 376, 411, 426, 430, 501
Douai 333, 349, 372
Dynjandi in Mosdal 329

E

Edinburgh 204
Einarsstaðir in Reykjadalur 208
England 23, 25-27, 30, 38, 40, 51, 144, 278, 300,-01, 318-19, 343, 347-48, 364, 371, 388, 416, 421, 423, 501
Eyjafjörður 161, 290, 313, 327-28, 378, 380, 388, 391, 408, 417, 419, 479

F

Faxaflói 378
Fellisendi in Miðdalur 354
Flatey in Breiðafjörður 408, 477
France 7, 21, 25-26, 30-31, 81, 237, 239, 287, 300-301, 342-43, 399-400, 406, 409, 411, 413, 426
Fremri Núpur 394

G

Gautastaðir 386
Germany 23, 26, 30, 69, 126, 159, 250, 472, 501
Giljar 322
Gilsbakki 314
Grenjaðarstaðir 250
Gröf 438
Grund 107, 327-28, 390, 408, 417-19, 479

1 The most common place names such as Iceland, Europe etc. are not in this index.

H

Hænuvík in Barðaströnd 390
Hafrafellstunga in Öxarfjörður 314
Hamburg 368-69
Hamrar in Reykjadalur 360
Haukadalur in Árnessýsla 52
Héðinshöfði 377
Helgafell 37, 57, 167, 380, 387
Helgastaðir 290
Hjörsey 396
Hof 200, 261, 322
Höfðaströnd 395, 438
Hofsjarðir 322
Hólar 45, 47, 60, 79, 82, 87, 89, 122, 125, 133-34, 136-39, 148, 156-57, 161, 165, 168, 177, 180, 187, 190-91, 196, 201, 236, 253, 261, 318, 330, 385-86, 388, 404, 501
Hóll 52, 389
Hóll in Bolungarvík 188
Hóll in Skinnastaðaþing 314
Holstein 141
Holt in Fljótum 391
Horn 329
Horn in Rennisey in Rygjafylki 309
Höskuldsstaðir in Skagaströnd 190, 394
Hrafnkelsstaðir 329
Hrafnseyri in Arnarfjörður 475
Hraun in Höfðaströnd 395
Húnavatnsþing 248
Hvalsey in Greenland 251
Hvammur in Hvammsveit 383
Hvassafell 139, 211
Hvassafell in Eyjafjörður 391

I

Italy 25, 26, 281, 343

J

Jutland 18, 353

K

Kalmanstunga 241
Ketilsstaðir in Vellir 327
Kirkjubæjarklaustur 143, 170
Kirkjuból 329
Kolding 366
Krísuvík 308
Kronborg 129

L

Lækjardalur 404
Lateran 68-69, 71-72, 82-83, 89, 180, 202-03, 428
Laufáss 250
London 137, 290
Low Countries 349, 422
Lund 8, 128
Lýtingsstaðir 322

M

Marðargnúpur 387
Maribo 282
Móberg 192
Möðruvellir 162, 211, 327, 331-33, 417-18, 479
Möðruvellir in Eyjafjörður 313, 327
Mýrdalur in Kjós 163

N

Neckerhausen 37
Niðarós 46, 54, 60, 77, 80-82, 87-88, 107, 119, 135-136, 139, 183, 186, 193, 215, 232-33, 428
Norway 25, 38, 46, 49, 60, 77, 81-82, 87-90, 99, 102, 104, 109, 111, 116, 129, 134-135, 187, 201, 223, 227, 249, 274-275, 278, 287, 301-302, 305,-306, 308, 332, 335, 348, 357, 359, 363, 381, 411-13, 415, 426, 501
Núpur 268, 329, 394

O

Oddi in Rangárvellir 52

P

Paris 26, 70, 250, 472
Pommerania 141

R

Refstaðir 404
Rennisey 309
Reykhólar 57, 183, 328-29, 414
Reykhólar in Reykjanes 52, 263, 313
Reykholt 141
Reykir in Miðfjörður 311
Reynistaðarþing 389
Rhone-Alpes 91
Ribe 123, 126
Rípur in Hegranes 385
Rome 135, 138-39, 180, 183-84, 193, 213, 428

S

Sæunnarstaðir 404
Saurbær 317
Saurbær in Rauðasandur 326
Sevilla 275
Sicily 84
Sjávarborg in Skagafjörður 327
Skagafjörður 251, 322, 327
Skálholt 18, 45, 53, 60-61, 79, 82, 87-89, 91, 114, 118-19, 121-22, 128, 133-37, 139, 141, 144, 146, 177, 183, 185-88, 192-93, 197, 200, 203, 251, 268, 287, 387, 501
Skarð 52, 57, 183, 188, 203-04, 258, 325, 327-28, 390
Skógar 329
Snorrastaðir 390
Spjaldhagi 193, 417
Staðarfell 394
Staður in Hrútafjörður 262
Staður in Reynisnes 192
Stafholt 146
Stokkahlaðir in Eyjafjörður 380
Strönd in Selvogur 52
Strútur 404
Svarfhóll 387
Svínafell in Öræfi 52
Sweden 26, 39, 302, 304, 362

T

Torfalækur 370-71
Torfustaðir 391
Trent 70, 73
Túná in Tálknafirði 368
Tunga 314
Tunsberg 113, 332

U

Urðir in Svarfaðardalur 261

V

Vallholt 391
Valþjófsdalur 316
Varðgjá 388
Vatnsfjörður 52, 57, 148, 183-84, 273-74, 316, 326, 328, 393, 416, 419
Vatnsholt 387
Vatnsleysa 308
Viðey 281
Víðidalsá 315
Víðidalstunga 392, 419
Vienna 136
Vík 389

Þ

Þingvellir 45, 61, 87, 114, 126,-28, 132-34, 139, 159, 175, 195, 202, 207, 210
Þórustaðir in Svalbarðsströnd 372
Þverá in Fnjóskadalur 211

Æ

Ærlækur in Öxarfjörður 380

Ö

Ögur in Isafjörður 186, 189, 258, 325, 330

Hóll
Ögur
Vatnsfjörður
Reynistaðir
Sjávarborg
Þingeyrar
Másstaðir
Ásgeirsá
Geiradalur
Reykhólar
Staðarhóll
Flatey
Skarð
Galtardalstunga
Helgafell
Vatnshorn
Hitardalur
Kolbeinsstaðir
Haukadalur
Innrihólmur
Þingvellir
Brautarholt
Viðey
Bessastaðir
Sandgerði
Hólmur
Skálholt
Strönd
Oddi
Mörk
Dalur
Þykkvibær
0
10
20
30
40
50 km